BLACK POWER

BOOKS BY RICHARD WRIGHT

FICTION

The Man Who Lived Underground

A Father's Law

Rite of Passage

Eight Men

The Long Dream

Savage Holiday

The Outsider

Native Son

Uncle Tom's Children

NONFICTION

American Hunger

White Man, Listen!

Pagan Spain

The Color Curtain

Black Power

Black Boy

BLACK POWER

Three Books from Exile: *Black Power*; *The Color Curtain*; and *White Man, Listen!*

RICHARD WRIGHT

WITH AN INTRODUCTION BY CORNEL WEST

HARPER**PERENNIAL** MODERN**CLASSICS**

NEW YORK • LONDON • TORONTO • SYDNEY • NEW DELHI • AUCKLAND

HARPER**PERENNIAL** MODERN**CLASSICS**

HarperCollins books may be purchased for educational, business, or sales promotional use. For information, please email the Special Markets Department at SPsales@harpercollins.com.

FIRST HARPER PERENNIAL MODERN CLASSICS EDITION PUBLISHED 2008.

REISSUED 2023.

Designed by Renato Stanisic

Library of Congress Cataloging-in-Publication Data is available upon request.

ISBN 978-0-06-144945-1 (pbk.)

23 24 25 26 27 LBC 8 7 6 5 4

CONTENTS

INTRODUCTION

By Cornel West

The unadulterated genius of Richard Wright has yet to be fully appreciated. His literary significance has been acknowledged—as in Irving Howe's famous quip that the day *Native Son* (1940) was published American culture was changed forever. Wright's political courage has been recognized primarily owing to his breaks from authoritarian Marxism and his fierce opposition to white-supremacist capitalism. But the very essence of Wright's genius, the sheer core of his artistic achievement, was his intellectual candor and existential honesty in his quest to be a free human being in the twentieth century. This painful though poignant quest made him the most secular of all modern African American writers. In short, his fundamental commitment to the rich legacy of the European Enlightenment and to the fecund heritage of Western humanism fueled his conception of himself and his art.

Wright's incredible journey from poverty-stricken childhood in Jim Crow Mississippi to world renown as an intellectual and freedom fighter is an epic one. This ninth-grade dropout had written a minor classic at twenty-nine years old (*Uncle Tom's Children*, 1938) and three major classics by the age of thirty-seven. (*Native Son*, 1940; *12 Million Black*

Voices, 1941; and *Black Boy*, 1945). Like his fellow Mississippian William Faulkner, who wrote *The Sound and the Fury* (1929) at thirty-two, Wright's self-made precocity was immense and undeniable. Yet unlike Faulkner, Wright's political views were direct and discernible. His secular conception of what it means to be a free human being always embraced political struggle for a just society and world. Similar to Enlightenment philosophes such as Diderot and Voltaire, Wright was first and foremost a cosmopolitan intellectual, a global man of letters, a Promethean figure in the life of the mind with international scope. His often overlooked nonfiction writings in the fifties—*Black Power* (1954), *The Color Curtain* (1956), *White Man Listen!* (1957), and *Pagan Spain* (1957)—confirm this highly deserved designation.

For Wright, to be a free human being meant to muster the courage to exercise one's critical intelligence in order to understand and change one's self and circumstances. His deep allegiance to intellectual candor and existential honesty yielded an unrelenting rootlessness and an empowering exilic consciousness. His principled rootlessness was inseparable from a transformative nonconformism that put a premium on critique and resistance to the powers that be. His exilic consciousness was driven by a countercultural and counterhegemonic orientation that refused the appropriations and seductions of any powers that be. For Wright, to be free was to be modern; to be modern was to make a radical disruption from a moribund past. Therefore, for him, to be deracinated with a courageous critical intelligence and a political commitment to justice was the highest badge of existential honor.

The three prose works in this indispensable collection are grand exemplars of Wright's existential journalism that reconstruct twentieth-century travel writings in light of his cosmopolitan deracination and political solidarity with oppressed people around the world. This peculiar paradox of his enactment of incessant global motions and his commitment to subaltern political movements produces its own rich insights and blindnesses. His fascinating reports on historic events in Africa and Asia, Ghana and Indonesia, cast a light on anti-imperial struggles in the middle of the turbulent twentieth century. And his Virgil-like role of guiding frightened and bewildered Europeans through the Inferno of their colonial possessions and legacies turns Joseph Conrad on his head. Now the colonized—as filtered through Wright's Western Enlightenment and Black gaze—look back at the colonizers with rage, resentment, and resiliency. Yet, in stark contrast to Frantz Fanon or Léopold Senghor, there is not an ounce of left romanticism or cultural sentimentalism in Wright. In his pioneering travel writings, his progressive secular humanism constitutes the lens through which he gazes at the colonizers and colonized. In short, he honestly acknowledges that he the traveler is the guide and measure of what we see and how we see. He wants us to see much and see through much owing to his deracinated and exilic perspective.

In his first book of travel writings, *Black Power: A Record of Reactions in a Land of Pathos* (1954), Wright explores the complex political and cultural dynamics of the decolonization of Ghana. His self-designated title of "Twentieth Century Western Man of Color" signifies his own oppositional stance against European imperialism and outsider status in Africa. Despite his claim and preference for rootlessness and aloneness, he never disavows his own experience of Black oppression and resistance. Hence, his personal struggle for identity and freedom is inseparable from, though never reducible to, the collective struggle for African dignity and liberty. He dedicates his book "to the unknown African," who though dehumanized by the Capitalist West created a vision of life "that was irreducibly human." His epigraphs are from two American poets, Countee Cullen (his famous query "What is Africa to me?") and Walt Whitman ("Not till the sun excludes you do I exclude you . . ."). His text ends with Whitman's praise of the slaves' revolt against American white supremacy and the American colonists' revolution against British colonialism.

As the exiled writer Chester Himes noted, "From beginning to end, deep in his soul, Dick identified with the poor and oppressed." Yet as in his powerful writings—fiction and nonfiction—on Black people in the United States, Wright loathed the white supremacy in Black people or internalized racism of subjugated peoples of color. He was convinced that freedom resided in a radical break from the premodern past for oppressed people. This fundamental belief led him to deploy what Anthony Appiah calls a "rhetoric of distance" that highlights a cultural chasm between the modern Wright and premodern Africans. This chasm is expressed in his basic claim that his Blackness does not help him understand Ghanaian thinking and feeling even given their Blackness. His candor shatters any romantic relation of Black Americans to Africans or sentimental attachments to African ways of life. Yet his frank distance also yields moments of Western condescension and modern revulsion at African bodies and religion. These problematic moments do not dehumanize Africans but they do blind him to the rich complexity of premodern Ghanaian culture and society. Again, as with his painful yet poignant critique of the Black American psyche, Wright holds that the African personality and mentality lacks a modern confidence requisite for the new industrial order. He hopes that President Kwame Nkrumah can bring Ghana into the modern world with dignity. Yet this must be done by sidestepping Western capitalism and Soviet communism. And what is this Third Way? He writes,

> **I'm speaking of a temporary discipline that will unite the nation, sweep out the tribal cobwebs, and place the feet of the masses upon a basis of reality. I'm not speaking of guns or secret police; I'm speaking of a method of taking people from one order of life and making them face what men, all men everywhere, must face.**

Wright calls for Nkrumah to feel free to improvise, industrialize, modernize, and militarize Ghana for peace, service, and production and "to free minds from mumbo-jumbo." He explicitly states that he opposes any form of "military dictatorship." Yet he also calls for a "firm social discipline" of "hardness" and "coldness" that builds a "bridge between tribal man and the twentieth century." The African path to modernity must create a "secular religion" that holds people together as they refuse to imitate the West or East.

> **Be on top of theory; don't let theory be on top of you. In short, be *free,* be a living embodiment of what you want to give your people. . . .**

Wright's controversial vision for Ghana is African in character and humanist in content. The African path to modernity must be experimental and improvisational yet it should be guided by Enlightenment ideals and humanist aspirations. As he notes in his introduction,

> **The Western world has one last opportunity in Africa to determine if its ideals can be generously shared, if it dares to act upon its deepest convictions. China has gone the desperate way of**

> **totalitarianism; India teeters on the brink; and now has come Africa's turn to test the ideals that the West has preached but failed to practice. . . .**

In *The Color Curtain* (1956), Wright examines the historic Bandung Conference in Jakarta, Indonesia (April 18–25, 1955) that brought together twenty-nine Asian and African nations intent on pursuing a Third Way. His epigraph is from the American poet Hart Crane's *The Bridge*—another gesture of decolonized peoples making the transition to modern freedom. Initially entitled *The Human Race Speaking*, the book shows Wright again attempting to lay bare a vision that goes "beyond Left and Right"—Soviet communism and Western imperialism—by counseling the nonaligned nations to confront race and religion equipped with global humanist ideals. His fascinating treatment of Carlos P. Romulo, chairman of the delegation from the Philippines, highlights the retarding effects of the white supremacy of Western imperialism on Asia and Africa as well as the liberating energy of Western ideas of science, political freedom, justice, and equality. For Wright, Third World unity pursuing a Third Way could possibly realize the grand humanist aspirations of the West—even as the practices of the West and East impeded this realization. In this way, *The Color Curtain* is a companion text for the much longer work *Black Power*.

The last of Wright's political travel writings—excluding his underappreciated book *Pagan Spain* (1957)—takes him back to Europe. Dedicated to Eric Williams, a public intellectual who became the leader of Trinidad and Tobago and to "the westernized and tragic elite of Asia, Africa, and the West Indies," *White Man, Listen!* (1957) posits exilic, rootless outsiders like Wright himself to be the guardians of freedom and caretakers of global humanist ideals. His epigraphs from the revolutionary poet William Blake and the melancholic poet Dylan Thomas set the tone for his defense of "that part of the heritage of the West that I value—man stripped of the past and free for the future." *White Man, Listen!* (1957) is a desperate plea for a racist West to turn to the "precious heritage—the freedom of speech, the secular state, the independent personality, the autonomy of science—which is not Western or Eastern, but human." The exilic outsiders enact a humanist tradition that builds on the best of the West and East.

> **For this elite in Asia and Africa constitutes islands of free men, the *FREEST MEN IN ALL THE WORLD TODAY*.**

Wright claims that "Europe missed the boat." So now the spirit of the Enlightenment that made Europe great is to be carried forward by courageous and compassionate rootless intellectuals of color like himself who must expose the lies of the West and East, speak the unpopular truths of our suffering world, and bear witness to justice for all. This grave prophetic role—often embodied in the work and life of poets—is the only hope for humankind. The longest chapter in the book—"The Literature of the Negro in the United States"—is a masterful and magisterial treatment of Black bards and poets whose humanist works are "rapidly becoming the most representative voice of America and of oppressed people anywhere in the world today."

The artistic genius and prophetic witness of Richard Wright—achieved at great cost and burden—is a grand example of his grandiloquent claim. The time is ripe to return to his vision and voice in the face of our contemporary catastrophes and hearken to his relentless commitment to freedom and justice for all.

Black Power

A Record of Reactions in a Land of Pathos

PRIME MINISTER
GOLD COAST

P.O. BOX 1627
ACCRA

TO WHOM IT MAY CONCERN:

This is to certify that I have known Mr. Richard Wright for many years, having met him in the United States.

Mr. Wright would like to come to the Gold Coast to do some research into the social and historical aspects of the country, and would be my guest during the time he is engaged in this work.

To the best of my knowledge and belief, I consider Mr. Wright a fit and proper person to be allowed to visit the Gold Coast for the reasons stated above.

Kwame Nkrumah,
Prime Minister.

Accra,
4th May, 1953.

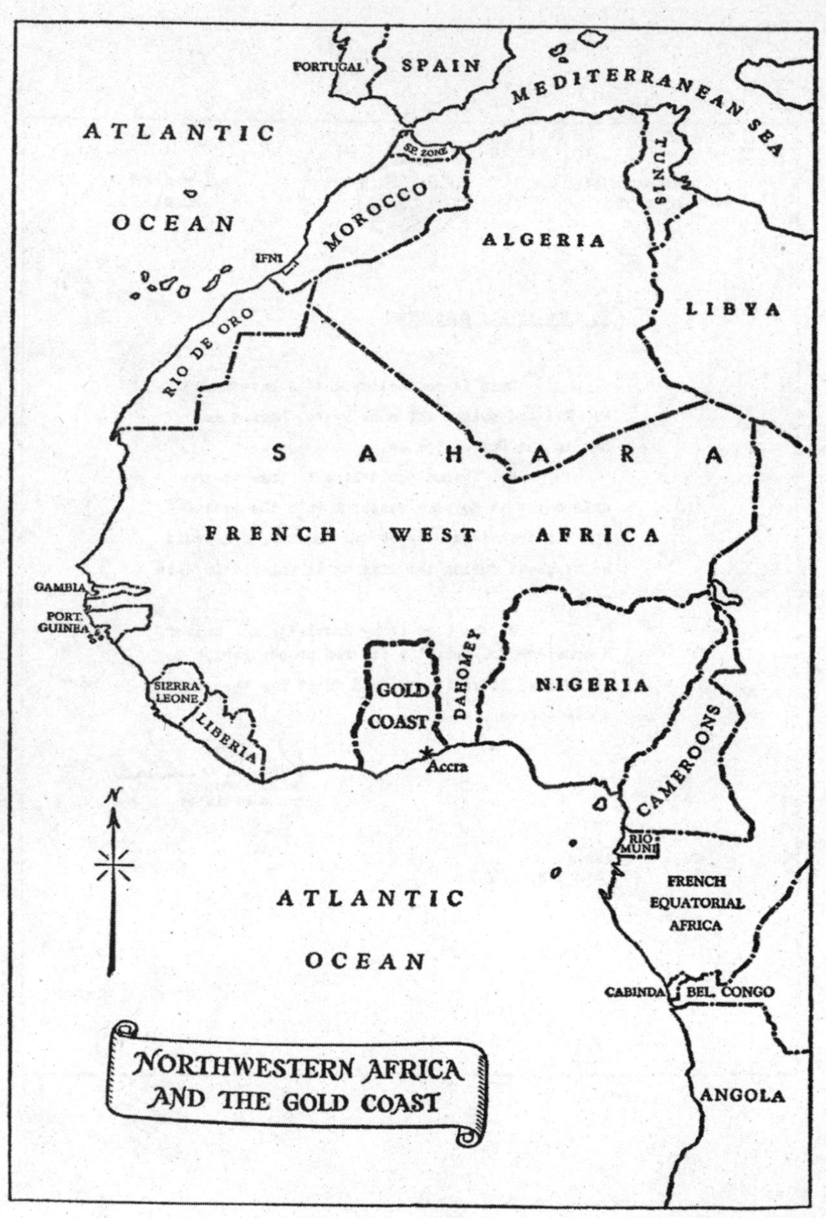

PORTUGAL
SPAIN
MEDITERRANEAN SEA
ATLANTIC
OCEAN
SP. ZONE
TUNIS
MOROCCO
ALGERIA
IFNI
LIBYA
RIO DE ORO
S A H A R A
FRENCH WEST AFRICA
GAMBIA
PORT. GUINEA
GOLD COAST
DAHOMEY
NIGERIA
SIERRA LEONE
LIBERIA
Accra
CAMEROONS
N
RIO MUNI
FRENCH EQUATORIAL AFRICA
ATLANTIC
OCEAN
CABINDA
BEL. CONGO
NORTHWESTERN AFRICA AND THE GOLD COAST
ANGOLA

To The Unknown African

who, because of his primal and poetic humanity, was regarded by white men as a "thing" to be bought, sold, and used as an instrument of production; and who, alone in the forests of West Africa, created a vision of life so simple as to be terrifying, yet a vision that was irreducibly human . . .

What is Africa to me:
Copper sun or scarlet sea,
Jungle star or jungle track,
Strong bronzed men, or regal black
Women from whose loins I sprang
When the birds of Eden sang?

One three centuries removed
From the scenes his fathers loved,
Spicy grove, cinnamon tree,
What is Africa to me?

—Countee Cullen

Not till the sun excludes you do I exclude you . . .

—Walt Whitman

The entire course of development of the human race, from whatever point of view it may be regarded, whether intellectual, economic, industrial, social, or ethical, is as a whole and in detail coincident with the course of transmitted social heredity.

—Robert Briffault

INTRODUCTION: APROPOS PREPOSSESSIONS

In today's intellectual climate—a climate charged with ideological currents in the service, paid or voluntary, of some nation, party, movement, or interest—it behooves a writer reporting in nonfictional terms on vital material to lay before the reader his working frame of reference, his assumptions and preoccupations. If the present writer were less serious or responsible, he would not be concerned about this, but since he knows that he is dealing with material out of which our destiny will partly be shaped, he is anxious to place himself in a position where the reader will have no doubts as to what he is up to.

During my lifetime I've witnessed a radical change engulf more than half of human society; some nations have disappeared and new ones have risen to take their places; some social classes have vanished and others have come into being. . . . These changes were not unexpected on my part; indeed, I labored to help bring them about. My belonging to a minority group whose gross deprivations pitched my existence on a plane of all but sheer criminality made these changes welcome to me. From 1932 to 1944 I was a member of the Communist Party of the United States of America and, as such, I held consciously in my hands Marxist Communism as an instrumentality to effect such political and social changes.

Today I am no longer a member of that party or a subscriber to its aims. Let it be said that my relinquishing of membership in that party was not dictated by outside pressure or interests; it was caused by my conviction that Marxist Communism, though it was changing the world, was changing that world in a manner that granted me even less freedom than I had possessed before. Perhaps, in time, I could have brought myself to accept this Communist suppression of freedom on a temporary basis, but when historic events disclosed that international Communism was mainly an instrument of Russian foreign policy, I publicly and responsibly dropped its instrumentality and disassociated myself from it.

Yet, as an American Negro whose life is governed by racial codes written into law, I state clearly that my abandonment of Communism does not automatically place me in a position of endorsing and supporting all the policies, political and economic, of the non-Communist world. Indeed, it was the inhuman nature of many of those policies, racial and otherwise, that led me to take up the instrumentality of Communism in the first place. . . .

Hence, the problem of freedom is still with me. The Communist instrumentality which I once held in my hands has built up a slave empire of 800,000,000 people; and the Western world, of which I am an uneasy member, has not materially altered many of its attitudes toward the aspirations of hundreds of millions of minority peoples caught by chance, time, and culture within its wide sway of power.

In this dilemma of a divided world one elementary fact stands out undeniably: the victories of the Communist instrumentalities were largely won by skilled Communist appeals to the Western sense of justice, by Communist exploitation of the thwarted traditional hopes of Western man. In fact, it can be definitely stated that Communist strength is predicated upon Western stupidity, moral obtuseness, foolish racial jealousies—of the abandonment by the West of its own ideals and pretensions. . . . ("Capitalistic contradictions," the Communists call it.)

If Western man has irrevocably decided that his record of dealing with the colored part of mankind is just and beyond criticism, that his way of life is perfect, that he has a godlike right to determine and time the development of mankind according to his own convenience, that his mere presence in this world is a blessing to the less fortunate, that he will make no meaningful concessions to the sense of justice and freedom which he himself helped to instill in men's hearts—if this is the stance of Western man, then the last and strongest weapon of the West has been voluntarily surrendered to the Communists, the most solid moral ground of the last two thousand years has been gratuitously vacated, and the chances of a Communist global victory thereby immeasurably enhanced.

The aim of this book is to pose this problem anew in an area of the world where the issue has not yet been decided, an area that is proving a decisive example for an entire continent. The Western world has one last opportunity in Africa to determine if its ideals can be generously shared, if it dares to act upon its deepest convictions. China has gone the desperate way of totalitarianism; India teeters on the brink; and now has come Africa's turn to test the ideals that the West has preached but failed to practice. . . .

Let me be honest; I'm not too hopeful. The Western world does not even yet quite know how hard and inhuman its face looks to those who live outside of its confines. One of the aims of this book is to show you that face in its characteristic historical expression, to show you that face in terms that maybe you can understand and recognize. I don't know. It may well already be too late. If you can feel that the person who presents these perhaps unwelcome facts to you does so with the desire of making you aware of your moral stance, of making you realize how others see and judge you, then you might read these lines with care.

In presenting this picture of a part of Africa, I openly use, to a limited degree, Marxist analysis of historic events to explain what has happened in this world for the past five hundred years or more. If anyone should object to my employment of Marxist methods to make meaningful the ebb and flow of commodities, human and otherwise, in the modern state, to make comprehensible the alignment of social classes in modern society, I have but to say that I'll willingly accept any other method of interpreting the facts; but I insist that any other method *must not exclude the facts*!

But my utilization of Marxist instrumentalities of thought does not necessarily commit me to programs or policies popularly associated with Marxist philosophy. The measures which I recommend at the end of this book do not derive from any programmatic theories of any political party. They are derived from my concern about human freedom, from what I know of the world, from what I saw and felt in Africa, and the concrete situation of the Convention People's Party of the Gold Coast.

This book seeks to provide Western readers with some insight into what is going to happen in Africa, so that, when it does happen, they will be able to understand it, so that they will not entertain the kind of illusions that held forth about China; my point is that if Africa today is in turmoil, it is not merely the omniscient hand of Moscow that is fomenting all the trouble; but that, given the harsh background of Africa and the numbing impact of the West that it has suffered, what is happening was bound to happen. Frankly, this current mania of ascribing *all* the world's unrest to Russian Communists simply credits the Russians with more intelligence than they actually possess.

The issue of who is to blame in a colonial nation that is determinedly actuated by Western ideals to throw off the yoke of foreign rule is a tricky one. The popular assumption is that colonial people are happy and that only evil foreign agents are stirring up strife, but the facts of life in the Gold Coast do not bear out such tortured contentions. Indeed, the greatest incentive to the growth of Communism in Africa today would be the attempt on the part of the West to throttle the rise of African nations; such an attempt at crushing African aspirations would drive the Africans straight down the road that China is so bloodily traveling. . . . That road began with Mau Mau.

The historical material in this book is drawn exclusively from bourgeois sources, if that is of any comfort to anybody. The interpretations of facts, their coloring and presentation, are my own, and, for whatever it is worth, I take full responsibility for them. And I think that time will bear me out.

This volume is a first-person, subjective narrative on the life and conditions of the Colony and Ashanti areas of the Gold Coast, an area comprising perhaps the most highly socially evolved native life of present-day Africa. The choice of selecting the Gold Coast for such an intensive study was my own and the judgments rendered are not comparative. I felt that it was time for someone to subject a slice of African life to close scrutiny in terms of concepts that one would use in observing life anywhere. Thus, some conclusions arrived at in these pages might well startle or dismay those who like to dote on "primitive" people. . . .

Africa challenges the West in a way that the West has not been challenged before. The West can meanly lose Africa, or the West can nobly save Africa; but whatever happens, make no mistake: THE WEST IS BEING JUDGED BY THE EVENTS THAT TRANSPIRE IN AFRICA!

RICHARD WRIGHT—PARIS: MAY, 1954

PART I

Approaching Africa

Only in one particular did the freedom accorded in the slave trade differ from the freedom accorded in other trades—the commodity involved was man.

ERIC WILLIAMS' *CAPITALISM AND SLAVERY*

One

The table had been cleared and the coffee was being poured. The Easter Sunday luncheon was almost over and we were stirring the sugar in our cups. It was so quiet that the footfalls from the tranquil Paris street below echoed upward. It was one of those moments when, for no reason, a spell of silence hangs in the air. I sipped my coffee and stared at the gray walls of the University of Paris that loomed beyond the window.

One of my guests, Dorothy, the wife of George Padmore, the West Indian author and journalist, turned to me and asked:

"Now that your desk is clear, why don't you go to Africa?"

The idea was so remote to my mind and mood that I gaped at her a moment before answering.

"*Africa*?" I echoed.

"Yes. The Gold Coast," she said stoutly.

"But that's four thousand miles away!" I protested.

"There are planes and ships," she said.

My eyes ranged unseeingly about the room. I felt cornered, uneasy. I glanced at my wife.

"Why not?" she said.

A moment ago I had been collected, composed; now I was on the defensive, feeling poised on the verge of the unknown.

"Africa!" I repeated the word to myself, then paused as something strange and disturbing stirred slowly in the depths of me. I am African! I'm of African descent. . . . Yet I'd never seen Africa; I'd never really known any Africans; I'd hardly ever thought of Africa. . . .

"Kwame Nkrumah, the Prime Minister, is going to table his motion for self-government in July," Dorothy said.

"It would be a great experience for you," my wife said.

I heard them, but my mind and feelings were racing along another and hidden track. *Africa*! Being of African descent, would I be able to feel and know something about Africa on the basis of a common "racial" heritage? Africa was a vast continent full of "my people." . . . Or had three hundred years imposed a psychological distance between me and the "racial stock" from which I had sprung? Perhaps some Englishman, Scotsman, Frenchman, Swede, or Dutchman had chained my great-great-great-great-grandfather in the hold of a slave ship; and perhaps that remote grandfather had been sold on an auction block in New Orleans, Richmond, or Atlanta. . . . My emotions seemed to be touching a dark and dank wall. . . . *But, am I African*? Had some of my ancestors sold their relatives to white men? What would my feelings be when I looked into the black face of an African, feeling that maybe his great-great-great-grandfather had sold my great-great-great-grandfather into slavery? Was there something in Africa that my feelings could latch onto to make all of this dark past clear and meaningful? Would the Africans regard me as a lost brother who had returned?

"Do you think that the Gold Coast will be self-governing soon?" I asked. I genuinely wanted to know about the political situation in the Gold Coast, yet another and far more important question was trying to shape itself in me. According to popular notions of "race," there ought to be something of "me" down there in Africa. Some vestige, some heritage, some vague but definite ancestral reality that would serve as a key to unlock the hearts and feelings of the Africans whom I'd meet. . . . But I could not feel anything African about myself, and I wondered, "What does being *African* mean . . . ?"

". . . and they are fighting for self-government," Dorothy was explaining. "It would be wonderful if you could be there when the first black Prime Minister in history asks the British for the freedom of his people."

"Yes," I said. "How long does it take to get there?"

"One day by plane and twelve days by ship," Dorothy said.

Was Africa "primitive"? But what did being "primitive" mean? I'd read books on "primitive" people, but, while reading them, their contents had always seemed somehow remote. Now a strange reality, in some way akin to me, was pressing close, and I was dismayed to discover that I didn't know how to react to it.

"Just what level of development have the people there reached?" I asked Dorothy.

"You must ask George about that," she said. "He's been there. . . . But you'll find their development mixed. You'll find Christians and pagans . . ."

"I want to see the pagans," I said impulsively.

"Why?" my wife asked.

"I know what a Christian African would have to say, but I don't know what paganism is—"

"It's *all* there," Dorothy said emphatically. "And if you're going to attend the session of the Legislative Assembly in which the Prime Minister will make his bid for freedom, you'd better see about passage."

"I'll go by ship, if I go," I said. "That would give me time enough to read up on the history of the country."

"You *must* go," my wife said.

The fortuity of birth had cast me in the "racial" role of being of African descent, and that fact now resounded in my mind with associations of hatred, violence, and death. Phrases from my childhood rang in my memory: one-half Negro, one-quarter Negro, one-eighth Negro, one-sixteenth Negro, one thirty-second Negro. . . . In thirty-eight out of the forty-eight states of the American Federal Union, marriage between a white person and a person of African descent was a criminal offense. To be of "black" blood meant being consigned to a lower plane in the social scheme of American life, and if one violated that scheme, one risked danger, even death sometimes. And all of this was predicated upon the presence of *African* blood in one's veins. How much of me was *African*? Many of my defensive-minded Negro friends had often told me with passion:

"We have a *special* gift for music, dancing, rhythm and movement. . . . We have a genius of our own. We were civilized in Africa when white men were still living in caves in Europe. . . ."

To me talk of that sort had always seemed beside the point; I had always taken for granted the humanity of Africans as well as that of other people. And being either uninterested or unable to accept such arguments, I'd always remained silent in such conversations. My kind of thinking was impotent when it came to explaining life in "racial" terms. On countless occasions I'd heard white men say to me:

"Now, you take the racial expression of the Negro . . ."

And I'd looked off uneasily, wondering what they meant. I was accounted as being of African, that is, Negro, descent, but what were these "racial" qualities that I was supposed to possess? While in the presence of those who talked confidently of "racial" qualities, I would listen and mull over their phrases, but no sooner had they gone than my mind would revert to my habitual kind of thinking that had no "race" in it, a kind of thinking that was conditioned by the reaction of human beings to a concrete social environment. And I'd ask myself:

"What are they talking about?"

Over the Easter Sunday luncheon table, I mapped out my voyage. I wanted to see this Africa that was posing such acute questions for me and was conjuring up in my mind notions of the fabulous and remote: heat, jungle, rain, strange place names like Cape Coast, Elmina, Accra, Kumasi. . . . I wanted to see the crumbling slave castles where my ancestors had lain panting in hot despair. The more I thought of it, the more excited I became, and yet I could not rid myself of a vague sense of disquiet.

I excused myself from the table and consulted the Encyclopaedia Britannica and the description of the Gold Coast it gave was vivid, replete with dangerous reptiles, gold, and diamonds. There were only three short paragraphs about the people who were described as being of the "Negro race." The Gold Coast was about four degrees from the Equator and teemed with mineral and agricultural wealth. I returned to the table.

"Do you think I'll have any trouble getting in?"

"You'd better apply for your visa at once," Dorothy advised. "If you have any trouble, get in touch with the Prime Minister. Meanwhile, George'll tell Nkrumah that you want to come. . . ."

"Just what's the setup in the Gold Coast? Are foreign affairs in the hands of the British?"

"Yes; and finance and the police too," she said.

"And the rest of the cabinet ministers are African?"

"Yes."

"I'm going," I said. It was decided.

Two

On the platform of Euston Station in London I saw swarms of Africans, Western in manner and dress, for the first time. The boat-train compartment in which I sat was cold and I huddled in my macintosh, longing for my heavy coat which was packed in my trunk. Outside the train window the landscape was as bleak as any described by D. H. Lawrence or Arnold Bennett or George Moore. . . . I drifted to sleep, then I was awakened by the train jolting, slowing. I looked out of the window and saw Liverpool. . . .

This was the city that had been the center and focal point of the slave trade; it was here that most of the slavers had been organized, fitted out, financed, and dispatched with high hopes on their infamous but lucrative voyages. Suffice it to say that the British did not originate this trading in human flesh whose enormous profits laid the foundations upon which had been reared modern industrial England. The honor for the launching of that crusade against Africa rested upon the pious shoulders of the Portuguese who had had the right, under a papal bull of 1455, to subject to servitude all infidel peoples. Later it fell to the daring of the English to rear that trade into a system whose functionings would in some manner touch more than half of the human race with its bloody but profitable agitations—the consequences of which would endure for more than four hundred years.

In dredging through books for material on the background of the Gold Coast, I purposefully confined my reading to the historical facts presented by the British themselves, many of whom, like Sir Alan Burns, Eric Williams, W. E. Ward, and K. A. Busia, etc., are still living and active. I found that though the British might at times be guilty of a kind of intriguing understatement, they never hid facts, even when those facts contradicted their own moral notions. The sketchy backdrop which follows came not from Socialist or Marxian, but from conservative British sources.

The search for short sea routes, the thirst for gold and spices, and Columbus' discovery of the New World set in motion international economic rivalries that have not subsided even to this day. I've often wondered why the assault upon Africa was called "imperialism" even by ardent revolutionaries, why such a mild word as "exploitation" was ever used to describe it. The simple truth is that it consisted of a many-centuries-long war waged by the peninsula of Europe, with the sanction of Catholicism, against the continent of Africa. In that campaign the odds were on the side of the superior organization and technical development of white Europe which, when pitted in war against the fragility of an essentially agricultural and tribal people, smashed those people, dealt them a blow from which they have never recovered. Indeed, so unimportant were Africa's millions deemed that no real account of that long campaign was ever fully or properly recorded.

True, forms of rigorous servitude existed even among European whites when the slave trade was launched, and, in those days, Liverpool had had but a modest share of it. Yet, there existed in England the conditions, the attitudes, and the impulses which would easily lend themselves with passion to the slave trade. The first slaves to toil for Europeans in the New World were not Negroes, but the indigenous Indians who, alas, were found to be temperamentally unsuited for arduous labor under tropic suns, and new sources of human instruments had to be sought. The next experiment in harnessing human beings to the plantations of the New World involved poor white indentured servants and convicts, and, during the sixteenth and seventeenth centuries, the word "convict" had a meaning that conveniently covered a wide area of people.

There existed a widespread system of kidnaping men, women, and children and spiriting them aboard ships bound for the colonies of the New World. England's feudal laws recognized three hundred capital crimes, and an Englishman could be hanged for picking a pocket of more than three shillings. Guided more by a sharp eye for the needs of the colonies than by humanitarian motives, many Englishmen, from 1664 to 1667, prayed for transportation to the colonies instead of death for those who stole more than four shillings' worth of goods, a silver spoon, or a gold watch. So vast and steady was the spawn that Newgate and Bridewell dumped upon the shores of the New World, especially in New York, Pennsylvania, Virginia, Georgia, etc., that even Benjamin Franklin protested.

But whence the ascendancy of Liverpool in this trade? With Spain and Portugal advancing conflicting claims to the newly discovered territories, the Pope stepped in, in 1493, and issued a series of papal bulls which gave the East to Portugal and the West to Spain. But the always protesting Anglo-Saxons were in no mood to recognize the right of even a Pope to divide up the world as he wished, and the English, the Dutch, the Swedes, the Germans, and finally even the French would accept no such papal edicts as binding. Every son of Adam felt he had a God-given right to share in the human loot—and share he did.

Slavery was not put into practice because of racial theories; racial theories sprang up in the wake of slavery, to justify it. It was impossible to milk the limited population of Europe of enough convicts and indentured white servants to cultivate, on a large and paying scale, colonial sugar, cotton, and tobacco plantations. Either they had to find a labor force or abandon the colonies, and Europe's eyes turned to Africa where the supply of human beings seemed inexhaustible. So the process of stealing or buying Africans to work the lands bought or stolen from the Indians got under way. . . .

If the Europeans were cruel to the infidel Africans, they were not much less cruel to their own Christian brothers. The African simply inherited a position already occupied by indentured white servants and criminals, and the nightmare called the Middle Passage—the voyage from Africa to the West Indies or America—had long been made by declassed Anglo-Saxons from England to America, and they'd been packed like herring in the holds of ships. . . . The tenure of the indentured servant was limited; for the African, this limitation was waived and he was bound for life. But, when the indentured white servant was eventually freed and settled on his own land, he found his lot doomed by the ever-increasing hordes of African slaves whose output reduced the conditions of his life to that of a debased class whose aims were feared by the slave-owning aristocracy. The plantation owners and the moneyed men of the mother country regarded these newly freed whites as constituting a threat in two directions: they didn't want those poor whites to advance claims for democratic rights which no colonial society could possibly tolerate; and the budding manufacturing interests of England feared that the rootless whites would turn to manufacturing and become their competitors. Thanks to slavery, the poor whites of the New World were retarded for more than two centuries in their efforts to gain political and social recognition, and it was not until the Civil War in America abolished slavery, thereby enthroning industrial production as the new way of life, that it could be said that the New World had had any real need of poor white people at all. . . .

The kidnaping of poor whites, developed in England, had but to be extended to the African shoreline and the experience gained in subjugating the poor whites served admirably for the taming of the tribal blacks. A hungry cry for sugar rose from all Europe, and blacks were siphoned from Africa to grow the cane. The colonial plantation became an economic and political institution that augmented wealth and power for a few aristocrats, spread misery for countless blacks, and imperiled the democratic hopes of millions of whites.

Eric Williams reports in his *Capitalism and Slavery* that the Stuart monarchy entrusted the slave trade to the Company of Royal Adventurers Trading to Africa, and these gentlemen, in 1663, incorporated themselves for a period of one thousand years! Hitler's clumsy dreams were picayune when compared with the sanguine vision of these early English Christian gentlemen. . . . The African trading companies were regarded not only as commercial enterprises, but as training schools for all those who wished to deal in slaves and African matters. The scheme, bold in scope and daring in design, enabled the English to establish a monopoly to steal or buy slaves from the Straits of Gibraltar to the Cape of Good Hope, unload British-manufactured goods in Africa, sell the slaves to the planters in the West Indies or America; they then would load their empty ships with plantation produce to keep the growing mills of England busy. It was foolproof; you couldn't lose. . . . The human bodies involved in this circular trade were incidental; it was just trade. . . . Of course, the colonial planters complained of the quality of the goods and the prices exacted by the English, just as the Africans complain today, but what could they do?

In 1698, however, this monopoly was broken and the right of free trade in slaves was equated to the natural rights of all Englishmen, and the English not only stocked their own colonial plantations with slaves but managed to supply black human beings to their imperialist rivals as well.

But Liverpool . . . ? Though London and Bristol exceeded Liverpool in importance as a slave port in 1755, Liverpool quickly forged ahead and, between 1783 and 1793, 878 Liverpool ships carried 303,737 slaves whose sterling value has been estimated as being over fifteen million pounds. This trade was a sky-dropped bonanza to the English, for it was conducted in terms of exchanging English manufactured goods for slaves whose sale in the West Indies and America supplied England with raw materials. English bullion had not to be touched to keep this vast circular movement going. Until 1783 the whole of English society, the monarchy, church, state, and press backed and defended this trade in slaves.

Out of the welter of this activity English mercantile ideas and practices grew up; a classic concept of a colony emerged and has endured more or less until this day: colonies are areas to be kept economically disciplined and dependent upon the mother country. Colonists were obliged to ship their produce to England in English bottoms, and they could buy no goods but English goods unless those goods had first been shipped to England. A colony, therefore, became a vast geographical prison whose inmates were presumably sentenced for all time to suffer the exploitation of their human, agricultural, and mineral resources. Then, as well as now, no native industry was tolerated; everything from sugar to shoes was shipped from the mother country, taxed by colony customs; and, after it had passed through many hands, it was sold to the native to enable him to enjoy the blessings of Christendom.

Once slavery had become a vested interest in Liverpool, its importance stretched far beyond the mere buying and selling of slaves. Britain's merchant navy was nursed and reared in the slave trade; her seamen were trained in it; shipbuilding in England was stimulated by this trade in flesh. . . . And Liverpool itself flourished. Eric Williams' *Capitalism and*

Slavery relates that: "In 1565 Liverpool had 138 householders, seven streets only were inhabited, the port's merchant marine amounted to twelve ships of 223 tons. Until the end of the 17th Century the only local event of importance was the sieging of the town during the English Civil War. In collecting ship money Strafford assessed Liverpool at fifteen pounds; Bristol paid two thousand. The shipping entering Liverpool increased four and one half times between 1709 and 1771; the outward tonnage six and a half times. The number of ships owned by the port multiplied four times during the same period, the tonnage and sailors over six times. Customs receipts soared from an average of £51,000 for the years 1757 to £648,000 in 1785 . . ."

In 1790 the abolition of the slave trade would have ruined Liverpool; her estimated loss from abolition was then computed at over seven and a half million pounds. Profits from the slave trade built Liverpool docks; the foundations of the city were built of human flesh and blood. . . .

Yet, how calm, innocent, how staid Liverpool looked in the June sunshine! What massive and solidly built buildings! From my train window I could catch glimpses of a few church spires punctuating the horizon. Along the sidewalks men and women moved unhurriedly. Did they ever think of their city's history? I recalled once having asked a lower-class Englishwoman what she thought of the colonies, and she had sucked in her breath and had told me:

"I'm sorry, but they'll have to go it on their own. We've bled ourselves white to feed them, to lift them up; now they've got to stand on their own feet. We've had enough of carrying them on our shoulders."

I went through immigration, customs; I was the only American on board. Despite the sunny sky, it was cold. I stood on deck and stared at the city. What a drably respectable face on this city that had had such a past. . . .

At five o'clock I heard a long, dull blast and felt the ship easing out to sea, heading, as thousands of English ships before her, toward African waters. . . . In those days those ships had carried cotton and linen goods, silks, coarse blue and red woolen cloths for togas, guns, powder, shot, sabers, iron and lead bars, hardware of all kinds, copper kettles, glittering beads, masses of cheap ornaments, whiskey, and tobacco. The cargo in the hold was not terribly different even today. Only this time there were no handcuffs, chains, fetters, whips. . . .

The dogged English had lost thousands of men, as seamen and soldiers, seeking gold and slaves in the hot climate of West Africa, and yet they'd kept sending their boys. Was it imagination or lack of it? Now that mercantilism was dead and industrialization was the cock of the walk, what would the English do with their colonies? What would they do with a surplus of 20,000,000 too many Englishmen reared on the easy profits of selling manufactured goods to backward peoples? Even Argentina today was industrializing herself and had but little need for English goods. The art of manufacture was no longer a secret, and machines had a nigger-loving way of letting even black hands operate them. Africans were talking boldly of hydroelectric plants and the making of aluminum. . . . True, the British could help technically in all of this, but British aid was timed by the capacity of Africans to absorb techniques which the world today knew could be mastered by anybody. . . .

Three

Next morning a steward seated me at a table at which sat a tall, slightly bald African. We exchanged greetings and he introduced himself as Justice Thomas of the Nigerian Supreme Court.

"You're American?" he asked.

"Yes."

"First trip to Africa?"

"Yes."

"You know, my grandfather was a slave in the West Indies," he told me. "He'd been stolen from Africa and sold. He managed to make his way back to Africa and he settled in Freetown. He was a Christian and gave his children an education."

"That's interesting," I said.

"My ideas are Left," he told me and waited.

That sounded strange to me. If you are a Leftist, you act it, you don't talk it. And I knew that I'd been farther Left than he'd ever dream of going. I nodded and waited.

"I believe in doing things for the masses, but it must be done with dignity," he told me. "I'm pro-British and pro-African. I'm for the United States."

"Uh hunh," I said and waited.

"You're going to the Gold Coast?"

"Yes."

"What do you think of Nkrumah?" he asked me.

"I don't know. I'm going down to find out," I said.

He launched into a description of one of his most recent cases; it seemed that he had presided at a trial of nineteen men and that he had sentenced them to long prison terms.

"Who were these men and what had they done?" I asked.

"They were Africans and they'd engaged in violent actions against the government," he told me. "By the way, what do you do?"

"I write," I said.

"What do you know about Communism?" he asked me.

"I was a member of the Communist Party of the United States for twelve years," I told him.

He blinked, sighed, and shook his head.

"Are you a Communist now?"

"No."

"Why did you leave?"

"I embraced Communism because I felt it was an instrumentality to help free the Negroes in America," I explained to him. "But, in time, I found that instrumentality degrading. I dropped it of my own accord. I was not driven out; I was not frightened out of Communism by American government agents. I left under my own steam. I was prompted to leave by my love of freedom. My attitude toward Communism is a matter of public record."

As breakfast ended, he hauled from his pockets several bottles of garlic tablets, yeast pills, and vitamin capsules; he was an ardent follower of Gayelord Hauser, blackstrap molasses and all. He continued to talk ramblingly, leaping from subject to subject. I listened.

"That Nkrumah's done a great job," he told me. "I know his secret. He embraced the masses. One neglects the masses at one's peril. . . . What do you think?"

"Embracing the masses seems to be a habit with politicians today," I said.

"You wouldn't mind if I asked that you be assigned to my table, would you?" he asked me.

"Not at all," I said. "It'd be a pleasure."

After breakfast I sat on the cold deck, mulling over Justice Thomas as the ship rolled gently through a wind-swept, leaden sea. I'd been told that we'd not find any warm weather for three days. The deck was quiet; the ship seemed to be settling down for a long run. The passengers were restrained, English, and so was the food.

At lunch, after we had greeted each other, Justice Thomas proclaimed:

"You see, we Freetowners have been in contact with Europe for a long time. We are called Creoles. It's from us that the English draw their best African leaders, teachers, doctors, lawyers. If we didn't have the help of the English, we'd be swamped by the natives in Sierra Leone. We in the Colony are but a handful, about 100,000, and the tribal people number almost 2,000,000. Against such numbers, we few literates rule by prescriptive right. It's not democratic; we don't pretend it is. What happened in the Gold Coast will never happen in Sierra Leone. No, sir! No tribal rabble will sweep us out of our positions!"

"Look, just what do you think of the tribal Africans?" I asked him.

"I like to live well," he said, grinning and looking at me frankly. "I love good food, good whiskey. . . . These natives running naked in the bush—" His nostrils wrinkled in disgust. "You don't know Africa." He lifted his right hand and cupped it to my ear and whispered: "There are men in Nigeria who still enjoy human flesh—"

"Cannibals?" I asked.

"God, yes," he assured me solemnly. "They are not ready for freedom yet. This business of having five and six wives . . . It's barbarous. I chose one wife and I stick to her. I can support more than one, but I want only one. I could have followed my people's customs, but I wanted to rise out of the mire. The British did *not* make me a Justice of the Supreme Court of Nigeria because they liked my black skin. They did it because of what I've got up here. . . ." He tapped his balding skull. "When Thomas sits on a case, the British know that it's useless to appeal against it. When a man appeals against a decision of mine, the British ask: 'Who tried that case?' If the answer is: 'Thomas,' the British will say: 'The decision is sound, for Thomas is a sound man.'" He laughed with self-satisfaction. "I know my English law. The British are hard but fair, and they trust me."

"Do you ever think of developing your country?" I asked him.

"No; my talent doesn't run in that direction," he said.

"What professions will your children follow?"

"Law and medicine," he said promptly.

"Suppose your son wanted to be a mining engineer. . . ."

"That would be difficult," he admitted.

"That's why we drove the English out of America," I told him. "Mr. Justice, it all depends upon how free you want to be. I'm neither anti- nor pro-British, but if I lived under British rule and wanted to develop and exercise my natural and acquired powers and the British said no, I'd be anti-British. Tell me, do you believe that the American colonies were right in taking their independence?"

He grinned at me.

"It's not the same thing," he said. "We are different. These boys in Africa want to go *too* fast. You and I have been in touch with the Western world for two, three hundred years—"

"Say, you know, if you were not black, I'd say that you were an Englishman. In fact, you are more English than many English I've met," I told him.

Reactions flickered across his face; then he decided to laugh.

"I *am* English," he said.

"But you cannot live like the English," I reminded him.

"What do you mean?"

"Do you have the British constitution in Sierra Leone?"

"No; but—"

"Why not?"

"They are not *ready*!"

"What do you call *ready*? Are people civilized and ready to govern themselves when they become so desperate that they put a knife at the throat of their rulers? Must the native rulers of all of Britain's colonies be graduates from prisons?"

He rubbed his chin and grinned at me. "But it mustn't go *too* fast," he mumbled stubbornly.

"Who's to time this development?" I asked.

We had reached an impasse. As we ate I looked past his shoulder and he looked past mine. We were still friendly, but we knew that we could not agree. It was not ideology that separated us, but fundamental attitudes toward life.

"I like Americans," he said as he left the table; there was something wistful in his eyes.

Four

We were in the Bay of Biscay and the ship pitched and rolled; I liked that, for it made me feel that I was really on the ocean. Heaving seas and tossing ships never made me ill. I always pictured in my mind the ship lurching forward and I could see the prow dipping, churning the sea, throwing up spray and foam as it lunged forward; and then I knew that the stern had to lift and, at the same moment, I knew that the huge ship had to roll to the right and I could feel it tilting—seeing it in my mind's eye—and then feeling the weight of the water of the ocean resisting and forcing it back into an upright position which it would hold for a moment, perilously balancing itself in the sliding waters; and I would wait for the ship to roll in the opposite direction, to the left; and I'd know that this same motion would have to be repeated endlessly, and I agreed with it, identifying myself with the ship and visualizing all of its motions as being necessary and natural, even when the pitching and rolling accompanied each other. . . .

That afternoon the sun came out for the first time and the sea turned from slaty gray to green; we were getting into deep waters.

It was my first voyage on a ship so purely English. With the exception of a Syrian or two, a German, some Africans, and a few vague Mediterranean nationalities, the ship's passengers were mostly men and women going to Africa to assume civil service jobs or returning from a few months' leave in England. Dull, repressed, stolidly English, they spent most of their days playing cards, ping-pong, or drinking. They were a mediocre lot to administer the destinies of millions of blacks. . . .

Each morning on deck, each Englishman had a cheery "Good morning," but evidently such a greeting exhausted him, for he'd remain taciturn for the rest of the day. It was just as well, for it was the Africans that I really wanted to talk to.

When I went up on deck Sunday morning for a stroll, I passed the forward foyer and heard that Anglo-Saxon, nasalized singing of psalms that had been so long familiar to my ears. A Church of England service was being conducted and, discreetly peering through the half-transparent curtains, I could see rows of white and black faces, heads lifted, mouths opened, giving praises to God. Several times I traversed the deck in order to observe without offending; I was curious as to how Africans and Englishmen served the same God.

I saw black faces well mixed with the white, which meant that, in confronting God, they drew no color line. I'd always accepted a Jim Crow Holy Ghost as being rather natural, indeed, inevitable; for, if God had entrusted the running of this earth to the white man, then He did so to prepare us all for the Jim Crow social stratification of life beyond the grave. Heaven had a color line and that was why white men, staunch Christians, reflected so much racial bias in their daily dealing with their fellow blacks. . . .

But why had the British drawn no color line in matters mystical and metaphysical? Upon reflection, however, I discovered that the British could not, in a black continent, draw a color line in religious matters and prove that God was a common Father. Jim Crow religious services would surely defeat the aims, economic, cultural, and political of *Pax Britannica*. So, on Sundays, the redeemed infidels stood shoulder to shoulder with their white masters to sing praises to "Him from whom all blessings flow . . ."

Upon the ship as a whole there was no color line, and yet it was strange how the English and Africans, after having closed ranks to acknowledge God on Sundays, kept more or less to themselves on weekdays. I didn't detect any desire on the part of the British to avoid the Africans; indeed, it was the other way around. The Africans, mostly returning students, were distant, reserved with the British. I learned later in Africa that they not only didn't yearn for the company of the British, but wanted them as far away from Africa as possible; they spoke their white tutors' language with an accent, entertained British values with self-consciousness, and seemed definitely to prefer the company of their own tribal folk to that of their alien overseers.

At lunch the judge remarked casually:

"I didn't see you at service this morning."

"That's right."

"Everyone is welcome, you know."

"I don't profess any religion," I said.

He stared at me. I don't think that he quite knew how to accept that; I doubted if he'd ever heard anybody say anything like that before in his life.

"You are an atheist then?"

"I couldn't even qualify for that. I'm nothing in matters religious."

"What reasons do you give for rejecting God?"

"I don't reject or accept Him."

"Who do you think made the world?"

"I don't know. *Must* I know that?"

"But how do you account for all of this—" He waved his hand to include the ship and the vast ocean beyond it.

"Look, Mr. Justice, please don't tell me that this universe is a kind of watch and that somebody just *had* to make it," I chided him, laughing.

"No; I wasn't going to say that," he smiled.

"I'm not proud, scornful, or anything like that. I just don't know and I don't feel compelled to say that I know about God," I told him.

"You have attended church services?"

"How could I have ever escaped such in my youth?"

"I don't know what I'd do if I didn't pray to God sometimes," he said.

"What do you tell God in your prayers?" I asked him.

"About myself, my worries—"

"Did you ever discuss the white man with God?"

He laughed.

"You are funny!" he said.

"You're funny too," I said. "If I prayed to God, that would be the first thing I'd take up with Him. Especially if I were an African. You see, I'm practical—"

"But don't you think that the African has been improved by accepting Christianity?"

"He's certainly more docile," I said.

That shook him, but he managed to confess:

"I don't doubt it."

Five

As we sailed from Freetown I saw my first real tropical sunset. From the blue-gray waters of the sea and the hills of Sierra Leone there rose a purplish mist that melted into the yellow and red and gold of the clouds that spread themselves for miles along the horizon. The dropping sun proclaimed itself in a majestic display of color that possessed an unearthly and imperious nobility, inducing the feeling that one had just finished hearing the dying, rolling peal of a mighty organ whose haunting chords still somehow lingered on in the form of those charged and spangled lances of somber fire. The ship sliced its way through a sea that was like still, thick oil, a sea that stretched limitless, smooth, and without a break toward a murky horizon. The ocean seemed to possess a quiet but persistent threat of terror lurking just beneath the surface, and I'd not have been surprised if a vast tidal wave had thrust the ship skyward in a sudden titanic upheaval of destruction.

As I watched the sea and the sky I knew that it was from feelings such as these floating in me now that man had got his sense of God, for, when such feelings stated themselves in him, he felt that some powerful but invisible spirit was speaking to him; and he fell on his face, asking to be saved from the emotion that claimed him, afraid, not so much of the sea or the sky, but of the fantastic commotion that bubbled in his heart. But I stood still, detached, watching the sea and the sky and at the same time hearing the echoing declarations that they roused in me. . . .

These feelings I do not deny, and I've not been the first to feel them. I do not know why they are such as they are, what they really mean, but I stand before them with the same attention that I stand before this sea and this sky. I refuse to make a religion out of that which I do not know. I too can feel the limit of my reactions, can feel where my puny self ends, can savor the terror of it; but it does not make me want to impose that sense of my terror on others, or rear it into a compulsive system. Detached, I contain my terror, look at it and wonder about it in the same way that I marvel about this sea and sky.

The sunset dies and is gone; I can no longer see it; I can only feel the feeling of wonder that still lives in me.

I admit the reality of the feeling; but I would not rig up devious forms of sacrifice to rid myself of it, for that would be the surest way of stifling it, killing it for all time.

At last, tropic weather. A blue horizon. Balmy breezes. A hot sun. The rustle of water filled the air as the ship glided forward through southern seas.

Night fell swiftly and overhead the stars, huge and chaste, glimmered faintly. One could now smell the sea.

I awakened one morning and looked out of my porthole and saw, looming through a warm mist, the Canary Islands. I shaved, showered, dressed, and went up on deck. Mr. Justice sauntered smilingly toward me, attired in tropic finery.

"Good morning!" he boomed. "Let's go ashore. . . ."

"Do you know Las Palmas?" I asked.

"Like the palm of my hand."

"All right," I said.

After breakfast the ship docked and the judge and I descended the gangplank.

"Once, when I was passing through Las Palmas," the judge rambled, "somebody offered to take me to a house of prostitution."

"Did you go?"

"I refused," Mr. Justice said with moral indignation. "I never let anybody take me to places like that. Things like that are to be found by yourself. I pity the man who can't find a woman."

I blinked, trying to keep abreast of his strange moral notions. Another African passenger joined us; he lived in the Gold Coast, but he'd been born in Togoland. I noticed that he was intimidated in the august presence of Mr. Justice, but he didn't seem to mind me. I was an American and he knew that I drew no class lines. This chap—I'll call him Mr.

Togoland—was careful at all times to walk just a few steps behind Mr. Justice, not to interrupt him as he handed down his lofty opinions, and to pay deference to his every move. We hired a taxi.

"Where're we going?" Mr. Togoland asked.

"I don't know," I said.

The driver turned and jabbered in Spanish, then grinned and drew with his palms the imaginary outlines of a plump woman-shape.

"Gurrls?" he asked in a thick accent.

"What do you say, Mr. Justice?" I asked.

Mr. Justice turned to Mr. Togoland and asked:

"You want to meet some girls?"

"Where?" Mr. Togoland asked.

"In a house," the judge said.

Mr. Togoland was a YMCA official and he looked at me and grinned.

"I'd like to *see* some," he ventured timidly. "Just to look at."

"I'll accompany you gentlemen," I said. "But I'm *only* looking. I didn't come thousands of miles to pick up diseases from Spanish women in the Canary Islands."

"Let's go then!" the judge shouted.

He was uneasy; he had changed his role and he was not certain as to how I was taking it. He placed his hand in a fatherly manner on my shoulder as the taxi bumped along in the bright sunshine.

"You know," the judge floated on, "my father used to make many trips here for business. In those days it was usual for a man to leave his calling card with the madam in a house of prostitution."

"Leave his calling card? Why?" I asked.

"That was to show other customers that only men of distinction went there," Mr. Justice explained.

"But I don't have any calling cards," I told him.

"You don't understand. Let me tell you a personal story," Mr. Justice said, relaxing, smiling. "Years ago, when I was a young man, I went into one of those houses. When I presented my card, the madam said: 'Why, your name is familiar to me. Wait a moment; I'll find a card with a name on it like yours. . . .' The madam pulled out from a closet a big glass bowl in which calling cards were kept. She fished around in it and a few minutes later she pulled out my father's calling card, all yellow and dusty—"

"No kidding," I protested.

"On my honor, she did," Mr. Justice swore. "Boy, oh, boy, was I proud!"

"A kind of following in your father's footsteps," I suggested.

"Yes! That's it exactly," he said and went into guffaws of laughter.

The taxi pulled up in front of a pale green cement house; the driver got out and rapped twice on a door panel—that, no doubt, was a signal. Well, I told myself, I'm a stranger, but I feel pretty safe in the presence of a judge of the Nigerian Supreme Court. No one will dare to pick my pocket in there; if they do, they'll find themselves tangling with the majesty of British jurisprudence. . . .

We were admitted by a squat, ugly woman. Nobody in our group spoke Spanish and I tried French.

"We want to drink some beer and talk to the girls," I told her.

She was more than agreeable; she let us in and ran down a dim hallway, knocking on doors and calling out girls' names. Mr. Justice, Mr. Togoland, and I sat down. In fifteen minutes twenty girls of all ages and sizes and personalities filed in sleepily, ranged themselves obligingly along the walls and looked at us with detached and casual eyes. I saw white matter at the edges of their eyelids and their faces appeared as though in dire need of a good wash. They yawned, but when our eyes caught theirs, they smiled shyly. The linoleum floor was littered with cigarette butts and a stale odor hung in the air. Some of the girls squatted on the floor; they wore thin pajamas but had no brassières. They asked for cigarettes and we passed some around. We drank, talked, joked, the madam doing the translating.

I watched Mr. Justice's eyes roving greedily among the girls.

"Don't let me cramp your style, Mr. Justice," I whispered to him.

"Oh, I'm happy," he said, laughing.

"Do what you want to do," I told him.

In comparison with the self-conscious stodginess of the British ship, this whorehouse was a citadel of simplicity, honesty, and straightforwardness. How relaxed everyone was! Even the haunting specter of Communism was absent. Since there was no need here of pretense or lying, one could afford to allow one's human impulses to come to the fore. It occurred to me that this shabby whorehouse was perhaps the only calm and human spot in this strongly entrenched Catholic city of Las Palmas where Franco's Fascism was in blatant evidence on so many billboards. . . . And perhaps these lost and sinful girls, pretty and always receptive, were the only free people in the entire islands. . . . Without doubt they were the only real democrats within reach. They were genial and they accepted everybody regardless of race, creed, or color; that is, for a price. . . . While we were talking and drinking, a black sailor came in and one of the girls rose promptly to serve him, taking him down the hall to a room.

Mr. Justice was nervous; he crossed and uncrossed his long legs. He drummed his tense fingers on the arm of the sofa. Too many wheat germs, I thought. At times he gazed thoughtfully at the ceiling, as though pondering some tricky point of law. Mr. Togoland's eyes shone as he looked from girl's face to girl's face, then glanced at their breasts which were like dim shadows under their sheer pajama tops. We ordered another round of beer and, as Mr. Justice tilted back his head to drink, I glanced shyly at him. When my eye caught his, he bent suddenly forward and laughed so loud and long that he spluttered beer spray across the room.

The girls were excited at his odd behavior and wanted to know what he was laughing at. I shook my head, knowing that moral subtleties of that genre were much too abstruse for prostitutes, no matter how generous they were.

"You are a knockout," Mr. Justice said to me, simpering.

"You are a killerdiller," I told him.

"It's wonderful being with you," he said.

"The pleasure is all mine," I said.

I knew that he was hotly longing to make a serious approach to one of the girls, but, out of deference to me—or was it the moral attitudes with which he had hemmed himself in during the past few days that was inhibiting him?—he was afraid to act and be himself. I could have easily put him at his ease, could have spoken a sentence and released him from the high-flown sentiments of honor and Christianity and he could have done what he wanted to do, but I was perverse enough to make him sit there on top of his platitudes and grin nervously. After all, I thought, it would certainly boost his chances in the other world if he could find enough self-control to forgo his impulse toward animal pleasure. And, if he persisted in building up his façade of pretense, if he must continuously fling Christianity and imperialism in my face, then let him squirm and wriggle a bit on the hook of his own hypocrisy—and that's exactly what he did. Every time he worked up enough spunk to start pawing one of the dusty-skinned Spanish girls, I'd look at him intently, reminding him with a reproving glance of his august position as a defender of British and Christian values, and he'd throw himself back on the sofa, slap his thighs, and let out a storm of embarrassed laughter. And I joined in his laughter, laughing at his predicament. Mr. Togoland looked from one to the other of us, wondering what was happening.

"What a life," Mr. Justice said, sheepishly wiping his mouth with the back of his hand.

"You can say that again," I assured him.

The girls chatted among themselves and threw out a few English words, urging us to drink. The squat madam hustled in with bottles of cold beer, anxious to drum up trade of a more solid nature. I drank and kept my eye on Mr. Justice, grimly determined not to give him a break. If he wanted a girl badly enough, he'd have to show me what a staunch individualist he was, how morally independent the British had taught him to be. But it was he who finally sighed and said:

"I guess we'd better go."

We paid for our drinks and climbed back into the taxi. Mr. Togoland was wistful and grateful, but somehow disappointed.

"Was that the first time you've ever been in such a place?" I asked him.

"Yes," he sighed. He glanced shyly at Mr. Justice. "And in such company," he murmured, deeply impressed.

Mr. Justice was silent, serious, reflective. The white Spanish-styled villas flew past the taxi window. We came in sight of the ocean where the sun splashed and glittered on the seascape. Ships idled at anchor. Gulls wheeled in the dazzling blue, crying hungrily.

"Listen," Mr. Justice began soberly, "those houses are safe, well run, clean. They're all right. I know that all of the leading British administrators, merchants, and soldiers in West

Africa go to such houses when they visit Las Palmas. . . ."

"Then it *must* be all right, if *they* go there," I said tersely.

Mr. Justice looked at me searchingly, surprised.

"Of course, it is," he said. "Did you *doubt* that?"

"I've *never* doubted the wisdom of the British," I said.

"Oh, come now," he chided me uneasily. "Be fair."

"I'm not a fair man, Mr. Justice," I informed him.

"I don't understand you," he said slowly.

"I understand *you*," I said.

Six

As we entered West African waters, the sea was choppy, with whitecaps showing. A blue mist hung on the horizon and, I was told, the humidity in the air was a foretaste of what I'd encounter in the Gold Coast.

At dinner I watched Mr. Justice take his wheat germ, his yeast tablets, his vitamins, and his laxative sticks. I struggled against an oblique sympathy that was dawning in me for the man. How England had mangled his soul! The truth was that the judge was living in the wrong century. His enslaved grandfather had desperately pulled himself out of servitude, had lifted himself above the tribal level, and, in doing so, he had been akin to the millions of Europeans and Americans of the nineteenth century who had so valiantly overthrown the remnants of feudalism. Mr. Justice represented the victory of enlightenment: he could read, he could vote, he was free; but he was adamant against the hungers of the new generation.

Mr. Justice's grandfather had been a hero to him, but I doubted if Mr. Justice's children would regard him in a heroic light. He wanted his children to be black Englishmen. But would his children want to be that? Were there not much bigger and more exciting battles for them to fight? Mr. Justice had succeeded at the moment when history was about to nullify his triumphs, and he was already confused and bewildered at the new social and political consents swirling about him.

We were now in tropic waters, almost opposite Dakar. The horizon was continually shrouded in mist. The sea was smooth, with a tiny whitecap here and there. Hourly the heat and humidity mounted and I imagined that the temperature on shore must have been very high.

That afternoon I wandered down into third class and found a group of young African students. I insinuated myself into their conversation and steered it toward politics. One undeniable fact informed their basic attitudes: Russia had made a most tremendous impression upon the minds of these world's outsiders. From where these colonial boys stood, Russia's analysis of events made sense. The first inescapable fact was that it was *only* from Russia—not from the churches or the universities of the Western world—that a moral condemnation of colonial exploitation had come. On this moral ground abandoned in embarrassment by the West, the Russians had driven home telling ideological blows.

The foremost conviction I found in them—or maybe you'd call it mood—was that nobody should strive for a unique or individual destiny. This was, of course, in essence, anti-Christian, even if the befuddled boys holding such notions did not know it. The historic events of the past forty years had made them feel that the only road into the future lay in collective action, that organized masses constituted the only true instrument of freedom.

This was not Communism; it was its impact; it was not the ideology of Marxism; it was its influence. The methods of imperialists have made it easy for these boys to embrace the idea of "masses," and the masses they have in mind are black masses. . . . Of Communism *per se* they wanted none, but they keenly appreciated the moral panic into which Russia had thrown the Western world. And they were aware of the huge mass of empiric material available about the techniques of making uprisings, general strikes, all kinds and degrees of actions that could paralyze the economic activities of imperialist powers. . . .

One rather heady young man expressed himself about Russia as follows:

"Russia's a gadfly! I'm not for her, but I'm not against her! Let her stay where she is and harass the West! Why are the British treating us a little better? They're scared of our going over to the Russians, that's all. If Russia were defeated tomorrow, a tide of reaction would set in in all the colonies. But, with the Cold War raging, even an Englishman, when he passes you on deck, is willing to say 'Good morning'!"

Their resentment against the British went far beyond economic issues. They swear that they'll rename many of their towns, rivers, villages and they'll christen them with names that their fathers gave them. They despise names like Gold Coast, Mumford, and Queen Anne's Point; and they are determined to rename their country Ghana. . . . I'm afraid that white Westerners will look on in dismay when they leave the Gold Coast and wonder what all their labors were for; they may go so far as to accuse the Africans of ingratitude. . . .

That night the ship washed through a steamy, tropic sea. A lighthouse whirled a powerful beam every few seconds through the velvet dark. The air smelled of rain. The winking red and green lights of a plane floated through the sky with a sound so faint that it emphasized the silence of the sea. Overhead the blackness was studded with points of star fire floating in a haze of silver; the sky seemed heavy, rich, about to swoop with a ripened load toward the heaving surface of the water.

Next day the sea was a flat, gray disc whose surface stretched toward a vague horizon. During the night it had rained and now drops of water clung to my porthole. The ship plowed through slaty seas that looked like viscous oil. The heat was so enervating that I felt sleepy, heavy, filled with unrest. The slightest exertion brought sweat to my face, yet the sky was never really bright; the sun's rays could not penetrate the overhanging mist. The day wore on and a kind of grayness pervaded the world and there was no line between the sea and the sky.

PART II

The Nervous Colony

Detribalization breaks down traditional ideas and introduces some of the Western; exploitation sharpens the ensuing restlessness into discontent; missionary education provides leaders and unwittingly furnishes much of the ideology and patterns of expression, for African revolts are frequently a mixture of religious fanaticism and anti-European sentiment.

The Marginal Man, by Everett V. Stonequist

Seven

When I awakened on the morning of the 16th of June, I was at once conscious of a strange, dead quiet. The ship's diesel engines had ceased to throb; stillness gripped my narrow cabin. We had docked! I leaped out of my bunk-bed and peered through the porthole and saw Africa. . . .

I dressed hurriedly and went on deck; an African city, under a blanket of blue mist, lay spread out before me. The heat was heavy, close, wet; and the city—Takoradi—seethed with activity at even this early hour. On the wharf was a forest of derricks, cranes, sheds, machines and, as I looked closer, I could see that they were being operated by black men—a fact that must have produced pain in the heart of Dr. Malan of South Africa, for he had sworn that black men were incapable of doing these things.

I studied the swirling crowd on the docks and found it hard to distinguish men from women, for practically everyone had a richly colored cloth draped about him, and almost everyone was barefooted except the policemen who, to my horror, were dressed in dark blue wool! I wondered how they could stand it. . . .

At the breakfast table I took my farewell of Mr. Justice who was continuing the voyage to Lagos, Nigeria.

"I wonder what you're going to make out of Africa," the judge said reflectively, chewing.

"I don't expect to find too much there that's completely new," I drawled.

"Africa's strange, *strange*," he assured me.

"My background's rather strange too," I informed him.

He laughed and shook his head.

"If you get to Nigeria, you must look me up," he said. "Don't forget me."

"I shan't forget you," I told him.

I descended to the customs shed where it was twice as hot as it had been on board. A young man approached me.

"Mr. Wright?"

"Yes."

"I'm meeting you for the Prime Minister."

He was Mr. Ansah, short, black, alert, a personal friend of Nkrumah. He guided me through customs and informed me that a government transport bus would take me to Accra, the capital. Emerging from the customs shed, I saw Africa for the first time with frontal vision: black life was everywhere. My eyes were riveted upon a woman wearing a brightly colored length of cloth which held a baby strapped to her back; the infant's legs were sprawled about the woman's hips and thighs, and the tiny head of the baby lolled in sleep with sweat beading on its forehead. The cloth held the weight of the baby's body and was anchored straight across the woman's breasts, cutting deeply into the flesh. Another woman was washing in a pan set on the ground; she was bent at an angle of forty-five degrees in the broiling sun, her black child also sound asleep upon her back. The babies of other women were awake, their wide, innocent eyes avoiding the broad blank expanse of their mothers' backs, looking at the world from side to side. Then I was startled by a European family threading its way through the black crowd.

"They are the minority here, hunh, Mr. Ansah?" I asked.

He roared with laughter.

"It's good *not* to be a minority for once, eh?" he asked.

"I admit it," I said. "Say, how do they behave?"

"All right," he said. "It's the high officials who need watching. Individuals like these are generally polite; they have to be. They're dependent upon us, you see."

We walked past black traffic officers, black policemen, gangs of black workmen; and, in the locomotive of a train, I saw a black fireman and a black engineer. The whole of life that met the eyes was black. I turned my attention to my host.

"You're a businessman, I take it?"

"Yes. I hope you're not opposed to businessmen."

"Not if they're working for the freedom of their country," I told him.

He laughed heartily and grabbed my hand.

"Just what do you do?" I asked him.

"Timber. I cut it, dress it, draw it, and ship it to all parts of the world."

"How many men do you employ?"

"About two hundred. Say, would you mind coming with me to the store? I must do a bit of shopping. . . ."

We entered a huge, modern store that reminded me of a unit in the American Atlantic and Pacific grocery chain; it was managed by the British but staffed with Africans. As Mr. Ansah shopped, I wandered about. I examined an enameled pot that would hold about a quart of liquid; it was priced at £1! Or $2.80! A salesman came up to me.

"You wish to buy something, sar?"

"No; I'm just looking."

"You're American, aren't you, sar?"

"Yes; how did you know?"

"Oh, we know, sar," he said. Another salesman joined him. "What part of Africa did you come from, sar?"

I stared at him and then laughed. I felt uneasy.

"I don't know."

"Didn't your mother or grandmother ever tell you what part of Africa you came from, sar?"

I didn't answer. I stared vaguely about me. I had, in my childhood, asked my parents about it, but they had had no information, or else they hadn't wanted to speak of it. I remembered that many Africans had sold their people into slavery; it had been said that they had had no idea of the kind of slavery into which they had been selling their people, but they had sold them. . . . I suddenly didn't know what to say to the men confronting me.

"Haven't you tried to find out where in Africa you came from, sar?"

"Well," I said softly, "you know, you fellows who sold us and the white men who bought us didn't keep any records."

Silence stood between us. We avoided each other's eyes.

"Are you going to stay with us, sar?"

"I'm visiting."

There was another silence. I was somehow glad when Mr. Ansah returned. We went back to the docks. It was so hot and humid that I felt that my flesh was melting from my bones. I climbed into the government bus and shook hands with my host. The bus rolled slowly through streets clogged with black life. African cities are small and one is in the "bush"—the jungle—before one knows it. Ten minutes out of Takoradi was enough to make Africa flood upon me so quickly that my mind was a blur and could not grasp it all. Villages of thick-walled mud huts heaved into view, tantalizing my eyes for a few seconds, and then fled past, only to be replaced by others as mythical and unbelievable. Naked black children sat or squatted upon the bare earth, playing. Black women, naked to the waist, were washing their multicolored cloths in shallow, muddy rivers. The soil was a rich red like that of Georgia or Mississippi, and, for brief moments, I could almost delude myself into thinking that I was back in the American South. Men, with their cloths tied at their hips, were cutting grass at the roadside with long cutlasses. Then I saw a crowd of naked men, women, and children bathing in a wide, muddy stream; the white lather of soap covered their bodies, and their black, wet skins glistened in the morning sun.

Then, to my right, the Atlantic burst in a wide, blue, blaze of beauty. Along this coastline Africa had been in contact with Europe for more than five hundred years. What kind of relationship had these people had with Europe that left them more or less what they were . . . ? Travelers' accounts in 1700 tell of having seen thousands of tracks of antelope, elephants, and other wild animals in the areas through which my bus was speeding. Wild life has vanished from here now. Those not slain by hunters have been driven deeper into the dense jungles. But the customs of the people remain almost unaltered . . .

In 1441 a Portuguese navigator, one Antonia Gonzales, launched the slave trade on these shores by kidnaping a few Africans; evidently the Christians of Portugal liked the services of those blacks, for Gonzales returned in 1442 for another shipload. Thus were inaugurated those acts of banditry which, as the decades passed, were erected into an institution that bled Africa and fattened Europe. In the beginning of the sixteenth century the slave trade took on a definite historic pattern and soon became the dominant passion of the Western world.

It had not, however, been for slaves that the Europeans had first sailed down the coast of West Africa; they'd been trying to prove that the world was round, that they could find a route to India, seeking to determine if Africa was a peninsula. They had become distracted by the incredibly rich gold dust to be found on the Guinea Coast and, in 1455, there had sprung up what was known as the "silent trade," a kind of coy and furtive bargaining between the predatory Europeans and the frightened but gullible natives. . . . Europeans would leave heaps of cheap trinkets upon the ground and then retire a half day's march away; the Africans would steal out, examine the shoddy merchandise, and place tiny piles of gold dust upon each heap. The Europeans would then return and try to determine if the gold dust left was an adequate payment for the goods; if they felt that it was not, they'd retire again and the Africans would sneak up. If the Africans wanted the goods badly enough, they'd increase the tiny piles of gold dust. . . . Confidence being somewhat established in this manner, the Portuguese, according to historical records, had once traded extensively for gold in the very neighborhood through which my bus now sped.

The kaleidoscope of sea, jungle, nudity, mud huts, and crowded market places induced in me a conflict deeper than I was aware of; a protest against what I saw seized me. As the bus rolled swiftly forward I waited irrationally for these fantastic scenes to fade; I had the foolish feeling that I had but to turn my head and I'd see the ordered, clothed streets of Paris. . . . But the string of mud villages stretched out without end. My protest was not against Africa or its people; it was directed against the unsettled feeling engendered by the strangeness of a completely different order of life. I was gazing upon a world whose laws I did not know, upon faces whose reactions were riddles to me. There was nothing here that I could predict, anticipate, or rely upon and, in spite of myself, a mild sense of anxiety began to fill me.

The bus stopped and I stared down at a bare-breasted

young girl who held a huge pan of oranges perched atop her head. She saw me studying her and she smiled shyly, obviously accepting her semi-nudity as being normal. My eyes went over the crowd and I noticed that most of the older women had breasts that were flat and remarkably elongated, some reaching twelve or eighteen inches (length, I was told later, was regarded as a symbol of fertility!), hanging loosely and flapping as the women moved about—and intuitively I knew that this deformation had been caused by the constant weight and pressure of babies sagging upon their backs and pulling the cloth that went across their bosoms. . . .

Some of the roofs of the huts were made of thatched straw and others were constructed of rusty corrugated tin. Many of the mud huts—commonly known as swish huts—had been fairly recently erected and were of a reddish-brown color; others were old, showing cracked walls half washed away by the torrential tropic rains, and their color tended toward a tannish yellow. I learned later that these swish huts had been known to withstand tropical weather for more than seventy years, so strongly were they built, and that they were cool and comfortable to sleep in. What fascinated me was the manner in which the swish hut structures ordered the manner of living; or was it that the African manner of living had preordained the odd structure of the huts . . . ? They were so constructed that they formed a vast rectangle, three sides of which were solid walls of clay rooms whose doors fronted a wide courtyard; the fourth wall of rooms had a narrow opening serving both as exit and entrance. A dwelling unit of this sort was referred to as a compound, and, in its enclosure, washing, cooking, mending, carpentry, and a score of other activities took place. A compound of this nature was a variant of a stockade and it was believed that the Africans resorted to this mode of building when they wanted to protect themselves from slave snatching.

Bit by bit my eyes became accustomed to the naked bodies and I turned my attention to the massive and green landscape, above which drifted that inevitable blue haze. I sped past plantations of banana trees, palm trees, coconut trees, orange trees, and rubber trees; then there loomed wawa trees and mahogany trees; cottonwood trees, white and tall and straight, stood like monuments amidst the green forest. Cocoa trees crowded the countryside with their red, brown, and yellow pods, then came patches of cocoa yam, cassava, and pineapple. But these plantations were like no plantations I'd ever seen before; there was no order, no fences, no vast sweeps of plowed earth such as one sees in the American Midwest—there was just a profuse welling of plants in a tangled confusion stretching everywhere, seemingly with no beginning and no end.

The bus rocked on through thick jungle; then, half an hour later, roared into another batch of mud villages. As we slowed for a crossroads, I stared again at the half-nude black people and they returned my gaze calmly and confidently. What innocence of instincts! What unabashed pride! Such uninhibitedness of living seemed to me to partake of the reality of a dream, for, in the Western world where my instincts had been conditioned, nude bodies were seen only under special and determined conditions: in the intimacies of marriage, in expensive nightclubs, in the clandestine rendezvous of lovers, in art galleries, or in the bordels of the kind that Mr. Justice liked to haunt . . . ; and only men of undoubtedly professional stamp—doctors, artists, undertakers—were permitted, by the tolerance of the state or the indulgence of society, to deal with nudity, and then only behind closed doors. Yet, as I stared out of the bus window, I was amazed at the utter asexuality of the mood and the bearing of the people! Sex *per se* was absent in what I saw; sex was so blatantly prevalent that it drove all sexuality out;

that is, it eliminated all of that evidence of sublimated and projected sexual symbolization with which Western men are habitually prone to decorate their environment in depicting to themselves the reality of the hidden bodies of their women. The hair of the women was plainly done, wrapped tightly in black strings and tied in plaited rows close to the skull; no rouge or powder showed on any woman's cheeks; no fingernails were painted; and, save for a few tiny earrings of gold, they were bare of ornamentation of every kind.

Undoubtedly these people had, through experiences that had constituted a kind of trial and error, and in response to needs that were alien and obscure to me, chosen some aspect of their lives other than sex upon which to concentrate their passions, and what that other aspect was and the manner in which they concentrated their passions upon it was something that I did not know, nor could I guess at its nature. Was it hunger? Was it war? Was it climate? Or was sex being *deliberately* brought into the open . . . ? Had it been from some taboo originating in their religion? Or had it risen out of the vicissitudes of natural catastrophes? And, again, faced with the absolute otherness and inaccessibility of this new world, I was prey to a vague sense of mild panic, an oppressive burden of alertness which I could not shake off. . . .

Fishing villages, quaint and bleak in the blinding sun, flashed by, then came Elmina, Cape Coast, Anomabu, historic Gold Coast place names that stirred me to a memory of dark and bloody events of long ago. The road twisted through plantation and forest and jungle and again, to my right, the green waves of the Atlantic leaped wild and free, rolling and breaking upon the yellow sands and the grayish rocks of the far-flung shore, and I knew that it was across those stretches of barren beach that hundreds of thousands of black men, women, and children had been marched, shackled and chained, down to the waiting ships to be carted across the ocean to be slaves in the New World. . . .

The bus stopped in a tiny village and I clambered down to stretch my legs; three or four Africans followed me, then the Europeans got off. . . . I strode around the market place and finally halted before a young woman who sat cross-legged and who was nude to the waist. Balanced on her head was a huge tray of peeled coconuts.

"I want to buy a coconut," I told her.

The flesh of her cheeks had been slashed by double marks in two places: tribal marks. . . . Though scarring the cheeks was being done less and less, it still occurred among the more backward elements of the population. In the old days all babies were thus marked at birth for purposes of identification, and some of the tribal marks were truly intricate; indeed, there were times when I had the impression that some delicate cobweb was covering a person's face, so many crossing lines traversed the jaws and cheeks, reaching from the temple to the chin, from the nostrils to the ears.

The young woman to whom I had spoken burst into embarrassed laughter, turned and beckoned to a girl friend, mumbled something to her in her tribal tongue, and pointed to me. Her friend sauntered over slowly, lifting her cloth and covering her breasts; she evidently knew something of Western ways. . . .

"You wanna buy?" she asked me, smiling.

"A coconut," I said.

She translated for her friend who, taking a coconut from her tray, whacked a hole in it with one deft stroke of her cutlass, and handed it to me, still giggling. I paid her and she tossed my coin upon the tray and, without looking, her fingers fished around on the tray and found my change. I stood to one side and drank the coconut milk, studying her. Her eyes were sloe-shaped; her feet were large and splayed, the soles coarsened by earth and rain and rocks. The skin of her arms held a slightly ashened hue. When she became aware of my gaze, she burst again into laughter, hiding her face. The Europeans standing nearby turned to look at me and the girl, and I wondered what they were thinking. . . .

En route again, we sped through several thriving commercial centers. Now and then, looming up from the beach, and fronting both the sea and the jungle, were huge white castles and forts, their lofty ramparts holding decaying gun emplacements that still pointed commandingly toward both the misty expanse of the Atlantic and the tropically green countryside. These forts and castles had been built centuries ago by the Portuguese, the Dutch, the Danes, and the Swedes and they had been designed not only to ward off attacks and raids of the hostile and desperate natives, but also those of other European imperialist rivals whose jealous hunger for gold and slaves made them a prey to be feared. For centuries these dominating structures had served as storage depots, barracks, military command headquarters, arsenals, and they also contained deep dungeons in which kidnaped, bought, or stolen slaves had been kept for overseas shipment. The iron rings and chains which had fastened their black bodies to the masonry were still intact.

How had the Europeans gotten a toehold upon this shore? Had they sneaked in? Had the naïve natives invited them in? Or had they fought their way forward in bloody battles? It was none of these; it had been through guile . . . ; a guile which enthroned distrust as a cardinal element in the African attitude toward Europe, a distrust that lives on in the African heart until this day.

The Portuguese set the pattern in 1481. John II, upon ascending the throne, organized a huge fleet for the purpose of establishing a European settlement upon the coast where it had been said that gold was an article of household use among the infidel natives. Historical records relate that the expedition carried "500 soldiers and officers and 100 masons and other workers"; they carried enough stones, cut, prepared, and ready to be fitted into place for the hurried building of a fort; also on board was ammunition, food, and a priest. . . . The idea had been, by ruse or force, to erect a fort strong enough to repel rival imperialist attacks and, at the same time, to compel the respect and obedience of the natives. The Portuguese strategy was to ask the natives to grant them the right to build a church in order that they might confer upon them the blessings of Jesus Christ; the force was to be held in reserve in case the natives refused to accept such blessings. . . .

Anchoring off Elmina in 1482, the expedition's commander, one Don Diego d'Azambuja, sought an audience with the native chief, using a Portuguese who had learned the tribal language as his interpreter. Concealing their arms beneath their imposing and gaudy clothing, they presented the chief with a sugared demand to establish a Christian church on the coast, extolling the benefits of heart and spirit that would ensue from such an institution.

The natives and the chief had but a hazy conception of Europe, but they were practical enough to doubt the word of men who came thousands of miles in ships to erect domiciles in their land; being naïve, they guessed erroneously that the white men had been driven forcibly out of their country, had been reduced to living in their ships, and now wanted to take their tribal lands for themselves. The Africans, mystical and fanatical lovers of their ancestral soil, could not conceive of people voluntarily leaving their homes and families and traveling vast distances merely for the sake of trade. A tragic misconception! Four hundred and thirty-one years ago, the first African to leave a record of protest, diplomatic yet charged with anxiety, spoke as follows:

"I'm not insensible to the high honor which your great master, the chief of Portugal, has this day conferred upon me. His friendship I have long endeavored to merit by the strictness of my dealing with the Portuguese, and by my constant exertions to procure an immediate lading for their vessels. But never until this day did I observe such a difference in the appearance of his subjects; they have hitherto been only meanly attired, were easily contented with the commodities they received; and so far from wishing to continue in this country, were never happy until they could complete their lading, and return. Now I remark a strange difference. A great number richly dressed are anxious to be allowed to build houses, and to continue among us. Men of such eminence, conducted by a commander who from his own account seems to have descended from the God who made day and night, can never bring themselves to endure the hardships of this climate; nor would they here be able to procure any of the luxuries that abound in their own country. The passions that are common to us all will therefore inevitably bring on disputes; and it is far preferable that both nations should continue on the same footing they have hitherto done, allowing your ships to come and go as usual; the desire of seeing each other occasionally will preserve peace between us . . ." (*A History of the Gold Coast*, by W. Walton Claridge, vol. 1).

But the Portuguese had long before made up their minds that it was well worth their while to risk the terrible climate, and, pretending to be spokesmen of the Gentle Jesus, they hankered not for peace, but for victory. Rebuffed, they soon resorted to threats, which caused the African chief to give an uneasy consent. But, next morning, as the Portuguese workmen were frantically hoisting the prepared stones into place, the natives of Elmina attacked them, wounding many of their men. D'Azambuja altered his tactics and rained presents and bribes upon the natives, offering profuse apologies. Despite this, the construction of the fort was pushed night and day and, in less than a month, a tower had been built against which the natives were helpless. The Portuguese flag was hoisted and a mass was said. . . .

The European campaign against the mainland of Africa, buttressed by a mixture of religious ideology and a lust for gold, had begun in earnest; there had been no declaration of war; there had been no publicly declared aims save those of soul-saving, which even the Portuguese didn't believe, and, as time passed, European governments *per se* were not even involved in these calculated assaults, for it was the right, endorsed by no less than the Pope, of any individual merchant, criminal, or adventurer to buy a ship, rig it out, muster a crew, and set sail for Africa and try his luck.

Fortified with the authority of a papal bull, publicly minimizing the loot to be had, and extolling the opportunities for Christian service, John II proceeded at once to safeguard his new possession by spreading the word that the natives of the coast of West Africa were cannibals and would eat Europeans; he caused rumors to be circulated that terrible storms rose four times a year and made the seas impassable; and he assured the world that no one ought to be foolhardy enough to venture into West African waters in any other than a ship of Portuguese construction, for others were definitely unseaworthy. . . . There followed a partial "blackout" of all information relating to Portuguese activities on the coast of West Africa until 1500 when other European nations, overcoming the psychological intimidations of Catholicism, disregarded the papal bull and pushed their way past bloody Portuguese resistance and into the trade in black slaves and yellow gold.

For 150 years there followed a period of free-for-all warfare among the Portuguese, the Dutch, the French, the English, the Swedes, the Germans and the African natives. . . .

Relying mainly upon the authority of their firepower, the Portuguese forbade the Africans to trade with any other European power, an injunction which the Africans, of course, resented. The Portuguese penalty for violating their wishes was to raze and burn African villages, and in time even worse reprisals were meted out. The French, being less strong at sea, were also dodging in and out of the coastal native settlements, trading and keeping a wary eye out for the Portuguese. The English made direct representations to the Africans, trying to dissuade them from trading with the Portuguese, and when the Africans failed to comply, they too burned and destroyed native villages and looted the countryside of goats, sheep, and fowl. Sometimes the English and the French formed uneasy alliances against the Portuguese, hoping that, with such a common front, they could drive them out of West Africa, but such alliances could last only so long as the two respective home countries were at peace with each other. Hence, on many occasions the English and the French, hearing that their respective home countries were at war with each other in Europe, would turn suddenly and attack each other in Africa, even though both of them were under attack by the hated Portuguese.

Toward the end of the sixteenth century the Dutch made a bid to share in the rich spoils by making an alliance with native tribes and arming them with guns (much to the fury of the Portuguese who loved the advantage of gunpowder over spears!) and urging them to fight against the Portuguese whom they had grown to hate. Meanwhile, Portugal became diverted by her rich colonies in the New World and allowed her forts to fall into disrepair and to become undermanned. In 1637 the Dutch made a determined assault upon the Portuguese fort at Elmina and captured it, and five years later they had driven the Portuguese, after 160 years of occupation, out of West Africa altogether.

The Dutch victory on the Guinea Coast went unchallenged for but a short time, for, in 1657, the Swedes built a fort at Cape Coast, which fell to the Danes soon afterward; after changing hands several times, the fort at Cape Coast fell to the English for keeps in 1664. The war between the English and the Dutch changed but little the *status quo* regarding the forts, and when peace came in 1667, the situation was about what it had been before the shooting started. Then, in 1655, the Germans horned in, building two forts at Sekondi and Axim.

In 1693 the natives around Accra attacked the Danes in their strongly fortified Castle Christianborg and defeated them through trickery and captured the castle, but, a year later, they sold it back to the Danes! From 1694 onwards the Dutch power began to decline slowly under the constant attack of native tribesmen, and, since most of the European interlopers were fighting each other in other parts of the world, forts changed hands only to be given back to their original owners when peace came about at spots far from Africa. When England, therefore, lost her American colonies, she was too weak, in 1785, to contest the Dutch ownership of forts in West Africa.

Eight

Though the distance from Takoradi to Accra was but 170 miles, it took us all of eight hours to make the journey; it was nearing six o'clock when Accra loomed through the sunset on the horizon.

A smiling but somewhat reserved mulatto woman who spoke clipped and careful English—she was the Prime Minister's secretary—was on hand at the bus station to meet me. The Prime Minister, she told me, was in the Northern Territories on an urgent political mission.

"What *is* the political situation?" I asked her.

"You'll see," she said cryptically, lifting her brows.

She drove me in her English car across Accra, and I could hear the faint sounds of drums beating in the distance, the vibrations coming to my ears like the valved growl of a crouching beast.

"What are those drums?"

"You'll find out," she said, laughing.

"I feel strange; I see and hear so much that I don't understand."

"It'll take you a few days to get into it," she said.

In the sun's dying light we came to a group of modernistic bungalows situated atop a chain of low-lying hills where the heat and humidity were more bearable. These beautiful bungalows, I was told, had been built expressly by the British authorities for the creature comforts of the new African ministers, many of whom had only recently been released from prison where they had been serving terms for sedition. But the wily black ministers, full of an old-fashioned distrust of Europeans, had had the unheard-of temerity to refuse to live in the bungalows, had stifled their natural yen for a modern domicile, and had remained, much to British astonishment, in the neighborhoods of their constituents. Their refusal to accept this British graciousness indicated that they suspected that the bungalows were bait to separate them from the common people and to keep them, as the British had always preferred to remain (as a matter of state policy), aloof and remote. But the African politicians had sensed that the most dangerous thing that they could do was to draw a class line between themselves and the masses of tribal voters who had endowed them with power. . . .

I thanked the young lady, bade her good night, and went to my room which had a screened-in balcony from which I could see the swarming, far-off, faint yellow lights of Accra twinkling in the valley below.

"Massa!"

I turned and saw a steward, dressed in white, black of face, barefooted, his lips hanging open expectantly.

"What is it?"

"Massa want chop?"

"What?"

"Chop? Hot chop? Cold chop?"

I hadn't understood anything; it was my first experience with pidgin English and I shook my head and confessed:

"I don't understand."

"Chop, Massa." He went through the motions of eating, carrying his hand to his mouth and chewing vigorously.

"Dinner?"

"Yasa, Massa. When you want."

When I entered the huge dining room I saw three black boys dressed in white standing at attention. I learned later that one was the cook, one was the steward, and the other was the steward's assistant; in addition there were a gardener, a laundryman, a night watchman (commonly known as "t'ief" man), a man who did the shopping, and an Englishwoman who acted as overseer.

As I sat at the table, my three men disappeared, their coarse-soled feet swishing over the highly polished wooden floor. I sighed. This was Africa too. These servants seemed to know their business; they had, no doubt, been trained in their duties by a tradition left here for a hundred years by English housewives. But that pidgin English! I shuddered. I resented it and I vowed that I'd never speak it. . . . I started; the steward was at my elbow, holding a platter of fried fish; he'd come so silently upon me that I was nonplused.

Early next morning I found a taxi at the roadside and went into the city. I got out at the post office. There were no sidewalks; one walked at the edge of a drainage ditch made of concrete in which urine ran. A stench pervaded the sunlit air. Barefooted men dressed in cloths whose colors were a mixture of red, green, yellow, blue, brown, and purple stood idling about. Most of the women not only carried the inevitable baby strapped to their backs, but also a burden on top of their heads and a bundle in each hand. I reached a street corner and paused; coming toward me was a woman nursing a baby that was still strapped to her back; the baby's head was thrust under the woman's arm and the woman had given the child the long, fleshy, tubelike teat and it was suckling. (There are women with breasts so long that they do not bother to give the baby the teat in front of them, but simply toss it over the shoulder to the child on their back. . . .)

The women's carriage was remarkably graceful; they walked as straight as ramrods, with a slow, slinging motion, moving their legs from their hips, their feet just managing to skim over the earth. When they glanced about they never jarred or jolted the huge burdens they had on their heads, and their eyes held a calm, proud look. In the physical behavior of both men and women there were no wasted motions; they seem to move in a manner that conserved their energies in the awful heat.

In front of the Indian, Syrian, and European stores African women sat before wooden boxes heaped high with red peppers, oranges, plantains, cigarettes, cakes of soap cut into tiny bits, okra, tomatoes, peeled coconuts, small heaps of matches, cans of tinned milk, etc. Men from the Northern Territories, dressed in long smocks, sold from carts piled with cheap mirrors, shoestrings, flashlights, combs, nail files, talcum powder, locks, and cheaply framed photos of Hollywood movie stars. . . . I was astonished to find that even the children were engaged in this street trade, carrying their wares on their heads either in calabashes or brass pans that had been polished until they glittered. Was it a lack of capital that made the Africans sell like this on the streets? One could buy bread from a little girl who carried a big box, screened-in, upon her cranium; one could buy a concoction called *kenke*—a kind of crushed corn that had been cooked and steamed and seasoned with pepper—from a woman who balanced an enormous, steaming calabash upon her head; one could buy baby bonnets from a woman who had layers of them stored in a brass pan that was borne aloft; yet another woman sold soap from a stack which held at least forty cakes perched atop her skull; one could buy lengths of colored cloth from a woman the top of whose head was a small dry-goods store; one could buy fish, eggs, chickens, meat, yams, bananas, salt, sugar, plantains, cigarettes, ink, pens, pencils, paper—and all of this was but "one flight up," that is, above the heads of the street women who were popularly known as "mammies."

The sun was killing. I sought shade at another street intersection where, around an outdoor water hydrant, a knot of men, women, and children were gathered. They had small tubs, gasoline tins, buckets, pans, anything that could hold water. Boys and girls of eight or nine years of age were balancing tins holding ten or more gallons of water upon their tiny heads and walking off toward their homes with careful strides. A girl, a cloth fastened about her middle, was bent over a basin assiduously doing the family wash. Still another girl, twelve or thirteen, was nude and standing in a small tub and bathing herself in full view. A tiny girl squatted over a drainage ditch, urinating. A man went to the hydrant, took a sip of water from the stream, rinsed his mouth, spat, then damned up the stream in his cupped palms and drank. The girl who had been bathing got out of the tub, dumped the water into the drainage ditch, went to the hydrant, took her place in line and, when her turn came, filled her tub, went a few feet away and dashed the entire contents of the tub over her head, rinsing the soapsuds from her body. She looked down at her gleaming, wet skin, her face holding a concentrated and critical expression. Taking her place in line once more, she filled the tub, lifted it to her head and went mincing off, presumably toward home. . . . A woman came leading a boy and girl by their hands; she carried a big galvanized bucket on her head. When she'd filled it with water, she proceeded to bathe the children with a bar of laundry soap and a sponge made of rough excelsior. She handled them rudely, jerking them this way and that, while she plied the sponge over their eyes, mouths, ears. . . . The girl wore a string of white and blue beads about her hips and a red cloth was pulled tight between her tiny thighs, each end fastened to the beads, front and back. The boy wore nothing.

(Over and above supplying needed water, these outdoor hydrants are really social clubs; it is here that the gossip of the quarter is spread and exchanged, where tall tales get embellished, where marriages, deaths, and births are announced. Sometimes fights take place, or romances are started. Sundry bargains and swappings are struck over petty merchandise. The intimacy of the African communal life can be witnessed in all of its innocence as it clusters about an outdoor hydrant.

(The crowds about the hydrants swell or diminish according to the time of day: there is an early morning crowd of men, women, and children; then a lull comes; toward noon the hydrant is patronized mostly by women who cook or wash; then the afternoon is slow; there are moments when the hydrant is completely deserted. Toward four o'clock the crowds collect again and they last until well into the night. Sometimes at four o'clock in the morning one can see a sleepy-eyed child filling a huge pail with water and walking slowly homeward. . . .)

Beggars were in thick evidence, their black, gnarled hands outstretched and their high-pitched voices singing out:

"Penny, Massa! Penny, Massa!"

So deformed were some that it was painful to look at them. Monstrously swollen legs, running sores, limbs broken so that jagged ends of the healed bones jutted out like blackened sticks, blind men whose empty eye-sockets yawned wetly, palsied palms extended and waiting, a mammoth wen suspended from a skinny neck and gleaming blackly in the hot sun—all of them were men and they sat nude to the waist with cloths draped modestly over their loins. I wondered if they were professional beggars, if they had deliberately deformed themselves to make these heart-wracking appeals? If they had, they had surely overdone it in terms of Western sensibilities, for I was moved not to compassion, but to revulsion. Perhaps for an African temperament conditioned to a belief that a beggar might be some distant relative in reincarnated disguise, such sights might impel donations, might induce a state of pity based upon dread. I don't know. . . .

I wanted to push on and look more, but the sun was too much. I spent the afternoon fretting; I was impatient to see more of this Africa. My bungalow was clean, quiet, mosquito-proof, but it had not been for that I'd come to Africa. Already my mind was casting about for other accommodations. I stood on my balcony and saw clouds of black buzzards circling slowly in the hazy blue sky. In the distance I caught a glimpse of the cloudy, grayish Atlantic.

Night fell and suddenly out of the blue velvet dark came the sound of African crickets that was like an air-raid siren. Frog belches exploded. A soft, feathery thud, like that of a bird, struck the window screen. Reluctantly, I climbed into bed. . . .

Next morning a phone call came from the Prime Minister's office; I was told that at four o'clock I'd be picked up by the Prime Minister's car and that I'd see "something."

And at four o'clock a sleek car entered the driveway. A uniformed chauffeur stepped out and saluted me; I climbed into the back seat. As we went through the city black faces jerked around, recognizing the car. We came to the Prime Minister's residence and pulled into a driveway. I got out and young black faces smiled at me. A few policemen hovered in the background. I was led forward into a red, two-story brick dwelling that looked remarkably like a colonial mansion in Georgia or Mississippi. I followed my guide upstairs, down a hallway, and into a living room.

The Prime Minister, dressed in a smock, was standing in the middle of the floor.

"Welcome!" he said.

"I'm glad to see you and your people," I told him.

"How are you?"

"Fine, but panting to see your party and your comrades."

He laughed. He presented me to a series of his friends whose strange names I did not recall, then we sat down.

"I want to take you on a quick tour of the city," he told me.

"I'm truly honored."

"Nothing has been prepared. I want you to see how these people respond to our appeals—"

"What's going to happen in July?" I asked, referring to the coming meeting of the Legislative Assembly.

The Prime Minister threw back his head and laughed. I got used, in time, to that African laughter. It was not caused by mirth; it was a way of indicating that, though they were not going to take you into their confidence, their attitude was not based upon anything hostile.

"You are direct," he said.

"Why not?" I asked.

"You'll have to wait and see," he told me.

I studied Nkrumah; he was fairly slightly built, a smooth jet black in color; he had a longish face, a pair of brooding, almost frightened eyes, a set of full, soft lips. His head held a thick growth of crinkly hair and his hands moved with slow restlessness, betraying a contained tension. His bodily motions were almost deliberate and at times his face seemed like a blank mask. One could almost feel the force of his preoccupations as he would jerk his head when his attention darted. His questions and answers were simple and to the point; I felt that he had much more on his mind than he permitted to pass his lips; he was the full-blown politician whose consciousness was anchored in concrete, practical concerns pointing toward a fondly sought goal. . . .

His colleagues drew him into a discussion that was conducted in tribal language; when it was over, he announced:

"Let's go!"

His personal bodyguard stood at attention; it was composed of hand-picked militants and faithfuls of the Convention People's Party. He led the way and I followed down into the street where his motorcycle escort, dressed in scarlet, stood lined up near their machines. The Prime Minister waved his hand to signal that all was ready. The motorcyclists raced their engines to a deafening roar; then they pulled slowly into the street, leading the way. The Prime Minister's car, with the Prime Minister seated on my right, followed.

The sun was still shining as we moved slowly forward. The drone of the motorcycles attracted the attention of people on both sides of the street and, spontaneously, men, women, and children abandoned what they were doing and fronted the car. Others rushed pellmell out of shacks, their faces breaking into wide, glad smiles and, lifting their hands upward with their elbows at the level of their hips, palms fronting forward—a kind of half-Nazi salute—they shouted a greeting to the Prime Minister in a tone of voice compounded of passion, exhortation, and contained joy:

"Free—doom! Free—dooooom!"

Ahead of the car the sides of the streets turned black with faces. We reached a wide roadway and the crowds swirled, shouting:

"Free—dooom! Free—dooom!"

"Kwame! Kwame!" They shouted his name.

"Fight! Fight!"

"Akwaba! Akwaba!" ("Welcome! Welcome!")

The road turned into a black river of eager, hopeful, glad faces whose trust tugged at the heart. The crowds grew thicker. The shouting sounded like a cataract. The Prime Minister, smiling, laughing, lifted his right hand as he returned their salute.

The road led into a slum area, and the Prime Minister turned to me and said:

"This is James Town. I want you to see this too. . . . I want you to see all we have, the good and the bad."

The narrow streets filled quickly and the car plowed slowly through nostalgic crowds of men, women, and children who chanted:

"Free—dooooom!"

Many of the women waved their hands in that strange, quivering gesture of welcome which seemed to be common to the entire Gold Coast; it consisted of lifting the hand, but, instead of waving the hand as one did in the West, one held the arm still and shook the palm of the hand nervously and tremblingly from side to side, making the fingers vibrate.

"Free—dooooom!"

My mind flew back to the many conversations that I'd had in Chicago, New York, London, Paris, Rome, Buenos Aires about freedom, and I could picture again in my mind the white faces of friends screwed up in disgust and distaste when the word "freedom" was mentioned, and I could hear again in my memory the tersely deprecating question shot at me across a dinner table:

"*Freedom*? What do you mean, *freedom*?"

But here in Africa "freedom" was more than a word; an African had no doubts about the meaning of the word "freedom." It meant the right to public assembly, the right to physical movement, the right to make known his views, the right to elect men of his choice to public office, and the right to recall them if they failed in their promises. At a time when the Western world grew embarrassed at the sound of the word "freedom," these people knew that it meant the right to shape their own destiny as they wished. Of that they had no doubt, and no threats could intimidate them about it; they might be cowed by guns and planes, but they'd not change their minds about the concrete nature of the freedom that they wanted and were willing to die for. . . .

The crowds, milling in and out of the space between the motorcycles and the Prime Minister's car, chanted:

"Free—dooooom!"

The passionate loyalty of this shouting crowd had put this man in power, had given him the right to speak for them, to execute the mandate of national liberation that they had placed in his hands; and, because he'd said he'd try, they'd galvanized into a whole that was 4,000,000 strong, demanding an end to their centuries-old thralldom. Though still mainly tribal, though 90 per cent illiterate, they wanted to be free of an alien flag, wanted the sovereignty of their own will in their own land. And they had melted their tribal differences into an instrument to form a bridge between tribalism and twentieth-century forms of political mass organization. The women who danced and shouted were washerwomen, cooks, housewives, etc.

"Free—dooom! Free—dooom!" rang deafeningly in my ears.

"They believe in you," I said to the Prime Minister.

"Would you believe that four years ago a demonstration like this was impossible?" he told me. "These were a cowed and frightened people. Under the British it would have been unheard of for people to sing and shout and dance like this. . . . We changed all that. When I came from London in 1948, the mood of these people was terrible. They trusted nothing and nobody. They'd been browbeaten so long by both the black leaders and the British that they were afraid to act."

"Who were the first in the Gold Coast to offer opposition to your efforts to organize your people?" I asked Nkrumah.

"The missionaries," he said without hesitation.

My mind raced back to my reading of the history of the early days of the Gold Coast and I recalled that, from 1553 to 1592, the merchants of England, all staunch Christians, had sent ships to the Gold Coast to engage in trading British trinkets for gold dust and slaves, and some of those ships had been named *John Evangelist*, *Trinity*, *Bartholomew*, *John Baptist*, and *Jesus*. . . .

That the missionaries should have been the first to manifest opposition was, in my opinion, as it should have been. If they had to, the industrial and mercantile interests could come to terms with a rising nationalism. Indeed, during the past five hundred years history has shown that nationalism is one of the necessary but transitional forms of an expanding industrial system, and there was no reason why industrialization and nationalism could not, for a time, coexist, mutually enriching each other.

Religious interests, however, were jealous by their very nature and felt an understandable panic at the emergence of a sweeping nationalism that was bent not only upon creating new institutions for the people, but also new emotional attitudes, values, and definitions. And what could have frightened the men of God more than this wild and liquid emotion that Nkrumah had channeled into a new political party? Religion needed all the emotion of a community allied to its own ends, and when a rival appeal was made for the loyalty of that emotion, religious people must needs be opposed, even if the counterappeal of religion meant a decrease in the basic welfare of the people. Mass nationalist movements were, indeed, a new kind of religion. They were politics *plus!*

"I want to see your party and how it works," I said to the Prime Minister.

He nodded but did not answer.

"Free—dooom! Free—doooom!"

The roar came from all sides. Gratitude showed in the eyes of those black faces for the man who had taken their hand and told them that they had no need to fear the British, that they could laugh, sing, work, hope, and fight again.

I was astonished to see women, stripped to the waist, their elongated breasts flopping wildly, do a sort of weaving, circular motion with their bodies, a kind of queer shuffling dance which expressed their joy in a quiet, physical manner. It was as if they were talking with the movements of their legs, arms, necks, and torsos; as if words were no longer adequate as a means of communication; as if sounds could no longer approximate their feelings; as if only the total movement of their entire bodies could indicate in some measure their acquiescence, their surrender, their approval.

And then I remembered: I'd seen these same snakelike, veering dances before. . . . Where? Oh, God, yes; in America, in storefront churches, in Holy Roller Tabernacles, in God's Temples, in unpainted wooden prayer-meeting houses on the plantations of the Deep South. . . . And here I was seeing it all again against a background of a surging nationalistic political movement! How could that be?

When I'd come to Africa, I didn't know what I'd find,

what I'd see; the only prepossession I'd had was that I'd doubted that I'd be able to walk into the African's cultural house and feel at home and know my way around. Yet, what I was now looking at in this powerfully improvised dance of these women, I'd seen before in America! How was that possible? And, what was more, this African dance today was as astonishing and dumfounding to me as it had been when I'd seen it in America.

Never in my life had I been able to dance more than a few elementary steps, and the carrying of even the simplest tune had always been beyond me. So, what had bewildered me about Negro dance expression in the United States now bewildered me in the same way in Africa.

I'd long contended that the American Negro, because of what he had undergone in the United States, had been basically altered, that his consciousness had been filled with a new content, that "racial" qualities were but myths of prejudiced minds. Then, if that were true, how could I account for what I now saw? And what I now saw was an exact duplicate of what I'd seen for so many long years in the United States.

I did not find an answer to that question that afternoon as I stared out of the window of the Prime Minister's car. But the question was lodged firmly in my mind, enthroned there so strongly that it would never leave until I had, at least to my satisfaction, solved the riddle of why black people were able to retain, despite vast distances, centuries of time, and the imposition of alien cultures, such basic and fundamental patterns of behavior and response.

We rode on through the cheering throngs. Whenever the car slowed, the black faces, laughing and excited, with heads thrown back, with white teeth showing, would press close to the windows of the car and give vent to:

"Free—doooom!"

But my emotions were preoccupied with another problem. How much am I a part of this? How much was I part of it when I saw it in America? Why could I not feel this? Why that peculiar, awkward restraint when *I* tried to dance or sing? The answers to those questions did not come until after I penetrated deep into the African jungle. . . . On we rode. The crowds surged, danced, sang, and shouted, but I was thinking of my mother, of my father, of my brother. . . . I was frankly stunned at what I saw; there was no rejection or condemnation; there was no joy or sorrow; I was just stupefied. Was it possible that I was looking at myself laughing, dancing, singing, gliding with my hips to express my joy . . . ? Had I denied all this in me? If so, then why was it that when I'd tried to sing, as a child, I'd not been able to? Why had my hands and feet, all my life, failed to keep time? It was useless to say that I'd inhibited myself, for my inability to do these simple things predated any desire, conscious or unconscious, on my part. I had wanted to, because it had always been a part of my environment, *but I had never been able to!*

"What do you think?" the Prime Minister asked.

"It's most impressive," I said.

"They're an unspoiled, a spiritually virgin people," he said.

We came at last to a block of cement houses; from windows and doorways black faces shouted and called:

"Kwame! Kwame!"

"Free—dooom! Free—doooom!"

The car stopped and the Prime Minister got out; I followed him.

"What is this?" I asked him.

"This is a meeting of the Women's Division of the party," he told me.

We entered a concrete compound and sat as the meeting, dedicated to reorganization and installment of new officers, got under way. A tall black woman led a chant:

"Forward ever, backward never . . ."

There was a relaxed, genial atmosphere; now and then an easy laugh floated over the crowd. The men, clad in their native togas, sat in the rear, rising occasionally to aid in making seating arrangements. In front sat about two hundred women also clad in their native cloths and, for this ceremony, they wore an enormous amount of gold in their ears, around their necks, on their arms and fingers. The yellow sheen of the gold against the background of black skin made a startling combination in the red rays of the dying sun. There was one fat, black woman who, I'd have said, had at least three or four thousand dollars' worth of gold on her arms and around her neck, and it was pure native gold, mixed with no alloy. . . .

A psalm was sung in English. Next, an African of the Christian persuasion stepped forward and, in English, led the group in prayer. Then came a pagan chief with his umbrella, his staff, his "linguist" and proceeded to pour a libation of corn wine to the dead ancestors. The two religions nestled smugly, cheek by jowl, and the setting sun shone as calmly as usual; there was not a tremor in the universe. . . . After he emptied the bowl by dribbling the corn wine upon the ground, the chief had the bowl filled again and he passed it around to each person nearby and they took three sips. (Three is the lucky number among many Africans of the Gold Coast.)

A series of speakers rose, both men and women, and, in a mixture of English and tribal tongues, exhorted the women to give all their support to the Leader, to the Convention People's Party, and to the struggle for national liberation. To this already turgid brew was added still another ingredient; a woman rose and proclaimed:

"I'm Mrs. Nkrumah!"

A howl of laughter rose from the women. Puzzled, I looked at the Prime Minister; he grinned at me, and said:

"It's a joke."

"I *am* Mrs. Nkrumah!" the woman said in a voice that sought to still all doubts.

The Prime Minister rose and, sweeping his arms to include all the women, said:

"You are *all* my brides!"

The women laughed and clapped. Nkrumah, of course, was a bachelor.

"I have to say that to them," he whispered to me as he sat again. "Now, tell me, do you understand what you are looking at?"

"You have fused tribalism with modern politics," I said.

"That's exactly it," he said. "Nobody wanted to touch these people. The missionaries would go just so far, and no farther toward them. One can only organize them by going where they are, living with them, eating with them, sharing their lives. We are making a special drive to enlist women in the party; they have been left out of our national life long enough. In the words of Lenin, I've asked the cooks to come out of their kitchens and learn how to rule."

The new women officials to be installed were called to come forward and stand fronting the Prime Minister. A short statement of aims and duties was read to them and, at the end, each woman was asked to raise her right hand and repeat the following oath (I'm paraphrasing this from memory):

"I pledge with all my life my support to the Convention People's Party, and to my Leader, Kwame Nkrumah; I swear to follow my Leader's guidance, to execute faithfully his commands, to resist with all my power all imperialist attempts to disrupt our ranks, to strive with all of my heart to rebuild our lost nation, Ghana, so help me God!"

I was thunderstruck. Nkrumah had moved in and filled the vacuum which the British and the missionaries had left when they had smashed the tribal culture of the people! It was so simple it was dazzling. . . . Of course, before Nkrumah could do this, he would first have to have the intellectual daring to know that the British had created a vacuum in these people's hearts. It was not until one could think of the imperialist actions of the British as being crimes of the highest order, that they had slain something that they could never rekindle, that one could project a new structure for the lives of these people.

But, an oath to a Leader? In the twentieth century? Then I reflected. Well, why not? This oath was perhaps the most rational pledge that these women had ever given in all of their lives. Before this they had sworn oaths to invisible gods, pagan and Christian, and now, at last, they were swearing an oath that related directly to their daily welfare. And would these illiterate and myth-minded women have understood an abstract oath taken to a flag or a constitution? In the light of their traditions and culture, this oath seemed logical to them, for the swearing of oaths was a common feature of their rituals. And, in a society ruled by chiefs decked out in gold and silk, what symbol other than that of a living man, a man whom they could see, hear, speak to, check upon his actions—what symbol other than a living one could make them feel that their oath was really binding . . . ? Indeed, the taking of this oath was perhaps the only act in their lives that they had performed over whose consequences they would have some measure of control. Nkrumah was tapping the abandoned emotional reservoir that Christian religion had no use for; he, in contrast to the Christians who called upon them to attend church service one day a week, was commanding the whole of their lives from day to day and they stood before him willingly, pledging to give. It was not a morality easier than that of the church that Nkrumah was offering them; it was a much harder one and they accepted it!

The slip of paper upon which the oath had been written was given to the Prime Minister and, at once, impulsively, I leaned forward and said to him:

"May I make a copy of that?"

I regretted asking the moment the words had escaped my lips; but I had spoken and there was no backing out.

"What did you say?" he asked me.

"I'd like to make a copy of that oath," I stated.

He glanced off without answering, still holding the slip of paper in his hand. I knew that he knew what I had asked and he seemed to be debating. Would my rash request make him distrust me? Would he think that I'd use the oath against him and his party, his people, his cause? I gritted my teeth, scolding myself for being too forward in my zeal to account for what I saw. . . . He was looking off into space; he had not answered me. Ought I ask him again? I decided not to. Nkrumah had been educated in the United States and he must have known instinctively how such an oath had struck me. And I knew that he couldn't imagine my being shocked and, at the same time, being in complete agreement! But, if he was reticent about this, what about the other things I'd see in the Gold Coast?

Another song was sung and, as we all stood up, the Prime Minister, looking off, slowly and seemingly absent-mindedly, folded the slip of paper containing the oath and put it into his pocket. I knew then that I'd never get a chance to copy it. . . . I was of a mind to remind him that I had asked for it, but discretion became the better part of curiosity and I inhibited myself. I'd be content with what I'd heard. Obviously the Prime Minister did not want me to attach too much importance, politically or psychologically, to that oath. How could I make him understand that I understood, and that in general I agreed to it as being an inevitable part of the twentieth century?

The meeting ended and we were escorted by the roaring motorcycle cavalcade back toward the Prime Minister's home. During the ride the Prime Minister was poised, aloof, silent. Intuitively, I knew that he was thinking of my reaction to that oath-taking. . . . We reached his house and sat upon the lawn under a starry sky and listened to an African band playing native tunes. Suddenly the Prime Minister spoke to me:

"Let's go upstairs and talk."

"A good idea," I said.

In his living room we sat on a divan; a steward served some drinks.

"Did you like what you saw?" he asked me.

"I'm stunned, amazed, and gratified," I told him truthfully. "Like is no word for what I felt. You've done what the Western world has said is impossible."

He threw back his head and laughed. A silence hung in the air for several moments. I felt called upon to say something, to explain, to justify myself.

"Look, I think you know something of my background," I began. "For twelve years I was a member of the Communist Party of the United States. I'm no longer a Communist, but I'm for black people. I know from history and from my personal life what has happened to us—at least, I know some of it. I don't know Africa intimately. That's why I'm here. I'd like to understand all of this. I think that my life has prepared me to do that."

"I'm a Marxist Socialist," he told me.

"I know that there are political things that have to be told with discretion," I went on. "But I'd like to see and know how you organized all this."

I wanted to be given the "green light" to look, to know, to be shown everything. I wanted the opportunity to try to weigh a movement like this, to examine its worth as a political instrument; it was the first time in my life that I'd come in contact with a mass movement conducted by Negro leadership and I felt that I could, if given a chance, understand it.

He gave me a mechanical nod, but I could see that his thoughts were far away. Then a crowd of men and women pushed their way into the room and there were more introductions.

"He is a novelist," the Prime Minister said, pointing to me.

"*A novelist?*" a tall black man echoed.

"Yes; a novelist," the Prime Minister repeated.

The tall black man's face was baffled; he stared at me, as though he doubted my existence. The Prime Minister saved the day by bursting into a loud and long laugh which was soon joined by all in the room. I sat silent and soon the crowd was talking among themselves in their tribal tongues. The Prime Minister rose and left; he returned a few moments later and sat next to me.

"The ideological development here is not very high," he said.

"Uh hunh," I grunted.

"There are but two or three of us who know what we are doing," he said.

"George gave me a list of your bright boys to talk to," I told him.

"Is Kofi Baako on that list?" he asked.

"Yes."

"Talk to him," the Prime Minister said. "He's my right-hand man."

"Is he here tonight?"

"No; he's in Cape Coast at the moment."

The Prime Minister disappeared and I struck up a conversation with some of the party militants. I wanted to break down their reserve and hear what they thought.

"Do you think that the English will shoot if you press your demands for self-government?" I asked.

A look of horror came over their faces.

"*They* can shoot, but *we* won't," a boy swore.

"They'll never get us in that sort of position," another told me.

Some of the boys who didn't understand English asked what I had said and they formed a knot debating and arguing my question. I was soon standing to one side. It was a strange household. People came and went. Presently a line of women edged into the room; at that moment a band downstairs began a dance tune and the women at once went into that same snakelike, shuffling dance that they had done on the streets earlier in the afternoon. The band boomed louder and the sound of dancing came from downstairs, upstairs, everywhere. . . . I wandered out upon the balcony and saw the Prime Minister dancing alone on the lawn with about ten women around him. African dancing is not like Western dancing; one dances alone if one wants to.

It was hot. I felt exhausted. It was near three o'clock in the morning when I met the Prime Minister entering the living room.

"I must go. I'm dead tired," I said.

"The car will take you home," he said.

We shook hands. A young man escorted me down to the car and soon I was whizzing through the humid night toward the government bungalow.

Nine

Next morning when I awakened my sense of amazement at what I'd seen was, if anything, stronger than it had been the day before. I'd seen something new under the sun. What a bewildering unity Nkrumah had forged: Christianity, tribalism, paganism, sex, nationalism, socialism, housing, health, and industrial schemes . . . ! Could this sweep Africa? I could well understand why the British, when they first saw it, thought it was a joke. They could not believe that a black man could take the political methods that Europe had perfected and apply them to Africa.

And, of course, only a native African could do what Nkrumah had done. Five hundred years of European barbarism had made it impossible for any European alive to claim the kind of frenzied assent from these black millions that Nkrumah claimed. To that degree, the Nkrumahs of Africa had something that the Europeans could never take from them. What had given Nkrumah the chance to do this was that the British concepts of education had misfired; they had thought that any African who earned a string of university degrees would never dare to stick his hands into this muck, would feel too much revulsion to do so. . . . From the point of view of British mentality, an education was a guarantee that the educated young African would side with the British, and, what is more, many of them did, especially the young Christians. And the British had never suppressed nationalist feeling *per se*; they'd merely shunted it into ineffective channels.

But the British had neglected to take fully into account that some of the Gold Coast boys would be beyond the confines of British influence, that some of them would soak up Marxism and would return home feeling a sense of racial and class solidarity derived from the American Negro's proud and defensive nationalism. Above all, the British did not take into consideration that the Gold Coast boys could take Marxism and adapt it to their own peculiar African needs. For three decades the Russian Communists had tried to penetrate Africa, sending agent after agent into the jungle, and Nkrumah had, in five short years, so outstripped them that their ideas had become, by comparison, backward!

The indirect rule of the British had, unwittingly, created the very conditions which Nkrumah had organized. And the British had adopted that indirect method of ruling so that the religion and customs of the masses would remain undisturbed. . . . To operate their mines, their timber concessions, and their mills, the British had regimented African tribal life around new social and economic poles, and the exhortation of the missionaries had slowly destroyed the African's faith in his own religion and customs, thereby creating millions of psychologically detribalized Africans living uneasily and frustratedly in two worlds and really believing in neither of them.

But could this liquid emotion be harnessed to modern techniques? And from where would come the men to handle the work of administration when self-government came? Would Nkrumah have to impose a dictatorship until he could educate a new generation of young men who could work with him with a willing heart? Or would he have to rely upon the dangerous collaboration of the British until such could come about? I'd seen the basis of power in the streets of Accra, but could it be used? And how?

And that fierce optimism? Where did it come from? What justified it? Of course, the Gold Coast had about 4,000 British in a population of 4,000,000 blacks, and one could actually forget that Europe existed.

Last night I hadn't had time to question myself closely regarding that snakelike, shuffling dance, that strange veering and weaving of the body. . . . That there was some kind of link between the native African and the American Negro was undoubtedly true. But what did it mean? A certain group of American anthropologists had long clamored for a recognition of what they had quaintly chosen to call "African survivals," a phrase which they had coined to account for exactly what I had observed. And now, as I reflected upon last night's experience, even more items of similarity came to me: that laughter that bent the knee and turned the head (as if in embarrassment!); that queer shuffling of the feet when one was satisfied or in agreement; that inexplicable, almost sullen silence that came from disagreement or opposition. . . . All of this was strange but familiar.

I understood why so many American Negroes were eager to disclaim any relationship with Africa; they were being prompted by the same motives that made the Irish or the Jew or the Italian immigrant more militantly American than the native-born American. The American Negro's passionate identification with America stemmed from two considerations: first, it was a natural part of his assimilation of Americanism; second, so long had Africa been described as something shameful, barbaric, a land in which one went about naked, a land in which his ancestors had sold their kith and kin as slaves—so long had he heard all this that he wanted to disassociate himself in his mind from all such realities. . . .

The bafflement evoked in me by this new reality did not spring from any desire to disclaim kinship with Africa, or from any shame of being of African descent. My problem was how to account for this "survival" of Africa in America when I stoutly denied the mystic influence of "race," when I was as certain as I was of being alive that it was only, by and large, in the concrete social frame of reference in which men lived that one could account for men being what they were. I sighed; this was truly a big problem. . . .

Restless, I sought the streets of Accra just to look at Africa. And while strolling along I found, for the first time in my life, a utilitarian function for nappy hair; the clerks and school children stuck their red and yellow pencils in their hair in order not to lose them, and they never did, so close and secure did their kinks cling to those pencils. Some children carried their ink bottles and schoolbooks on their heads, their arms swinging free as they walked. I saw a little girl peel an orange to eat it; she broke the orange in two, put one half of it upon her head and proceeded, as she walked along, to eat the other half; when she had devoured it, she reached up nonchalantly and got the remaining half of the orange and commenced to nibble away at it.

Bracing myself to encounter rebuffs, I strayed off the main thoroughfares and entered a maze of warrens—compounds—enclosed by stone walls. I blinked; before me was a scene crowded with scores of men, women, children, and everything seemed to be happening at once. . . . The over-all impression was that the black human beings had so completely merged with the dirt that one could scarcely tell where humanity ended and the earth began; they lived in and of the dirt, the flesh of bodies seeming to fuse insensibly with the soil.

On a nearby stone wall were scores of lizards, red, green, gray; and, when I moved, they scuttled to safety. Chickens moved slowly and unafraid among the children and pecked at piles of refuse. Here and there a sheep or goat stood sleepily. Mangy dogs lay in the sun. A woman was kneeling upon the ground, frying some kind of meat in a smoking pot of deep fat. A girl was pounding *fufu* with a long wooden pole, plunging the pole into a wooden vat in which was a mixture of boiled plantains, yams, and cassava; now and then she paused and added a little water to the yellow, doughlike mass, then pounded again. . . . Still another girl, just a few feet from the *fufu*-pounder, was squatting and tending a bubbling pot that cooked over a pile of stones enclosing a tiny flickering fire. Two men, standing opposite each other, were washing a huge tub of clothes, running their hands down washboards that rested in the same tub. . . . Another was mending a pair of shoes. A tiny little nude girl was grinding red pepper on a stone. A fat woman sat nursing a baby at her right breast while she idly and unconsciously, staring off into space, toyed with the teat of her left breast with the fingers of her left hand. A tiny boy minded some ears of corn that were roasting over an iron grill. Off to one side a group of little girls was playing a strange game that consisted of jumping up and down and clapping their hands—a game called *ampe* which fascinated me no end as long as I was in Africa. The legs of the girls were skinny, their black shoulder blades stuck out at sharp angles, and yet their supply of physical energy seemed inexhaustible.

I took out my camera to photograph the scene and the children let out a warning yell that made every face jerk toward me. At once the women began covering their breasts and the boys rose and ran toward me, yelling:

"Take me! Take me!"

Chances of a natural photograph were impossible, and, not to disappoint the children, I snapped a picture or two of them. I turned to leave and they followed me. I walked faster and they began to run, yelling:

"Take me! Take me!"

I hastily turned a corner, hoping that they'd fall behind; but they came on and on, their ranks swelling as they ran. It was not until I was some five blocks from the compound that they began to fall out, one by one, and return. Didn't their mothers miss them? Wasn't there anyone to look after them? To let tiny children of four and five years of age have that much freedom filled me with wonder. . . .

I entered a store to buy a black bow tie and I found that I could barely make the African clerk understand me. My American accent must have indeed sounded strange to his ears which were used to British English spoken with a tribal accent. I had to repeat myself several times before he could grasp what I meant.

"Who owns this store?" I asked him.

"A Syrian," he said, pointing to the rear.

"Do Syrians own most of the stores?"

"Naw, sar. The Indians own some too."

"How are they to work for?"

"All right *now*," he mumbled, eying his Syrian boss.

"What do you mean by *now*?"

"I mean since the CPP, sar," he said, referring to the Convention People's Party.

"How was that? Why did they change?"

"They were scared that we'd take power and chase 'em out of the Gold Coast if they didn't behave, sar," he told me.

Before the coming of Nkrumah there had been much racial tension between the Africans and the Syrians, but, with the mounting tide of clamor for self-government, the Syrians had abruptly changed their attitudes toward the masses of the Africans, and the Syrians were now considered the largest and steadiest contributors of cash to the coffers of the Convention People's Party. . . .

When I was back upon the streets again I was impressed by what I felt to be a sense of fragility, of delicacy almost, of the physique of the people. For the most part they were small-boned, of medium height, well-developed muscularly but tending toward slenderness. I had an intuitive impression that these people were old, old, maybe the *oldest* people on earth, and I felt a sense of melancholy knowing that their customs, laboriously created and posited for thousands of years, had been condemned as inferior, and shattered by a strong and predatory nation. The delicate strands of that fragile culture, so organically dependent upon the soil and climate of West Africa, so purely woven out of the naked impulses of naked men, could never be reconstituted. We had to depend upon guesses and folklore to determine what that culture had once meant to them. True, they still clung, in secrecy and shame, to the ways of their fathers; but, surrounded by a new order of life, they didn't and couldn't believe in them as they once had.

I was pleased to see that, with but a few exceptions, they did not deliberately disfigure or deform their bodies, distend their lips, or force huge holes in their ears or nostrils. Once or twice I did see women who had induced strange swellings on their skins in order to beautify themselves, but that was rare. (I divined later that their religious customs made such deformations abhorrent to them, for they felt that one's chances of passing, when one died, into the other world depended somewhat upon the degree to which one's body was intact. Circumcision was taboo among the Ashanti, and, among those close to the royal family, the spilling of a woman's blood was also strictly forbidden. An intelligent African doctor told me that no wife of the King of Ashanti could submit to any operation, no matter how urgently needed.)

Wilted from the heat, I made my way back to the government bungalow and found a strange young African waiting at the door to talk to me.

"What can I do for you?" I asked him.

"Dr. Wright—" he began.

"Please, I'm no doctor of any kind," I told him.

"Well, sar," he said, smiling. "I work for the English family next door. . . ."

"Yes?"

"You're an American, sar? Aren't you?"

"Yes; I am."

"Maybe you can help me, sar? Please," he begged.

"I'll try. But what is it?"

"You see, sar, we don't like the British. I met American soldiers during the war and they were nice, sar," he explained. "Now, sar, I want to educate myself. I want to take a correspondence course from America and I need help, sar."

"Just what sort of help do you need and what kind of a course do you want to take?" I asked.

"I want to be a detective, sar," he said.

"What?" I thought that I hadn't heard him.

"A detective, sar. Like the ones you see in the movies," he made himself explicit.

"And you want to take all of this in the form of a correspondence course from America?"

"That's right, sar," he said, smiling, glad that at last I'd understood him.

"Now, just how can I help you in that?"

"Well, sar, money is controlled here. I went to the post office, sar, to buy dollars and they wouldn't sell them to me. They said that I'd have to go to a bank, sar. Well, I went to the bank and they said no; they wouldn't sell me dollars, sar. They said I'd have to get the government to okay my application for dollars. Then I went to the government, sar, and talked to a young Englishman."

"And what did he say?"

"Sar, he said I couldn't have any dollars. . . . You see, sar, the English are jealous of us. They never want us to do anything, sar. . . ."

"Why wouldn't the Englishman let you have the dollars?"

"He just wouldn't, sar. He said that I could take a course in how to be a detective from London, sar."

"From London?" I echoed.

"Yes, sar; that's exactly what he said, sar."

I looked at him, at his pleading eyes, at those half-parted, waiting lips, at the slight stoop of respect in his bodily posture.

"Come onto the terrace," I told him.

He followed me and stood respectfully as I sat.

"Sit down," I said.

"Thank you, sar," he said, sitting.

"From where did you get this notion of becoming a detective?"

"In a magazine. . . . You know, sar. One of these American magazines. . . . They tell about crimes. I got it right in my room now, sar. Shall I get it for you, sar?"

"No; no; that's not necessary. Now, just why do you want to become a detective?"

"To catch criminals, sar."

"What criminals?"

He stared at me as though he thought that I'd taken leave of my senses.

"The English, sar!" he exclaimed. "Sar, we Africans don't violate the law. This is *our* country, sar. It's the English who came here and fought us, took our land, our gold, and our diamonds, sar. If I could be a good detective, sar, I'd find out how they did it. I'd put them in jail, sar."

It was all clear now. But the pathos of it stilled my tongue for several moments.

"Didn't the British tell you not to spend your money taking courses in detective work from either New York or London?" I asked him.

"Naw, sar. They just wanted me to take the courses from London, sar," he said. "But the English courses wouldn't tell me all the truth about detective work, sar. They know better than to do that, sar. Oh, sar, you don't *know* the English!"

"In other words, the English wouldn't give you the *real* lessons in detective work? Is that it? They'd keep the really important secrets from you . . . ?"

"That's it, sar! You can't trust them, sar!"

"To whom would you give this evidence of the criminality of the English?"

"To all the people, sar. Then they'd know the truth. And I'd send some of it to America, sar."

"Why?"

"So they'd know, too, sar."

"And if they knew, what do you think they'd do?"

"Then maybe they'd help us, sar. Don't you think so, sar?"

"Why don't you try studying law?" I asked him, seeking some way to get his feet upon the earth.

"Law's all right," he said hesitantly. "But, sar, law's for property. Detective work's for catching criminals, sar. That's what the English are, sar."

"Just how did you get hold of this magazine?"

"My Massa brought it home, sar."

"And when he got through with it, you read it?"

"Yes, sar. But he threw it away before I took it, sar. I got it out of the dustbin in back," he told me circumspectly.

"Look, let me tell you how most detectives get to be detectives," I said. "They start out as policemen and work their way up. Or they start out as stool pigeons. . . . Do you know what a stool pigeon is?"

"Yes, sar. I know that from the movies, sar."

"American movies?"

"Yes, sar. I see a lot of them, sar."

"Well, a stool pigeon tells stories on his friends, on anybody and everybody. In that way the police come to trust him. In time, if he's really good, he might become a detective. It's not really a good job for you."

He was baffled; for a moment he hung his head in thought.

"But I *want* to be a detective, sar," he said insistently.

"But how can I help you?" I was dejected.

"Well, sar, you can sell me some dollars," he said. "I need seventy-five dollars to pay for the first course, sar."

Where could I start with the boy? His view of reality was warped; it was composed of fragments of Hollywood movies and American pulp magazines and he had lived his life so far from such manufactured dreams that he was unable to tell what was plausible or implausible in them. And all of this was fed by an inflamed sense of national oppression; he felt that the least move he made to better his condition would be thwarted by the British who were the focal point of the organization of his hate, a hate that would always be his excuse if he failed, no matter what he tried to do or how badly he did it. As long as the Union Jack flew over his country, he could always blame the British for everything.

"Why don't you ask some of the rich Africans to help you?" I suggested.

"Oh, *them*, sar?" He actually repressed a sarcastic laugh.

"Why not?" I demanded.

"They are *worse* than the British, sar."

I saw now that I had to be careful in talking to him, for he had a ready category in which to put anybody with a black skin who disagreed with him. The black man who opposed him was a British collaborater.

"How are they worse?"

"They keep away from their black brothers, sar."

"Look, I don't have any dollars with me in cash. I've only travelers' checks. And they can't do you any good," I told him.

I studied him. Maybe he had been prompted by the police to ask me for dollars? No; his story sounded too pathetic to be false, too understandably human to have been calculated.

"Can't you do something, sar, please? I'm not begging; I've saved the pounds, sar. I can give them to you."

How could I get at the boy? He was hugging to his heart a delusive dream and he was determined not to surrender it; if he had to let that dream go, he'd hate whoever robbed him of it. But that false dream stood between him and his seeing reality for what it was, colored his vision regarding the value of being a detective. . . .

"I'll have to think about this," I told him with a sigh.

He thanked me and left; I went upstairs and sat in a chair and shook my head. Good God. . . . Did the men who had administered this colony before the coming of Nkrumah know that this sort of rot was simmering in the minds of boys? Maybe they had known it and had not cared? No; I was inclined to feel that they had not known it, for, if they had, I was sure that they would have been frightened. But what stunned me most about the boy was his absolute distrust of the British; it was by far the deepest emotion of his life.

Next morning the Prime Minister's office phoned to tell me that I'd be called for at four o'clock and taken to a huge outdoor political rally to be held at the Westend Arena. The Prime Minister was scheduled to speak upon his forthcoming motion for self-government and he indicated that he wanted me to greet his followers with a short speech.

As I was driven toward the rally that afternoon, I could hear the roar of the vast crowd five blocks before the arena came into the line of my vision. Arriving at the edge of the throng, I heard a speaker addressing the audience in Ga, the language of a tribe close to the Accra region. I was led through packed black bodies to the platform where the Prime Minister sat surrounded by his ministers and aides.

Fanning out in front of the platform were more than ten thousand faces whose brown, reddish, and black skins were lit to a blatant distinctness by the long red rays of the setting sun. There were practically no women present, a circumstance that I was to get accustomed to in all public affairs of the Gold Coast. Many of the men were barefooted and most of them wore their native togas. An impression of earthiness rose up from those tense, lifted faces that stretched so far away that they became dim to the eye—faces that seemed like a reality conjured up by a sorcerer from the early days of mankind; they appeared unsubstantial, like figments of a dream that would vanish upon close inspection. Then, at that moment, a roar welled up from ten thousand throats and the crowd's reality not only became real, but suggestive of a menace, a threat. . . .

The speaker threw a challenging question in English requiring a yes or no answer, for he wanted the audience to participate in the meeting, and the crowd hurled a rolling "NO!" that made my eardrums tingle. The speaker switched to Ga and hammered on and on; then he swung back to English, declaring:

"Nkrumah has led you this far and he will lead you on! If you don't support him, he cannot have the power to act for you! You must believe that he'll never let you down! He went to prison for you; he suffered for you; hell lay down his life for you! You must have faith and trust him! Do you trust him?"

"YES!" the crowd roared.

"Will you follow him?" the speaker asked.

"YES!" the crowd answered.

"Do you believe that he fights for freedom?"

"YES!" the crowd answered.

"Who organized the CPP?"

"NKRUMAH!"

"Who raised the slogan for self-government NOW?"

"NKRUMAH!"

"Who?"

"NKRUMAH!"

"I asked you who?"

"NNNKKKKRRRUUUMMMMAAH!"

"Will *he* fight for you?"

"YES!"
"Will *you* fight for him?"
"YES!"
"And what are we fighting for?"
"FREE—DOOOOM! FREE—DOOOOOM!"

At times the dialogue between the speaker and the audience became so intimate, so prolonged, so dramatic that all sense of distance between leaders and followers ceased to exist, and a spirit of fellowship, of common identity prevailed among faces young and old, smooth and bearded, wise and simple. . . . The speaker lifted his voice in song and the mass joined in, and the collective sound seemed to rise as high as the skies:

There is victory for us
In the struggle of the CPP,
There is victory for us!

Sons of Ghana, rise and fight!
Girls of Ghana, rise and shine!
In the struggle of the CPP
There is victory for us!

Forward ever, backward never;
In the struggle of the CPP
There is victory for us!

My turn came to greet the audience and I rose and spoke somewhat as follows:

"Men of Ghana: Your great and respected Prime Minister has extended to me an invitation to see your country, its people, and the rapid rate of development that you are making. It is with pride that I've come to look upon the labor of a man who attended our American schools and who has dedicated his life to the struggle for the freedom of his country.

"I'm one of the lost sons of Africa who has come back to look upon the land of his forefathers. In a superficial sense it may be said that I'm a stranger to most of you, but, in terms of a common heritage of suffering and hunger for freedom, your heart and my heart beat as one.

"Centuries ago the living bodies of our forefathers were dragged from these shores and sold into slavery; centuries ago the bodies of our forefathers formed the living instruments which the white men of Europe used to build the foundations of the Western world; centuries ago we were reduced to nameless, stateless pawns shuffled by the will of Europeans and Americans across the chessboards of history; centuries ago our tribes were so mauled, mixed, and scattered that we could not even speak to one another in a common tongue.

"This is indeed a turgid, cloudy past, a past not of our making or choosing; yet, despite all this, this heritage has brought us a sense of unity deeper than race, a sense of humanity that has made us sensitive to the sufferings of all mankind, that has made us increasingly human in a world that is rapidly losing its claim to humanity. . . .

"Under the leadership of your Leader, the Convention People's Party has roused immense interest throughout America and the world at large. You men are, of all the teeming millions of Africa, the first to step upon the political stage of the twentieth century. What you do will have consequences that will roll down the years. What you achieve in the coming months will to a large degree define the character of the coming struggle for the redemption of Africa.

"Today, in your struggle for self-government, you are presenting to the men of England a political promissory note which the English have declared to be the real moral currency of mankind, and now the world is watching to see if the English will honor their own currency! They asked you to build political parties, and you did! But you did it so much quicker than they thought you could! You are making your bid for freedom in terms which your teachers in England and America told you were correct. Now, in your struggle for self-government, you are presenting for redemption a promise made to you by the heart of England. Will she honor it? The world is waiting to see. . . .

"From the 30,000,000 sons and daughters of African descent in the New World, both in North and South America, and in the many islands of the Atlantic, I bring you deep-felt greetings.

"I am an American and therefore cannot participate in your political affairs. But I wish you victory in your bid for freedom! Ghana, show us the way! The only advice that I can give you is two thousand years old and was uttered by a Man Whose name is frequently used but Whose moral precepts millions choose to ignore. To a great and despoiled Africa, to an Africa awakening from its slumber, to an Africa burning with hope, I advise you: TAKE UP YOUR BED AND WALK!"

The handclapping was weak and scattered. Perhaps they were not used to hearing speakers who did not raise their voices, or maybe they had not understood . . . ? I sat. The Prime Minister rose to speak. The chairman asked the crowd to pledge their personal loyalty to the Leader and I saw twenty thousand palms shoot willingly upward and their colors—orange, brownish, dark yellow, and dingy gray—made me feel that I was gazing upon a sweep of newly turned earth. . . . And from the rapt look on their faces I knew that these men had never before in their lives made such a pledge to a secular cause. Here was religion melting into politics; prayers were becoming pledges; hope was translating itself into organization; devotion was becoming obedience; trust was turning itself into discipline; and reverence was being converted into vigilance. . . .

In his speech the Prime Minister was quiet, restrained; he informed his followers that it was necessary from time to time to report to them upon progress. He reminded them that if they were displeased with him that they could dismiss him. He asked for their trust for the future.

"It was Clausewitz who said that politics is war by other means," he told them. "Because our struggle now has entered a quiet phase, do not think that we are not fighting. We are fighting the same old battle for freedom with other weapons. . . ."

I watched the faces closely. Did they understand such concepts? I wondered. . . . Could such sophisticated language be grasped by men so new to party struggles? How would this party behave in complicated situations? Could these pledges of loyalty withstand the many snarling currents ahead in the sea of politics?

The Prime Minister spoke on, and the sun, as it went down in the west, was a huge blue-gray ball showing through folds of straggling clouds. Again the vast crowd was asked to pledge its loyalty to the Leader by raising its hands, and again those clay-colored, orange, red, yellowish, brown, and grayish palms lifted skyward, extending as far back in the fading purple light as my eyes could see. . . . And I realized that sprawling over this vast continent were millions of other black people just as eager, as submissive, as trusting, who wanted to hold up their hands and pledge their loyalty to a leader—eager to die, if need be, for their redemption, their justification in the eyes of the world.

The Prime Minister finished and there was applause, singing, chanting. On the platform there was some milling around and talking. A newspaperman came to me and asked:

"We'd like to run your speech in tomorrow's paper. I'm with the *Graphic*. Can we have it?"

Instinctively I turned to the Prime Minister.

"There's a reporter asking to print what I said."

"Have you got it written down?" he asked.

"Yes," I said.

"Let me see it," he said.

I gave him my notes. He took them, looked off solemnly, then folded them slowly. The reporter waited. I waited. Then the Prime Minister came close to me and pushed the notes into the top breast pocket of my suit; he said no word and I said no word. I looked at the reporter and he looked at me. Then the Prime Minister moved silently away. . . . The reporter took a few steps backward, looking around with embarrassment. I did not understand what was happening and I did not want to ask for any explanation in public. Had I said something wrong in my speech? No one had asked to read what I had proposed to say. If they had, I'd have gladly submitted my ideas to be censored. But why had the Prime Minister taken my notes and given them back to me with such a meaningful gesture? I wanted to know, but, in the end, I resolved that I'd do nothing; I'd wait. . . .

I made my way back to the government bungalow in a deeply thoughtful mood.

Ten

Next morning I resolved to move at once into the center of the city and I made the round of the three available hotels. I finally settled on the Seaview which stood at the edge of the beach and fronted James Town, the slum area.

The Seaview was grim, with dingy mosquito nets over the beds; there were flies, greasy food, spattered walls, wooden floors whose cracks held decades of filth. The cold-water faucets gave forth water that was almost hot, so exposed to the tropic sun was the plumbing of the establishment. It was the kind of hotel that one read about in a Joseph Conrad novel and, what intrigued me most, I had only to go to the balcony and look down and there was Africa in all its squalor, vitality and fantastic disorder. . . .

No breezes blew here to freshen the air. My skin was always oily and wet and tiny mosquitoes bit deeply into my arms and ankles. The humidity was so dense that each time I shaved I had to clean a film of sweat from the mirror. An army of stewards was in attendance, dressed in white, their naked feet swishing to and fro day and night. No one hurried; voices were never raised; the hotel seemed in the grip of the heat, mastered by it.

At mealtimes fried food, prepared by a chef whose god seemed to have been named grease, was served. The mattresses on the bed were damp and stained by God knows what. The locks, keys, and latches on the doors were rusty and worked with difficulty, so damaged had they become by the ever-present moisture. The lavatory, when it was flushed, set up a groaning, howling noise that penetrated every room of the hotel at all hours. And almost always one could hear the continuous and mysterious beating of drums deep in the maze of the streets of James Town. . . . The hotel's veranda was constantly crowded with Africans and Europeans guzzling beer which was used instead of the uncertain and sometimes dangerous drinking water. It was amazing how quickly I got used to the medley of odors; the early morning stench of homemade soap, the noon-hour cooking smells, and the vapors of excrement drifting into the hotel from the open drainage ditches outside.

The hotel was owned by a Greek; there were three hotels in Accra and all of them were owned by foreigners. Africans seemed to have the notion that there was something immoral about a hotel, and when you explained to them how needful hotels were to travelers, to those who had no relatives, they'd only smile or giggle. Pride would have kept any African, if he had had the capital, from operating a hotel, even though he had a Western education from Oxford or Cambridge. Living in tribal families, boasting "brothers" and "sisters" by the hundreds in far-flung towns and villages, an African had only to seek out his tribe to be housed, fed, and taken care of.

Using the Seaview as a base, I made many long excursions into the alleyways and compounds of James Town, in and out of the narrow paths between crummy shacks, and even down to the seashore where the strangely painted canoes of the fishermen lay upon the hot sand. Those inhabitants of James Town who lived near the water front were fisherfolk, and their drying nets, dark brown or purple, could be seen draped over wooden trestles in the sun. If a good catch of herring had come in the night before, the women, their cloths tied at their hips, would be arranging the fish in the sun to dry, laying them in rows side by side upon the red earth, upon palm leaves, or upon the rusty tin roofs. . . . And the cured fish would be shipped into the interior.

In shady places the men could be seen standing or squatting, mending nets, or talking politics, or arranging the details of their next fishing expedition. Now and then, stepping calmly among the sprawling men and women, would come a chief, togaed, sandaled, surrounded by his "linguist" and his elders, a young boy holding a vast umbrella above his head. . . .

Practically no grass grew in James Town and there were but few trees. Above all, there were no flowers. So denuded of blooming things was the African's environment that one wondered if it was by intent. (Someone told me later that the lack of vegetation was to keep down the invasion of snakes, but I doubt if that can account for the scarcity of green stuff around African homes.) It might well be that the nearness of the jungle and its lush creepers have made the African feel that he could derive all the delight he needs in growing and blooming things without bothering to plant anything in front of his door.

I turned down a narrow path and saw a woman bent over, resting on her knees, washing her hair in a tin pan, lathering the soapsuds over her head, her eyes closed. Evidently she had heard my footsteps on the hard red clay, for she paused, cocked her head, and listened for a second with her eyes still closed; then, as I walked on, she resumed her vigorous massaging of her hair. . . .

I came upon a group of old men sitting upon their wooden stools, their naked backs resting against a stone wall; they were talking and their bony black bodies reminded me of those wooden carvings now so rare in Africa and which can be seen only in the drawing rooms of rich Europeans. As I passed them I caught the low, soft murmurs of the Ga language flowing from their lips. They knew undoubtedly from my dress that I was a stranger, yet they evinced no overt curiosity. After I'd gone about twenty yards I turned my head and found them gazing at me. But the moment they knew that I knew that they were staring at me, they turned their eyes away. A stranger incited Africans to a high pitch of interest, but they were sensitive and always tried to hide that interest.

I barged into a crowded compound, walking slowly, as though I had a right to be there. The women, as they saw me approach, stopped their work, reached down and took hold of their cloths and covered their naked breasts. I walked on for a few yards and glanced back; they felt that I had gone and had let their cloths fall again to the ground, not slackening the performance of their domestic duties. . . . It was not because I was a man that they had covered themselves, for there were many men in evidence everywhere. It was not only because I was a stranger that they had exhibited such modesty; it was because I wore Western clothes, shoes, a sun helmet, that they had shrunk and covered themselves. They had performed a gesture in which, according to their customs, they did not really believe. But they had been long taught by the missionaries that it was considered shameful—that *others* considered it shameful—to be naked, and so when they had caught sight of me, they had hastily sheltered themselves. My approaching presence had been like the shadow of the Cross falling athwart the innocence of their simple lives, and, because of their conditioning, they had paid deference to that Cross; but the moment I had gone, they had reverted quickly and naturally to their traditional behavior. The words of St. Paul, that arch inhibitor of men, came to my mind:

> **What shall we say then? Is the law sin? God forbid. Nay, I had not known lust, except the law had said, Thou shalt not covet.**
>
> **But sin, taking occasion by the commandment, wrought in me all manner of concupiscence. For without the law sin is dead.**
>
> **For I was alive without the law once: but when the commandment came, sin revived, and I died.**

As I walked on in the hot sun I could sense vast emotional impactions taking place; I could feel dammed-up physical hungers straining like jungle plants for the heat of the sun; and, in the end, I could see that Africa too some day would exhibit those strange and fantastic patterns of Western neurotic behavior that would necessitate the uncovering of all of that which religion was now covering up, that there would be doctors to coax these people to believe again in that which religion had taught them to repress. I could feel the mental suffering and emotional anguish that had yet to come into those innocent lives. . . .

I paused before a young woman selling tin pans and, by pointing, I indicated that I wanted to buy one. At once a group of women gathered about; it seemed that my buying a pan made them feel that they had the right to examine me at close quarters. The woman to whom I had pointed out the pan seemed baffled; she called hurriedly to a friend. Soon a crowd of no less than fifteen women were ranged about me, chattering excitedly. Finally they called an old man who spoke a little English and he translated. The pan cost seven shillings and I paid, sweating, wondering why the women were evincing such interest. As I started off with the pan under my arm, the old man called me back.

"What is it?" I asked.

The women chattered even more loudly now.

"What you do with pan, Massa? Women wanna know."

I looked at the women and they hid their faces, laughing.

"I'm going to use the pan to boil water. I'm making a chemical solution in which to develop films . . ." My voice trailed off, for I could see that he had not understood me.

"They wanna know if you buy it for wife?" the man asked.

"No."

There was another outburst of laughter.

"They wanna know if Massa cook chop in pan?"

"No. I eat in a hotel restaurant," I said.

The women conferred with the man again and he shook his head. Finally he turned to me and asked:

"Massa, women wanna know if Massa make peepee in pan?"

I blinked in bewilderment. The women were howling with laughter now.

I pushed away, hearing their black laughter echoing in my ears as I tried to lose myself in the crowd. I learned afterward that it was considered a disgrace for a man to purchase pots, pans, or food, that it was an open confession that he had no woman to do such things for him, and that no decent, self-respecting African would ever dare be caught buying such a thing as a pan in the public market. In the eyes of those women I'd lost caste, for they'd been conditioned in a hard masculine school of detribalized thought whose slogans regarding women were: keep 'em ignorant, keep 'em pregnant, and keep 'em ten paces behind you.

That evening the Prime Minister's office called and informed me that I'd be picked up and taken to Cape Coast to watch the Convention People's Party campaign in a by-election. It seemed that Kwesi Plange, one of the youngest and brightest members of the party, had died and that it was now necessary to fill his post with a man upon whom Nkrumah could rely in the Legislative Assembly. The Plange seat was being hotly contested by the opposition parties led by the English-educated old guard. Cape Coast was the educational center of the nation and most of the best educated families lived there. A Gold Coast slogan went: as Cape Coast goes, so goes the country. Hence, the Convention People's Party was most anxious to win. But, so many wild and hot charges had been made by both the Convention People's Party and the opposition that the outcome was a tossup and an opposition victory was being predicted in some quarters.

Next morning at ten o'clock a string of about twenty automobiles halted in front of my hotel; the cavalcade consisted of sound trucks, private cars filled with the party's ablest speakers and organizers. There was one car filled with women only. . . . This rigorous separation of the sexes seemed to prevail in almost everything the Africans did; you never saw their women until the time came for them to make their appearance, and then they moved ghostily, doing their chores, and, it seemed, at some prearranged moment, they would vanish as quickly and silently as they had come.

I sat in the car with the Prime Minister and we roared out into the countryside. A blue haze hung over the green stretches of forest. Much of the conversation that went on was in tribal language and it didn't seem to bother them that I couldn't understand; it may be that they talked their tribal tongue so that I *wouldn't* understand. . . . I felt that some of them regarded me as an outsider who'd scorn their habits, their manners, and their attitudes. I found the African an oblique, a hard-to-know man who seemed to take a kind of childish pride in trying to create a state of bewilderment in the minds of strangers. Only a man who himself had felt such bewilderment in the presence of strangers could have placed so high and false a value upon it. They seemed to feel that that which they did not reveal to me I could never know, but nothing could have been more erroneous.

On this journey I had an opportunity to observe the Prime Minister in action at close range. Among his own people he was a democrat, self-forgetfully identifying himself with the common masses in deed and word each passing hour. He slept, played, and ate with them, sharing his life in a manner that no Englishman or missionary ever could. . . . It was his lapsing into a sudden silence that drew a line between himself and them. His prescriptive right to leadership was derived from his demonstrating the correctness of his political tactics. I'd not witnessed any evidence of the fury of which I'd been told that he was capable, but there was a hidden core of hardness in him which I was sure that no one could bring to the surface quicker than an Englishman. . . .

The cavalcade halted in a coconut grove just outside of Cape Coast, in sight of the rolling Atlantic which sent white-capped waves breaking in foam upon the rock-strewn beach. Standing to one side and flanked by his trusted aides, the Prime Minister organized his entry into the town, indicating which car was to enter first, who was to ride in each car. The loud-speakers of the sound trucks were tested; an agenda for the day was drawn up; the route to be taken was mapped out.

To Nkrumah's orders the party men reacted quickly, keenly; here, less than five hundred miles from the Equator, amidst an appalling heat and humidity, these blacks whom the world had branded as being lazy and indifferent went about their duties with a zeal that would have put even Communists to shame. While this organizing was transpiring, a crowd of barefooted black boys clustered around. The Prime Minister asked me:

"How about a drink of coconut milk?"

"That'd be fine," I said.

At his signal the boys raced toward the trees; they did not climb them; they walked up, so adroitly did they scale the tall, slick tree trunks. Soon they were nestling in the tops of the trees and coconuts rained earthward. A tall boy picked them up and, with a cutlass, whacked holes in them. I was handed one; the juice tasted sweet, cool, and delicious.

I noticed that the women's contingent stood discreetly to one side. Such separateness, I was now convinced, must have a deep basis, a religious origin. At no time did the women mingle with the men; they kept in one compact group, to themselves. I spoke to one and she replied shyly, edging away. . . . She was a fully mature woman and surely she was not afraid of talking to a man. This exclusiveness of the women was undoubtedly due to some powerful tribal taboo too deep for even the Convention People's Party to overcome. . . .

The cavalcade was ready; we got into the cars; the Prime Minister stood up, lifted his hand in the party salute. I sat behind him in the open convertible car. . . . The loud-speakers of the sound trucks blared:

"FREE—DOOOOOM!"

And the procession was off on its political mission. Already the people of Cape Coast, hearing the roar, were crowding into the streets, rushing from their mud or concrete houses to salute and scream:

"FREE—DOOOOOM!"

The Prime Minister knew where his votes were; he hit the slum section first. The people, many of them half naked, flowed out of the warrens and mazes of compounds into the streets and their reactions were vital. They waved their hands in that queer, trembling vibration of the outstretched palm, giving a rolling, veering motion with their bodies as they sang and yelled:

"FREE—DOOOOOM! FREE—DOOOOM!"

"All for you, Kwame!"

"FREE—DOOOOOM! FREE—DOOOOOM!"

The procession wove in and out of the narrow, dusty streets, up and down hill. We passed Cape Coast Castle, built by the Swedes in 1657; it stood white and awesome in the hot sun. It was here that most of the slaves of the entire Guinea Coast had been assembled to be shipped to the New World. With loud-speakers screeching, we finally entered the Cape Coast residential section which fronted the sea; here lived some of the oldest and most respected families of the nation. They boasted a Sir or two, a few Orders of the British Empire, scornfully dubbed by the nationalists as: Obedient Boys of the Empire. . . . It was here that the African elite attitude held forth with bitter mien; it was here that the colony's most famous schools were located; it was here that Drs. Danquah and Busia, the intellectual leaders of the opposition, had raised the nostalgic but futile cry: "Preserve our traditions!"

There was less shouting for "FREE—DOOOOM!" in these quiet and sedate streets. Indeed, a skinny black man with a *pince-nez* athwart his nostrils, a chuck of graying mustache upon his upper lip, wearing his toga like that of a Roman emperor, stood on the wooden steps of his house and shouted again and again:

"I HATE HIM! I HATE HIM! I HATE HIM!"

The loud-speaker grated:

"VOTE FOR WELBECK! VOTE FOR THE CPP! VOTE FOR SELF-GOVERNMENT NOW! FOLLOW NKRUMAH TO VICTORY!"

After two hours of emotional blitzkrieg upon the inhabitants of Cape Coast, the tour ended; later in the afternoon would come the ideological assault in the form of words hurled in an open-air rally in the center of the city. As we drove toward a private home for lunch, the Prime Minister told me some of his problems.

"We really don't know the exact mineral resources of this country," he said. "The British were only interested in getting rich quick, exporting those minerals which could be carried away to England or some other place. One of our urgent tasks is to find out just what mineral wealth we have locked in our soil.

"We have a wonderful soil out of which to make bricks. We've also found locations with soil from which we can make cement. But the British ship us cement from England. . . . And nothing is done about the natural advantages of making cement here. We'd like to, say, in housing, evolve a distinctly native style of architecture that would be suitable both to our people and to the climate. . . .

"Until today England has decided what was good for us and shipped it to us at prices that they determined. For example, woolens, which are far too hot for this climate, were shipped here and sold. Even now they make our local police wear woolen uniforms in this awful heat. . . .

"Take another example. . . . Our climate is good to grow almost anything, yet 80 per cent of our staple food is imported. No one has really ever tried to experiment and determine what foods this soil will grow best. Why should the English care about things like that? They don't live here. They came here to make money in government or business and then they go back. And, of course, they never dreamed that one day the native would arise and say:

"'*No more of this!*'"

We sat down to lunch and the Prime Minister warned me:

"Take it easy with that food. You're not used to it."

I ignored him and served myself generously with groundnut soup, *kenke*, *fufu*, all of which tasted wonderful except for the fiery red pepper which pervaded everything.

"It may give you trouble," somebody else cautioned me.

"What harm can this good food do me?" I asked challengingly.

The next morning I knew. . . .

After lunch the cavalcade set out for the center of town where a vast crowd had congregated. There was no shade and the tropic sun beat down without mercy, making me squirm, sweat; finally I put my handkerchief, dampened with water, to my face to keep from feeling faint.

An African band—composed mostly of drums—played music and a group of singers chanted a dirge for the dead Kwesi Plange; then speaker after speaker lashed out at the crowd in Fanti and English. It seemed that the oppositionist, Dr. Busia, had allowed himself at some time or other to be quoted as saying that he did not think that the country was ready for self-government and this was used for all that it was worth against him. Even if people were not ready to govern themselves, they certainly would not want to be told so in such snobbish terms. . . . Nkrumah's orators were no novices; they were consummate politicians and they played upon the crowd's emotions with great skill. But from where had they gotten this art . . . ?

Again, as it had been in Accra, the meeting was a mixture of tribal ancestor worship, Protestantism, Catholicism—all blended together and directed toward modern political aims. One speaker, for example, trained his audience to respond verbally by telling them: "When I say——, then you say——!" The speaker then chanted his words and the audience responded, not knowing where the seemingly innocent words were leading. It went something like that game that children play when they recite: "One nis ball, two nis ball, three nis ball . . ." And ending in: "Ten nis ball. . . ." And when the crowd discovered that they had been unknowingly led into chanting a political slogan or hurling a stinging insult at the opposition, they literally howled their approval. One man, clad in a toga, rose, lifted his hands skyward; his eyes glazed and dreamlike, he sang out with orgiastic joy:

"What a wonderful life! What a wonderful life!"

Never before had that man had a chance to express himself, or to hear others state what he felt to be true, and the mere hearing of someone recount his hopes and dreams was enough to make him feel free. England was reaping the results of keeping these people from trying to manage their own lives and now they were relishing freedom, savoring it, so to speak.

The Prime Minister advanced to the microphone. He was in form; he was sharp, unyielding in his condemnation of the opposition. He hissed:

"I don't care how many university degrees that Busia and Danquah have between them! The truth is: they don't know politics! Why, they are scared of you, as scared of you as the British are!"

The crowd laughed.

"Danquah ought to be an assistant librarian and leave politics alone! I'll give him such a job, if he wants it!"

The audience listened, open-mouthed, smiling in agreement.

"Busia? He's a goat! Let him keep to his sociology! As a politician, why, he's not worthy to stoop down and untie my shoestrings!"

This was hard fighting and the crowd roared their appreciation.

"We prefer self-government with danger to servitude in tranquillity!"

"FREE—DOOOOOOOM! FREE—DOOOOOOM!"

The crowd chanted as their dark and emotion-spent faces left the meeting; wistfully I watched their toga-draped bodies wander off in the fading light of the setting sun. . . . I sat brooding. How had he conquered them? He had held them in the palms of his hands; he had poured scorn on the claims of the opposition; he had allowed no mercy for a contrary opinion; and it seemed that that was what his followers wanted. Prolonged British evasion and aloofness had made them ready to embrace certainty, definiteness. . . .

Back in my hotel room that night in Accra I tried to analyze what I'd seen. One could argue that Nkrumah had learned such tactics from observing Communist activities in London and New York, but there was the problem of determining how his aides, in five short years, had developed such a high degree of political dexterity with the masses. I had had enough experience in the Communist Party of the United States to know that what I had seen in Cape Coast had not been Communism. Communism was, above all, ideological; and what I had seen was the quintessence of passion.

My tentative answer was that, with the multitude of revolutionary examples before their eyes to indicate a general sense of direction, Nkrumah and his boys had doped out the rest, had guessed it, had fumbled and found how to organize their people; moreover, back of it all was, I believe, something much deeper and more potent than the mere influence of Marxist thought. It was my conviction that the twentieth century was throwing up these mass patterns of behavior out of the compulsive nakedness of men's disinherited lives. These men were not being so much guided as they were being provoked by elements deep in their own personalities, elements which they could not have ignored even if they had tried. The greed of British businessmen and the fumbling efforts of missionaries had made an unwitting contribution to this mass movement by shattering the traditional tribal culture that had once given meaning to these people's lives, and now there burned in these black hearts a hunger to regain control over their lives and create a new sense of their destinies. White uplifters were generally so deficient in imagination that they could never realize how taunting were their efforts to save Africans when their racial codes forbade their sharing the lives of those Africans. . . .

What I had seen was not politics proper; it was politics *plus*. . . . It bordered upon religion; it involved a total and basic response to reality; it smacked of the dreamlike, of the stuff of which art and myths were made. . . . The number of men around the Prime Minister who knew Marxism were few in number, and how could they have instilled so quickly such abstruse ideas into illiterate masses? What I had seen was a smattering of Marxism plus the will to be, a thirst for self-redemption! And I suspected that Nkrumah himself was but an *agent provocateur* to the emotions of millions—emotions which even he did not quite grasp or understand in all of their ramifications. . . .

Eleven

At last the Prime Minister's political secretary, Kofi Baako, called at my hotel to talk to me. He was a short, brownish-black man, thin, restless, intense, nervous. So well did he know the story that he had to tell that he had no need of notes; he got down to work at once, the words coming fluently from him. I recapitulate his story:

In August of 1947 the leaders of the Gold Coast met at Saltpond and inaugurated an organization called the United Gold Coast Convention, the declared aim of which was self-government. To carry on the work of the organization, a full-time secretary was sought and Nkrumah, then in London, was recommended for the post.

Arriving in December of 1947, Nkrumah defined the political character of the organization as being "the people's nationalist movement," and at once a deep conflict of interests arose. The wealthy Africans in the organization, lawyers and doctors educated in England, did not regard their efforts as representing the aims of the "people." They wanted to rule in *their* name; Nkrumah wanted the widest strata of the *people* to become involved. . . .

Nkrumah set about at once broadening the basis of the organization and his drive coincided with the efforts of Nii Bonnie II, a subchief of the Ga states who had launched a nationwide boycott of imported goods in an attempt to force foreign firms to reduce prices. The boycott terminated in a meeting at which members of the government and foreign merchants pledged to Nii Bonnie II to reduce prices.

But, on the morning of the 28th of February, 1948, when the people went into the stores, they did not find a reduction of prices and spontaneous demonstrations broke out against a score of European firms. In the afternoon of the same day a delegation of ex-servicemen marched on the Governor's castle in Christianborg to present grievances and a clash developed between the ex-servicemen and the police, the latter charging that the demonstrators had deviated from the agreed-upon line of march. When ordered to disperse, the demonstrators refused and the police opened fire and killed three veterans of British campaigns in India and Burma. . . . The news spread and an infuriated populace began a looting of foreign firms; arson and street fighting ensued and, during the following days, violence gripped the southern half of the country. Twenty-nine people were killed and about two hundred and thirty-seven were injured.

These disturbances prompted the leaders of the United Gold Coast Convention to send cables to London petitioning the British to create a commission of inquiry to study the underlying causes of the disorders; they also demanded an interim government. A few days later the leaders of the United Gold Coast Convention, Kwame Nkrumah, J. B. Danquah, Ako Adjei, Akufo Addo, Obetsebi Lamptey, and William Orfori Atta were arrested and banished to the Northern Territories; they were incarcerated separately for fear they would meet and plot.

The Governor declared a state of emergency and a curfew was imposed. Suspicion rose in the minds of the British that the local soldiers and police were not loyal and they imported troops from Nigeria.

The Colonial Secretary in London appointed a commission to investigate the causes of the violence and to recommend constructive measures. The Watson Commission—so named because of its chairman, Aiken Watson—took testimony in April of 1948 and the six arrested leaders were released so that they could give evidence. In June of that year the commission issued a report which declared the old constitution outmoded, urged a new constitution embodying the aspirations of the people, and endorsed a ministerial type of government patterned on those obtaining in the dominions.

But, when the Governor appointed a constitutional committee of forty Africans under the chairmanship of Mr. Justice Coussey, apprehension set in. The committee was composed entirely of upper-class chiefs and lawyers and the younger elements of the population were completely ignored.

When the committee began work on the 20th of January, trade-unionists, students, "mammy" traders of the streets, and the nationalist elements launched a protest against their representatives being excluded. Nkrumah hastily formed a youth committee and sent young men touring the nation to raise three demands: (1) universal adult suffrage; (2) a fully elected legislature with a fully representative cabinet; and (3) collective ministerial responsibility.

The traditional leadership of the United Gold Coast Convention now felt that Nkrumah was deviating from the organization's policies and an inevitable class split developed. Nkrumah was determined that the people should know what the real issues were and, accordingly, on September 1, 1948, he founded the *Accra Evening News*. The split widened as Nkrumah's journal vehemently demanded a democratic constitution. Attempts to bridge the differences between the right-wing old generation and the left-wing new generation served but to sharpen the conflict. Failing to achieve a satisfactory agreement with the leaders of the United Gold Coast Convention on points which he felt too vital for compromise, Nkrumah publicly announced his resignation.

The Convention People's Party took actual shape from that point on and Nkrumah announced his intention of staging positive action based on nonviolence if the people's demand for a democratic constitution was not granted.

The British Government now actively entered the campaign against Nkrumah, filing a series of libel suits. On September 15, 1949, Nkrumah was charged with contempt of court and fined three hundred pounds. This sum was quickly raised by the voluntary exertions of the street "mammies." This incident, more than any single thing else, convinced the leaders of the new Convention People's Party that they had the solid support of the masses of the common people, and they intensified their protests.

Upon the release of the Coussey Committee's report, Nkrumah summoned a monster mass meeting composed of trade-union leaders, farmers' organizations, and other political parties to study the report and to decide to what extent it was acceptable. This meeting took place on November 28, 1949, and the crowd was estimated at over 80,000. . . .

This mass meeting declared immediate self-government as its aim; it objected to the three ex officio members representing British vested interests being included in the cabinet; it protested against the suffrage age limit being set at twenty-five years; it demanded a legislature composed of fully elected members instead of, as the report recommended, some being nominated and others being elected.

The organizers of the Convention People's Party now took to the field and urged the people to prepare for country-wide civil disobedience and nonco-operation if the British refused these demands.

This campaign brought about a conference, on January 5, 1949, between British government officials and the leaders of the Convention People's Party. At this conference the British informed the nationalist leaders that they were studying the proposals and asked that positive action should not be evoked. When, however, the next day, the British announced on the radio that an "agreement" had been reached, Nkrumah felt that the British were merely playing for time and he announced that positive action would begin.

On the morning of January 8, not a train ran; no one went to work; busses and transportation trucks stood still. The nationalist leaders agreed to the functioning of essential services: water, electricity, health, medical care, etc. For twenty-one days, despite threats of dismissal of workers from jobs, numerous warnings and curfews, and the full evocation of the emergency powers of the Governor, positive action continued. When it became evident that such action could continue almost indefinitely, the British ordered the arrest of the leaders of the Convention People's Party. Nkrumah and about twenty others were seized, charged with sedition, and refused bail. . . . The trial, which lasted two months, ended with all of the leaders being convicted and sentenced to prison terms varying from three months to four years.

Yet, in 1950, during the imprisonment of the leaders of positive action, elections for town councils took place in Accra, Cape Coast, and Kumasi and the condemned party won majorities in all three cities. It began to look as if the real leaders of the nation were in prison.

In April, 1950, Gbedemah, one of the leaders of the Convention People's Party, came out of prison and became acting chairman of the party and took charge of organizing for the coming general elections, presenting candidates in all of the thirty-eight constituencies. And from the imprisoned leaders came smuggled-out directives as to how the campaign should be conducted! It was in prison that the greeting of "Freedom" and the salute of the elbow-resting-on-the- hip-and-the-palm-fronting-outward was conceived of. . . . Nkrumah himself, in his cell, wrote the party's song which the marching Africans sang: "There Shall be Victory for Us."

On February 8, the Convention People's Party swept the nation, winning thirty-five out of thirty-eight seats. The people of the Gold Coast had elected as leaders of the new government men who were lodged in prison cells and the British had a new headache on their hands.

A few days later the imprisoned nationalists were told to get dressed in civilian clothes, an order that aroused their suspicion, for they thought that the British did not want the populace to see their newly elected leaders being transferred to another prison. . . . But it was freedom, an act of "grace," as the British quaintly called it.

Convoking the national executive committee of the Convention People's Party, Nkrumah made it plain that the party would enter the new government as a representative of the will of the nation. "We are going into the government to show the world that the African can rule himself. We want the chance to fight for the political, social, and economic improvement of the country from both within and without the government." He warned the people that self-government had not been achieved and he described the constitution under which he would be acting as "bogus and fraudulent."

Nkrumah had won the election, but his thirty-five seats represented a minority, for nineteen representatives had been named by the Territorial Council, and there were seventeen chiefs or representatives of chiefs, and there were also three ex officio British members representing special interests, such as mines, commerce, etc.

Appointed Leader of Government Business by the Governor, Nkrumah was then elected to the same post by the Assembly in a vote that carried seventy-eight out of eighty-four voices. His ministerial colleagues, five in number, were also elected by the Assembly. Three other cabinet posts were filled from three other territorial councils: one from Ashanti; one from the Northern Territories; and one from the Colony.

Eight months later, in October, 1951, the Convention People's Party, through the Legislative Assembly, smashed the old system of Indirect Rule (Native Authority) which had given the chiefs statutory powers to maintain order, collect taxes, and dispense justice, etc. In place of Indirect Rule there was erected a system of District, Urban, and Local Councils elected on the basis of universal suffrage. . . . With this one stroke religion was swept out of government and the will of the people took its place.

"This, in short, is how the first determined bid of Africans to rule themselves turned out," Mr. Baako told me. "We know that we're not through, that victory has not been won. This is only the first step. . . ."

"Suppose the British do not grant full self-government? What then?" I asked Mr. Baako.

"Our program has the full support of the masses," he told me. "And the British know it. They have co-operated so far. If they do not continue, we shall declare ourselves a republic."

After Mr. Baako had gone I marveled how, in one historic leap, the Gold Coast African had thrown off his chains. Though the conditions of his life were harsh, ridden with fetish and superstition, he would eventually be free, for he was determined and tough. . . .

Twelve

Next morning I resumed my trudging through the winding mazes of James Town's slums. And this time, as each time I sauntered out, I saw something that had escaped my notice before. The streets, doorways, and the little compounds were jammed with able-bodied men lounging the hours away. How was it possible that so many men were idle when ships, filled with manufactured goods from Britain, were docking every hour? Having spied these loafing men, my eyes traveled farther and I saw that men were cooking most of the meals in all the European homes and hotels, that men did all the washing, scrubbing, dusting, sweeping, kindling of fires, and making of beds. . . . These black men did everything except the wet-nursing of European babies. It seemed that it was beneath the dignity of a tribal African woman to work in a European home, and only a declassed woman would do so. Maybe this was the manner in which the African male saved his honor, kept his women out of reach of the Europeans?

As I entered the offices of the United States Information Service to look over the recent newspapers from America, I was stopped by a young lad.

"Dr. Wright, may I speak to you, sar?"

"Certainly. What is it? But I'm no doctor, son."

"I want a camera like that, sar," he said, touching the instrument I held under my arm.

"Well, they are rather expensive, you know."

"But I've an idea, sar," he said. "You see, sar, if you gave me a camera like that, I'd take pictures with it here and I'd send you the pictures in Paris and you could sell them, sar."

I blinked, trying to grasp what he was saying.

"I don't understand."

"You see, sar, when you sell my pictures, I wouldn't want you to send me any money until you had sold enough to get your own money back *twice*. . . ."

It was obvious that he had no intention whatsoever of trying to defraud me; he simply did not quite grasp the reality involved in his scheme.

"That's very kind of you," I told him. "But don't you

know that they sell these cameras right here in Accra? Have you any money?"

"I could get the money, sar," he told me. "But they wouldn't sell me a camera like *that*, sar."

I finally understood what he meant. He was trying to tell me that he believed that the British would, say, take out some valuable part of the camera before they sold it to him, an African. He was convinced that every move of the British contained some hidden trick to take advantage of him. (Many Africans, I was told, ordered their goods directly from the United Kingdom and paid duty on them, believing that the goods would be of better quality than those sold by foreign merchants in local stores. And an African boy, wanting a bicycle, has been known to beg a Britisher to buy it for him, feeling that the foreign storekeeper would cheat him, but wouldn't dare cheat the Britisher. . . . A sodden and pathetic distrust was lodged deep in the African heart.)

"Look, I'd like to help you, but, honestly, I don't know how. . . ."

He seemed to be about twenty-one years of age. . . .

"But I'd pay you back; I'd send the pictures to you; I swear, sar," he begged me.

I sighed. I was angry, but I didn't know with whom. I tried to avoid his pleading eyes. I was not angry with him.

"I'd suggest that you go to a school of photography," I advised him.

He looked crestfallen. He did not accept it. But he nodded and allowed me to pass. I sat down to read, but my mind was trying to fathom how these young boys saw and felt reality. The boy had seemed to feel that he had a claim upon me that I could not accept. I was for him, but not in the direct way he seemed to feel that I ought to be. Did he think that I was naïve enough to make him, a stranger whose merits I did not know, a present of an expensive camera? Obviously, he did. But why? I had never in my life dared ask anybody for a gift so exorbitant.

That evening I discussed this boy's demand with an African who had been educated in the United States.

"That boy thinks that you are his brother—You are of African descent, you see," he told me.

"But you don't give expensive cameras to boys even if they are of your color," I protested.

"You don't understand. The boy was trying to establish a sort of kinship with you. In the Gold Coast, a boy can go and live with his uncle, demand to be fed, clothed, and the uncle cannot refuse him. The uncle has a sacred obligation to comply. Tribal life has bred a curious kind of dependence in the African. Hence, an uncle, if he has four or five nephews, can never accumulate anything. His relatives live on him and there is nothing that he can do about it."

"But what right has the nephew to make such claims?"

"The uncle's sister's blood flows in the nephew's veins. . . . Look, if an African makes £100,000, do you think he can keep it? No. His family moves in and stays with him until that money is gone. You see, the family here is more of an economic unit than in the West. . . . Let's say that an African family has gotten hold of a few thousand pounds. They'll hold a family meeting and decide to send Kojo, say, to London to study medicine. Now, they are not giving that money to Kojo; they are *investing* it in him and when he masters his medical subjects, returns home, and starts practicing, the family stops working and goes and lives with Kojo for the rest of their lives. That's their way of collecting their dividends, a kind of intimate coupon clipping, you might say. . . .

"African society is tightly, *tightly* organized. . . . No one is outside of the bounds and claims of the clan. You may never get rich, but you'll never starve, not as long as someone who is akin to you has something to eat. It's Communism, but without any of the ideas of Marx or Lenin. It has a sacred origin—"

"What sacred origin?" I asked.

"It all starts with the sun. . . . Say, you must read Dr. Danquah's book; it's called *The Akan Doctrine of God*."

I jotted down the title of the book, but realized that curiosity in Africa led one not to any immediate satisfaction, but only toward ever-winding avenues of searching. . . .

Next afternoon Mrs. Hannah Cudjoe, the propaganda secretary of the Women's Division of the Convention People's Party, called upon me at the suggestion of the Prime Minister. She was a pleasant, soft-spoken woman, diffident in manner, slow-moving, coy-eyed, short, heavy, black, with a shrewd, placid face. She spoke English with a slight tribal accent. We sat in a shady spot on the hotel veranda and I ordered two bottles of beer. She seemed ill at ease, kept her knees tightly pressed together, and seemed not to know what to do with her hands. Despite her self-consciousness, I felt that in certain circumstances she would know how to throw herself forward, for there slumbered beneath her evasive eyes a restlessness, a superfluity of hard energy. I questioned her about her work and she laughed, fell silent for several moments and sat in an attitude of deep repose, reflecting, staring off.

I discovered later that this shyness indicated that she was afraid of saying the wrong thing; above all, it meant that she did not completely trust me, did not *know* me. . . . Western "knowing" and non-Western "knowing" were two different things. It was impossible for a European to "know" somebody in the sense that an African "knows" somebody; "knowing" a person to an African meant possessing a knowledge of his tribe, of his family, of the formation of his habits, of the friends surrounding him, of being privy to the inmost secrets of his culture. While Western "knowing" was limited to a more rational basis—to a knowledge of a man's profession, of his ideas, and perhaps some of his interests.

So often had the Africans been deceived that distrust had become enthroned in the very processes of their thoughts. I could feel Mrs. Hannah Cudjoe's distrust of me; it came from no specific cause; it was general. I was a stranger, a foreigner, and, therefore, must be spoken to cautiously, with weighed words. Distrust was in full operation before any objective event had occurred to justify it. A stranger confronting an African and feeling this distrust would begin to react to it and he'd feel himself becoming defensively distrustful himself. Distrust bred distrust; he'd begin to watch for evasion; he'd begin to question a flattering phrase. So, with no basis in immediate reality, both sides would begin regarding the other warily, searching for hidden meanings in the most innocent statements. In the end, what had begun as a stranger's apprehension of the African's wariness would terminate in a distrust created out of nowhere, conjured up out of nothing. This fear, this suspicion of nothing in particular came to be the most predictable hallmark of the African mentality that I met in all the Gold Coast, from the Prime Minister down to the humblest "mammy" selling *kenke* on the street corners. . . .

I had literally to pull Mrs. Hannah Cudjoe's words out of her, so cautious was she; finally, she told me frankly:

"You know, we black people have to be so careful. We don't have many friends. Everybody wants to hurt us. They come here and grin in our faces, and then they go away and make fun of us. . . ."

"I understand," I said. "But you must learn to control your reactions; you mustn't let others see that you are afraid. You must never show weakness, for weakness invites attack—"

"You think so?" she asked me.

"Absolutely," I told her.

She was silent for a few minutes, then she relaxed and began to talk slowly. She told me that she had enlisted in the Convention People's Party in the early days when the party had been young and the going hard. She had stood alone and many of the women of the Gold Coast had reviled her for daring to enter the political field. . . . She had once married one of the top party leaders, but she was now divorced. She worked hard, making four or five speeches a day, always on the move.

"Please, be careful what you write about us," she begged me. "We are poor and we must learn to live the modern way. So many people have hurt us."

Her answers were simple, direct, and factual, but she could not grasp abstract ideas and could not give me broad, coherent descriptions. She related how she had gone into the "bush" and had recruited hundreds of women into the party, how she had taken food to them and had made them feel that others cared about them, how she had shown them how to wash and feed their children.

"Just what is the position of tribal woman today?" I asked her.

"We are chattel," she said frankly. "Under our customs the woman is owned by the husband; he owns even the clothes on her back. He dictates all of her moves, says what she can and can't do. That's why we don't have as many women in the party as we would like. When a woman tells her husband that she wants to attend a political meeting, the husband tells the wife to stay home, that he'll go to the meeting and he'll tell her what she needs to know. A tribalized African simply cannot, will not believe that a woman can understand anything, and the woman alone can do nothing about it. Tribal law is against her; her husband has the right to collect all of the wife's earnings. . . ."

"But, despite that, some of them are joining the party, aren't they?"

"Yes. Slowly," she said. "Almost all the women in our party are illiterate. In their homes, the women cannot speak about politics. But once they join the party, they find that life can be different. So some of our best defenders are women. They give their lives to the party and will stand and fight as nobody else will."

"Listen, Mrs. Cudjoe," I asked her, "do you think that it's possible for me to become a paying guest in an African home? You see, I'd like to get closer to the people, like to know how they live in families. What do you think?"

I watched her face grow thoughtful and I knew that it was not a question of whether she could find an African home that would accept me as a paying guest; the question in her mind was: what would be my reactions to the life I'd see in an African home? She feared my scorning that life, laughing at it; she was afraid of me; I could feel distrust welling up in her. . . .

"I'll ask around," she mumbled without enthusiasm.

And the lame tone of her voice told me that I'd never hear from her about my request, and I never did. What had been done to these people? That they had had and still had a lot of enemies, I had no doubt; but how could they ever win sympathy or friends if they were afraid to honor a simple, human request, if the most casual questions evoked grave doubts? Or were they so childlike as to imagine that they could hide the entire life of the Gold Coast from strangers? With the exception of the work of one or two of their educated men, all the history of their country and the interpretations of their customs had been written by Europeans, and those interpretations had shamed and angered them, but it was only to Europeans that they could talk really, that they could try to communicate.

When Mrs. Cudjoe had gone, I fought against a horrible realization that was seeking to make itself manifest in me:

these people could never really trust me. They had a tradition of nearly a hundred years of trusting—even against their will—the British and they had grown used to British authority, so used to it that they kept on trusting the British even when they hated them. For a long time to come it would be only to their British masters that they could really open their hearts. They'd grown used to British snobbery, curtness, aloofness and, even though they loathed it, they missed it when it was absent and felt loose and uncomfortable. I gritted my teeth and shook my head in dismay. Centuries of foreign rule had left their marks deep, deep in the personalities of the people, deeper than the people themselves had any idea of. . . .

The Africans I met knew that I knew something in general of the conditions of their lives, the disorder, the polygamy, the strange burial customs, etc.; these were the things in which they most deeply believed, yet they were ashamed of them before the world. How could one believe in something that one was ashamed of? Perhaps it was because it was all that they had? Western civilization had made them want to hide their traditional lives and yet that civilization had given them no other way to live. . . .

All that the African personality seemed to have gotten from the West so far was a numbed defensiveness, a chronic lack of self-confidence. How could even that which the Africans were ashamed of be changed if they never wanted it shown or talked about? Their contact with the West had been so negative and limited that they could not objectively determine what in their lives they could be proud of or ashamed of. They were uncertain, uneasy, nervous, split deep within themselves. I wondered if the British were sensitive enough to know what they had done to these people? Crimes have been committed in this world of so vast a nature that they have never been recorded in any criminal code.

Thirteen

Next morning I paid a visit to the headquarters of the Convention People's Party. It was housed on the second floor of a stone building in a thriving trading quarter of Accra. It looked exactly like any political headquarters of any political party in the world: that is, dingy, humdrum, ill-lighted, and bare. Mr. Kwame Afriyie, the general secretary of the party, was presented to me and at once he said:

"We won in Cape Coast, you know."

I congratulated him. During my entire visit the phone rang; every party member was wanting to know the results of the Cape Coast by-election. Streams of people flowed in and out of the office, asking questions, seeking help in their party work, and offering themselves to be assigned to duties. A chief came in with his "linguist," his umbrella, and all; he was taken into a private room. . . .

"Do chiefs come here too, especially after your party has clipped their political wings?" I asked Mr. Afriyie.

"Oh, yes," he said, laughing.

"But why do they come?"

"They're sensible," Mr. Afriyie told me. "They're adjusting themselves to the new situation. Some of them come here to beg the Prime Minister to address audiences in their local areas. You see, when a chief feels that he is losing prestige, he wants our help. Then sometimes a chief is the president of a local council and he wants our advice on some point or other. And a lot of chiefs are now wanting to become presidents of town councils; you see? We don't bother with the chief's sacred, religious, or ceremonial functions, but we see that he keeps out of politics. The smart chiefs see the handwriting on the wall and are trying to get adjusted to the new social order that is in the making.

"Since we have come to power, the old tribal spirit and cohesiveness have declined. Many of the old chiefs were corrupt, holding their positions by right of the British under a system of indirect rule. Many people were deeply dissatisfied with them. Chiefs pitted their little tribes against other little tribes in senseless disputes, and the resulting debilitating atmosphere was discouraging to the masses who wanted something concrete and practical done. Then many of the chiefs were illiterate and would co-operate with no one. They could understand nothing."

"And did the British try to correct that?"

"Why should they have tried to do that?" he asked me. "It wasn't in their interest. The British wanted things to stay just as they were."

I examined the membership book of the Convention People's Party and saw that the Prime Minister's name headed the list. The party had a membership of about 400,000, the average age being about thirty-five. The rank and file were carpenters, students, clerks, seamstresses, goldsmiths, photographers, tailors, pressmen, watch repairers, printers, chauffeurs, barbers, teachers, building inspectors, electricians, foremen, masons, draughtsmen, traders, nurses, blacksmiths, fitters, mechanics, and storekeepers—essentially a petty bourgeois class.

Tribally they derived from Wangara, Wassaw, Ajumaku, Asdna, Shai, Prampram, Grushie, Ga, Fanti, Twi, Ashanti, Ewe, Akan, Guang, Nzima (the Prime Minister's tribe), Akwapim, Kwahu, Efutu, Demkyira, Anum, Krobo, Adangme, Nkronyo, Ada, etc.

"Tell me, how do you get discipline in the party?" I asked Mr. Afriyie.

His genial smile wavered. I saw distrust flicker across his face. The moment I touched upon some vital question, I could feel the African's emotions running away. . . .

"We follow the Leader," he said evasively.

I knew that it would have been useless to persist. Yet I could sense tense dramas taking place in the life of the party: expulsions, chastisements, factional battles, etc. I was once a Communist and I knew that those things were inevitable in any vital organization. But all of that was hidden and, so far as I was concerned, would stay hidden. Yet, I could guess at the concealed reality. I studied Mr. Afriyie and could see that he felt that he had fooled me. To have insisted would only have roused his doubts and suspicions of me. I found that the African almost invariably underestimated the person with whom he was dealing; he always placed too much confidence in an evasive reply, thinking that if he denied something, then that something ceased to exist. It was childlike.

I shook hands all around and took my leave. Didn't Africans know that their elusiveness simply whetted people's curiosity the more? The African had a mania for hiding the facts of his life, yet he hid those facts in such a clumsy way that it made others know that he was hiding them. In short, African secretiveness defeated itself by calling insistent attention to what was being secreted.

I wander through the Accra streets. . . . Is it because I see so many men and women urinating publicly, in drains, on the sides of roads, in bushes, behind hedges, that I've begun to think that Africans urinate oftener than other people . . . ? That, manifestly, is not true. Then, what is it? Is it that the African urinates, as it were, so unconsciously that one is forced to the conclusion that he urinates oftener than other people? It cannot be that, as a nation, they have weak bladders; "racially," no such fact could be proved. A woman suddenly pauses at a corner, leans a little against a wall, opens her legs, and urinates, standing up. . . . Then she walks blithely off. Men will squat with their backs to the roadway, their heads turned to watch the traffic or passers-by, and urinate. At cocktail parties the British have an expression for wanting to urinate; they say, mindful of African habits:

"I must go and water the garden."

One wonders what such constant urination does to the plants, flowers, grass, etc.

One evening I accompanied a young, American-educated African to an outdoor dance arena, the Weekend in Havana. The specialty of this establishment, as with all the dance spots in the Gold Coast, was a shuffling, lazy kind of somnambulistic dance step called High Life. Curiously enough, even here I observed that tendency of the African sexes to segregate themselves. Little knots of women—they all wore European dress to these social affairs—clustered together. I was informed that this avoidance of the opposite sex was but an extension of the rituals of the tribal African family life; in the home men and women slept under different roofs and ate their meals separately, even when they were married. And so ingrained had those habits become that even when they were participating in non-African activities they tended to keep to their fundamental patterns of behavior. Perhaps it made them feel more at ease, quieted a sense of guilt for deserting their traditional ways . . . ?

I compelled myself, out of politeness to my host, to watch the dancing. Nothing could have been more boring to my temperament than such spectacles and I sat with a fixed smile on my face, nursing a bottle of beer, wishing I was somewhere else. I'd seen better and more spirited dancing among the Negroes of New York's Harlem and Chicago's South Side, but since it was expected of me to watch Africans demonstrate that they could imitate Europeans or Americans, I thought that I'd better pretend to be interested.

Then my eyes caught sight of something that all but pulled me up out of my seat. Two young men walked slowly across a corner of the dance floor, each with his arm tenderly about the waist of the other, their eyes holding a contented, dreamy gaze.... What was *that*? Had I misjudged the African capacity for the assimilation of Western emotional conditionings? But maybe those two boys were from Oxford or Cambridge . . . ? They didn't look like it. I wanted to question my friend about this, but I feared appearing too indelicate. But, just as I repressed my impetuosity, the two young men glided gracefully out upon the dance floor and moved with all the sexual suggestiveness of a mixed couple to the catchy music. Again I inhibited myself, not wishing to wade too abruptly into such matters with people whose reactions I could never predict. After all, I was a stranger in a strange land. I sat quietly, watching, wondering. Had the British brought homosexuality to Africa? Had the vices of the English public-school system somehow seeped through here? Just as the African had taken inordinately to alcohol, had he taken to this too? Then I was startled to see two more young men, holding hands, walk leisurely across the dance floor, heading, it seemed, for the bar. A deep, calm togetherness seemed to exist between them. Was this more evidence of that innocence of instinct that I had previously observed? I could no longer restrain my curiosity. I leaned toward my host and whispered:

"Look here. What's going on?"

"I don't get you," he said; but I saw an ironic twitch on his lips as he suppressed a smile.

"If what I see happening here tonight between young men happened in New York, the police would raid the place and throw the people in jail. . . ."

My friend guffawed.

"What do you *think* you see?" he demanded.

"I think I see some pretty overt homosexual behavior," I said quietly.

"You *don't*," he said flatly.

"Then what am I looking at?"

"You're looking at nice, manly tribal young men who love dancing," he explained in a somewhat aloof voice.

"Look, I'm no moralist; I don't care what they are," I said. "But I want to make sure."

"And I'm making no moral defense of Gold Coast boys," he said. "But you don't see any homosexuality. Listen, I wanted you to come here to see this. I could have called your attention to it, but I was waiting for you to notice it—"

"How could I escape it?" I asked him. "Now, why are they acting like that?"

"It's a bit complicated," my host explained as the music jumped all over the dance floor. "These young boys are still mainly tribal. They speak English; they go to school, to church; and they work as clerks, perhaps, in European offices. But their deepest reactions are still basically tribal, not European. Now, in tribal dances men dance with men, women dance with women, or they all dance together, or each person alone, if he wants to. . . . Tribal dancing is not uniquely sexual. Sometimes they dance for a god, to please him, to coax him, to tell him something. Sometimes they dance to please each other. Long habituation to this kind of dancing makes them, when they dance in public to Western tunes and rhythms which are replete with sexuality, still follow their tribal conditioning. There is no homosexuality here. In most tribal dancing men get used to touching or holding other men; they think nothing of it; and they'd be morally shocked, hurt, if they thought that you saw something perverse in it. So you have here a strange synthesis of seemingly disparate elements—young boys dancing together, embracing ardently, holding hands, with no thought of sex. They are brothers."

"I see," I said.

Each hour events were driving home to me that Africa was another world, another sphere of being. For it to become natural to me, I'd have to learn to accept without thought a whole new range of assumptions. Intellectually, I understood my friend's all too clear explanation of why boys liked to hold hands and dance together, yet the sight of it provoked in me a sense of uneasiness on levels of emotion deeper than I could control.

Later that evening the dance gradually reverted more and more to African patterns. The drums in the orchestra took over the tunes and beat out wild, throbbing notes. Around two o'clock in the morning there were but a few mixed couples on the floor—mostly everyone was dancing alone, his eyes half closed, his lips hanging slightly open, his right hand pressed to his heart, as though lost in the sheer physical joy of movement. Presumably each person was dancing for himself or whatever friend or god he felt was near him, or for whoever wished to observe his ecstasy. The African seemed to feel that whenever he experienced something vital, he had to share it; his joy had to arouse joy in others, even though those "others" were unseen. It was to that which was not present to sight or touch, sometimes, that the African seemed to want to talk, to plead, to trust. There was in him a tinge of otherworldliness even when he danced to sexy jazz tunes; he seemed chronically addicted to a form of physical lyricism. He spoke with physical movement, protested with a stiffening of his neck, argued with his legs, cajoled with his arms, said yes with his hips, and no with a slow roll of his head. . . .

Fourteen

There are no mail deliveries. You went to the post office each morning for your letters; if you lived in Accra, you kept a post-office box, that is, rented one. If you didn't, you asked a friend to receive your letters for you in his box.

When I inquired why mail could not be delivered, the explanation was that the problem of illiteracy made it impractical to assign the delivery of mail to literate men when there were far more important jobs for those literate men to do. It would have been, I was informed, an abuse of the value of the few literate men to impose delivering mail upon them. In banks, stores, and shops there was a desperate need of clerks, and such men could not be spared to sort or handle mail.

The more I probed into the problem of illiteracy, the stranger it became. It was generally stated that there was a 90 per cent illiteracy in the Gold Coast; that is, only 10 per cent of the people could read and write *English*. All of which might well be true. A few of the natives read and wrote their own tribal languages, but such proficiencies were almost useless in the daily business world where English was not only the official language of the country, but the dominant language of the most vital trade areas of the earth.

Yet, despite this vast illiteracy, an average "mammy" who buys and sells staples in the open markets handles, during the course of a year, a turnover amounting to £50,000! But how does she know this, since she cannot read or write? She keeps it all in her head! It's possible that tribal African customs have conditioned her to perform these feats of memory for such a multitude of details.

The great majority of the Africans buy not from the European stores, but from each other, and one feels, when looking at the bustling activity in the market places, that almost the whole of the population is engaged in buying and selling. Just how this strange method of distributing products came about is a mystery. Perhaps it can be partly explained by the manner in which British firms ship their products to the Gold Coast. The British exporting firm generally deals through a certain *one* firm; that firm in turn sells to another, and *that* firm to *yet* another. . . . An African "mammy" finally enters this elaborate process, buying a huge lot of a certain merchandise, which she, in turn, breaks up and sells in fairly large lots to her customers. And her customers now sell directly to the public or maybe to other sellers who sell to the public. African wives are expected to aid in augmenting the income of the household and they thus take to the streets with their heads loaded with sundry items. . . . Naturally, this fantastic selling and reselling of goods drive the prices up and up until finally poor Africans must pay higher prices than a Britisher for a like product! Capitalism here reaches surrealistic dimensions, for even an ordinary match gains in value if it must afford profit to each hand through which it passes. This frantic concentration of the African mind upon making a profit out of selling a tiny fragment of a bar of soap or a piece of a piece of a piece of cloth is one of the most pathetic sights of the Gold Coast.

Of late there has been an effort to establish co-operatives to eliminate this senseless and self-defeating trading, but a casual glance at Accra's market places reveals that the whole process of buying and selling is anarchy calling for the sharpest wits imaginable. Haggling over a penny enlists the deepest passion, and you have the impression that the African trader is dealing in life-and-death matters. One wonders if such a manner of trading could have grown up in any society other than an illiterate one. It's likely that traditional tribal customs can account to some degree for this seeming preference for direct cash dealing on the part of the African, for his passion for visible, tactile methods of exchange of goods; I don't know. . . . All I know is that the African seems to love a petty financial game of wits and he'll ask you ten times the value of any object he's selling without batting an eye. Of course, the true explanation might be much simpler; the African might have learned all of this innocent chicanery from the Europeans during five hundred years of trading with them. The Portuguese, the Danes, the Swedes, the Germans, the French, and the English had some pretty sharp and unsavory methods of trading cheap trinkets for gold dust, a transaction which allowed for a wide leeway of bargaining. . . . But I leave this question of accounting for the "economic laws" (I don't believe that there's any such thing!) of the Gold Coast to other and more astute minds.

And yet a smart "mammy" will let a moneylender cheat her. . . . Since an African, when he is short of cash, thinks nothing of borrowing as much as he needs to tide him over, the Gold Coast moneylender will charge two, three, or four hundred per cent interest. I was told of a case in which a cocoa farmer borrowed money on his farm and pledged the yield of each year's crop as interest; of course, since his farm did not bring him any income, he could never pay off the principal!

Marriage and adultery too operate on a "cash and carry" basis. Tribal Africans do not like to admit that they buy their wives, but obtaining a wife amounts to no more or less than just that. And if your wife commits adultery, you can be compensated for it. There exists a regular fixed scale of fines to be paid by those either trapped or caught in the act of adultery. Or if your wife runs away, you can claim from her family—that is, the ones from whom you bought her—the return of your money. I'm reliably informed that some chiefs urge their many wives to commit adultery so that they can collect large sums of money by fining the culprits gullible enough to commit fornication with them.

The following is a list of fines leveled against all sections of society in a given Gold Coast area for the crime of adultery:

	£	S.	Plus
Any Akan man or indigene	5	5	1 bottle of gin
The wife adulteress	2	2	2 fowls
Any clerk	7	4	1 bottle of whiskey
All artisans, carpenters, blacksmiths, etc.	7	4	1 bottle of whiskey
Linguists for divisional chiefs	7	4	1 sheep and 1 bottle of gin

As the delinquents rise in the social scale, the fines increase. For example, men high in the tribal hierarchy, members of royal families, etc., are fined for adultery as follows:

Divisional chiefs without stool	10	—	2 bottles of gin
Divisional chiefs with stool	25	—	2 sheep and 2 bottles of gin
Divisional chiefs	100	—	3 sheep and 1 case of gin
Divisional chief's wife	7	4	2 sheep and 1 bottle of gin

The most severe penalty is meted out to royalty. For example, an Omanhene's adultery fee is fixed at

200	—	7 sheep and 2 cases of gin

It is reckoned that the committing of adultery with an important person's wife amounts to a defilation of his stool and those of his superiors, hence sheep are slaughtered to sanctify the stools or fetishes. A person's ultimate importance to the state, in the Akan tribal society, is judged by the amount of his adultery fee. The above amounts of fines are in force as of this moment in the Gold Coast, having been enacted by a state council (which will remain unidentified) on the 12th of May, 1953.

Marriage fees are likewise fixed. (This does not refer to what the man pays to the family for his wife.) The following prevails today:

new marriage	£ 1.10/
secondhand marriage	£ 1. 2/

> **Every woman should give her husband one fowl at a new marriage**
>
> **When a man marries a new wife, he should pacify his old wife with 8/.**

Funeral expenses are also fixed by the state; it was decided that at the death of a man, all women should pay 6*d.* and men 1/. But when a woman dies, all women should pay 3*d.* and men 6*d.* When a young man dies, the chief should pay 3*d.* and the men 6*d.* When an adult dies the chief should pay 4/.

These rules were made in an attempt to keep down the cost of funerals, for it has been known for funerals to plunge families in deep debt for years. The motives for spending so much money on funerals are simple: the deceased is about to enter the other world and he has to go there in style, with dignity, etc. One costly item for funerals is alcohol; most funerals are occasions for an inordinate degree of drinking. Attempts are being made to limit the drinking to palm wine, which, God knows, is potent enough. Some chiefs. influenced by Christianity, are actually arguing for lemonade. They constitute a "still small voice" as yet. . . .

So great is the propensity of Africans to celebrate death that many local councils have sought recently to impose drastic time limits upon funerals. For example, in an unnamed but prosperous Gold Coast state, the local council has decreed that:

A. Funerals for young men should be strictly limited to one week.

B. In the case of a child, there should be no funeral. (This is a rather involved and metaphysical point, for when a child dies it is assumed that the child did not wish to stay in the world of the living. It is said that the child's ghost mother in the other world has persuaded the child to return. In the old days the dead child was actually beaten and punished for not wishing to stay.)

C. Funerals for adults should be strictly limited to two weeks.

Funerals for chiefs, etc., are special occasions and the local council determines the duration of the funeral; the expenses are arrived at by a consultation between the chief's subjects and the chief's family. After the funeral the amount spent is shared among all the chief's subjects.

Adultery fines meted out to Gold Coast people of different religious persuasions often involve odd and incongruous items. For example, a Mohammedan caught in adultery is fined:

£5.5/–, 100 kola nuts and 1 piece of white shirting material.

Further items relating to marriage state:

To the woman he marries, a man owes: £1.10/–, plus a pot of palm wine, 3 headkerchiefs, 2 good cloths, 1 ordinary cloth, 1 hoe, 1 cutlass, 1 wooden tray and also a £2 dowry.

Any marriage contracted after that, the man owes the new wife £1.2/–, plus 1 pot of palm wine,

3 headkerchiefs, 2 good cloths, 1 ordinary cloth, 1 hoe, 1 cutlass, 1 wooden tray and also £2 dowry.

The codification of marriage rules, expenses, etc., runs into fine detail. Nothing is left to chance. For example, the seduction of a young girl who does not go to school is reckoned in terms of fine at £7. But if the girl is in school, the fine is fixed at £50. (Missionary influence?) If a man lives with a young girl as man and wife and refuses to marry her, he can send her off with £5. But if the girl refuses to marry the man, she can send him off with £7.

There is no sighing, longing, or other romantic notions in a young African seeking a wife; kissing is not a part of courtship, and is unknown except among chaste Christians. A man regards a woman as an economic investment; she must be sturdy, able to do a hard day's work, bear many children, and, above all, obey. . . . He may aid her in the heavier parts of her field labors, but his aid is limited to providing certain essentials for the household, such as meat which he obtains by hunting. The basic drives reveal themselves not as romance or love, but children and crops.

What desperate coping with nature dictated the African's concentration upon these elements? Maybe we will never know. Some of his greatest festivals center, until this day, around celebrating the harvest of yams. Another deep regard of the African heart is toward water, for it was water that kept his fields growing. Around ponds, lakes, rivers, and lagoons are likely to be found many myths and legends, and any untoward event occurring in connection with water is at once enshrined in memory. The whole of tribal life is pitched on a sacred plane, and the imposition of any other religion is likely to give them not more but less religion.

This dense illiteracy and the astonishing oral tradition—transmitted from generation to generation—upon which it feeds, its roots sunk in tribal memory, has formed a barrier, has erected a psychological distance between the African and the Western world and has made it increasingly difficult for the African to be known. This distance has not lessened with the passage of time; indeed, it has widened, for the tempo of progress of the West has qualitatively made the difference between the Western and non-Western world almost absolute. The distance today between tribal man and the West is greater than the distance between God and Western man of the sixteenth century. Western man could talk to his God in those days; today illiterate tribal minds are numbed when they hear of the atomic weapons of the Western world; and even when those tribal people revolt against the West and its technical mastery of the earth, they oftime find themselves, ironically, more dependent upon their white masters than before they launched their nationalistic revolutions. . . .

A Westerner must make an effort to banish the feeling that what he is observing in Africa is irrational, and, unless he is able to understand the underlying assumptions of the African's beliefs, the African will always seem a "savage." And yet the African too is struck by what seems to him the irrational nature of the world that is non-African, for he too does not often know the assumptions of that non-African world. And when those assumptions are revealed to him they are just as fantastic to him as his are to the West.

In such areas of compounded involvement the chances for self-deception are enormous. For example, the African fondly believes that there is another world beyond this world, and he predicates his most practical actions upon its validity. Therefore Westerners who live or work among Africans, for religious or business purposes, cannot escape lending a degree of recognition to the nonexistent world that the African projects in his living, thereby adding weight to the African's delusions.

Conversely, the Western assumption of the inferiority of the African compels the Westerner to constrict the African's environment; so, in time, African psychological attitudes and conditions of life come to reflect the West's assumptions. And the African, anchored amidst such degrading conditions, cannot help but reinforce them by accepting them; and what was, in the beginning, merely a false assumption, becomes a reality. Men create the world in which they live by the methods they use to interpret it. . . .

Even the astute men of the British Colonial Office, classic imperialists though they are, are no exceptions to this involved process of self-deception. Indeed, after holding the Gold Coast in their complete power for decades, having had access to the entire life and customs of the people, they reacted until very recently to the beliefs of the Africans more or less on the same basis that the Africans themselves reacted.

For example, in March of 1900, Sir Frederic Hodgson, Colonial Secretary of the Gold Coast, addressing the King of Ashanti and his chiefs and aides, asked for the surrender of the Golden Stool in the following words:

". . . Where is the Golden Stool? Why am I not sitting on the Golden Stool at this moment? I am the representative of the paramount power; why have you relegated me to this chair? Why did you not take the opportunity of my coming to Kumasi to bring the Golden Stool, and give it to me to sit upon? . . ."

The Africans had sunk the harpoon of their own indigenous assumptions deep into the Englishman's heart! The Golden Stool, of course, was not a seat to be sat upon; not even the King of Ashanti did that. Says W. E. F. Ward, in his *A History of the Gold Coast*, (London: Allen and Unwin, 1948, p. 304): ". . . It [the Golden Stool] contained the soul of all Ashanti; and the Ashanti could no more produce it to be sat upon by a foreigner than a Christian bishop in the Dark Ages could be expected to invite a barbarian conqueror to feast off the communion plate at the high altar of his cathedral . . .".

It seemed that Sir Hodgson believed in the magic of the Golden Stool, that is, in the mystic power presumably inherent in its possession, as much as the poetic Africans did, and his rash demand brought war between the English and the Ashanti in its wake. . . .

It was in 1923 or thereabouts that Capt. R. S. Rattray, an English anthropologist, uncovered some of the complex meanings of the Akan rituals and ceremonies and gave English governors and civil servants an inkling of the nature of the beliefs of the Akan people; but, by the time that that knowledge had shed some belated clarity upon the nature of Akan customs, Gold Coast lives and institutions had been so mauled and truncated that the knowledge was all but useless, and any *healthy* revivification of Akan customs in whole or part was beyond hope.

The Ashanti, being thus conquered, had to dilute his indigenous religious customs with Christian ones, had to pretend to be Christian in order to live and be left alone. . . . And the pattern of evasion, doubt, and distrust was set.

Hence, no one was more surprised than the British, in 1948, at the sudden and violent upsurge of nationalist feeling in the Gold Coast, for it contradicted not only the observations of the trusted civil servants on the spot, but its existence found no explanation or support in British academic circles. Until the coming of Nkrumah, the Gold Coast had been referred to as the "model colony," that is, a place from which a fabulously high return could be gotten on modest investments without a need to fear native unrest or reprisals.

Informal conversations with the Gold Coast Information Service officials elicited the following facts: At the very moment when Nkrumah was launching his positive action program that would paralyze the economic life of the colony, a British professor of anthropology in London was briefing a group of civil servants bound for the Gold Coast. He spoke to them somewhat as follows:

"The Gold Coast is a kind of colonial Eden. You'll find the natives gentle, satisfied, and deeply grateful for what we have done for them."

But when the shipload of civil servants docked at Takoradi, they could hear gunfire raking the streets and they were informed that violence had gripped the entire colony. . . . It seems that imperialists of the twentieth century are men who are always being constantly and unpleasantly surprised. The assumption of the inferiority of the African, which gave the British the courage to conquer them, was now the very assumption that stood in the way of their seeing what was actually taking place. To enforce docility, they had rammed down African throats religious assumptions which they themselves believed in more deeply than the Africans ever did, and the basic mood of the Africans, of course, always eluded them.

Fifteen

One afternoon, after lunch, I walked down to the seashore where the stevedores were unloading freighters. I had to identify myself and get a pass before being allowed into the area where swarms of half-naked men were carting huge loads upon their heads. The nearer I got to the men, the more amazed I became. I paused, gazing.

Coming toward me was an army of men, naked save for ragged strips of cloth about their hips, dripping wet, their black skins glistening in the pitiless sun, their heads holding pieces of freight—parts of machines, wooden crates, sacks of cement—some of which were so heavy that as many as four men had to put their heads under them to carry them forward. Beyond these rushing and panting men, far out on the open sea, were scores of canoes, each holding twelve men who paddled like furies against the turbulent surf. Save for the wild beat of the sun upon the sand of the beach, a strange silence reigned over everything. I had the impression that the tense effort of physical exertion would not permit a man to spare enough breath to utter a word. . . .

The wet and glistening black robots would beach their canoes filled with merchandise and, without pausing, heave out the freight and hoist it upon their heads; then, at break-neck speed, rush out of the sea, stamping through soft, wet sand, and run; finally, they would disappear over a dune of sand toward a warehouse. They ran in single file, one behind the other, barely glancing at me as they pushed forward, their naked feet leaving prints in the soft sand which the next sea wave would wash away. . . . On the horizon of the sea, about two miles away, were anchored the European freighters and between the shore and those ships were scores of black dots—canoes filled with rowing men—bobbing and dancing on the heaving water.

Another canoe came toward the beach; the men leaped out, grabbed its sides to steady it until it touched the sand; again I saw that wild and desperate scrambling for the merchandise; again they lifted the boxes or crates or sacks or machine parts to their heads and came rushing toward me, their lips hanging open from sheer physical strain. My reactions were so baffled that I couldn't tell what I felt. What I saw was so useless, so futile, so inhuman that I didn't believe it; it didn't seem real. I felt no protest; I was simply stunned, feeling that someone had snatched back a curtain and I was contemplating half-human men as they had labored in the hot sun two thousand years ago with the threat of death or physical torture hanging over them. But I saw no whips or guns; a weird peace gripped the scene. . . .

The harbor here, I was told, was much too shallow to allow ships to dock; they could dock, of course, at Takoradi, 170 miles away, but that would mean that the various shipping companies would have to send their freight by rail to Accra. That was why this beastly work had to take place; it allowed a higher profit to be made on the merchandise.

Each of the twelve men in each canoe held a short, splayed oar with three prongs; each man had to dip and pull this oar through the water sixty times a minute if the canoe was to keep afloat and move through the raging current, and each stroke of each man had to plunge into the water at the same time. There were some children working too, but not in the canoes; they waited at the water's edge and helped their fathers or friends or brothers to lift the heavy loads to their heads.

Nearby was a young black clerk dressed in Western clothes; he held a sheet of paper in his hands, and, as each canoe came in, he checked it off. I went up to him.

"Do they make much money working like that?"

"Each boat earns twelve shillings a trip; that's a shilling for each man, sar."

"How many shillings can a man make a day?"

"If he works hard, sar, he can make seven."

"But why do they rush so?"

"It costs a ship a lot of money to stay out there, sar."

"When do they start work?"

"At daybreak. Not much sun then, sar."

"Do you have trouble finding workers?"

The young man looked at me and laughed. Then he turned and pointed to a far crowd of half-nude men huddled before a wooden stairway leading up to an office.

"Do you lose many men in the sea?"

"Oh, no, sar! Those men are like fishes, sar. But we do lose merchandise—the company and the ships can stand it, sar. They're insured. Oh, sar, if you saw the beautiful automobiles that go down in that sea—"

A man passed with a sack of something lumpy upon his head, running. . . .

"That looks like a sack of potatoes," I said.

"It is, sar."

"Why aren't they grown here?"

"I don't know, sar."

"Is seven shillings a day considered good pay?"

"Well, sar, for what they buy with it, it's not bad."

He wandered off, jotting down figures on his sheet of paper. I'd seen men tending machines in frantic haste, but I'd never seen men working like machines. . . . I'd seen River Rouge and it was nothing compared to this hot, wild, and hellish labor. It was not only against exploitation that I was reacting so violently; it frightened me because the men did not seem human, because they had voluntarily demeaned themselves to be spokes in a wheel.

I walked toward the exit, then paused and stared again at the fantastic scene, seeing it but not believing it. I felt no hate for the shipowners who had contrived that this should be; there was something here amiss deeper than cheating or profit. . . . My reactions were elementary; the ships could have remained at anchor until they rotted, I wouldn't have cared. There are circumstances in which human life is no longer human life, and I'd seen one of them. And for this particular barbarity I had no answer, no scheme; I would not have gone on strike if I had worked there; I simply would not have worked there in the first place, no matter what. . . .

I returned to my hotel and lounged in my room. Water seemed to stand in the air. I got up and went into the bathroom and picked up my nail file. Good God. . . . It had turned red. I looked farther. All the metal in my toilet kit was a deep, dark red. I rubbed my fingers across the metal and a soft mound of wet rust rolled up. What a climate. . . . What could last here? Suppose the Gold Coast was cut off from the Western world, for, say, ten years? Would not the material level of existence be reduced to that which existed before the coming of the white man? Practically nothing, under British colonial policy, was manufactured in the Gold Coast. Indeed, the only ostensible difference between the environmental conditions of the bourgeois blacks and the tribal blacks consisted in the possession by the upper-class blacks of a mass of imported British products in their homes. The British argument until now has been that the climate ruled out industrial production, but I was convinced that this was a British "rationalization" to keep down potential industrial competition. I was sure that if the British *had* to industrialize the Gold Coast, they would have found a way of doing it. . . . Until some effort was made to preserve metal against corrosion, this place was under a sentence of death. And I realized that whatever history was buried in this hot and wet earth must have long since decayed, melted back into the red and ravenous clay. No wonder that archeologists, no matter how long and earnestly they dig, could find little or nothing here. Throw the whole of Detroit into this inferno of heat and wetness, and precious little of it would be left in a hundred years.

Restless, I wander again into the streets and am struck by the incredible number of mere tots engaged in buying and selling. I've begun to feel that, as a whole, there is no period of "youth" here in Africa. Here, at one moment, one is a child; then, almost overnight, at the age of eight or ten, one assumes the status of an adult. Children toil at minding smaller children, cooking, carrying water on their heads, trading in the market place, assuming responsibilities long before the children of the West. Perhaps "youth" is a period of luxury which middle-class Westerners alone could give their children?

Maybe that was why one so seldom encountered what might be called "idealism" in Africa? Perhaps there was no time for dreaming—and how could one get the notion that the world could be different if one did not dream? Though the African's whole life was a kind of religious dream, the African scorned the word "dream." Maybe the plant of African personality was pruned too quickly, was forced to bear fruit before it had a chance to grow to its full height? What would happen to a romantic rebel in an African tribe? The African takes his religion, which is really a waking *dream*, for reality, and all other dreams are barred, are taboo.

In the late afternoon a rainstorm broke over the city; it had been threatening for some hours and when it did come, it came down with a violence that made you feel that some malevolent being was bent upon harm. Nature here acts with such directness, suddenness, that the mind, in spite of itself, projects out upon natural events animistic motives. After the first cloudburst the rain settled down to a long, steady downpour. The air was still; I could almost feel the moisture enter my lungs as I breathed. It was not until after ten o'clock that the sky cleared and the stars could be seen, distant, mingled with clouds.

Again I poked about the alleyways of James Town. Now that the rain had stopped, the gregarious natives were returning to the streets. At corners women were lighting candles and huddling themselves beside their piles of staples. Plantains were being dropped into cauldrons of boiling fat. Finding myself out of cigarettes, I paused in front of a woman.

"A can of cigarettes," I said, pointing.

She stared, then opened a can and took out one cigarette.

"No; I want to buy a can," I said.

She turned and called, summoning help. Cigarettes were sold in round tin cans of fifty each and they were vacuum-packed against the moisture. A young girl came; she and the woman chatted.

"No; she sell you *one*." The girl was emphatic.

"Why won't she sell me a can?"

"She can't." Again she talked to the woman in tribal language, then she turned to me once more. "She sell can for one pound."

A tin can of cigarettes cost but seven shillings. Was she trying to cheat?

"That's too much," I protested.

"You can buy *three*; that's all," the girl said.

I finally understood the crisis that I'd brought into the woman's life. In this poverty-stricken area rarely did a native buy more than one cigarette at a time, and I had confronted her with a demand for fifty, which was wholesale business!

I pushed forward in the dark, down lanes of women sitting beside their boxes, their faces lit by flickering candles. As I strayed on I heard the sound of drums. Yes; I'd find them. . . . Guided by the throbbing vibrations, I went forward until I came to a vast concrete enclosure. The drums were beating behind that high wall. . . . Could I get in? I went around the wall until I came to a narrow opening. Discreetly, I peered through and saw, far back in the compound, a group of people dancing to drums; kerosene lanterns lit up the tableau. Ought I go in? They were black and so was I. But my clothes were different from theirs; they would know me for a stranger.

A young man came toward me; he was about to enter the compound. He paused and asked:

"What do you want?"

"Nothing," I said, smiling at him. "What's going on in there?"

"You're a stranger, aren't you?"

"Yes; I'm an American."

"Come on in," he said.

I followed him in, noticing as I passed a row of dim-lit rooms that in some rooms only men were seated and in others only women. . . . We came to a swirling knot of men and women; they were dancing in a wide circle, barefooted, shuffling to the demoniacal beat of the drums which were being pounded by a group of men near the wall. The ground was wet from the recent rain and their bare feet slapped and caressed the earth.

"Why are they dancing?" I asked the young man.

"A girl has just died," he told me.

There was no sadness or joy on their faces; they struck me as being people who had to go through with something and they were doing their job. Indeed, most of the faces seemed kind of absentminded. Now and then some man or woman would leave the ring and dance alone in the center. They danced not with their legs or arms, but with their entire bodies, moving slowly, undulating their abdomens, their eyes holding a faraway look.

"Why are they dancing?" I asked again, recalling that I'd asked the same question before, but feeling that I hadn't had an answer.

"A young girl has just died, you see," he said.

I still didn't know why they were dancing and I wanted to ask him a third time. An old man came to me and shook my hand, then offered me a chair. I sat and stared. The lanterns cast black shadows on the wet ground as the men and women moved slowly to the beat of the drums, their hands outstretched, their fingers trembling. *Why are they dancing . . . ?* It was like watching something transpire in a dream. Still another young man came and joined the two who now flanked my chair. They mumbled something together and then the young man who had brought me in stooped and whispered:

"You'd better go now, sar."

I rose and shook hands with them, then walked slowly over the wet earth, avoiding the rain puddles. *Why are they dancing . . . ?* And their dancing was almost identical with the movements of the High Life dancing that I'd seen in the outdoor dance hall. . . . At the entrance I paused and looked back; I was surprised to see that the young man had discreetly followed me.

"You say that a young girl has died?"

"Yes, sar."

"And that's why they are dancing?"

"Yes, sar."

I shook his hand and walked into the damp streets, my eyes aware of the flickering candles that stretched to both sides of me. Jesus Christ, I mumbled. I turned and retraced my steps and stood again in the entrance to the compound and saw that the men and women were now holding hands as they circled round and round. The young man stood watching me. . . .

"Good night!" I called to him.

"Good night, sar!" he answered.

I walked briskly and determinedly off, looking over my shoulder and keeping in the line of my vision that dance; I stared at the circling men and women until I could see them no more. The women had been holding their hands joined together above the heads of the men, and the men, as though they had been playing London Bridge Is Falling Down, were filing with slow dignity through the handmade arches. The feet of the dancers had barely lifted from the ground as they shuffled; their bodies had made sharp angles as they moved and I had been surprised to see that they were moving much quicker than I had thought; they had given me the impression of moving slowly, lazily, but, at that distance, there was a kind of concentrated tension in their gyrations, yet they were utterly relaxed. I had been looking backward as I walked and then the young man pulled the wooden gate shut and it was gone forever. . . . I had understood nothing. I was black and they were black, but my blackness did not help me.

Sixteen

One heard the word "palm" all day long; you were invited out for "palm chop," that is, a meal cooked with palm oil. Or you were offered a drink of palm wine or palm gin. I began inquiring into the uses to which the palm tree had been put, and here's what was revealed: The palm tree bears red berries called palm kernels which, if boiled and cracked open, yield a red and white oil. The red oil is used for cooking and the white oil for the making of many kinds of pomades, soap, etc. The red oil is called palm butter.

Many of the articles sold by the "mammies" on the streets are wrapped in palm leaves, and the plaited palm leaves are used in erecting fences and screens to keep out the prying eyes of strangers. Roofing of a sort is made from the leaves, and so are decorations, toys, and dishes. The stems of the palm leaves are used to make a short kind of broom with which the African women sweep their houses and yards.

When a palm tree is cut down, the heart of the palm is eaten and is considered a rare delicacy. Palm wine is made by fermenting the whitish fluid which the tree yields; also palm gin is made, though both palm wine and palm gin are declared illegal, for their alcoholic potency is considered dangerous to health. The tree's wood itself is used for fuel or building.

I sat at the table in the hotel's dining room, eating lunch, staring moodily out of the window. In the distance I saw a bright, shining object moving erratically. It looked like a brass pipe or pole; then I became aware that there was a mass of people clustered about the gleaming brass object. What could it be? Sounds of drums, of shouting, of shooting came to my ears. Was there a political disturbance? I rose and ran to the balcony; the mass of people was drawing near and the shooting and the drums sounded sharp and clear through the bright sunshine. A businessman, a German who stayed in the hotel, joined me.

"What is it?" I asked him.

"A funeral," he said. "And it's a big one. Must be for a chief."

"But why are they shooting?"

"They always do that. . . . Say, you'd better get your camera and go down—"

"Yes!" I said, tearing off to my room.

When I returned to the balcony, a wave of flowing robes, red, yellow, brown, scarlet, and russet was rolling down the street. Huge drums were being pounded by men who sweated and whose faces were tense. Men bearing vast red umbrellas marched and behind them came men holding red flags aloft, then more flags. Men and women came rushing madly from all directions. My eyes darted, trying to encompass the many things that were happening all at once. The men, dressed in red, formed a huge circle in a vacant lot and began firing the muskets they held. A funeral? How was that possible? It seemed more like an advertisement for a circus. Another round of firing into the air made a pall of light blue smoke drift over the field and the acrid scent of gunpowder smote my nostrils. The procession flowed on below me; then my eyes looked to the left. My mouth dropped open. A group of men bore aloft on their shoulders a brass coffin, gleaming and polished until it glittered in the sun. The coffin went round and round. . . .

"Is that really a coffin?" I asked the German.

"It sure is."

I was afraid that the coffin would fall and smash against the concrete pavement, but, evidently, the men had had long experience bearing whirling coffins on their heads and the coffin spun slowly, the men rushing with it seemingly at random from spot to spot. For example, they'd run to a corner, stop, twirl the coffin, then, amidst shouting, singing, chanting, they'd turn and race with the coffin spinning above their heads in another direction. . . .

I ran from the balcony; I had to see this at close range. Some ritual whose significance I could not understand was taking place. A thousand questions popped into my mind and no answers could even be imagined. I reached the street just as a young chief, borne aloft on a palanquin decorated in brightly colored silks, came by on the bare black shoulders of his carriers. Above him was the usual vast umbrella being twirled by a panting and sweating boy. Now the brass coffin came again, the black men running as they turned it round and round on their heads, and this time I noticed that in front of the men bearing the brass coffin was a half-nude woman, wearing a skirt made of raffia; she had a huge black fan made from feathers and she was swishing that fan through the air with hurried, frantic motions, as though trying to brush away something invisible. . . .

The parade or procession or whatever it was called was rushing past me so rapidly that I feared that I would not get the photograph I wanted; I lifted my camera and tried to focus and when I did focus I saw a forest of naked black breasts before my eyes through the camera sight. I took the camera from my eyes, too astonished to act; passing me were about fifty women, young and old, nude to the waist, their elongated breasts flopping loosely and grotesquely in the sun. Their faces were painted with streaks of white and sweat ran down their foreheads. They held in each of their hands a short stick—taken from packing boxes—and they were knocking these sticks furiously together, setting up an unearthly clatter, their eyes fixed upon the revolving coffin of brass. . . .

Then came another palanquin upon which sat a young boy about nine years old; his face was sad, solemn, and over him too was held a wide, spinning red umbrella. There followed a long stream of women dressed in native cloths, most of them bearing babies strapped tightly to their backs; they sang some weird song in staccato fashion. . . . Again came the turning coffin of brass and this time I noticed that it too had an umbrella of its own, that a man was rushing and trying to keep up with it, to hold the umbrella over it to shade it from the sun. . . .

The men in red were firing muskets again, and blue, thin rings of smoke hung in the sunlit air. I tried to keep up with the procession, but the men carrying the coffin changed their direction so abruptly and so often that I gave up and stood feeling foolish and helpless in the hot sun, sensing sweat streaming down my face.

I had understood nothing, nothing. . . . Why were they rushing so quickly and seemingly at random with that brass coffin? The funeral still flowed past me; there must have been five thousand people in it. I looked closer and saw that the faces of the women and children were marked with a reddish paint on the left cheek. . . . My mind reeled at the newness and strangeness of it. Had my ancestors acted like that? And why?

The men rushing with the turning coffin ran past me again and I stood aghast. I was nervous, feeling that maybe the poor dead man would fall out of the coffin, and I could imagine his being there jolted and bumped as they tossed the coffin round and round. . . .

These people were acting upon assumptions unknown to me, unfelt, inconceivable. Slowly I mounted the steps of the hotel and stood again on the balcony. The funeral was far away now, but I could still hear the vast throng shouting, the muskets firing, the women chanting. . . .

I found myself standing next to an African dressed in Western clothes.

"That's some funeral, all right," he said.

"But who's dead?" I asked.

"It's a chief," he told me.

"I can't understand it," I confessed.

"It's not simple," he said.

"Why do they fire those muskets?"

"Who knows? Some say that they got that firing of muskets from the Europeans during the fifteenth century," he said. "They have forgotten, maybe, just where they got it from."

"But the dead man, won't he fall out of that coffin?"

"There's no dead man in the coffin," he said.

"What? It's *empty*?" I asked, dumfounded. "Then why are they rushing about with it like that?"

"The coffin has the dead man's hair and fingernails in it," he explained. "The body is buried somewhere in secret, that is, after the brain has been taken out—"

"Why bury it in secret?"

"So no one will find it."

"But why would anyone want to find it?"

"Well, there are several reasons. . . . You see, a chief's body is sacred. . . . If somebody finds it, they can use it, take its power and use it—"

"Then why don't they stand guard over the body?"

"They've *got* to hide the body; they're hiding it from the man's spirit—"

"But the man's *dead*," I protested.

"Yes; but they claim that the man's spirit is hanging around, wanting to re-enter the body. . . . The spirit doesn't want to leave; you see? The body's the home of the spirit. If the spirit can't find its home, it'll keep on traveling—"

"And the man's brain . . . ? Why do they take the brain out of the skull and hide it?"

"Because they believe that the brain's the seat of the man's power. They hide the brain for fear that the dead man's enemies will get hold of it and take over the role that the dead man played in life. . . ."

"And the hair and fingernails in the coffin?"

"They are substitutes for the body. By putting the hair and fingernails in the coffin, the spirit is fooled. When the spirit seeks the body and can't find it, it then finds the fingernails. . . . It knows then that the body is gone. . . ."

"And why were those women beating those sticks?"

"That's to scare the spirit on its way. . . . And to announce to the spirit world that the spirit is coming."

"And the running and twirling of the coffin? What does that mean?"

"It's the same thing. . . . It's a kind of farewell that they're giving to the dead man, you see. But they are trying to fool the spirit away at the same time. Now, they take the coffin, running with it, back to all the places in the city where the dead man had enjoyed himself. The dead man is paying his last respects to his relatives, his friends, and so forth. Now, when they turn, change their direction, zigzag this way and that—that's to lose the spirit which is supposed to be trying to keep up with the body. The man's spirit, of course, will haunt the houses of the man's friends. So, when they rush up like that, spin the coffin, and then rush off, going from left to right, the spirit becomes confused. . . . You understand?"

Yes; if you accepted the assumptions, all the rest was easy, logical. The African's belief in the other world was concrete, definite. If there was another world, then the African was about the only man really believing in it; and if there was no other world, then one could maintain an attitude of indifference toward the idea. But if there was one, then evidently one should do something about it. The African sincerely believed that there was another world and he was desperately trying to do something about it.

The tropic night fell suddenly and there was complete darkness; then, after a bit, the sky turned a pale, whitish color and the moon came out, a glowing yellow sphere. My room was damp, hot; I tried to sleep, my mind filled with tumbling brass coffins. I awakened the next morning feeling more fatigued than when I had gone to bed.

It was Sunday and the idea occurred to me to visit a Christian church and see, for the sake of contrast, how the followers of Jesus behaved themselves. The word "pagan" was beginning to have a real meaning for me now; it was against these desperate pagans that St. Paul had fought. . . . I could understand a Christian service; I knew its assumptions. In my wanderings I'd seen a Wesleyan Methodist church and I was determined to go there.

The service was under way as I entered rather timidly. I didn't know if they had any special rules or not, so I stood discreetly at the back. A preacher was talking in a tribal tongue, quietly, with no gestures, no passion. To my astonishment the congregation was segregated: men sat on one side and women on another; young boys sat together and young girls did the same.

An usher showed me to a seat. I saw that the congregation wore their native clothes. The church was built of stone, but it had no panes in the windows; there was no need for any, for it never got cold here. The interior of the church was dim and I noticed that the ears of the women glowed softly with gold earrings. What a contrast to paganism! At the forefront of the church was the Cross, the symbol of Christianity, just as the Golden Stool was the symbol of the Akan religion. I recalled that frenzied pagan funeral I'd seen and I was kind of surprised that Protestant religion still existed. There was no fierce joy here, no dread, no anxiety; everything was taken for granted. The preacher's voice droned on sedately, mildly. If religion partakes of the terror stemming from the proximity of human life to eternity, to an absolute otherness, then there was, by a hell of a long shot, much more genuine religion in that barbaric pagan funeral than I could feel in this quiet, bourgeois Christian church!

The choir rose and sang and I was disappointed. There was none of that snap and zip (and a little sexual suggestiveness!) which American Negroes manage to inject into their praises to God. The tones and volumes fell flat, and the singing was namby-pamby, singsongy, nasalized. The mood of their worship was a longing to be socially correct, and I felt that it was a crime to take a vital and earthy people like these and thwart and blunt their instincts—instincts which they sorely needed in their struggle to live against the odds of nature *and* the British! Even though the men and the women wore their native clothes, it was easy to see that they were striving to be middle class. Why was it that Christians always seemed to have money and comfort, when the symbol of Christ, half naked and bleeding on the Cross, evoked a sense of suffering in the world?

Being areligious myself, I preferred the religion I looked at to be interesting, with some of the real mystery, dread, and agony of existence in it. I'd much rather have heard the kind of singing that Paul Laurence Dunbar described in his poem "When Malindy Sings":

She just opens her mouth and hollers,
"Come to Jesus," 'til you hear

Sinners' trembling steps and voices
Timidlike a-drawing near;
Then she turns to "Rock of Ages,"
Simply to the Cross she clings,
And you find your tears a-dropping
When Malindy sings.

But that Gold Coast hymn evoked in me merely a cough of embarrassment behind my cupped palms. . . .

Of course, the pastor no doubt would have unctiously told me that there was no need now to suffer, that Christ had felt it all for us, had suffered the supreme penalty and had set us free by an act of grace. But was there not somewhere in such a rationalization a sneaking evasion, a dodge? How the Christians had their cake and ate it too! O poor pagans who lived the naked terror of life, spurning all the symbolic substitutions, without steady incomes, without comfortable clothes! They had no Christ to die for them; they had to sweat and suffer it all. My sympathies were with the pagans; the pagan was my kind of a Christian, the kind that the Christians hated and feared. . . .

I left the church and got out into the sinful streets where naked little boys confronted you, begging for pennies. It would be to these that the future would have to look, these whose souls had not been stunted, whose sense of earthly pride had not been intimidated, and in whom the will to live still burned with undiminished fervor.

Religion has been only one aspect of the means by which the Gold Coast has been maintained as a captive nation for more than a hundred years. Just as the early Portuguese traders had sought to keep out sundry strangers, so the British have not been unmindful of stray foreigners or alien ideas knocking about in a domain so rich in gold. This isolation of even the Gold Coast intellectuals from the currents of modern thought has kept them from realizing how universal were their predicaments. With the exception of Nkrumah, the actions of their politicians were not informed by lessons drawn from other peoples and other countries; and, until the coming of Nkrumah, there was no attempt on the part of the British government officials to dramatize or publicize local events and enlist the comment or scrutiny of interested outsiders.

Another means by which the Gold Coast African had been led astray was by the British insistence, almost to the point of absurdity, upon the highest possible academic standards and qualifications for all kinds of work. This in itself, of course, was not at all bad; but the manner in which it was used was more a means of control than a means of enlightenment. Prior to 1948, education in the Gold Coast was not even remotely related to practical accomplishment or functional efficiency, or even to a comprehensive grasp of life; it smacked more of status, manners, class standing, "character," and form. . . . The African leaving Oxford or Cambridge found all doors in Africa open to him; in an illiterate society, he was at once at the top of the heap; he did not have to accomplish anything to merit his position; it was his by right of his having absorbed certain acceptable qualifications. . . . Education therefore assumed a kind of religious tone capable of conferring upon its devotees, like the act of conversion, all the boons of life, of civilization. The result was that the psychological distance between the educated and uneducated became almost absolute in character, and among the illiterates there developed an attitude toward education that reeked of yearning, of pathos, of a ludicrous waiting. . . .

Conditioned to give as little of himself as possible when working for the British, living amidst a prodigious jungle abounding in great heat and humidity, the Gold Coast African has never been too strong an advocate of manual labor; and the British stress of "education" and "qualification" tended to reinforce in him the feeling that the most humiliating thing that could possibly happen to him was that he would have to work with his hands for a living. One of the first lessons that Nkrumah had to drive home was that technical education was not only respectable, but that it was one of the indispensable conditions for national freedom.

Of the value of the teachings of the missionaries as a technique of colonial control, Mr. W. E. G. Sekyi, president of the Aborigines' Rights Protection Society, said explicitly:

"I've no way of telling what the average individual missionary was thinking when he preached his white paganism to us. All I can tell you is that such teaching and preaching supplemented and complemented the schemes of the merchants and the men of the colonial office. Its effect was to break the military traditions of our tribes. The missionaries used to inveigh against 'Black Christmases,' human sacrifices, etc., but they knew that our society was one organic whole, and that if you broke one part of our customs, you influenced them all. Their aim was to destroy our capacity for self-defense. Wherever the seeds of the Christian doctrine fell, the will to resist was weakened. And the missionary was careful in propounding his 'glad tidings' to us; he never went so far as to instruct us in regard to the concrete steps that we could take to become self-sufficient. His propositions dealt with the soul and obedience. Always he stopped short of imparting that kind of information that would lead to activities that made for self-reliance and the independence of our people. . . ."

Seventeen

My money is melting under this tropic sun faster than I am soaking up the reality about me. For two days now I've moped about my hotel room with no visitors or telephone calls. In the newspapers are items telling of monster mass meetings, of vast educational rallies; I'd have liked to have attended those events, but I hear of them only after they have taken place. My frequent visits to the Convention People's Party's headquarters do not elicit any information about what is transpiring, and I cannot escape the feeling that my seeking information has somewhat frightened the African politicians.

I'm of African descent and I'm in the midst of Africans, yet I cannot tell what they are thinking and feeling. And, without the help of either the British or the Africans, I'm completely immobilized. Africa sprawls far inland and my walking jaunts about Accra are no way to see this life. Yet, I cannot just take a train or a bus and go; the more I ask about jungle conditions, the more I'm dismayed. The general state of affairs in the country is not conducive to the safety of wandering tourists. There are but few hotels in Accra, Takoradi, and Kumasi, and their accommodations are of a sort to discourage the heartiest of travelers. Trekking into the interior can only be done with the aid and consent of the government, for, without it, one does not have access to the government resthouses that are stationed at intervals in the jungle. Beyond that, one must depend upon the willingness of the Africans or the British to put one up in their private homes! This does not mean that the British would forbid anyone's going off alone into the jungle to trust his luck, if he was fool enough to want to do it. . . . Neither do I say that this has been expressly arranged; it just works that way.

Each time I entered a store, the Indian or Greek or Syrian merchant wanted an account of my opinions. I suspect that my attitude caused a lot of background talk, for my reactions were open and direct and I could not order them otherwise. When something struck me as being strange, I erupted with questions; when something seemed funny, I laughed; and when I was curious, I dived headlong to uncover the obscurities. . . . Moreover, being obviously of African descent, I looked like the Africans, but I had only to walk upon a scene and my difference at once declared itself without a word being spoken. Over and above these liabilities, I had a background steeped in Communism, yet I was no Communist.

My thought processes were of interest even to the British banker who cashed my travelers' checks.

"Well, sir, what do you think of all this?" he asked me.

"You know, I've only been here a few days," I tried to evade him.

"I mean, don't you think that the people are happy?"

"I've seen so little—"

"Don't you think that we've done a lot for them?"

"I haven't seen very much of life here yet," I stalled.

He knew damn well what I thought, but I was determined not to give him the satisfaction of letting him hear me say it. He leaned forward as he spoke and his tone was low, urgent, confidential:

"You American chaps are three hundred years ahead of these Africans. It'll take a long time for them to catch up with you. *I* think that they are trying to go too fast, don't *you*? You see, you American chaps are used to living in a white man's country, and these fellows are not."

In his attempt to influence my attitude, he was using the old tried and trusted British technique of divide and rule.

"I don't know about that," I said, smiling at him.

He counted out my pound notes through the barred window.

"Thank you," I said.

"Good morning, sir," he sang out.

"So long," I said.

There was no room for jockeying or making tactical moves in a colony; the European was at close grips with the native who was trapped in the European net of trade and religion. Every casual remark of the dubious stranger had an implied bearing upon policy. Whether you danced or not, whether you were interested in a given scene or not, whether you laughed or not—all of these items were weighed, examined, and filed away in the minds of the upper-class African or British civil servant. A sort of living dossier was kept on you: what you said casually at Mr. So-and-so's luncheon table was discreetly and questioningly served up to you at Mrs. So-and-so's dinner table on the evening of the same day. It was check and double-check.

So far my random observations compel me to the conclusion that colonialism develops the worst qualities of character of both the imperialist and his hapless victim. The European, on duty five hundred miles from the Equator, in the midst of heat and humidity, can never really feel at home and the situation breeds in him a kind of hopeless laziness, a brand of easygoing contempt for human life existing in a guise that is strange and offensive to him. Outnumbered, he feels safe only when surrounded by men of his own race and color. Since, for questions of policy, he cannot live with the native, he develops an indifference for the land that grows the food. *His* food is transported over vast distances and at great cost for which the native must pay in the form of taxes. Hence, the European tries without success to convince himself that he is worth all of this bother and care, but he never quite can. His basic concerns are centered upon the wealth of the country, upon doing his job so that no crass criticisms will be heaped upon his head. The social setting produces a chronic suspiciousness about the ultimate meanings of the most ordinary ideas and remarks of the natives, and there is a continuous undertow of concern about the possibility of the native's developing a mood of rebellion, for, at bottom, no matter how jaunty the European pretends to be, he cannot rid himself of the idea that what he and his kind are doing is stealing. . . .

And the native, when he looks at the white man looming powerfully above him, feels contradictory emotions struggling in his heart; he both loves and hates him. He loves him because he sees that the white man is powerful, secure, and, in an absentminded and impersonal sort of way, occasionally generous; and he hates him because he knows that the white man's power is being used to strip him slowly of his wealth, of his dignity, of his traditions, and of his life. Seeing that there is nothing that he can do about it, he loses faith in himself and inwardly quakes when he tries to look into the future in terms of white values that are as yet alien to him. Charmed by that which he fears, pretending to be Christian to merit white approval, and yet, for the sake of his own pride, partaking of the rituals of his own people in secret, he broods, wonders, and finally loses respect for his own modest handicrafts which now seem childish to him in comparison with the mighty and thunderous machinery of the white man.

In the end his own land lies fallow, his skills waste away, and he begins to prefer menial jobs with white families which will enable him to buy tinned food shipped from Europe. He no longer fishes for herring; he buys them in a can; he no longer burns local fats; he depends upon kerosene; he abandons his weaving and buys cloth from Lancashire; he goes to mass and learns to cross himself, and then he goes to the Stool House to propitiate the spirits of his long-departed ancestors.

This afternoon, after taking a nap, I went upon the veranda to escape the humidity of my room. A young African boy was there, wrapped and bundled in his cloth, stretched upon a bench; he glanced at me, then leaped quickly to his feet and hurried off. He turned his head and stared at me as he went around a bend of the veranda. . . . Why had he been so apprehensive? I sat and looked about; the veranda was empty. I had forgotten my cigarettes and went inside my room to fetch them; when I returned the young African was there upon the bench again. Seeing me, he rose at once and walked quickly off. There was no doubt about it; he was afraid. . . . He had thought that I was a European and would be offended at his presence. But what could I say to him? Merely to speak to him might well frighten him even more. . . .

Eighteen

I decided to try something on my own; I'd rent a taxi and start making short trips out of the city and into the neighboring villages. Good God, whoever heard of seeing Africa by taxicab?

I knew that barging out into tribal villages alone in a taxicab was rash. Being alone and with no knowledge of the language, I'd miss a lot that I'd want to know, but, being alone, unannounced, with no guide or interpreter, I'd catch the native African without warning; he would have no chance to dress up or pretend; the chiefs would have no opportunity to get out those big and ridiculous umbrellas. The idea appealed to me.

Wearing a sun helmet and a T-shirt, with a camera slung over my shoulder, I ambled out to a line of waiting taxis at the hotel entrance. The drivers began honking their horns, trying to attract my attention. I went to an elderly man, feeling that he would think twice before trying any tricks or cheating. . . .

"What's the nearest village that's worth looking at?"

"Don't know, Massa."

"You know some villages. You live here, don't you?"

He scratched his head and eyed me speculatively.

"There's Labadi, Massa."

"What kind of a village is it and how far is it?"

"Three miles, Massa. It's where the beach is. . . . And they fish there. Cost you two pounds, Massa."

"What do you think I am?"

He guffawed and his eyes avoided me.

"Three shilling an hour and one shilling a mile, Massa."

"All right," I agreed. "Let's go."

Labadi lay athwart the highway to Tema, the big port that was under construction. The driver raced along with a carelessness that made me wonder if he saw the cars coming in the opposite direction. Before I knew it, he was pulling up alongside rows of wooden huts with rusty tin roofs.

"Labadi, Massa."

"Lock your car and come with me," I ordered him, expecting him to demur. But he didn't. I found that that was the only way to get any consideration out of a native; he'd been conditioned by the British to being ordered and would obey only when ordered.

Labadi was a small fishing village and was a mixture of the primitive and the modern. The houses that fronted the highway were mostly of wood or cement, but when I poked behind them I came across the usual mud hut crowned with thatched straw. I walked as though I knew where I was going and the taxi driver followed me.

"Massa know somebody here?"

"No. Why?"

"Better see chief, Massa," he advised me.

"Why?"

"Always see chief, Massa."

"Where is the chief?"

"Don't know, Massa."

I knew that his counsel was sound, but I decided to ignore it. I pushed on and saw compounds alive with black men, women, and children. They glanced up at me, pausing in pounding their *fufu*, grinding pepper, or mending fish nets. Sheep, goats, turkeys, guinea hens, and pigs mingled with the naked, dirty children. Here the women did not bother to cover their breasts; they must have thought that I was an African schoolteacher or some government worker. I walked down winding paths bordered by tall weeds.

"Any snakes around here?"

"Yasa, Massa. Snakes all round here—"

I paused, hearing a droning, dashing sound.

"Is that the sea I hear?"

"Yasa, Massa."

I headed for the sea, not knowing where I was going, but not wanting to give the impression that I was wandering. I noticed that the men stared at me long after I had passed. Then suddenly, a voice yelled:

"Hey, sar!"

I turned and a brown-skinned boy ran up to me.

"Where're you going, sar?"

His voice had a hard, direct quality. He confronted me with purpose.

"I'm just looking around," I said.

"Oh," he said, studying me. "Are you an American, sar?"

"That's right."

"Oh, sar. What do you want to see?"

"First, I want a drink of coconut milk from one of these coconuts on that tree," I said.

He was taken aback for a moment, then he turned to one of the crowd of men who had gathered behind him. He spoke to them in his tribal language and one of the boys ran toward a coconut tree and scaled it, monkeylike.

"Where did you learn such good English?" I asked him.

"At missionary school, sar," he said proudly.

"Do you work?"

"Yes, sar. I'm an electrician," he said.

A mass of shy black children began crowding about. Playfully, without attempting to take a picture, I pointed the lens of the camera at a boy and he shuddered, burst into tears, and ran off screaming.

"What happened to him?" I asked the young electrician.

"Nothing, sar. He's just scared."

"How many people are in this village?"

"I don't know, sar."

"You live here?"

"Yes, sar. With my mother and father."

I noticed that many of the children's entire heads were gripped with sores and that yellow matter streamed from their eyes.

"What are those sores on their heads?" I asked.

"Yaws, sar," came the prompt reply.

"Are many of them like that?"

"Yes, sar. Most all of them, sar."

"Are they being treated?"

"They are talking about it, sar."

"How many babies die here during the first year of their lives?"

"I don't know, sar."

(I was afterward informed, in Accra, that the infant mortality rate was more than 50 per cent during the first year of life.)

"What's your nationality?" I asked him.

"Fanti," he said proudly. "Oh, sar, here's your coconut."

"Aren't you a Gold Coast man?" I asked pointedly, accepting the coconut. "Thank you. . . ."

He grinned at me; he knew what I meant. At no time did I hear an African identify himself as other than belonging to a tribe. It was only after I had prodded him that he would identify himself as a Gold Coast citizen. They wanted their country to be free, but the idea of a national identification was too new to have sunk home in their minds so that they could give an automatic reply.

"What's your profession, sar?" he asked me.

"I'm a writer," I said.

"You write for the newspapers, sar?"

"Sometimes. But mostly I write books."

"Do you think somebody in America would give me a scholarship, sar?"

"Perhaps; but you have schools here."

"But I want to go to America, sar."

"What makes you think they give scholarships in America?"

"They're rich, sar."

"I was born there and nobody ever gave me one," I told him.

He stared, then looked off. He turned to me with a timid smile.

"But you are rich, sar; aren't you?"

"No. I'm not. I was born as poor or maybe poorer than you are now," I told him. "I'm not rich."

"But you went to a university, sar?"

"No."

"Then how did you become a writer, sar?"

"Because I wanted to be a writer."

He could not understand that. He yearned for an education, but he did not associate personal will with it. He felt that only the generosity of somebody else could open the door to education for him.

"You can study right here in Labadi and be anything you want to," I told him.

He shook his head and smiled doubtfully.

"What kind of mission school did you attend?"

"Methodist, sar."

"Did you like your teachers?"

"Yes, sar. They were very kind."

"May I see where you live?"

"Oh, yes, sar," he said eagerly. "Come along, sar."

I told the taxi driver to go back to his car. I followed the boy, and a swarm of black children trailed eagerly after me. We went past stagnant lagoons that stood but a few yards from thatched mud huts.

"There are a lot of mosquitoes here, aren't there?"

"Oh, yes, sar."

"Why don't they fill in these lagoons?"

He stared a moment before answering. I suspected that the reason was that some god was connected with the lagoons. . . .

"I don't know, sar," he said.

"Is there much malaria and yellow fever here?"

"Yes, sar. We have it all the time. But there's not so much right now."

I noticed that the children's bellies looked like taut, black drums, so distended were they. Almost every child, boys as well as girls, had monstrous umbilical hernias. We came to a broad lagoon across which a few rotting logs had been placed as a bridge. He walked surefootedly across and I hung back, going slowly, balancing myself. The children, for some reason, stopped at the water's edge. We skirted a small pond in which men and women were bathing, their black skins streaked with white lather.

"Tell me, in school did they tell you not to worship fetish?"

"Oh, yes, sar," he said, his eyes round with seriousness.

"And if they caught you doing fetish, what did they do?"

"They whipped you, sar."

"And would they put you out of school for it?"

"No, sar. I don't think they ever do that."

"Your family—Is everybody Christian?"

"We're all Christians, sar," he said emphatically.

We were now passing between swish houses. The yards were of red clay and clean-swept. Women sat pounding that inevitable *fufu*. . . . I paused and watched a mother dart her black and gnarled fingers in and out of a huge wooden mortar into which her daughter rammed a long wooden pole, pounding boiled yams, cassava, plantains. They both looked at me and smiled; the daughter glanced down each time she sent the end of the pole plunging into the soft, yellowish mass of *fufu*; but the mother, confident that her hand would never be crushed, stared at me and then burst into a laugh, hanging her head.

"How many times a day do they make this *fufu*?" I asked.

"In the middle of the day and at night, sar."

"Now, look—you are an electrician. Why don't you invent a machine to pound that stuff?"

His mouth dropped open and he stared at me, then he tossed back his head and laughed.

"I'm serious," I said.

He spoke hurriedly to the two women and they laughed so heartily that they had to abandon their work. The daughter lifted her cloth to her mouth and yelled, then ran away, laughing hysterically. But the mother quickly grew solemn; her supper was being delayed. She called sternly to her daughter and the pounding began again, but the daughter continued to giggle.

"What are they laughing at?" I asked the electrician.

"They say machines can't make *fufu*, sar," he told me.

"Do you believe that?" I asked him.

It was evident that he did believe it, but he was too polite to want to contradict a stranger.

"You'll have to believe it before you can invent the machine," I told him. "We make bread in America with machines."

"Really, sar?"

"Of course. And *you* can make *fufu* with a machine," I said.

There was silence. I felt that it would be a long, long time before machines made *fufu* here. It was not that the young electrician could not make the machine, but I felt that the women would surely have had none of it. . . . Making *fufu* with a machine would have been the work of evil spirits. As we moved along, the boy was pensive. I turned and tried imitating that queer, African hand wave and the people waved back at me, smiling, their fingers trembling. Women passed, carrying those huge tins of water on their heads, their necks straight, their eyes proud, somber, and bold, and their lips ready to give vent to an embarrassed giggle. Yet no movement of their bodies so much as caused a tremor of the huge tins of water, which must have weighed thirty pounds. . . .

We were passing a magnificent woman who sat nursing a fat black baby. The long red rays of the setting sun lit her ebony torso to a soft distinctness. I requested the boy to ask her to let me take a picture. He spoke to her and she nodded her head.

"Penny, Massa," she said, extending her hand.

I fished a shilling out of my pocket and gave it to her. She rose, laughed. I tried to focus my camera and she lunged past me, holding the baby with one hand under its belly, and made a beeline for the mud hut; she was out of sight before I could utter a word. A howl of black laughter echoed through the compound. I stood looking like a blundering fool. She had outwitted me. I laughed too. She had won.

I walked past compounds filled with black life, naked, dirty, diseased, shy, friendly, curious. . . . Was it possible that Great Britain had had the power to rule here for 104 years? Three generations had passed and things were like this? Obviously, no one had really tried to do anything. I felt that these people could have created conditions much better than this if they had been left completely alone. It couldn't have been worse. Yet, from the soil of these people had come an untold fortune in gold, diamonds, timber, manganese, bauxite. . . . Truly, Nkrumah had a job to do. . . .

We reached the top of a hill and I stared down at a cluster of compounds. The sky was gradually darkening, but there was still enough sun to light up the black bodies, to make the rusty tin roofs distinct, and to outline the sleepy lagoons. And suddenly I was self-conscious; I began to question myself, *my* assumptions. I was assuming that these people had to be pulled out of this life, out of these conditions of poverty, had to become literate and eventually industrialized. But why? Was not the desire for that mostly on *my* part rather than *theirs*? I was literate, Western, disinherited, and industrialized and I felt each day the pain and anxiety of it. Why then must I advocate the dragging of these people into my trap?

But suppose I didn't? What would happen then? They would remain in these slavelike conditions forever. . . . The British would continue to suck their blood and wax fat. Of that there was no doubt. Yet, there was an element of sheer pride in my wanting them to be different. With what godlikeness we all thought of the lives of others! I yearned for them to break away from this and master machines, dig the minerals out of the earth, organize themselves, grow strong, sovereign. . . . And why? So that the British would not exploit them, so that they could stand equal with others and not be ashamed to face the world. I wanted them to redeem themselves. . . .

But was not this, my yearning for them, predicated upon the premises of the British? Was it merely for that that I wanted their lives changed, their beings altered? Well, their lives had been already altered; the faith of their fathers had been taken from them. True, they'd not been admitted into the world that had decreed that their past lives had not been good, and they had played no part in the world that had condemned theirs as being bad. And their participation in that world was what I was hungering for. . . . Why? Was it just my pride? Just to show the British that these people could do what the British had done . . . ?

But, if not that, then what? I didn't know.

I brooded over the young electrician who walked ahead of me. In that boy lay answers to questions. But could he tell me what he felt?

"Look, you want your country to be free, don't you?"

"Oh, yes, sar," he answered, amazed that I should ask.

"Did the missionaries ever tell you to dedicate your life to freeing your country?"

He looked at me thoughtfully, then shook his head.

"No, sar."

"But they taught you to read, didn't they?"

"Yes, sar."

"And after they had taught you to read, you read, didn't you? And when you read you found out that the British had taken your country? Is that it?"

"I think so, sar," he said slowly and evasively. "I know the history of my country, sar. We were conquered."

"Did the missionaries ever tell you that you were conquered?"

"No, sar."

"Did they ever tell you to fight for your freedom?"

"They didn't talk about that, sar."

"But the reading that they taught you, you used it to learn about freedom, didn't you?" I hammered at him.

He was beginning to understand. He had understood it before I spoke to him about it, but he had just never put it into words, into ideas.

"We'll be free some day, sar. We'll drive them *all* out," he said grimly, under his breath.

His footsteps had slowed. His eyes were wide and unblinking. Over and over again I found that same reaction: the Gold Coast African loved the white missionaries as long as he thought of them in the category of their teaching him to read and write, but when the same reading and writing brought home to him a knowledge of what the British had done to him, a knowledge of how his country and his culture had been shattered and exploited, he felt a rising tinge of resentment against the missionaries. Unwittingly, the missionaries had placed themselves in a strange position, a delicate position in the minds of the African people. Toward the European missionaries the African held that somewhat ambivalent attitude of love and hate that he held toward almost everything Western. It was easy to love and hate at the same time, but it was hard to talk about it.

When we came to his home, which was a tin-roofed swish house whose outer walls had been covered with a coating of cement, he introduced me to his mother, then to his grandfather, an old man who was partly blind. His father—the boy was almost tearful about it—was absent. I stood and waited, for no one spoke English but the boy.

"Who makes the money to pay the bills?" I asked.

"My father and I work, sar," he said.

I longed to go inside the house and look at the rooms, but I felt that I would have been trespassing. One room, he told me, was a kitchen in which his mother washed and cooked when it rained; otherwise, she worked out of doors. I saw that she had finished her *fufu* and it was laid out in earthen dishes in round yellow balls covered with palm leaves. Everything was neat here; all tools and utensils could be accounted for. The little short broom—made from the veins of palm leaves—was lying against a wall near a pile of rubbish. The *fufu*-pounder—I never did learn the name for it—was washed and lying atop the tin roof. Zinc washtubs were turned upside down in one corner of the yard. Nearby was an orderly okra patch. Farther out was a garden of tomatoes which had not yet begun to ripen and each plant was tied to a stake driven into the earth.

"How old is your grandfather?"

"Seventy-eight, sar."

"Have you any brothers and sisters?"

"No, sar."

"Just you, your mother, father and grandfather?"

"Yes, sar."

"What kind of electrical work do you do?"

"I'm an apprentice, sar."

"And what do you make?"

"£2. 10/- a month, sar."

"Is that all?"

"Yes, sar. And I pay 15*s*. a month for transportation, sar."

I wanted to stay here and learn this life, to feel it, to try to find out the values that kept it going. But I didn't like prying out the details. The African had been violated often enough in the dark past. And I had a taxi waiting. The light of the sky was growing darker.

"Your grandfather, does he remember a lot of history?"

The grandfather was consulted; when he understood what I had asked, he laughed loudly and nodded his woolly head. The boy translated:

"He says, sar, that he's seen a lot of things. Wars and fighting, sar."

"You've been very kind," I told the boy.

I gave him some shillings and shook hands all around. I started back toward the taxi.

"I'll come with you, sar."

The compounds were noisier now; it seemed in Africa that the days were quiet, but, as night drew on, a clamor set in, increasing as the hours passed. Even the children, who had been somewhat listless all day, now began their games. Was this because of the heat?

"Tell me: is there any difference in the way the pagans and the Christians live?" I asked the young electrician.

"I don't understand, sar."

"Do pagans and Christians live together? Or separately?"

"Oh, we all live together, sar."

"How does one tell a Christian from a pagan?"

He was silent for a moment, looking at me, puzzled.

"We all live together, sar. Christians go to church on Sundays—"

"Do *you* follow pagan ceremonies?"

"Oh, no, sar!"

"But when you have holidays, you enjoy them with the pagans, don't you?"

"Yes, sar. We do that, sar."

I walked slowly beside the boy in the dying light. The swish houses of the landscape were now bathed in soft purple shadows. A candle flickered here and there. So this was the White Man's burden that England had been so long complaining about? How cleverly the whole thing had been explained to the outside world! How wrapped up and disguised in morality had this lust for gold become!

"Sar, perhaps you could come and see my father?" the boy asked me shyly.

I promised him that I would try. When we reached the roadway he was a little downcast that I was leaving him.

"Study hard," I told him.

"Yes, sar," he said.

I could see the wistful smile on his shy, tight little brown face as my taxi pulled off into the deepening night.

Well, paganism and Christianity were all mixed up, blended. It seemed that being a Christian didn't mean giving up all of one's former outlook. Then I wondered how a pagan could really surrender all of his paganism when the community in which he lived was still basically pagan. It was a halfway world, all right. There were in both religions elements that the people needed in their lives; the only way paganism could really vanish would be for the total pagan environment to be transformed, and that was manifestly impossible. It would have been demanding of the pagan something that even the Christian had not demanded of himself.

The more I reflected upon the work of the missionaries, the more stunned I became. They had, prodded by their own neurotic drives, waded in and wrecked an entire philosophy of existence of a people without replacing it, without even knowing really what they had been doing. Racial pretensions had kept them from sharing intimately the lives of the people they had wanted to lift up. Standing outside of those lives, they had thrust their doctrines into them, gumming them up, condemning them, and yet they had failed to embrace those pagans who had turned Christian and who now yearned so pathetically to follow them into their world. . . .

What would happen when the native began to realize all of this clearly? Some were already doing so, and they felt a deep and sullen anger that was almost speechless in its intensity. I recalled Nkrumah's having told me with suppressed emotion that the missionaries had been his first political adversaries.

For centuries this sugared duplicity had held forth; and, because there were so many European national philosophies to justify it, so many European interests involved in it, there had been no one to come forward and call the deed by its right name. Indeed, so intertwined was Christianity with this getting of gold and diamonds that it was not until now that any real crime has been felt—and even by a *very* few—to have been committed! In Sunday schools all over the Western world little boys and girls were giving their pennies to help save the "soul of the heathen"!

Yet, as I saw and felt it, the looting of the country of gold and diamonds and slaves had not been the greatest crime that had been committed against these people. Diamonds have no great value when weighed in the scales against human life; and gold, though it figured symbolically in the Akan religion, could be done without and the Akan people haven't suffered mortally from losing it.

The gold can be replaced; the timber can grow again, but there is no power on earth that can rebuild the mental habits and restore that former vision that once gave significance to the lives of these people. Nothing can give back to them that pride in themselves, that capacity to make decisions, that organic view of existence that made them want to live on this earth and derive from that living a sweet even if sad meaning. Today the ruins of their former culture, no matter how cruel and barbarous it may seem to us, are reflected in timidity, hesitancy, and bewilderment. Eroded personalities loom here for those who have psychological eyes to see.

And even when, as Nkrumah's valiant efforts are directed now, they did finally rebel and strive to throw off the psychological shackles of foreign misrule, they were compelled to attempt it in terms of the values and on the moral grounds of their conquerors . . . ! In a certain sense, even if the Gold Coast actually won its fight for freedom (and it seems that it can!), it could never really win. . . . The real war was over and lost forever!

I do not say that the impact of the missionary was deliberately made to coincide with the military and commercial conquering of the Gold Coast people, or that the missionary was a conscious handmaiden in subjecting them to the yoke of economic imperialism. Frankly, I doubt if the oldtime English mercantile pirates were that smart or foreseeing. Their aims, I suspect, were much more limited when they struggled so desperately for a foothold on the Guinea Coast.

However synchronized or not were the motives of the missionaries with those of the imperial financial interests, their actions could not have been more efficient in inflicting lasting psychological damage upon the personalities of the Africans who, though outwardly submissive, were never really deeply converted to a Christianity which rendered them numb to their own dearly bought vision of life, to the values for which they had made untold sacrifices.

Nineteen

My next taxi sortie took me to Tema where a modern port was being built. The government, I was told, has great plans for the transformation of this all too sodden place.

I got out of the taxi and threaded my way between dark yellow swish huts with thatched roofs. The fishermen had just brought in a huge catch and wherever my eyes fell I saw herring neatly laid out in rows to dry: on roofs, on the red earth, on planks, on stretches of cement. Everywhere were huge black iron vats three or four feet in diameter; across the tops of these vats were stretched metal slats or screens which held herring being smoked, a process that caused a blue mist to rise through the blinding sunshine and hang over the entire village. The stench of fish mingled with the odor of urine and excrement that flowed in an eroded gully down through the center of the village. Flies, satiated, buzzed in lazy clouds. Naked children, gripped by disease, followed me for a mile as I walked to the seashore and looked at the gray and misty Atlantic. . . .

Returning through the village, I came across a huge black woman sitting in front of her hut; she was obviously ill, her eyes cloudy and her head bent forward. At her side was a bottle of patent medicine and a bottle of gin, both imported from England. I spoke to her through my taxi driver.

"Is it your stomach that's bothering you?"

"Yasa, Massa."

I picked up the medicine bottle and examined the label which read: BILE TONIC. . . . The woman's stomach was enormous and she was no doubt suffering from some liver complaint.

"Why do you drink?"

"It helps me, Massa."

"Is it your liver that's bad?"

"Yasa, Massa. Doctor say so. Bad liver."

I sympathized with her; alcohol was good, but not for what was ailing her. I gave her a few shillings and left. Time and again I had to choke back feelings of compassion in these mudholes. If one allowed one's feelings to become identified here, one could no longer see anything; in fact, one could no longer think.

I came across a tiny wooden structure which, I learned, was the village school and church. The children were out at sports and the schoolroom was deserted. I entered and found that clothes had been discarded hastily and thrown upon desks. Desks? I stooped low and examined the strange objects. They were made of soapboxes, had rough, jagged edges, and the sides and ends of the boxes still bore the name and address of the English manufacturer stenciled in black letters. Most of the boxes were about 18 inches in length, about 6 inches high, and about 2 feet across; some of them were so arranged that the opened side ran lengthwise, facing the child, and thus provided storage space for books, etc. Nailed to the bottom of these boxes were four slats of wood chopped from the same kind of packing cases.

Such a "desk" must have given a child a great deal of discomfort. The remainder of the seating accommodations was comprised of chairs, but chairs not as we know them. The seats were about nine inches from the floor and the backs were so sloping that they could give little or no support to the back of any child optimistic enough to expect it. These chairs were miniature in every respect, and just how the children managed to adapt their limbs to the whims of these desks and chairs is difficult to imagine.

Hovering over this evil-looking litter of a schoolroom was a swarm of slow-moving flies. . . .

At the head of the classroom was an altar set upon a dais and rising above this was a heavy, gilded cross. . . . I saw no books, no evidence of this being an educational institution other than a soiled sheet hanging on a wall with a few clippings from illustrated journals pinned to it. Under these clippings was a timetable that showed that the children received one-half hour of religious instruction each day.

Outside of the school building, about a hundred yards away, a group of about thirty children sat in rows upon benches. Their average age seemed to be about six years. I stood discreetly to one side while an African man conducted the class; with a pointer he indicated the following words which were chalked in white upon a blackboard:

I go
I go up
I go so
I no go

Beside each expression was the vernacular equivalent. I couldn't believe it, but there it was.

This, of all things, was a church mission and, as such, I wondered just what the mission thought it was doing. . . . Saving the heathen? In my opinion it would have been far better to have left those children alone; either one gave them a decent education or none at all. I would have preferred to have seen them retain their tribal heritage intact than to have had drilled into them this travesty of a Western education. These children, when they grew up—if they could possibly survive amidst this appalling filth—would come in time to hate what had happened to them, especially if they turned out to be intelligent and had the capacity to reflect.

It was, of course, the European traders who first brought the missionaries to the Gold Coast and helped to establish these churches; those traders were the Portuguese, the French, the English, the Dutch, the Swiss, and the Germans, in short, most of western Europe. From about 1687 to 1820, companies ruled the colony and had the final and decisive say in everything, including the education of the natives. In 1843, with the aid of some West Indians, the missions became firmly established and began to work closely with the government, and, by 1848, a girls' school had been established. At Akropong, in the same year, a seminary was set up for catechists.

In 1876 the Methodists opened a high school for boys in Cape Coast; this was followed by the establishment, in 1909, of Mfantsipim Secondary School, which was a union of the Wesleyan Collegiate School and the Fanti Public School.

In 1880 the Roman Catholics began religious teaching at Elmina, and by 1900 the Catholics had opened six or seven schools. . . . The government aided these schools somewhat, but it must be remembered that it was not until 1900 that fighting between Britain and Ashanti ceased and allowed some steady and continuous progress to be made in educational work.

In 1924 the Methodists opened a college at Kumasi and thereafter the government became active in opening trade schools for artisans; but it was only in 1930 that "national" schools came into existence. These schools represented the efforts of native rulers, chiefs, etc., and were administered by Africans. In 1924 the government established Achimota College. . . . Education in the Gold Coast has been a slow, torturous business. Indeed, "business" itself—gold, diamonds, timber—fared far better than education, and, though businessmen exploited the Africans, I believe that their impact, in the final analysis, was far less detrimental to the personalities of the Africans than that of the religious teachings of the missionaries.

The conducting of mines and timber camps brought the African into contact with the most progressive and dynamic aspects of the Western world and, though it cheated him, at the same time it roused his sense of achievement, challenged him to emulate the undertakings of white men and free himself. Those African leaders who today fight courageously and without stint for their country are those who have been impressed by the techniques of Western exploitation, by the manner in which the West produced. It was not what Nkrumah learned about God in his Catholic mission school that urged him to struggle for the liberation of his country, but his grasp of the role played by economic forces in the modern world that launched him on his path to grapple with the British, and when he did come to grips with them, he knew the exact spot where they were most vulnerable; that is, he knew how to paralyze the economic life of the colony. It was an economic vision rather than a metaphysical one that had organized the personalities of the young men I met in the Convention People's Party.

On the other hand, the religious teachings of the mission schools, though it did impart the three R's to a few hundred thousand in a hundred years, tended to develop quietism in the African personality. More detrimental to the personality of the African than the religious instruction *per se*, perhaps, was the strange, neurotic temperament of the missionary—kind but impersonal, near but aloof, anxious but superior; in brief, it was a relationship calculated unconsciously to arouse hatred and jealousy. Few or no really independent African personalities emerged from the nervous ministrations of these missionaries who, because of racial feelings which even religion could not help them to overcome, could never actually identify themselves completely with the people.

It seems that the world cannot leave Africa alone. All of Europe is represented here in Africa, to kill or save Africa. The businessman, the missionary, and the soldier are here, and each of them looks at the question of the meaning of human life on this earth when he looks at Africa. The businessman wants to get rich, which means that African suffering to him is an opportunity. The soldier wants to kill—for the African is "different" and is, therefore, an enemy. The missionary yearns to "save," that is, to remake his own image; but it is not the African that he is trying to save; it is himself, his sense of not belonging to the world in which he was born. . . . (No one should be allowed voluntarily to enter Africa; one should be *sentenced* there to service. . . .)

One does not react to Africa as Africa is, and this is because so few can react to life as life is. One reacts to Africa as one is, as one lives; one's reaction to Africa is one's life, one's ultimate sense of things. Africa is a vast, dingy mirror and what modern man sees in that mirror he hates and wants to destroy. He thinks, when looking into that mirror, that he is looking at black people who are inferior, but, really, he is looking at himself and, unless he possesses a superb knowledge of himself, his first impulse to vindicate himself is to smash this horrible image of himself which his own soul projects out upon this Africa.

In the future men will die, as they have died in the past, about the meaning of Africa; the only difference in that future fighting and dying will be that the Africans themselves will be wholeheartedly involved in the fighting and dying from the beginning, for they too have now caught a sense of what their problem is; they too have seen themselves reflected in the mirror of their misery and they are aroused about the meaning of their own lives. The European white man made Africa what he, at bottom, thought of himself; it was the rejected and the self-despised of Europe who conquered and despoiled Africa. But today Africa is not alone in her misery. She is keenly aware that there are others who would solve their problems at the expense of her misery. . . .

To ask if Africa can be changed is to ask if man can be changed. Africa must and will become a religion, not a religion contained within the four walls of a church, but a religion lived and fought out beneath the glare of a pitiless tropic sun. The fight will be long, new, unheard of, necessitating a weighing of life in terms that modern man has not yet thought of.

Life in Africa must handle life; life here is just bare, sentient life; life is all that life has in Africa. This might sound strange to Western ears, but here it is so plain and simple and true. No wonder men killed and enslaved others in Africa; no wonder they sacrificed human beings; no wonder they invented fantastic religions—they did these things because they were really reacting to themselves, their sense of themselves.

Africa, with its high rain forest, with its stifling heat and lush vegetation, might well be mankind's queerest laboratory. Here instinct ruled and flowered without being concerned with the nature of the physical structure of the world; man lived without too much effort; there was nothing to distract him from concentrating upon the currents and countercurrents of his heart. He was thus free to project out of himself what he thought he was. Man has lived here in a waking dream, and, to some extent, he still lives here in that dream.

Africa is dangerous, evoking in one a total attitude toward life, calling into question the basic assumptions of existence. Africa is the world of man; if you are wild, Africa's wild; if you are empty, so's Africa. . . .

These were the thoughts that ran through my mind as I bathed and dressed the next morning. I felt tired, as tired as when I had gone to sleep. I was gripped by an enervation that seemed to clog the pores of my skin. I was about to pull on my shoes when I discovered, to my horror, that my clothes were getting mildewed, that my shoes were beginning to turn a yellowish green color. I scraped at it; it was mold. I called the steward and asked him what caused it.

"That's the heat and the sea water in the air, Massa."

"Well," I sighed, "try and do something about it."

"Yasa, Massa. I put clothes in sun."

"Okay."

I took a taxi to the Prime Minister's office to see if I had any mail there. The Prime Minister's secretary looked at me and asked:

"How are you getting on?"

I felt depressed. She knew what was happening and I resented her asking me to tell her what she already knew.

"I feel like the Africans have put their *juju* on me," I muttered, trying obliquely to let her know that I was dissatisfied.

She whirled in her swivel chair and stared at me.

"You must be careful of *that*," she said in a deadly serious tone.

"What?" I exclaimed, coming fully aroused now.

"There's something to *juju*," she said to me sternly.

I wanted to howl with laughter, but a Prime Minister's office was not the place to act like that.

"You're kidding," I said.

She shook her finger solemnly in my face and said:

"Watch it!"

"My God, *you* don't believe that," I said.

"There's more to it than you think," she snapped.

I sank weakly into a chair and stared at her. I'd met this cool, intelligent, and efficient woman in London and Paris and we'd had long discussions about the state of the world; and I had respected her opinions. And now, here in this heat and humidity, she was hinting to me that *juju* was real and not just a psychological delusion.

"What do they do to people down here?" I asked her. I walked slowly out of the office, feeling defeated. Lord, *juju*...? Let 'em bring on their *juju*. . . . If you didn't believe in it, it could never influence you. . . . And that *juju* was real was being hinted to me in the Prime Minister's office! Oh, no! Oh, no!

I hailed a taxi and climbed in. Just as the taxi got under way, I saw a tall, well-dressed black girl running wildly toward the car, waving her hand at me.

"Hold it, driver," I said.

The girl came panting to the car window.

"Say, please. . . . Give me a ride into town with you?"

"Why not?" I said.

She got into the taxi and settled into a seat. She was dressed in stylish European clothes, high-heeled shoes. She was deeply rouged and her hair was piled high on top of her head, like that of a woman who was imitating photographs of European women in fashion magazines.

"Where would you like to be dropped?" I asked her.

She looked at me and smiled slowly. I felt *juju* coming; but it was not that of the Gold Coast or anywhere in Africa. It was as old as mankind; the Africans could not claim it. . . .

"Where are *you* going?" she asked me.

"To my hotel. Why?"

She still continued to smile at me. The sun flickered through the taxi window as we sped past tall trees and I could see that her hair was soaked in grease. She edged closer to me and I felt her naked arm touching mine. Here it comes, I thought. They have this in Africa too. I sat still and stared determinedly out of the window. Then I glanced at her and she laughed. She grasped my hand. I pulled away from her.

"Look, what is this?" I asked her.

"It's *me*," she said.

"Are you working for the government?" I asked.

"No. I'm a social worker," she said.

"And are you now performing a part of your duties?"

She giggled.

"Do you live in Accra?" I asked her.

"No. Not now. I was born here. But I've been in school in Cape Coast. I'm leaving shortly for England to study."

"I see. I doubt if England has anything to teach you," I told her.

She took hold of my hand again, holding it tightly now, glancing at me out of the corners of her eyes. I looked full at her and she bent over laughing.

"Did someone send you to my taxi?"

"No."

"Then why did you pick *me* out to ask for a ride?"

"I just liked the way you looked," she said simply.

The taxi bumped along in the hot sunshine.

"Where are you going *now*?" she asked me again.

"I told you. To my hotel—"

"Take me there—"

"I can't. I've an appointment—"

"Later, then," she insisted.

"No. Really, I'm busy today."

I wondered how long she had been practicing this kind of approach to men; and, above all, where she had learned it? She could not have been over twenty-one and her English was fluent.

"Are you a Christian?" I asked her.

"Of course," she said.

Asking a person if he were a Christian or not in Africa does not mean what it does in the West; it is asking if the person belongs to a certain social status. It has little or nothing to do with morals, ethics, or metaphysics.

"You live with your family?" I asked.

"Yes."

"You like movies, don't you?"

"Yes," she said, surprised. "How did you know?"

"Oh, I know," I said.

I could not tell her that she was acting like a very bad movie. Again and again in Africa I found natives trying to imitate American movies, but, having no idea of the distorted context of life in which Hollywood actions take place, they vulgarized those actions, making them even more fantastic, which was no mean accomplishment. She was accepting a shopgirl's escape dream as a realistic vision of life!

"You know," I said seriously, "you are young and you ought to be careful. You'll get into trouble, maybe, if you do anything like this in London."

She was suddenly sober; I had made her a little doubtful, but not for long; she still believed in her goal but was searching for new means. She looked yearningly at me and tried to talk convincingly.

"I need a friend," she said. "I've never had a friend."

"Do you say that to all the men you meet?"

She laughed, surrendering her tactic. But undismayed, she switched to another one.

"I've spent so much money buying things for my trip," she explained. "Four days ago I had seventy-five pounds. Today I've only three pounds."

"What did you do with your money?"

"I bought a trunk and a winter coat. . . . They say it's cold in England. . . . God! If I had a friend, I could have some money."

"Do all of your girl friends have friends?"

"All of them except me."

"Where did you get seventy-five pounds?"

"My family."

"And why won't they give you more?"

"They haven't got it. I need forty pounds."

"That's a lot of money," I said.

"Well, twenty pounds, then."

"How did you get the idea of asking for money like this?" I asked her. "It was from a movie, wasn't it?"

She looked at me and giggled again. And I knew that it was from either a movie or a novel that she had gotten the notion.

"What school did you go to in Cape Coast?"

"The Methodist Mission," she said.

Well, Christianity had changed her. Before professing Christ, she might have slept with a man for the sheer physical pleasure; now, she still wanted to sleep with a man, but she wanted to be paid, and, moreover, being out of touch with reality, she had placed a fantastic overestimation upon herself.

"You're selling and I'm buying, is that it?" I tried to shock her.

She brushed it off. Her eyes moved frantically as she thought of ways and means.

"Haven't you got a friend who'd be nice to me?"

"I have no friends in Africa," I told her.

"Come home with me."

"But aren't you with your family?"

"My aunt. But she'll leave if I ask her to."

"Listen, this is no way to study social work," I argued.

"Can't you let me have ten pounds?"

"No."

"Five pounds?"

"No."

"Would you take me to the movies tonight?"

"No, no. This is no way to live, sister."

"I'm trying to go to school," she explained.

That justified it all. I desisted. I could see nothing in her that I could appeal to. She was using tribal methods in order to latch herself onto the twentieth century. . . . She was somehow terribly innocent, and, at the same time, hotly and crassly determined to put her life on a cash-and-carry basis to buy an education. Hers was a mixture of Christian and tribal values.

"Do you smoke?" she asked me.

"Yes. Pardon me. Do you want a cigarette?"

"No. I don't smoke. Do you drink?"

"Yes; sometimes. . . . Do you?"

"No; I never drink," she said.

She looked off in wonder. She was trying to become quickly acquainted with the most elementary things of life.

"Your family and the teachers at that mission school watched you pretty closely, didn't they?" I hazarded.

"Yes; but all that's over now," she said.

I looked at her and she hung her head and giggled, then she lifted her knuckles to her lips, thinking intensely.

"I have a sister in America," she said suddenly.

"And you want to go there?"

"If I can."

"You go to the movies too much," I said.

"But I like movies," she said defensively.

The taxi spun round curves. The hot sun splashed on the rickety houses and the crowded streets where young black women, wearing native cloths, carried unbelievable burdens upon their heads. The taxi stopped; I got out and held the door for her.

"Won't you come in, please?"

"I can't, really."

"Meet my aunt, won't you? She's there."

"I'm sorry, little lady."

Her eyes were baffled. She turned suddenly and walked off across the street and entered a vacant, littered lot; she paused and looked back at me, laughing nervously in the hot sun. The taxi driver stared at me, waiting.

"Come in for a moment," she begged.

I shook my head, forcing a wry smile.

"Good luck to you and be careful," I called to her.

She stood still. I moved backward toward the open door of the taxi. Then she turned and ran; she reached a corner of a cement house and paused again, standing a little sideways; she smiled, laughed, then beckoned me with her finger. I shook my head, filled with pathos. She ran out of sight.

I climbed into the taxi and settled down. The driver sat, not moving.

"To the Seaview," I told him.

"Massa no go with girl?" he asked me.

"No," I said.

He laughed and started the motor.

"Mary, she want too much money, hunh, Massa?" he asked, wagging his head.

"Do you know her?" I asked him.

"Oh, naw, sar!" he said.

"Then why do you call her Mary?"

"They all named Mary, Massa," he told me, and he laughed until his shoulders shook.

Late that afternoon I visited, in the company of some young Africans, the famous Korle Bu Lagoon, a center of legend and fetish worship situated on the outskirts of Accra. The lagoon was a wide stretch of gray, stinking mud over which a modem concrete highway ran. You could smell the lagoon's awful stench a few moments before your car reached it, and you also believed that you could smell it for an hour afterward when you were miles away, so nauseating was its odor.

"But why don't they do something to cover the thing up?" I asked of my companions in the car.

"Oh, that's a problem," I was told.

"Won't the government act?" I asked.

"Oh, yes. If they could—"

"It's a simple job. Isn't there money enough for that?" I asked. "At least they could cover all that slime with a coat of thick oil and mosquitoes couldn't breed in it. That stagnant water causes typhoid and yellow fever and malaria. . . ."

"We told you that there's a story—"

The story I heard went something like this: Years ago, according to legend, the Fanti tribe was fighting the Accra tribe. The Fanti tribe, so went the story, advanced with a powerful army to the edge of the lagoon but, since it was nearly night and they were tired, they decided to camp and rest till morning. . . . The Accra tribe, seeing that their enemies, the Fanti, had given up hope of launching an attack, took heart, mobilized their forces, made a few sacrifices, called on their gods, and attacked and won a smashing victory. . . . And, of course, that victory, according to the calculations of the tribal mind, had come from the helpful spirit of the lagoon which had confounded and confused the Fanti and prevented them from fighting! Since that day the Korle Bu Lagoon has been held in deep reverence; it is thought that a god resides in it. So, when the government decided to drain the lagoon, a crowd of thousands of angry and terrified Accra people gathered, headed by the fetish priests and priestesses, and dared the government authorities to act! And, so far, the government authorities have not acted. . . . And this reeking lagoon lies within a stone's throw of the most modern tropical hospital in all West Africa!

Twenty

On the tenth of July the Legislative Assembly convened, presided over by the brown-skinned, wigged, robed, and spectacled Sir Emmanuel Quist, distinguished lawyer and elder statesman. The Prime Minister, clad in a smock of the Northern Territories, submitted a motion calling for drastic modifications of the constitution—modifications which would eventually mean a large measure of self-government for the people of the Gold Coast.

The session was impressive, colorful, but restrained. Most of the Convention People's Party members of the Assembly wore their tribal costumes; the opposition members were dressed strictly in Western style. Nkrumah, as well as all of his aides who had been imprisoned with him for sedition, wore peaked white caps, the same kind that they had been forced to wear when behind bars; and on the front of those caps was printed in red letters for all to see: P.G., meaning: Prison Graduate.

The high-ceilinged room in which the Assembly met had been consciously modeled on the British House of Commons and the mood that prevailed was more British than the British themselves could have provided. Most of the speakers droned in voices so low that I could barely hear one half of what was being said.

At once I was aware of the contrast between this prim atmosphere, this staid gathering, this chaste room and the screaming and dancing crowds that I'd seen in Accra and Cape Coast. Would these men fulfill the hopes of those hopeful people? I was not doubtful or cynical; I was just wondering and skeptical. I was for these men and I found myself hoping that the British, uncannily politically astute, had not already snared this revolution in a net of politeness and parliamentary maneuvering. . . .

All around the grounds outside of the Assembly were thousands of Gold Coast citizens clad in their native togas and waiting behind long cordons of Northern Territory police. Every time a car rolled up bearing some Convention People's Party functionary, the crowd would let out a long roar of applause. These were the masses; they had put Nkrumah in power and now they were waiting to see if he would fulfill the mandate that they had given him.

Inside, with the help of an African newspaperman, I spotted the key Britishers who held the decisive cabinet positions and the balance of power for Britain. There was Sir Charles Arden-Clarke, the Governor of the Colony: short, stumpy, aloof, detached, hiding his tension. There was broad-browed, spectacled R. H. Saloway, the Minister of Defense and Foreign Affairs. There was P. Branigan, Minister of Justice, Queen's Counsel, tight-lipped, sharp of features, partly bald, and with the subdued air of a detective. And there was R. P. Armitage, the Minister of Finance, a wisp of hair dividing his bald dome, reserved, determined. . . . These four Britishers had the armed forces, the money, the administration of the courts, and the foreign affairs of the colony in their hands. The rest of the power was in the hands of Africans. It was truly a delicate balance.

In the galleries there were almost as many Europeans as Africans and that reminded me that Nkrumah, so far, has had to rely, ironically enough, mainly upon the British for the burden of administering most of the departments of government. The black intellectuals from Oxford and Cambridge were, almost to a man, with the opposition and were, therefore, unacceptable. In coming to power Nkrumah had to import more Britishers to serve in technical capacities than had ever been in the Gold Coast before; the drive toward self-government had not lessened but increased the number of British officials. . . . If Nkrumah had not followed this line, his new and varied programs of social reform could not have gotten under way so quickly; in short, he'd not have been able to keep the many promises that he and his party had made to the masses. . . .

As the preliminaries began, I mulled over the strange facets of this political situation: had the British, having faced many similar situations of revolt in other lands with other people, known the exact moment when to call these black boys into power? There was no doubt but that Nkrumah's acceptance of responsibility in the government had been to demonstrate to the world the African's capacity to shoulder the burdens of office. But had he accepted these responsibilities too *soon*? Might not the famous British gesture of an "act of grace," the releasing of Nkrumah and his aides from prison, have concealed a knowledge on the part of the British that the new political party and its leadership were not yet quite ripe to rule, and that they would have to depend upon the British? The British would not have been able to rule the Gold Coast without force had they not invited Nkrumah and his party into the government as partners. But the black brother who had been invited into partnership was a weak one, inexperienced. . . . In other words, the victory of the Convention People's Party, as astounding and unheard of as it was, had not been really and truly decisive. The British, having their hands upon the money and the police, and having the right to say who could or could not enter the colony, could bottle up the country any time they wanted to. And, though they were quiet about it, the mining, timber, and mercantile interests, all foreign, had their own ideas about what was happening.

Nkrumah's speech petitioning Her Majesty's Government to enact the necessary legislation for Gold Coast self-government was calm, competent, and calculated to appeal to the traditional British pretensions of self-rule for colonies. His most telling point came when he stated that as long as the British ruled the Gold Coast, all the mistakes of the Africans could be laid at British doors. He said nothing to frighten foreign capital; he expressed a desire to remain within the Commonwealth; and I could not escape the feeling that the speech implied an almost formal understanding with the British. . . . There was nothing inherently shameful in that; any smart politician would have done it. But I could not help but ask myself if it should have been done *now*—with the national front broken, with the most able men of the country sulking in their corners . . . ? I did not disagree with Nkrumah; I simply and honestly feared for him and his people.

At the conclusion of the Prime Minister's speech, prolonged applause broke forth and the Prime Minister was taken outside and lifted upon the shoulders of his comrades and paraded to and fro. The surging crowds behind the cordons of police cheered and chanted:

"FREE—DOOOOOM! FREE—DOOOOOM!"

Their faces streaked with white clay as a sign of victory, decked out in wild and gay colors, the women did that slow, snakelike dance, shuffling their feet over the ground, their fingers lifted and trembling in the air, chanting songs, clapping their hands in offbeat rhythms. But I was apprehensive about a reality that lurked behind the reality I saw. I could feel the fragility of the African as compared with the might of the British, the naïveté of the African when weighed against the rancid political insight the British possessed, the naked plea of the African when pitted against the anxieties of man holding the secrets of atomic power in their hands. . . . And a phrase from Nietzsche welled up in me: the pathos of distance. . . . The Africans were grappling with a new and different kind of god that could be propitiated only with raw materials: uranium, bauxite, gold, timber, and manganese. . . . It was not what Nkrumah had said but what he had left unsaid that induced in me a mood of concern, of uneasiness.

How would the black bourgeois opposition handle this? I'd heard a lot about Drs. Danquah and Busia. I'd been told that they were able men when it came to handling words and this was pre-eminently a battle in which words were the decisive weapons.

While waiting for the opposition speakers to get under way, I wondered if it would not have been wiser for Nkrumah to have refused to share power with the British, to have allowed the black bourgeois opposition to rule while he enlarged and strengthened his party. . . . In a nutshell, what was bothering me was the manifest shallowness of the African foundation for the efficient exercise of power. If Nkrumah could have postponed his entering the government, he could have had, when he did come to power—as he inevitably would have!—a power that would have been *African* power, a control over the country so complete that he could have ruled in the name of his party until he could have trained a new legion of like-minded young men to help him.

The disruption of the class and social relations of a tribal country that has long been under the fumbling tutelage of a Western imperial power throws up a variety of possibilities, the crux of them being: for whose benefit will the turnover in power be made?

There could have been a narrow, nationalist revolution made for the benefit of the chiefs, the intellectuals, and the not too numerous black middle class. Such a realignment would have been a restoration, at a higher level, of the tribal power which the British had once smashed, and this power would have had to depend upon foreign mercantile interests. Under such a regime the masses of the people would have fared no better than they had fared before.

Yet, another revolution could have been made in the name and for the benefit of the Gold Coast and the whole of West Africa; such a revolution, of course, would have been attacked at once by the combined forces of both Britain and France; but, if such a revolution could have maintained discipline within its geographical boundaries and denied the exploitation of its natural resources to foreigners, it would eventually have been able to deal with the Western powers on a new basis. Such a revolution would have been difficult, costly in human life, would have entailed great sacrifices; but, in the end, whether it won or not, the entire black population of West Africa would have been forever committed to the new course, and the fetish-ridden past would have been killed beyond recall. . . .

Africa needs the West and the West needs Africa; the

problem is: How can this exchange of values, services, and materials between Africa and the West be made on a basis that will not outrage the African sense of justice, a basis that assumes the equality of needs on both sides?

The revolution that was actually made was for the benefit of British capital, the interests of the Commonwealth interlaced with the interests of the Gold Coast; and this revolution necessitated a sharp ability on the part of the participating Africans to know where their interests *began* and where those of the Commonwealth *ended*. Already the clash of interests, the ceaseless bickering over definitions of power was a lawyer's paradise!

The British-educated, black bourgeois opposition opened with an attack delivered by Dr. J. P. Danquah, lawyer, philosopher, politician, dramatist, and long-time nationalist leader. Short, slow-moving, he rose, shuffled his pile of notes; then, in a well-modulated baritone, he charged Nkrumah with converting the Gold Coast into another Malta. He pecked away at Nkrumah's motion without ever once getting beneath the surface of the situation. It was evident that he was innocent of the meaning of the twentieth-century industrial world. His concepts were dragged from the nineteenth century and hell and high water were not going to shake him loose from those prepossessions. England had laid her hand upon his spirit and, in spite of himself, he hated England but could not tell how England had grabbed hold of him. . . . He had no idea how hard and cold were both the white and black men with whom he was dealing, men who were professional politicians and who labored at their craft every waking hour. . . . (Dr. Danquah gave only his spare time to politics!) He argued as though he were exhorting, say, on behalf of Shell Oil. Not once did he indicate that he felt that the fate of millions of his fellow countrymen was at stake, that they had passionately asked for something for which they were willing to die, that they actually were massed and waiting out there in the hot sun to hear their aspirations put into words.

I left the Assembly before Dr. Danquah finished his speech.

After lunch I recalled that I'd noted many American movies being shown in the city. I'd come across the influence of Hollywood so often in the mentality of the Africans that I was curious to see how they absorbed these artificial dreams. I took a taxi and went to the biggest movie house in Accra. One entered the theater from the rear; I suppose that was necessary because of the absence of sidewalks in front. I bought a ticket for the gallery, for I wanted to be close to the side of the black boys and girls whom I'd seen on the streets.

The interior was vast, barnlike, undecorated. To find a seat you had to grope your way forward in the dark, bumping into walls and colliding with other people until your hands encountered vacant space. Smoking was allowed and the air was stale. I sat and became aware that an uproar was going on about me and I looked at the screen to see what was causing it. An advertisement was being projected; a bottle of beer was leaping and jumping on the screen as a British voice extolled its merits. The beer bottle tilted and foam gushed from its neck, demonstrating the beer's wonderful qualities of nourishment, and the audience howled with laughter. Then a black boy was shown drinking from a bottle and the audience hooted and yelled. They seemed amused no end to hear an alien voice telling them about something that was a daily familiarity in their lives.

This quality of uproarious detachment continued when the main feature was projected. Indeed, the laughter, the lewd comments, and the sudden shouts rose to such a pitch that I could not hear the shadowy characters say their lines. I could not follow the story amid such hubbub and came to the conclusion that they could not either; it soon became clear that the story was of minor interest to them. It was upon each incident that they were concentrating with such furious noise. If a man accidentally fell, they screamed with delight. If a love scene was portrayed, they hooted:

"Take her! Take her!"

And when a frustrated man rested his head tenderly upon a woman's breast, they jeered:

"Don't break 'em! Don't it hurt!"

It was a Western movie, packed, as they say, with action. In the Legislative Assembly the Africans had made believe that they believed in Western values; here, in this dark movie, they didn't have to pretend. Psychologically distant, they mocked at a world that was not their own, had their say about a world in which they had no say. . . . When a cowboy galloped across the scrubby plains, they shouted in chorus:

"Go, go, go, go, go . . . !"

During stretches of dialogue, they chatted among themselves about the last explosion of drama, waiting for the action to begin again. It was clear that the African was convinced that movies ought to move. . . . A fist fight took place and each blow that landed brought:

"Swish-um! Swish-um!"

Throughout the film the audience commented like a Greek chorus, and when the heroine was trapped I was sure that they wanted the villain to violate her. They applauded when the hero rushed his panting horse to the rescue; but their applause was not because they were concerned about the poor girl's virginity, but because his horse was beautiful and fast and strong. I dare say that these boys must have wondered, years ago when these films were first being projected in the Gold Coast, why the hero rushed so in such cases. . . .

And it did not matter too much whose hands held the smoking guns—the hand of the law or outlaw—for they helped to speed the bullets on their way with:

"BOOM! BOOM! BOOM!"

When a character made his reappearance, they greeted him like an old friend. (The same film is shown over and over again, for the audiences derive great joy from seeing the same action performed time and again!) Scenes filled with suspense caught them up totally; a thunderous drone would fill the air until the moment of climax and then, as the net closed tighter and tighter about the hero, or as the villain moved in for the kill, they went wild. . . . Elements of surprise delighted them; when the hero's bullets had run out and the trigger clicked on empty chambers, the tongues in the audience went:

"Click, click, click. . . ."

The impossible made them stand up and cheer, as when the hero, stealthily creeping around the villain in the semi-darkness, climbed a tree, waited for the villain to lift the blond virgin in his arms, and then plunged headlong down upon the villain—the pandemonium that erupted drowned out the soundtrack.

Not a little dazed, I made my way back to the hotel and tried to sort out what I had seen and heard. It was quite obvious that the African's time sense was not like our own; it did not project forward in anticipation; it oscillated between the present and the past. And at once I knew why there had been no literature in the Gold Coast, no novels or dramas even from those who had been educated in England. (Mabel Dove has written some short stories and Dr. Danquah has written a drama; but I've not read them.) The great adventure of the Western world, the rise out of feudalism of a new bourgeois class that thirsted to explore experience, that felt that it had a future that had to be ransacked for sensations, had not touched these people.

The African did not strain to feel that which was not yet in existence; he exerted his will to make what had happened happen again. His was a circular kind of time; the past had to be made like the present. Dissatisfaction was not the mainspring of his emotional life; enjoyment of that which he had once enjoyed was the compulsion.

I did not regard this as wrong; it was just different. By implication, it could make for a deep sense of conservatism. That which had occurred was holy, right, just, natural. . . . Why not? It was human. One did not leave the past behind; one took it with one; one made the past the present. I could not get beyond that, for it was alien to me; it was intriguing, but beyond the bounds of my feelings. I could understand it, but I couldn't experience it.

Twenty-One

As detached and resistant as I try to be, I find myself sometimes falling heir to the reaction pattern which lingers on here as a kind of legacy of British imperialism. One morning I wanted to take a batch of film to the Photographic Section of the Gold Coast Information Service and I got into a taxi and told the driver:

"Photo Section of the Gold Coast Information Service."

"What, Massa?"

"The Photo Section on Boundary Road," I said.

"Yasa, Massa."

He set his car in motion and drove for some time. I noticed that he had taken a route that was not familiar to me.

"Where are you going?" I asked him.

He stopped the car and looked at me, his face flashing a white grin.

"Where Massa wanna go?" he asked me.

"I told you the Photo Section. It's on Boundary Road."

He drove off again; then once more he slowed the car and said to me:

"Massa, tell me where it is. . . ."

"What are you doing?" I demanded. "You drove off like you knew where it was—" Houses have no street numbers in Accra.

"Yasa, Massa," he said, picking up speed.

What was wrong with the guy? The taxi sped past buildings that were strange to me; soon I saw the green landscape of the suburbs of Accra.

"Say, boy! Where're you taking me?" I yelled at him, leaning forward.

"Massa, I don't know where it is," he mumbled, slowing the car.

"Then why didn't you *tell* me? Why are you driving about aimlessly?" My voice was so sharp that he winced; the heat and the humidity held me in a grip. I noticed the lazy, relaxed manner in which he sat slouched behind the wheel and I was suddenly angry. "For God's sake, ask somebody where the Photo Section is," I directed him. "It's somewhere on Boundary Road. You know where that is, don't you?"

"Yasa, Baas."

He drove on. I sat back and swabbed sweat off my face, chiding myself. I oughtn't to speak to a boy like that. . . . The car rolled on and I watched for familiar landmarks. I saw none.

"Where are you taking me?" I begged of him.

"I don't know, Massa," he said and stopped the car.

"I want to go to the Photo Section on Boundary Road," I said, talking slowly, making sure that he heard every word.

"Yasa, Massa."

He started the car up again and sped off. The landscape was still strange. But perhaps he's taking a roundabout way to get back into the city? I held myself in. But, no; the city was getting farther and farther away. . . .

"Where are you going?" I asked him.

"I don't know, Massa," he said, slowing the car.

"Ask somebody," I told him.

We went forward slowly and, at the sight of a policeman, he stopped the car and spoke to him in his native tongue. The policeman pointed elaborately and again we were off. I waited, tense, sweating. I looked at my surroundings and saw a huge sign that road.

BRITISH MILITARY COMMAND FOR WEST AFRICA

"Boy, stop!"

The car skidded to a halt, the tires screeching on the concrete pavement.

"Turn this car around!"

He turned the car.

"Now, take me back to my hotel!"

"Massa wanna go back?"

"Yes!"

He started off. I relaxed. I'd get another taxi and start all over again. Jesus. . . . The British might have thought that I was trying to spy on them if they had found me wandering amidst their military installations. . . . A good five minutes passed and when I looked out of the window of the car I saw the Photo Section of the Gold Coast Information Service as we were speeding past it. I'd found it by accident!

"Stop!" I yelled. "There it is!"

He jammed on his brakes and I went forward against the back of the front seat. I got out and told him to wait. Ten minutes later I emerged and told him to drive me to the Seaview Hotel. At the entrance of the hotel, I got out.

"What do I owe you?"

"Eighteen shillings, Massa," he said, his face averted.

That did it. I got mad. I felt that I was dealing with a shadow.

"Don't be a fool, man! Tell me what I *owe* you!"

He looked at me and grinned shyly.

"Fourteen shillings, Massa."

"Talk sense," I muttered, feeling sweat running on my face.

He waited a long time, scratched his head, looked at me out of the corners of his eyes, his brows knitted, weighing me.

"Twelve shillings, Massa."

"Are you charging me for taking me out into the country? That was your fault—"

"Ten shillings, Massa." He was still bargaining.

"What was the actual price of my trip? You charge a shilling a mile, three shillings an hour, don't you? Did you drive me nine miles?"

I was determined not to be cheated. He looked at me fully now, grinned again, and said imperturbably:

"What Massa wanna give me?"

"Here are eight shillings," I said; I felt that that was too much, but I was willing to settle for that.

"Thank you, Massa," he said, bowing and smiling.

I stood watching him, wanting to tell him that was no way to act, that he should have been honest with me. He looked at me and burst into a wild laugh, a laugh of triumph. I was on the verge of cursing him, but I controlled myself. Suddenly I too laughed, lifted my arm in the Convention People's Party salute, my elbow resting on my hip, the palm of my hand fronting him.

"FREE—DOOOOM!" I roared at him.

He jerked to a surprised attention, gave me a salute in return, shouting:

"FREE—DOOOM!"

I spun on my heels and went to my room. More than once did I find myself slipping into the pattern left here by the British. The Africans had been so trained to a cryptic servility that they made you act a role that you loathed, live a part that sickened you.

Twenty-Two

At midday when the tropic sun weighs upon your head, making you feel giddy, you discover that there are no parks in Accra, no water fountains, no shade trees, no public benches upon which one can rest from a weary walk. There are no public cafés or restaurants in which one can buy a cup of tea or coffee; there are, of course, a few private clubs, but they are either far from you when you need them or you have to be a member to use their services.

This lack of amenities stems from two sources: first, the habits of African tribal life do not call for these tiny, civilized services; second, the British administrators retire to their homes for refreshment and relaxation. There are but a few hundred Britishers in a city like Accra and they do not feel that the city in which they are living temporarily or the country from which they draw their profits or salaries will be the place where their children will stay and grow up.

I strode into the bourgeois section of Accra and passed home after home of rich blacks; they were huge structures, pale pink, light blue, pastel shades of brown, cream, yellow, and red and they were enclosed by high concrete walls the tops of which held barbed wire and jagged shards of glass to keep out intruders. Each house stood a great distance from the others and was surrounded by a wide expanse of ground which usually was overgrown with weeds or was bare or littered with rubbish. Not once did I observe an attempt at making a garden or landscaping. The entire section had about it a garish but bleak air. A little attention would have converted the area into a park, but, even though many of the wealthy Africans of this section had once lived in England, they evidently didn't care for that sort of thing.

I left the paved streets of the rich African section and, leaping over the ubiquitous open sewage drains, wandered into the dusty compounds alive with the usual clutter of children, goats, sheep, and chickens. I stepped cautiously around sedentary but ever-busy women. . . . What could they be doing all the time . . . ? Their housework was no doubt easy; there was no dusting to be done; no floors to scrub or wax; no washing of windows; no lace curtains to be laundered. . . . I peered discreetly into interiors as I passed and only here and there did I see a bed or a cupboard. The windows were square, gaping holes. A roll of straw represented a pallet for the body when placed on the floor at night. And, as closely as I could observe, there didn't seem to be any set time, any scheduled hour for anything; one ate, slept, cooked when one felt like it, and there was no reason for the keeping of rigid hours.

My prying walks ranged as far as the suburbs and, one afternoon, I found myself in Christianborg, an outlying upper middle-class quarter in which both Africans and Europeans lived. While rounding a corner I saw the ruins of a huge building facing me. I stopped, interested. From the atmosphere of settled decay that lay upon the heaps of crumbling stone, I guessed that the structure must have dated from the early nineteenth century. All of its upper floors had long since caved in and a greenish mold clung to the jagged masonry. I climbed upon some rocks and peered over the edge of a rotting wall and saw fallen columns lying athwart mounds of debris, stone stairways that halted abruptly in mid-air, vacant spaces that terminated in masses of rubble.

I sought an entrance into the ruin and was amazed when I came to a vast doorway. A man emerged and, seeing me, he came forward.

"You know what this is, sar?" he asked me.

"No; what is it?"

"It's the Old Slave Market Castle, sar."

"Does anybody live here now?"

"Oh, yes, sar. It's full, sar. Come along. I'll take you to Mr. Hagerson."

"Who's he?"

"He's the head man of the compound, sar."

I looked up at the top of the entrance and saw a faded inscription that read: 1803. . . .

"You live here too?"

"Yes, sar. I'm Mr. Hagerson's assistant, sar."

The interior was more spacious than I had thought. The ruins extended over the area of a city block. At the edge of the mounds of crumbling stone and against the thick walls were crudely constructed rooms in which people lived, cooked. . . . As I penetrated farther I became aware of scores of black families quietly going about their duties. Through the debris were narrow dirt paths that skirted many rooms in which stooped women prepared meals over charcoal fires. . . .

Mr. Hagerson was a brown-skinned man of seventy-odd, clad in a pair of baggy trousers and a frayed shirt. He was barefooted and it seemed that a part of the flesh of his toes had worn away. He stretched out a shaking, skinny hand, greeted me with a smile, obviously delighted to meet a stranger.

"Glad to meet you, sir," he said, lifting a gnarled walking stick to help him stand.

He led me toward his room, hobbling, turning his head now and then to point out a wall or a place where some large room had once existed. I entered his sleeping quarters which were dirty and musty. Pushing the only chair to me, he sat himself upon the edge of a box. On an old sun helmet to my left an eighth of an inch of dust had gathered. Had Mr. Hagerson been a bit taller, he could have been my grandfather. He had the same angular features, the same proud bearing, the same patient dignity that my grandfather had had.

"I'm interested in this place, Mr. Hagerson. Could you tell me a little about it?"

"Be glad to," he began cheerfully.

I wondered why he was so eager to talk. Most Africans are not very communicative unless it's for material reasons. I learned later that Mr. Hagerson was presenting "his case" to me.

"There was a man named Henry Richter," he began leisurely enough. . . .

It seemed that in the early days of the Gold Coast there lived a Dutch family of Richters. One member of that family had been governor for a while; when he left the governorship, he went into the slave trade, took himself an African wife by whom he had several children, mulattoes. When the old man died, he left his mulatto children a fortune in gold dust which they had used to build the Slave Market Castle on whose ruins we now stood. . . .

"Were slaves quartered here?"

"Oh, yes. They sold many, many slaves to America."

"Were any records kept?"

"Yes. But they are hard to find. You see, there are people here in the Gold Coast with records of the sale of slaves in their possession. But nobody likes to show such things. Nobody likes to say that their family dealt in slaves. . . .

"The people who now live here in this ruined castle are the descendants of John Richter, the son of Henry Richter. He too had an African wife. Now, John had a brother, Bob.

John and Bob had a dispute and finally John drove Bob out. John continued to live in the castle until his death. The slave descendants put in a claim to the effect that they owned the castle, and the brother, Bob, who lived at that time in Accra, put in a counterclaim. The slave claim won in the courts."

"You are a descendant of John Richter, Mr. Hagerson?"

"Yes."

"But your name is not Richter?"

"My name comes from my mother's side. We have a matrilineal system, you know," he told me.

I was baffled. The men and women I had seen moving about in the compound had been all black and the descendants of the Richters had been mulattoes. So how could these people, 150 years later, after marrying far and wide, claim to be the descendants of the Richters? And what had become of the white blood?

I learned that in the ruins of this Slave Market Castle lived a compound tribal family of some forty-odd men, women, and children, that Mr. Hagerson, the family's only literate member, had been elected some three years previously as its head and spokesman. Though governed by tribal law in secular matters, the family had divided its religious loyalties among Presbyterians, Anglicans, Church of England, and Catholics; a substantial majority were pagans.

The Castle is regarded as being "owned" by this family; no rent is paid; and the government tax rate is met by a communal pooling of funds. All of the children are being sent to mission schools, but the adult pagans follow the instructions of their fetish priest. Reckoning kinship in African tribal terms, Mr. Hagerson told me that, though only a part of the actual family lived here, many outstanding Gold Coast citizens had their family roots here, that no less than Sir Emmanuel Quist, the Speaker of the Legislative Assembly, came from the original family of this compound. . . .

"Who was head of the compound before you?" I asked him.

"A Mr. Cochrane. . . . But he's been set aside by the family."

"Was there a dispute?"

He did not answer. I sensed that he did not want to go into the disposition of Mr. Cochrane and I did not press the matter. I was resolved to see Mr. Cochrane later.

"Now, when do you call a meeting of this compound family?"

"Whenever cases arise."

"What kind of cases? Crimes? Marriages?"

"Oh, no. Crimes are handled by the police. Marriages are under the customs of the tribal people. Christians marry in church. I call a meeting when land has to be leased. For example, we own the land on which the petrol station is operating across the street. The people who own that station leased that land from us and pay us rent."

"Now, Mr. Hagerson, suppose a pagan girl here wanted to get married. Or a pagan boy, for that matter. . . . What would happen?"

"With the boy," Mr. Hagerson said, "it's simple. He goes and lives with his wife. But the girl's case is different. If a man falls in love with a girl living here, he must send two of his relatives to the girl's parents to ask if the girl is free, that is, if she's engaged or not. In coming, they must bring a guinea apiece with them, that is, two guineas. If the girl's family says that the girl is free, the two relatives leave and go back and when they return, they bring four guineas and a ring with them. . . . If the girl happens to be engaged, they leave and they forfeit the two original guineas they had brought. . . . If the girl is free and the two relatives have left the additional two guineas apiece and the ring, the bridegroom has to send the following:

6 guineas
30 shillings for the mother and father
2 bottles of gin
2 bottles of whiskey
1 dozen bottles of mineral water
1 dozen bottles of beer

"These are gifts from the bridegroom and his family and they are given to the family of the bride. But the parents of the bride give back to the bridegroom's family a shilling out of each guinea which has been given. The womenfolk change a pound into penny pieces and they send these to all the members of the bride's family with this message: 'Here is drink. Your niece or granddaughter is engaged.'"

"What politics do the members of your family believe in, Mr. Hagerson?"

Mr. Hagerson and his assistant tilted back their heads and roared with laughter.

"Convention People's Party, sir," Mr. Hagerson told me.

I gave Mr. Hagerson some shillings for "drink" and made my way past Christianborg Castle to the home of Mr. W. T. Cochrane. It was a gaunt structure enclosed by a stone wall. Mr. Cochrane was a man of sixty-odd, tall, mulatto, gracious. I told him that I wanted to ask about the Slave Market Castle and he regarded me with caution.

"What do you want to know about it?"

"You were the former head man there," I said. "Why aren't you the head man now?"

"You've talked to Mr. Hagerson?"

"Yes."

Finally Mr. Cochrane cleared his throat and said:

"You see, there's a fight going on in our family. There's a case in the courts—"

"What's it about?"

"Well, you see, it's a fight over the ownership of the land there. These people, who were once slaves—that is, their ancestors were—think that they own that land. They are fighting us about it. They are contesting the ownership of the land in court—"

"Who is 'us' in the case, Mr. Cochrane?"

"Well, *our* side of the family—"

"The mulatto side?" I ventured cautiously.

"I wouldn't put it that way," he said quickly.

Mr. Cochrane was staring thoughtfully before him. I had at last put my finger on the heart of the problem. The black side of the family was fighting the white side of the family for possession of the land. That was not an unusual thing, but the manner of the fight, as Mr. Cochrane revealed it to me, was unique. Convinced now that I, a stranger, had no part in the fight, he talked freely.

"Those people think that because they've lived there all these years, they own that land," he argued. "It's a hangover from slavery. They argue their claim under tribal law. They say the land is theirs just because they are on it. But they can't prove it in court—"

"And what would constitute proof in court in a case like this?"

"Records and testimony," he said.

"Are there records?"

"There are some," he said slowly.

It was the old war of race and class being fought all over again in a new guise; it was Europe against Africa, Christianity against paganism; freedom against slavery; law against custom; white against black; the rich against the poor; individuals against the tribe. The black side of the family had been born in slavery (that is, their ancestors had been), and they were now contending that they, by custom and traditional right, owned and controlled the land; and the mulattoes were contending that the documents and legal instruments in their hands gave them the clear right to the land. . . .

I couldn't guess who would win that fight, but, in a sense, it was the same fight that Nkrumah had made in the Legislative Assembly a few days before. Nkrumah had had no legal right to the land in which he had been born; he had pled that since his people had been living for centuries on that land, they had the right to rule it. . . . That fight, that claim, that plea went straight through the heart of all black Africa.

Twenty-Three

I spent the afternoon visiting the newspaper offices. There are about twenty daily and weekly newspapers in the Gold Coast but none of them, with the exception of one—the *Daily Graphic*—is a newspaper in the sense that the West uses that term. They are broadsheets, badly printed, dingy, smeared, horribly written, with atrocious layouts and unreadable editorials. The two official papers of the Convention People's Party, the *Ghana Evening News* and the *Ashanti Sentinel*, though suffering from being printed under primitive conditions, are at least coherent and militant, reflecting the basic moods and hopes of the people.

The printing shops are tiny and cluttered; many of the presses are hand-powered; the staff, in terms of quality, is extremely poor; and the salaries of the reporters are unbelievably low. Sometimes when a press breaks down, the paper does not appear on the streets for days. . . .

It was Nkrumah who founded the *Ghana Evening News* (formerly the *Accra Evening News*) in 1948, and it has a circulation of more than 15,000; it is the most influential single newspaper in the Gold Coast. Then there is the *Daily*

Graphic, owned by the West Africa Graphic Company, a subsidiary of the *London Daily Mirror*, the British Labour Party paper. Launched in the fall of 1950, the *Graphic* has evoked intense local African opposition which dubs it the "white press." It is technically the best newspaper in the Gold Coast, having a circulation of more than 40,000. It is equipped with linotype machines and has a number of Europeans on its staff.

The most influential of the opposition press is the *Daily Echo*, one of the two publications of the Independent Press, Ltd. Its editor in chief is Daniel George Tackie, a member of the royal family of James Town with the title of NII Arde Nkpa. Other Gold Coast papers are the *Spectator*, the *African Morning Post*, the *Ghana Daily Express*, the *African National Times*. . . .

Nothing short of a miracle gets these papers printed at all. In one shop I talked to the editor and his co-workers; I asked them why many of the city's papers did not merge their resources and circulation, etc., and try to lift up the standards of the Fourth Estate. I was informed that such co-operation among educated Africans was impossible, that each African was fiercely independent. I countered by reminding them that the Africans were reputed to be communal-minded. . . . Well, it seems that newspapers here are generally owned by families, and these families in turn are tied up with tribal interests, politics, etc.

Strictly speaking, there is no independent press in the Gold Coast; each paper is violently partisan and libel suits are many and ludicrous. One of the devices for squeezing out unwelcome competitors is to sue, and the one to whom the court decision is awarded has the right to seize the press of the loser!

Here is a short news item taken from the *African Morning Post* (Wednesday, September 16, 1953):

ODIKOR'S DEATH BEING INVESTIGATED

The Kedwai Police are investigating the death of the Odikor of Senfi near Bedwai, Nana Kwami Booba, who was found dead in the bush recently with a gun shot on his chest.

It is said that the Odikor left home early in the morning with a gun to see his animal traps. In the evening when it was discovered that the chief had not returned a search party was organized. He was found lying dead in the bush.

The government, trying to aid the press, has suggested that a national printing press be set up on which all of the newspapers can run off their editions. Such a press would seek to teach the basic essentials of the modern newspaper, how to increase circulation, how to devise a strict libel code, etc., but, so far, the African editors will have none of it. They feel that the opposition would have an opportunity to learn what they were printing and would, therefore, steal their news if all the papers were printed on a common press. . . .

The Gold Coast press differs sharply from the press of the American Negro. If one ignored the names, one would never know that the press was giving news of black people. Words like discrimination, lynch, race, Jim Crow, white people, etc., are conspicuously absent.

Most African papers carry no foreign news at all; the *Daily Graphic* usually devotes two or three paragraphs to "World News." The Gold Coast African feels that he is at the center of the universe and a conversation about world affairs is likely to elicit silence. The African newspaper, like the African himself, is a local thing. African ideas and culture do not fare well on alien soil, and the African has no hankering for foreign parts.

Twenty-Four

I was invited by the Gold Coast Information Service to hear Mr. Gbedemah, the Minister of Commerce, deliver a talk upon one of the pet schemes of Nkrumah's government. The scheme, known as the Volta Project, is to be launched with the creation of one of the world's largest inland lakes. There is a vast basin, sparsely populated, in Ashanti; this basin is surrounded by hills and if the Volta River were dammed up at a certain point, a lake, in about three years' time, would rise, making a body of water some two thousand square miles in area.

The main object in creating this lake would be to obtain cheap electric power with which to manufacture aluminum. Fabulously rich Ashanti has not only timber, gold, and diamonds, but also deposits of bauxite estimated at 200,000,000 tons. . . . Enough to last for two hundred years! The trapped waters of the Volta River are expected to turn turbines and generate enough electric power for the production of aluminum cheap enough to be sold on world markets.

At present the Gold Coast Government, the British Government, and the Canadian Aluminum Company are trying to find a formula to pool their joint funds and build the dam, control the flow of water, and produce 600,000 kilowatts of electricity per year. Of these 600,000 kilowatts of electric power, 500,000 will be earmarked for the production of aluminum, and 100,000 will be allocated to the Gold Coast for industrial and agricultural purposes. Hence, there is expected to spring up on the Accra plains a light industry under African leadership. Also experiments are being made to determine if the arid coastal plains will grow quantities of food if sufficiently irrigated. . . .

The British are asking the right to buy aluminum from such a project at rates prevailing in the dollar areas of the world. It is estimated that many thousands of workers will have to be moved from their present living sites and this will entail a vast job of resettlement of people who are not used to leaving the lands of their ancestors. It is also hoped that the edges of this great lake will provide marshes in which rice can be grown. This last item sounds attractive inasmuch as the Gold Coast now imports much of its rice supply from Liberia. It is also contended that the new project is needed to balance the economy of the Gold Coast, for at present the mainstay of the farmers is the one-crop system of cocoa. If one year the cocoa crop should fail, the Gold Coast would face famine or worse and the country would be engulfed in economic chaos.

All of this sounds wonderful, but for whose ultimate benefit is it? If the Africans are able to swing such a mammoth project with the British and the Canadians, and if the British civil servants can be trusted not to try to be civil masters, it would be a step toward the twentieth century for the Gold Coast. But does not this Volta scheme sound as though the British were exchanging political for economic control?

After I'd left Mr. Gbedemah's lecture, I was talking with a group of young Africans about the fantastic wealth of the Gold Coast, and one of them told me that some Americans were skeptical of such wealth. I told him that I saw no reasons for American skepticism in such matters, and that I was certain that he was mistaken. He then showed me the following document, laughing uproariously as he handed it to me.

It read as follows:

Faith in God! Hope in Immortality! Charity to All Mankind

OFFICE OF
UNITED AFRICAN MISSIONARY ALLIANCE
747 East 62nd Street
Chicago 37, U. S. A.

July 5, 1952

The British Embassy
3100 Massachusetts Ave., N.W.
Washington, D. C.

Honorable Sir:

The United African Missionary Alliance is interested in purchasing the British Gold Coast Colony in West Africa as a homestead for those of our members in the United States who are desirous of going to Africa to do missionary work.

Please inform your government at London immediately of our intentions, and if your government is willing to sell this territory to us, please notify the United African Missionary Alliance at once. Tell us how much money your government will accept in exchange for this territory. We will pay your price, if it is reasonable.

Looking forward to hearing from the Embassy just as soon as you can get a reply from your government.

Yours truly
United African Missionary Alliance
(signed) Rev. J. H. Edmondson

JHE:mc
Encl-DP

All of which indicated how remote America was from Africa, from colonies, and the realities that govern the lives of the people who live in them. The gentleman who showed me the above letter was a responsible man and he obtained the document from government files. I have no way of gauging the intentions of this particular organization to buy the Gold Coast and send missionaries to lift up the poor African to something lower; I can only hope that the Africans can be spared more interference of that kind.

When I awakened one morning, damp and enervated as usual, the steward came to tell me something and I could not understand him; then and there I took my first lesson in pidgin English and found that it consisted of a frightful kind of baby talk.

The first principle was that the African never referred to the European in the second person; it was always the third person that he had to use. For example, "Massa go now?" Never: "You go now?" When an African houseboy is asked to fetch something, he replies: "I go bring 'em, Massa." A child is always called "piccin," which is short for pickaninny. Lunch, dinner, eating, a meal, and food of all kinds are designated by the word "chop." The word "little" must have caused them great pains, for it has been replaced by the word "small." Everything that is little is "small"; something very little is "small small." It is used in a great variety of ways. For example, instead of saying, "Wait a little," one says "Wait small." If one does not wish much whiskey to be poured into one's glass, one says: "Small whiskey. . . ." If one does not wish to eat much, one says: "Small chop." "Dash me, Massa," means, "Give me a tip, sir." If you call, asking for the master, and he has gone upstairs, you are supposed to understand when the houseboy tells you: "Massa, he catch topside, sar." The stewards have been drilled into a clownish form of exaggerated politeness. "Yes" is always said as, "Yes, please. . . ." "No" is uttered as: "No, please. . . ." If a steward dares give a European a bit of information, he must not be so presumptuous as to speak it straight out, but he begins with: "Excuse me, please, to say . . ." One hears the word "pass" all day long and all night long; that one word takes care of the entire range of comparatives, material or psychological. For instance: "I like this pass that . . ." A man who is more important socially than another "passes" him. A building that is taller than another "passes" the other building. A youngster who is impertinent to an older person is trying to "pass" that older person. To look for something is to "catch" it. Thus, if you ask for the master of the house, the houseboy will tell you: "I go catch 'im." And if the master is not in, you are supposed to know that fact from the following sentence: "Massa, I see Massa, but he not there." The first time I heard a boy say that I thought he was trying to talk religion. . . .

It was amazing how much one could communicate by juggling these simple words. I suspected that the African had adopted these words on a basis that rested in his own language, Twi, which is fundamentally tonal, and one word can mean many things, depending upon how it is said, its context, etc.

I was still in the dark as to how the African mind functioned and I wanted to come to closer grips with it. I appealed at last to a white missionary, Lloyd Shirer, telling him that I wanted to ask an African, a cook or a houseboy, his beliefs. Mr. Shirer worked for the Department of Welfare in the Northern Territories and knew the Gold Coast well, having spent some thirty years in the "bush." He told me that what his cook could tell me would relate only to his cook's part of the country, that is, the North, but that the basic psychological reactions were mostly the same everywhere. Since Mr. Shirer spoke the language, he promised me a word-by-word translation.

"Come to dinner tonight, and after we've eaten, I'll call in the cook and you can ask him anything you want," he said.

I went to dinner and, after we had eaten, Mr. Shirer called in his cook. He was a tall man of about forty, jet black, slightly bald and skinny. Mr. Shirer told him that I was an American of African descent, that I'd come back to see the land of my ancestors, that I wished to ask him about his life. He had been a little nervous, but now he smiled, sat on a little stool, and nodded.

"Black man's country mighty sweet, sar," he told me; Mr. Shirer was translating.

"Where are you from?" I asked him.

"The North, sar."

"Why are you in Accra now?"

"I'm cooking for Mr. Shirer, sar."

"You are away from your tribe. Do you miss your sisters and brothers?"

"Oh, yes, sar! It's hard to be away from my tribe. But I go back as often as I can. This is *not* my home, sar! My home is with my tribe."

"What do you do to keep up your spirit while you are away from your tribe?"

"I observe all the customs, sar. I sacrifice a sheep or a goat at times of feasts or celebrations and I implore my ancestors to watch over me. If I die, I want to be taken back to my tribe and buried with my ancestors."

I questioned him about his dying so far from the land of his ancestors and his expression darkened. It was obvious that it was something that distressed him acutely. He told me:

"A stranger died far from home, sar. We buried him, but not like we bury our own. We dug a grave in a pathway pointing toward his home. Then we sacrificed a sheep and let the blood drip on the grave and we said a prayer to the spirits. We said:

"'Spirits and gods, this man had every intention of going home to die. You can see that, for his grave points in the *direction* of his home.' So you see, sar, his ancestors must forgive him. He wanted to do right, but he didn't have a chance."

"And do you think that that prayer fixed everything?"

"Oh, yes, sar."

"Now, tell me . . . Do you ever think of going far away, to America, for example?"

"Oh, no, sar! Never!" he said, shaking his head slowly. "I couldn't leave the land of my ancestors. There is land here for me to cultivate and watch over."

(As he spoke I wondered what terror must have been in the hearts of the slaves who had been, through the centuries, shipped to the New World? It is highly possible that the psychological suffering far outweighed the physical!)

"Now, suppose a great calamity overcame a man? What would that signify?"

His eyes widened and he shook his head, staring at me as though he thought that I was mad.

"Why, sar, it means that a witch has got 'im," he told me with conviction. "And he'd have to go to a witch doctor and get something to counteract the evil eye."

"So when someone dies, it is caused by someone else?"

"Of course, sar. If he is old and has had many children, then he dies a natural death. But if he is young, it is certain that someone has killed him, done something to him. For a young man or a young woman, there is no natural death. It is only when you are old and have had many children that your ancestors call you to join them."

"What do you think happened to the millions of your black brothers who were sold into slavery and shipped to America?"

He was thoughtful for a long time, then he answered, speaking slowly:

"They were being punished, sar. Their dead fathers had no thought for them. Their ancestors did not afford protection for them, abandoned them, did not defend them as they should have—"

"Why?"

"It's hard to tell, sar."

"Is there anything that those slaves could have done to avoid being sold into slavery?" I asked him.

"Oh, yes, sar!" he said, brightening. "Listen, sar, if you are bound in chains, helpless, and if you swear an oath, your ancestors will turn into lions or tigers or leopards and come to your aid. Why, you could ride one of those lions or tigers or leopards six hundred miles in one night. Now, sar, these lions or tigers or leopards that your ancestors turn into are not the kind of animals that a hunter shoots at in the forest. No, sar. . . . They are *magical* animals. . . . You can't see them. But you can hear them crying at night. And if you hear one of those magical animals crying at night, it means something bad will happen. It might even mean that the fetish priest will die."

I next asked him:

"Now, look at me. You can see from the color of my skin that I'm of African descent. Now, after all of these years, why do you think I've come back to the land of my ancestors? Do you think that they called me back for some reason?"

Again the tall, serious cook was deeply thoughtful; he scratched his head and said soberly:

"It's hard to tell, sar. Such a long time has passed." He looked at me and shook his head pityingly. "I'm afraid, sar, that your ancestors do not know you now. If your ancestors knew you, why, they'd help you. And, of course, it may be that your ancestors know you and you don't know them, so much time has passed, you see, sar. Now if, by accident, you happened to go back into the section where your ancestors are buried, they'd perhaps know you but you wouldn't know them. Now, if, while you are in Africa, your ancestors should recognize you, then something strange will happen to you and then, by that token, you'd know that you were in touch with your ancestors."

"What sort of strange thing would happen to me?"

"It's hard to tell, sar," he said.

I gave him a few shillings for "drink" and told him goodbye. I sat brooding. Mr. Shirer watched me and then broke into a soft laugh.

"Does that interview satisfy you?"

"Yes," I told him. "Is he typical?"

"Quite typical," he said. "You see, in my work in the Department of Welfare, I have a lot of trouble with beliefs of this sort. This concern with ancestors makes it difficult for the government to launch schemes of resettlement. For example, if, in a certain region, the land is poor and if it's thought that it's better for a tribe to move into a new area, the people will resist, because they do not want to leave the ground on which their ancestors lived and died. To the grave of his ancestors a man will go each year and kill a chicken and drop the blood on the earth, hoping that this will appease his ancestors, hoping that his ancestors will rest in peace and not come into this world and take him to keep them company in the world of spirits. The ground in which his ancestors are buried is charged with spirits whose influence is both good and bad. Therefore, to leave a spot in which ancestors are buried creates terror in some African tribes. . . . They feel that they are leaving their very souls behind them. It is only after making many sacrifices to the earth, to the dead ancestors, that they are able to leave at all."

The illiterate cook had given me, by implication, answers to many questions. It was now obvious why Africans had sold so many millions of their black brothers into slavery. To be a slave was proof that one had done something bad, that one was being punished, that one was guilty; if one was guilty, one was a slave; if one was not guilty, one would not be in the position of a slave. . . . To be sold into slavery meant that your ancestors had consigned you to perdition! To treat a slave harshly was a way of obeying the spiritual laws of the universe! Hence, he who has misfortune merits it. Failure is a sign of badness; winning is a sign of goodness and indicates that the man who wins has a good cause. If you take something from a man who has lost, whom luck has deserted, you are doing right and adding to your own power and goodness. . . .

"I wonder," I said to Mr. Shirer as I sipped my coffee, "what would happen to that cook if he died here in Accra?"

"Let's see what he has to say about that," Mr. Shirer said. "I'll ask him; I'll call him back—"

"Oh, don't bother—"

"Hell be glad to tell you," Mr. Shirer said, rising and going to the door and calling the cook.

He entered again, wiping his hands on his apron. The question was put to him by Mr. Shirer and the cook answered:

"Oh, that's easy, sar. My son would take me back and bury me in the land of my ancestors."

"But what if your son were not here?" I suggested relentlessly.

That one bothered him. He studied the floor for some minutes, and then he said:

"Then my friends would bury me and then they'd watch my grave for those black ants who are called God's slaves. Now, you take one of those ants when he is crawling over my grave, wrap that ant in a bundle of three stones, and then take that bundle to the land where my ancestors are buried and bury it and my soul will be there. I'll be with my ancestors then."

These, of course, are but dreams, daylight dreams, dreams dreamed with the eyes wide open! Was it that the jungle, so rich, so fertile, was it that life, so warm, so filled with ready food, so effortless, prompted men to dream dreams like this? Or was it the opposite? These dreams belong to the African; they existed before the coming of the white man. . . . One thing was certain: their sense of reality was but a dream. It may be, of course, that dreams are the staunchest kind of reality. . . . It may be that such beliefs fit the soul of man better than railroads, mass production, wars. . . . And the African is not alone in holding that these dreams are true. All men, in some form or other, love these dreams. Maybe men are happier when they are wrapped in warm dreams of being with their fathers when they die . . . ?

Twenty-Five

Upon my return to my hotel, I found an invitation to visit Dr. Ampofo of Mampong. After being in Africa for a month, this was the first invitation I'd received from the black bourgeoisie. I was anxious to meet Dr. Ampofo, for his personality was of a kind that evoked extreme reactions; there were those who liked him and those who felt that he embodied something evil.

Half an hour's drive up the escarpment through dense forest brought me to a neat village where, for the first time, I saw flowers blooming. . . . Dr. Ampofo's home could be seen a hundred yards away: a design of stone and serried windows, long lines, terraced landscape, trees, color. . . .

Dr. Ampofo was forty-five years of age, black, short,

nervous, thin, alert of body and agile of mind. He smiled quickly, *too* quickly, as he shook my hand. And he laughed. . . . I was beginning to wonder about that African laugh; it did not stem from mirth, as many people have erroneously thought. It was to bid for time, to hide one's reactions, to reflect, to observe, to judge, to make up one's mind! He was most gracious and showed me his beautiful new home which, he said, had been designed and built by his wife. He next showed me a collection of his wood carving which he himself had carved. He had a medical degree; he was the head of a huge African family; he had acted in the movies; and he conducted a thriving business in timber. . . .

With drinks at our elbows, the doctor and I got to work at last.

"Do you mind talking about yourself?"

"Not at all," he said.

He'd come to Mampong in 1919 after four years of schooling in his father's village; he had lived in Mampong until 1922, then he'd attended boarding school at the Annum Presbyterian Senior School until 1926. He related how he and his friends had had to walk for three days and nights to reach this school, for there was no transportation in those days. His schooling continued at Cape Coast in the Mfantsipim's Boys' Secondary School. In 1930 he got a scholarship to study art for his B.A., but, halfway through, he gave it up for science. He won a competitive scholarship for study in England, and in 1932 he went to Edinburgh and completed his studies, obtaining his medical degree in 1939.

Touring Europe, he was caught in Sweden by the outbreak of war; he was forced to remain in Stockholm until February, 1940, at which time he returned to Africa. . . .

"Doctor," I began, "I want to ask you about life in the Gold Coast. I came here because of the reputation of the Convention People's Party. It's the one thing here that seems somewhat familiar to me; it's a modern political movement and operates in terms of concepts that Westerners can understand. Now, this movement is not Communist, for the Communists are opposed to it; they have branded it as 'corrupt, bourgeois nationalism.' Yet, when I try to account for this national liberation movement, I'm baffled. Some aspects of this movement seem to partake of Leftism; other aspects are almost religious in their emotional expression. Sometimes one must use Marxist ideas to aid one in trying to grasp what one is looking at, but Marxism cannot satisfactorily account for this. . . . You don't have in this country a great deal of industrialization which would have created a rootless mass of men ready for such a movement. Neither do you possess a great deal of class consciousness out of which such a movement could be created. The race consciousness here is not as sharp as that of the American Negro. Yet you have a rip-roaring political movement. How did it happen?"

He hesitated, then laughed.

"It has a background. It's not only Nkrumah, I tell you. These things do not just burst out of the blue. There's a creative energy in these people, the Akan people. The Akan is a stubborn and proud man. There is in him a consciousness of national humiliation and there is a deep race consciousness, deeper than you think. . . ."

"How does this race consciousness manifest itself?" I asked. "Both Britishers and Americans have assured me that no such thing exists here—"

"It *does* exist." He was adamant. "The men who organized our people into nationalistic organizations were educated abroad. It was in foreign lands that they learned the meaning of what was happening to our people. The men who went to America and to England came back and injected, and rightly so, the concept of our subjection and the concept of race consciousness into our lives. It came from without.

"The prime event that spurred us to action was the fall of the price of cocoa in 1940–43. Cocoa was so plentiful, the market was so rigged, that the farmers were burning it; there was no good price for it. Cocoa was withheld to lift the prices, and during the war the world market was bad. . . .

"Then the Europeans made a move that brought violence. . . . A group formed a monopoly which was known as the Association of West African Merchants. They aimed to buy cocoa as cheaply as possible from us and sell it as high as possible on the markets of the world. These same merchants sold us imported goods at terribly high prices. We were trapped. . . .

"This led to the events of 1948 when the national boycott was launched and white business firms were looted and burned. . . ."

"So far, it's clear," I said. "But that does not explain the Convention People's Party. Why did it arise in the Gold Coast? I've attended political meetings and I've seen some strange things. I've seen chiefs pouring libations; I've heard prayers, both Christian and pagan; I've heard oaths of personal loyalty taken by vast throngs of people to obey and serve the Leader—"

"You saw oaths administered?" he asked me quietly, seriously.

"I'd not lie to you. Why should I? I saw it on two occasions."

"Yes. It happens," he said, sighing.

"What does it mean?" I asked him.

He looked at me and laughed.

"You're touching on something—"

"An oath in Africa is a terrible thing, I'm told," I said, trying to urge him on.

He laughed again, rose, walked the floor, then scratched his head and whirled to me. He shook his finger at me, saying:

"When you talk of oaths, you're touching on *juju*—"

"Oh, come now," I said.

"You don't believe in *juju?*" he asked.

"Hell, no! You're a doctor. You *can't* believe in such; not literally," I said.

He studied me and wagged his head.

"There's something to it," he said solemnly.

"It's purely psychological," I said.

"I've seen it work," he told me.

"It works only for those who believe in it," I said. "It's a psychological problem."

He was silent again, looking at me and then looking off.

"You're strong-minded," he said.

"Oh, no. It's just common sense. If the African had any damned *juju*, he'd have used it a long time ago to free his country," I said.

"I've seen men who had been sentenced to death by *juju*," the doctor said. "And they died."

"They believed that they would die," I said. "It's suggestion, self-hypnosis, that's all."

"Yes; if you keep in mind that it's psychological, you can escape it," he conceded. "But it gets a lot of people. . . ."

"I've found evidence of that," I agreed. "Now, this business of the compound family and the head of that family to whom the members owe loyalty. . . . Does that have anything to do with the foundations of the Convention People's Party? *Juju*'s out of the way; let's talk sense. Tell me what you think."

He still walked restlessly about the room, glancing at me now and then. Then he gave another laugh. I did not know him and he did not know me; and I *was* breaking in on him rather unceremoniously.

"Look, don't be afraid of me," I tried to reassure him. "I want to get at the bottom of this reality. But each time I've tried to talk a little, when I begin pressing questions, the Africans—"

"They close up like clams," he said.

"Exactly. But they ought to know that I know that something is being hidden here. . . ."

"What do you want to know?" he asked me, sitting suddenly.

"The official line is that this is just pure and simple nationalism," I resumed. "It is, but it's more than that. Yet it's not Communism. I'd know it if it was. . . . Now, explain this to me in terms that I, a Westerner, can understand, can grasp."

His wife entered the room at that moment. She was a tall, handsome woman, poised, Western in her manner. I congratulated her in her taste in the building and furnishing of her home and she was modest and polite. She and her husband spoke briefly in their native tongue and she invited me to lunch. I accepted, but warned her that African pepper was too much for my stomach. She promised that the lunch would be mild and simple. . . . When she had gone, I turned again to politics.

"I see the great influence of the tribe in politics," I said. "But how is it done? How does the party latch onto the tribal life?"

"All right. . . . We live in a queer way in Africa," the doctor began his explanation. "Our inheritance is matrilineal, coming from the mother's side of the family. When a man takes a wife, he cannot leave the family and live with her; he has to bring her into his family. She becomes a daughter in his family in addition to being a wife. She comes under the authority of the family. The family is supreme in Africa; its authority is unquestioned. That is why no European girl can fit into our families. They are acceptable, but they find it impossible. . . .

"When a head of the family joins the Convention People's Party, the entire family joins. And families in Africa are large. The head of the family has the final say; his word is law. If a chief is Convention People's Party, then the entire town is Convention People's Party. . . . Say, did you know that Nkrumah is a Tufuhene . . . ?"

"A *what*? What's that?" I asked.

"It's a Fanti term. . . . It means Warrior Chief."

"But that's just an honorary title, isn't it?"

"No."

"It's serious?"

"Of course it is," the doctor said. "Now, the origin of the Convention People's Party came from the Gold Coast Youth Organization, which was led by Gbedemah, Ako Adjei. . . . Nkrumah was the spirit of the group. He knew how to set off herd reactions, and the clan and the family formed the basis for his drive for power. His aim is to replace the chiefs entirely, and eventually the British also. . . .

"I believe that Nkrumah believes in the same qualities that he arouses in others. I've tried to question him about these things, and when I did, he evaded me, he hemmed. He has seen clearly the kind of life we lead and he is out to organize it. . . . He has learned how to sink roots into this tribal life and he intends to rule. He is on his way to wipe out the identity of people like me. . . . It's not democracy. I know he has the masses with him, but it's not democracy. The real center of power in our society was in the hands of the chiefs, but Nkrumah has smashed all that. . . ."

"Why are you opposed to this, Doctor?"

"I'm not a political man, but I'm opposed to it."

"Why? Why don't you serve the people? The people need you, men like you. . . ."

"It's not right," he said.

"What are you saying?" I asked him. "Whatever power there is in the Gold Coast, they'll need men like you. They are your people; serve them—"

"The people must be educated—"

"Granted," I agreed. "But why not let them be free first? It would have taken a thousand years to educate them at the rate the British were going. The Americans were once a colonial people too. But they didn't wait until all of their people were educated to make their bid for freedom. They took their freedom and then educated their people. This is a question of power. . . . Either you feel that you ought to be free or you do not."

"Educate the people and then let them be free," he said and laughed.

And I knew that that laugh was to cushion the shock of his attitude.

"What do you think's going to happen here, then?"

"There'll be a blowup, a sudden change," he argued. "This cannot go on. You cannot build anything solid on a basis of mass hysteria."

"In what way will it blow up?" I asked. "It's certain that the country's united against the British. The British have no roots or parties here. Therefore, if there's to be a blowup, it'll have to come from either African opposition or British-supported African opposition. You know that the African opposition's too weak to act alone. Would bourgeois Africans fight Nkrumah for the British?"

"I don't know how it's going to happen; but it won't last," he reiterated. "This is no way to build a nation—"

"Doctor, my mind is open about that," I told him. "You know what happened in Russia. Ideology aside. You know what happened in Germany. In Spain. In Italy. In China. In Argentina. Those were not accidents or the actions of evil men. And a lot more is involved than the problem of education. People are tired of the old, traditional forms of living. All about them they see and sense the possibility of change. The people who should make that change—men like you—do not make it. Then along comes someone who sees that it can be done and he does it. You cannot expect a vacuum to remain unfilled. Don't blame Nkrumah. I'm not partisan. I'm objective. Nkrumah's doing what should have been done long ago; that's why he was able to do it so quickly and easily. The cost of that kind of social change comes high; many things go by the board. . . . This seems to be the reality of the twentieth century. . . . Now, since other nations have proved that the masses can absorb education quickly, why not the masses of the Gold Coast . . . ?"

"I'm willing to admit that the masses can absorb technical education quickly. . . ."

"Isn't that decisive?"

"What about the values—?"

"The old values go," I argued. "The new ones are created as men strive to live, as men's needs prod them forward. . . . I'm not so much for Nkrumah as I am for the right of the masses of people to cut loose from the past, and since Nkrumah's leading them from the past, I'm for him. Man, I've looked at your villages. They and the people in them are rotting. . . . It's a living death. Only when men break loose from that rot and death and plunge creatively into the future do they become something to respect. Life then becomes a supremely spiritual task of molding and shaping the world according to the needs of the human heart—"

"That's not going to happen in Africa soon," he told me, shaking his head.

"And did you think that Nkrumah could happen so soon?" I countered.

"It's a matter of time—This is too *fast!*"

"How do you know how *fast* people can develop? Has it ever really been tried? Tested? All right, make Africa a test and see. No matter what you do here in your fight for freedom, as long as it's for freedom, you can't lose. . . ."

We were going at it so hot and heavy that I didn't notice that it was almost one o'clock. During lunch there was a lull. I'd at last talked freely to my first intellectual African; he didn't agree with me, but at least he knew what I was talking about. My position in the Gold Coast was indeed strange; the Convention People's Party was afraid to talk freely and frankly to me, yet I was for them in a more fundamental sense than they could accept. And it was only with the opposition that I could talk freely, and they disagreed with me!

Must it always be that the middle class must go down to defeat complaining and rejecting reality . . . ? I'd seen the same thing in Buenos Aires. . . . There I'd had to consort with the decadent nobility who sat huddled and afraid in their huge houses, cursing, swearing that peons could not operate telephones, could not run railroads. . . . Industrialization had made the world simple, yet those who opposed the masses operating that world dared not oppose industrialization. Why, their profits came out of it. . . . One's respect for man sank as one watched this same stupid drama re-enact itself from country to country, almost without variation.

Was Dr. Ampofo's attitude the only contribution that English education and missions had given to the upper-class Africans of the Gold Coast? The doctor knew, of course, what Britain had done to his people, how it had shattered their culture; he knew, deep in his heart, that Nkrumah's overthrowing the chiefs came only after Britain had long undermined the very basis of tribal life, that Nkrumah had only deliberately and self-consciously dealt that system its last blow. . . .

What bitter pathos churned in the hearts of the African middle class! How they felt that Britain, their idol, had let them down! Yet, what could Britain do? She had no roots among the masses of African people and yet she had heavy investments in gold, timber, diamonds, bauxite, manganese. . . . She had denounced Nkrumah as dangerous, but, when faced with losing her material interests, she, like Jesus, conferred upon the black rebel an "act of grace" . . . Britain had acted to save not right, not hope, not honesty; she acted to defend her interests. And that is as it should have been. One's real quarrel is that the British could never say so frankly. Maybe they didn't know how to. . . .

Twenty-Six

If I was to continue my taxi excursions into the "bush," it was now clear that I would have to rent a car for a long period. I finally approached a Swiss car-rental agency whose officials told me that a car that could withstand a "bush" trek would cost me twenty pounds a month, plus the driver's salary, plus the cost of gas and oil; and, beyond a twenty-five-mile radius of Accra, I'd have to pay a premium of a shilling a mile because of bad roads; further, while on trek, I'd have to maintain the driver's food and lodging. . . . I resolved to rent the car and keep rolling until my money melted, and then I'd go home.

While in the offices of the car-rental agency I noticed that the Europeans dressed much more simply and comfortably than the Africans. The whites were striving to keep cool in the torrid heat, but the petty bourgeois black clerks and secretaries, etc., wore heaps of woolen clothes to draw a highly visible line of social distinction between themselves and the naked, illiterate masses. An educated African could not afford to be seen dressed comfortably, that is, in sandals and a toga; he had to dress like the British dressed in Britain! And the Britisher wore shorts and T-shirts!

Having rented a car, I began to plan a tour of the triangle enclosed in the lines drawn between Takoradi, Accra, and Kumasi, an area that held three-fourths of the nation's wealth and population; and, what was more, it comprised a big slice of the high rain forest, the real jungle.

But, if I went on trek, where would I sleep, what could I eat? The Americans I questioned had no suggestions. I approached the Prime Minister's office and was urged to talk to the British. I balked. I'd come to be with Africans and I was being shunted into the hands of the British! I brooded for a couple of days and, in the end, I knew that I either had to depend upon the British to see the interior or go home. . . .

I presented my request to the Gold Coast Information Service and was told that they would draw up an itinerary for me in a few days' time. Meanwhile, I hired a chauffeur, an ex-middleweight champion of the Gold Coast, Battling Kojo, black, quick, and loyal. I was advised that I needed someone of his pugnacity if I was to be on my own in the jungle.

I waited, fighting against a never-ending sense of enervation. I was eating a normal amount, but the food seemed to give me no strength. I was told that vegetables grew so swiftly in this hot and red earth that they were not really nourishing! Lettuce refused to form a head here. Corn shot up so quickly that the ears became full-sized before the grain matured on the cobs. Other vegetables turned into soft, pulpy masses. Among the Europeans, tropical ulcers were common and they were forever dosing themselves with vitamins. Fresh milk and butter were unknown, being shipped from Europe in tins. The threat of sleeping sickness from the tsetse fly was so acute to both cattle and humans that no large herds of cattle were kept. From the Northern Territories cattle were marched five hundred miles down to the coastal area and when they arrived they were gaunt, tough, and weak-eyed from the long trek in the awful heat. . . . In the hotel restaurant I've never been able to tell from the taste the kind of meat I'm eating.

The heat makes insect life breed prolifically: mosquitoes, ants, lizards, and myriads of other creatures swarm in the air and underfoot. A lump of sugar left in a saucer will draw ants in an hour even to the second floor of a stone building in which stewards are constantly cleaning. Everything seems to develop faster here; life gushes up in a careless profusion; the universe seems in a state of biological hurry, as though nature were prodding and driving all living organisms beyond their normal rate of reaction.

The cheapness of labor clutters the landscape with odd sights. One sees gangs of black workmen cutting grass with long cutlasses. Couldn't it be done with machines? Sure; but labor is cheaper than machines, and machines get rusty and wear out. The problem of the repair and upkeep of the laterite roads has also been solved in a fashion that indicates that men are cheaper than materials. The torrential rains wash out the roads periodically and, instead of anchoring the roads in beds of rock or cement, which is expensive, large gangs of workers are kept constantly busy shoveling the soil back into place.

I've not seen a single wood carving or art object since I've landed in the Gold Coast. The advent of the missionary has driven underground much of the religious expression of the tribal people; they no longer allow it to be known that they fashion those odd, elongated ebony figures that Europeans seek so ardently. In the eyes of the new black Christians those figures hold no value; they are obtainable, I'm told, but you will have to convince a chief or a fetish priest that your interest is favorable to tribal life. Instead of many gods, the Gold Coast African now has one Who is nailed to a cross and Whose image is stamped out by mass production.

Just as he has been shamed into hiding his religion, so has the Gold Coast African attitude toward political symbols become more Western than the West's. One day I was asked to comment upon the unofficial (of course!) designs for the new flag which the Gold Coast will adopt when freedom comes. After examining all kinds of newfangled geometric patterns, I said that I could not conceive of a Gold Coast flag without a "stool" upon it. What? My African listeners were speechless with rage and indignation. The "stool"? Never! They were sick and tired of "stools"! But, I argued, look at America. The thirteen original colonies had hated their colonial status, but, when they designed their flag, they were confident that they would eventually be free and they included in their flag a symbolic representation of their original colonial status. . . . You too, I argued, will some day be so far removed psychologically from this struggle that you will look back and want to acknowledge your early religious and national symbols. . . . But, no, *never* . . . !

I was invited to a party and did not want to go, but somebody whispered that I'd meet some of the local CID men and the head of the Accra police, a Mr. X. That decided me. I've long been interested in the psychology of policemen; of all the functionaries in a country, they share the outlook, the fears, the aims, and the attitudes of the group holding power. Enforcers of the law generally partake of the impulses both of the lawmakers and the lawbreakers, and they are mostly men devoid of illusions.

Mr. X was about my height, nervous, talkative; in fact, he resembled a foreman in a factory; he looked anything but a policeman. We were immediately drawn to each other: he wanted to know what I was doing and I wanted to know what he was doing, and we spent most of the evening talking together.

"Just what do you do here?" I asked him.

"My job is to keep law and order in this city," he asserted with pride.

"Is it difficult?"

"No more difficult here than it is anywhere else," he told me.

"But I thought that Africans were so *different* that you'd have to use special methods to catch them. . . ."

"Not a bit of it," he argued. "The same thing that makes an Englishman steal makes an African steal. There's but one slight difference: the African is more prone to be prouder of his theft than the Englishman—"

"How do you account for that?"

"I don't know," he said. "But he just is."

"Maybe the black criminal thinks he's right. . . ."

He blinked, then asked:

"In what way?"

"Well, it's *his* country, you know. Maybe he thinks he's evening up scores."

"Maybe," he said thoughtfully. "But, for my part, it *is* his country. I'm here just to do a job—"

"Does that include training Africans to take over the enforcement of law and order?"

"Absolutely. We've got them right now studying in Scotland Yard."

"Do they have much chance to get experience in London?"

"No; they're sent back here for that."

"Do you find any emotional differences between an African murderer and an English one?"

"Well, what I told you about stealing goes also for killing. The African feels that he has done right, most of the time," Mr. X explained. "If an African kills his woman, it's because he feels that she deserves it. He'd scorn running off and hiding. He even takes a kind of pride in telling why he did it. You don't get much of a sense of guilt out of them."

"Does that stem from tribal influence?"

"Maybe. He kills her because what she did was not right—"

"Under what law would he be tried? Tribal or English?"

"Under our laws."

"I don't want you to divulge any of your confidential matters, but tell me: suppose a crime has been committed and you are called in. What do you do?"

He thought a moment.

"I'll tell you about one. . . . A few weeks ago a safe was robbed here. The safe belonged to a European auto firm. They had a repair shop. The metal of the safe was cut through—"

"With an acetylene torch?"

"Exactly."

"That smacks of New York or Chicago."

"Of course it does. Now, my job was to catch the criminal. Who did it? I can't be bothered with fancy theories. I have a practical job to do. Who cut into that safe and took the money? Now—"

"Maybe a European or an American safe-cracker came ashore. . . . Truly, no black boy could do that, unless he has had experience. It's a daring feat—"

"That's where you are wrong. First of all, we know pretty well who comes into this colony. There are no American or European safe-crackers within reach. So, I must concentrate upon the Africans.

"Now, finally everybody is cleared but one boy. He's average; he's never been out of the colony. He has only recently been hired. He works on the bodies of the autos; he has just recently learned to use the acetylene torch. . . . We take fingerprints. It was *his* job. . . . We confront him. He confesses—"

"No coercion used?"

"None whatsoever."

"But did he put two and two together so *quickly*?"

"You'd be surprised how bright these boys really are," he assured me.

"Do you think that brightness is confined to crime?"

"God, no!"

This policeman was, ironically, the most liberal-minded Englishman I'd met so far in Africa! As a law-enforcement officer, he had to admit that it didn't take years or months, but only days, for that young boy to see that if he could cut through the steel of auto bodies, he could also cut through the steel of the boss's safe and take the money. It was strange that this man who had served for years in Scotland Yard should turn out to be so frank and intensely perceptive! His mind was not encumbered with bulky theories of sociology or anthropology that insisted that certain spans of time had to elapse before people could absorb knowledge. He didn't complain that Africans were progressing too fast. If he'd allowed his attention to become cluttered up with such nonsense, he'd have lost his job pronto. A policeman has to assume the equality of man; hence, he sees the possibilities of Africa, especially on the level of crime, much more clearly than the Colonial Office or the professors in English universities.

Now that I'd rented my car, I decided to find out how rapidly the pounds would mount up at the rate of a shilling a mile. Prampram had been pointed out as a typical ancient village and I directed Kojo to drive there. It was raining and the roads were under water most of the way. As we heaved in sight of the village, I saw the usual mud huts with thatched roofs and a few cement houses built up out of blocks. I heard drums beating and I looked out and saw a group of men clad in togas and dancing in the cloudy light of the rainy morning. It was a funeral; an elder had just died. Not far from the men was a group of women, some sitting, some standing, some dancing. I waved and smiled at the men and they waved and smiled in return. There seemed to be no grief; they were all relaxed. Now and then a man would leap out in front of the drums and do a frenzied dance, signaling the gods to look down with favor upon his tribe. Then I started violently, for a musket had gone off right behind my back. . . . I spun to see what was happening; a man was kneeling, holding a gun from which wisps of blue smoke curled. The gun was pointing toward the sky. . . .

A black young man came up; he spoke English.

"Why do they fire those guns?" I asked him.

"It's custom," he said.

"But there must be some *reason* for it," I insisted.

"Why do you send flowers to a funeral in America?" he asked me, laughing.

I stared, unable to answer.

"It must be custom," I said and laughed too.

The young man seemed intelligent and willing to answer questions, and so I waded right in.

"Why are they beating the drums?"

"The drums 'talk,'" he explained. "Not everybody now can interpret drum language. But those drums are announcing to the spirit world that the elder is on his way."

"Don't the women sing?"

"Yes; they sang this morning. They wailed too," he said.

The funeral ritual flowed on; they danced war dances, the muskets fired, and the drums beat on and on.

"Where is the dead elder?"

"He's on his bed. Do you want to see him?"

"Yes."

I followed the young man to a paneless window through which I saw a long, black man wrapped in a brightly colored shroud; he was stretched out upon a bed and a white strip of cloth was bound over his mouth.

"What's that cloth for?"

The young man said that he didn't know.

"Who handles the dead, that is, prepares them for burial?"

"The women handle the dead, wash them, dress them, and make them ready for the grave," he explained. "The women bring us into the world and they see us go out of it."

I saw women going to the foot of the dead man's bed and whispering a few words into his ears. I could not hear or understand what was being said.

"Are they praying?" I asked.

"Well, not exactly," he told me. "They are telling him good-bye. They are giving him messages for their relatives in the spirit world, you see."

It was not death as we know it; in fact, it was not death at all. It was a departure.

The "talking" drums recounted the man's life, celebrating the trouble he had seen, and they also sought to pacify the "dead" man for the perils he had to encounter in the world of spirits. For there was a transition period from the world of the living to the world of the dead. For a certain number of days the "dead" man's spirit was supposed to hover in the vicinity of the living as it climbed a steep hill toward the land of his ancestors, and that climb was long and hard. Hence, as the "dead" man had been breathing his last, his soul had already begun, in terms of native imagination, to pant and heave with effort. The death rattle was interpreted as physical exertion; therefore, as the old man was "dying," his relatives poured water down his throat to help him quench his thirst. (Maybe it actually hastened the poor man's end. . . .)

In Africa the "dead" live side by side with the living; they eat, breathe, laugh, hate, love, and continue doing in the world of ghostly shadows exactly what they had been doing in the world of flesh and blood. The Akan feel that the "dead" get lonely in that world and are anxious for the living to come and keep them company. Thus, the pacification of the "dead" constitutes one of their biggest problems of life.

The drums of state beat on, encouraging the "dead" man to mount the steep hill of the other world. Naked black children stood about, their mouths agape in awe. Already the other world was as real to them as this one. . . . Instinct ruled here; fear and guilt and doubt and hope held sway in the dismal morning air.

How did this come to be? It looked simple, but it had its origins in a complicated and subtle balancing of many emotional factors. On my way back to the hotel, I visited a bookstore and bought a stack of literature; I wanted to see what the "authorities" had to say about this. And was there a better way to spend a rainy afternoon in Africa than in reading what they say about their "dead"?

Thumbing through old pages, one learns that the African does not believe idly in another world; for him, there *is* another world. Every object in existence has a twin, itself and its ghostly shadow. (Plato seems to have been somewhat primitive too!) The origin of this motion came from his dreams. Did he not move about and see people and objects many miles away when he slept? Just as he is convinced that spirits dwell in trees, rivers, in fact, in all inanimate objects, so a spirit, he is persuaded, dwells in man.

From this point on, matters become a little complicated. The spirit, known as *kra*, that dwells in man is distinct from him. In death, when *kra* leaves a man, it has two possibilities: it can, if the man was old, go straight to the world of spirits. If, however, the man died before his time, if he was unaccountably ill or accidentally killed, his *kra* would linger on in the world of the living for an indeterminate length of time.

With the normal "death," all goes well; the family places food, water, tobacco, alcohol, clothing, etc., at the side of the grave. (Weapons are expressly excluded, for fear that the "dead" would use them harmfully against the living.) But with the *kra* that lingers, for whatever reason, trouble starts. This *kra* can "embrace" children and induce illness in them. Indeed, *kra* have been known to enter into newborn babes, thereby reincarnating themselves. It is, therefore, a matter of conjecture when someone has just died in a family and when someone has just been born in that family if that "dead" man's *kra* has returned in the form of the new baby. . . .

Life in the ghost world is an exact duplicate of life in this world. A farmer in this world is a farmer there; a chief here is a chief there. It is, therefore, of decisive importance when one enters that world of ghostly shades to enter it in the right manner. For you can be snubbed there just as effectively and humiliatingly as you were snubbed here.

From this belief that the "dead" live as we live, the following deduction is simple: to the degree that we love, honor, and revere our "dead," we must help them to establish themselves in the world of shadows. So, in the end, the extreme sacrifice will be made. If a chief had slaves in this world, his slaves would be sent to serve him in the beyond; and so would his several wives be dispatched to comfort him. Fortunately, most Africans are poor and their duties in the next world will be as modest as they were in this world and they will have no need of many slaves or wives to keep them happy. . . .

All of these seemingly gruesome duties are performed with awe and tenderness. Make no mistake about that. . . . Even human sacrifice is solemnly ritualized. What strikes us as being monstrous is done by them with a sense of exaltation. Yet, suppose it's not done? Ah. . . . The "dead" do not like neglect, and they are quick to revenge such by returning to the world of the living and snatching you into their dreaded domain. Why the "dead" insist upon acting in this vengeful manner is a question to which the Akan has no clear-cut answer.

How did these strange notions come about? Yes; it was about time that I dipped into the muddy metaphysical waters of those African intellectuals who had tried to explain these spiritual riddles. And I selected as my guide a learned African who was still living, a man to whom I could talk after I had read his ideas. That man was none other than the leading political opponent of the Convention People's Party, Nkrumah's Nemesis, Dr. J. B. Danquah; and forthwith I plunged at last into his *The Akan Doctrine of God*.

I hastened to confess that I'm far from being the most suitable person in the world to report on metaphysical doctrines. A fair report on such subtleties requires a man who, through empathy, can follow the curling and dipping of such notions with anxious love. I possess no such love. . . . In relating the following, I am, no doubt, doing a degree of violence to the astute learning of Dr. Danquah; but, since I'm of another culture, another time sense even, and since I cannot express myself other than directly, this is how it must be.

The first fact that impresses one in Dr. Danquah's exposition is his unjustified feeling that he must demonstrate that the African has a religion whose concepts are on par with that of the religion of the Western world. In a manner that smacks of an unconscious apology, he assumes that Christianity is believed superior and that the devotees of that religion are too filled with racial prejudice to acknowledge that the religion of the African is just as good, in fact, according to Dr. Danquah, it is, in some respects, better. I'd agree with the good doctor about this; the African religion has no hell and no sin, and hell and sin have always struck me as boresome and static conceptions. Africans manage to fuse hell and sin in an organic and concrete manner, and their lives thereby become as charged and exciting as the moving tables and floating trumpets in a séance in a dreary London flat.

Each race, says Dr. Danquah, apprehends God through a "seed"-quality of ideas; thus:

". . . When the family is the chief idea, things that are dishonorable and undignified, actions that in disgracing you disgrace the family, are held to be vices, and the highest virtue is found in honor and dignity. Tradition is the determinant of what is right and just, what is good and done."

The Akan regard the sky and the earth as great gods. The sky-god is the Saturday Sky-God, *Nyame*. The earth-god is the Thursday Earth-Goddess, *Asaase Yaa*. But the most important gods to which the people appeal daily are the spirits of the departed ancestors of the clan. Over and above this there are hundreds of minor gods, who, when appealed to, act as intercessors to the higher gods; these higher gods, in their vast concern with other worlds and other matters, do not have the time to give full attention to the prayers of millions of ordinary men. . . .

The Akan believe that the spirits of his ancestors find a repository in the Golden Stool, which represents the soul of the nation. The head of a Stool is called Nana, and this meaning, rising from the Nana who is chief of the family, goes right on up to the Nana of the Universe, this final Nana occupying the great Stool of all existence. There is, then, a direct line of relation from the head of the family, rising by degrees, to the great god who rules all things. And the bridge between the head of the family and the head of the universe is to be found in the friendly or baleful spirits of ancestors who hover about the families in which they once lived.

To show how the Akan concept of God operates in a real social sense, Dr. Danquah addresses himself to the baffling problem of the "omnipotence" of God, for, if each head of a family, clan, tribe, or state partakes of God, are they too "omnipotent"? Dr. Danquah says: ". . . The Akan idea is of a community, continuous with the past, present, and future of his relations of blood. The 'omnipotence' of the high-father cannot be greater than the reality of this community. A father, of necessity, is what all his children are."

On page 82 of *The Akan Doctrine of God*, Dr. Danquah clearly, in the name of the West African, rejects some of the most central concepts of Christian religion. Sin and remission of sin are tossed out of the window. Original sin is flatly rejected. The notion that, because two remote ancestors had sexual relations and bore a child, there was imposed upon all mankind a threat of suffering, is, to the African mind, simply ridiculous. And that one can only be saved through God's grace from this "sin" is something that the African cannot conceive. (He may pay lip service to such in the face of white Christians, but in his heart he knows that it is not true.) That the world is "worldly," sinful, a place to abhor, is a joke to the African mentality. And that one must belong to a certain church in order to be saved merits a smile from black lips.

The Akan believe that one comes into the world to try to perfect his soul, and, failing one try, he returns again and again until his soul is ready to join that of the universal. Closer and closer does Dr. Danquah approach the linking of man and God until finally, through incarnation, he sees a blending. On page 95 of *The Akan Doctrine of God*, he states: ". . . we have a superman born, but not born as a superman by his parents, but because, and in virtue, of his own previous achievement in a previous incarnation . . . he may have lived in that same community in his previous life, or he may have chosen or been assigned that community for his present essay in life, believing that a new country, a new environment, lacking in some of the opportunities, and some, possibly, of the resistances of his previous life or community, may afford him just that beneficial advantage and accommodation for actualizing his soul for an accelerated progress towards the good . . ." And when a man overcomes great odds, distinguishes himself, "that superior nature shines through the superman, as if a god had revealed himself in him . . ."

The religion of the Akan is not primitive; it is simply terrifying. And even Dr. Danquah seems to feel that what he claims for the African is a little too tall, for he modestly asserts (page 116): "I do not, of course, recommend to modern European thought to follow the Akan and worship this mystery that explains why any man, at his choice, has it in him to become a god or a beast."

Death does not round off life; it is not the end; it complements life. Dr. Danquah's theories of death are expanded (page 156): "To the Akan, therefore, death is less than a negation of life . . . It is but an instrument of the higher consummation, a planting or fruition of it." And then Dr. Danquah gives philosophical dignity to the African mood about death (page 160): "Death, therefore, is not a natural thing. Basically, there is no reason why any man, any being, should die. . . ."

The door is now wide open for any man to become suspicious when death strikes a loved one; the cause of death seems inexplicable, due either to witchcraft or poison. Dr. Danquah spells it out clearly: "Deep down in the natural being of man there appears to be an instinct that man is not a dying animal, that he was not made to die, and that he has that in him which ought to keep permanently his vital function working interminably."

I come up for air, to take a deep breath. . . .

These are the broad religious propositions underlying the beliefs of the Akan people of the Gold Coast.

Twenty-Seven

I at once, of course, bent my efforts to meet this man. I had the good luck to see him a few days later at a great formal gathering, and, alas, it was to an Englishman that I had to appeal for an introduction to him. And, uninhibited, I told him:

"I want to talk to you."

"What about?" he asked me.

"About your ideas about the people of the Gold Coast."

"What do you want to ask me?" He was equally direct.

"I'd like to know why you hold such views," I said. "Why are you with the opposition? What are you really trying to do? What is this business of the African being so different?"

"How long have you been in Africa?" he asked me.

"About two months," I said.

"Stay longer and you'll *feel* your race," he told me.

"*What?*"

"You'll *feel* it," he assured me. "It'll all come *back* to you."

"What'll come back?"

"The knowledge of your race." He was explicit.

I liked the man, but not as a Negro or African; I liked his directness, his willingness to be open. Yet, I knew that I'd never feel an identification with Africans on a "racial" basis.

"I doubt that," I said softly.

"What specifically do you want to ask me?"

"What's going to happen here? I'm trying to figure it out. You have lived here; you are African. Can this last? Why are the masses following Nkrumah? He talks a language that they have no background to understand, except his campaign for national liberation. Now, you talk about their religion, the religion they live each day. Why do the masses follow Nkrumah and not you?"

That got him; he stared off above the heads of the crowds of people dancing over a glassy floor. Then he said:

"All right. Come to see me Thursday. At four."

I was there on the dot of four. I met a trained lawyer, gracious, affable, generous-hearted, a man who was deeply baffled and tried to hide it, a man whose mind was desperately trying to grapple with a new and alien reality which he hated. He had the bearing of an aristocrat, relaxed, poised; he was on his mental toes each moment I spent with him. No honest Englishman could ever really quarrel with this man; he personified, alas, exactly what England wanted to make every African into. . . . And yet they had unceremoniously ditched him! And he felt it; he never said one word about it; but it was deep and bitter in him. He had been betrayed by England, the land that had given him his ideals and his sense of honor.

"What are the differences between you and Nkrumah?"

"We really have no differences," he said blandly.

"Oh, really, now. You are at each other's throats!"

"We are one in our aim for self-government for the Gold Coast," he said.

"But you are not together," I said.

He took a deep breath, looked off, then glanced at me and said:

"Nkrumah is selfish. With wiles and tricks he stole power. We sent for that man to come and help us. Then, while pretending to work for us, he secretly built up his own following within our ranks. Ruthlessly, he split the national front, then made a filthy deal with the British. . . . One day he said that he wanted national freedom, and the next day he compromised with the British."

"Do you think he'll keep power for long?" I asked.

"Yes; until the illiterate masses wake up," he said.

"Why don't *you* try to win the masses to your side?"

I watched a grimace come over his face; he looked at me and smiled ruefully.

"Masses?" he echoed the word. "I don't like this thing of masses. There are only individuals for me—"

"But masses form the basis of political power in the modern world today," I told him.

"You believe that?" he asked me. "I know you fellows dote on this thing of masses. . . . I've read that you claim that this mass unrest comes from the industrialization of the Western world—"

"Where else could it come from?" I asked him. "Look, how did Nkrumah learn his techniques of organization? In New York, in Chicago, in Detroit, and in London he saw men organizing and he studied their methods. Then he came to Africa and applied them. . . . You're facing the twentieth century, Dr. Danquah."

He shook his head. Every word that I had uttered clashed with deep-set convictions. And it suddenly flashed through me that this man was not a politician and would never be one.

"Why is it that you cannot appeal to the masses on the basis of their daily needs?" I asked him. "You're a lawyer; you're used to *representing*. . . . Well, *represent* them. As we say in America: Be a mouthpiece for them—"

"I can't do things like that—"

"It's the only road to power in modern society," I said. "No matter how deeply you reject it, it's true."

"It's emotion," he protested.

It was the lawyer speaking. He was used to those facts which the tradition of law said were admissible; all other facts had to be excluded.

"I heard your speech," I told him. "I'd like to make a suggestion—"

"Go ahead," he said.

"Had I been you," I began, "I'd have stood up there and told those people: 'I'm Her Majesty's Opposition. I do not agree with the methods of Nkrumah. But, today, gentlemen, we have heard a motion for self-government. I'm an African. I want, above all things, to see my country free. So, for what it's worth, I hereby vote for this measure. And, in so doing, I challenge Nkrumah to keep his word and drive for self-government. I'm here to see that he does not lag, does not tarry. . . .' Dr. Danquah, had you said that, you would have become the hero of that hour. Those masses outside of that Assembly would have been galvanized. Nkrumah himself would have been speechless. And the British would have been thunderstruck; it would have put them on the spot. . . . Don't you see?"

He stared at me and shook his head slowly.

"I can't say things like that," he protested.

"Why not?"

"I don't believe in it," he said.

"It's not a matter of believing; it's politics! You would have voiced the demands of your country's masses, and you would have, with one stroke, pushed the British to a point where they would have had to act. . . ."

He was shaking his head. . . . It was no use. He was of the old school. One did not speak *for* the masses; one *told* them what to do. . . .

"You are a Christian?" I asked him, switching the subject.

"Yes," he said.

I was dumfounded.

"But I've read your book, *The Akan Doctrine of God*. You are a pagan too?"

"Yes," he said.

"Don't you find a conflict in the two religions?"

"No. Not at all. I go to church and serve God, and then

I go to the Stool House and worship my ancestors," he explained. He was on familiar ground now and he grew expansive. "You see, the Christian worships the Son. We worship the Father. It's the same thing."

I wanted to ask him why he felt the need to worship both the Father and the Son in that manner, but I shied off digging into delicate areas. It was evident that he knew nothing of the impact of the industrial West; the destiny of the disinherited would never be his; he was anchored for always in the calm waters of belief. . . . Our apprehensions of reality were too profoundly different to permit of much talk along religious lines. With a promise to meet and talk again, I took my leave.

It bothered me that I couldn't find among educated Africans any presentiment of what the future of their continent was to be. The more highly educated they had been, the more unfit they seemed to weigh and know the forces that were shaping the modern world.

It must not be thought that I did not give a full measure of respect to the ideas of Dr. Danquah. It's rare in our world today to feel that the sky has a value over and above that of space to be conquered, and that the earth means something more than an object out of which to dig minerals, or that human personality is something beyond a mere consumptive-productive unit. . . . The good doctor's grasp of life was essentially poetic; it was close to that which our fantasies and daydreams would have reality be; its essence was woven out of what we call human traits. Yet, if he would pit himself against his political adversaries, if he would win a struggle for the liberation of his country, he would have to lay aside such poetic preoccupations and adopt more realistic measures. He could, of course, declare that he would have no truck with such methods, that they were beneath him; but, if he did that, he would go down to defeat as so many others had gone before him.

What amazed me was that men like Dr. Danquah saw and knew each day what the British wanted from the Gold Coast; they knew that the hunger for raw materials and the opportunity to sell merchandise at high prices constituted the crux of British imperialism. An educated African might well curse those mysterious forces of geography that had made his country so fabulously rich in those raw materials that served as the fulcrum of world power politics. . . .

Twenty-Eight

I had long wanted to come to grips with the chiefs of the Gold Coast and finally one evening one was served up to me at the dinner table of the American Consul. This chief was a tall, gentle black man with a delicate face, sensitive fingers; it was obvious that he was burning to have his say, but he inhibited himself, declaring that he was not a political man. He was a Christian from the town of Odumase, the state of Manya Krobo. Gently, I steered the conversation toward native religious practices.

"Really," he told me, waving his hands a little impatiently, "our religion is basically the same as that of all other people. You mustn't get the idea that there's anything fantastic in ancestor worship."

"I agree with you," I said, anxious that he should talk freely. "All people have in them the germs of ancestor worship. The Russians are always talking of Marx, Lenin, and Stalin as being the *fathers* of the Russian Revolution. In America, we speak of our *Founding Fathers.* What they did in establishing the foundations of our country has assumed almost a magical sanctity." I could see the chief relaxing, and that was just my aim.

"There is nothing that we do in a Stool House that is

strange," he explained. "There are stools there. To us they are sacred. Just as other churches have holy things, so do we. And you must realize that even in the illiterate masses there is a certain wisdom. By trial and error, they have learned a lot. For example, there is a certain leaf of a certain tree. If you hold it in one of your hands, you can catch a scorpion in the other, and the scorpion cannot sting you—"

"How was that discovered?" I asked.

"I don't know how these fetish men found it out, but they did," he said.

It was strange how his mind seemed to prefer to deal with such magical manifestations. The African places mystery between cause and effect and there is a deep predilection toward omnipotence of thought, of spirit acting on spirit. The more I listened to Africans describe their achievements in the realms of the magical, the more I felt that it was how one related fact to fact that constituted the real difference between the Western and non-Western mind. When the chief had saturated my understanding with mystery, I launched into a discussion of politics where, I was certain, he could give me no facts tinged with mysticism.

"What do you think of the Convention People's Party?" I asked him.

"I'm not a political man," he began, "but, of course, politics influence my life. I'm a chief. Nkrumah has reduced the power of the chiefs, but he could not have done it unless the British had consented to it. You must understand that. I'm not bothered about all this talk about the wicked British imperialists. It's against their code of action that I inveigh. They betrayed a sacred trust that we chiefs had given them—"

"Tell me more about that," I urged him.

"It's simple," he explained. "Most of us chiefs gave the British our power. They didn't conquer all of us. Our tribes had been fighting one another. Now, for decades we'd watched the British and we liked the way that they did things. . . . Then, orally and in writing, we made agreements; we surrendered our power to them; we told them to establish peace. . . . Now, I contend that that power was *not* theirs to give away. . . . They should have handed it back to the men from whom they had got it. But they went and gave it away; they didn't even consult us; we knew nothing about it; they just did it and told us that we had to like it. Our ancestors had no notion that some day the power that they had tendered the British would one day be given away to people who are our enemies. . . . The British could not have ruled this country for the past hundred years without the consent of the chiefs. . . ."

"I see your point," I said. "But listen to another side of the story. What did the British give your people? In the light of the gold and diamonds and manganese and timber that they took out of the country, and all for a pittance, could they not have built roads for you other than in those areas where they had to bring their raw materials down to the ports? Could they not have built more schools? Could they not have improved the health standards of the people?"

He didn't answer. He knew that the real responsibility for those matters had rested, in the last analysis, with the chiefs. . . . And those chiefs had not been anxious to bring reforms into the lives of the masses of the people. They knew that widespread literacy marked the termination of chieftaincy. Under the British the chiefs had had it soft and they'd wanted to keep it soft. Now, in looking back, they were wishing that they had acted a little differently; but that time had gone. . . . A new political party had condemned them on the very grounds which they had claimed were their own: moral grounds.

In the old days the chiefs had, through the hereditary

rights of royal families, formed the sacred instruments of rule and had ordered the lives of the people; now Nkrumah had insisted that the instruments of rule be made secular, elective, that the entire legislative body of a given community could not be completely hereditary. And the young men of the nation had marched in agreement with that democratic aim.

"Don't you think," I asked him, "that the new schools that will be built, the new health measures now in operation, will outweigh the claims of those who lost power?"

"Our ancestors, to help us," the chief said, "made a gentleman's agreement with the British, then the British broke their promise and leveled their guns at us. They let us down. That was not *right!*"

The concept of honor was being evoked against the right of men to live and breathe without fear and poverty. The black elite was asserting its claims against the younger men who yearned to toss off the yoke of imperialism and banish the blindness of centuries of illiteracy. Blacks against blacks!

"We are not used to political parties, central governments," he lamented.

"Look," I argued gently, "all nations have central governments. A central government is an absolute necessity if man is to live at all rationally. How can you trade with nations of the world, how can you educate your children, how can you wipe out disease, how can you defend yourself against aggression unless you have a strong central government?"

"But we are not educated; we don't know how—"

"Then learn," I said. "Make your mistakes. A central government is simply national housekeeping. Why let another government do this for you? Your people are passionately anxious to try. Then let them try. Common people rule elsewhere; why not here?"

The chief sighed. What pathos! He was a "decent" man, but it seemed that all "decent" people were being driven out of power in the world today.

In the old days a chief's children had, by hereditary and prescriptive right, first choice to enter what limited schools existed. Now, all students, regardless of background or social origin, had to pass an entrance examination to be admitted to the universities of the nation. . . . And the chiefs, the old and great families, did not like it. Their blood was the best blood in the land, hallowed by the stools containing the souls of their ancestors—stools that had gradually turned black by the constant dripping of sheep's blood upon them. Now that the magical authority of those blackened stools over the minds of their subjects had gone, they didn't like it; they wanted a chance to turn the clock back; they didn't want history to catch up with Africa. . . . But the past had gone; the magic wouldn't work any more; the sheep, goats, chickens, and even human beings, when slain as sacrifices, were of no avail. . . .

The Gold Coast was being strait-jacketed into the future; events were moving fast to overcome the inertia of the chiefs. But was the pace so swift that the native genius of the people was not being taken into account? In olden times the undertakings of the people had been communal; they had labored to the sound of drums and music. Today prefabricated houses were being thrown up overnight. . . . Was enough thought being given to what had happened in other industrial countries?

The pathos of Africa would be doubled if, out of her dark past, her people were plunged into a dark future, a future that smacked of Chicago or Detroit. . . . But how can these harassed politicians, working in such a heated and partisan atmosphere, battling both the British and the black elite, have time to think and plan? What would be the gain if these benighted fetish-worshipers were snatched from their mud huts and their ancestor idolatry, and catapulted into the vast steel and stone jungles of cities, tied to monotonous jobs, condemned to cheap movies, made dependent upon alcohol? Would an African, a hundred years from now, after he has been trapped in the labyrinths of industrialization, be able to say when he is dying, when he is on the verge of going to meet his long dead ancestors, those traditional, mysterious words:

I'm dying
I'm dying
Something big is happening to me . . . ?

Twenty-Nine

To find opinions on these questions, I sought to talk to Dr. K. A. Busia, one of Africa's foremost social scientists. He was with the opposition, but he had indisputable facts in his grasp.

I called at his office in the Department of Social Sciences at Achimota University. Dr. Busia turned out to be a short, medium-sized, affable man who had about him a slightly worried and puzzled air. He was the author of *The Position of the Chief in the Modern Political System of Ashanti* and *Social Survey Sekondi-Takoradi*. I could tell at once that he was orientated and could express himself with ease.

"Dr. Busia, to just what degree are the traditional rituals and ceremonies of the Akan people still intact?" I asked him.

"They are completely intact," he told me. "The people hide them from the West, and they make peripheral concessions to Western opinion. But the central body of our beliefs and practices still functions and is a working frame of reference from day to day."

"You are with the opposition, are you not?"

"I am."

"Do tribal rituals play a part in the Convention People's Party?"

"They most certainly do," he snapped.

"Why has not this been pointed out before? Why has no one shown the vital link between modern politics in Africa and the religious nature of tribal life?"

"Westerners who approach tribal life always pick out those manifestations which most resemble their own culture and ignore the rest," he said. "That which they recognize as Western, they call progress."

"What is the significance of the oath-taking and libation pouring at Convention People's Party's rallies?"

"It's to bind the masses to the party," he said. "Tribal life is religious through and through. An oath is a great thing to an African. An oath links him with the past, allies him with his ancestors. That's the deepest form of loyalty that the tribal man knows. The libation pouring means the same thing. Now, these things, when employed at a political meeting, insure, with rough authority, that the masses will follow and accept the leadership. That is what so-called mass parties need. . . . The leaders of the Convention People's Party use tribal methods to enforce their ends."

"I take it that *you* wouldn't use such methods?"

"I'm a Westerner," he said, sucking in his breath. "I was educated in the West."

I had the feeling that he was speaking sincerely, that he could not conceivably touch such methods, that he regarded them with loathing, and that he did not even relish thinking that anybody else would. My personal impression was that Dr. Busia was not and could never be a politician, that he lacked that innate brutality of force and drive that makes a mass leader. He was too analytical, too reflective to even want to get down into the muck of life and organize men. I sensed, too, that maybe certain moral scruples would inhibit him in acting. . . .

"What has been the influence of Christianity?"

"Despite all the efforts of the missionaries, the Akan people have not changed their center of cultural gravity. Where you do find changes, they are mainly due to the church and the factor of urbanization. But even there you find a curious overlapping, a mixture. You have literate chiefs, for example, who practice an unwritten religion; you have lawyers trained in England who feel a tie to the tribal legal conceptions of their people. Such mixtures go right through the whole of our society. It's not simple."

"Have any psychological examinations been done to determine how this mixture is reflected in the minds of the people?"

"Nothing has been done in that direction," he said.

I next inquired of Dr. Busia the reasons for the low population level of the Gold Coast. I pointed out to him that the geographical area of the Gold Coast was more or less the same as that of England, but the Gold Coast had less than one-tenth of England's population. . . .

"Two things have kept the population level low," he said. "The lack of water and the tsetse fly. Seventy-five per cent of our population live in the forest area. If we could banish the tsetse fly from that area, we'd have horses to draw our carts and cows for meat and dairy products. Now, in the Northern Territories there is no water; it's filled with scrubland that can barely support its meager population."

"Dr. Busia, if you don't want to commit yourself on the question I'm going to ask, you can just tell me," I told him. "How do you, a British-trained social scientist, feel about the British recognizing the Convention People's Party . . . ?"

"Sure; I'll tell you," he said readily. "I'll tell you exactly what I told Sir Arden-Clarke, the Governor of this Colony. . . . The British here care nothing for our people; they are concerned with their political power which enables them to defend their financial interests. They sided with the Convention People's Party in order to protect those interests. It's that simple. We educated Africans looked to the British for but one thing: the maintenance of standards. Now that they have let that drop, what are they good for?"

Again I heard that echo of pathos. . . . A scientist had been trained by Britain to expect certain kinds of behavior from Britishers; now British behavior had turned out to be something that even their best pupils found somewhat nauseating. . . .

"The British call such abrupt changes 'flexibility,' do they not, Dr. Busia?"

Dr. Busia laughed ruefully.

"But tell me . . . In your book, *Social Survey Sekondi-Takoradi*, you show pretty clearly the disintegrating forces of urbanization at work in the cities of the Gold Coast. Now, is there any widespread awareness of this?"

"No," he said.

"Is there any plan to see that the growth of your cities can take a new direction?"

"There is no plan," he said.

"I feel, from reading your book, that when tribal life and rituals break down under the impact of urbanization, and when no new sense of direction takes the place of what tribal culture gave, you will find a new kind of pagan among you: a pagan who feels no need to worship. . . ."

"The germs of that are making their appearance in our country," he admitted. "It's not widespread as yet; but it's evident."

"Do you think that Nkrumah can easily wipe out the old habits of the people—?"

"The African will react in that matter just as all people react," he said. "In the crucial moments of life, people fall back upon the deepest teachings of their lives; hence, in matters like politics, death, childbirth, etc., it's the teachings and beliefs of the tribe that all people—even those who are literate—turn to, give support to and trust. . . ."

There were other questions that I wanted to ask Dr. Busia, but I felt that they were too delicate. Had I not been afraid of wounding his feelings, I'd have asked him how was it that he, a social scientist, who saw so clearly the forces that were breaking down tribal life, could oppose those forces? If those forces had given way under the impact of industrialization in other countries, would they not do so in the Gold Coast? And, knowing that, why did he take his stand with the opposition? But I'd been told that Dr. Busia came of royal stock, that his brother was a chief, that he too might possibly some day be a chief. . . .

I'd now talked to enough educated Africans of the Gold Coast for there to emerge in my mind a dim portrait of an African character that the world knew little or nothing about. . . . I could imagine a young boy being born in a tribe, taking his mother's name, belonging to the blood-clan of his mother, but coming under the daily authority of his father, starting life by following his father's trade. I could well imagine this boy's father's coming in contact with missionaries who would tell him that his religion was crude, primitive, that he ought to bring his family into the church of the One and Living God. . . .

I could imagine that family's trying to change its ways; I could sense conflicts between husband and wife, between the father's family and the mother's family over the issue of Christianity; and I could readily picture the father, in the end, winning his argument on the basis of his superior earning power gained from working for Christian Europeans.

Let us assume, then, that the boy is the first child that the family has consented to send to the mission school. . . . There, he learns how "bad" is the life of his tribe; he's taught to know what power the outside world has, how weak and fragile is his country in comparison to the might of England, America, or France. Slowly he begins to feel that the communal life under the various stools is a childlike and primitive thing, and that the past of his tribe reeks of human sacrifice.

He now begins to identify himself with his mentors; they teach him to eat a balanced diet; he becomes ashamed to go about half nude; he feels that painting the body with lurid colors signifies nothing; he grows to loathe the mumbo-jumbo of the chiefs and the incessant beating of those infernal drums of state; and, above all, he squirms in the grip of the sticky compound life where every man is his brother and every woman is his sister or mother and can lay claims upon him which, if he refuses to honor them, can make him an outlaw. . . .

He develops a sense of his own individuality as being different and unique and he comes to believe that he has a destiny, a personality that must not be violated by others. He cringes in his heart at the memory that he once had to obey orders but confusedly heard and dimly understood from the shades where his ancestors dwelt.

Christ is offered and he accepts the way of the Cross. He now has a stake in the divine; he has a soul to save, and there seeps into his young and yearning heart that awful question: Where will I spend Eternity? The future looms before him in terms of a romantic agony: he can either live forever or be consigned to a lake of fire that never ceases to burn those whose sins have found them out. . . .

Yes, he must redeem himself; he must change; he must have a career. He reads of the exploits of the English and the Americans and the French, and he is told that they are strong and powerful because they believe in God. Therefore, finishing his mission studies, he elects to go to England or France or America to study. . . . He is baptized and his name is changed from Kojo or Kwame or Kobina or Kofi or Akufo or Ako or Kwesi, to Luke or Peter or Matthew or Paul or Mark or John. . . . He adopts a Western style of dress, even if it does not fit his needs or the climate. He no longer eats with his brothers, squatting on the floor about a common dish and lifting the food with his fingers; he insists upon sitting at a table and using a knife and fork.

If he goes to America to continue his studies, he is elated upon arrival. What a country! What a people! The seeming openness, the lavish kindness, the freedom of the individual, and the sense that one can change one's lot in life, the lightheartedness, the almost seeming indifference with which religion is taken, the urban manner of Negro living and what the Negroes have achieved against great odds—all of this contrasts with the bleak mud huts and the harsh life of the African compounds. For the first time in his life he sees black men building and operating their own institutions in a Western manner, and a sense of social romance is disclosed to him, and he yearns to emulate it. . . . All of this makes him apply himself to the study of his chosen subjects with a zeal that is second only to the religion that he'd been taught back in his African mission school. But . . .

He begins, as the years pass, to detect that the Americans are not a happy or contented people. He learns how to be afraid, how to decipher the looks of desperation on the American faces about him. He learns how it feels to be related to nobody. What at first had seemed a great romance now seems like a panting after money with a hotness of emotion that leaves no time to relax. And he begins to wonder what would happen to him in such a life. . . .

And he learns the meaning of the word "race." What he had failed to notice before now strikes home: he is free, but there are certain things he cannot do, certain places where he cannot go, all because he's black. A chronic apprehension sets up in him; the "person" in him that the missionaries had told him to develop is reduced, constricted. He'd never thought of being rich, and now he knows that if he is not rich in this land, he's lost, a shameful thing. . . .

That sense of poetry in him that even religion had not dulled makes him ask himself if he wants to be defined in terms of production and consumption. The feeling of security he had first felt is gone; the more he comes to know America, the more he, stammeringly at first and more forthrightly later on, begins to ask himself: "Where's it all going? What's it all for?"

And the only answers that make sense to him are heard in Union Square or Washington Park. Yes; he'd go back home and try to change things, to fight for freedom. . . .

And if he went to England for his education, his sense of alienation would be the same, but differently arrived at. Indeed, his blackness is swallowed up in the vast grayness of London. Perhaps he might have difficulty getting a room in which to live because of his blackness, but he soon meets another Englishman who feels free to do what he likes with his own home. But what puzzles him is the English assumption that everything that is done in England is right, that the English way is the only way to do it. He sees that no black man could ever sit in the House of Commons, that he is not expected to participate in English life on any level except that of a doctor. It seems that the English entertain a quaint notion that all Africans have sensitive hands that can heal the sick!

At Oxford or Cambridge he is far from the world of "race." He is a black gentleman in a graded hierarchy of codes of conduct in which, if he learns them, he can rise. He can, even though black, become a Sir. . . . The more he learns, the more Africa fades from his mind and the more shameful and bizarre it seems. But, finally, he begins to gag. The concepts that are being fed to him insult him. Though he will have a place of honor, that place will be with the lower and subject races. . . . Every book he reads reveals how England won her empire and this begins to clash in his mind with the codes of honor that he's learning so skillfully to practice. Soon he knows that he has to avoid saying certain things; for example, if it's known that he's a nationalist, he will surely not pass his bar examinations. Inhibition sets in and he has to choose whether he's to be among the favored or the scorned.

He learns that his blackness can be redeemed by service, but this service is not in the interests of his people; it's against them. . . . He begins to wonder why his missionary teachers never hinted at all about this. Were they parties to this deception? At the bottom of English society he sees servility and suffering and he senses that what has ensnared the people of his country has also ensnared these poor whites, and the first blow to his confidence is received. He could have been like those drab and colorless millions of London's slums; indeed, his mother and father are like that in far-off Africa. . . . He becomes afraid of his choice, and slowly he begins to sympathize with the fear and insecurity of the poor whites around him and, in the end, he begins to identify himself with them. It's not in the schoolrooms or the churches that he can hear moral preachments denouncing what is being done to his country; he hears it only in Hyde Park. But he's too afraid as yet to agree with what he hears; it sounds too violent, too drastic; it offends those delicate feelings that the missionaries instilled in him.

His first clumsy criticisms are addressed to religious people and he's disturbed that they defend the system as it is. He's secretly enraged that the English do not feel that he is being dishonored. Just as the missionaries taught him just so much and no more, he finds that the English accept him just so much and no more. He's praised when he's like the English, but he sees that the English are careful to make sure that he's kept at arm's length and he begins to feel that he's a fish out of water—he's not English and he's not African. . . .

If he chooses to go to France, he will encounter the same theme, but with even subtler variations. Indeed, in France he'll need all of his will power to keep from being completely seduced by the blandishments of French culture. None of the blatant American racism or that vague social aloofness which so often prevails in England will meet him in Paris. Instead, he'd be eagerly received everywhere, but . . .

He senses that the Frenchmen he meets are sounding him out about the national liberation movement in his country. If he makes the mistake of being forthright about his country's demand for freedom, he'll encounter no overt racial discrimination; he'll simply find everything suddenly becoming extremely difficult. He'll learn, as he talks to animated and polite Frenchmen, that they feel that they have worked out, in the last two thousand years, just about the most civilized attitude on earth; he'll be obliquely but constantly discouraged to think in any terms save those of extreme individualism.

Suppose he discovers that the French know nothing of his country and its culture, and, to remedy this lack, suppose he tells his French friends that he plans to launch a magazine in which young Africans can express themselves to the people of the Western world . . . ? A good idea! But, *mon ami*, you don't need to create a new magazine! You have the freedom to contribute to any magazine published in Paris! In fact, *mon vieux*, we'd welcome any contribution you might make. By the way, we'd like to make you a co-editor of our review!

The more intelligent the French think he is, the more he'll be watched; but this surveillance is not done in terms of crude spying, not yet—but in terms of social cultivation. He'll hear his professors in the classrooms constantly asking him: "What do you intend to do when you get your degree?" And if he says he's seriously thinking of settling down in France and pursuing his profession, marrying, no matter what woman of what race, his professors nod and smile their encouragement. But if he says that he wishes to return to his homeland and fight to lift up the standards of living, to free his country from foreign rule, from French domination, he feels a coolness of attitude that, in time, will change to freezing. . . .

He sees that many of his fellow blacks are obtaining university degrees and that almost all of them are at once put into civil service where they can be effectively controlled!

The black colonial Frenchman in Paris, like his counterpart in London or New York, will encounter the men on soapboxes preaching revolution, but, to his surprise, he'll find that the French are fairly indulgent toward his budding interest in Marxism! It's only upon nationalism that they frown. . . . Hell find, in Paris as in the colonies proper, that the French will prefer his becoming a Communist rather than his embracing the cause of his homeland. In time he sees that the French have a great deal of experience in dealing with Communists, but that they shy off in a state of terror when confronted with nationalists.

He learns that in French eyes nationalism implies a rejection of French culture, whereas they regard Communism as a temporary aberration of youth. Let him yell for revolution all he can; he might find a few French millionaires at his side, helping to spur him on . . . !

Alone in Paris, he'll take up with some French girl and she'll sympathize with him, but will tactfully point out how hard and long will be his fight, that there are so many pleasures to be savored, and he'll be lucky if he does not yield. He sees that many of his black brothers who came to France are sophisticated, successful black *Frenchmen!*

Still thirsting for self-redemption, thwarted in pride, he dreams of showing the French that he too can build a nation. He realizes now that his resolution to do this must be ten times as strong as that of an African in New York or London; also he begins to realize that the culture of France is so profound that it can absorb even Communism and pat its stomach. . . .

It's a desperate young black French colonial who resolves to return to his homeland and face the wrath of white Frenchmen who'll kill him for his longing for the freedom of his own nation, but who'll give him the *Legion d'honneur* for being French. . . . Through books he finds that other men have forged weapons to defend themselves from the domination of the West; he learns that the Russians, the Chinese, the Indians, and the Burmese saved themselves and he begins to master the theories of how they did it.

Strangely, he now yearns to build a land like France or England or America. Only such a deed will assuage his feelings of shame and betrayal. He too can be like they are. That's the way to square the moral outrage done to his feelings. Whether America or France or England have built societies to the liking of his heart no longer concerns him; he must prove his worth in terms that they have taught him.

But when he arrives in his tropical homeland, he is dismayed to find that he's almost alone. The only people who are solidly against the imperialists are precisely those whose words and manner of living had evoked in him that sense of shame that made him want to disown his native customs. They want national freedom, but, unlike him, they do not want to "prove" anything. Moreover, they don't know how to organize. They are willing to join him in attempting to drive out the invaders; they are willing, nay, anxious, on the oaths of their ancestors, to die and liberate their homeland. But they don't want to hear any talk of ideas beyond that. . . .

So, the young man who spurned the fetish religion of his people returns and finds that that religion is the only thing that he has to work with; it's muck, but he must *use* it. . . . So, not believing in the customs of his people, he rolls up his sleeves and begins to organize that which he loathes. . . . Feeling himself an outsider in his native land, watching the whites take the gold and the diamonds and the timber and the bauxite and the manganese, seeing his fellow blacks who were educated abroad siding with the whites, seeing his culture shattered and rendered abhorrent, seeing the tribes turned into pawns that float about the harbor towns, stealing, begging, killing—seeing that the black life is detribalized and left to rot, he finally lifts his voice in an agonized cry of nationalism, *black* nationalism!

He's the same man whom the missionaries educated; he's acting on the impulses that they evoked in him; his motives are really deeply moral, but pitched on a plane and in a guise that the missionaries would not recognize. . . . And almost the only ones who answer his cry of nationalism-at-any-price, nationalism as a religion, are the tribes who are sick of the corrupt chiefs, the few who share his emotional state, the flotsam and jetsam of the social order! But, things being as they are, there's no other road for him; and he resolves: "So be it. . . ."

The strange soil of the Western world, composed as it is of individualism, hunger for a personal destiny, a romantic sense of self-redemption, gives birth to fantastic human plants that it is ashamed of!

PART III

The Brooding Ashanti

Not only might human development have never overstepped the pre-scientific stage and been doomed never to overstep it so that the physical world might indeed retain its truth whilst we should know nothing about it; the physical world might have been other than it is with systems of law other than those actually prevailing. It is also conceivable that our intuitable world should be the last, and "beyond" it no physical world at all . . .

Ideas, by Edmund Husserl

Thirty

At last I've got from the Gold Coast Information Service an itinerary that will take me up into the high rain forest, to Kumasi, Kumawu, Bibiani, etc. The British were, in the end, kind enough to allow me the use of the few government resthouses which were dotted here and there in the jungle area. I had a long list of personalities to see: doctors, lawyers, chiefs, and politicians. . . . The Britisher who gave me the itinerary cleared his throat and said casually:

"I say, old chap, it'd be better to stick to the itinerary, you know."

I assured him that I would, that I had no desire to wander at random in the jungle.

I bought a half-gallon thermos jug for water, about £30 of tinned food, a bottle of germicide to put into the water before using it for washing, a big box of DDT, cigarettes, and a five-yard length of colored cloth to use as a sheet at night when I'd be bunking in out-of-the-way places. I examined my budget and decided that I'd go as far as a shilling a mile would take me. I'd no notion that I was to find the jungle the most expensive place on earth!

On the morning of August 4, with Battling Kojo behind the wheel, I took off. Ahead of me, across the flat plains of Accra, I could see the bluish-green escarpment rising towards a misty sky. Half an hour later we began to climb the escarpment itself on a red laterite road that mounted and wound amidst palm and coconut trees. Gradually the sky began to darken a little and the vegetation became a deeper and more prolific green. Suddenly the sky seemed to lower itself to the tops of the tall trees and the air became clogged with humidity. As we lifted still higher, I could feel the temperature dropping sharply. I turned my head and stared out of the rear window of the car and saw the coastal plain drenched in sunlight, with here and there, gleaming balefully, a mud village or two—and I knew it was sizzling hot down there. . . .

The vegetation turned a still darker green and I could sense the jungle beginning, becoming dense. The car churned up steep hills and to either side of the road loomed walls of dark green from which, now and then, appeared black faces of men, women, and children, half nude, carrying vast burdens of plantains, bananas, or wood upon their heads. Their faces were stolid, set, humorless; once or twice I saw a startled expression leap into someone's eyes as he glimpsed my face staring at him. Some waved at me and I waved back, wriggling the palm of my hand in that salute which is so native and which, by now, I had come to feel was normal.

As we crawled still higher, the trees became taller: the wawa, mahogany, palm, and cocoa trees flanked both sides of the road with leafy curtains of brooding green. Jutting skyward were a few gigantic white cottonwood trees. Thick creeping vines, three and four inches in diameter, entwined themselves amid the branches and leaves of the trees, giving the impression of some hovering mystery, some lurking and nameless danger. What was down those narrow paths leading into the jungle—paths so shaded and black and wild . . . ?

Past Mampong we still mounted; the road was good, the earth was red, and the vegetation denser still. The people had a quieter look than those of the Accra plains. We sped past villages of mud huts; men and women were sitting and staring calmly into space. Yams were piled before doorways. Africa was a dark place, not black but somber, not depressing but slightly haunting—moody, with a kind of dreaminess floating over it. We were in the thick jungle now and moisture clung to the car windows.

This is, it is said, the home of the true Negro—whatever that means. Speaking a poetic language which, ironically, they feel describes reality, the Negroes themselves claim that they came out of holes in the ground; the white anthropologists contend that they came from farther north, Timbuktu or above the Sahara. Who knows? So much prejudice has entered into these calculations that perhaps nobody will ever know what the truth is. One thing, however, is true: an astounding religion, complicated and abounding in taboos, came to birth here and no one has ever really fully traced its growth or origin. It is not definitely known if the Akan religion influenced the Egyptian religion or if the Egyptian religion influenced the Akan religion. Briffault feels that the Egyptians got the moon-worshiping phase of their religion from the Negroes; some authorities feel that the Negroes never produced anything original but borrowed everything they've got. Other authorities contend that they can find traces of Ethiopian religious practices among the Ashanti. Yet the manner in which the Akan wears his native toga is exactly the way in which the ancient Romans wore theirs. How is that possible? Did the Romans penetrate this far before the days of Christ? Or did Negroes get as far as Rome? Or did the two peoples evolve the same kind of dress independently, without coming in contact with each other? No one really knows. It might well be that people in ancient times had much more social intercourse than we now suspect, that they were much less conscious of "race" than we are. . . .

At last we came into Koforidua, a small, clean-looking town of about 25,000 people. It has paved streets and the inevitable open sewer drains at each side of the road. Trees are everywhere and a relaxed atmosphere pervades the town. Koforidua is the center of a once rich cocoa-producing region and, under the auspices of the United Africa Company, many agents from many European countries are stationed here to buy cocoa from the African farmers. The Gold Coast produces more cocoa than any other country in the world and its sale abroad makes the Gold Coast the single largest dollar-earning area in all of Africa.

I put up in the modern home of Mr. R. A. O. Eccles, the district manager of the United Africa Company. Mr. Eccles was not at home, but word had been left to feed me. . . . While at lunch the sound of bells and drums came from the green and hazy distance. I asked the inevitably barefooted, white-jacketed steward boy what was happening and he told me:

"Somebody dead, Massa. So drums beat."

A young Englishman, a friend of Mr. Eccles, called; he was a buyer of cocoa in an area about sixty miles square.

"How do you go about buying this cocoa?" I asked him.

"Well, we have subagents. They get the stuff from other agents who, in turn, buy directly from the farmers."

"What local business group gets the cocoa in the end?" I asked.

"It works like this," he explained. "The Gold Coast Government has created a Cocoa Marketing Board to buy up the cocoa crops from the agents and then this Cocoa Marketing Board sells the cocoa on the world markets at prices advantageous to the farmers, always keeping a pool of money in reserve, so that if there is a break in the cocoa market, the farmers will have some money to fall back upon."

"How, in a concrete way, does one of these agents buy cocoa?"

"At the beginning of the cocoa season—and we're getting into it right now—an agent looks over a crop of cocoa, estimates the yield and by that the value the crop will have when it ripens. He then advances cash against the crop. Generally, when the time comes to harvest the crop, the farmer's money has been spent. Hence, most of the cocoa farmers are about a year in debt, even though the Cocoa Marketing Board helps them in many ways. This is an area rich in money, though the appearance of the streets and houses and stores would not indicate that such is true," the young man went on.

"But what do they do with all the money they get from selling the cocoa?"

"Well, it's funny, you know," the young man said, twisting his mouth into a wry smile. "What happens to the money earned by an enterprising African cocoa farmer is something that economists have never been able to grasp. In this town you'll see no huge, rich-looking houses, no green lawns, little attempt at conspicuous consumption, etc. In fact, the town is, as you can see, rather shabby. Well, this is the way it works. . . . When an African earns a pile of money, it is not his alone. He belongs to a tribe and a family. That money, under tribal law, is as much his sister's children's as it is his own. In fact, his first duty is toward his sister's children. Now, let's suppose such a man got a thousand pounds. At once, before he can derive any personal benefit from it, his relatives descend upon him, making demands which, under the family system in Africa, he cannot refuse. They cling to him like leeches, demanding bicycles, sewing machines, radios, clothes, phonographs, etc. The man is soon broke. But he does not worry. The system of native African communism saves him from want, for all he has to do is go to another relative and sponge on him. Individual initiative is not very popular in Africa. Why amass a lot of money? You'll have to give it away anyhow. . . ."

"Has there been any attempt to change this right of the relative to take a share of the wealth of another relative?" I asked.

"It's hard," he explained. "Religion is law in Africa. How can you change religious beliefs?"

"And what do you think of those beliefs?"

He looked at me, then raised his forefinger and shook it in my face.

"There's more to it than meets the eye," he said solemnly. "I've heard things that cannot be sneered at."

"Like what, for example?" I asked him. "Really, all of this *juju* stuff has a simple, psychological explanation. Now, tell me something that has no such explanation."

"Well," he began gently, cocking his head. "I've an educated young African working for me. He speaks English as well as I do; he speaks French too. Now, he told me the following story . . ."

I sat hunched, trying to suppress a smile. It was impossible for the English to live side by side with the Africans without becoming infected with the African's religious beliefs. The African had projected an invisible world out of himself and he was living in and reacting to that world, and the English found themselves, in the end, obliged to give a certain kind of assent to that nonexistent world. . . .

"One day this young African and his wife went to a nearby town to do some shopping. Now, the husband had to return home before the wife and he waited for her. The wife was supposed to return around six o'clock and when she didn't put in her appearance, the husband began to worry.

"Well, late that night the wife came in, looking deeply

disturbed. The husband upbraided her and demanded to be told what had happened. Now, the wife told the following story . . .

"It seems that while on the bus en route home, the wife had been in the center of a violent argument. A woman's purse had been stolen on the bus and there had been a hue and cry about it. Finally, the driver of the bus declared that every passenger on the bus had to go to the police station. This was done and the police questioned everybody and could arrive at no solution.

"The people were dissatisfied with the work of the police and then somebody suggested that only a fetish priest could find out who the culprit was. They argued pro and con and, in the end, the whole crowd went to the house of the local fetish priest. This priest made the entire crowd sit in a circle on the ground and he placed a bowl of water in the center. He then placed a reed in the water, making it stand up—"

"No!" I exclaimed.

"That's what my friend told me and I believe it," the young Englishman swore. "Now, I don't know how that priest managed to make that reed stand up; but he did. . . . My African friend wouldn't lie to me. Now, the fetish priest had an old knife that had been owned by an ancestor. He told the crowd that each person must hold the knife over the standing reed and when the guilty man's turn came, the reed would fall. . . .

"That knife was passed from hand to hand and it was held over the standing reed. The reed still stood. Finally, when one man took hold of the knife, the reed promptly fell. . . . The man got excited and declared that it was all a mistake, that he had not stolen the woman's purse. . . .

"Three times the knife was passed around, and each time the guilty man took the knife and held it over the standing reed, the reed fell. The crowd was so angry that it wanted to lynch that man. But the fetish priest calmed them down, took the trembling young man into a room and asked him to give up the woman's purse or he'd turn him over to the police. The man produced the purse—"

"Where had he been hiding the purse all the time?" I asked. "Why didn't the police find it in the first place?"

"I don't know," the suave, clean-shaven, intelligent, well-dressed young Englishman told me. Then he concluded: "This is a true story. What do you say to that?"

"Did you ever personally see anything like that?"

"No."

"You're telling me, no doubt, exactly what the young African told you," I said. "But I doubt the whole thing. The only trouble with these wonderful tales is that you can never check them. I'm convinced that the story has a psychological explanation. The guilty man believed in the power of the priest. By the way, where is this young African? I'd like to talk to him."

"Unfortunately, he's on leave," he said.

"And the man's wife?"

"She's gone too," he said. "But there's something to this *juju*."

Yes; this nonsense had caught him too. I decided to haul the conversation down to a practical level.

"Look, if these Africans have some powerful, wonderful, deep secrets, why in hell did they wait so long to kick the British out? Why didn't they use their knowledge to defend themselves? They had to wait until a man trained in Western thought came to lead them before they could even dream of fighting for their freedom. Is that not so?"

He grinned at me, shook his head, then stared at the floor.

"That's true," he admitted.

That afternoon I had Kojo drive me about the town; the

sky was gray and a fine drizzle of rain was falling. Ringing the town was a chain of green hills and the clouds were so low that their edges were entangled in the treetops. I could feel a somber mood of mystery lurking up there in those high, dim hills.

"Massa wanna see the chief?" Kojo asked me.

"Exactly," I told him. "Drive me there. Do you know where it is?"

"Yasa. Chief's house biggest house in town; it passes 'em all, sar," Kojo said.

The house of the chief was a huge yellow structure built in a strange style of architecture, half Western and half Oriental. Timidly, I walked up the long, wooden steps, hoping that Kojo would follow me, but he did not. And I did not want to betray my nervousness by asking him to. . . . I had heard those funeral drums beating and I hoped that no African of importance had died. I'd been told that the sacrifice of a stranger to accompany the dead was looked upon with particular favor by the ancestors. . . . I walked into a vast rotunda that reminded me of the pictures I'd seen of early Roman buildings. Under a high dome to the left was a dais upon which—I was later informed—witnesses stood when the chief was conducting court with the aid of his elders.

"Hello! Hello!" I called.

A young boy, dirty and badly dressed, came up to me.

"Is the chief in?"

"Yes, sar."

"May I see him?"

"You American, sar?"

"Yes."

"Wait, sar."

He left. Five minutes later I heard footsteps behind me; I turned. A slight, brown man of about forty came forward. He had on an old dark-colored cloth and he wore sandals.

"Good afternoon, Nana," I said, addressing him according to custom.

"Welcome," he said.

I took his right hand in both of my hands, which, I'd been told, was the proper way to greet a "father of the people." He spoke English with a tribal accent and was most polite, gracious. He bade me sit and we talked casually. A group of toga-clad young men drifted in and seated themselves on the floor around us, listening, smiling. Meanwhile, the chief was observing me closely. A boy brought in two bottles of beer. The chief poured out several glasses. As he handed me a glass, he said:

"Pour a libation for us."

"*Me?*"

"Yes," the chief said. "*You*. You are African."

"But I've never done it before."

"Then try."

"But what am I to say?"

"Anything that's in your heart."

I tilted my glass and let a few drops of beer fall into a huge wooden vat in which cigarette stubs and trash were collected. As the beer dribbled downward, I declaimed in a tolling voice, calling upon our common ancestors to witness that I had come from America, that I wished health and happiness to everybody, that I yearned to see Africa free, that I was a stranger who bore no ill-will toward anyone; I beseeched the ancestors to watch with care and love over those who were present; I begged them to bless the fields, to make the women fertile, and to protect the children. . . . My glass was empty.

"You did fine," he said, filling my glass again.

We drank and when our glasses were empty, the chief took me gently by the hand and said:

"Come with me."

"Yes, Nana," I said, following him obediently.

As we walked down the long veranda, he whispered to me:

"I want to show you a mystery."

We came to a corner of the veranda that overlooked a dismal courtyard. He caught my arm, stopping me. I wondered what he was about to reveal. Then he pointed off into some shadows.

"Do you see that box?" he asked me.

I squinted and saw a dark, oblong metal box about eight inches thick, about two feet long, and about a foot wide.

"Yes."

"What's in that box?" he asked me.

"I don't know," I said.

"Look at it. . . . Go closer and look at it," he urged me.

Maybe it contained some foolish, but, to his mind, powerful fetish? I wanted to burst out laughing, but I inhibited myself. I bent forward and examined the box and saw that it seemed to be covered with flies or some other insects. Then I knew; they were bees, crawling. . . .

"What's in the box?" he asked me.

"Honey's in the box," I said brightly.

"You think that those are bees?" he asked me.

"Yes," I said, puzzled at his insistence.

"They are *not* bees," he said.

"Well, maybe you've got some insects in Africa that I don't know about," I ventured. "What are they?"

"That's a mystery," he said.

I stood looking at him and he stood smiling at me, watching me. He led me back to the group of young men. I was trying to think hard, but the material I had to think with was slippery. Maybe a joke was being played on me?

"Say," the chief asked me suddenly, "do you like riddles?"

I felt that I was playing a game with little boys and I said:

"Well, yes. But I'm not too good at them. . . ."

"I'd like to ask you one," the chief said.

"Well, try me."

"What's smaller than an ant's mouth?"

I thought a moment and said:

"The ant's finger."

There was a moment's silence. The young men began asking, I gathered, what I'd said and, when the chief translated my answer for them, they burst into wild laughter, clapping their hands. The chief poured me another glass of beer.

"You are clever," he said.

"Was that the right answer?" I asked.

"It *could* be," the chief conceded. "The right answer is the food that goes into the ant's mouth. But if the ant had a finger, his finger would have to be smaller than his mouth."

A furious discussion took place between the young men and the chief; they spoke in their tribal tongue and finally the chief rose, pushed his forefinger into his mouth to demonstrate that what I had said was true. Evidently the chief won the argument, for the young men lapsed into silence. The chief sat and looked at me with admiration. I felt enclosed by a dream.

"You are *too* clever," the chief said.

"Oh, I'm not," I said. "But what's the mystery in that box?"

There was silence. Beyond a paneless window I saw a dark green mountain rising and melting into a gray and lowering sky. Was this the normal, day-to-day reality of a chief's entourage?

"Say," the chief asked me suddenly, "did you ever see a dwarf?"

"A what?"

"A dwarf. A little man. . . . You know what I mean?"

"No," I said.

"But you have heard of them?"

"Yes."

He rose and crossed to the paneless window, then called to me.

"Come here."

I rose, crossed, and stood beside him.

"You see that mountain?"

"Yes."

"Well, there are dwarfs on that mountain."

I held very still. Was he pulling my leg? I studied him; his face was intensely solemn.

"Really?" I asked, letting my voice spill over with curiosity.

"Yes."

I decided to pretend to believe it all.

"How big are they?"

"Well, they are so tall," the chief said, holding up his hand to show the height. "They have feet that are turned around—"

"Backward?"

"Yes."

"Do they talk?"

"No: they whistle."

"Are they friendly?"

"Yes; very friendly."

"You've seen them?"

"Yes; I've seen them," the chief said.

"But this is wonderful," I said, wondering what the meaning of it all was. Did he think that I would believe this? "What do they look like?"

"They have long, silky hair."

"Do they wear clothes?"

"Yes; of course."

"If I went up there, would I see them?"

"No. You're a stranger," he said, shaking his head. "You mustn't go up there."

"Why?"

"The dwarfs would beat you up—"

"But you said that they were friendly—"

"They are. But to *us*—"

"But suppose I took a gun to protect myself?"

"But *you* can't see them," he told me.

"They're invisible to strangers, is that it?"

"Yes. And they'd beat you up. And when you came down, you'd be covered with sores and bruises."

Well, that was that. But that mystery box . . .

"Now, tell me about the mystery in the box?" I asked him.

"That box is my protection," he told me.

"What's in it? Guns?"

"No. Bees—"

"But I *said* that they were bees—"

"No; no. . . . You don't understand," he said. "My army's in that box."

"What?"

"I have an *army* of *bees* in that box. The bees protect me," he said with deep conviction.

Silence. Was the man mad or pretending?

"Say, Nana, how many people are in your town?"

He looked surprised and spread his hands in a wide, helpless gesture.

"We are many, many, *many*," he intoned.

"But you don't know *how* many?"

"No."

"All right. Now, why do you say that those bees are your army?"

He thought a moment, then told me the following story:

"Two years ago I had a hard fight with some of the chiefs in this town. It was a long fight, but I won it. The night after I'd won that fight, I went into my room and saw that box. I'd never seen it before and I didn't know who put it there. . . . I saw those bees on it and it puzzled me. I asked the fetish priest why a box with bees on it had been put in my room. . . . You see, I knew that there was some reason for it. The fetish priest told me that the bees had been sent by God to take care of me. They were my army.

"Now, that was why I took you to see that box. . . . If you had been an enemy of mine, those bees would have buzzed you out of here. . . . They sting and drive out all of my enemies. Only last week a man came here with evil intentions against me. Those bees drove him out; he ran away, screaming. . . ."

"What did the man say to you?"

"Nothing. He didn't have a chance—"

"Then how do you know that he had evil intentions?"

"Because the bees attacked him!"

Yes; the bees had attacked the man. That was proof. . . . What could I say? He was sincere. I sat confronting men who were dreaming with their eyes wide open. Beyond the paneless window I could see the upthrusting cross of a Christian church. Yes; Christianity was here in Africa. For centuries the missionaries of the Western world had tried to alter the mental habits of these people, and they had failed. But had they really tried? There were missionaries in Koforidua, isolated, apart, white. . . . These people were black. . . . Only a fool could not see the simple lesson of that. But why had the missionaries tried at all? It may be that the motives that made them try could explain why they had failed.

And it was more than clear now why Nkrumah had to get rid of these old chiefs. Here was a man who was the head of a town of 25,000 people and he didn't know that there were 25,000 people in the town! No modern political organization could possibly have need of a man like that; only the British could use him. . . . It was chiefs like this who had, for more than a century, bartered away the mineral and timber resources of the nation for a few paltry pounds and a few cases of gin. . . . Indeed, I felt, after having talked with this chief for an hour, that the Convention People's Party had been rather kind. The party was offering men like him "honorary" positions.

I learned later—in Kumasi—that the chiefs had been demanding a second house, a sort of senate, in short, a bicameral system of government in which their "voices" could be heard. But when they were informed that they would, in that setup, be in a position to veto the legislation passed by the lower house, and that, if they did veto the wishes of the people, they would find themselves no longer "fathers" of the people, but just plain, ordinary politicians and that they would be treated as such, attacked in public, criticized, and opposed at the polls, the chiefs had thought it over and had finally said:

"No, thank you."

They were wise. They knew in their hearts that their authority came from mumbo-jumbo and not from rational thought; that it came from spells, mystery, and magic which could not possibly succeed at the polls. . . .

I stood at the front door and the chief identified himself to me proudly: he was Barima Osei Kwesi, Omanhene of New Jauben. He asked me if I had a place to stay, if I was being properly fed, if there was anything that he could do for me. I realized then why the old tribal setup in the Gold Coast had had no need of hotels. The chief was generously offering me the hospitality bred of the long traditions of his people, but he didn't know how many people were in his town. . . .

Before taking leave, I asked him:

"Those dwarfs . . . How can they walk like you and me if their feet are turned backward?"

"That?" he said. "It's easy. Watch me. . . ."

He walked rapidly backward several feet.

"See?"

"Yes."

"It's simple," he said.

"Yes; I see it is. Good night, Nana."

"Good night," he said. "And keep well."

I held his right hand between my two hands.

"Good luck to you."

"The same to you."

"Good night."

"Good night."

Thirty-One

It has been raining steadily now for several hours; there is so much moisture in the air that a piece of paper grows quickly limp. Outside the colors are white and green: white mist and rain and dark green of the foliage of the trees.

It's about six o'clock and all's quiet. The green hills, haloed by clouds, bend broodingly over the town. No wonder the mind of "primitive" man felt that there were spirits in this jungle, for it does seem that some presence, some living but invisible being is hovering here. It is, of course, the weather, a weather that dominates everything, seeping into the senses, creating a mood. One feels that one is not living in the world; one feels—Yes; I've got it. . . . I feel more or less the way I felt long ago when I first made a visit to witness a Catholic mass. . . . Imagine living in a world whose dramatic setting evoked in you a continuous mood of wonder and awe and dread! And imagine being unable, because of a lack of the capacity of reflection, to step outside of that mood and question it . . . ! One would be trapped. I'm not saying that the weather accounts for everything here; but I swear that it helps. . . . The mist and rain of these jungle hills complement and stimulate those feelings in one which one always tries to ignore: that sense of something untoward about to erupt, that feeling that one's unwanted moods are about to intrude upon one's waking, rational thoughts. At any moment a big, shiny-eyed cat might leap out of the rainy black jungle, just as an impulse toward impiety might leap compulsively out of the unconscious of a deeply devout Christian. . . .

It's only natural that a man, misapprehending the nature of cause and effect, should think that his dead father was somewhere out there in the depths of that unpredictable jungle, that that father was still watching over him, ready to encourage or censor his thoughts and actions, to bring down upon his head praise or blame. Especially would this be so if he'd both loved and hated that father, wanted his guidance and rejected it when it came as being too severe. No wonder he feels that he must pour libations continuously, offer gifts, make sacrifices. He views his ancestors as being huddled together in loneliness in that other world, seeking the most unheard-of ways and means of re-entering life, ready at any moment to find an excuse for snatching one of the living into their dreadful world of shades, of nonbeing. . . .

Is this not merely a turning upside down, a reversal of what the African lives and feels each day? To put it plainly: are not these living men projecting their hostile impulses upon the dead and converting those dead into a dead that can never die? For every tree in the jungle forest there is a taboo in the tribal home; there are a hundred thousand don'ts which they long to violate.

But they cannot violate them: the menstrual taboo must

be observed; one must turn one's stool over when leaving it, for fear an evil spirit might possess it; one must never give another something with the left hand, for the left hand is used in cleaning one's self after answering calls of nature; a portion of each meal must be set aside for the dead, or else the dead will be displeased; men must never plant seeds, for the planting of seeds is the task of women: seeds are more likely to grow if women put them in the ground; boys of a certain age must not be with their mothers; girls of a certain age must not be with their fathers; and so on. . . . Wild savages? No! Just too afraid, overburdened, too civilized. . . .

Yesterday, amidst a green and towering nature, the distinction between the objective and the subjective was wiped out; one lived, nervous and afraid, in two worlds and one could not tell them apart. The urge to kill the beast stalking in the green and wet jungle, the urge to kill the enemy who was trying to kill you and take your wife, the urge to kill the chief who was sending you to death in war or captivity—the urge to kill must have been ever-present. And how the heart must have fought against killing, felt that killing was wrong, loathed and dreaded killing; and, finally, the heart found a way to stop killing and at the same time to kill with justification, that is, kill with ritual. . . . The heart then killed to satisfy the demands of the heart, but it deluded itself into feeling that it was killing to satisfy the demands of the angry and dead father, to appease and keep him quiet. And killing like that made the heart feel better, safe once more, for the heart was really killing for its own sake, for itself—killing for itself but in the name of another. . . .

What a contagious quality of emotion must be in the lives of men who live like that. There is no way to check one's perceptions or feelings against any objective standard. What one feels, one's neighbor also feels instantaneously by the mere fact of communication, for, in that state, to feel something is to make it true. What one imagines instantly exists. What one fears comes immediately into being. Thought and feeling become omnipotent.

Hour after hour it rains and I hear the water dripping from the roof of the house. . . .

Thirty-Two

Next morning at breakfast my host, Mr. Eccles, put in his appearance. He was a tall, affable young man with English public school mannerisms. He immediately told me that he'd arranged a cocktail party at which would be all the "important" people of the area. I protested, but he said that they would be disappointed if he did not give a party.

At nine o'clock about twenty guests, English and African, stood around with glasses filled with scotch and soda and talked. British CID men, businessmen, and government men tried to get me to commit myself on the question of colonialism; I talked for three hours and said absolutely nothing. It was exhausting. . . .

After the party we drove a long way in a heavy rain to a bar where Mr. Eccles introduced me to an African businessman. He was a dour, huge, black fellow; he was in his shirt sleeves and his collar was open. He was drunk; his breath smelled like a brewery.

"You know," the black money-maker began, "after you leave the Gold Coast, you mustn't say anything that'll hurt these people."

"What do you mean?"

"We're getting along all right," he assured me. "Many people don't understand Africa. And we'll be so hurt if people laugh at us—"

"What do you want me to say about Africa?"

"Tell 'em we're getting along," he said. "You can make money. These English boys here—they're my friends—"

"What kind of business are you in?"

"Timber."

"What's your attitude toward self-government?"

"It's all right, but—" He belched. "Look, what's the use of making trouble always? We're progressing fast. . . ."

"What do you call *fast*?"

"Now, don't take that attitude—!"

"What attitude? I've only asked you a simple question."

He grew nettled, hostile. He rose and walked a few feet off and returned and sat again.

"You want a drink?" he asked me.

"All right."

"I asked you do you *want* a drink?" He was belligerent.

"Sure. Okay. I'll drink one with you."

The waiter brought over two scotch and sodas.

"You don't always know what you're looking at," he told me. His tiny red eyes glittered malevolently.

"That's true," I said. I felt that he could have slit my throat without a single qualm.

"Do you realize that these Englishmen wouldn't be here in this town if it was not for *me*?"

"I didn't know that," I said.

"My family owns timber and cocoa farms here," he said.

"I see."

"Just because you meet me in a bar, drinking, don't think that I don't know what I'm doing," he argued.

"I've no doubt about your capacities," I said.

"Now, look," he said. "Take these chiefs . . . I don't give a damn about 'em. They say that they are masters of men. All right. How do they prove that they are masters? By letting men carry them on their shoulders. You ever see a palanquin? Four men carrying one man? Well, when four men are carrying you on their shoulders, that's a visible sign that you are a master of men. . . . The world sees and knows that a man being carried like that is a master. Now, I'm no chief. I'm a businessman. How do I let the world know that I'm a master? I have a hundred men working for me. But they don't carry me on their shoulders. Now, come here and let me show you something. . . ."

He rose and went to the door; I followed him. He drew aside a dirty, tattered curtain and pointed out into the rainy night.

"See that car?" he asked me.

At the edge of an open sewer ditch was a long black sleek car whose soft white and red lights gleamed in the wet darkness.

"Yes."

"That's my car. It's a Jaguar."

"It's beautiful," I said. It was.

"That's *my* palanquin," he told me. "Understand? I've got a hundred and fifty horsepower to carry me around. And these people round here, black and white, know I'm a master of men when they see me in that car. . . . I'm *modern*. I'm no chief with half-naked men sweating and carrying me on their shoulders. . . ."

"I get the point," I said. I clapped him upon his back. "You know your way around."

We sat again; he sipped his drink and glared at me from under his eyelids.

"You don't always know who you're talking to," he said.

"That's right," I agreed.

"Have another drink."

"All right." I didn't want to offend him.

Halfway through emptying his glass, he dozed, tilting the drink in his hand. I took the glass from his numbed fingers and set it softly on the table. He sagged against a wall, mumbling. Mr. Eccles passed and I signaled to let him know that I had had enough.

"You don't know who you're looking at," the black businessman mumbled.

Well, he had made it. It was the first time I'd heard an African express his sense of how to make the transition from tribal life to the twentieth century, from tribalism to capitalism, from manpower to horsepower!

With Kojo behind the wheel, I started out next morning in a downpour of rain for Kumasi. Leaving Koforidua, we plunged into deep jungle. Steadily we mounted the curving road with red earth and dark green vegetation flanking both sides of the car. The road slanted, dipped, lifted; at times, when I stared out of the rear window of the car, the undulating highway seemed like a bridge strung between high green poles. Mile after mile rain splashed against the car windows. Suddenly there were spots of sunshine and the jungle glittered evilly. The rain came again, then stopped. The metal inside the car breathed sweat. The backs of my hands were damp. When the rain stopped, moisture still formed on the car windows and Kojo had to turn on the windshield wipers in order to see the roadway. There was not much difference between rain and sun; moisture hung in the air in any case.

The jungle reared thickly sixty feet into the air. Out of the virgin green, cottonwood trees jutted up like white sentinels. Drenched villages of mud huts, each with its rusty tin roof, flashed by. Along both sides of the road were droves of Africans walking in the rain, wearing those somber-colored cloths, black shoulders wet and bare, black breasts wet, uncovered, heads supporting huge piles of wood or charcoal or yams or cassava or vast calabashes of steaming *kenke*—walking barefooted with short, jerky, almost dainty steps. It was odd how they would stop suddenly in their tracks at the sound of the approaching car, leap nimbly into the muddy ditches at the side of the road, and stand immobile until the car had passed, their eyes staring bleakly. . . . Had they been conditioned to leap out of the way like that? Or were they simply afraid? And it was strange how the women always walked with the women, the girls with the girls, the men with the men, and the children with the children; they did not mix. African society seemed to divide, like unto like. They walked in single file, their naked feet barely lifting from the wet ground, their insteps flat, their necks straight, their shoulders square, their heads erect. . . .

Ahead the horizon was a stretch of blue mist and the rearing hills were half lost in the brooding clouds. Near Nkawkaw, some sixty-six miles from Kumasi, the jungle reached smack to the top of a tall mountain. The air was wet, sticky, yeasty. This earth and climate could grow anything; indeed, here man must wage an incessant battle against this vegetation in order not to be smothered by it. For two minutes the sun breaks through a rent in the sagging clouds, lighting up the drops of water on the palm leaves and jungle grass, and then, without warning, the world is plunged again into green gloom.

I tried to imagine the state of life that existed here before the coming of the white man. According to R. S. Rattray, who interviewed aged Ashanti men and women during the 1920's, there was little or no war among the widely scattered tribes. With the coming of the Europeans, the Ashanti began to dream of selling their slaves directly to the white men in the coastal forts, thereby avoiding the middlemen and augmenting their profits. They launched a series of crushing attacks upon neighboring tribes and conquered them and were on their way to building up a formidable kingdom when the combined forces of the coastal tribes and the British, in war after war, bled them white and laid them low. . . .

Before that, what . . . ? Life was family life. When the

head of the family died, he passed his authority on either to his younger brother or to his sister's son, and his dying words of caution, advice, admonition were remembered and followed with a tenacity which today we can scarcely conceive of. The dead ancestor was buried under the floor of the hut and when the members of the family slept at night, he visited them in their dreams, reprimanding, cajoling, demanding, complaining. The belief that the other world was thronged with spirits was the order of the day.

Yet, there was something inherently modest about these jungle children; theirs was a chastened and sober mood. The pre-Christian African was impressed with the littleness of himself and he walked the earth warily, lest he disturb the presence of invisible gods. When he wanted to disrupt the terrible majesty of the ocean in order to fish, he first made sacrifices to its crashing and rolling waves; he dared not cut down a tree without first propitiating its spirit so that it would not haunt him; he loved his fragile life and he was convinced that the tree loved its life also.

So violent and fickle was nature that he could not delude himself into feeling that he, a mere man, was at the center of the universe. It was not until the meek and gentle Jesus came that he waxed that vain!

Above all, the sight of blood exercised a magical compulsion upon the emotions of the Akan and does so to an inordinate extent even to this day. The monthly menstrual flow of women made them feel terror and dread, made them think that a child was struggling futilely to be born. The woman was believed to be the nexus of a battle between the visible and invisible worlds, and what man, in his right mind, would have sexual truck with a woman so involved with the dark and abysmal forces of a deified and polytheistic nature. And no doubt in those early days they lived a life of sexual communism, like so many other tribal people, and did not connect coitus with conception, and when a woman was menstruating or pregnant, she was a deadly creature whom one had better avoid—a tabooed being coming directly under the influence of the unseen. . . . Far, far back there must have been cults of moon worshipers among the women, for there are traces of moon images in their decorations and ornamentations even today. Silver is for women; silver symbolizes the moon; and does not the moon make the women bleed and pull the tides of the sea? On one of the trucks on a highway I saw a painted sign which proclaimed: FEAR WOMAN AND LIVE LONG. . . .

What symbols did they have in those bygone days, symbols of wood and iron which have long ago rotted in this hot and humid earth?—symbols whose forms and meanings flowed from an order of emotional logic forever lost to our minds and feelings? The ego felt continuously threatened by ghosts and goblins against which resistance had to be offered night and day. Food, and children to help to grow more food, were the crux of existence. Pray the ancestors to let us have more children so that there will be more hands to grow more food. . . .

People were valuable *per se* as people; indeed, they were a kind of currency; one could pawn one's children, one's nieces or nephews. You gave people in exchange for goods, in exchange for land; you gave people in exchange for other people; and, to own another person to help you with your daily chores was, of course, natural. When the West saw these pawns in the African households, they called them slaves and felt that these people would be fit to labor on the plantations in the New World.

Arriving at Nkawkaw at midday, I ate, rested, went out upon the narrow veranda of the resthouse. . . . Emotionally detached, I feel the spell of this land. Those still, stagnant clouds snared in the tops of those tree-clad mountains—

must not that have been an ominous sign in the old days? And that blood-red sun at sunset, what did it mean? That crawling line of ants, was it not pointing the way to a guilty man? Was not the veering flight of that bird the gesture of an unseen ancestor trying to communicate something? Why did the wind blow down that tree and make it point northward? That huge rock tilting at so strange an angle, what did it mean? And that child dying so young? Who did that . . . ? What punishment was being visited and for whose sins?

Night comes suddenly, like wet black velvet. The air, charged with too much oxygen, drugs the blood. The scream of some wild birds cuts through the dark and stops abruptly, leaving a suspenseful void. A foul smell rises from somewhere. A distant drumming is heard and dies, as though ashamed of itself. An inexplicable gust of wind flutters the window curtain, making it billow and then fall limp. A bird chirps sleepily in the listless night. Fragments of African voices sound in the darkness and fade. The flame of my candle burns straight up, burns minutes on end without a single flicker or tremor. The sound of a lorry whose motor is whining as it strains to climb the steep hill brings back to me the world I know.

Thirty-Three

These shy people of the mud villages seem to live lives extending more into space than into time. They are static; they move and have their being, but it's a kind of being that bends back upon itself, rests poised there, settled. . . . For housing, they do not build a house; they erect a shelter. For food, they do not eat for taste, but from hunger, habit, from what they recall of what their fathers ate.

There is not enough foundation to this jungle life to develop a hard and durable ego; more than ever do I know that that sudden burst of laughter which they give forth when my eyes meet theirs is acute embarrassment, a yearning to vanish, to have done with their personalities while someone is looking at them—a shyness that would fain give up and have no more dealings with strangers—a laughter that is so sweet of sound and yet so bitter in meaning. I look at a black child and it sinks right down upon the floor and hides its face, giggling. I look at a boy and he looks at me as though hypnotized, startled, awed, then he breaks into a wide, still, scared grin which he holds as he keeps staring at me, as though I'd put some kind of spell upon him. A black girl comes into a liquor store and when I glance at her, she pauses, smiles, gathers her cloth tightly about her, tucking and twisting it across her chest, bends in her knees, laughs, ducks her head, and moves forward in a shuffling and stumbling manner which keeps up until she vanishes around a corner; and her laughter is caught up and contagiously echoed by others who guffaw loud and long. . . .

The tribal mind is sensuous: loving images, not concepts; personalities, not abstractions; movement, not form; dreams, not reality. . . . Hence, institutions based upon royalty of blood are natural to that mind. Endow a thing or a person with a rolling, sonorous name, and the tribal African must needs feel that there is something noble about it. "Fine!"; "A big, big man!"; "I want a wonderful life!"; "I like your emotion!"; "I'd like to serve you.": "I like you too much!"—all of these are phrases of full-bodied emotion, passion, joy as they roll from black lips. From a strictly tribal point of view, they cannot really conceive of a political party except in the form of a glamorous leader. When they honor, adore, obey it's toward a person and it is absolute in its intensity. The tribal African does not really love, he worships; he does not hate, he curses; he does not rest, he sleeps; and when he works, his work becomes a kind of dance. . . . He transforms that which he touches into something else which is his and his alone; he dreams naturally, spontaneously, without even being aware that he does so. To live, with the tribal African, is to create.

System is the enemy of the tribal mind; action proceeds on a basis of association of images; if feeling is absent, the tribal African mind is in doubt. There is something which is lord over him and there are things over which he would be a lord. . . . A chief whom I met casually could give me but a few moments of his time; as he shook my hand warmly, he told me:

"I must go now. I must preside over a ceremony and I must make myself gorgeous for my people. . . ."

He meant that he was going to deck himself out in silk and gold. . . . The tribal African feels caught between greater and lesser powers, feeling that some are harmful and some are helpful. Hence, he evolves the notion of propitiation to aid him in controlling those powers. Since he likes to receive splendid gifts, he reasons that the spirits of rivers and trees and rocks and wind would also like to have gifts; and especially do the dead love gifts. . . . Imagine four hundred gods! Every possible combination of impulse and desire are projected and symbolized; the subjective and the objective melt; through ritual, man and nature fuse. . . . Jesus Christ? God number 401. . . .

But maybe the Africans are so biologically different that no matter what they are taught or what influences they are subjected to, their attitudes will remain unaltered. Is the African less adaptable than other races to change?

In America anthropologists have long debated what is in academic circles referred to as "African survivals." But when one sits in Africa and observes African people, the problem of "African survivals" takes on a new dimension and becomes possible of statement in terms that admit of a solution. The truth is that the question of how much of Africa has survived in the New World is misnamed when termed "African survivals." The African attitude toward life springs from a natural and poetic grasp of existence and all the emotional implications that such an attitude carries; it is clear, then, that what the anthropologists have been trying to explain are not "African survivals" at all—they are but the retention of basic and primal attitudes toward life.

The question of how much African culture an African retains when transplanted to a new environment is not a racial, but a cultural problem, cutting across such tricks as measuring of skulls and intelligence tests. Barring a racial prejudice which keeps the African at bay, he, when transplanted, identifies himself with the rational, urban, industrial (for whatever it's worth!) order of things, and, to the extent that his basic apprehension of the universe is coincident with that of the Western environment in which he finds himself, he changes as would other human beings. In short, he remains black and becomes American, English, or French. . . . But, to the degree that he fails to adjust, to absorb the new environment (and this will be mainly for racial and economic reasons!), he, to that degree, and of necessity, will retain much of his primal outlook upon life, his basically poetic apprehension of existence.

There is no reason why an African or a person of African descent—in America, England, or France—should abandon his primal outlook upon life if he finds that no other way of life is available, or if he is intimidated in his attempt to grasp the new way. (It must be said, however, that the African, in his effort to assimilate the Western attitude, starts from a point of reference that is not completely shared by the Irish, the Italians, the Poles, or other immigrants. The tribal African's culture *is* primally human; that which *all* men once had as their warm, indigenous way of living, is his. . . .) There is nothing mystical or biological about it. When one realizes that one is dealing with two distinct and separate worlds of psychological being, two conceptions of time even, the problem becomes clear; it is a clash between two systems of culture.

If the American Negro retained, in part and for a time, remnants of his background of traditional African attitudes, it was because he couldn't see or feel or trust (at that moment in history) any other system of value or belief that could interpret the world and make it meaningful enough for him to act and rely upon it. What the social scientist should seek for are not "African survivals" at all, but the persistence and vitality of primal attitudes and the social causes thereof. And he would discover that the same primal attitudes exist among other people; after all, what are the basic promptings of artists, poets, and actors but primal attitudes consciously held?

Thirty-Four

I left Nkawkaw in rain pouring from a sky that was at the level of the treetops, and the dark green vegetation filled the universe. Rice fields, rubber and coffee plantations, men, women, and children heaved into sight and vanished. I asked Kojo the meaning of those oblong smoking packages held high above the heads of the people and he told me that there were many farmers who, living far back of the highway, had no matches and came down to seek homes having fires; and, when they found one, they lighted their dry sticks or charcoal, wrapped them carefully in palm leaves as protection against the rain, and walked, holding them aloft, going home to make a fire. . . .

The area through which I was passing was thickly populated and was about forty miles from Kumasi, the capital of Ashanti, the home of the most stubborn and warlike of all the Akan people. But, if they were belligerent, they revealed none of it in their facial expressions which, if anything, seemed detached. The hard red clay road was dangerously slippery during rain and the car lurched and skidded. The Africans trudging in the rain had no covering for their heads except those lucky enough to be carrying ballooning burdens of yams or calabashes which, of course, they balanced upon their skulls. . . .

At about eleven o'clock in the morning I came to Ejisu, a village some ten miles from Kumasi. This quiet, drowsy cluster of houses was known in the old days as the "fetish capital" of Ashanti. It was from this village, in 1900, that Queen Ashantuah, the Queen Mother of Ejisu, emerged to lead a vast army against the British in what was to be the fifth and last British-Ashanti war.

In 1896 the British had entered Kumasi with a strong military force whose object was, to quote Wynyard Montagu Hall, a British officer who participated in that campaign, to "put an end to human sacrifice, slave trading, and raiding, to secure peace and security for the neighboring tribes, and to exact payment of the balance of the war indemnity of 1874." The real aim, of course, was to bring Ashanti into the British Empire by force and to forestall the imperialistic aims of France and Germany. But such intentions could not be publicly stated.

Sir Francis Scott, the leader of the expedition, informed the King of Ashanti, King Prempeh, that he was to submit himself and his people in accordance with "native forms and customs" to the Governor of the Colony, who was then en route to Kumasi.

The Ashanti knew that this meant the end of the sovereignty of their kingdom, but, the British military forces pitted against them being formidable, they complied. King Prempeh bared his body to the waist, the Ashanti sign of humility, and embraced the Governor's feet, an act of abject surrender which the Ashanti had never suffered before. The British then read a long list of demands which the Ashanti, though conquered, claimed that they could not fulfil.

The King, the Queen Mother, the King's father, his two uncles, his brother, the war chiefs of Mampong, Ejisu, and Ofinsu were at once seized by the British and shipped to the coast. The Ashanti population was numb with amazement. With King Prempeh in captivity, the British now proceeded to break up the African kingdom, making separate treaties with the tribal states.

The population seethed at what they felt to be a gross betrayal and proceeded forthwith to prepare for war. On March 28, 1900, Sir Frederic Hodgson—with Lady Hodgson, a party of Europeans, and a few native soldiers—entered Kumasi and made his famous demand for the Golden Stool, a demand which the assembled chiefs listened to in silence. The Governor sent a military expedition to hunt for the Stool and, on the 24th of April, the Ashanti signaled their determination to resist with force by cutting the telegraph line between Kumasi and Cape Coast. . . . The Governor and his party fled to the fort which was quickly surrounded by enraged Ashanti. Natives seized the Ashanti Goldfields Corporation, one of the richest in the world.

Many of the Ashanti states remained neutral or actually helped the British, but the tribes around Kumasi answered the call of black Queen Ashantuah of Ejisu and made an unsuccessful attack upon the fort. Meanwhile, the British sent out a frantic call to Central and West Africa for troops. In London the press played up the rescue of the Governor and the "besieged white ladies and missionaries," but the journalists omitted to mention that the freeing of the Ashanti

Goldfields Corporation was the most immediate objective of the British military forces. . . .

With an army of 20,000 men fanned out and blocking the approaches to Kumasi, Queen Ashantuah's aim was to stall and harass the British troops pending the arrival of the rainy season. If, however, the British tried to force their way to Kumasi to free the Governor and his party, she would trap them. . . . In fact, the holding of the Governor was a deliberate attempt to entice the British to attack the Queen's army. . . . The Queen, with her drums of state, her loyal chiefs, and her soldiers, lay athwart the road to Kumasi at a point about a mile from Esumeja.

From the fort the Governor sent native runners with frantic appeals for help. Food and water were dwindling daily. Would those desperate appeals lure the British into the old sly Queen's trap? She waited in sun and rain, praying for time, offering counsel to her chiefs and soldiers. But the British were wary; they knew that a trap had been laid for them and they camped and waited for reinforcements.

The jungle and the rain, the allies of the Ashanti, created in the British a sense of dread, making them feel that the enemy was everywhere. Illness too took its toll of the white men who looked upon West Africa as "the white man's grave." Against the Dane guns of the Ashanti, the British had carbines, incendiary shells, and 75-mm guns. The only advantages of the Ashanti were their numbers and a fanatical love of their country.

As the British troops huddled in the jungle rain at night, they could hear the war drums of the Ashanti and they could not sleep. Continuously threatening attack, with her war drums vibrating twenty-four hours a day, the black Queen launched a war of nerves against the enemy. It was rumored that she was sacrificing human beings to her ancestors, propitiating them for victory. (I checked this in Kumasi and highly placed Africans told me that it was true!) And the British soldiers knew that if they were captured, they would be decapitated and their blood would be smeared on the sacred skeletons of the long-dead Ashanti kings that lay in the dreaded mausoleum at Bantama . . .!

Throughout the rainy jungle nights the Death Drum of Queen Ashantuah would sound three times:

"BOOM! BOOM! BOOM!"

That meant that a victim had been selected, his cheeks thrust through with knives to keep him from hurling a curse at his executioners or the Queen.

An interval of time would elapse, and then the Death Drum would sound:

"BOOM! BOOM!"

And that would mean that the victim was prepared.

"BOOM!"

This single dreadful sound would indicate that the head had rolled from the victim's body. Most of these victims were captured enemies, slaves, and convicts saved for the express purpose of sacrifice. But this did not lessen the terror struck in the hearts of British troops who shivered and wished that they were home in London or Leeds. . . . Night after night they listened to those drums and they knew what was happening. And the Governor's letters appealing for aid, smuggled out by native runners, continued to pour in upon the British troops and commanders.

April and May passed. June came. From Southern Nigeria, Northern Nigeria, Sierra Leone, from England, and from Central Africa British troops were rushing. Above all, the British yearned for the arrival of white troops, for it had long been proved that black troops fared badly against the ferocious Ashanti warriors. But how long could the Governor and his party of missionaries and white ladies hold out?

At daybreak on June 23, the Governor, feeling that he could wait no longer, took his soldiers and his party and stole out of the fort, plunging into the jungle, heading for the coast. The Governor felt that any jungle fate was better than falling into the hands of the determined Ashanti.

It was on the 22nd of July that the British threw their fully assembled forces against the Ashanti and finally routed the old Queen and her army, though fighting continued in different parts of the country until the end of the year. It was no accident that a black Queen was the last Ashanti to stand against the forces of Europe in the Gold Coast, for, in the hands of Ashanti women the religion of the nation rested. It was they who instilled in the young the meaning of their rituals, their festivals, and their sacrifices. . . .

Though the Ashanti were defeated, it is doubtful if the British aim of modifying the tribal religion was actually achieved; indeed, one could ask if the British attack did not have as its final result the driving of the tribal religion deeper into the people? Just how many human sacrifices Queen Ashantuah made to propitiate her ancestors to come to her aid are not known; but, if she was offering these hapless victims as atonement to her ancestors, might she not have been led to do so because the British were attacking? It might well be that British policy stimulated precisely what it sought to defeat.

Had the Akan people been able to look objectively upon British achievements, had they been in a position to weigh and judge the value of British institutions without fear of British aggression, they might have voluntarily altered many of their religious practices without outside threat or persuasion. I'm inclined to believe that Nkrumah will achieve in months what the British failed to achieve in many long decades with their smoking guns and "indirect rule."

Thirty-Five

How different Kumasi is from Accra! A brooding African city, hilly, sprawling, vital . . . You get the feeling that the white man is far away. The population is about 70,000 and there is a mood of quiet confidence in the air. This is the heart of historic Negrodom; it was from here that hundreds of thousands, perhaps millions of slaves were marched down to the coast and sold to white traders; it was here that the Negroes stood stalwart against the British in war after war; it was here that the idea of a black empire once agitated the minds of Negroes; it was from here that raids, fierce and unmerciful, were visited upon neighboring tribes—raids that left no hut standing, no men free, no children living, no women unchatteled, no crops growing. It was from here that tribute was levied upon the outlying tribal states—states that were subjected so long and steadily that in time they felt that their loyalty to the Asantehene was being given of their own free will.

It was here that the great fetish men of the kingdom lived, each with his special array of gods, his strange powers; it was here that the bones of the dead kings reposed in brass coffins, each coffin having a "ghost wife," that is, a woman whose life was dedicated to cooking and serving food to the bones of the dead king. . . . It was here that the sacrificial victims were brought, their heads lopped off, their blood caught in huge brass pans and laved lovingly over those dead kings' bones, presumably to give them life, to propitiate their care and love for the stability and prosperity of the Ashanti kingdom. It was from here that calls went out for war—and woe to the chief who refused to furnish his quota of troops, slaves, carriers, gold, and sacrificial victims. . . .

The Ashanti, short, black, reddish of eye and quick of

tongue, is a hard man to deal with. He stands rooted in the world of his strange culture and looks out at you, waiting, judging. He kowtows to no standard but that of his own pride. Christian church steeples rise through the white mist from the hills of the city, but the mood of the people is pagan. The symbol of the Golden Stool—upon which no man sits but which itself lies upon its side upon a special throne of its own—is the magic that makes more than a million people one. Ashanti is vaguely Oriental; there is something hidden here, a soul that shrinks from revealing itself. The Ashanti are polite, but aloof, willing to do business with you, but when business is over, they turn from you. They will learn the codes of the Western world and will practice them; but when day is done they go back to their own.

Kumasi is the core of what young Africans love to term "Divine Communism"; it is here that the matrilineal conception of the family rules in matters pertaining to inheritance and descent, where the nephew or brother inherits the stool, where, even if you don't work, you can eat, that is, if you're black and belong to the clan. It's here that even until today society is basically religious, military, and political—all one organic whole under a fierce patriarchal leadership sanctioned by the "mystic" powers of woman. The law that obtains in the family is the religion and the constitution of the state. In that society all men are soldiers and are sworn from infancy to die for the state; all women are destined by the magic of the moon and the stars to bear many children, to rear them and transmit to them the religion of the state. No man is free unless he accepts society's grim mandates; and no man would dream of violating the taboos, which are many and varied; if he did violate them, he'd be put beyond the pale. . . .

With the exception of a mission society here and there, the main streets are lined with European stores: The United

Africa Company, the United Trading Company, Barclays Bank, the British Bank of West Africa, Kingsway Stores, etc. As in Accra, there are many Indian and Syrian establishments. African business firms are conspicuous by their shabby triviality. Less vibrant than Takoradi, moodier than Accra, dreamier than Koforidua, Kumasi has huge black vultures wheeling in its cloudy sky all day long.

I stopped at a dank and musty African hotel. Night fell and a clamor rose from the street below my window. Children screeched and played games. Downstairs a band played Western dance music. From far off came the dull throb of a beating drum. Tired, I closed my eyes and, it seemed, a moment later I was awake and staring at a dull, daylight sky.

It's six o'clock, but the streets are alive. Out of my hotel window I see an African family beginning the day in their front yard, which is a combination of bathroom, kitchen, dining room, and living room. The mother, nude to the waist, is bent over washing dishes in a tin pan that rests upon the red clay ground. An old woman sits on her stool and is combing her hair. Another woman kneels and is fanning a charcoal fire. A man is chopping kindling. Three children are squatting on the red earth, playing. A tall black girl is pounding corn in a vast wooden vat.

Enervated from the heat and dampness, I had to urge myself against my will to visit the offices of the leading opposition paper, the *Ashanti Pioneer*. The editor turned out to be fluent, putting himself at my disposal.

"How are things looking to you?" I asked him. "How do you feel about these impending changes?"

He drew a deep breath, shot me a glance, then laughed an African laugh; but at once he was solemn.

"What progress we make ought to be built upon our own institutions," he said. "We have our own traditions. It's a bad policy to impose the West upon us. Leave us alone to work out our destiny, to develop as our inward bent directs us."

Mr. John Tsiboe is in his early forties; he is the owner and publisher of his paper which has been appearing for fourteen years.

"What do you think of political parties as instruments of the popular will?"

"For us, the introduction of the party system was much too soon," he declared. "And that's the consensus of opinion in Ashanti. Now, it's not widely known, but the British offered us the party system before Nkrumah came along. We refused it. It clashes with our deepest traditions. We rejected it because it divides us. Our outlook upon life is based upon social cohesion.

"The Convention People's Party won, but the British are now using that party in the same manner that they once used the chiefs. The present government is for British interests; it's the same situation with the chiefs in reverse. . . .

"Until recently, I didn't know what politics was. We Africans still don't know. In its election campaign, the Convention People's Party painted everybody black and white; all who were for the Convention People's Party were white, those who were against it were black bribe-takers, agents of imperialism. . . . Our simple tribal people believed it all.

"Do you realize that, for six weeks during the positive action period, my home and office had to be protected by the police? The Convention People's Party so incited the population that I lived in fear of my life. . . ."

The more I talked with the Ashanti, the more I sensed tension. These people had once ruled themselves for centuries and now they were embroiled in something which they did not understand, something which they had no preparation to accept. Bewildered and disillusioned, they thought one moment of out-Nkrumahing Nkrumah, of going to the masses and organizing against him; but the next moment they remembered their hallowed traditions of unity and they shrank and felt guilty. They knew that the victory of the Convention People's Party had multiplied their enemies: they now had the modern, streamlined Convention People's Party against them *and* the armed might of the British.

Next morning I visited the British District Commissioner's office to pay my respects, a formality with which foreigners were supposed to comply. I found a stoutish, brisk, pleasant enough man. Our chat was interrupted when his telephone rang.

"Excuse me a moment, will you?" he asked me.

"Go right ahead," I said.

He listened at some length on the phone, then sighed and said into the transmitter:

"I say, let me call you back, eh? Good-bye."

He hung up and turned to me.

"Here's a typical problem," he told me. "That was a call from a Fanti delegation. Now, they want to send a petition to the Prime Minister. But, in the Fanti language, there's no concept for Prime Minister and they've addressed him as: Otumfuo. . . . That means The All Powerful One. Well, to say the least, that's not an accurate designation for a Prime Minister. They realize that, but they don't know what other expression to use. They're asking me to help them. . . ."

"In other words," I said, "when the Fanti language evolved, there was no concept for Prime Minister, and the Fanti people want to call the Prime Minister the name they used for their king. . . ."

"Exactly," the Commissioner told me.

It was a problem, all right, and it was not the first time in the history of the Gold Coast that these cultural differences had manifested themselves. Happily, this was a rather innocent misunderstanding.

I recalled reading that, in 1863, a subject of the King of Ashanti, the Asantehene, found a big nugget of gold and, instead of surrendering it, as was required by Ashanti law and constitution, to the Asantehene, he kept it for himself. The Asantehene, upon hearing of this, summoned the culprit to Kumasi to stand trial. The man hid his gold nugget and fled to Cape Coast and begged the protection of the white Governor.

The Asantehene sent a delegation to the Governor, and this delegation took with them a famous Ashanti symbol: a Golden Ax. Now, in Ashanti, a Golden Ax is a symbol of peace; it signifies: Let us cut down trees and clear the land and make farms in common. . . .

But the British Governor, a Mr. Pine, grew frightened at the sight of the Golden Ax. The only associations that that ax evoked in his mind was that he, Mr. Pine (maybe he was reacting to the magical relationship between the words *tree* and *ax*? After all, his name was *Pine* . . .) would be cut down from his place of power; to him the Golden Ax was a symbol of war. Accordingly, he invented on the spot a tall tale of a nonexistent treaty between him and the Asantehene; this treaty, he declared, stated that he did not have to return an Ashanti criminal to the jurisdiction of the Asantehene.

As a result, the Ashanti declared war and invaded the colony in three columns and, after a costly and protracted campaign, won the war. So serious did the British position grow that the House of Commons debated withdrawing from the Gold Coast *in toto*. . . .

Two worlds did not understand each other's symbols and they tore at each other's throats, each convinced that the other was a devil and had to be killed!

That afternoon I told Kojo to drive me to one of Ashanti's most sacred bodies of water, Lake Bosomtwe, a lake which is second only to the River Tano in the degree to which it inspires ritual, dread, devotion, and sacrifice from those who live near it. Viewed from the surrounding hilltops, it is a beautiful lake, calm, majestic, gleaming like a jewel amidst the dark green forest hemming it in. Tiny mud villages lay humbly about its almost perfectly circular rim. I was told that those villages were filled with leprosy. . . .

Clinging to Lake Bosomtwe is that same halo of legend that clusters about so many rivers and brooks and ponds among the Akan Africans. Though local legend holds that the lake has no bottom, British scientists have measured its greatest depth, which is about 233 feet. . . . It is a fresh-water lake and was no doubt formed by a meteor. The lake's most astonishing manifestation of "spiritual" action is that every three or four years there is an "explosion" deep in the depths of the water and dead fish, floating to the surface, can be caught by the thousands. . . . This so-called "explosion" is referred to by the natives as "Bosomtwe's firing his gun."

The scientific explanation of the "explosion" is quite simple. The organic matter at the bottom of the lake—rotting leaves, etc.—would form from time to time masses of gas which would, because of mud and slime, be gathered and held down. When a sufficient volume of such gas was collected, it would force its way upward rather violently to the surface of the water, creating the "explosion" that the natives so much feared and loved. The reeking odor of the gas was what made them believe that some mystic gun had been fired.

The dead fish that could be so easily gathered would be the lake's "gift" to the people. (Psychoanalysts would clap their hands in joy over this one!) So, when the lake failed to "explode," it was said that the lake's taboos had been violated. These taboos included: no metals, no oars, no paddles, no strings, and no poles could be used on the lake.

Despite the mass of written material that exists on the lake's natural idiosyncrasies, even literate Europeans as well as Africans love to dote on the lake's "mysteries." Everybody likes to dream.

I intercepted a fisherman coming up the steep slope of the lake and examined his catch. The string of fish he held in his hand looked and smelled like ordinary fish from an ordinary lake.

Thirty-Six

I was a guest at a dinner attended by the King of Ashanti, the Asantehene, officially known as Otumfuo Sir Osei Agyeman Prempeh II. He was of medium height, slender, about sixty years of age, not quite black in color but definitely Negroid of features, quick of expression, and flat of nose. His skin was pitted with smallpox scars; his lips were clean-cut, his head slightly bald. He was poised, at ease; yet, like other men of the Akan race, he smiled *too* quickly; at times I felt that his smile was artificial, that he smiled because it was required of him. During the meal he had an occasional air of preoccupation and there was something definitely cold deep down in him. He was the kind of man about whom I'd say that, if there was to be a fight, I'd wish that he was on my side and not against me. . . .

He was installed by the British in 1931 as Omanhene of Kumasi, and, in 1935, upon the restoration of the Ashanti Confederacy, as Asantehene. He struck me as a man who had suffered much in silence, as one who could really talk frankly only to his trusted and intimate friends. Though a king, a British Commissioner really ruled over him. I asked him to grant me an audience and he was kind enough to consent at once.

From a young, intelligent African I heard a queer story.

When I asked him why so many of the women who were scantily clad had markings of various sorts cut into the flesh of their stomachs, he told me that there is a legend that when women die and go to heaven, God carefully examines all the skins of women's stomachs to see if they are good enough for Him to use in His making of drums. Only women whose stomach skins are smooth, taut, and strong can be used. Hence, when God looks for a skin and sees that the skin of a given woman's stomach has been deformed, marked, cut into, He will pass it by. . . . I was so intrigued with this story that I forgot to ask my friend just why God had need of drums. . . .

Mornings dawn gray and damp. There is little or no sun. Somber is the word for the sky over Kumasi during the season of rain. Weather broods over the city; always it feels like rain, looks like rain, smells like rain; and then, suddenly, a fine drizzle falls. I'm sure that a few hundred feet in the air this city and its surrounding vegetation are invisible. Outside of my hotel window the ranging hills recede and fade in mist; now and again a slight wind agitates the tops of the stately palm trees.

To my hotel this morning came a young photographer whom I'd met in London; he is a grandson of the Asantehene and has agreed to accompany me to Mampong, a village about thirty-six miles from Kumasi. I was delighted to have him along because he, being of royal blood, could help to make the dour and brooding Ashanti open up.

Upon our arrival in Mampong, a typical mud village, we went to the local council over which the chief was presiding. We were admitted and sat while the council members conducted their business in their native tongue. The meeting adjourned and we followed the chief, Nana Asofo Kamtantea II, Mamponghene, to his office. The entourage surrounding the chief was amazing. One little boy held the big state umbrella, another carried the stool, and still another carried a bushy fan of some kind.

"Who are these boys who follow the chief?" I asked the Asantehene's grandson.

"They just follow him," he told me with a shrug of his shoulders.

But I knew better. I'd inquired to check his answer against what I'd read about entourages of this sort; I was convinced that he knew the answer. Then why was he lying? He was Catholic and was evidently ashamed to tell me that one boy was an umbrella carrier, another was a stool carrier, and that the third boy was a "soul" carrier, that is, the chief had selected this last boy for his innocence and had asked him to serve him so that he could be constantly reminded to keep his own soul in a state of innocence. . . . I looked at the Asantehene's grandson and he grew uncomfortable, then he smiled and said:

"I must show you where Okomfo-Anotchi, the great fetish man, drove a sword into the ground and no one can pull it out."

"Why can't anyone pull it out?" I asked.

"They just can't," he said. "Okomfo-Anotchi is the man to whom God sent down the Golden Stool from heaven on golden chains."

"The Golden Stool originated in that way?"

"Absolutely. And it must never touch the ground," he explained.

"And what else did Okomfo-Anotchi do?"

"Well, there's a sacred tree on which his footprints are still visible. You see, he climbed that tree and wherever his feet touched, they left impressions. You can see them."

But why had he not told me the truth about the roles played by the little boys? And he was willingly telling me about the supernatural origin of the Golden Stool!

"What has the Catholic Church to say about the Golden Stool?" I asked him.

"Oh, they say it's all right," he explained. "It has been Christianized."

I began to understand. Some things he was ashamed of because the church forbade them; other things he could accept because the church had endorsed them. I learned later that the strength of the Catholics was five times that of other Christian sects in the Gold Coast.

In the chief's office I met the Queen Mother; she was a daughter of the Asantehene and was accompanied by a tall, black woman who, I was told, was Head Woman of the Queen Mother's household. I noticed that when the Queen Mother rose to speak to me, she turned over her silver stool to make sure that no evil spirit would take possession of it.

"Why did she turn over her stool like that?" I asked the Asantehene's grandson in a whisper.

"Oh, that . . . ? It just fell over; that's all," he said lamely.

He had again evaded telling me the truth, and yet I held under my arm a volume by a British anthropologist which explained the turning over of the stool! I was to encounter this shame and shyness many times in Ashanti; they believed in and practiced their customs, but they were ashamed of them before the eyes of the world. . . .

The chief sat silent, waiting for his elders; he could not talk to me until they were present as witnesses—a universal practice among the chiefs of the Akan. I met many chiefs who refused to say more than "good morning" or "good evening" for fear that their elders would accuse them of misinterpreting the customs and traditions of the people to strangers. The Mamponghene's elders never came and we took our leave without talking to him. The Queen Mother, ever gracious, saved the hour by inviting me to her "castle" for a drink. I accepted. Her "castle" looked like a tenement on Chicago's South Side.

Seated in the Queen Mother's living room, I was struck

by the number of men and women wandering in and out without being introduced. They sat and looked at me out of the corners of their eyes, then would rise and hurriedly perform some order of the Queen Mother. While the Queen Mother and the others were chatting among themselves, I whispered to the Asantehene's grandson:

"Who are these people? Are they guests of the Queen Mother?"

"Oh, no."

"Are they friends?"

"No."

"Are they servants?"

"Well, no."

"They all live in the same household?"

"Yes."

"Are they paid?"

"Well, no; we don't pay them."

"But they work for her?"

"Yes."

"Can they leave when they want to?"

"They'd never want to leave."

"Are they slaves?" I asked him finally and bluntly.

He was irritated. He bit his lips and looked off.

"You don't understand," he said. "They wouldn't want to leave us. They live with us all of their lives. If they left, they wouldn't have anywhere to go. We feed them, clothe them; they live with us till they die. They are like members of the family; you see?"

"But other people would call them slaves, wouldn't they?"

"Yes; but that's not right; it's not the right word. It's not right to call them that."

It was slavery, all right; but it was not quite the Mississippi kind; it fitted in with their customs, their beliefs. There was no lynching. . . . I stared at the slaves. I tried to swallow and I could not. The Asantehene's grandson seemed to be worried at the impression I was getting and he said:

"We live differently; you see? We take care of these people. We give them all they need. You see?"

"Yes; I see," I said.

After a lunch of hard-boiled eggs, beer, bread, and tinned butter, we drove out along the roadside to look at the stool-makers. Entire families were engaged in this ritual-like profession, for the making of a stool was a complicated affair. They were carved whole out of tree trunks, with long knives attached to tree limbs for handles. There were no nails, screws; no measurements were taken. The black boys hacked at the wood and their aim and precision were amazingly accurate. Families selected a certain type of stool and commissioned the stool-makers to carve them for each member of the family. No one was supposed to sit upon your stool; it was yours, personally, and it was believed that, since you sat on it all of your life, some of your spirit adhered to it. When you died, your stool was placed in the Stool House along with other stools of the dead members of the family. If you were a chief or a king, sheep's blood would be dripped on your stool to revivify it; in the old days the blood of human beings was dripped or smeared on the stools. Such stools, in time, were referred to as "blackened stools."

I returned to my hotel in a heavy downpour. My room was as damp as an underground cave. Water pounded on the roof like somebody beating a big drum. Now and then a European car sped through the wet streets, making a swishing noise. I glanced out of the window and there was no sky. For hours the rain tumbled. Weather dominated everything, created the mood of living, framed the passing hours, tinted the feelings with somberness, with an unappeasable melancholy. . . .

Most of the Akan people, I've noticed, have a peculiar way of making odd mouth and head noises when engaged in conversation. For example, when we would say, "Unh hunh," an Akan would say, "Haaaan," to let you know that he was following or agreeing with what you were saying. Hence, when listening to a roomful of Ashanti talk, your ears are startled by a succession of "Haaaans" uttered sometimes with the mouth open and sometimes with the lips closed.

And why do most of the people spit all the time? Young and old, men and women, people of high and low stations in life, spit. I observed a young girl of about twelve years of age for about five minutes and she spat six times; and this spitting is not just ordinary spitting; it's done in a special manner. First, taut lips are drawn back over clenched teeth and from out through the clenched teeth comes a jet of saliva, straight, clean, strong, like a bullet from a gun, never touching the lips. The people do not seem to be ill; I've seen no one chewing tobacco or dipping snuff. Is this spitting at all times and in all places a kind of reflex? Or does the climate here engender a universal catarrhal condition . . . ? I tried, before my mirror in my hotel room with the door locked, to spit like that and I succeeded only in soiling the front of my shirt. . . .

Thirty-Seven

I spent the next few days visiting chiefs and there formed in my mind an image of a vast purgatorial kingdom of suppliant and petitioning multitudes ruled by men wielding power by virtue of their being mediators between the guilty living and the vengeful dead. What a fabulous power structure these chiefs have built up through the ages, a structure whose essence consisted of a kind of involuntary emotional slavery! Only in an illiterate society could these "fathers" of the people have derived so much absolute authority from their exploitation of the loyalty, of the love and fear that men feel for their mothers and fathers. How these poor, half-naked beings rushed compulsively to obey their chiefs' interpretations of a menacing and vindictive shadow world whose emotional claims they could not conceive of questioning or denying . . . !

One chief's house was like another. One part of a vast, sprawling rectangle was given over to the living compound, another to the women and children. (Each chief, according to his wealth, had a houseful of wives; he also had wives who did not live with him.) Then there was the inevitable meeting hall, and, lastly, a police station. . . . And, somewhere usually more or less out of sight, was the Stool House holding the precious ancestral trinkets about which the spirits of the long dead were supposed to hover or could be persuaded to do so. In full view were the huge state drums used to summon the populace in tonal rhythms of joy, anger, or alarm. . . . No one was supposed to play upon those drums unless authorized to do so; to tamper with them irreverently merited a penalty of imprisonment. (In the old days the penalty was death.)

Some of the chiefs were literate; most of them were not. Inside of his rectangular building was a courtyard in which, at most all hours, large or small crowds of natives gathered, arguing, or waiting for an audience with the chief. The so-called "enstooling" and "destooling" of chiefs provided one of the most popular, passionate, and chronic activities of the colony. Hardly a day passed but what some chief somewhere, on a cloudy pretext whose density would be difficult to grasp by an outsider, was tossed out of his august spiritual position and some other aspirant placed on the stool in his stead. Though the chief, in theory, partook of the divine while he was in a position to mediate between the living and the dead, the moment he was off the stool he was no longer considered divine; indeed, he was someone to fear, for he might begin scheming at once to regain possession of the stool. "Destooled" chiefs, therefore, were urged to get as far as possible from the scene of their former divine activities. . . .

It struck me that the attitude toward these "destooled" chiefs was remarkably like that of their attitude toward the dead itself: nothing but harm could be expected from them, it seemed. And, being alive, they were not nearly as easily propitiated as the dead. It often occurred to me, while in the Gold Coast mulling over these mystic matters, that a dear dead friend, or brother, or father would be of much more benefit to the living than a living, sentient dear friend, or brother, or father. The dead had access to spirits that, for a reason no one could really satisfactorily explain, insisted on hanging around and haunting the living. I was certain that there was some gross misinterpretation here, for I could not conceive of a dead Ashanti, if he had any real intelligence at all, wanting to hover spiritually amidst these mud huts and rain and poverty and disease when he had entry to all the vast and interesting worlds far from the sodden high rain forest of British West Africa. . . .

There is, however, one great stroke of luck which the Akan dead have performed for the living. Since it is supposed that the dead and not the living own the land upon which the living dwell, the living are not at liberty to dispose of that land. If there is any issue about which an Ashanti will fight, it is about the disposition of the land upon which he lives, for he does not feel that it belongs to him. He is merely holding it in trust, cultivating it, and, when he dies, it is to be passed on to his or the tribe's children. This fact, plus that of the climate, has kept the white settler out of the high rain forest and has spared the inhabitants of the Gold

Coast the agony of Kenya's Mau Mau making a war to recapture stolen ancestral lands. . . .

The dubious nature of land ownership has, however, mitigated against social and economic development in other directions. Since nobody in particular owns the land, no bank will advance money upon it. Land can be leased only, except in certain sections of the Colony area where Christianity has taken shallow root. Hence, though the British have gobbled up most of the rich gold and diamond mines, their right to those properties is limited to designated stretches of time.

The tracing of boundaries between plots of land was always a matter of sharp conflict. Land litigation is, therefore, one of the most widespread sources of legal activity in the Gold Coast. Lawsuits over narrow and almost profitless bits of land have been known to drag on year after year and the legal expenses would rise far beyond the value of the land in dispute.

The African attitude in legal matters is strange, one might almost say, idealistic. When he goes to law it is not only to obtain what he thinks is his right, but he wants that right done in a certain and particular manner. There was a story of an American who gave his "t'ief" man, that is, the man who slept on the porch of the American's house at night and watched for thieves, a Sears, Roebuck catalogue. A friend of the "t'ief" man borrowed the catalogue and, after many warnings, refused to return it. The "t'ief" man approached his American employer and told him that he was forthwith starting legal proceedings against his friend for the recovery of the catalogue. The American, feeling that such massive legal machinery was not needed to recover so trifling an object, offered to replace the catalogue, but the "t'ief" man would have none of it. He insisted upon going through with his legal action and did eventually repossess his valued catalogue, much to his pride and joy. He felt that he had vindicated himself, had proved his "right," which, to him, was a precious thing indeed.

Typical of a broader outlook and a more intelligent order of chiefs is one called the Efiduasihene, Nana Kwame Dua Awere II. Efiduasi is a little village (population indeterminate) of swish huts and is the center of trade and agriculture for an area which has a radius of ten miles. Sitting in his stuffy little office surrounded by his illiterate elders, the chief complained bitterly that his people were leaving the land in droves to go to the cities where life was more interesting. He frankly admitted that life in the villages was hard, that there were no modern amenities to lighten the burden, no conveniences for transportation, communication, etc. Yet, he pointed out, the government was crying out for the villages to grow more food.

The chief is president of the local council which has a membership of twenty-one, all of whom are members of the Convention People's Party. He has achieved a rare sort of psychological detachment about his position and spoke about it without lamenting.

"It's hard for people to understand that what has happened to us in the past was done by the chiefs. The rise of our way of life was inspired by the chiefs. All crafts were under their leadership; the goldsmiths, the silversmiths, the blacksmiths—all trades were at the behest of the chief, and the people were loyal to him." He paused and pointed openly to the half-clad men who sat around him, smiling and not understanding a word of what was being said. "Now, take these men . . . All of them are older than I am. Yet I'm their chief. They serve me willingly. I don't ask them to; their serving me is the meaning of their lives. They want me to dress up in these bright garments. It's their sense of what's good; they yearn for something to serve, to fight for, to maintain. . . . You see? Their loyalty to the Stool is deep and genuine. They cannot grasp politics. Yet, history is making severe demands upon us and we are not prepared. How will this illiteracy fit into the machine age?

"Yet, I don't see the end of the chief. He's closer to the people than anyone else. I'm convinced that it will take a long time for the social habits of the people to die out. The clan spirit is strong. We must find a way to bridge that gap. . . ."

As the chief propounded the problem, there were in full view his huge state drums which he used to call his people together. And he knew that telephones and wireless and newspapers were taking the place of those drums. But could the new means of communication equal in emotional value the things that the drums said, drums which could, at a moment's notice, throw a people into anger, joy, sorrow, or the stance to fight and die? That was the problem. The base upon which the new order had to build was so slight. . . . How could these people be taken from these ancestral moorings and be made to live contented lives in a rational industrial order?

"You are an American," the chief said to me. "You fellows are, in a sense, our brothers. You've made the leap. What do you think of our chances?"

He was an intelligent man, an ex-schoolteacher, and I didn't want to misguide him. He had me stumped. The problems involved were stupendous. Above all, I had to disabuse him of the illusion that American Negroes had attained a kind of paradise, had solved all of their problems.

"Nana," I said, "you don't have a race problem as severe as ours. Your problem is much simpler and yet much harder, and much more important. . . . The American Negro has done no reflective thinking about the value of the world into which he fought so hard to enter. He just panted to get into that world and be an American, that's all. The average American Negro is perhaps the least qualified person on earth to guide you in matters of this sort.

"I'm black, Nana, but I'm Western; and you must never forget that we of the West brought you to this pass. We invaded your country and shattered your culture in the name of conquest and progress. And we didn't quite know what we were doing when we did it. If the West dared have its way with you now, they'd harness your people again to solve their problems. . . . It's not of me, Nana, that you must ask advice. You men of Africa must be able to tell the West something about how to live. Get it out of your head that we are all happy and have no problems. That's propaganda. . . .

"If you go into the industrial world, Nana, go in with your eyes open. Machines are wonderful things; love them for what they can do for you; but remember that they cannot tell you how to live or what aims you should hold in life. If you have no sense of direction before you embrace the world of machines, machines will not give you one. . . ."

I was convinced that the meaning of the industrial world was beyond that chief. He could grasp it with his mind, but he could not feel or as yet know the emotional meaning of the lives of wage workers in Chicago or Detroit. The question facing him was a bigger one than merely becoming modern. Must he leave behind him his humanity, such as it was, as he moved into that industrial world, as he built his Volta Projects? Or could he take it with him? Must his culture, though condemned by the West—a culture evolved under unique conditions and over long centuries—be cast unthinkingly aside as he embraced plumbing, printing, and politics?

And what would the Akan religion be if grafted, in its present state, onto the techniques of atomic energy? The West had taken hold of the world of modern techniques with its old humanity intact, and now, in Paris where I lived, men were huddled together in indecision, numbed with despair, facing a myriad of possibilities, none of which they wanted, all of which sickened them. . . .

The pathos that rose from my talking to Africans about their problems was that their minds were uninformed—thanks to the contribution of a British education—about the bodies of knowledge relevant to their situation, bodies of knowledge which other peoples had erected at a great cost of suffering, toil, and sacrifice. Hence, I felt that almost any decision that the Africans would make, perhaps for some time to come, would be a hit-or-miss proposition, that they would have to tread ground already laboriously trampled by others. But there was no turning back; historic events had committed the Africans to change. . . . For good or ill, the die was cast. The game was up. What had been done, could not now be undone. Africa was moving. . . .

Thirty-Eight

Most of the Africans I've met have been, despite their ready laughter, highly reserved and suspicious men. It would be easy to say that this chronic distrust arose from their centuries-long exploitation by Europeans, but that explanation would not elucidate the total African attitude. They never seem to feel that they have judged a man rightly unless they project some ulterior motive behind his most straightforward conduct. I'm willing to admit that, through the centuries, the Africans have had to bear the brunt of coping with the cream of Europe's confidence men; but I'm persuaded that Europe's smooth chicanery served but to augment elements that were already lodged deep in the heart of African culture. I submit that the African's doubt of strangers, his panic in the face of reality has but peripheral relations to objective reality. Behind the most ordinary happenings the African is inclined to suspect the miraculous; to him casual signs point away from present facts.

Unless you exhibit strong, almost passionate emotion, the African is never quite sure that you are honest. Consequently, he possesses an inordinate faith in the force of mere words to dispel or hide facts. With many Africans words assume an omnipotent power. . . . Knowing that the outside world is curious and perhaps scornful of their magical beliefs, being devoid of a written history, they have devised, out of psychological necessity, methods of verbal jockeying to cast doubt into the minds of those who would try to know them. For example, in questioning one of the chiefs about the rituals of his people, I was told with a superior smile that:

"You don't know all of our secrets. You can't know them all."

"But," I told him, "Rattray and others have written pretty clearly about your religious practices."

"Oh, Rattray. . . . We didn't tell him *everything*. We told him *some* things. But we *never* tell *anybody everything* . . ." he said.

I was convinced that the many anthropologists who had studied Ashanti had put down, by and large, the basic truth of their religious customs, and I think that the chief knew this. He was trying to make me believe that the Ashanti had secrets *behind* secrets; and if I pried out *those* so-called secrets, he could at once allude to still other and more dreadful secrets behind *those* secrets, and so on. But what value have these secrets? Obviously, to his mind, a "secret" possessed the psychological value of intimidating others, of making them think that any move they might make against him would be met with some countermove of a surprising nature. . . . In short, in his eyes, you were an enemy until, by his own standards, he had decided that you were not.

At times this denial of plain facts on the part of chiefs became laughable. One chief would tell me a story that was flatly and passionately contradicted on the same day by another chief in a neighboring state. These effacings of reality went so far as to include objective evidence. For instance, with an anthropological volume under my arm showing clear photographs of "blackened stools," one chief defiantly informed me:

"There are *no* such things as blackened stools! There are no such things and there *never* were any! That's a fiction invented by the British to smear us!"

All of this dodging and denying is, of course, aided by the fact that there is no written history. If the Ashanti had a concrete manner of ascertaining what went on yesteryear, they might have escaped the more bizarre aspects of their religion, its more bloodthirsty phases. With a vivid account of what they had done, uncolored by the emotionally charged recital of a "linguist," they might have been able, perhaps, to remember their bare, objective actions and, in remembering them, they would have been made to pause and wonder, would have been able to get beyond the circling coils of abject fear. . . .

Dr. R. E. Armattoe of Kumasi, an African doctor educated in England and Germany, and who has lived in the United States for a time, told me:

"You have to open your mind to believe that these people believe some of the things that they do believe."

"Does human sacrifice still exist?"

"It does."

"It's hidden, then?"

"Yes; they don't want the British or outsiders to see or know about it."

"What do the British do about it?"

"Nothing, as long as it's kept out of sight."

"What reasons do the Ashanti offer for doing it now, this killing of innocent people?"

"It's to appease the dead ancestors. They fear that their ancestors will return."

"That sounds like a psychological compulsion."

"Could be."

"What method do they use in this killing, that is, sacrificing?"

"You see, they have a way of seizing you quickly, running your cheeks and tongue through with a long knife so that you cannot speak. They cut off your head and take your blood in a brass pan and bathe the bones of their ancestors with that blood, mumbling and praying the while:

"'Dear father, here is some blood for you, to strengthen you. . . .'"

"Do they seem calmer after such deeds?"

"My friend, I've never got that close to it. . . . I can only tell you what they have told me about *that* part of it. But when they speak of it, they're exultant, adamant. They get some kind of conviction out of it."

"Does the mood vanish after the deed, or can you detect traces of it in their everyday life hereabouts?" I asked.

"Well, when you talk to some of these people, you might notice that often they have a calm, abstracted air. That means that even while they are talking to you, they are listening, waiting to hear the advice of their ancestors. . . . Now, if you should telephone anybody here in Kumasi at night, late—and if that person is an oldtime African—no one will answer your ring until after you've rung at least *three* times."

"Why is that?"

"It's said that the dead ring twice. Only a living person will ring three times," Dr. Armattoe told me.

"Is that, then, why they don't want to talk about this thing?"

"Yes, and as long as they don't and can't talk openly about it, it means that they are still under the spell of it," he said.

Later, in talking to a British doctor who asked to remain anonymous, I learned that Dr. Armattoe's words were true.

"We don't publicly acknowledge it," the British doctor said. "But we try to interfere as little as possible with the religious habits of these people. Of course, all kinds of persuasion are brought to bear upon the local Africans to stop this business of human sacrifice; but it happens. When a big chief dies, the local police collect a barrel of human heads and haul them, like carting furniture, to the police stations. What can we do?"

If you fear your ancestor, it's because, psychologically, you feel guilty of something. But of what? That guilt, no matter how confused or unconscious, stems from one's having wanted to kill that dead ancestor when he was alive. In the life of the Akan people the thought that is too horrible to think finds its way into reality by identifying itself with the dead ancestors. Killing for that dead ancestor is a way of begging forgiveness of that ancestor; their own murderous conscience assumes the guise of their ancestor's haunting them. . . .

If the human sacrifice—and that of animals: bulls, sheep, goats, and chickens—does not represent displaced hate of the living, why then is blood the gift that will appease the dead ancestor? The staunch conviction that the dead ancestor wants blood is their inverted confession of their own lust for blood. So they feel that by killing a stranger and bathing the bones of an ancestor in the blood of that stranger, the ancestor will, for the time being, hold off haunting them, will leave them in peace. Through such collective compulsive murders their emotional tensions are resolved.

Their homicidal attitude toward the stranger is evidence of their present but deflected lust to kill the not-yet-quite-dead but prospective ancestor whose edicts they hate deep in their hearts. The tight vise of taboo-ridden tribal life, holding the hearts of simple, non-reflective men in a strait-jacket, finds its apogee of protest, its psychological balance in venting its hate and lustful rebellion upon the stranger, but that stranger is symbolically the living dead which that heart hates and fears. So crime and forgiveness for crime are magically combined in a single act of ritualized violence. . . . Men whose hearts are swamped by such compounded emotional problems must needs be always at war with reality. Distrust is the essence of such a life.

There is too an element of vicarious suicide in this psychologically complicated business of human sacrifice. The millions who support this bloody ritual know in their hearts that they too might be killed, know that they have no control over the selection of victims. Terror reigns when a king or a queen mother dies, for anyone might be seized and dispatched for service in the shadowy world of ghosts. So the sense of guilt lingers on, becoming a palpable and public thing that spreads and grows and enshrines itself in ritual and ceremony. . . . The wild and dark poetry of the human heart!

I'm in my hotel room. There is still no sun. A faint, humid wind blows in, bringing the smell of rain. Then it begins to drizzle; soon the fuzzy water thickens and slanting strings of rain are drenching the red clay. The city is hushed. The rain slackens, then stops; people emerge and cook and wash and talk. At this moment, in a space twenty yards square, I see: carpentering, nursing of babies, pounding of *fufu*, a game of checkers, children leaping and jumping *ampe*, a barber shaving a man, a man repairing a pair of shoes, a public letter writer scribbling a missive for a customer, etc.

Until now I'd not seen the central market of Kumasi at close range; today I decided to descend into the maelstrom. But, before going, I mounted four floors into a European commercial establishment to get a full view of it. It was a vast masterpiece of disorder sprawling over several acres; it lay in a valley in the center of the city with giant sheds covering most of it; and it was filled with men and women and children and vultures and mud and stagnant water and flies and filth and foul odors. Le Marché aux Puces and Les Halles would be lost here. . . . Everything is on sale: chickens, sheep, cows, and goats; cheap European goods—razor blades, beds, black iron pots three feet in diameter—nestle side by side with kola nuts, ginger roots, yams, and silk *kente* cloths for chiefs and kings. . . . In these teeming warrens shops are social clubs, offices are meeting halls, kitchens are debating leagues, and bedrooms are political headquarters. . . . This is the Wall Street of the Gold Coast.

Coming on foot, you are aware of a babble of voices that sounds like torrents of water. Then you pause, assailed by a medley of odors. There is that indescribable African confusion: trucks going to and fro, cooking, bathing, selling, hammering, sewing. . . . Men and women and children, in all types of dress and degrees of nudity, sat, lay, leaned, sagged, and rested amidst packing boxes, metal barrels, wooden stalls, and on pieces of straw matting. As far as my eye can reach is the African landscape of humanity where everybody did everything at once.

I paused at a place where native medicines are sold in the form of various gnarled and blackened roots. Kojo, who accompanied me, swore solemnly that these roots could cure almost any ailment; you boiled a root—a special root for each illness—in water and you drank it.

"Did your family ever give you any medicine like that?" I asked him.

"Nasa, Massa. Not yet."

"Well, if your relatives ever give you anything like that, they'll be making sacrifices to you, asking you to forgive them."

Kojo was startled for a moment, then he burst into a loud and long laugh.

The market's most amazing stall contained about two hundred black men, women, and children squatting upon many mounds of charcoal. At first I could not make out what was happening, so generally black did the scene seem; only after a few moments' gazing did I see that the color of the charcoal was blending so evenly with the black skins as to create an over-all impression of pall. Slowly I distinguished whites of eyes staring at me as I stood gaping. . . .

One part of the market is set aside for the manufacture of the African toothpick, known locally as chewingstick; it's about four inches long and is kept in the mouth for hours. Men or women walk, talk, work, or just stare off into space, slowly and carefully worrying the end of the stick with tongue about teeth and gums. It's publicly done, no shame being attached to cleaning the teeth in this manner. Africans regard it about as we regard chewing gum.

It rained and cleared; then rained and cleared again; now it looks as though it would rain once more. . . . It rained.

The rain stops. Gray clouds hang behind the stately palm trees—clouds that glow with a touch of red and gold and silver, turning dark purple as the light fades. . . .

The evening arrived for my audience with the King. He received me in his palace, dressed in a native costume, a dark blue silk *kente* cloth draped gracefully about him. He was accompanied by his secretary and he spoke slowly, in a low voice, and again I had an impression of melancholy from him. He was a sensitive man and knew that his day had gone. I wondered how much of a *prisoner* he was of the rituals and ceremonies of his people. He was well informed: we talked about England, Russia, France, America, the atom bomb, and American Negroes. I asked him about the chance of the institutions of his people weathering the political storm, and he told me emphatically:

"I warned my people—I told them that they had to learn!"

While sitting and talking with him, sipping a glass of orange juice, feeling the essential pathos of his position, I remembered that if this old man, seemingly kind, fatherly, should suddenly have a heart attack and die in my presence, I'd be killed, no doubt, by his executioners and dispatched forthwith into the world beyond. . . . I'd be commissioned, perhaps, to write his biography for the ancestral ghosts of Ashanti!

Could that happen? Yes; I'd been assured by prominent Ashanti men that if the King died, every paramount chief of Ashanti would be called upon to send his quota of victims and that those victims would be furnished. . . . Lawyers, doctors, serious politicians, men of sober judgment told me that they would not venture out upon the streets of Kumasi if the Asantehene or any of his relatives died, or if any of the paramount chiefs died; they were convinced that such foolhardiness on their part would be worth a first-class ticket to the other world.

"What about the Golden Stool?" I asked him.

He spoke in a low tone to his secretary who rose and got a mimeographed sheet of paper which he handed to me. I glanced at it and it stated clearly that the stool system was a "political fiction" . . . He made no attempt whatsoever to cling to the old symbols in terms of their supernatural potency.

"I've told my people to *change*," the Asantehene said solemnly. "I've told them that they've got to *change!*"

I was more or less convinced now that he was an unwilling prisoner of the religious traditions of his people! He was a Methodist; he had been a clerk in a mercantile establishment before he'd been elevated to his position. He was no doubt struggling to find ways and means to let his people know that he was not akin to any mystic powers; but *could* he . . . ?

He showed me his portrait painted in oil by a European artist; it depicted him dressed in his most formal regalia and the canvas gleamed as it reflected the huge masses of gold about his arms, his head, and his legs. I was told later that, on festive occasions, he was so burdened with gold that he could not move, that he had to have help when he stood or walked.

"It's our culture," he told me softly.

Yes; that was the way the transition was made; religion turned into culture; holy days turned into holidays. . . .

After an hour I shook hands with him and left, heading in the car for Berekum, which lay about a hundred miles to the north and west. I was accompanied by a local member of the Gold Coast Information Service who, while we lurched over the laterite road, regaled me with information about the royal family. We were entering the tsetse fly region and the forest jungle was not as thick as it had been about Kumasi; the air was less heavy and I felt almost normal for the first time in many days. The heat was there, all right, making you feel that it would push you down, but a horizon opened out to all sides, relieving me of that hemmed-in feeling that the jungle gives.

We passed a funeral procession in a tiny village and we stopped to observe. A young man had died and he lay upon a litter wrapped in a brightly colored shroud. The women were chanting a funeral dirge and the men who carried the litter all had unlighted cigarettes in their mouths, the significance of which I was unable to determine. The procession marched slowly over the bare red earth and the colors of the cloths seemed to blend with the bloody red soil and the green vegetation. A brass band blared out a jazz tune and I was startled to see that some of the chanting girls were shuffling their feet in time to the beat of the music. I mingled with the procession for a while and I could smell palm wine on the breaths of the young men. The sun beat down pitilessly, lighting up the somber procession, outlining it against the sky as it moved off with dragging feet, threading its way past sheep, goats, and chickens. The mourners descended into an eroded gully and began to go downhill. I watched them until the vegetation screened them from view. . . .

"Tell me," I asked of the young gentleman of the Gold Coast Information Service, "is there a committee or somebody who decides who is to be sacrificed when a member of the royal family dies?"

"Oh, no," he told me. "It's all arranged in terms of ritual. You see, the executioners go about their work at the silent bidding of the Queen Mother. When death strikes one of the members of the royal family, the theory is that the bones of the sacred dead are not satisfied, that they are restless, that they are hungering for life. Now, the ritual goes something like this. The Queen Mother paints her mouth red, which is the Akan sign of acute sorrow. She then enters the room where the executioners are stationed. She does not speak. She sinks slowly to the floor and weeps. That is all. She does not open her mouth; the rest is understood. She is telling them by her silent sorrow that death has claimed one of royal blood. . . . Death is hungry and must not be allowed to devour another member of her family. Death must be fed the blood he wants, and quickly, or he would take yet another one. . . . The weeping of the Queen Mother is the signal for the dreaded executioners to go into action. . . ."

"Just how many deaths are needed?" I asked.

"That depends upon who dies," he told me. "And the exact number is a secret. I've heard some say that twelve deaths are needed for a paramount chief. Undoubtedly more are needed for the King himself."

The car lurched on. I remembered those Bible verses that my grandmother used to quote (Exodus, 29:20):

> **Then thou shalt kill the ram, and take of his blood, and put it upon the tip of the right ear of Aaron, and upon the tip of the right ear of his sons, and upon the thumb of their right hand, and upon the great toe of their right foot, and sprinkle the blood upon the altar around about.**

And (Leviticus, 17:11):

> **For the life of the flesh is in the blood; and I have given it to you upon the altar to make an atonement for your souls; for it is the blood that maketh an atonement for the soul.**

The voice of the Ashanti joins that of the human race in testifying that the human heart has need of blood. And, in the matter of this peculiar need, there is no difference between the agony of the Ashanti and the Christian. With Christ the human sacrifice is offered up symbolically; you merely have to feel it and not do it. Yet, the compulsion derives from the same burden of fear and guilt, a longing to go down and placate the dark powers of one's heart. The Ashanti sacrifice human beings; Christians offer up Christ maybe 300,000,000 times a day in the form of the mass. . . . But the blood that flows from the Cross is imaginary blood, magic blood, make-believe blood, and the blood that flows from the knife of the Ashanti is no less magical, but all too real. . . . The advantage of the white Westerner is that he found a way of killing and dodging the consequences of it; he found a way of stifling that awful need in a socially acceptable way. The African believes straightforwardly; his heart lacks the artful sophistication of the white man who shrank from the direct demands of the heart and found a substitute. Who is right here: the Ashanti or the Christian? I think that both are lamentably right, terribly childlike, and tragically human. Neither has the inner strength to stand aloof from himself and wonder at his dread; neither distrusts his irrational feelings, feelings as wild as the heaving ocean, as demanding as the sweeping and tearing wind. Neither can resolve not to spill blood to still that churning in him which he does not want. . . .

Thirty-Nine

Another sultry morning. The sun cannot be seen, but its heat can be felt through the white mist that overhangs the sky. Scores of black vultures wheel silently over the city, moving their revolving circles from spot to spot on the horizon. Sometimes they are high up and far away, sometimes they are very low, so low that you can see their scaly heads and long, sharp beaks.

I entered Barclays Bank and took my place in a queue before a teller's window. Before and behind me were cloth-draped Africans. One man had a bundle wrapped in newspaper; it was filled with pound notes; there must have been hundreds of them and they made a gigantic heap. I looked at him; he was unshaven, barefooted, and wore a tattered cloth. I was never able to tell the wealth or social position of an African by his dress. Had he entered a New York bank, dressed as he was and with such a pile of notes, I'm sure that he would have incited the suspicion of the officials of the establishment.

I started, hearing a noise behind me. I turned and saw a

young African leap into the bank through an opened window. I tensed, thinking that maybe a holdup was about to take place. But he walked smilingly forward and took his place in line. Then another African leaped through the window. . . . I relaxed. It was no holdup; it was simply some Africans' way of entering a bank. The door was too far and so they just jumped calmly through the window and went about their business.

At lunch today I was told that the Gold Coast Government was importing prefabricated wooden houses from Sweden. I said that I didn't believe that, not with all the huge forests that I'd seen in Ashanti. But a young African volunteered to take me to see the houses.

We drove to the edge of the city and, amidst a plot overgrown with tall weeds, I saw rows of neat, new wooden houses.

"Is Swedish wood better than Gold Coast wood?" I asked the young man who had accompanied me.

"No. Our wood is the best in the world," he said. "We export it everywhere."

I approached the houses and examined them; they seemed well put together, solid, but they were uninhabited.

"With such an acute housing shortage, why are these houses standing empty?"

"They cost too much; Africans can't buy or rent them."

"Haven't you got wood like this in the Gold Coast?"

"Yes; we have plenty of it."

"Then it's possible that this very wood could have come from the Gold Coast?"

"That's right."

"So, other than cut it in lengths, etc., what did the Swedes do to this wood?"

"I think that they spat on it," the young man said, laughing. "All we know is that the government awarded contracts to some Swedes to build these houses for us."

"Why wasn't this work done here in the Gold Coast?"

"I don't know. There's a lot of whispering about graft," he said, pulling down the corners of his lips. "Look, I want to show you something else. . . ."

We drove to the heart of the city, upon a hill, overlooking a race track.

"See that big white house over there?" he asked me, pointing.

I saw a vast structure that looked like a hospital surrounded by a high cement wall.

"Yes. What is it?"

"That's a home of one of the new members of the black government."

"He must be rich," I said.

"Well, he wasn't rich four years ago."

"Then how did he get that house? Did he inherit it? And what's a house like that worth?"

"Nobody knows how he got that house," the young man said. "But there's plenty of speculation. . . . He didn't inherit any money. A few years ago he was making two pounds a week as a newspaper reporter. The house cost fifteen thousand pounds. . . ."

"You seem to be hinting at widespread corruption in politics here."

"I'm doing just that."

"How does it work?"

"It's done mostly through the awarding of contracts for the building of roads, schools, hospitals, etc."

"Good God! And who awards these contracts?"

"A special board created by the government."

"How many members are on that board?"

"Eight."

"How many Africans?"

"Three."

"Ah, then the Africans cannot really be guilty of all this

corruption. At least, not alone. Do the Africans and the English work together?"

"No; the Africans manage to do it alone."

"But how's that possible? They're outvoted five to three."

"It's complicated and when I explain it to you," he said, "you'll have to admit that the African boys are smart. Now, there's a lot of undercover tension on that board between the Africans and the English. On the surface, you'd think that everything was all right, but it's not. Each side distrusts the other. Now, let's say that a hospital is going to be built. This board lets it be known that it will accept bids from firms all over the world to do the job. The bids flow in. Meanwhile, the African boys approach the firms submitting bids and tell each firm that it can have the job for, say, three thousand pounds. Of course, the firm wants the job. It pays."

"But the Africans can't *guarantee* that a firm will get the job," I protested. "The white members of the board will outvote them—"

"That's all been figured out," he said. "When the board votes the contract (the African boys don't care *which* firm!) to a certain firm, they keep the three thousand pounds from *that* firm and to the unlucky firms they return all the other batches of three thousand pounds!"

"Is this widely known?"

"It's talked about here and abroad."

"But how could they risk their drive toward self-government with such petty thieving?"

"Well, for one thing, they're cynical," he explained. "They've watched the British grab and conquer, so they've grown to think that anything that you can get away with is right. And, strangely, tribal customs encourage such attitudes. If one wants a favor, one gives someone something. They deal that way even with their dead. . . .

"But the African thief is not nearly as clever as his European counterpart. The African is still dealing in pennies. What is really bad about it is that the African can't be made to feel that his stealing is wrong; you can make him cautious, but not repentant. His being conquered and plundered are the two central facts of his life. He feels that he's an amateur in these matters; after all, he's never grabbed a country of four million people and milked them for his benefit for over a century. . . ."

Wherever I probed in the Gold Coast I found this sense of having been violated by a stronger power, and that the actions of that stronger power proved that might made right. . . . And too there was always this question: Can we trust that stronger power to teach us? Since so many of the moves of Europeans have been tricky, must not *all* of their moves be tricky . . . ?

This distrust manifested itself in a novel manner in Elmina, in 1953, when the local authorities told the people that they were going to "give" them "free" education, good roads, etc. The people agreed quite readily to accept these gifts. But when they learned that they had to pay an increase in taxes for them, they felt that they had been tricked! They were being asked to pay for what had been promised as "free," as a gift.

Outraged, they massed and moved on Elmina Castle to protest. The British official in charge, serving under a black cabinet, ordered them to disperse. They refused and answered with a shot that killed the white official. The police returned the fire and several natives lay dead. . . . The rest of the mob was driven off with rifle butts.

A rather peculiar economic structure has served to blunt the sense of the Gold Coast population to the realities of modern industrial life. Out of a population of 4,500,000 (1952 census), there are roughly about 1,500,000 able-bodied males of working age. Yet, the total number of actual wage earners number but 250,000. There are about 1,000,000 petty traders and farmers. Out of the 250,000 wage earners, 93,000 work for the central government, which makes government the most thriving industry in the nation. There are about 40,000 employed in mining gold, diamonds, manganese, bauxite, etc. The strength of the army is roughly 10,000. The United Africa Company employs nearly 6,000.

Most of the menial labor is done by non-Gold Coast Africans. The Krus from Liberia move the night soil; the Nigerians work in personal services. In Accra, Cape Coast, and Kumasi there is a fairly large middle class composed of teachers, preachers, doctors, lawyers, etc. It's estimated that about 200,000 migrants from French territories come each year to work in the mines, to help harvest the huge cocoa crop, and, once they have earned the amount of money that they have their hearts set on—enough to buy a wife or a cow—they return to their native haunts. Next year another and almost entirely new flood of migrants come to take the place of the old wave. . . . This almost 100 per cent turnover does not, of course, make for efficiency in modern industry. The lessons learned last year are washed down the drain of tribal life. . . .

Capitalism has to buck a strange set of conditions in the Gold Coast. Besides the land being owned by the dead and the widespread distrust of outsiders, there is the jungle in which a man can snatch a living straight from nature herself. If you drive an Akan at a pace that he thinks is too hard, he'll drop his work and head for the "bush" where he can live, maybe not as well as he could on a monthly wage, but he'll be living just the same!

In the south, in the Colony area which holds the Ga and the Fanti tribes, one finds many Western attitudes, a high rate of literacy, etc. These people have been in contact with

Europe for centuries. The Northern Territories, mostly Mohammedan, contain the most backward elements of the population, though they number more than a million. To the north is grim poverty, nakedness. . . .

The most important native industry is cocoa farming, which accounts for the bulk of the nation's income. Cocoa was introduced into the country in 1879 by a Gold Coast African returning from the islands of Fernando Po and San Thomé. Beginning with an export of eighty pounds of cocoa in 1891, the Gold Coast today supplies a third of the world's demand. In 1935 there were 950,000 acres under cultivation; cocoa farming gives employment in all to some 195,000 people, including labor communally derived from African family groups. If the cocoa industry should fail, the nation's attempt to rise out of its tribalism would be strangled. Farmers, therefore, are today battling desperately to save the industry from a blight called swollen shoot, a disease which reduces the yield of trees and finally kills them. In 1944 the disease had spread over such a large area of the country that it was feared that the industry would be wiped out. The government called in scientists who discovered that swollen shoot was caused by a virus which was being spread by mealybugs traveling from tree to tree, drinking the sap.

The only method found so far to check the growth of this disease is to cut out the infected trees, a method which aroused the opposition of the semi-literate farmers and caused a nationwide political uproar. But it was found that by controlled methods of cutting out infected trees over an eleven-year period, only a loss of about 7 per cent of the trees was sustained.

The government is now seeking a method of registering workingmen, providing them with identity cards, taking their fingerprints, etc. At first the tribal-minded suspected a white man's trick in this attempt to introduce standards of efficiency and classification of trades; they felt that the government was about to conscript them into a new war and they would not co-operate. But, as time elapsed, they saw the advantage of being identified; from tribal nonidentity, the working masses are now moving slowly toward personal identity, individuality, and responsibility.

An amusing tribal habit came to light in the mines of Takoradi, Kumasi, and adjacent regions. The clan spirit prevailing among the workers made them share and share alike in all details of life. Thus, if a boy felt that he didn't want to go to work one morning, he asked his tribal brother to work in his stead, telling his pal to use his name. The European bosses didn't know one African from another; all blacks looked alike to them. This widespread system of masquerading was not employed to cheat; its aim was simply to rest and while away the hours. And the boy substituting for his loafing comrade would not know how to do the work properly. . . .

One of the most serious employment problems in the country concerns the illegal recruitment of labor, a practice which constitutes a hangover from the slavery that was once widely (and to some extent, still is) exemplified in the institutions of the Akan. A loose sort of trade in human beings still goes on; it's not as blatant as in the old days, but it's serious enough to make trouble. This illegal recruitment is so skilfully organized along clannish lines that it's well-nigh impossible, so far, for the government to stamp it out.

At most of the northern borders, beginning with autumn, are unofficial labor agents with trucks, waiting to intercept the half-famished migrant who longs for food and work. These labor agents "buy" these hapless tribesmen by promising them food and lodging for as long as they remain under the tutelage of their "buyers." The agents finally "sell" the migrant to a cocoa farmer, for, say eight pounds.

If the migrant does not like the work, he runs off, though the farmers watch these migrants most carefully. If a migrant succeeds in escaping, the farmer has to "buy" another migrant. In some remote districts there are migrants who have been with cocoa farmers so long that they do not know where to go; in a land of tight clannishness where everybody is related to somebody, these migrants feel that they do not belong to anybody; they become resigned and quite willing to work indefinitely for their keep.

There is an obscure but potent psychological element abetting slavery; the Akan has a terror of his family line becoming extinct, which means, in terms of his religion, that an ancestor's desire to return to the world through a reincarnation of the family blood stream would be impossible. . . . Hence, slaves occupy a strange and privileged relationship with African families. The offspring of masters and slaves are considered as a legitimate part of the family. If the family line is threatened with extinction, a slave can and has been elevated to the head of the family, enjoined to keep the property intact, to pass on the heritage to succeeding generations.

There are factors in the attitudes and habits of African workers that make them rather inefficient from a Western point of view. Conditioning, stemming not from a racial, but from a cultural background makes them feel that it is not necessary to measure up sharply to certain standards of performance. This does not mean that the African is lazy; he can work, can extend himself as much as any man when he wants to, but his grasp of the world is as yet too poetic and he is reluctant to pant and sweat to earn a living, especially if the work involves digging gold out of the soil of his own earth for Europeans!

African capitalism is practically nonexistent; it seems that the African possesses little or no desire to launch ambitious financial schemes. He distrusts long-range plans; he is the most materialistic of men, wanting his share now, cash on the line. He is a close and practical dealer in small and petty trading for a quick turnover. Many Africans do not trust banks; life insurance is rare among them. But when they feel that they are working or fighting for themselves, there is no limit to their exertions. . . .

Forty

I must plead guilty to a cynical though cautious attraction to these preposterous chiefs, their outlandish regalia, their formal manners, the godlike positions that they have usurped, their pretensions to infallibility, their generosity, their engaging and suspicious attitudes, their courtliness, and their thirst for blood and alcohol and women and food. . . . Their huge umbrellas are foolishly gaudy, their never-ending retinue of human slaves is ridiculous, their claims about their ability to appease the dead is a fraud, their many wives are a seductive farce, the vast lands that they hold in the name of the dead are a waste of property, their justice is barbaric, their interpretations of life are contrary to common sense; yet, withal, they are a human lot, intensely human. . . . Let no one suppose that the knowledge that they possess about human life was lightly gained. Insights of that order are bought dearly, with streams of blood. As rulers of men, they know something that many twentieth-century rulers do not know, or are afraid to acknowledge.

I'd like to feel that, in the hoary days before the coming of the white man, they were superbly conscious of what they were doing in that fetid jungle. But, really, I cannot. . . . These chiefs dote too obviously on rituals involving babies, adolescent girls, women, mystery, magic, witchcraft, and war. I'd like to feel that they laughed to themselves when they were alone at how they duped their illiterate followers —or did they? Really, I doubt it. They were as illiterate as their simple-minded victims, so how could they have had that degree of reflective knowledge that would have given them the freedom to laugh? The odds are that they believed in it all.

But that guy (He intrigues me no end!) called Okomfo-Anotchi, that joker who evoked the Golden Stool from the sky on golden chains, that guy who drove that sword into the earth and nobody can pull it out, that chap who climbed that tree and left footprints that can be seen even now—he could not have been completely serious all the way! His deceptions are of so high an order that they imply a cosmic sense of humor. I'd like to regard him as being knowing, humanly cynical, compassionate, and deeply mindful of his people's future; I'd like to feel that when the time came for him to die, he turned his head discreetly to the wall and tried as hard as he could to repress a sad smile. But I'm afraid that that's hoping for too much. Most likely, when dying, he picked out ten or twelve people to serve him, to keep him company in the beyond. . . .

These chiefs are and were, one and all, scoundrels, some consciously, some unconsciously, some charmingly, and some with ill-humor. Yet, in a world where cause and effect rested upon a basis of magic, they were needed as mediators between the visible and the invisible. It must not be thought, though, that this propensity toward magic originated solely with the chiefs; it was there before they came; in fact, they were thrown up as functionaries as the result of the widespread belief in magic among the common people.

It is striking that all the cases of attempts at magic or witchcraft I heard about in the Gold Coast dealt with someone's trying to make something *concrete* happen. By that token, it would seem to me that the best possible demonstration against this thirst for magic would be, at all costs, an overt and highly publicized *increase in material production!* The African mind works logically, but, in the confines of tribal life, it works with the wrong material: spirits, bones, blood, funny little dolls and sticks. . . . The will to accomplish is there without doubt, and what makes verbal admonition so futile against belief in magic is that, on the emotional and psychological plane, magic does work, really accomplishes something in terms of suggestion and hypnosis. Omnipotence of thought makes it possible for the native mind to believe that it is transferring these subjective manipulations to the objective realm. . . .

Kobina Kessie, a young African lawyer, a member of the royal family of Kumasi, has lived long in England and views his country's culture with an admirable measure of objectivity; yet he assures me that the spell of the Stool House, its dread, gloom, awe, dampness, and silence are really impressive and moving things, that while in the Stool House something actually comes over you so deeply and penetratingly that you feel that you are in the presence of the departed. I do not doubt this. Confront me suddenly with a moldering pile of skulls and bones in a dank and narrow room and I would, too, for moments, feel the same. The tribal African thinks that when he confronts you dramatically with a detached human head, and you fall down in a faint, he has demonstrated some awful spiritual power. He divines that it is the spirit in that decapitated head and not the sheer horror that it evokes in you that makes you back up with a look of revulsion.

My last day in Kumasi dawned sultry and sunless. With Kojo behind the wheel, I set out for one of the big gold mines in Bibiani. Again green jungle loomed to left and right as the car lurched, dipped, slanted, curved, and mounted red laterite roads. Swish hut villages swung by, lost in the green uproar of vegetation. Occasionally we crossed a shaking wooden bridge spanning a small, stagnant river. The journey alternated between miles of cascading rain and miles of dazzling sunshine. Flanking the road were those streams of filing Africans, stripped to the waist, plodding along with gigantic and unbelievable loads floating atop their skulls.

Lying amidst dramatically plunging hills, Bibiani is a large-sized village divided into four main parts: the gold mine, the European community, the African community attached to the gold mine, and a native community rotting away in an unhealthy depression beside a huge, muddy, scummy lagoon. One can see the native section, called Old Town, a veritable city of mud, before arriving; it stretches out, dark brown and yellowish, fading toward the towering jungle. Its one main street is gouged with gullies and lined with stores selling cheaply made European goods. Lifting one's eyes, one sees the European community nestling high up in the cool hills: white bungalows gleaming among the dark green trees. Before the gold mine came, there was no village here; the natives who huddle here now work for the Europeans in their white homes high up in the hills or in their black mines deep down in the hot earth. Bibiani is a company town. . . .

In this gold mine some hundred Britishers direct a labor force of some four thousand Africans. Each year about half of the workers leave and a new batch take their places. Underground as well as above, so many different tribal dialects are spoken that sometimes as many as three interpreters are needed to know what one native is saying. When a mine sucks in natives from British and French West Africa, a Tower of Babel is truly created. The task of organizing, for political or industrial purposes, such a variety of tribes is stupendous. Floating fragments are these tribal men when they are compared with the tight, corporate unity of the Europeans above them.

I wandered down the narrow, winding lanes between the mud huts in Old Town and saw the bleakness, poverty, and dirt. Indeed, sanitation, just simple animal cleanliness, is the crying need here. The gullies, cut into the red earth by eroding water, were filled with excrement. Flies buzzed lazily in the still, hot air. Physical disorder was rampant; nothing repeated itself; the only time I saw anything in series was when I came across a batch of flashlights for sale.

I glanced up the hill at the gold mine; I could hear the faint, regular, rhythmic clang of the machinery even down here. In the mud huts life was being lived by the imperious rule of instinct; up there, instinct had been rejected, repressed, and sublimated. I passed a tall, naked black boy; he stared at me, at my camera, my sun helmet; then, seemingly unaware of what he was doing, he squatted and evacuated his bowels upon the porch of his hut, still staring at me. . . . It was clear that the industrial activity upon that hill, owned or operated by no matter what race, could not exist without the curbing and disciplining of instincts, the ordering of emotion, the control of the reflexes of the body. Again I felt that pathos of distance!

I was told that *juju* interferes with the working day of the men in the mines to a surprising degree. If a boy has a curse put on him by another boy, the cursed boy becomes terrified and must forthwith leave for his tribe to become purified. No persuasion of his more learned brothers or Europeans is of any avail. When ill, though the company maintains a hospital, many African workers prefer their own native witch doctors, believing their illnesses to be the results of spells cast by someone. They do not trust the "white man's" medicine. And, often, it is only when they are so ill that they cannot resist that many of the miners in this area will accept modern medical treatment.

That afternoon I watched the elaborate mechanical and chemical processes by which gold was extracted from rock. Endless tons of crushed ore ran over conveyer belts and poured into huge revolving bins which emptied into vast steel drums that whirred and groaned, pulverizing the ore for twenty-four hours a day. From crusher to crusher I followed the ore until finally I saw vats in which the ore had been reduced to the consistency of talcum powder. At last I came to that section where, from a shaking table covered with corduroy, water washed down a trickling stream of golden flakes into a metal pail over which stood, stripped to the waist and barefooted, a black boy keeping track of the wet gold dust. Behind him stood an armed Britisher.

"You chaps must have a time keeping track of this gold, hunh?" I asked my guide.

"How did you guess that?" he asked me.

"Because if I were that boy, I'd swallow that gold if I had a chance," I told him.

The guide laughed uneasily.

"The anxiety we have keeping track of this gold!" he exclaimed. "As soon as we discover one method they use in taking the gold out of here, they've got another. Talking about eating gold: now and then we *do* have to have a man assayed. If the armed man at that table simply sneezed, that boy would swallow a handful of that gold dust. . . . By swallowing a bit each day and recovering it, he'd make a lot of money. It's smelly but highly profitable. . . ."

The white and black men lived in separate worlds; the blacks felt that the white men were powerful interlopers from whom to steal was regarded as "getting even." Though practically all the African workers were illiterate, they had devised many shrewd schemes of getting the gold out of the mine. Those working at the tables from which gold dust trickled had to present themselves for duty completely nude; the company gave them something to cover their bodies. Despite that, they found ways of taking "their share" of the gold.

One ingenious method the Africans used in getting the gold out of the mine involved the utilization of rats. The boys would catch rats—the mine was full of them!—and kill them and disembowel them and secrete their corpses in nooks and crannies. While working, they would come across bits of gold, or sometimes they'd dig gold out of the quartz with their penknives—I saw veins of gold as thick as pencils!—and hide it until they had a pile worth getting out. They'd take the dead rat, fill his rotting carcass with gold dust, and toss his reeking body atop a heap of debris to be carted upward and thrown away. Bound by clannish ties, they could work like this with little risk of detection by the British.

One day a British guard saw such a moldering rat arrive at the surface atop a pile of rubbish. He saw a black boy pick up the dead rat with the tips of his fingers, wrinkle his nose in disgust against the foul odor, and fling the rat away. But this time there was something just a little odd about how the rat fell upon the ground. It landed with a thud and lay completely still. . . . Despite the repelling scent, the guard went to it and kicked it with his foot. The dead rat did not budge; it was too heavy! Examining the rat, the guard found it stuffed with gold. . . . It was never known which boys had been involved.

The most typical story of gold stealing related to a tribal boy working in a department where the gold was cast into bars. One day, after a bar of gold had been cast, the African boy—a model worker who had been employed for many years—walked slowly and boldly up to the counter upon which the golden bar rested, lifted it, and started unhurriedly, confidently toward the door. . . . For a moment the African guards and the European officials were too stupefied to move. When the boy, clutching the bar of gold, reached the door he was, of course, stopped by an armed guard. What puzzled everybody was that the boy exhibited utmost surprise at being interfered with and, gently, tried to disengage himself from the guard. His lips were observed moving soundlessly; he squinted his eyes; but, when he was shaken sternly, he relaxed and surrendered easily enough.

Questioned as to what he thought he had been doing, the boy told a pathetic story of a long and futile attempt to learn how to become invisible! For a hundred pounds a witch doctor had told him that, if he followed instructions faithfully, he could become invisible and be able to walk out of the mine with a bar of gold. . . . Having adhered to the witch doctor's routine, the boy reached that point where, he thought, by saying a certain combination of weird sounds, he could become unseeable to the naked eye. That was why he had so slowly and calmly lifted the bar of gold, why he had walked with such confidence with it to the door, why he had at first ever so gently tried to disengage himself from the guard, and why he had been seen moving his lips soundlessly—he'd been reciting the magic formula to make himself totally invisible!

The company has made itself completely self-sufficient, self-contained; it has its own water supply, its own powerhouse, its own schools, churches, movies, hospital—in fact, it is more than a company; it's a little city. Black life and white life flow daily around each other, not touching, yet generating charged currents of cooperation and hostility. There is no doubt but that the black boys who are working here are learning trades, slowly absorbing the techniques of the Western world. Though the government taxes the mines almost 50 per cent, the wages paid are fantastically low and the profits make it well worthwhile for these British to be here.

It is not the profits that this company makes that worries me; there is a profound wrong here creating a sense of tension and uneasiness. This black world is reflected in the minds of the white world in a strange and warped way, and the white world is reflected in the minds of the black world in a manner that is just as distorted. In the hearts of both races there rages a silent war of pride, of face-saving, of jealousy; attitudes on both sides tend to become total in their hate or distrust.

I don't say that this company ought to be made to leave the Gold Coast; the elaborate methods of industrial chemistry, the vast machine shops that are maintained, the punctuality, the order, the cleanliness—all of these are qualities that the African must learn to master. But can he learn them under conditions whose objective configurations smack of intimidation? Of black against white? Of master against slave?

I observed orders being given an African; I saw him listen, nod his head to signify that he had understood. Five minutes later the African returned and asked for his instructions again! The first time the African had not been listening; he had been exhibiting what he felt was the necessary degree of servility; he had returned the second time for the actual instructions! The emotional and psychological factors involved in the mere confrontation of the African by his white master is enough to reduce his efficiency and intelligence immeasurably. Europeans will *never* be able to command the same degree of skill, loyalty, devotion, and intelligence of the Africans that the Africans can command of their own people. Centuries of invasion, war, plunder, indirect methods of exploitation have enthroned themselves in tradition, structuralized themselves in institutions, and kept alive the sense of the conquered and the conquerors.

Repeatedly Europeans of the Gold Coast told me how

amazed they were at the manner in which the black politicians of the Convention People's Party drove themselves night and day. Naïve attitude! Those politicians were working for themselves and they knew no limit to their devotion save sheer exhaustion. It can be said that the presence of this company getting the gold out of the earth with its complicated machinery is helping the African to understand just what he most needs to learn. I've no doubt about it. In the compounds erected by the company for the African workers to live in, there is a visible improvement in local standards of living; but the same cannot be observed in the Africans' moral attitude. . . . They know that the company leased the land for a song from their illiterate chiefs. In their hearts they do not respect the British.

For several days now I've been observing, without quite knowing it, a living example of clannishness, its meaning, its merits, and limitations. Kojo, my driver, is a man of the Ga tribe. Whenever we arrived in a village or city, Kojo would disappear at night to seek lodging. But when we entered Bibiani's company town, a crisis arose. Kojo approached me, frowning, and a little intimidated.

"Massa, small complaint," he said.

"What's the matter? You run out of money?"

"Nasa. Like to find my people, Massa. I need help."

"Your people?" I asked, bewildered.

"Yasa, Massa."

"You mean your family?"

"Yasa, Massa. My brothers and sisters."

"I didn't know you had relatives here."

"Nasa, Massa. Not proper, you know. But my tribe—"

"Oh! But how can I help you?"

"Massa ask big white man where Ga people live."

I got the point. I put the problem up to the officials of the gold mine who quickly located a Ga settlement, and Kojo, smiling and happy, was sent there. . . . The members of all tribes save that of the Ga were strangers to him; he could not quite trust them and would rather have slept in the car than to have stayed among them. Kojo told me that his "family," when he appeared suddenly like that, fed him, entertained him, took him around to meet and make friends. If you are a tribal stranger, you seek out your tribe and you are taken care of. If you are a European, you seek the shelter of the European community. But an American Negro is an oddity; he has one foot in both worlds and he pays through the nose for what he gets from each.

The gold-mining officials informed me that the diet of mostly starch that the African workers eat definitely lowers their productive efficiency. After some astute figuring, the mining bosses felt that they could safely open a cafeteria and sell solid food that made a balanced diet at very cheap prices. They made no bones about the fact that it was to increase their profits that they made this charitable gesture; but, to their chagrin, the pumping of more vitamins into the African did not obtain the sought-for aim. The mining officials had failed to reckon with the temperament of the swarms of "mammies" who, with calabashes and boxes atop their heads, waited at the gates of the mine to sell the traditional *fufu* and *kenke* to the workers. When the miners began taking their meals in the company cafeteria, they naturally ceased patronizing the "mammies" who forthwith called a meeting and passed a resolution to demand that each wife exact a promise from her husband not to eat in the cafeteria! The cafeteria closed down and the mining officials are now trying to devise other means of eradicating *fufu* and *kenke* from the miners' diet, in short, some subtler means of getting more vitamins into the workers so that the production of gold bars can be increased!

Forty-One

On a sunless, sultry morning I struck out for Samreboi, the world's largest plywood and timber mill, built by the United Africa Company in 1945. I was entering an area where rain had not fallen in two weeks and red dust coated the leaves of the trees and turned them a dull, brownish tint, making the jungle green seem even more dreamlike, unreal. It was around three o'clock in the afternoon when the jungle terminated abruptly and before me lay a vision of paved streets, electric-light poles, painted houses, stores. . . . I'd arrived in Samreboi.

"Kojo, drive around a bit. I want to see what it looks like," I said.

"Yasa, Massa."

It was a vast industrial plant; everything had a look of newness. The roads had been but recently cut through hills; steel structures reared toward the misty sky; paint gleamed on wooden doorways; European cars were parked row upon row; and even the Africans I saw walked with a quicker stride.

We came to a wooden bridge and Kojo slowed the car to a stop.

"Important river, Massa. Tano," Kojo said.

"Really?"

I leaped out of the car. The word "Tano" had evoked in my mind a sense of mystery, of ceremonies of purification, and rituals of sacrifice. This was the most sacred river of all Ashanti and I wanted to see it. But, being a stranger, it looked just like any other river to me. It was about the size of the Seine or the Tiber; I walked to the bank and watched the swift, muddy current and tried to feel what others could have felt about this all too ordinary stream. I felt nothing.

I later learned that, because of this river, no goats could be kept in this area; they were taboo. Only sheep were allowed to graze and to be sacrificed. A person bringing in a goat would find himself in serious trouble.

I was the guest of an English couple, a Mr. and Mrs. Y, both of whom rushed themselves with almost frantic anxiety to show me this sprawling industrial town. Interspersed between questions of: "Have you had enough coffee?" or "Is there anything you want?" were questions touching upon politics. Mr. Y was delicate and knew that it was considered bad taste to press such matters, but Mrs. Y waded boldly in where even British officials felt it wise not to tread. . . . Her attempts to determine if I were a Communist or not almost made me laugh out loud at times.

"The poor company's losing so much money, you know," she told me.

"Oh, really? I didn't know that."

"Oh, yes. They haven't recovered their initial investment."

"I'm sure they will eventually," I assured her.

"People do not realize what it takes to build a big plant like this," she confided in me. "Now, there's the union talking about higher wages already. But they are being paid more money than they've ever had in their lives. . . . What would they have if we had not come here? Don't you think we're fair?"

"Really, I know nothing about local economic conditions," I lied.

"Managers of businesses are human beings, just like anybody else," she said stoutly.

"I'm sure of it," I agreed.

"I say," she asked me suddenly. "When you are riding from place to place here in the Gold Coast, do you sit up in the front seat with your chauffeur?"

"Oh, no. I sit in the *back*," I told her as if she had affronted me. "He's my driver."

She'd been trying to determine if I felt that Kojo was as "good" as I was! And in such a transparent manner! She had the queer notion that a Communist would have ridden up in the front seat with his chauffeur! And she felt that if I had been a Communist, I'd have told her that I did!

"Frankly, are you for or against colonies?" she asked me directly at last.

"When you put it that way, I don't know what to say," I told her.

After all, I was her guest; she was feeding me three meals a day. . . . How could I tell the lady that I thought that she ought to be back in England . . . ?

Though the officials at Samreboi were fluently vocal about how much money they had invested in this gigantic undertaking, how efficient was their medical care, how fair their wage scales, etc., they were always silent about their secret methods of regulating the ceilings of wage rates. A shy, well-spoken black boy had whispered some information to me and I checked its accuracy; it was correct. . . . There existed an unwritten agreement between the mining industry and the timber industry that each would not *exceed* certain wage rates paid to workers. In short, wages had been fixed through inter-industrial agreements.

The company holds a ninety-nine-year lease and it employs some four thousand Africans and about sixty Europeans. In the beginning, in 1945, in trying to establish itself here, the biggest problem faced by the company had been the obtaining of food for the African workers, their kind of food; cocoa yam, cassava, groundnuts, palm oil, corn, and pepper had to be brought in each evening. If this diet was not available, the workers left.

The tribal workers had to be taught how to use complicated machinery. Formerly, I was told, only Europeans operated the huge saws that sliced the many-tonned mahogany trees and a theory prevailed that Africans could not possibly do such work with precision. But now, they were proud to tell me, the Africans were handling all the machines, though the Africans were not being paid what their European predecessors had been paid!

This timber concession spreads over an area of a thousand square miles; just what had been given the chiefs in return for this vast tract, I could not learn. The region was virgin forest and the jungle was so filled with elephants and leopards that it was not safe to go alone for more than two miles, unless one was prepared to defend one's life against sudden attack. The loggers, as they penetrated deeper into the jungle, came across scattered human bones, blackened and half buried in a carpet of rotting leaves. These bones were no doubt the remains of people devoured by jungle beasts.

En route to my British host's home a woman came yelling and running across a field. She was a European.

"Hold it a second, won't you?" Mr. Y asked me.

I called to Kojo to stop.

"What's the trouble?" my host asked the woman.

"Oh, God, I'm so scared," the woman whimpered.

"What happened?"

"They just killed a big snake in Mr.——'s living room—"

"Really?"

"Oh, I'm so frightened, I'm weak," the woman sighed. "They say that snakes travel in pairs, husband and wife. Now, maybe the husband'll come back and bite somebody. . . . Do you think so? I'm scared to go home. . . ."

Overhearing this, I grew slightly suspicious. Maybe the public-relations department of Samreboi was putting over a "big one" for my benefit. Killing a snake in the living room seemed fantastic to me. I'd see. . . .

"I'd like to see that snake," I said.

"But it's dead," my host told me.

"That makes it perfect," I said. "Let me get a glimpse of this—"

"All right."

We drove about half a mile and came to a white bungalow. A scared steward came from behind the house.

"I'd like to see that snake that you killed," I told him.

"He dead, Massa."

"Well, where is he?"

"In a bucket, Massa."

"Well, bring me the bucket."

The stunned steward disappeared and a few seconds later he came carrying a bucket that was obviously heavy. The top of the bucket was covered with a white towel. Why? I did not know and forgot to ask. The steward set the bucket gently upon the earth and backed off, as though he felt the snake still lived. . . .

"Uncover it and let me see the snake," I said.

Trembling, he yanked the towel off and leaped away. It was a monstrous reptile, bluish black, curled round and round, coil upon coil.

"What kind is it?"

"He black mamba, Massa."

"Dangerous?"

"Oh, he bad, Massa."

"Did *you* kill 'im?"

"Yasa, Massa."

"How did it happen?"

"Well, Massa—*my* Massa—he chop and he sleep in living room in chair. He sleep 'fore he go to work. Massa wake up 'cause he hear swish-swish-swish. . . . Massa, he open eyes and snake coming for Massa. Massa, he jump outta window. . . ."

"And what else?"

"Massa call me. He say, 'Kill snake!' I catch stick and I kill snake, sar."

From the jerky, nervous movements of the steward's body, he was still killing that snake. No; it was no put-up job; the jungle snake had come right into the living room of the European man. . . .

Establishing a town in a dense jungle was not easy; there were no roads; to send tractors to clear away the bush was not possible. The jungle roots were so tough that even steel would bend under the pressure of tearing them from the earth. Armies of workmen, carrying their tools on their heads, had to whack with cutlasses for each inch of space. Once an area was cleared by hand, fires were lit to the east, west, north, and south to keep snakes away. In the clearing a base would be set up so that they could send another army of workers ahead still farther into the jungle. The men were inexperienced and the accident rate was high.

When they finally reached the spot where they wanted to establish the town, they offered ten shillings to the natives for each bamboo hut that was erected. Place names originated in a most interesting fashion. When gangs of workmen were building a road, they would come to a spot on a hill where, say, many monkeys were perched high up in trees, whole colonies of them. . . . The workers would send word back to headquarters that they were located on Monkey Top Hill, and such names stuck.

As in Bibiani, so in Samreboi, all the needs of the European staff had to be anticipated; water, schools, movies, electricity, all of the appliances of modern life had to be brought here or the many European workers needed would not have come.

Then there was the task of getting the tribal people integrated into the project, or else they would have simply stood by and looked on with amused detachment. The chiefs had to be assembled, sheep had to be slaughtered and blood offered to the ancestors, libations of gin had to be poured, promises had to be made. . . . When the Europeans asked for African women to work as cooks, none was forthcoming. The tribal African male fondly believed in keeping his women out of sight. The educated Africans working for the company slowly persuaded the women to come forth, and I saw them cooking in public canteens. . . .

That night I attended a party at the home of the general manager; some fifteen company officials and their wives were present. With the exception of the white-clad, barefooted, slow-moving African stewards serving drinks and sandwiches, one could have thought that one was in New York, London, or Paris, so freely did the cognac, scotch, and sherry flow. The party got under way with a blanket introduction of me to the group; the general manager intoned:

"I know that we are all glad to have Dr. Williams from the States here with us tonight!"

I was of a mind to protest my being identified as Dr. Williams, but I thought, what the hell . . . ?

Amid wild hilarity, they began telling jokes about the natives. A man began:

"You know, one of those savages working at a saw this morning had an accident. . . . He was there cutting a slab of timber and the damned fool looked up and off went a finger. I heard a commotion and went running to see what had happened, and there stood the fool staring down at his hand, blood spurting out. . . . I was so angry that I could have spat lizards. I said:

"'How in hell did you do that?'

"He rolled his eyes up at me and said:

"'Like this, Massa. . . .'

"He stuck his hand near the whirring saw and another

finger came off, flying up in the air over the machines. . . ."

The heads of men and women tilted back and laughter gushed up in the room.

"I was about to ask him how he had managed to lose that second finger, but I didn't want him to lose a third one; so I just took the monkey gently by the shoulder and led him to the doctor."

A relaxed silence ensued, then another man cocked his head, smiled, and began:

"That reminds me of the time when I was general manager of UAC. . . . The cocoa crop had come in and the place was swimming in money; those 'ink spots' had so many pounds they didn't know what to do with them. . . . One bugger came in one morning and wanted a sack of cement to make a floor for his bathroom, and he wanted a sack of fertilizer for his yam patch. . . . He laid down cash for the two sacks and hoisted them atop his head and off he went. . . . Well, the damn fool couldn't read. He plowed the sack of cement into his yam patch and mixed the fertilizer with water and smeared it over the ground of his bathroom. . . ."

Happy laughter went around the room. . . .

"So the next year he came to see me, looking all sad and bewildered. He said:

"'Massa, there musta been something wrong with that cement and fertilizer you sold me. 'Cause when I take a bath, my feet get muddy and I'm standing in weeds. And that fertilizer was no good; my yam patch didn't grow a single yam this season.'"

Laughter and the serving of more drinks. I sat with a tight smile. I was wondering if Kwame Nkrumah knew the kind of British friends he had. . . .

Another man launched forth:

"Say, did I tell you about the half-educated guy who organized a reception for Winston Churchill? Well, Churchill came to this particular colony to make a major address. This African monkey worked day and night to organize the thing, and he was perfect. . . . Everything was just right. . . . Churchill rose to speak and, as he started, a naked African woman ran into the crowd, holding one of her breasts. . . . Churchill paused and the woman ran away. Churchill resumed and the naked woman came running again, holding her breast. . . . This time Churchill ignored the woman and continued speaking. . . . But, when his address was over, Churchill sent for the African who had arranged the meeting.

"'My good man,' Churchill said, 'I know that you have a lot of customs here that we don't know about. But why did that woman run into the meeting hall holding one of her breasts, like that . . . ?'

"The African frowned, surprised. And he said:

"'But don't you know, sir? That happens every time you make a speech in London, doesn't it?'

"'Why, man, you're mad,' Churchill said, flabbergasted. 'Never at any meeting in London at which I spoke did a naked woman run into the hall holding onto one of her breasts—'

"'I beg your pardon, sir,' the African scholar protested, his eyes bright and knowing. 'I recall reading, sir, that at your last public meeting in London, at which, sir, you spoke, that, as you spoke, a *titter ran through the crowd . . . !*' "

That one brought the house down and they laughed loud and long. The guffaws would die down for a moment, then swell forth again as each person present visualized the foolish joke. They sat sniffing, sipping their drinks, well satisfied with themselves; finally silence prevailed, one of those silences which, for no reason, settles upon a group of people.

At that moment the newly installed plumbing was heard throughout the house; a coughing, sucking sound went through the pipes. One of the young men lifted his eyes cynically toward the ceiling and announced in stern tones, struggling against the laughter that tried to break through his lips:

"SOMEBODY IS BEING DESTOOLED!"

The room actually exploded with laughter. The men stood up, holding onto their drinks, and yelled. The women bent over, clutching their stomachs. It was fully five minutes before the thigh slapping and the yells died down.

"That's a hot one, eh, Dr. Williams?"

"That's a hot one, all right," I said. "God, I never thought I'd hear one as hot as that!"

I forced a smile, sitting tensely, holding my drink. Why were they acting like that? Did they think that they'd win me over to their point of view? Or were they trying to see if I'd object? Or did they take it for granted that I was on their side? (In talking over this incident with Africans in Accra, I was informed that the Britishers felt that they had been acting quite normally, that they were used to black Sirs and black Orders of the British Empire sharing such jokes and attitudes.) Well, this was Africa too; the conquerors were godlike, aloof; they could derive their entertainment from the lives and gropings of the people whom they had conquered. . . . These were cold, astute businessmen and I knew that self-government for the Gold Coast was something hateful to their hearts. On and on the storytelling continued until the small hours of the morning. At last we all stood in the humid darkness on the veranda, saying good-bye. The general manager shook my hand warmly and said:

"It was a pleasure, Sir Williams, to have you with us."

"It was an *unforgettable* evening," I said.

We shook hands again. An hour later I was in my mosquito-proofed room in a modern bungalow. My emotions and my body felt bleak. I got ready for bed, then stood at the window and looked out into the blackness. . . . Jungle lay out there. Then I started, my skin prickling. A sound came to my ears out of the jungle night; something—it was a tree bear, I was told afterwards—began a dreadful kind of moaning that stabbed the heart. It began like a baby crying, then it ascended to a sort of haunting scream, followed by a weird kind of hooting that was the essence of despair. The sound kept on and on, sobbing, seemingly out of breath, as if the heart was so choked with sorrow that another breath could not be drawn. Finally, a moan came at long intervals, as though issuing from a body in the last extremities of physical suffering. And when I could no longer hear it, I still felt that it was sounding in my mind. . . .

Forty-Two

It's said that the Tano, the sacred river, requires one human victim each year, and if it does not get it, there is trouble. About six weeks ago, it seems, there was an unusually heavy rain and the river rose to the level of the only bridge spanning it in this area. It was across this bridge that the native workers had to come from their compounds each morning. The officials of the company became alarmed because, if the bridge was swept away, the vast mill would have to close down until another bridge was built. In that event the loss of man hours would be stupendous.

Both Africans and Europeans gathered on the bank of the swollen river and anxiously watched the progress of the rising water. It was disclosed through gossip among the natives that the chief, a new one, had forgotten to sacrifice a sheep to the river that year, and that, they said, was why the river was behaving so angrily. Tano would claim a victim in revenge for its neglect; then, as the crowds stood watching, the current uprooted a huge tree which fell athwart the stream and inched its way slowly toward the bridge. . . .

The European engineers got busy at once; that tree had to be anchored or the bridge would be lost. After much desperate work, they succeeded in tying a rope about one end of the tree; but would the tree, so big and heavy, hold with just *one* rope? No! It was decided that another rope was needed, and it had to be tied onto the tree at its middle. The Europeans called for volunteers from among the Africans and none was forthcoming. The raging torrent frightened them. Finally an African from another tribe, to whom the god Tano meant nothing, said that he would try. The Europeans fitted him with a lifebelt; the man was an excellent swimmer; and, to make sure that he would assume no risks, the Europeans secured the man with an extra rope tied about his waist.

Cautiously, I was told, the man waded out toward the tree, then swam. He actually made it, tied the rope about the middle of the tree. The tree budged and the rope grew taut, like a violin string. His work done, the man reached up and caught hold of the taut rope; then a strange thing happened. Just as the man was ready to launch himself into the water, he let the weight of his body suspend from the rope; he was seen bobbing, then the taut rope shot the African into the river, like an arrow from a bow. . . . Frantically, the workmen began hauling on the rope that was tied to the man's body; they pulled it out of the river, but the man's body was not tied to it. He was lost. . . . The man's body was never recovered.

That was proof! A lamentation set up at the riverside. Tano had had its victim! You see, you can't ignore that river! These Europeans, they don't know what they're talking about, the Africans said. They think that they are so smart, but look at what they did. . . .

I went out into the jungle to see how those huge trees,

weighing many tons, were cut down. The ground was sodden with decayed leaves. In the jungle proper it was so cool that a faint vapor came from my mouth as I breathed. Solid walls of leaves and branches and creepers and plants whose names I did not know rose from sixty to a hundred feet all round me. It was so quiet that the voices of the workmen seemed muted. All kinds of insects swarmed; it was there that I saw my first soldier ant, that black, almost inch-long creature which, when sufficiently mobilized, could wipe out human life on this earth, could devour man and animal. I did not see them at their worst; there were simply long black lines of them, busy tunneling, making bridges of themselves for their brothers to pass over, frantically rushing about on their mysterious errands.

Trees, some of them forty feet in diameter, towered skyward. I was told the names of some of them: the African Walnut, Mahogany, Cistanthera, Gedu Nodor, Guarea, Cedrata, Idigbo, Opepe, Sapelewood, Iroko, Abrua, Omu, Colawood, Piptadenia, Akomu, Antiaris, Canarium, Celtis, Limba, Mimusops, Apa, Ekki, Ochrocarpus, Okan, Avodire, etc.

An eagle swooped through the skies; there came a sound like someone pounding an anvil with a hammer; it was a bird cry and it kept up for a moment, then stopped. There is a jungle denizen called the golden spider who spins a vast golden web, the strands of which are thick, wet, sticky, and glisten brightly.

That evening I had an interview with the leaders of the African Plywood Timber Employees' Union. The organization had a membership of about a thousand; it was two and one-half years old; the illiteracy rate was established at 75 per cent. The wage rates ran from four to six shillings a day; the workers got free rent, medical care, etc.

I could detect no special problems about the workers' being able to relate themselves to industrial conditions. The management informed me that they were punctual, diligent. There was but one terror: the manner in which the African drivers handled the trucks carrying logs weighing fifteen tons or more along the dirt highways. The accident rate was appalling. The logs were chained to the trucks and a sudden putting on of brakes would send the fifteen-ton logs plunging forward against the driver's cab, crushing the driver to death. Also there were hundreds of Africans, bedeviled by the problem of transportation, who would sneak rides atop the logs. I was shown a blotch of blood on the roadside where one such rider had been caught beneath a twenty-ton mahogany log. . . .

"But doesn't this awful accident rate make them want to be more careful?" I asked one of the more intelligent union leaders.

"With a Westerner, yes," he told me. "But the African believes that when an accident occurs to him, it's because of *juju*. . . . So he goes right on speeding, not caring, with death loaded behind him in the form of a tree weighing twenty tons. . . ."

The union members were athirst for technical education; the hammering of this point by Nkrumah had sunk home in their minds. Yet, almost every question they asked me about education was couched in terms of somebody somewhere beyond the Gold Coast giving them something. Does this curious attitude of dependence stem from tribal life?

"Self-reliance is the only sure way to freedom," I told them over and over again. But I doubt if they grasped what I meant.

Politics was the one topic about which they were most vocal. In a colony, trade unions are not and cannot be simply economic organizations; they must, of necessity, if they are to hold their membership, enter politics in a vitally active way. The drive toward self-government was more urgent to them than wage rates. Most of their meetings, I was told, were taken up with questions of nationalism and political strategy. Their standard of living could not be thought of as being separate from their colonial status, and nobody could ever fool them on that fundamental point.

Adhering, according to my instructions, to my itinerary, I had to leave Samreboi and head for Takoradi, that most industrialized of all Gold Coast cities. The opportunities for employment had caused this port to become clogged with migrants for whom living space had not been found. Indeed, migration was so great that there was some unemployment. The process of urbanization was reflected in the attitude of the people, their speech and walk.

Economic activity dominates life here: the building and repairing of locomotives, fishing, furniture making, house construction, leatherwork, and the fashioning of gold into ornaments, transportation, etc. Almost one-tenth of the population of forty-odd thousand work for the government or public services. Poverty is acute and stares at you from the overcrowded compounds. Detribalization has proceeded further here than at any other spot in the Gold Coast.

The inflation of prices that took place during the war has not been adjusted and the laboring masses find it almost impossible to make their scanty wages cover the bare cost of existence. Dr. Busia's *Social Survey Sekondi-Takoradi* indicates that many of the young people cannot marry in terms of their tribal customs; their wages simply do not permit it. In some instances laborers earn barely enough to feed themselves and must take on extra work after the work day is over in order to pay rent. A great part of the food that is eaten in this city comes from either the interior of the country or from Europe, a condition which augments the prices of staples.

The impulse to organize for economic betterment has

thrown up a multitude of occupational organizations whose membership is composed of fish sellers, carpenters, shoemakers, chauffeurs, seamen, sugar sellers, cooks, stewards, gold- and silversmiths. . . . (Busia's *Social Survey Sekondi-Takoradi*). It seems that these organizational efforts are really an attempt to fill the emotional void in their lives left by their former tribal identification. The African, even when he comes to the city, hangs onto his feeling about death for a while; hence, large funerals are a much desired end to one's life. Dr. Busia reports that two recent funerals in the city cost £85 14*s.* 10*d.*, and £87 12*s.*, respectively. Items for these funeral celebrations included: whiskey, beer, mineral water, palm wine, gin, food, a silk shroud for the corpse, etc.

Upon my arrival I ordered Kojo to drive me around so that I could get the "feel" of the city. Riding through what seemed a respectable quarter, I heard the yelling of men, women, and children.

"Find the place where that noise is, Kojo," I said.

"Where they act wild, Massa?"

"Yes."

The car turned and drove into a crowded compound. I got out and stood stockstill, unable to believe my eyes. Though the streets were paved and the houses were made of cement, I was witnessing the wildest funeral I'd yet seen. . . . There was an unpainted coffin in the background, near a veranda, resting on the bare red earth. Around this coffin about twenty men were running and sweating and panting and jabbering furiously. Their eyes were smeared with some black substance and their mouths were dabbed with red. Crisscrossing their foreheads were white strings of cowrie shells, cutting deep into the flesh. In each right fist was a long, evil-looking knife. They were naked to the waist and a grass skirt covered their buttocks. Around and around in a circle they went, chanting; but, at some signal, they would all halt, crowd about the coffin, pointing to it, stamping their feet; they puffed their cheeks and swung their heads from side to side with intense passion. Then they would resume their running in a circle. . . .

A woman, presumably the dead man's wife, went to the coffin and pointed to each nail. Strangely, the nails had not been driven home; it was as though they were expecting the dead man to push aside the lid, rise, and live again. Then the woman knelt and placed a small bottle of clear liquid at the head of the coffin.

To one side was a row of men beating drums, blowing horns, and brandishing sticks. Some people were prancing, others dancing, while the onlookers made wild and meaningless grimaces with their faces. I jumped; several muskets had gone off in back of me. I took out my camera and focused. A painted man came running to me.

"You take no picture!" he said, turning hurriedly away.

But another man yelled:

"No; no. . . . Stay here! We want you take picture!"

I stopped. I explained that I was an American, that I wanted somebody to explain the meaning of the funeral rite to me. I waited while they consulted among themselves. Finally they said that I could take two pictures. But, as I tried to focus my camera, the first wild man who had objected rushed forward, waving that awful knife. . . .

"Take no picture! I kill you!" he screamed.

The others caught him and held him. I stood, undecided.

"You work for British!" the wild man yelled.

"I'm an American!" I yelled back.

"You lie! You work for British!"

"I'm an *American!*" I screamed, hoping that the crowd would sympathize with me.

But the crowd looked on with detached curiosity and I knew that they would not have moved a finger if that crazy man had got ever so close to me with that knife. I started backing discreetly off.

"Naw; don't go— Stay and take pictures!" another man said.

I thought hard. People who carry on in this manner over a dead man's body might just as well get the idea into their poetic heads that I was some kind of a ghost, or a prospective sacrificial victim. One flick of one of those monstrous knives would yank me straight into the other world. I managed two more shots with the camera, but my sweaty hands were trembling. The wild man was struggling to get free from his pals.

"He be drunk, Massa," Kojo warningly whispered to me.

"Let's go," I said.

I turned and started toward the car, almost colliding with a tall, handsome woman.

"Take me," she said.

"Hunh?"

"Take me," she said again, putting her hands on her hips.

I got out my camera; I'd take a shot of her just to show this wild and mean-tempered crowd that I was a sport, a well-meaning sort of fellow. . . .

"No, no," the woman said, blocking my lens with her hand. "Take me, *me*," she repeated.

I blinked. Then I understood. She was selling and she thought that I would buy.

"Nuts," I said, whirling and making for the car.

The crowd guffawed. The painted men were still rushing in circles about the coffin. I got into the car, slammed the door and locked it. The "take me" woman was smiling invitingly.

"Let's get away from here, Kojo," I said.

A fairly well-dressed man came to the door of the car and tapped on the window glass. Cautiously, I lowered the window an inch.

"You'd better go," he said.

"I'm going," I said. "But what in God's name are they doing?"

"They're trying to frighten away the dead man's spirit," he said.

"Thanks," I said, rolling the window up again, tight.

The motor roared; the car pulled off and I felt better. I lay back and closed my eyes and tried to relax. I don't know if those painted men with their long knives were successful in scaring away the dead man's spirit or not; all I know is that they sure scared the hell out of me. . . . Next day at noon I told Kojo to drive nonstop to Accra.

Forty-Three

I cast my accounts and found that I was near the end of my pounds. Since the 4th of June I'd been reacting to the reality of Gold Coast life every waking hour.

Through a travel agency I booked passage for Liverpool for the 2nd of September, which gave a few days' breathing spell and allowed me time to visit the forts and castles on the way back to the port of Takoradi.

In response to an advertisement I had inserted in a local newspaper asking to buy an out-of-print book, R. S. Rattray's *Ashanti*, I received a neatly written reply informing me that the book was to be had; and, at once, I set about locating the gentleman who held the book I so urgently wanted. His address was in care of an educational institution; but, when I applied there, I was told that:

"This gentleman comes here for his mail sometimes, but we don't know him."

"You receive his mail and don't know him?"

"We do that for many people, sir," a mild black man told

me. "You see, many people have no fixed place of abode."

"But I thought that that only applied to juvenile delinquents—"

"Oh, no, sir. Many respectable people have no work and, consequently, no home."

"How can I locate a man with no fixed place of abode?"

"You can't, sir. You'll have to wait. He'll show up."

"But I need him urgently."

"Why do you need him urgently?"

"He has a rare book for sale. I want to buy that book."

"Oh, just a *book*, sir?" he asked, surprised.

"Yes."

"Well, I can't help you, sir," he said.

I left my address, which was a post-office box number, with the official and told him to tell the man possessing the book that I wanted to see him at once. A few days later I got a note asking me to telephone a certain number; I did. It was my man with the rare book. I instructed him to meet me in a bar.

He came wearing a dirty native cloth, holding an oblong, flat package wrapped in frayed newspaper under his arm. It was the rare book. I'd thought that maybe a thin, hungry-looking professor would have come; I hadn't expected this rather rough-looking fellow. . . . I bought the book, then asked him:

"Haven't you got an address?"

"No, sar."

"Where do you sleep at night?"

"I got a big family, sar."

"Where does your family live?"

"All along the coast, sar."

"Your family, your clan, or your tribe?"

"My family, sar. I've many brothers—"

"Blood brothers?"

"Yes, sar."

"Are these brothers sons of your mother?"

"Not quite, sar, you see. . . . But men are brothers to me, sar, blood brothers."

"What's your tribe?"

"Ashanti, sar."

"And your blood brothers are Ashanti men?"

"Yes, sar. We know and help each other, sar."

"But, why?"

"Because we are brothers, sar."

"But how did you *get* to be brothers?"

"We grew up together, sar."

The men with whom he had shared life were his brothers; men of the same generation were brothers. They knew a look and feel of the world that other men of other generations did not know. I watched him stuff the money somewhere under his dirty cloth, pull on his battered hat, and walk out. A man with no address? A nomad. . . . I regretted that I had not had time to talk with him. . . . And he hadn't seemed worried. He had brothers, not the sons of his mother, but men to whom he felt a blood relationship, brothers who fed him when he was hungry, let him sleep when he was tired, consoled him when he was sad. . . . He had a large "family" that stretched for miles and miles. . . . I tried to visualize it and I could not. . . .

Forty-Four

To think about Africa is to think about man's naïve attempt to understand and manipulate the universe of life in terms of magical religion. Africa, until now, was religious. Africans hold their lives as being sacred. And it is ironical that the men of Europe who plundered this continent for four hundred years did it in the name of religion! It was religion against religion. That is the only manner in which the insane thirst for gold and slaves could possibly have felt itself justified. The white masters of Africa were and are remarkably akin, emotionally and spiritually, to their black slaves.

The African conception of life is neither evil nor criminal; it is simply pitiably human. His conception of the state is symbolically derived from his love and reverence for the family. The state as well as the universe are symbolically conceived of in a way that is but a sweeping projection of his concept of and feeling for the family. To understand the Akan idea (and it's a pretentious, inordinately vain one!) of the state, one has to unite two distinctly different ideas: the family and the universe.

The African does not distinguish absolutely between good and evil. No matter how malignant he thought some of the "spirits" of the universe were, he never succumbed to feeling that the world as a whole was evil. Maybe he has more than paid for that mistake, a mistake that was squarely on the side of the angels.

It was only when adversity drove him to feel evil that he felt it, and the white men of Europe contributed more than their fair share to that psychological process by their wars and oppression. One would have thought that Christian Europe, discovering people serving God in an Old Testament style, would have been deeply mindful of the fact that only a nuance separated their religious beliefs from those of the African. Compassion could have served here better than scorn or bungling uplift. . . .

The state is owned by a female king, just as a child is regarded as being owned by its mother; the state is ruled by a male king, just as a family is headed and its affairs managed by a father. Hence, female kings are founders of states, the "mother" of everybody in the state; the female companion of the king is called queen mother, though she is not actually the mother of the king at all; she is either his sister or some other worthy female.

The symbolic nature of these relationships have been rather well worked out in a book entitled *The Sacred State of the Akan*, by Eva L. R. Meyerowitz (London: Faber and Faber, 1951). Though some Ashanti intellectuals sneer at what this book has to say, it does fill a void when one tries to explain what meets the eye in the Gold Coast. Thus, to the queen mother the emblem of the spiral, the sign of birth and motherhood, has been assigned. The female king is also considered as the daughter of the moon, for the moon is regarded as having given birth to the sun. The sun is then the king and the moon the queen. . . . Now, I don't believe any of this, but I see nothing barbarous in it.

The moon (that is, the sense of woman) created the universe and in that universe are seven aerial bodies—the Moon, the Sun, Mars, Mercury, Jupiter, Venus, and Saturn. Consequently, any state or universe that wants to rule must have seven parts. . . . The universe is regarded as being a mother and the basic origin of all things, families as well as solar systems. A woman's giving birth, her menstrual period, her moodiness and irrationality—all of this tended to envelop women in an atmosphere of general awe, justifying the Akan mind in projecting out upon her a contradictory and dubious mixture of honor, fear, worship, and loathing.

The moon, being the color of silver at times, made them feel that the mother must be symbolized by silver; and the sun, being yellow, made them think that the man was symbolized by gold. When a queen died in the old days, silver dust was stuffed into all the opening of her corpse: eyes, ears, nostrils, mouth, anus, vagina. And when a king died, gold dust was packed into his eye-sockets, etc.

These primal symbols, derived from the reality of mother and father, female kings and male kings, created many of the Akan details of life. The female kings introduced lamps, codes for women and girls, laws governing sexual offenses, etc., and the male kings and his advisors, in the name of their ancestors, elaborated laws and rules for the state, war, trade, etc.

The Akan people *believed* these poetic conceptions, the only conceptions available to them. Blood relations were replaced by mystical ones which were believed to be based upon "blood." In this manner came about the matrilineal conception of descent and inheritance. It was an intuitive grasp of life dictated by endemic wisdom, tracing relations between objects that really had no relations, but establishing such relations by similarity, proximity, succession, etc. I still do not believe a single word of all of this, yet I do not endorse the killing of a single flea if that flea happened to believe it. I cannot say that imperialism is right because it blasted the lives of people holding such notions. . . .

The king is the son of the sun, and is, thus, sacred. The king's greatest dangers are death and unclean women in their menses; hence, the king's food must always be cooked by men; if a menstruating woman touches a king, rites of purification and sacrifices must be made. The king wears sandals to keep his feet out of touch with the earth which contains the countless bodies of the dead.

Since he partakes of the divine, the king never really dies; his soul becomes a part of that in which it resided before it was born, that is, the sun; and that "blood" part of him becomes an ancestral spirit which can, with proper ritual, words, and sacrifices, be evoked to enter those things which were once the intimate possessions of the king. Indeed, these spirits are conceived of as being capable of eating and drinking. All of which explains libation pouring, etc.

The corpse of the king in the old days was allowed to decompose under ritualized conditions. It was placed in a coffin which had holes in its bottom and then the coffin was set over a pit; when the body fluids had all dripped out, the remainder—the sodden bones—was taken from the coffin and scraped, dried, oiled, and the skeleton was strung together, bone by bone, with thread spun of gold. These skeletons were then wrapped in costly cloths and taken to Bantama where they were jealously guarded. A stranger intruding into such a place would be instantly slain. . . .

All of this seems bizarre to me; I can't conceive of myself ever believing any of it; but, still, I don't agree that people who do believe in such ought to be declared biologically inferior!

It is thought that forty days after the death of a king, his soul reaches heaven or the African counterpart of such a place; and a great deal of joy is evinced at that period by the general populace.

The Akan, acting upon the division of the sexes, erected two corresponding attitudes to denote them: *ntoro* implies the male principle of life, and *abusua* the female principle. *Ntoro* is the semen of the male and it is believed to possess the power of bestowing spiritual qualities of a male sort. *Abusua* is the blood of the woman and it is transmitted to the offspring, and, it is believed, it is *only* the woman, in conception and birth, who transmits blood and all of its magical qualities to the child. This is the erroneous conception that buttresses the matrilineal descent and inheritance, and the practice of exogamy to some degree in some clans of the Gold Coast.

The *ntoro* outlook actuated the impulse to create armies, to wage war, etc.; the *abusua* outlook prompted the religous role of woman. Both outlooks, hedged about with numberless taboos, account for the sexual segregation that cleaves African society in twain. Out of *ntoro* and *abusua* have come a multitude of gods and rituals and ceremonies, the dreaded apex of which is human sacrifice. For example, from *ntoro*, meaning semen, comes a deep and mystical regard for water, lakes, lagoons, rivers, etc. From *abusua* springs the conviction that blood, menstrual and otherwise, possesses powers allied to the hidden energies of the universe. With the fiery sun and silver moon as an eternal background, gold and silver assumed powerful meanings. Throughout Akan society emotional values are attached to these colors and projected onto objects, natural or fabricated, having those colors or some shades of them. Kola nuts, being red (like blood or gold), occupy a higher place of esteem than just ordinary nuts; brass, resembling gold, is used to decorate state chairs if gold itself is not obtainable. This is why Africans regarded the worthless trinkets of the Europeans with such delight. It wasn't simple-mindedness that made them feel that the beads were something for which one exchanged gold. It was religion. . . .

The moods born of this apprehension of existence gave birth to a high order of simple poetry. Thus, the Earth Goddess *Assaase Afua* is addressed as follows on the Talking Drums:

Spirit of Earth, sorrow is yours,
Spirit of Earth, woe is yours.
Earth, with its dust,
Earth, while I am yet alive,
It is upon you that I put my trust,
Earth, who receives my body.

A funeral song goes:

I am an orphan, and when I recall the death of my father, water falls from my eyes upon me.

When I recall the death of my mother, water from my eyes falls upon me.
We walk, we walk, O Mother Tano,
Until now we walk and it will soon be night.
It is because of the sorrow of death that we walk.

Before the coming of the white man, matrilineal institutions conferred upon the African woman a special and mystical position. The queen mothers had the right to veto much of the men's actions. In the event of the death of the chief or king, she, in consultation with advisors, selected the new head of the clan or state. . . . With the establishment of the religously patrilineal English power, the chiefs were recognized and the women ignored. Institutions were smashed and no new ones were devised to perform their functions. The coming of the white man spelled the doom of the African woman; as Christianity gained a foothold, she became "free" but with far less real power than she had before. It is not without its meaning that the last military effort of the Ashanti was led by a black woman! And this same fact might well account for the great popularity of the Convention People's Party among the women of the Gold Coast.

Forty-Five

I visited Christianborg Castle which was built by the Swedes in 1657 and taken by the Danes in 1659. In 1679 it changed hands again, being bought by the Portuguese from the Danes, and in 1682 was bought from the Portuguese by the Danes. This swift change of ownership reflected the desperate struggles that went on between European powers in the early days of the Gold Coast. The castle was captured by

Gold Coast native tribes in 1693 and resold by them to the Danes a year later. In 1850 it was bought by the British. . . .

It is at present the official residence of the Governor of the Colony, Sir Charles Arden-Clarke. White, vast, standing at the edge of the Atlantic, it dominates the tropic, sandy, palm-treed landscape. As I entered the castle grounds, the armed Northern Territory guards came to attention. I explained that I wanted to look over the castle. Six of them spoke at once:

"Me, Massa."

They were eager because they wanted that inevitable "dash" at the end of the tour. I mounted the broad, white, spick-and-span steps and stood looking out over the rolling sea. . . .

"The ships that took the slaves to America and the West Indies . . . Where did they anchor?"

The guide pointed to the sandy seashore. "Right out there, Massa."

"And where were the slaves kept?"

"Follow me, Massa."

I was led down winding steps until I came into a narrow and dank passageway, then into small dark rooms whose only light came through barred windows.

"Are these the same windows that the slaves looked out of?"

"The same, Massa."

The walls were incredibly thick.

"Just how thick is that wall?"

"Fifteen feet, Massa."

I was told that the same iron bolts which secured the doors to keep the slaves imprisoned were the ones that my fingers now touched.

"How did they take the slaves to the ships? Is there a passageway?"

"Yasa, Massa. Come."

He pointed out the route the slaves had taken when they had been led in chains to the waiting ships.

"It was that simple?" I asked.

The guard showed his white teeth in a sad grin.

"Yasa, Massa. Very simple. But it gone now," he told me.

"And maybe you'll be free, really free soon?"

"We hope, Massa."

I looked at the chapel—it was quiet, dim, ready to cast its spell of awe and wonder. . . .

"Did you ever worship in there?" I asked the guard.

"No, Massa."

"Are you Christian?"

"I'se Moslem," he said.

"And what about the Christian's God?"

"He all right, Massa," the guard said, laughing.

I "dashed" him a few shillings and left. Outside, I gazed at the grim stone walls. The dramas that once took place in that castle were forever lost. The slaves sickened and despaired and the white men died of yellow fever and malaria. . . . I tried to picture in my mind a chief, decked out in cowrie shells, leopard skin, golden bracelets, leading a string of black prisoners of war to the castle to be sold. . . . My mind refused to function.

A few days later, with Kojo behind the wheel, I set out to see Cape Coast Castle which was built by the Swedes in 1657, captured by the Danes in 1659. Stormed by the local Fetus tribe, it was taken in 1660; in 1662 the English captured it, lost it to the Dutch, and recaptured it from them in 1664. Less impressive than the castle at Christianborg, it nevertheless shows by its moldering gun emplacements what went on in those days. It is now occupied by state officials, the post office, etc. Slaves had been kept here in dungeons, and then marched to the great slave headquarters of the Gold Coast, the Elmina Castle, and thence shipped to the New World.

I reached Elmina just as the sun was setting and its long red rays lit the awe-inspiring battlements of the castle with a somber but resplendent majesty. It is by far the most impressive castle or fort on the Atlantic shore of the Gold Coast. Built originally by the Portuguese in 1482 with stones prepared in Portugal, it is approached by a drawbridge which, when lifted, foiled any attack from either natives or Europeans in the old days.

I crossed the vast courtyard and entered the auction room in which countless slaves had been sold. One had to know how to pick a good slave in those days, for slave traders were tricky men. They shaved all the hair off the Africans, oiled their bodies, making the ill look as good as the healthy. I stood in a tiny enclosure which had slits in the wall; it was here that African chiefs would hide themselves while their captives were being bid for by Europeans. The chiefs didn't want their victims to know who was selling them. . . . I saw the dungeons where the slaves had been kept—huge, bare rooms with stone floors.

No one will ever know the number or identity of the black men, women, and children who passed through these walls, but there is no doubt but that the men who dealt in this human flesh waxed rich. Even today the castle bears marks of crumbling luxury; there are marble sills at many of the doorways; there are lofty, spacious rooms which you know at a glance no slaves had ever entered. The mighty guns that still point toward the horizon and the misty landscape must have cost heaps of gold dust; and the mere upkeep of such an establishment must have necessitated a staggering turnover in human flesh each year. . . .

Some of the walls are thirty feet thick. Towers rise two hundred feet in the air. What spacious dreams! What august faith! How elegantly laid-out the castle is! What bold and plunging lines! What, yes, taste. . . . King Prempeh I was kept in a large bare room in one of the towers by the British. I stood gazing into that room and wondered what could have passed through his mind. . . . How he must have prayed to his ancestors for help!

Rumor among the natives has it that there is a vast treasure trove buried somewhere in the depths of the castle fortress. I don't think there is; but the native, remembering the horrible tales of what went on within these walls, likes to think that there is gold dust here, thousands of tons of it. If there is any treasure hidden in these vast walls, I'm sure that it has a sheen that outshines gold—a tiny, pear-shaped tear that formed on the cheek of some black woman torn away from her children, a tear that gleams here still, caught in the feeble rays of the dungeon's light—a shy tear that vanishes at the sound of approaching footsteps, but reappears when all is quiet, hanging there on that black cheek, unredeemed, unappeased—a tear that was hastily brushed off when her arm was grabbed and she was led toward those narrow, dank steps that guided her to the tunnel that directed her feet to the waiting ship that would bear her across the heaving mist-shrouded Atlantic. . . .

Dear Kwame Nkrumah:

My journey's done. My labors in your vineyard are over. The ship that bears me from Africa's receding shore holds a heart that fights against those soft, sentimental feelings for the sufferings of our people. The kind of thinking that must be done cannot be done by men whose hearts are swamped with emotion.

While roaming at random through the compounds, market places, villages, and cities of your country, I felt an odd kind of at-homeness, a solidarity that stemmed not from ties of blood or race, or from my being of African descent, but from the quality of deep hope and suffering embedded in the lives of your people, from the hard facts of oppression that cut across time, space, and culture. I must confess that I, an American Negro, was filled with consternation at what Europe had done to this Africa. . . .

Yet, as grim as the picture is, its grimness is somewhat relieved by the fact that African conditions are not wholly unique. The suffering that your people bear has been borne triumphantly before, and your fellow countrymen have shared that burdensome experience of having had their destinies dictated by alien powers, from above, an experience that has knit together so many of the world's millions in a common consciousness, a common cause.

Kwame, let me put it bluntly: Western lay and academic circles utter many a hard saying against Africa. In defending their subjugation of Africa, they contend that Africa has no culture, no history, no background, etc. I'm not impressed by these gentlemen, lay or academic. In matters of history they have been more often wrong than right, and even when they have been right, it has been more by accident than design, or they have been right only after facts have already been so clearly established that not even a fool could go wrong.

I found only one intangible but vitally important element in the heritage of tribal culture that militated against cohesiveness of action: African culture has not developed the personalities of the people to a degree that their egos are stout, hard, sharply defined; there is too much cloudiness in the African's mentality, a kind of sodden vagueness that makes for lack of confidence, an absence of focus that renders that mentality incapable of grasping the workaday world. And until confidence is established at the center of African personality, until there is an inner reorganization of that personality, there can be no question of marching from the tribal order to the twentieth century. . . . At the moment, this subjective task is more important than economics!

Manifestly, as in all such situations, the commencement of the injection of this confidence must come from without, but it *cannot* and *will* not come from the West. (Let's hope I'm wrong about that!)

Have no illusions regarding Western attitudes. Westerners, high and low, feel that their codes, ideals, and conceptions of humanity do not apply to black men. If until today Africa was static, it was because Europeans deliberately wanted to keep her that way. They do not even treat the question of Africa's redemption seriously; to them it is a source of amusement; and those few Europeans who do manage to become serious about Africa are more often prompted by psychological reasons than anything else. The greatest millstone about the neck of Africa for the past three hundred years has been the psychologically crippled white seeking his own perverse personal salvation. . . .

Against this background one refrain echoes again and again in my mind: *You must be hard!* While in Africa one question kept hammering at me: Do the Africans possess the necessary hardness for the task ahead?

If the path that you and your people had to tread were an old and tried one, one worn somewhat smooth by the past trampings of many people; had Europe, during the past centuries, dealt with Africans differently, had they laid the foundations of the West so securely that the Africans could now hold Western values as basic assumptions—had all this happened, the question of "hardness" would not have presented itself to me. (I know that some Europeans are going to say: "Ah, look, a black man advocates stern measures for Africa! Didn't we tell you that they needed such as that?") But Kwame, the truth is that nothing could have been more brutally horrible than the "slow and sound" educational development that turned into a kind of teasing torture, which Europe has imposed so profitably upon Africa since the fifteenth century. . . .

The accomplishment of this change in the African attitude would be difficult under the best of circumstances; but to attain that goal in an Africa beset with a gummy tribalism presents a formidable problem: the psychological legacy of imperialism that lingers on represents the antithesis of the desired end; unlike the situations attending the eruptions of the masses in Russia, China, and India, you do not have the Western-educated Africans with you; in terms of mechanization, you must start from scratch; you have a populace ridden with a 90 per cent illiteracy; communication and transportation are poor. . . .

Balancing these drawbacks are some favorable features: West Africa, thanks to climate, is predominantly *black!* You can pour a libation to the nameless powers that there are no white settlers to be driven out, no knotty land problem to be solved by knocking together the heads of a landed black bourgeoisie. And, though the cultural traditions of the people have been shattered by European business and religous interests, they were so negatively shattered that the hunger to create a *Weltanschauung* is still there, virginal and unimpaired.

If, amidst such conditions, you elect, at this late date in world's history, to follow the paths of social and political evolution such as characterize the history of the institutions of the Western powers, your progress will go at a snail's pace and both of your flanks will be constantly exposed and threatened.

On the one hand, just as you organized against the British, so will other Nkrumahs organize against you. What Nkrumah has done, other Nkrumahs can do. You have made promises to the masses; in your heart of hearts I know that you wish hotly to keep those promises, for you are sincere. . . . But suppose the Communists outbid you? Suppose a sullen mood sets in? Would not that give the Communists *their* opportunity?

On the other hand, I cannot, as a man of African descent brought up in the West, recommend with good faith the agitated doctrines and promises of the hard-faced men of the West. Kwame, until they have set their own houses in order with their own restless populations, until they have solved their racial and economic problems, they can never—no matter *what* they may say to you at any *given* moment!—deal honestly with you. Given the opportunity, they'll pounce at any time upon Africa to solve their own hard-pressing social and political problems, just as you well know that they have pounced in the past. And, also, I'm convinced that the cultural conditioning of the Africans will make it difficult for them to adjust quickly to values that are solely Western, values that have mocked and shamed them so much in the past, values that go against the grain of so much in the African heart. . . . After all, you have already been down that road.

Your safety, your security lie in plunging full speed ahead!

But, how? What methods? Means? What instrumentalities? Ay, there's the rub. . . . The neurotically fluttering attempts of missionaries, the money lust of businessmen, the cool contempt of European soldiers and politicians, the bungling cynicism of statesmen splitting up families and cultures and indigenous national groupings at their pleasure—all of these have left the task of the redemption of Africa to you and yours, to us. . . . And what a task! What a challenge! What an opportunity for creation . . . !

One simple conviction stands straight up in me: Our people must be made to walk, forced draft, into the twentieth century! The direction of their lives, the duties that they must perform to overcome the stagnancy of tribalism, the sacrifices that must yet be made—all of this must be placed under firm social discipline!

I say to you publicly and frankly: The burden of suffering that must be borne, impose it upon *one* generation! Do not, with the false kindness of the missionaries and businessmen, drag out this agony for another five hundred years while your villages rot and your people's minds sink into the morass of a subjective darkness. . . . Be merciful by being stern! If I lived under your regime, I'd ask for this hardness, this coldness. . . .

Make no mistake, Kwame, they are going to come at you with words about democracy; you are going to be pinned to the wall and warned about decency; plump-faced men will mumble academic phrases about "sound" development; gentlemen of the cloth will speak unctuously of values and standards; in short, a barrage of concentrated arguments will be hurled at you to persuade you to temper the pace and drive of your movement. . . .

But you know as well as I that the logic of your actions is being determined by the conditions of the lives of your people. If, for one moment, you take your eyes off that fact, you'll soon be just another African in a cloth on the streets of Accra! You've got to find your *own* paths, your *own* values. . . . Above all, feel free to *improvise!* The political cat can be skinned in many fashions; the building of that bridge between tribal man and the twentieth century can be done in a score of ways. . . .

You might offer ideology as an instrument of organization; but, evidently, you have no basis for that in Africa at this time. You might, by borrowing money from the West, industrialize your people in a cash-and-carry system, but, in doing so, you will be but lifting them from tribal to industrial slavery, for tied to Western money is Western control, Western ideas. . . . Kwame, there is nothing on earth more afraid than a million dollars; and, if a million dollars means fear, a billion dollars is the quintessence of panic. . . .

Russia will not help you, unless you accept becoming an appendage of Moscow; and why should you change one set of white masters for another . . . ?

There is but one honorable course that assumes and answers the ideological, traditional, organizational, emotional, political, and productive needs of Africa at this time:

AFRICAN LIFE MUST BE MILITARIZED!

. . . not for war, but for peace; not for destruction, but for service; not for aggression, but for production; not for despotism, but to free minds from mumbo-jumbo.

I'm not speaking of a military dictatorship. You know that. I need not even have to say that to you, but I say it for the sake of others who will try to be naïve enough to misconstrue my words. I'm speaking simply of a militarization of the daily, social lives of the people; I'm speaking of giving form, organization, direction, meaning, and a sense of justification to those lives. . . . I'm speaking of a temporary discipline that will unite the nation, sweep out the tribal cobwebs, and place the feet of the masses upon a basis of reality. I'm not speaking of guns or secret police; I'm speaking of a method of taking people from one order of life and making them face what men, all men everywhere, must face. What the Europeans failed to do, didn't want to do because they feared disrupting their own profits and global real estate, you must do.

Above all, Africans must be regimentalized for the "long pull," for what will happen in Africa will spread itself out over decades of time and a continent of space. . . . You know as well as I that what has happened in the Gold Coast is just the beginning; and there will be much marching to and fro; there will be many sunderings and amalgamations of people; there will be many shiftings and changes of aims, perspectives, and ideologies—there will be much confusion before the final redemption of Africa is accomplished.

Do I sound gratuitously hard, cruel? How I wished I did not have to think of such measures! Yet, what could make such measures unnecessary? Only a West that could come forth and admit that it didn't do the job, that the job has to be done, and that it was willing to help you to do it. . . . Yet, I cannot conceive of the West acting in that manner, even though all the common sense of history, moral and material, is in favor of it. In its fight against Communism, Europe could bind Africa to her by such an act of help and understanding. . . . Of course, when this is pointed out to Westerners, they shrug their shoulders and say that they have timed African development according to their conceptions of what Africans can do; but, in saying this, they forget that they are not free to indulge in such fantasies. Western time today is being timed by another time: *Communist* time! It would seem that the issue of self-preservation alone would jolt Europeans out of their infantile dreams about Africa. . . .

And in exchange for aiding honest Africans to shake their people loose from their tribal moorings, the West could have all the raw materials it wanted, a larger market for its products. . . . And an Africa deliberately shaken loose from its traditional past would, for a time, be a more dependent Africa than the angry, aimless Africa of the present day. Such an Africa could menace nobody.

Why do I bring up the question of "menace"? Because the mere thought of a free Africa frightens many Europeans. Europeans do not and cannot look upon Africa objectively. Back of their fear of African freedom lies an ocean of *guilt!* In their hearts they know that they have long tried to murder Africa. . . . And this powerful Europe, with atom bombs in its hands, is haunted by visions of an eventual black revenge that has no basis in reality. It is this subjective factor, among others, that makes the West brutally determined to keep Africa on a short chain. . . .

Will the West come forward and head up these nationalist revolutions in Africa? No; it's a dream. If it comes true, I'd be the first to hail it. But since we cannot wait for dreams, let us turn to reality. . . . That is, the militarization of African life.

The basis, concrete and traditional, for the militarization of African life is there already in the truncated tribal structure. The ideological justification for such measures is simple survival; the military is but another name for fraternalization, for cohesiveness. And a military structure of African society can be used eventually for defense. Most important of all, a military form of African society will atomize the fetish-ridden past, abolish the mystical and nonsensical family relations that freeze the African in his static degradation; it will render impossible the continued existence of those parasitic chiefs who have too long bled and misled a naïve people; it is the one and only stroke that can project the African immediately into the twentieth century!

Over and above being a means of production, a militarized social structure can replace, for a time, the political; and it contains its own form of idealistic and emotional sustenance. A military form of life, of social relations, used as a deliberate bridge to span the tribal and the industrial ways of life, will free you, to a large extent, from begging for money from the West, and the degrading conditions attached to such money. A military form of life will enable you to use *people* instead of money for many things and on many occasions! And if your people knew that this military regime was for their freedom, for their safety, for the sake of their children escaping the domination of foreigners, they will make all the sacrifices called for.

Again I say: Would that Western understanding and generosity make these recommendations futile. . . . But if the choice is between traditional Western domination and this hard path, take the hard path!

Beware of a Volta Project built by foreign money. Build your own Volta, and build it out of the sheer lives and bodies of your people! With but limited outside aid, your people can rebuild your society with their bare hands. . . . Africa needs this hardness, *but only from Africans.*

You know as well as I know that politics alone is not enough for Africa. Keep the fires of passion burning in your movement; don't let Westerners turn you away from the only force that can, at this time, knit your people together. It's a secular religion that you must slowly create; it's that, or your edifice falls apart.

There will be those who will try to frighten you by telling you that the organization you are forging looks like Communism, Fascism, Nazism; but, Kwame, the form of organization that you need will be dictated by the needs, emotional and material, of your people. The content determines the form. Never again must the outside world decide what is good for you.

Regarding corruption: use fire and acid and cauterize the ranks of your party of all opportunists! *Now!* Corruption is the one single fact that strikes dismay in the hearts of the friends of African freedom. . . .

In your hands lies the first bid for African freedom and independence. Thus far you have followed an *African* path. I say: *So be it!* Whatever the West or East offers, take it, but don't let them take you. You have taken Marxism, that intellectual instrument that makes meaningful the class and commodity relations in the modern state; but the moment that that instrument ceases to shed meaning, drop it. Be on top of theory; don't let theory be on top of you. In short, be *free*, be a living embodiment of what you want to give your people. . . .

You and your people need no faraway "fatherland" in either England or Russia to guide and spur you on; let your own destiny claim your deepest loyalty. You have escaped one form of slavery; be chary of other slaveries no matter in what guise they present themselves, whether as glittering ideas, promises of security, or rich mortgages upon your future.

There will be no way to avoid a degree of suffering, of trial, of tribulation; suffering comes to all people, but you have within your power the means to make the suffering of your people meaningful, to redeem whatever stresses and strains may come. None but Africans can perform this for Africa. And, as you launch your bold programs, as you call on your people for sacrifices, you can be confident that there are free men beyond the continent of Africa who see deeply enough into life to know and understand what you *must* do, what you *must* impose. . . .

You have demonstrated that tribes can be organized; you must now show that tribes can march socially! And remember that what you build will become a haven for other black leaders of the continent who, from time to time, long for rest from their tormentors. Gather quickly about you the leaders of Africa; you need them and they need you. Europe knows clearly that what you have achieved so far is not confined to the boundaries of the Gold Coast alone; already it has radiated outward and as long as the influence of your bid for freedom continues to inspire your brothers over the teeming forests of West Africa, you can know that the ball of freedom that you threw still rolls. . . .

With words as our weapons, there are some few of us who will stand on the ramparts to fend off the evildoers, the slanderers, the greedy, the self-righteous! You are not alone. . . .

Your fight has been fought before. I am an American and my country too was once a colony of England . . . It was old Walt Whitman who felt what you and your brother fighters are now feeling when he said:

Suddenly, out of its stale and drowsy lair, the lair of slaves,
Like lightning it le'pt forth, half startled at itself,
Its feet upon the ashes and rags—its hands tight to the throats of kings.

O hope and faith!
O aching close of exiled patriots' lives!
O many a sicken'd heart!
Turn back unto this day, and make yourself afresh.
And you, paid to defile the People! you liars, mark!
Not for numberless agonies, murders, lusts,
For court thieving in its manifold mean forms, worming from his simplicity the poor man's wages,
For many a promise sworn by royal lips, and broken and laugh'd at in the breaking.
Then in their power, not for all these, did the blows strike revenge, or the heads of nobles fall;
The People scorn'd the ferocity of kings.

INDEX

The Color Curtain

A Report on the Bandung Conference

With a Foreword by Gunnar Myrdal
and an Afterword by Amritjit Singh

Under thy shadow by the piers I waited:
Only in darkness is thy shadow clear.
The City's fiery parcels all undone,
Already snow submerges an iron year . . .

O Sleepless as the river under thee,
Vaulting the sea, the prairies' dreaming sod,
Unto us lowliest sometime sweep, descend
And of the curveship lend a myth to God.

HART CRANE'S *THE BRIDGE*

FOREWORD

This book does not pretend to be a heavily documented analysis of the Bandung Conference and of the forces of world history in the making which converged there. It is, rather, Richard Wright telling us what he, a visiting stranger and a good reporter, heard and saw there, and what he himself thought and felt.

His interest was focused on the two powerful urges far beyond Left and Right which he found at work there: Religion and Race. These urges unite the peoples—keep them apart from, and against, the West—and at the same time divide them internally and in their mutual relations; they call to concerted action but tend also to frustrate such efforts. Religion is their cultural heritage from many thousands of years of living and dying, longing and fearing, and it has molded their institutions and loaded their valuations. Race is the explosive pressure of their reaction to West European prejudice and discrimination, stored and accumulated under centuries of colonial domination. Asia and Africa thus carry the irrationalism of both East and West.

In Richard Wright's own individual development from a childhood amongst the remnants of slavery to his present life as a free and lonely intellectual lie the foundations for his absorbing interest in these matters and his deep and spontaneous understanding. The specific objectivity of his observations and inferences is determined by the clear definition of the very personal point from which he views things. As a writer—and this is his approach to greatness, giving distinction also to the collection of snapshots in the present volume—he is the scrupulously honest artist who gives himself fully, without any opportunistic reserves.

GUNNAR MYRDAL

GENEVA, 18 SEPTEMBER, 1955

PART I

Bandung: Beyond Left and Right

In order to spend Christmas with my family, I'd returned to Paris from a long, tiring trip in Spain where I'd been gathering material for a book. The holidays had passed, but, in one corner of the living room, sheltering a pile of children's presents, the glittering pine tree was still up. It was evening; I was alone; and my mind drifted toward Andalusia where I had work to finish. . . .

Idly, I picked up the evening's newspaper that lay folded near me upon a table and began thumbing through it. Then I was staring at a news item that baffled me. I bent forward and read the item a second time. *Twenty-nine free and independent nations of Asia and Africa are meeting in Bandung, Indonesia, to discuss "racialism and colonialism"* . . . What is this? I scanned the list of nations involved: China, India, Indonesia, Japan, Burma, Egypt, Turkey, the Philippines, Ethiopia, Gold Coast, etc. My God! I began a rapid calculation of the populations of the nations listed and, when my total topped the billion mark, I stopped, pulled off my glasses, and tried to think. A stream of realizations claimed my mind: these people were ex-colonial subjects, people whom the white West called "colored" peoples. . . . Almost all of the nations mentioned had been, in some form or other, under the domination of Western Europe; some had been subjected for a few decades and others had been ruled for three hundred and fifty years. . . . And most of the leaders of these nations had been political prisoners, men who had lived lonely lives in exile, men to whom secret political activity had been a routine matter, men to whom sacrifice and suffering had been daily companions. . . . And the populations of almost all the nations listed were deeply religious. This was a meeting of almost all of the human race living in the main geopolitical center of gravity of the earth.

I tried to recall what I knew of their leaders and my memory dredged up: Ali Sastroamidjojo, Prime Minister of Indonesia: exile, prison, war . . . Jawaharlal Nehru, Prime Minister of India: long years in prison . . . Kwame Nkrumah, Prime Minister of the Gold Coast: ex-political prisoner and gifted organizer of tribal masses . . . Chou En-lai, Premier of China: a disciplined Communist of the classical, Bolshevik mold, a product of war and conspiracy and revolution . . . Ho Chi Minh, Prime Minister of the Democratic Republic of Viet-Nam: soldier, staunch Bolshevik, sagacious and pitiless leader of guerrilla armies. . . . The despised, the insulted, the hurt, the dispossessed—in short, the underdogs of the human race were meeting. Here were class and racial and religious consciousness on a global scale. Who had thought of organizing such a meeting? And what had these nations in common? Nothing, it seemed to me, but what their past relationship to the Western world had made them feel. This meeting of the rejected was in itself a kind of judgment upon that Western world!

I rose, walked the floor for a moment, then sat again and read the aims of the twenty-nine-nation conference:

a. to promote good will and co-operation among the nations of Asia and Africa, to explore and ad-

vance their mutual as well as common interests and to establish and further friendliness and neighborly relations;

b. to consider social, economic, and cultural problems and relations of the countries represented;

c. to consider problems of special interest to Asian and African peoples, for example, problems affecting national sovereignty and of racialism and colonialism;

d. to view the position of Asia and Africa and their people in the world of today and the contribution they can make to the promotion of world peace and co-operation.

It was simple; there were no hidden jokers. . . . The nations sponsoring the conference—Burma, India, Indonesia, Ceylon, and Pakistan—were all religious. . . . This smacked of something new, something beyond Left and Right. Looked at in terms of history, these nations represented *races* and *religions*, vague but potent forces.

It was the kind of meeting that no anthropologist, no sociologist, no political scientist would ever have dreamed of staging; it was too simple, too elementary, cutting through the outer layers of disparate social and political and cultural facts down to the bare brute residues of human existence: races and religions and continents. Only brown, black, and yellow men who had long been made agonizingly self-conscious, under the rigors of colonial rule, of their race and their religion could have felt the need for such a meeting. There was something extra-political, extra-social, almost extra-human about it; it smacked of tidal waves, of natural forces. . . . *And the call for the meeting had not been sounded in terms of ideology.* The agenda and subject matter had been written for centuries in the blood and bones of the participants. The conditions under which these men had lived had become their tradition, their culture, their *raison d'être*. And they could not be classed as proletarians; they comprised princes and paupers, Communists and Christians, Leftists and Rightists, Buddhists and Democrats, in short, just anybody and everybody who lived in Asia and Africa.

I felt that I had to go to that meeting; I felt that I could understand it. I represented no government, but I wanted to go anyhow. . . .

I called my wife and when she came into the living room I said to her:

"Look here, twenty-nine nations of Asia and Africa are meeting in a place called Bandung."

"Why are they meeting?"

"Read this," I said, giving her the newspaper.

When she had finished, she exclaimed:

"Why, that's the human race!"

"Exactly. And that is why I want to go."

"But you are going to Spain."

"Sure. But when I'm through in Spain, I could go to Bandung.

"What would you do there?"

"I'd try to report this meeting, what it means—"

"For whom?"

"I don't know. For somebody . . . I know that people are tired of hearing of these hot, muddy faraway places filled with people yelling for freedom. But this is the human race speaking . . ."

"But how would you report twenty-nine nations meeting together?"

"I don't know. But I feel that my life has given me some keys to what they would say or do. I'm an American Negro; as such, I've had a burden of race consciousness. So have these people. I worked in my youth as a common laborer, and I've a class consciousness. So have these people. I grew up in the Methodist and Seventh Day Adventist churches and I saw and observed religion in my childhood; and these people are religious. I was a member of the Communist Party for twelve years and I know something of the politics and psychology of rebellion. These people have had as their daily existence such politics. These emotions are my instruments. They are emotions, but I'm conscious of them as emotions. I want to use these emotions to try to find out what these people think and feel and why."

There was silence. Then my wife said:

"If you feel that way, you have to go."

I applied forthwith for a visa at the Consulate of Indonesia. The Press and Cultural Attaché told me with a smile:

"You can go. And I'm not going to try to influence you one way or the other. Go and see for yourself. All that I ask is that you be honest and tell the truth."

"That's fair enough," I said. "Tell me this: how has the press reacted to the Africans being invited to this conference?"

"They don't understand it," he told me, laughing, celebrating the bewilderment of the world's press.

But the Frenchmen and Americans I met on the streets or in the cafés of Paris were more decided, suspicious, skeptical.

"But is not this Asian-African Conference merely racism in reverse?" a young white American asked me; he was obviously worried.

"I think that the Asians and the Africans are trying to gang up on the Western world," a young woman, a journalist, told me.

"Isn't this a racism inspired by the Communists?" an American professor asked me.

"It's those Indonesians!" a young, conservative but fiery

Dutch girl said. "The Communists have agitated them so much that they are 'Dutch crazy.'"

(It was the first time that I'd heard the phrase "Dutch crazy," and, when I investigated its origin, I found that it was the Dutch description of all those Indonesian nationalists who had refused to compromise with the Dutch and had insisted upon national freedom. For three hundred and fifty years the Dutch had so rigged the governing of the colony that there was but a handful of people out of a population of eighty million who could read and write; and, naturally, when that handful demanded taking over the country, they were regarded as "crazy" . . .)

My interest in the Asian-African Conference was not shared by personal friends of mine.

"What on earth have African Negroes and Burmese Buddhists in common?" a young, ardent Frenchwoman asked me, with her eyes wide with images of global racial revenge.

A day or so later I met a young Dutch girl whom I'd known for some time; she was liberal, anti-racist. Ah, I must tell her that I'm going to Indonesia.

"Oh, D.!" I called to her; she was walking ahead of me.

She stopped, turned, smiled, and held out her hand.

"How are you?" she asked me.

"I'm happy," I said.

"Good! What's happened?"

"I'm going to one of your ex-colonies, Indonesia. They are holding a conference there, a meeting of Asian and African nations—"

"Oh, my God!" she exclaimed.

Her brown eyes were wide in surprise, her lips parted. She reached forward and impulsively seized the fingers of my hands.

"You're actually going to Indonesia?" she asked me breathlessly.

"Yes."

"Oh, God! Then maybe you can bring me some spices?"

I hid my shock, remembering that spices were what Christopher Columbus had been looking for in 1492 when he had sailed forth . . . Even before leaving Paris, I was discovering how the reality of Eastern nations was reflected in many European minds: the islands of the Atlantic and Pacific, and the millions of people who lived on them, still meant spices. . . .

I was ready to fly to Bandung, to fly from the old world of Spain to the new world of Asia. . . . My work in Spain was over and I was sitting in a café with a Spanish friend; he was liberal, anti-Franco, a bitter man who longed passionately for freedom.

"When are you leaving us? "my Spanish friend asked.

"Tomorrow," I said.

"You are returning to Paris?"

"No. I'm going to the Orient."

"Really? Where?"

"Indonesia."

"Why are you going there?"

"On the eighteenth of April there is a great conference taking place."

"What conference?"

I stared at my Spanish friend in disbelief.

"There are twenty-nine Asian and African nations, all free and independent, meeting in Bandung, Indonesia."

"Why are these nations meeting?"

"They are going to explore problems of colonialism and racialism."

"Good God!" he exclaimed. "I hadn't heard of that!"

"It's in the newspapers," I said.

"Not in the Spanish newspapers," he said, bringing down the corners of his mouth and shaking his head. He cupped his palms to his eyes and moaned: "Once we Spanish were great; now we are nothing. . . . If Franco decides not to let us know what is happening in the outside world, how can we know?" He stared at me a moment, then his eyes fell upon my brown hands that lay upon the tile-topped table. "You know, we Spanish have a bad reputation. You've heard of it? The Black Legend . . . ?"

"Yes," I said, understanding now why he had stared so intently at my hands. He had suddenly grown color-conscious.

"We did bad things in South America," he drawled with a sad smile. He shrugged his shoulders. "But what can these nations do about racialism and colonialism?"

"Well, they are free, you know."

"And just a bare ten years ago they were not free—"

"That's it."

He laughed uneasily, then looked at me with a twinkle in his eyes.

"We Spanish were different from the British, the Dutch, the French, and the Belgians. . . . We married the colored peoples. Look at the mixed-bloods in Mexico and Peru. . . ." He sighed wistfully.

"You sure did," I said.

So it went; worlds were being born and worlds were dying. . . . In Asia and Africa the leaders of the newly freed nations were meeting to find ways and means of modernizing their countries, to banish fear and superstition, while only yesterday in Sevilla I'd seen thousands of Spanish men, women, and children marching in pagan splendor behind jeweled images of Dying Gods and Suffering Virgins. . . .

I bade my Spanish friend goodbye and took the night express to Madrid. Once I had settled in my compartment, my mind turned toward the vastness of Asia and its unknown life. Since I had resolved to go to Bandung, the problem of getting to know the Asian personality had been with me day and night. Knowing that I had no factual background to grapple with the swirling currents of the Asian maelstrom, I had weeks before devised a stratagem to enable me to grasp at least the basic Asian attitudes. I had compiled a list of what I felt to be relevant questions to elicit responses bearing on broad, general issues. Ensconced in the *wagon-lit*, I unpacked my notes and reread my questionnaire and the answers that my Asian informants had given me. My questionnaire had included the following queries:

How far did you go in school? Were you educated in your youth by missionaries? Have you attended European schools?

What religion did or do your parents profess? What religion do you profess? Do you feel that the state should sponsor religion? How important was the introduction to Christianity in your country?

How did you become interested in politics? Did you participate in the liberation movement of your country? Were you ever arrested for political activity? How much time have you served as a political prisoner? Have you ever served in the armed forces of any Western power? Do you think that your country has an enemy? If so, how would you describe him?

How many international conferences have you attended? What does the Bandung Conference mean to you?

Do you feel that there is a naturally allotted, irrevocable geographical space for each race on earth? Do you believe that Asia is for Asians, Europe for Europeans, America for Americans, Africa for Africans? How frequently do you read European newspapers? What have your experiences revealed to be the attitudes of Europeans and/or Americans toward your people? How do you think that such attitudes originated? How do you feel that your contacts with the Western world have affected you personally? Have Westerners ever made you feel self-conscious because of your race, religion, color, or culture? Do national inferiority feelings find expression in your country? If so, in what forms? Do you recall in what connection you first heard the phrase "White Man's Burden," "Yellow Peril," "lynch," "nigger"? What, in your opinion, is the best way to eliminate racism?

Do you want to see your country industrialized? What do you value most in your culture and how do you propose to save it? How do living standards in your country compare with those of the Western nations?

Is the racial purity of your family blood important to you? Did you ever desire to marry a European woman (or man)? If so, why didn't you? Should intermarriage between races be regulated by law? Will you send your children to "national" or European schools?

Do you feel that Asian and African nations should act as a political bloc?

How much contact have you with your people? Do you still speak your "native" language fluently? Is or was your city divided into "native" and European quarters? In which quarter have you lived? When the European occupation of your country was over, did your people rename any of your towns, cities, rivers, etc.?

What is the literacy rate in your country?

What are the relations today among the new countries of Asia and Africa? If there are tensions, how did they come about? How, in your opinion, can such tensions be kept from developing?

What, in your opinion, is the most urgent problem on the international scene? What do you think of the United Nations? Do you feel that the white nations of the Western world constitute a racial and/or political bloc? Why?

Stalin is reputed to have once used the phrase, "We Asiatics . . .": In your opinion, does that mean that the Russians regard themselves as belonging to Asia? What, in your opinion, do Europeans mean by the designation "colored countries"? Do you regard your country as being "colored"?

What does Left mean to you? What does Right mean to you?

Do you feel that a nation is ever justified in using the atom or hydrogen bomb as a military weapon?

What kind of aid does your country need from Western industrial nations? In what form do you think that such aid should be obtained?

What, in your opinion, is the meaning of the phrase "democratic opinion"? What, in your opinion, is a "democratic institution"? What, in your opinion, justifies the exercise of state power?

Do you believe in the possibility of world government? Should the state create trade unions for workers? What, in your opinion, is the best form of government for your country? In your opinion, does social or political change stem from economic or psychological causes?

Are there any secret societies in your country? If so, are they political or religious?

Do you think that there is a conflict between the younger and the older generations in your country? If such a conflict exists, what are the causes?

Do you think that a classless society, in an economic sense, is possible?

What was the single most important event of the twentieth century?

If your country were fully developed, what European country would you like your country to resemble? What, in your opinion, was the West's greatest effect upon your country?

What, in your opinion, should be the aim of education?

What is your idea of a great man? What men now living do you call great?

Do you believe in capital punishment?

Why, in your opinion, did not the European working class revolt and make revolutions when the Russian Revolution occurred? What do you think of Lenin's appeal to the people of Asia and Africa for help to defend the Soviet Union?

Do you feel that the removal of oppressive conditions makes men happy? Do you feel that man needs a universal humanism that can bind men together in a common unity? If so, what culture in the world today seems the most promising candidate to champion such a humanism?

I had sought reactions to this list from two typical Westerners living in Paris, and I had been surprised to learn that they felt that no or but few Asians would know what the questions were all about. I had seriously doubted that. I had reasoned that if I, an American Negro, had thought of them, then an Asian, meeting the West from the "outside," so to speak, must surely have thought of them even more. How naive I had been! Little had I suspected that I would have to do no questioning at all, that all I had to do was to show up and the Asians would gush, erupt, and spill out more than they knew. I had used the questionnaire five times, then I had thrown it away. . . . If I, an American Negro, conscious of my racial and social and political position in the Western world, could misjudge the Asians' willingness to bare their feelings so completely, how much more, then, must white Westerners misjudge them?

In my questioning of Asians I had had one tangible factor in my favor, a factor that no white Westerner could claim. I was "colored" and every Asian I had spoken to had known what being "colored" meant. Hence, I had been able to hear Asians express themselves without reserve; they had felt no need to save face before me. . . . (As a frank and sometimes bitter critic of the Western world, I've been frequently dubbed "extreme." . . . Well, what I heard from the lips of many Asians startled me, reduced my strictures to the status of a "family quarrel." . . . I found that many Asians hated the West with an absoluteness that no American Negro could ever muster. The American Negro's reactions were limited, partial, centered, as they were, upon specific complaints; he rarely ever criticized or condemned the conditions of life about him as a whole. . . . Once his particular grievances were redressed, the Negro reverted to a normal Western outlook. The Asian, however, had been taken from his own culture before he had embraced or had pretended to embrace Western culture; he had, therefore, a feeling of distance, of perspective, of objectivity toward the West which tempered his most intimate experiences of the West. . . .)

As the express train bumped along over the Spanish mountains toward Madrid, I recalled having asked myself how would I be able to tell how important the Asian responses evoked by my questionnaire would be. For a while that problem had me stumped. Then I had hit upon a general solution, a rule-of-thumb guide: I had decided to try to interview an Asian-born European who had once lived in Asia. I had felt that in that way I would get European attitudes to the same realities that constituted Asian life.

I had been lucky enough to find a young Indonesian-born Dutch journalist who had readily consented to be my guinea pig. He had been more European in attitude than most Europeans; having been born in Indonesia but educated in Holland, he had felt a high degree of consciousness about his European values and possessed a detachment that made for straight answers.

I summarize his answers to my list of questions in order to make a coherent statement:

He is twenty-four years of age, married, his wife and children in Holland. He is a university graduate, a Protestant. His ancestors were French Huguenots. He professes no religion and is of the opinion that religion is "an instrument of war, of fighting." He feels that the introduction of Christianity into Indonesia influenced the people to lead a moral life, yet he says that religion has made the people militant. (When questioned as to whether Indonesians had any idea of "the good" before the Europeans brought in their idea of "the good," he was quite confused. He assumed a natural European superiority in all phases of life.)

His interest in politics derives from his concern about what happens to people. He did not participate in the liberation movement of Indonesia, nor did he serve with Dutch troops when those troops tried to put down that movement; he was a student in Holland when those events took place. He has never experienced any penalties, legal or moral, for his political opinions. He has traveled widely in Europe, has dabbled in European philosophical theories, but he has not served in the armed forces of any European nation.

He does not think that Indonesia has an enemy. The Asian-African Conference concerns him only from a journalistic point of view: it is a project he has to cover.

Though Indonesian born, he believes in Asia for Asians, Europe for Europeans, America for Americans, and Africa for Africans and feels that such an order of things is "natural." But, as a European, he prefers to live in Asia! He has many Dutch and Indonesian friends and feels that the Dutch were mainly interested in trade in Indonesia and that that was what conditioned Dutch attitudes towards Indonesians. Contact with the West made the Indonesians feel something that they "had never felt before, made them feel different, that they were not as important as they had thought they were; but the net result of the Indonesians' contact with the West has been to broaden their outlook on the world and life in general." He admits that Western contacts have made the Indonesian very self-conscious, but he does not think that there is any evidence of inferiority feelings on the part of the Indonesian, that Indonesian culture does not reflect any such expressions. . . .

The word "lynch" is English but has been adopted into Dutch and is used to signify that someone must be got rid of by some means, legal or otherwise. He first heard of the phrase "White Man's Burden" in connection with Dutch colonial policy; the word "nigger" came to him from reading done in an American context; he had never heard of "Yellow Peril." The best way, in his opinion, to eliminate racism is to find out what causes it and fight it.

He wants to see Indonesia thoroughly industrialized, but he wishes that the wood-carving, music, and dancing skills of the people could be saved. "But I'm afraid that that won't be possible."

He feels that the "difference in climate makes impossible any comparison between Indonesian and European standards of living."

The purity of his family blood was not important to him; he once wanted to marry an Indonesian girl, but he never found the one he really loved. He does not feel that marriage between the races ought to be regulated by law. He'd never send his children to Indonesian schools. "That's why they are in Holland now."

If necessary, especially if it means peace in the world, Africans and Asians should act as a political bloc. He does not know what the literacy rate is in Indonesia. He says that the Indonesians renamed many of their towns, cities, streets, etc., when the Dutch were driven out. (He attached no importance to this.)

He knows nothing of the relations between the new Asian countries; he feels that the most urgent problem on the international scene is peace. War is the deepest fear of his life; Communism comes next. The United Nations is a means for keeping peace, but he does not think that it can do so.

He feels that Asian and African nations have had their fair share of say-so, authority, and influence in the deliberations of the United Nations. White Western nations should act as a political or racial bloc in order to defeat Communism. Flatly, Russians are Asiatics. European workers felt far too superior to Russian workers to have helped them in their revolution. Lenin's turning to Asia for help was a "smart move."

Countries inhabited by nonwhites are "colored" countries; Indonesia thus is a "colored" country. He is sure that the Indonesians feel this.

Communist ideology is Left; those who do not like Communism are on the Right.

There can never be any justification, he feels, for using the atom or hydrogen bomb as a military weapon.

Indonesia, in his opinion, needs technical aid, loans, machines, exchange of students, etc., from the West. Trade is the means by which these things should be obtained.

"Democratic opinion" is government by the people; a "democratic institution" exists with the consent of the people; the state derives its power from the people. The state should have nothing to do with creating trade unions for workers. Indonesia needs a dictatorship; it is not ready for democracy. Political change stems from both economic and psychological causes.

There are many secret societies in Indonesia; some are political and others are just gangs. In his opinion, there is no conflict between the younger and older generations in Indonesia. A classless society, in an economic sense, is impossible.

The single most important event of the twentieth century was the social revolution; this revolution has not yet reached Indonesia, or anywhere in Asia for that matter. He knows of no country that he would like Indonesia to resemble if it were fully industrialized. The impact of trade is the greatest influence of the West upon Indonesia.

There are no men now living whom he would call great. Simple men are great men; therefore, there are many great men in the world. "Greatness is how you live your personal, individual life." The aim of education is to enlarge one's understanding of life.

He does not believe in capital punishment. The removal of oppressive conditions can make men happy. Man needs a universal humanism, but there is no culture in the world today that can serve as a model.

I lifted my eyes from my notes and, to the rocking of the train, I reflected: This young white journalist was certainly not as excited about Bandung as I was. His casual attitude toward that pending conference made him an ideal model which I could place at the head of my continuum of Asiatic subjects. Against his nonchalant, normal personality I could measure, compare, and judge the "pure" Asian personalities I would encounter. In fact, I could safely eliminate him from my immediate consideration, that is, I would not include him except negatively in my search for the emotional landscapes of Asia. . . .

Yet, his being in but not of Asia, his sheer detachment yielded some information. The most that he seemed to be aware of was that Asians were slightly embarrassed in the presence of their Western superiors, and, to him, that was as it should have been. To me, his conviction that Indonesia needed a dictator, that the people were not ready for democracy, seemed to be the product either of a sense of pity for the plight of the Indonesians or of an attitude of scorn. It was like saying that a delinquent child needed a stern father. I was convinced that his attitude represented more disgust with the disorganization of Indonesian life than any insight into the needs of that life. By prescribing dictatorial methods for Indonesian needs, he was endorsing drastic measures that he never would have sanctioned for any Western nation. . . .

The one surprising element in the Indonesian-born European's outlook was his characterizing the Christian religion as an instrument of war, and I suspected that he had absorbed that idea from talking to his Indonesian friends. Being Indonesian-born and having kept his Western attitude intact, he was wrestling with an experience that but few Westerners knew: he was white, but he saw and felt, to some degree, how the West looked from the *outside*. . . . There was no doubt but that he was concerned about the meaning of the Christian religion as the historical reality of that religion had impinged upon non-Christians, and, had he known or felt the central psychological reality of that religion and what made it function so militantly, I am sure that he would have been honest enough to have mentioned it. He felt its warlikeness, but he didn't know why it was so.

Otherwise, the racial state of things seemed quite natural to him: if black people lived in Africa, then Africa was naturally a black man's land, ordained by nature to be so. And so on with China, America, Europe, etc.

There seemed to be in him no need for a sharp racial consciousness, though he was dimly aware of the existence of that phenomenon and felt that it was a regrettable defect derived from lack of education. Differences in the standards of living between East and West were natural, due to climate. He was vaguely liberal and humanist, willing to marry an Indonesian girl; indeed, he was naive enough to feel the possibility of an ideological solidarity with yellow, brown, and black men and could conceive of their uniting with him to fight Communism! To designate a country as being "colored" carried no stigma.

To him the problems of the Eastern nations were simple: give them technical aid, loans, permit the exchange of students, and all would be well. There was nothing urgent; business as usual could contain any tensions arising. . . .

He rejected capital punishment—a rejection that implied, since he was not religious, that circumstances accounted for men's actions. This same slightly romantic streak manifested itself in his belief that the removal of oppressive conditions could make men happy. He possessed no messianic sense; he wanted no atom or hydrogen bombs used as military weapons, and the concept of "greatness" had, for him, no golden halo around it. Education was his key to the future and man was bound to improve with time. . . .

The express pounded on into the night as I pored over my notes. . . . My luck had held and, earlier that spring, I had met in Madrid someone who had fallen naturally in line after my Indonesian-born European: a subject who had reflected, with enthralling interest, the psychological landscape of a mixture of Asian and European values, that is, the Eurasian mind.

Informant was a girl, highly intelligent, nervous, articulate, with a kind of repressed charm. Tall, about twenty-six years of age, she came of mixed parentage, her mother being Irish Catholic and her father an Indian of Moslem faith. Her skin had just a touch of copper; she had been in Spain for six months and I wondered if she'd not come to Spain because she resembled Spaniards? Attempting a new identification? Most Spaniards, she said, took her for one of them until they heard her speak. She described herself as being "a rather bad Roman Catholic."

Single, Singapore-born, a journalist by profession, she had completed the equivalent of an American high school training. She was entirely educated by missionaries, having lived her youth in a convent. Afterward she spent ten years in school in Australia. She is thoroughly Westernized in manner and speech. (I questioned this girl in the presence of a white American and she, to my observation, never betrayed the slightest hesitancy or embarrassment in replying. Other subjects were questioned in private, with no whites, American or European, present. Experience taught me that the presence of whites constrained Asians to a startling degree!) Her father is a lawyer and helped to frame the constitution for Malaya; he is, she says, an easygoing man who takes his religion lightly.

She feels that no state ought to sponsor religion; Christianity has had no deep effect in her country. (Throughout my questioning of this girl, I had to make sure just what country she was alluding to, for it was not always clear whether it was Britain or Malaya she was referring to. . . .) The role of religion in history is to her an open question; she takes her religion for granted.

She identifies herself with her father, and her intense interest in current politics flows from her father's activities on behalf of his country's freedom. Having never participated in politics, she has never been molested because of her political views. She has traveled extensively in Europe.

She feels that Malaya has an enemy: Red China. Since she has never attended an international conference, she holds no opinion about the Asian-African Conference. Because of her lack of racial and national identity, she does pay more than ordinary attention, she says, to political events reported in the press.

There is a natural, allotted, irrevocable geographical space for each race on earth: Africa for Africans, America for Americans, Europe for Europeans, and Asia for Asians. She says: "It is just and right like that."

She has many white friends and associates with them without any emotional disturbances; she confesses, however, that she has had racial feelings. Working as a newspaperwoman in Singapore, she frequently was in the company of white friends who asked her to visit their clubs, and she had to tell them that she was not "acceptable, much to their astonishment." Some offered to make her an exception and get her a membership, but she refused such offers, feeling that she would be playing false with herself.

Color lines are sharp in Malaya, she says, and sister has been known to deny sister in public on the basis of color. She fled Malaya because she did not fit in, because she was neither Indian nor European. She does not like Eurasians or "the Eurasian atmosphere. They are full of complexes; they are sick people, *sick*, I tell you, *all* of them. I feel pain when I see the neurotic attitude of the Eurasians." She maintains that color, race, and religion have not given birth to any expressions of cultural inferiority feelings in Malaya. "Malayans are dull, easygoing; now and then they are reminded by someone that the country is really theirs, and they blink and say, 'Yes'; but that is all."

She has felt the life of the Malayan from both sides. "Europeans regard us as exotic when they meet us in Europe, but in the East they stick together against us. They have fixed ideas about us, and such ideas enable them to exploit the natives." (In one sentence she switched from "us" to "natives.")

She is visibly Eurasian and her mother sometimes openly expressed doubts about the way she was rearing her and her sister and her brother. Her mother felt that perhaps it would have been better if the children had remained in India. But the children had not wanted that; though dark, they felt European.

Ten years' residence in Australia conditioned her against respecting Asians; but, working as a newspaperwoman in Singapore, she had comrades who were Malayan and, slowly, she began to feel their humanity. Her father's fighting for the freedom of his country helped her to overcome many of her doubts, to believe that Asians could do what Europeans did.

Her father and his friends are dark and, when she is in their presence, she feels "outside," feels that they "feel" her white blood, and she is hurt. By exchanging her British passport for an Indian one, she could work for UNESCO; but qualms hold her back. Because she has never done anything for India, she does not want to pretend to be Indian in order to obtain a well-paying job. Her father agrees with her decision. It is her love for her father that keeps her from "passing" into the white race; she does not want to "pass" if her father cannot do so. . . .

She first heard "nigger," "Yellow Peril," "White Man's Burden," and "lynch" while in school in Australia, read them in novels like *Gone with the Wind*, in nursery rhymes like *Ten Little Niggers*, etc. During the war of Japan against China, she heard of "Yellow Peril" and it made her feel strange, for her complexion is yellowish. Comic strips made her conscious of her background, for Asians were always depicted as villains. She has no idea how racism can be eliminated; she simply longs "for people to live together in peace."

She does not want her country (Malaya) to become any more industrialized than it is right now. In Malayan culture she values dancing, and she thinks that the state ought to take steps to see that it is preserved.

There is an upper class in Malaya that lives from profits gotten out of tin, rubber, fisheries, and shipping; these people possess as high a standard of living as Westerners.

The purity of her family blood is not important to her. She once desired to marry an Englishman, but she felt that they were incompatible. People told her that the Englishman was a "rotter." "I was too immature at the time to make up my mind." She is definitely against the regulation of interracial marriage by law. She feels that her personal conflicts will eventually be resolved either in marriage or religion;

though she is a writer, she has little hope of resolving her conflicts through art. . . . Most definitely she will send her children to European schools.

She fears Asians, yet she knows how much they suffer. Hence, she does not want to see Asian and African nations act as a racial or political bloc. "I feel for both sides. I love Asia and I love Europe and I don't want to see a clash. . . ."

She does not speak Malay. In her childhood she lived with her mother and father in a "mixed" district, though there existed both "native" and European districts in her city. She does not know the literacy rate in Malaya.

She has a deep curiosity about Japan and longs to go there; they are a powerful, civilized, "yellow" people. "Maybe I could fit in there." She reacted strongly to the Japanese occupation of Malaya; her feelings were ambivalent: she respected the Japanese and feared them.

The Japanese worked up much racial feeling in Malaya, but they did not originate that racialism. She says: "The racial feeling was already there; the British brought it in and the Japanese simply exploited it and organized it."

She knows nothing of the relations among the new Asian and African countries and she has no notion as to how those nations can avoid the development of tensions. . . . Toward China she holds a deep fear. "They are helping the Malayan Communists in the jungles right now!" she wails. "When I was in my house in Singapore, I could hear the Reds shooting. Each night a guard was placed before our door. Any stranger was instantly arrested. Those Chinese come to a country and, before you know it, they have opened a business. My mother called them 'counter-jumpers,' because they made money so quickly and took up other professions. They make slums wherever they go. They're awful." (Bourgeois and Communist Chinese are all the same to her!)

She feels that peace is the most urgent problem now; the

United Nations is a terrible disappointment to her, but the idea is good. "Maybe if we all had faith in it, it might avert war," she says. The Asian and African countries really have no voice in the United Nations, she says.

Fear makes the white Western nations act as a racial and political bloc against the Asians and Africans. When Stalin called the Russians Asiatics, he was trying to win the sympathy of Asians. . . . "Colored" countries, she feels, are countries like the West Indies, African countries, etc. "Colored" *races* include Asians, she feels. Expressly, she does not regard Malaya as being a "colored" country. She was uncertain about Indonesia.

"Left" means anyone inclined toward Russian Communism; but being Left in England means being pro-Labor Party. She would not express herself about the meaning of the word "Right." She strongly feels that no nation should ever use the hydrogen or atom bomb as a military weapon.

Her country (Malaya) needs machinery and it should be obtained in the course of normal trade.

"Democratic opinion" to her means the free expression of ideas, "democratic institutions" are forums for such ideas. The exercise of state power is justified by the amount of power entrusted to a government by the masses of people.

In regard to world government she says:

"I hope never to live to see it. I hate the idea of a super-government dictating to people. No state should create trade unions for workers. I'd like a democratic form of government in Malaya. I believe that social and political change stems from both economic and psychological causes."

The Chinese have secret societies in Malaya, but she knows nothing of them.

There is a conflict in Malaya between the younger and the older generations; the origins of this conflict come from the family structure. Traditional forms of living conflict with the desires of the younger people who are stimulated by American movies, big cars, and the general influence of the West. . . .

A classless society in an economic sense is impossible. The First World War, in her opinion, was the single most important event of the twentieth century; it gave birth to Communism. If Malaya were fully developed, she'd like to see it resemble Britain. She has no ideas about how the West has affected Malaya.

Her idea of a great man is someone who is true to himself. The aim of education is to make people think for themselves. She believes most strongly in the need for capital punishment. "During the Japanese occupation there was much looting in Malaya, much rioting. The Japanese penalty for such was to chop off heads and impale them on poles to warn others. It worked. I tell you, Asians need such as that. As a last resort, capital punishment is good. At this moment in Malaya we welcome the idea of the British remaining. Of course, we want self-government, but we are not ready for it."

The European working class felt itself far superior to Russians and would not support the Russian Revolution. Lenin's turning to the poor masses of Asia was clever, she says. She is convinced that the removal of oppressive conditions makes men happy.

The world needs no universal humanism, surely not in the form of world government or Communism or Fascism. Books, ideas, etc., are the only valid psychological or spiritual food that people need. No control from above is her motto.

It was nine o'clock; in the corridor of the train, the bell sounded for dinner. As I made my way, swaying with the rushing train, down the narrow aisle to the dining car, I reflected:

This Eurasian girl's replies shed more light upon a personal dilemma than upon the causes of that dilemma. At bottom, a simple and firm choice on her part could have eradicated her problem. She could have become either British or Malayan and that would have been the end of it. Whatever her choice, she would have eventually inherited new problems, but they would have been objective ones and she could have dealt with them in terms of action based on reality. Fundamentally, I felt that she was reveling in an emotional enjoyment of clinging to the sweet agony of an infantile situation. . . .

Though some superficial observers would have said that her "nervousness" was caused by her mixed blood, it was evident that it was rather the result of a mixed environment, of divided loyalties, of opposing values warring in her heart. Catholic norms of respect for authority clashed with nationalistic Malayan norms that prompted rebellion against the British. . . . At the expense of shame for herself, British norms won. Her dilemma, however, did reveal the irony of educating colonials in Western schools: her education had conditioned her for a situation other than the one in which she lived. Her impulsiveness of speech might have been the product of the clash of the two worlds of values that swirled in her.

Though she said that she took her religion for granted, there resided deep in her a latent, unconscious ambivalence towards that religion that found expression in her questioning attitude toward Malaya and her father. She was hostile toward authority; she wanted no part of world government; no state should sponsor religion (no father should have created the kind of problem that her father had created for her! There were times, when I was questioning her, that I felt that she wanted to be her own father; there was a strongly repressed masculine drive, though she was ostensibly feminine in manner . . .).

She, like the Indonesian-born European, felt that some vague, metaphysical principle in nature had decreed that Africa was for the blacks, China for the yellows, Europe for the whites, etc. (It was amazing how widespread this feeling was in Asia and Europe, but less in Asia than in Europe. Those who took their racial environment for granted seemed to feel that nature had ordained the present arrangement; and those who had been shaken up, as it were, by war, racial prejudice, or religious persecution, had become awakened and felt that the world belonged to all of those who lived in it.)

Her insistence that Eurasians were full of complexes was but an oblique recognition of her own perturbed state, and some of the doubt and distrust that she felt for Malayans she also felt for herself. Her outlook being divided, she held toward Malayan culture a vacillating attitude, respecting parts of it and disparaging others. As highly color-conscious as an American Negro, she felt the racial insults thrown from both sides. Her individualism made her family blood unimportant to her, yet, concerning love objects, she leaned first toward the whites and then toward the group with which her father was identified. . . . It was significant that the Japanese attracted her mightily because of their "pride" and "strength" and "development," and she would certainly have liked to belong to a "colored" nation if that nation resembled, say, the British or the American. Her *bête noire* was the yellow races, be they bourgeois or Communist. And she was careful to exclude Malaya from the category of the "colored" countries.

The social aspects of Catholicism made her distinguish between the Leftism of Russia and that of the British Labor Party; her refusal to describe what Right meant to her indicated that that was her position. Though no nation should use the atom or hydrogen bomb as a military weapon, she passionately believed in capital punishment, especially as a protection against Communism and the yellow races. Her belief in democracy was limited by national boundaries; to her mind, world government, though supported by all the people of the earth, was as bad as Communism.

To her most problems were subjective ones, and "thinking" could solve them; "greatness" was being true to one's self. Though ostensibly conservative, this girl could almost as easily have been a revolutionary, for the crux of her problem was a question of identification. . . . Her agonizing position was born of accident, and her emotional rootlessness aggravated it. Had Communism been presented to her before she embraced Catholicism, she might well have accepted it. . . .

After dinner, back in my compartment, I resumed perusing my notes:

Moving from the European-born Indonesian and the Eurasian, I had encountered an Asian, but, strangely, a Westernized one. Mr. X was an extraordinary man, one of the leading educators of his country. He was no marginal man; he was more Western than most Westerners. Self-made, partly self-educated, rich, he stood alone and unique among his kind. Each question posed elicited a psychological reaction (I might say a physiological one!): a quick smile, a tensing of his muscles, a faraway look, then halting words that cut across the distilled wisdom of many cultures.

He is married, fifty years of age, has six children. His rooms are lined with shelves of books from all the Western countries. Widely read, widely traveled, he reacts sharply to my questions and I have the impression that ideas are more real to him than reality. His parents are Moslems, but he shies off committing himself too definitely in religious matters.

He feels that the state should not have anything actively to do with religion, but perhaps the state ought to try to keep alive the sense of the religious, the attitude and feeling of religion without regard to sects or ideology.

He feels that the overrunning of the continents of Asia and Africa by the white Western nations was a mixture of good and bad. Objectively, the impact of the West had a liberating influence. He is inclined to feel that short-range views tend to emphasize the damage done to Asia and Africa; five hundred years from now the bad effects will be forgotten and the good effects remembered.

He is interested in politics in spite of himself. "I'm impatient with politicians; they take such short views. My aim is to make people think correctly. At this moment, politics is the negative thing in my country. . . ."

He participated in the liberation movement of his country in the field of publishing; he was a member of the first parliament and he would like to sit in parliament again. The Japanese imprisoned him for three months when he opposed their trying to ram the Indonesian mind into a strait jacket. When the Japanese banned the Dutch tongue, he saw his opportunity and came forward with his own native language, Indonesian, which is now the official language of his country.

He has traveled in Europe and America, but he has not served in the armed forces of any non-Indonesian power.

"The only enemy of Indonesia is Indonesia herself," he says.

He attends many international conferences but feels that the Asian-African Conference is but a political gesture to bolster the local political regime in Indonesia. He does not feel that there is a naturally allotted, geographical space for each race on earth; the earth is for everybody. . . . He has many white friends. His wife is German. He feels that Western contact has had an emancipating effect upon him and his people, smashing the irrational ties of custom and tradition. "But the West failed to replace these ruptured relations with anything positive," he says. Dutch colonial oppression kept the Indonesians stupid, did not give the people a chance to develop their personalities. The only justification of Dutch rule in Indonesia was the superiority of the Dutch. . . .

Inferiority feelings in his country have been copiously expressed in novels, plays, poems. As proof of the intense inferiority feelings engendered in his people after three hundred and fifty years of Dutch rule, he cited the passion with which the Indonesians rejected the Dutch language and insisted upon resurrecting their own long-buried native tongue, a tongue which now, under enforced conditions, they seek to modernize and make serviceable. Japanese occupation helped to stimulate the desire on the part of the Indonesians to break with the West.

He first heard the word "lynch" in connection with what the United States did to American Negroes; he first encountered the phrase "White Man's Burden" in connection with Dutch rule over Indonesia; he came across the phrase "Yellow Peril" in connection with Western attitudes toward Japan and China. "It's racial snobbery," he says. He believes that racism can be eliminated by education, by informing people of its baleful effects.

He yearns to see Indonesia industrialized. He says: "We must have a most fundamental change in every department of life. That part of the past that can be synthesized with the future will be saved." The purity of his family blood is not important to him; he will not send his children to either "national" or European schools; he will send them to *modern* schools.

Maintaining close contact with his people, he not only speaks his native language fluently, but he helped to create and develop that language. Under Dutch rule he lived in the "native" quarter of his city; today he lives in the "European" quarter. The literacy rate is about 30 per cent in Indonesia. When the Dutch were driven out, his people "reclaimed" their country by renaming many of the towns, cities, etc. He feels that the relations between the new nations of Asia and Africa are cordial.

He disdains slogans, propaganda. We must, he says, rethink and revalue the whole of history. We must recontemplate the role of ethics and morality in the light of modern knowledge; the conflict between morals and the advance of science is something that must be thought through and enthroned in our educational system.

He could not answer yes or no to the question as to whether Indonesians were dissatisfied with the United Nations. "Indonesia is not as yet sufficiently developed to make herself felt. She cannot handle the facilities offered her."

He does not feel that the West constitutes a racial or political bloc against the Asian and African peoples. "Sometimes it might look as though such a bloc existed," he says. "But if one takes a long view, it's not entirely true. One must always remember that one of the deepest traits of the West is its anti-Western attitude. Take our fight for national independence, for example. A part of the West sided against the West in our favor. A characteristic of the West is its restlessness, its changeability. Most Easterners overlook this."

Regarding Stalin's identifying Russia with Asia, he says:

"Stalin used such a phrase because he felt that it benefited the policies of his country at that moment." He has no ideas about the impact of the Russian Revolution in either Europe or Asia.

When asked what the words "Left" and "Right" meant to him, he answered sharply:

"They are misused words. 'Left' is a word that is an instrumentality in political struggles. The same is true of the word 'Right.' In reality, there is not much difference between the Left and Right today. Again I say that we badly need a redefinition of words that will link words with reality. To garner votes from emotionally conditioned and ignorant masses, politicians use terminologies from the last century. The character of the world has changed radically, but we are using an old, outmoded terminology to describe that world. Many of the world's problems are simple, but we use words to describe those problems and the problems become complicated. The phrases on the lips of most people have little or nothing to do with the new times. Words like 'Left' and 'Right' denote psychological attitudes rather than objective realities. . . ."

Is a nation ever justified in using the atom or hydrogen bomb as a military weapon? "What a question! Such a question has meaning only when there is no war. Once you are in a war, you use what you have got."

He says that Indonesia needs all kinds of aid. "We need all those things that will help us to stand shoulder to shoulder with other nations, things that will make us the equal of others. But this is not simple. For one nation to help another is to assist in the development of a competitor. True planning is possible only on a world basis. For that we need a superparliament filled with men of the highest skills. The insistence upon state sovereignty is what blocks world planning, and world planning is the only way to aid nations to develop."

He balked when I asked him what the phrases "democratic opinion" and "democratic institutions" meant to him.

"These are difficult questions. Maybe my attitude will be misunderstood, will shock people. Like so many other phrases we use so much and do not think about, these phrases ought to be re-examined and reinterpreted. . . ." He paused, stared off. "The best way to explain my whole attitude to you is to tell you a story. I was interned by the Japanese for opposing what they wanted to do with our educational system. There were some twelve of us in a tiny cell. For a window, we had only a small hole high up in the wall. It was hot. . . . We suffered. Spiders and lice crawled on the floor. I hated it; we all hated it; I hated it in particular, for I could never be alone. I refused to take exercise; it was only when the others went out to take exercise that I could be alone and *think*. . . . When alone, I sat and thought. What could I do? What was my role here? Would I die? Would I live? At last I came to feel what the true worth of a man was. I survived only because I could *think*. . . . I mastered my situation with my mind. That was the main thing. Thinking is what marks off man from the animal kingdom. The Japanese conquered me, but not really. . . .

"How can a man's worth be measured when he votes? If Democracy means the opportunity of each man to develop to his highest capacity, then a mere counting of heads is no Democracy. Really, Fascism is the logical outcome of Democracy as it is practiced in the world today. I ask you: Do people really know what they are voting for at the polls? The world is not simple, yet simple men vote. Is there any wonder that they vote for things that they never get? Some men are just naturally quick, and some are just naturally dull-witted. . . . And the quick rule; the mobile get to the top, get power and riches. That is the law of the jungle. . . . So when we trust the running of government to a counting of heads, the vast majority cannot vote for their rights; they do not know them. I don't know of any system of government that can defeat the general welfare more thoroughly than what we call Democracy. Democracy is a means of protest, not a method of construction.

"I feel that men ought to have the right to vote for only what they can understand. I'd not have the franchise go further than village voting. But there are problems that village folk cannot understand, so why ask them to vote on them? Only a scoundrel bent upon duping ignorant people would urge those people to vote on issues too big and complicated for them to understand.

"In the world today Democracy is the greatest enemy of the true democrat. The so-called democratic process keeps the real democrats from being in a position to help the people. People have been lulled into believing that they are wise, that they know all things, that there is a kind of divine wisdom in their collective decisions; so, when these simple people try to think and vote, the quick and the unscrupulous outwit them and cheat them.

"That is why I insist that all of these questions must be re-examined. I know that people will quail before such probing. The problem of ethics must be brought up again; today we live in a world that is modern and our ideas about that world are obsolete. That is the origin of most of our trouble. . . ."

I felt there must have been a factor of Asian skepticism in that man's outlook. Compassion for man was the keynote of his life. Such a mind refused to accept the means for the end. His outlook was grounded in a tough-souled pragmatism. My questionnaire was not designed for such as he. He stared at me and smiled. "I'm alone in my country," he mumbled sadly. I desisted in my questioning.

This subject's replies, especially his disdainful skepticism toward Democracy, came as a complete surprise, and I jokingly dubbed him the H. L. Mencken of Indonesia. . . . He had an acute mind, yet he was atypical and he ruefully admitted it. But, as drastic as he sounded, he was by far the most impractical of all the Asians I talked to. He was logical, but his logic was not of the life that surrounded him. Because he could easily spot fraud, he had concluded that that fraud had no valid reality.

He took the view that, in the long run, the impact of the West upon the East would undoubtedly be entered upon the credit side of the historical ledger. I was inclined to agree with him. But that was not what the individual Asian colonial victim felt about that Western impact while he was undergoing his torturous "liberation" from his irrational customs and traditions, his superstition and folklore. It may be perfectly true that there was absolutely no synchronization between the aims and actions of the Western merchants, soldiers, and missionaries when they swarmed out of Europe and overran Asia and Africa; but, from where the victim stood, the impact of the West had as its main effect a result that could come about only if those Western forces had been synchronized in their aims and actions: that is, his culture had been smashed by what he felt to be hostile forces and he had been cast into a void. . . .

On the other hand, compassion was this Asian's hallmark. If the future of the masses of Asia were to be in the hands of aristocratic spirits such as this Indonesian educator, then one could say that the bridge between lives anchored in mysticism and lives built on secular and industrial reason could be erected with a minimum of tragedy and human waste. But neither Asia nor Africa nor Europe was ruled or was likely to be ruled by compassionate aristocrats; instead, there were millions of folk-minded masses trapped in the nets of fear, hunger, and impossible dreams—masses at the mercy of irresponsible interpretations of their plight. Such masses, under the leadership of messianic men, would be induced into situations whose final outcome would spell more of glory for the messianic leaders than of welfare for the millions of expendable lives involved.

There was no doubt, in my mind, that my Indonesian educator was correct on the plane of abstract logic, but logic cannot solve problems whose solutions come not by thinking but by living. His approach implied a denial of collective thought-processes, of mass organic experiences embedded in the very lives and social conditions about him. His people, eighty million strong, had fought and died for the right to vote, and now they were going to vote whether they voted right or not and there was nothing that anybody could easily do about it. Regrettably, one could safely assume that his influence upon Asian reality would be nil.

My eyes were heavy; the Madrid express was rocking me to sleep and I could hold out no longer. . . . When I awakened the next morning, daylight gleamed through the curtain of my train window. After breakfasting, I went into my notes again. . . .

My fourth subject had been a more typical and basic Asian, whose attitude was less conditioned by abstract considerations; from the outset, I had been able to feel in his reactions the pressures of history and environment:

He is full-blooded Indonesian in his twenties. Single, restless, a student of political science, he is supported by his government, and he openly says: "I belong to the backward nations of the world, the underdeveloped nations." And his manner of saying it indicates how deeply a sense of his people's inferiority weighs upon him. He has a quick smile that hides bitter knowledge; already he is an actor: for the outside world that is white, he laughs; for the nonwhite world he drops his smiling mask and his eyes stare with the unblinking fixity of the fanatic.

He is Moslem and so are his parents. He has broad artistic interests and boasts of the cultural contacts of his people. He is, he says, too busy with his political studies for organizational activity, and he is too young to have participated in the liberation movement of his country.

"The West came to us to get what they could out of us," he says. The Christian religion, he believes, did not have a great influence upon his country. Proudly, he drew me a rough map and pointed out that the Moslems and the Hindus had influenced the Indonesians "long before the Christians ever came. It was in the southern islands, where pagans live, that Christianity has had its influence."

Yes; the state should support religion. "The Moslem religion, unlike the Christian religion, is coherently social. We have a variety of religions; we even have a ministry of religion."

The nations of Asia and Africa have a common colonial experience that binds them together and gives them common interests; they should consult together often. The relations obtaining today between the new Asian and African countries have been conditioned by attitudes instilled by the late imperial powers; hence, relations between these powers are very sensitive. Nations like China, Japan, and the Philippines are inclined to feel that they are the natural leaders of Asia and are prone to say: "Don't you tell us what to do. You are a new country and without experience." He says: "We don't like such attitudes. They reflect the influence of the West."

That the state should regulate marriage is something that he expects, though he and his family are in revolt against such state measures when pitched on a narrow plane. There exist customary laws in Indonesia that regulate the marriage of one blood clan with another, but this custom does not rest on racial identity in the Western sense of that term: it has religious sanction. His brother has married a Dutch girl; his father married out of the clan. He describes himself as a marginal man. "It's up to us; we have a free choice in marrying or doing anything we want to do, if we'd only take the choice." But he is not concerned at present about marrying a European girl. "It's possible, but it's in the future."

He has no Dutch friends; he is self-conscious about it. I'd touched a complex. "I've no time to find Dutch friends, really. I'm busy."

His contacts with the West have left scars. "I remember once at military school something happened. We were together there, Dutch and Indonesians. I was invited to a birthday party by one of my Dutch classmates. But the parents of my classmate did not want me to come to the house. There was a big row in my classmate's home about it. At the last moment the boy's parents said that I could come along. I went and pretended that I was having a good time, but I was self-conscious. . . .

"My father is a doctor and holds a high position. But the Dutch who live next door would never call on his services unless they could not get a white doctor. The rich Dutch would never ask for his services, and the poor Dutch would call him only when there was no Dutch or German doctor to be found. . . .

"My political awakening came one day at school when I colored the face of Queen Wilhelmina with my pencil. I didn't know what I was doing; I was sitting in class with my book open before me and when I saw her face on the page, I made it dark, dark like mine. . . . When the Dutch teacher saw that, he beat me, but he didn't tell me why. . . . It seemed natural to me for my queen to have a dark face. My father had to explain to me the meaning of what I had done. . . .

"I first heard the word 'lynch' when I was very young; we were at lunch and my father told of a lynching in the United States. I first heard the phrase 'White Man's Burden' just before the war between the Japanese and the Chinese. The word 'nigger' came to me from the English and the Americans. 'Yellow Peril'?" He laughed to hide a nervous reaction. "I heard it in connection with the Western attitude toward the Chinese. . . . You know, it reminds me of the phrase 'Yellow Fever' . . . It makes me think of disease, something that has to be stamped out, cured—something formidable, dreadful . . ." (He had looked at me slyly, winking his eye, and I had been shocked to realize that he had been referring to the two million Chinese who lived in his country and who were widely hated!)

He would send his children to European schools only after they had gotten their B.A. degrees. "By that time their characters will have been formed and they can resist the bad influences of the West much better."

His people renamed many of the towns, cities, and mountains after the Dutch had been driven out. "After all, the country belonged to us."

The United Nations cannot stop war as it is now set up. The big powers have too much influence. The United Nations can postpone war but not stop it.

Indonesians, he feels, cannot conceive of Europe. "Our people think that Europeans live more or less as we do. But, of course, European standards of living are much higher."

European workers felt superior to the Russians and never wanted to identify themselves with the Russian Revolution. Lenin was smart to appeal to the Asians. "But one must not think that the idea of Communism is new to us. What impressed us about Communism was its technique of struggle, organization—its methods. We borrow a lot of those ideas, but we use them in our way. With us land has always been communal. For example, China has always had large collectives in terms of large families. . . ."

In his country, he says, there is a conflict between the younger and the older generations; the older generation is more dependable than the younger. "Our youth has never known anything but war and revolution. They've lived in anarchy. The older people have the habit of work and they make the best administrators in our country at the present time. We made a revolution and now our revolutionists are unemployed and they turn bandit. We don't know what to do with them.

"I want to see my country industrialized, but too much of

it is bad. What I would like to save in my country's culture? We don't have a national culture yet; we have many cultures. We are trying to find a culture.

"There is no country in the West that I'd like to see my country resemble.

"The biggest event of the twentieth century was the defeat of Russia by Japan in 1905. It was the beginning of the liberation of the Asian mind. . . . Social and political change comes through economic factors. The greatest impact that the West has made upon Asia was in the form of gunpowder. Trade came next.

"There are no great men in the world today.

"Education should teach men to live together. . . . That's why we got rid of the Dutch. They didn't belong in our country, so we drove them out. We didn't have any ideas or feelings beyond just getting rid of them."

What I had read in books, what I'd seen in the daily press told me that I had touched the real, contemporary Asia. . . . What struck me first of all in this student's attitude was his ready acceptance of reality, the "given" in his environment; he was quite content to work and struggle with what was at hand. To him reality was what it "seemed" to be, and he was determined to grasp hold of it and follow its processes and try to mold them in the direction that he desired. He knew that his attitude was carrying the day in Asia, and he felt that he was preparing himself to enter a world whose lines of battle had been mapped out by his revolutionary predecessors. He spoke with that nonchalant confidence that betokened a conviction that, though hostile Westerners might brand his words as mere chatter, he knew that his words were the stuff of reality for hundreds of millions of his fellow Asians. . . .

He impressed me as having the feeling that, though his government had taken power, the fight was not over; the objective situation about him might spell freedom, but his subjective issues were still unresolved. (That was why he had said that there were "several" cultures in his country, and not a national culture.) He had escaped a world that he did not want, but he did not know what kind of a world he did want. There was in him a fund of passion which he had to spend somehow, someway. . . . The world was a problem to him, and he was a problem to himself. His reactions were strong but not simple, though, had he been pushed, I suspect that he would have modestly described himself as a simple man. . . .

No missionary had tampered with his Moslem beliefs and he was, therefore, outside of the Western world, objective about it in a way that no Jew, Gypsy, or refugee could ever be; he could hate, that is, he could reason passionately toward the aim of destroying a loathsome enemy.

He was totalitarian-minded, but without the buttress of modern Communist or Fascist ideology; he did not need any, for his totalitarian outlook was born of his religious convictions. Allah was his dictator. Hence, preachments against the separation of church and state, for the liberty of the individual, sounded like so much alien, diabolical propaganda to his ears. But he was sophisticated; he met arguments directed against his beliefs with a smile. He knew both East and West, without really believing in either of them. There was another and other world that he and his kind had to create.

Personal relations were not important factors to him; his affective identifications were with nations, movements, religions, cultures, races. . . . Personal insults meant nothing; only when those aims in which he fondly believed were maligned or threatened did he react with passion.

Racially, the Dutch had put him through the mill, and an element of iron was already deep in his heart. Confronting whites, he would have bent a million times, but he would never have broken. He was willing and ready to die for what he felt to be the value of himself, that is, his sense of dignity. . . . His people's inferiority rankled in him, and he passionately longed to see his country industrialized. But such a longing was not related to the benefits of industrialization *per se*. To him industrialization was a means, the only one he knew, to hoist the West off of his back. Of Western values he wanted none.

Great men? There were no such things. How could there be, when he and his kind were suffering . . . ? The aim of education? Ah, he was true here. . . . "That's why we got rid of the Dutch," he had told me. His eyes had shone as he had shot that bolt home. *He meant that the West had been stupid and had taught him enough to make him know that the West was his enemy!*

In the morning's light I stared at the tilting olive groves on the Spanish mountainsides; the train jolted toward Madrid. . . . I frowned, trying to judge just what coefficient I could have given him as a representative of Asian reactions. . . .

The next and last Asian subject had been a young journalist from Pakistan. He had been eloquent, bitter, with a fund of fire smoldering in his heart. Like all uprooted Asians, talking had seemed with him a compulsion: it had been as though he had felt that talking would have helped him to find answers to questions that were plaguing him. . . . He had spoken in quick, clipped, tense tones. . . .

Born in a small town, he'd been educated by missionaries, had also attended European schools. With a wry smile, he called himself a Christian. He had grown up in a home that had a mixture of Christian and Hindu influences. "Religiously, I'm really nothing," he confessed. "But among my people at home I can't own to that."

"Should the state sponsor religion? No!" he snapped. "Let religion be a private affair. The Christian religion helped the British to gain power. Christianity divided my country, sundered an already greatly sundered people. The Christian religion, as it operated among us, was a political instrument, an instrument used by the West to rule my country. I was born in the Christian faith, but I feel that that faith was used against me and my country."

His father was educated in the United States and returned to Pakistan with a heightened political consciousness; so, as a young boy, he breathed an atmosphere of political discussions that raged in his home. He learned early that he was a member of a subject nation and race. While still in his teens, he participated in the liberation movement of his country, but he has not served any time as a political prisoner. He refused to serve in the British Army.

Now that Pakistan is free, he does not feel that his country has an enemy. He has attended international conferences. "But I won't tell you how many and I won't identify them. I don't want any country to refuse me a visa. One must be careful these days, you know.

"The Asian-African Conference will be a great thing. In the past, the West always took the lead; now it is time for Asia and Africa to lead mankind. We have been objects; now we can be subjects."

He has traveled and read widely; he does not feel that there are any hard and fast racial lines in the world and he is not in favor of any geographical limitations upon where people should dwell, despite the fact that he has felt racial hostility from whites. He has many white friends but he feels that they hold toward him patronizing attitudes which imply: "We are white and we showed you the way." He feels that such attitudes are traditional with whites. "The impact of the West was to awaken me, to make me feel the ways and values and manners of both worlds, the East and the West. We Easterners are more conscious of these things than the Westerners," he says. The West has made the Easterner feel a sense of shame, and this shame is very widespread and is really an inferiority feeling that finds expression in such books as *Mother India*. Such cultural expressions seem to him an attempt on the part of his people to defend themselves against the shame-engendering impact of the West.

He encountered the word "lynch" in reading British and American periodicals; he met "Yellow Peril," "nigger," and "White Man's Burden" in a like manner. When he was a child in India the British called him nigger. (He is as dark as a Negro.) "The only way to eliminate racism is to eliminate imperialism. The structure of imperialism means racism; the two are one thing. Racism is an instrument of the West, an instrument used to control Asia and Africa."

He feels that the only way for his country to become free of the West is to industrialize, but he is afraid of too much industrialization. "The one item I value most in my culture is religion for the masses; we can keep religion for the people if we don't industrialize too much."

There is no comparison, in his mind, between the living standards of his country and the Western countries. "We are far, *far* behind," he says sadly, shaking his head.

In the past the racial purity of his family blood was very important to him, but he has changed his mind about all of that now. "I've seen too many alien lands and alien people. And the West has used that idea about blood to divide us. Definitely, I'd not support any legislation to regulate marriage between the races. I look at any idea that seeks, for whatever reason, to divide us with distrust."

Would he ever marry a European woman? "No!" he exploded bitterly. "Why should I do that, after the way they regard me?"

He was ambivalent about the value of a Western education; he felt that it was necessary for him and his generation to learn Western values and methods to aid them in liberating their country, but, now that his country was free, he'd want the next generation to learn more about their own values. He would want his children to learn about the West, but from an entirely different point of view than the one that was taught him.

He feels strongly that the new Asian and African nations should act, for the time being, as a racial and political bloc. "This should happen until a balance has been achieved," he says.

Because he feels that the West has striven to erect an elite as an instrument of rule in subject countries, he has deliberately kept close contact with the common people of his land. He speaks his native tongue fluently. During British rule, there was a "native" and European quarter in the city in which he lived; his father was a civil servant and it enabled him to move and live in both worlds.

He is sensitive about the West's description of the high rate of illiteracy in his country; he feels that these European standards are unfair to the quick intelligence of his people. "We are judged entirely in terms of British standards," he complains.

His people quickly renamed many towns, mountains, etc., when the British left.

He feels that the relations between the new countries of Asia and Africa are very good, except for those countries dominated by Western capital. He cites Siam as an example of such a country. He admits that religious tensions exist between the new countries, but he has no idea about how these tensions could be lessened. "All intelligent Asians now know that the Western white man is praying for us to fight among ourselves, and that we'll never do," he declares. "Fighting among ourselves is the white man's only chance of getting back. We're closing ranks. The white man will be disappointed."

To him the colonial problem is the most urgent and

important thing on the international scene. "I agree with Nehru," he says. "Colonialism and not Communism is the main danger. Get rid of colonies and you'll not have a trend toward Communism. Russia was in effect a colony when she went Communist. The American thesis is shortsighted and unhistorical. The next explosion of Communism will come out of some colony. . . . I distrust anybody's policy that is based on Communism as the main danger; it is a dishonest policy; if it is not, then it's worse, because it's stupid."

To him the United Nations is an instrument of United States foreign policy; it won't succeed, he thinks, in preventing war. The Asian and African nations have not enough authority and influence in that body. He is convinced that the white nations of the West act as a racial and political bloc even in and through the United Nations. . . .

Russia pretends to belong to Asia in order to win the sympathy of the Asian people. Lenin's call to Asia was realistic. "But we would have risen without the Communists."

The West calls some nations "colored" in order to impose a separation between the dominator and the dominated. A Leftist is someone with Russian Communist sympathies; a Rightist is a propagator of imperialism.

He does not feel that any nation is ever justified in using the atom or hydrogen bomb as a military weapon.

His country urgently needs factory and farm equipment from the West. "But we won't take these needed items in exchange for granting political concessions. We are alert that the West tries to gain influence by such means. We must get what we need from the West in the course of normal trade. We'd rather suffer than let the West steal back in that way."

In general all state power should be derived from the people. "But I suspect all phrases like 'democratic opinion' and 'democratic institutions'; too many people have been hoodwinked and enslaved by those slogans. I say, Live and Let Live. That's simple and honest."

The state should organize trade unions for workers; he wants a democratic government in his country; he feels that social and political change comes through economic forces. . . . There are no outright secret societies in his country; there are political groups which wear a religious guise. A classless society in an economic sense is definitely possible.

The older men lead in his country and the younger men follow. If his country were fully industrialized, he would want it to resemble Sweden or Switzerland. To him the greatest effect of the West upon his country was the bare fact of occupation.

A great man is a man concerned about mankind. Gandhi was such a man. . . . The aim of education should be to create a greater understanding between peoples. The word "civilization" means to him big cities, comfort, fine cars, movies. . . .

Europe, in his opinion, has "had" it. The European working class was selfish and felt itself too superior to heed the meaning of the Russian Revolution, felt no sense of identity with it. The liberation of Asian nations is more important than revolution. "The Africans should take help from anywhere, if that help will enable them to build free nations."

To him the removal of oppressive conditions does not necessarily make men happy.

He feels that some culture should lead the masses of the world in establishing a universal humanism and that Buddhist cultures can do this for mankind.

I lifted my eyes; the pastel-colored apartment buildings of Madrid were flashing past. I sighed.

By far, this Pakistanian journalist had disclosed the deepest chasm between East and West that I had yet come across. His bitterness had been edged directly by his contact with missionaries. He felt that he had to rebel twice as passionately against the West to overcome "alien" influences lingering in him. Indeed, his most curious attitude involved religion: he was willing to allow religion to exist in his country in the future, but not for himself; he wanted the *masses to believe.* He feared a too-drastic industrialization of his country would result in those masses' lives being as stripped of tradition and meaning as his had been. If he were restless, how much more would be the illiterate millions when cast into the void . . . ?

It was clear to me that the East held by the West as a fond image does not exist any more; indeed, the classical conception of the East is dead even for the Easterner. . . . He lives in his world, but he does not believe in it any longer; he holds on to its values with too much self-consciousness to live by them. In fact, his pretentious clinging to those old values signifies that he is trying to save face. This Pakistanian journalist knew in his heart that the West had been irrevocably triumphant in its destruction of his culture, but he insisted that when he embraced a new way of life he was going to do so on his own terms, with no monitoring or overlordship from Westerners.

I was discovering that this Asian elite was, in many ways, more Western than the West, their Westernness consisting in their having been made to break with the past in a manner that but few Westerners could possibly do. The elite of the East was now the restless, the changeable, the critical. . . . It would be naive to suppose that this journalist, having broken with the past, would now proceed to try to build a world that would be a duplicate of ours, and he could no more know the kind of world that he wanted to build than we knew when we started building ours.

Unless it was brought pointedly to his attention, the average white Westerner could never suspect how emotionally charged the Asian really was, how chronic his state of perturbation. The centuries-long dominance—military, political, religious, and economic—of the West over Asia had purged the Asian outlook of its naturalness and innocence. While the European, when he was in Asia as an administrator or businessman, did not regard the Asian as his enemy, the Asian almost inevitably looked upon the European as his prime antagonist.

The journalist's vehement objection to marrying a white woman was not based upon a fear of adulterating his family blood stream; it was a matter of hot pride. The West had kept their women out of reach, and he would prove, by spurning such women, that he did not react to them, did not want them. . . .

Believing that the removal of oppressive conditions does not make men happy, he would not perhaps resort to a violent attempt at overthrowing what he felt to be oppressive conditions. . . . Yet his disinherited state makes him expect an over-all, universal culture; he dreams of men like Gandhi banishing the conditions that make for diversity and establishing unity. . . .

The reactions that I had been able to gather could not possibly describe Asian reality; the questions that I had posed had not been designed to elicit that. But those replies did, to some degree, illuminate that narrow zone where East met West, and that zone was hot and disturbed.

The first general conclusion that could be drawn was that not one Asian had taken pains to defend that most sacred of all Western values: property.

The second conclusion: to justify his dominance, the European had sought to make his superiority seem historically natural; he had cited examples of the cruelties of Asians and Africans to one another to show how his long control over Asian and African destinies was merely what man had always done to man. What the European generally overlooked in his attempts at self-justification was that the Asian and African had indeed been cruel to one another but that they had practiced their barbarities and brutalities within the confines of common cultures and religions which even the victims, in some measure, shared.

The trampling by a powerful West upon the traditional and customary Asian and African cultures, cultures sacred and beyond rational dispute, left vast populations at the mercy of financial and commercial relations which compounded the confusion in Asian and African minds. Attempts on the part of the sundered and atomized "coloreds" to reconstitute their lives, to regain that poise and balance that reigned before the coming of the white man, were regarded as a warlike threat by the powers originally responsible for the atomization of the customs and traditions. Present Asian and African mass movements are the frantic efforts on the part of more than one and one-half billion human beings to reorganize their lives. . . .

Still another and, to the Western mind, somewhat baffling trait emerged from these Asian responses. There seemed to be in their consciousness a kind of instinct (I can't find a better word!) toward hierarchy, toward social collectivities of an organic nature. In contrast to the Western feeling that education was an instrument to enable the individual to become free, to stand alone, the Asian felt that education was to bind men together. Underlying most Asian tenets was a hunger for a strong leadership, for authority, for a sacred "head" toward which all eyes could turn for guidance and final sanction. The Asian seemed to have a "picture" of life and wanted to find out where and how he fitted into that "picture." He sought no separate, unique, or individual destiny. This propensity toward the organically collective might be the residue from his past family, cultural, or religious conditioning, or a reflecton of it; it's hard to tell. . . . In any case, it certainly propelled him, irrespective of ideology, toward those collectivistic visions emanating from Peking and Moscow. . . . And all the fervid adjurations of Washington, London, or Paris to strive for individual glory and achievement left him cold and suspicious. And past colonial experience made him feel that unity with his own kind, the only strength he could visualize, was being threatened when he was asked to follow the lead of Western individualism.

To the Asian mind industrialization was not a project whose growth came with time, but a dogma in a religion, something to be experienced here and now with emotionally charged words; "race" was no longer a simple designation, nonscientific, of a people and their physiological differences, but an instrument of subjugation, a badge of shame, a burning and concrete fact that was proved instantly by the color of one's skin. . . . Religion was no longer a delicate relationship of a people to the world in which they lived, a relationship wrought through centuries and embodied in ritual and ceremony, but a proof of one's humanity, something to defend and cling to (even if one did not believe in it!) passionately, for the sake of one's pride, to redress the balance in the scales of self-esteem.

That elementary instinct that had made man conquer his environment, that right to name the items that surround one, was eagerly seized upon again as soon as the "white invader" had gone; then, like a child, he walked about his domain and touched his old playthings and called them again by the names that his father and his father's father had called them.

Rendered psychologically uncertain as to motive, the uprooted Easterner did everything self-consciously, watching himself, as it were. Behavior was spontaneous only when passionate action lifted him to the plane of self-forgetfulness.

Hence, to feel a thing deeply made that thing the worthwhile thing to do, indeed, made it the *right* thing to do. He felt that history now coincided with his feelings, for he knew that what he did was now making history; he might be right or wrong, but what he did would count historically for good or ill. He could not lose, really. A sort of depersonalization took place in his thinking, and this buttressed his personality toward an attitude of irresponsibility. Worlds of infinite possibility opened up before the eyes of the new, young Asians and Africans and they felt as gods. . . .

In Madrid, on Easter Sunday, I boarded a TWA Constellation for Rome where I made connections with a KLM Cairo-bound plane. I was heartened when a batch of French newspapermen hailed me. They were Bandung-bound and had the latest news.

Through the hot night we flew high over Africa, and Cairo was but a far-flung lake of shimmering lights when the plane landed for passengers and refueling. I heard an explosion of the French language; I turned my head and saw red-fezzed North Africans from Morocco, Algeria, and Tunisia climbing aboard: revolutionaries and nationalists from the turbulent areas of French rule along the life line of Western European imperialism. . . . I told myself: There's gonna be a hot time in old Bandung. . . . I studied the newcomers: they were a hotly nervous lot, tense, talkative. As the Constellation roared into the dark toward teeming Asia, I heard excited voices discussing Palestine.

"No matter what they do, they won't be able to keep the Jews off that agenda," a man said.

"Whether they let us raise the question of Jewish aggression or not, we are going to raise it!" another man shouted. "Their crimes will not be covered up—"

"The Jews are the greatest racists on earth and I'll prove it!" a dark-faced man with a thin mustache shouted above the roar of the plane's four engines.

He reached above his head and pulled down his brief case; from its fat bulk he withdrew a stack of photos which he began passing around. A batch was shoved into my hands and I glanced at them.

"What are these?" I asked.

"Photos of Arab refugees driven by Jews out of their homes!" he said. "There are nine hundred thousand of them, homeless, starving. . . ."

"Are you a delegate to the Asian-African Conference?" I asked him.

"No. I'm a journalist."

"Is Palestine coming up for discussion at Bandung?" I asked.

"We are going to try to raise it," he swore. "The world must know what has been done! It's our duty to make the world know. . . ."

I leafed through the bundle of photos; they were authentic, grim, showing long lines of men, women, and children marching barefooted and half-naked over desert sands, depicting babies sleeping without shelter, revealing human beings living like animals. I peered up into the face of the journalist; his eyes were unblinking, hot, fanatic. This man was religious. It was strange how, the moment I left the dry, impersonal, abstract world of the West, I encountered at once: *religion* . . . And it was a passionate, unyielding religion, feeding on itself, sufficient unto itself. And the Jews had been spurred by religious dreams to build a state in Palestine. . . . Irrationalism meeting irrationalism . . . Though the conversation about the alleged aggression of the Jews in Palestine raged up and down the aisles of the plane, I could hear but little of it; all I could make out was that the

Jews would come under sharp and bitter attack at Bandung, and that they had enemies who had a case and knew how to present that case at the bar of world opinion. . . . I recalled that six million Jews had been gassed, hounded, slaughtered, and burned by German Hitlerites, and I knew that that people, hapless and haunted, had yet more suffering and trials to bear in this world.

Later that evening (or rather morning), before the plane landed at Baghdad, I got into a conversation with a shy young man who had Oriental features. He turned out to be Indonesian, a student returning from Holland. He had spent four years studying sociology at Leiden.

"You're going to find your newly gained knowledge useful," I told him.

"Yes," he said. "My country is very backward."

"Do you have a large bourgeois class among the Indonesians?" I asked him.

Until that moment he had not asked who I was; now mental pain flickered over his sharp, brown face.

"You are an American?" he asked me.

"Yes."

"Negro?"

"Yes."

He relaxed. I was to get to know that reaction very well. The Asian had many truths to tell. He had one truth for the British, one for the Dutch, one for white Americans, and still another and a special kind of rueful truth for American Negroes, who shared a background of racial experience that made them akin to the Asian.

"No. We have no rich class among our people," he said. "We have no bourgeois to knock over."

"But in a nation of eighty million people, somebody has all the money. The Dutch are gone. Now who has the money?"

He stared at me with a strange, hard smile on his lips.

"For the *time being*, the Chinese have all the money," he said.

In his words I caught echoes of hate and a determination to have done with the two million Chinese of dual nationality who lived in his country. All you had to do was to touch an Asian, and out spewed hate, bitterness, and a long-nursed desire for revenge.

"How did you enjoy your stay in Holland?" I asked.

"I didn't," he said, and he would not look at me.

He was anti-Western, all right. And I wondered why Western nations insisted upon bringing these boys to their universities. . . . The young man I looked at was neither Eastern nor Western; he had been torn from his warm, communal Eastern environment and had been educated in a tight-laced, puritanical Teutonic environment which he could not love or accept. Where would he fit in now, being a stranger to both worlds . . . ?

High up in the skies of Asia, I lost track of time; day skies alternated with night skies and I cat-napped when I could. We landed briefly at Karachi and Sikhs mounted the plane; they had bushy black beards, Oxford accents, and they sat together in a knot. Black silken cords undercut their jaws and held black silken skull caps tightly to their heads. Wherever I looked in Asia I saw signs or symbols of religion and it made me silent. There is nothing that can be said when one faces men in whom there is a total mobilization of all the irrational forces of the human personality to a point of organized militancy. . . . It was rapidly dawning upon me that if the men of the West were political animals, then the men of the East were religious animals. . . .

It was night when we landed in Calcutta, and sleepiness made the airport a blur. Hindus entered the plane; they wore Western clothes and seemed urbanized. . . . Groggy from lack of sleep, I took Nembutal and did not awaken until the plane jolted me, landing in Bangkok; it was morning and Japanese and American newsmen swarmed aboard, chatting, their eyes puffy from lack of sleep. While the plane was on the ground, I stared at throngs of barefooted men who wore orange-colored robes; they were Buddhists and were making a pilgrimage. Here religion came before all else. . . .

Aloft again, I got into a conversation with a young Japanese newspaperman. Despite his bookish English, he made me understand that he was terribly interested in Africa.

"Why?" I asked him.

"We know nothing about Africa in Japan," he said. "Yet Africa is a vast continent."

"Even we of the West know but little of certain parts of Africa," I told him. I recommended some titles for him to read.

"What about this Belgian Congo?" he asked.

"I can't tell you a thing," I said. "I've never been there and I've never in my life met a man from the Belgian Congo."

"Why?"

"The Belgians do not allow them out," I informed him.

He stared and fell silent.

"What will be Japan's role at this conference?" I asked him.

"Our position is very delicate," he murmured.

Yes; the Asian-African Conference was the kind of get-together that the Japanese had undoubtedly once dreamed of holding. . . . The most Westernized and industrialized of all the Asian peoples, they must have felt that they were eating humble pie indeed to come and sit down with Burmese and Ceylonese and Indonesians. . . .

We were high over the jungles of Malaya, and political discussions raged. Rumors were sorted out, accepted, abandoned. Was it true that the Japanese were going to offer a public apology for their role in World War II? Was Sir John of Ceylon going to carry the ball for the West? Was a Peking-

Delhi-Cairo Axis forming? Were the Moroccans and the Tunisians and the Algerians uniting as a block against France? Would anyone from South Africa be at the conference to report on the racial tensions there? Would Red China launch an attempt to capture the offshore islands during the conference? What the hell did Nehru think he was doing flirting with Communist China's Chou En-lai? The delegations from the Philippines, from Iraq, from Syria would sound the call for freedom, would they not? Would Red China take advantage of the conference and use it as a propaganda tribunal? A group of American newspapermen had made a list of all the delegates going to Bandung and had checked them all off according to their political leanings and had come to the conclusion that the West would emerge victorious from its clash with China's evil genius, Chou En-lai. . . . I was baffled. Were we going to a football game?

These men, affable and relaxed, representing some of the world's biggest and most powerful newsgathering agencies, knew less, perhaps, than even I about what was going on. To them Bandung was a contest of personalities. I soon realized that American newsmen had at least two grave disabilities in trying to grasp what was happening: one, they had no philosophy of history with which to understand Bandung; two, they were trying to understand actions initiated by someone else and they could not quite grasp the nature of the terms in which those actions were being projected. . . .

In fact, the comments of the world's press upon the Asian-African Conference had been simply astonishing. From an English daily had come the following tidbit, written by one Sefton Delmer:

"They are holding a jamboree in the sun-drenched Indonesian hill town of Bandung next month. It is a political jamboree, an anti-Colonial gathering of Asian and African nations. What a pity President Sukarno and the Indonesian

Government are being so very exclusive and colour conscious about it!"

This was the beginning of a press tirade against the conference; the sponsoring powers had not invited any white Western powers, and the above writer seemed to have forgotten that for centuries Asian and African nations had watched in helpless silence while white powers had gathered, discussed and disposed of the destinies of Asian and African peoples—gatherings in which no Asian or African had ever had any say. The writer was protesting that the Asians and Africans were acting as the West had acted, had learned their lessons too well!

Two eminent Australians, Dr. John W. Burton, former Secretary of the Department of External Affairs, and Prof. Charles Patrick Fitzgerald, holder of the Chair of Far Eastern History at the Australian National University, Canberra, issued a statement that reflected Australia's dilemma in confronting the reverse of the racial policy she had so long and proudly practiced in the Pacific. In part the statement declared:

"It is our view that Australia should have been invited to this Conference and should have accepted; and should on all future occasions be invited and attend."

Yet most of the men who would attend the Bandung meeting could not have been admitted to Australian soil solely on the basis of their color and race; indeed, the mere presence of Australians and South Africans would have had an inhibiting and perhaps intimidating effect upon many of the Asian and African delegates who, above all, wanted to speak their minds freely and frankly among themselves.

The Launceston *Examiner* of Tasmania (Australia), December 30, 1954, gave vent to real fear when it stated:

Decisions by the "Colombo Premiers" are of deep significance to Australia and the Western world.

> **Their invitation to twenty-five nations, including Communist China, but excluding all Western countries, to a conference in April, could be the beginning of an upsurge of racial hatreds against the West. The decision to support Indonesia in its claim for sovereignty over West New Guinea, though not unexpected, should show Australians where the sympathies of most of their neighbours lie.**

Speculation about the role of Red China was voiced on December 28, 1954, by the Delhi *Times* of India. It stated:

> **. . . Much will depend on whether Peking considers itself more Asian than Communist or vice versa. If the Asian-African Conference accomplishes nothing more than reveal to what extent the Communist is willing to cooperate with its Asian neighbours and Arab States, it will be a worthy attempt on behalf of Asian solidarity. Peking will then be given an opportunity to establish its bona fides and if possible to confound those sceptics who feel that, by the fact of being Communist, China is nearer to its fellow Communist States in Europe than to its Asian neighbors with which it has racial and cultural ties.**

The *Globe and Mail* of Toronto, January 1, 1955, observed:

> **What can bind these scattered countries together? What is the common interest of Red China and Ethiopia, of the Philippines and Lebanon, to name four of the invited? The answer is plain. These Asian and African states, with few exceptions,**

recently were or still are dependencies. With no exception whatever, they have a lower standard of living, measuring welfare by the distribution of material goods, than is enjoyed in other countries. This, of course, is obvious. What is significant about the call to Bandung is that the common plight of Asians and Africans has been recognized and proclaimed—in Asia.

Said *Newsweek* bluntly, January 1, 1955:

"Everybody knows what must come to pass between Asia and the West, the *yellow and the white.* It is imbecile folly for us to close our eyes to the inevitable. . . . All the world understands that the gravest crisis in the destiny of the earth's population is at hand. . . ."

Western statesmen last week unhappily recalled these words of Kaiser Wilhelm II, popularizer of the phrase 'Yellow Peril.' They could reflect that the onetime German emperor was right as rain—and wrong as sin. He was right in foreseeing a crisis that now threatens in a more virulent form than he envisaged—an Afro-Asian combination turned by Communists against the West. The problem, according to those who have to deal with it today and tomorrow, is to prevent its formation. . . .

The *Christian Science Monitor* of Boston, January 23, 1955, summed up the meaning of the conference in terse phrases:

. . . The West is excluded. Emphasis is on the colored nations of the world. And for Asia it means

> **that at last the destiny of Asia is being determined in Asia, and not in Geneva, or Paris, or London or Washington. Colonialism is out. Hands off is the word. Asia is free. This is perhaps the great historic event of our century.**

Reflecting a feeling of long isolation, the *Burma Star* (London), January 29, 1955, declared:

> **The Afro-Asian conference is decidedly of vital necessity from the standpoint of many countries who have agreed to lend their participation. The least value it can have is a true forum of Afro-Asian opinion which does not always find its proper outlet in the United Nations and other world councils where Western political sway is indisputably in evidence.**

On March 3, 1955, came an undisguised sneer from Portugal. Said *Diario Popular* of Lisbon:

> **. . . this spectacular conference is actually a kind of a vast whirl of panic, as happens in ant hills on the approach of some collective danger. Let us forget appearances and even the perturbing possibilities for our particular interests and let us face the problem of the West. It consists in calming that immense flock before it delivers itself up to bad shepherds and before it is too late to influence it.**

On the same day, ten thousand miles distant, the *Times* of Manila, playing possum, said in a voice whose studied naïveté did not ring true:

> With the best will in the world it is difficult to understand what Premier Jawaharlal Nehru expects of the Afrasian conference at Bandung next April.

Said Walter Lippmann in the Paris *Herald Tribune* for March 1, 1955:

> The list of the states they did not invite makes it very evident that this is no mere attempt to make a neutral bloc or a third force in between the giant military powers. Red China is no neutral and no third force. What this is, to put it plainly, is the most formidable and ambitious move yet made in this generation to apply the principle of Asia for the Asians.

The words that cut and hurt the Asian-African delegates most came from no less than the American Secretary of State, John Foster Dulles. In a radio-television address in Washington on the 8th of March, 1955, he referred to the conference as follows:

> Three of the Asian parties to the Pacific Charter, Pakistan, the Philippines and Thailand, may shortly be meeting with other Asian countries at a so-called Afro-Asian conference.

(This single phrase, "so-called Afro-Asian conference," echoed and re-echoed at Bandung as proof of American contempt; and the people who called attention to it were not Communists. . . .)

On March 13, 1955, the Central African Federation, which is affiliated with the British Commonwealth, decided not to participate in the mammoth conference. Speculation had it that since a white man, Sir Godfrey Higgins, was the Prime Minister, he could not possibly speak in the interests of his African constituents. His presence at Bandung would have been a curious spectacle, to say the least.

On March 25, 1955, this announcement came from New Delhi; it was published in the New York *Times*:

> **India will ask the conference of Asian-African nations to put the problem of nuclear weapons on its agenda.**

Then, from an unknown quarter, came sensational news that set off a frenzy of fear and speculation. On March 26, 1955, the New York *Times* carried the following item:

> **A significant change in policy and defense planning is under consideration here in the belief that Red China will begin its campaign to capture Matsu and Quemoy about the middle of April.**
>
> **There is as yet no sign that President Eisenhower has decided to intervene militarily to prevent the capture of the islands.**
>
> **On such a basis the United States would be committed to the use of precision atomic weapons against purely military targets even in a limited Far Eastern war.**

The pending Asian-African conference began to loom more and more as a war council of the nations attending. The New York *Times*, March 27, 1955, quoted Senator Walter F. George, Chairman of the Senate Foreign Relations Committee, as saying:

. . . some credence was being given to the possibility of a Communist attack after the Asian-African conference. He was not prepared to say, Senator George added, whether the United States would become involved.

Burma's Buddhist Premier U Nu sought to allay war fears in a New York *Times* article, March 27, 1955:

. . . Communist China was afraid that as soon as the United States bases in Asia were 'completed' an attack would be launched against the China mainland.

Premier U Nu said he had not met many leaders of the United States but those he had talked with had told him of their fears of continued aggression from Peking.

Premier U Nu said he did not think the forthcoming Asian-African conference was an 'anti-Western' meeting. But he made it clear that he thought some Western powers would take a verbal slamming on the issue of colonialism.

On March 28, 1955, William Humphreys analyzed Nehru's probable relation to Communism in the Paris *Herald Tribune* in the following words:

Mr. Nehru spent ten days in Peking as the guest of Communist party leaders Mao Tse-tung and Premier Chou En-lai, and on his return to India, November 2, he extolled his 'peace and progress' mission as 'an historic event certain to influence all of Asia.' Rumors of the conference then began to circulate.

Thus, when the idea of the Afro-Asian meeting

> was formally projected a few weeks later, it appeared to be a reasonable conclusion that Mr. Nehru had set an international stage on which Red China would be presented as a peace-minded nation militarily intent only upon resisting United States' 'aggression.'

Behind all this frenzied speculation was, of course, something else. An American admiral, Carney by name, Chief of Naval Operations, predicted that the Chinese Communists were likely to attack Quemoy and Matsu in mid-April. On April 7, 1955, the Manchester *Guardian* reported:

> In his opening remarks Admiral Carney said that the Chinese Communist leaders Mao and Chou had made a straightforward pitch on what they intend to do.
>
> He went on:
>
> "They have a series of unbroken successes and they are flushed with victory. They should feel safe in continuing to probe and they will probe. The first two things they will go after are the off-shore islands. They can take Matsu and Quemoy from the Chinese Nationalists. It could be expensive for them but they will take the islands by expending enough. They probably will initiate the attack on Matsu in mid-April. The significance of the timing is that it would tie in with the Afro-Asian conference in Bandung, Indonesia, from April 16 to 24. The all-out attack on Quemoy would be some weeks later than that on Matsu. The build-up around Matsu includes the air near Foochow.
>
> "The attack on Matsu may begin on April 15 or later during the conference. A month later, maybe

in May or June, they could launch an attack on Quemoy. . . .

"If the decision is made to participate it should not be on a localized tactical basis. We have to carry the thing to a conclusion and find what will wreck the enemy's efforts. That involves enlargement far beyond that tactical area of Quemoy and Matsu. We have to engage China in an all-out war. If we go in with the restricted view we will find ourselves about to lose all of Asia."

In the Manchester *Guardian*, April 13, 1955, Adlai Stevenson, leader of the Democratic Party in the United States, speaking in subtle, ironic tones, tried to draw attention to the essential horror involved in the whole discussion by asking a series of pointed questions:

Are the off-shore islands essential to the security of the United States? Are they, indeed, even essential to the defense of Formosa—which all Americans have been agreed upon since President Truman sent the Seventh Fleet there five years ago? Or is it, as the Secretary of Defense says, that the loss of Quemoy and Matsu would make no significant military difference?

Can they be defended without resort to nuclear weapons? If not, while I know we now have the means to incinerate, to burn up, much of living China, and quickly, are we prepared to use such weapons to defend islands so tenuously related to American security?

It should be remembered that these quotations fit into a real, concrete, historical context. These molten words, dealing with the incineration of continents, were related to a process that began directly after World War II when Western Europe, prostrate from Hitlerian domination, was anxious to stem the tide of Stalinist revolutions that were sweeping into Europe. America, leader of the West, then launched a campaign, the intensity of which it did not appreciate, to frighten the men of the Kremlin, and month after month that campaign kept up, flooding the world on all levels of communication. And it was successful, too successful; it not only scared and deterred Russian Communists, but it frightened the living daylights out of the human race. It was a campaign so fierce, so deadly, so unrelenting that it created precisely what it sought to defeat, that is, an organization of Asia and Africa around a Communist cell on a global scale: BANDUNG. . . . The dialogue of events had reached a pitch that involved the totality of man on earth.

Such was the atmosphere, brooding, bitter, apprehensive, which greeted the projected conference. Everybody read into it his own fears; the conference loomed like a long-buried ghost rising from a muddy grave. . . .

On the afternoon of April 12, we landed at Jakarta airfield, which was decorated with the flags of the twenty-nine nations attending the conference. As soon as I became entangled with the bureaucracy of Indonesian customs and immigration, I discovered a great deal of smiling good will but an appalling amount of inefficiency. The brown young men seemed at a loss as they fumbled with papers, searched about for rubber stamps. It was clear to me that these young men had not had much previous experience in administration; under Dutch rule few Indonesians did such work. Ten minutes sufficed to reveal the void left here by the much-vaunted Dutch imperialists.

The heat was like a Turkish bath; the humidity was higher than in the African jungle. I was met by P.E.N. club officials and Mochtar Lubis, editor of the *Indonesia Raya*, an independent Socialist daily. Lubis took me in tow, loaded my luggage into his car, and we nosed into the wide streets of a chaotic, Oriental city. Jakarta, like Accra in the Gold Coast of Africa, presents to Western eyes a commercial aspect, naked and immediate, that seems to swallow up the entire population in petty trade—men, women, and children. . . . The spectator who is acquainted with colonial practice knows at once where this feverish activity comes from: one must sell to earn money to buy products shipped from Europe. Family relations have been replaced by factory and financial relations, and the resulting picture of brutal and direct commercial activity is of a nature unknown even in cities like London, New York, or Paris, where tradition, having survived through gradual transitions of one culture overlapping another, forming a synthesis of stability, is still a force making for regularity and a degree of humanness in daily relations between people.

I passed those famous canals which the Dutch, for some inexplicable reason, had insisted upon digging here in this hot mudhole of a city. (Indeed, the site of Jakarta itself must have been chosen for its sheer utility as a port and with no thought of the health of the people who had to live in it.) I saw a young man squatting upon the bank of a canal, defecating in broad daylight into the canal's muddy, swirling water; I saw another, then another. . . . Children used the canal for their water closet; then I saw a young woman washing clothes only a few yards from them. . . . A young girl was bathing; she had a cloth around her middle and she was dipping water out of the canal and, holding the cloth out from her body, she poured the water over her covered breasts. . . . A tiny boy was washing his teeth, dipping his toothbrush into the canal. . . .

Lubis' car snaked forward through throngs of strange contraptions that resembled huge tricycles; they had one big wheel behind upon which was perched a native boy who sweated and pumped the pedals; in front were two smaller wheels and a seat large enough for two people.

"What is that thing?" I asked Lubis.

"That's our Indonesian taxicab," Lubis explained. "There are about forty thousand of them in the city. They are called *betjas.*"

"A sort of Indonesian rickshaw, eh?"

"Yes, and we are ashamed of them," he confessed. "Many Indonesians refuse to ride in them; it reminds them of imperialism. . . . You understand? Brown or yellow men hauling white men . . ." He sighed. "A boy who works on one of those things gets ill after about two years. But we have no money to import taxis."

"How much does a boy make a day driving one with his feet?"

"About ten rupiahs, or a dollar. He is required to have a license, but he pays no taxes."

Lubis' words made me wonder about the over-all reality of his country.

"Say, just how many islands are there in this archipelago?"

"About fifteen thousand; but only about three thousand are inhabited."

"And how large in area is the space covered by these islands?"

"Roughly, it is the size of the United States."

"What about natural resources?"

"This nation is potentially the third richest on earth."

"And what language do the people speak?"

"Indonesian," he told me. "But we have two hundred languages." He worked his car through a crowd of Chinese children. . . .

"There must be a strong central government to keep order in such far-flung islands and amid so many diverse peoples—"

"The government is weak," Lubis told me. "Bandits are everywhere. There are daily clashes between government troops and bandits."

"That's a kind of civil war," I said.

"Exactly," he said.

"The literacy rate?"

"About 30 per cent."

"Is education compulsory?"

"Well, the government wants to pass a law making education compulsory," Lubis explained. "But what would such a law mean? We don't have enough school buildings, enough teachers, enough school books."

"Is it true that the Dutch used compulsory labor here during two hundred of the three hundred and fifty years that they held these islands; is that true?"

"Compulsory labor actually stopped here about fifteen years ago," he said.

Lubis' dark facts clashed with the blindingly bright sunshine. Jakarta is a vast, sprawling city, disordered, bustling, overcrowded. Wide ornate boulevards alternate with districts called *kampongs*, the equivalent of the African compound. These *kampongs* were formerly villages and the rapidly growing city swallowed them up; now Indonesian peasants still live in them within the modern city, following the ways and the manners of their forefathers, oblivous of the rage of alien ideology that circles about them. The Chinese section was a nightmare, overflowing with shops, stores, warehouses, and restaurants.

"How is the housing situation?" I asked Lubis.

"Desperate," he said. "Before the war, this city had four hundred thousand people. We now have about three million people jammed into it. People flock here for jobs, or because they are bored in their villages."

"What's holding up the building of houses? I see that

many houses here are made of bamboo. Why can't people build more houses like that?"

"It takes about fifty dollars worth of Western materials to build a house. And we have no dollars, no hard currency. We don't even have nails; we can't make them."

"Before the coming of the Dutch, I bet these people had houses, maybe not modern houses, but houses . . ."

"That's true."

"So the introduction of the Western way of life has not helped in the matter of housing?"

"No," Lubis said, smiling ruefully.

"I'm not anti-Western," I assured him. "But can't a way be found to by-pass this kind of dependence upon the outside world? Can't Indonesia make nails, pipes, etc.?"

"No. Not yet."

"What do you export?"

"Copra, tin, rubber . . ."

"And that does not give you enough foreign exchange?"

"No. And production is falling day by day. Our foreign exchange is less and less."

"Why?"

"We are still fighting a revolution, nationalizing; there are strikes and much government control."

"Why are the people doing that instead of rebuilding?"

"Sentiment, politics. . . . They are trying to sweep out the last of Western influence. They have their own ideas about what they want."

The car edged on through narrow streets. I noticed that the Indonesians seemed a delicate people, thin, small. . . .

"What about health?" I asked Lubis.

"We have much malaria and yaws. Infant mortality is high—"

"And your population is falling?"

"No. Rising. . . . We have much rice and the soil is rich."

"How many doctors have you?"

"We have one doctor for about every seventy thousand people. We have fourteen hundred doctors for eighty million people."

"And education?"

"It's out of control. The Dutch kept education from us and now the people believe in education like a religion. . . . There is a vast thirst for learning. Universities are springing up everywhere, faster than they can be properly manned. The year the war broke out, we had two hundred and forty high school graduates. We had only ten Indonesians teaching in our high schools. Today nobody knows just what the figures are. . . . The Dutch left us in the lurch and we had to start from scratch."

It was a grim picture, yet quite typical. These conditions were the gift of three hundred and fifty years of Dutch rule.

"Just how is the national budget divided?" I asked Lubis.

"Well," he said, "we have about two million people on the pay roll. Soldiers, policemen, and hordes of government functionaries. The army and the government personnel take 70 per cent of our national budget. Education takes only 7 per cent."

"From what you say, government is the biggest business here."

"That's right," Lubis said.

"A country in which men make careers and fortunes out of government is a sick country."

"Right," Lubis said.

He had been in America twice and now and then an American phrase crept into his speech.

"What about this so-called Communist menace I've heard so much about? Word has it in Paris that the Communists are about to pull off a Prague coup here any minute, any hour—"

"No!" Lubis said. "That's not true. We have Communists, and at the moment they hold the balance of power in the government. But they are not even our largest political party. The present government accepts the support of Communists. But don't forget that this country is 90 per cent Moslem and these people are not going Communist."

"Who puts out the story that the country is almost in the hands of Communists?" I asked him.

"There are people who were once here and they want to come back," he said tersely.

It was strange, but, in this age of swift communication, one had to travel thousands of miles to get a set of straight, simple facts. One of the greatest ironies of the twentieth century is that when communication has reached its zenith, when the human voice can encircle the globe in a matter of seconds, when man can project the image of his face thousands of miles, it is almost impossible to know with any degree of accuracy the truth of a political situation only a hundred miles distant! Propaganda jams the media of communication.

I was lodged in the home of an Indonesian engineer. Mr. P. and his young wife were ardent nationalists, their home modern to the *n*th degree.

"What kind of an engineer are you, Mr. P.?" I asked my host.

"I'm an oil man," he answered.

"You got your training and experience in Europe?"

"My training I got in Europe," he told me. "But I'm getting my experience now here in my country. You see, before the revolution, they would not hire me to do what I'm now doing—"

"You mean the Dutch?"

"Yes. Now I'm head of my department. It took a revolution to do that. Killing, fighting . . . I'm a major in the Indonesian Army. By nature, I hate war. But what is one to do?

The Dutch attitude was that I was not and could never be intelligent enough to do what I'm now doing. So it was with men of my generation; so it was in all of the other sections of Indonesian life. If we had not fought the Dutch, we'd still be in slavelike conditions, not allowed to do anything."

Mrs. P. nodded her head affirmatively as her husband spoke. These people had been put through a hard school. Mr. P. had spent sixteen years in Europe; he loved Europe, but—

"Your home is in a beautiful section of the city," I told him.

"This used to be the European quarter," he told me with a wry smile. "The revolution gave me the right to live here."

"How many engineers have you in Indonesia?" I asked him.

"About a hundred and sixty, forty of whom are in government service. The rest work for themselves, for they make about three times more than the ones who work for the government."

"How will your country get through this bottleneck? You need articles, skills, technicians—you need many things from the Western industrial world. How will you get them?"

There was a silence. Mr. P. looked at me and smiled wryly.

"I'm a technician," he said slowly. "So I know what we need. It's America or Russia. There's no middle ground."

"Which do you choose?"

"I don't know," he said.

"You can work for either side," I reminded him. "You are a technician."

"I know," he said.

"What about Russia?"

"I was in Europe during the war. I met many Communists. It's a dictatorship and it's hard."

"And America?"

Mr. P. sat staring at me silently.

"I've been in America, you know," he said softly, smiling again.

"I didn't know that. For how long?"

"I was there for three months. I wanted to stay. I worked as an engineer. I lived in New York."

"Did you go to Harlem?"

Mr. P. looked at me without answering. His wife nudged him and said:

"Tell him, darling."

"Mr. Wright," Mr. P. began, looking off into the corners of the room, "I never went to Harlem. Indeed, I never went out—"

"What do you mean? You had some racial experiences?"

"No. That's what I avoided. I was scared," he said simply.

He was as dark as I was. I understood. He could not take it.

"I came from my job and stayed in my room," he explained. "I never went anywhere. Every night I stayed in my room. Then I left."

He had "had" it. Fear had kept him from exposing himself to the experience of American life; the idea of what he would encounter had immobilized him, and he had given up without even trying. . . .

After dinner Mr. and Mrs. P. took me for a tour of the city in their car. I noticed that the sidewalks were thronged with children who carried books under their arms. It was past ten o'clock.

"Where are those children going this time of night?" I asked.

"To school," Mrs. P. told me. "We don't have enough schools, not enough teachers. So these children are going to the night shift."

The suburbs of Jakarta are studded with lovely, newly built bungalows erected by the *nouveaux riches* from money gained in black market operations. There is no doubt that a new Indonesian middle class is rising and it is focusing attention, mostly unfavorable, upon itself.

"It's all wrong," Mr. P. said wearily. "We made a revolution and the common people fought and died to drive out the Dutch. Now the common people are not getting benefits from that revolution. That's why today we are threatened with another revolution. . . . Why should one part of our population get rich and the rest get poorer? We drove out the Dutch to build a good society, now we have a class of Indonesians who are acting more or less like the Dutch."

"When was your Republic proclaimed?"

"In August, 1945."

"And when did your people actually get control of the country?"

"In December, 1949."

"And between 1945 and 1949?"

"There was much fighting, bitter fighting between us and the Dutch."

"Now, just what is the present government?"

"We have a President, a Vice-President, a House of Representatives, and a Supreme Court."

"But you have had no elections as yet?"

"No. Elections are pending for November, 1955."

"How, then, did the present government get into power?" I asked him.

"That's a little complicated," he said. "On the 18th of August, 1945, after the Republic had been proclaimed, our Independence Preparatory Committee designated Sukarno as President of the Republic and Hatta as Vice-President. . . . This committee was composed of outstanding leaders in all fields of Indonesian life. After full sovereignty was gained, the following bodies were welded into a House of Representatives: the Senate of the United States of Indonesia; the members of the Provisional Parliament of the United States of Indonesia; the members of the High Advisory Council of the Republic of Indonesia; and the Working Committee of the Provisional Parliament of the Republic of Indonesia. . . . This House of Representatives has confirmed Sukarno as President and Hatta as Vice-President."

"It's a little baby country," I suggested to Mr. P. with a smile.

He laughed and agreed:

"Yes. We are a baby country with many little childhood diseases."

The next morning I got hold of a copy of the Provisional Constitution of the Republic of Indonesia and leafed through it. One could tell the past fears and sufferings of the people of Indonesia by what was emphasized in that Constitution.

It provided that all were "entitled to equal protection against discrimination and against any incitement to such discrimination." It stated explicitly: "Slavery, the slave trade and bondage, and any actions in whatever form giving rise thereto are prohibited." It declared: "No one shall be subjected to torture, or to cruel, inhuman or degrading treatment or punishment." One could feel the fear of men who had been seized and shipped off to exile in the following: "No transgression or crime shall be made punishable by total forfeiture of the property of the offender." One could feel the anxiety of men who had not been allowed to govern themselves in Article 15 of Section IV: "No sentence may cause civic death or the loss of all civic rights." The vast inequalities in the population left by Dutch rule prompted: "Differences in social and legal needs of the various groups of the population shall be taken into consideration." Then Section VI spells out in Article 38 a vague kind of socialism derived partly from ideology and partly from the tenets of the Moslem religion: "The national economy shall be organized on a co-operative basis. Branches of production of importance to the State and which vitally affect the life of the people, shall be controlled by the State. Land and water and natural riches contained therein shall be controlled by the State and used for the maximum prosperity of the people." Article 38 says: "The family is entitled to protection by society and the State. The State shall provide for the needs of the poor and waifs." In Article 40 one finds: "The authorities shall promote the spiritual and physical development of the people. The authorities shall in particular aim at the speediest possible abolition of illiteracy. Freedom of religion and speech are guaranteed." It was a brave document filled with pathos.

I hired a *betja* and, perched upon a rickety seat, spent an afternoon looking the city over. I noticed that each home in the bourgeois section kept huge, vicious dogs; one move on the part of a stranger created a loud snarling and barking. These dogs, I was told, defended the inhabitants against the all-too-frequent visits of bandits who infested near-by mountains and suburbs. Try as I could, I was never able to resolve the mystery of the Indonesian bandit. One person would tell me that the bandits were just lawless gangs; another would swear that they were Communists; yet another would claim that they were Moslems who did not like the Communist participation in the present government; still others said that they were youths who had fought in the revolution and had never learned to work and were living in the only manner known to them. I suspected that the bandits were all of this, plus hordes of young men who were, in the daytime, respectable wage earners and who found it impossible to make ends meet in a nation where the government printing presses were grinding out a whirlwind of all-but-worthless paper money; I suspected that during the nighttime a good part of the population, resentful of the *status quo*, took to the byways with guns to get what they felt society owed them.

As in most countries gripped by inflation, one saw vast numbers of bureaucrats searching for contraband and one wondered whether, if those same bureaucrats had been put to work producing commodities, the necessity for searching for contraband would have obtained . . . ? In any case, large areas of Java and Sumatra were overrun with bandits and smugglers, and it was not safe to drive upon the highways after dark.

Next day I called upon one of the best-known Indonesian politicians, Sutan Sjahrir, Socialist, patriot, intellectual, and one of the country's ablest students of Western political thought. Unlike many other opportunistic Indonesian politicians, Sjahrir had absolutely refused to collaborate in any form with the Japanese invaders. He is a short man, plump, affable, and about forty-five years of age. Educated in Holland, he is the idol of a considerable section of the younger generation. He was the first premier of Indonesia, and it was he who conducted most of the delicate negotiations with the Dutch, who were hankering to regain their control over the potentially third richest nation on earth. It was this same modest, smiling Sjahrir who presented Indonesia's case before the United Nations, and he convinced that august body of the Indonesians' right to govern themselves.

"What is being done to organize the energies of the people to rebuild the nation?" I asked him.

He smiled, shot me a quick glance, and then answered in a manner that left no doubt of his courage to be truthful:

"We have not got that far yet."

"What's being done about housing?" I asked.

He laughed and stared at me. Then he spoke in a quiet, chuckling tone:

"The government's building houses; they call them 'workers' houses.' But they turn out to be ornate ministries.

There's practically no building of houses for poor people."

"Many people are blaming the present attitude of Indonesians upon the Japanese. What was the attitude of the Indonesians toward the Japanese?"

"The Japanese were not loved here," he told me quietly. "We killed more Japanese than we did Dutch. One of the most decisive factors in the Indonesians' winning of independence is something that is not well known abroad, not at all. And that was how the Dutch behaved when the Japanese came in. They caved in. The Dutch were scared; they bowed; they wept; they begged; they all but crawled. . . . And we Indonesians said to ourselves: 'If the Dutch are that scared of the Japanese, then why ought we be scared of the Dutch?' Dutch fear of the Japanese was a powerful psychological element in our resolve to fight the Dutch for our freedom."

Sjahrir told me that the Dutch "could dish it out, but that they could not take it." When released from the notorious Japanese internment camps, the Dutch, completely lacking in imagination, and looking like wretches, went back to the homes in which they had once lived and to the factories that they had once managed and were amazed to find that the Indonesians had taken over. . . . They demanded their homes, their factories, and their jobs back and were stunned when no one obeyed them.

"Will you be at the conference at Bandung?" I asked him.

"No. I'm with the opposition, you know," he said. Then he laughed and added: "I don't want to embarrass the government."

"Is there a Communist coup pending here?" I asked him.

"No!" he said flatly.

"Why is such an impression being created abroad?"

He laughed and did not answer.

I next asked Sjahrir if he considered himself a professional politician and he replied:

"I suppose you could say that I am. I've never had any other job than that of fighting for my country in my life. The only steady employment I've ever had was when I was Prime Minister. Most of the other years of my life were spent either in exile or in prison."

"What about production?" I asked, already surfeited with gloomy facts.

"It's dropping month by month," he admitted. "Things are not good."

"It's politics," I suggested.

"Yes; politics and too many parties," he confessed.

I respected Sjahrir. I felt that his heart was wedded to the cause of his country. We chatted for more than an hour, but he was affably cautious. He was one of the leading opposition men, and he did "not want to embarrass the government." In Europe it was rumored that men like Sjahrir lived in daily fear of their lives; if that were true, then Sjahrir gave me no confirmation even when I asked him bluntly if he feared for his life. An hour's friendly conversation is not enough time in which to get to know a man, and, when that man is an experienced politician, a man surrounded by enemies, an intellectual, one has to be careful in making hasty judgments. Sjahrir was sane, balanced, poised, yet I could not escape the impression that he was basically a *Western* Socialist, honest, fair, good-hearted, and filled with a love of freedom. But was he the man to tame the Indonesian tiger? Could he unite eighty million half-tribalized human beings, 70 per cent of whom were illiterate, most of whom were sunk either in a theistic Moslem religion that had yet to bear the acid test of modern industrialization or in an animistic grasp of life that riveted the attention more upon the poetic than the practical aspects of existence? Were housing, health measures, finely spun concepts of freedom the implements that could spur a nation that had been for three hundred and fifty years under the iron heel of Dutch rule to an attitude of alert pragmatism? I had the feeling that he wanted to build soundly, solidly, yet the situation in which he found himself reeked of urgency; the people were not waiting for the government to build schools, they were creating them themselves; their loyalties were being bid for by America and China; the future and its shape were uncertain and the people felt that they had to choose *now*; the Constitution had not been implemented and a kind of civil war was going on against both Indonesian bandits and foreign capital. . . . What would happen in the next few years would surely set the mold for the future of Indonesian life. Was not Sjahrir a man for a future time, when these basic problems had been solved? I could not imagine Sjahrir instilling in these millions a sense of their historic destiny. . . . It would take other and specal kind of men for that work.

That evening I inquired of my host, Mr. P., what was there that one could do or see in Jakarta at night, and he informed me that there were no night clubs, no bars in the city.

"We are Moslems and we are not a drinking people. We dance, but not in night clubs. There are but few Europeans in the city now. They are going home, or being sent home, at the rate of twenty thousand a year. There'll be but fifty thousand Dutch left at the end of this year. Night clubs are definitely European establishments; so, when the Europeans go, so do the night clubs."

As I had discovered in Africa's Gold Coast, so I found in Indonesia that almost every item in the home in which I was staying had been imported from faraway Europe. There is a nervous kind of dependence bred by imperialism: not only are the people taught Western law, ethics, and finance; but they are encouraged to develop a taste, yea, a need, for goods which are only to be had from the European mother country. Then, when the natives rise and make a revolution in the name of the values of the West, they find themselves trapped, for they cannot build even a modern house without Western aid. The psychological agony that Indonesia suffers was created by a situation compounded of a fear of the return of Western technical capacities which they feel they need, which in their hearts they adore; yet, how can they have the co-operation of the West and at the same time fend off what they feel to be the desire of the West to dominate? In some Indonesian hearts the fear of the West is so great that they are willing to forego all advantages of Western technology, but they know that in doing so they are leaving themselves open to re-enslavement. . . . It is not an easy attitude to hold when you feel that, when you reach out for something you want, you will be clutching bait embedded upon a sharp and cruel hook. . . .

One morning I went into the Ministry of Information for my press card; all the faces behind the desks were dark, as dark as mine. . . . At one desk I saw a white American newspaperman leaning forward intently and putting up an argument, and the dark Indonesian official to whom he was so urgently talking was obviously not listening and had already made up his mind as to the kind of negative answer that he was going to serve up to the white American. . . . But the moment that the Indonesian official's dark face turned to me there was another and different attitude. His manner changed at once: I was one of his kind; I'd endured the humiliations that he and his people had endured. So, while the white American waited, I got my press card at once. I was a member of the master race! Well, there it was. . . . I'm not proud of it. It took no intelligence, no courage; in the situation that obtained, it was the easiest thing to do. It was racism. And I thought of all the times in the American South when I had had to wait until the whites had been served before I could be served. . . . All you have to do in a situation like that is relax and let your base instincts flow. And it's so easy, so natural; you don't have to think; you just push that face that is of an offensive color out of your mind and forget about it. You are inflicting an emotional wound that might last for years, that might be handed down to other generations; but why worry about that? You are safe; there are thousands around you of your color and, if the man who's been offended should object, what the hell can he do? I was disturbed. I was not proud of what had happened, but I understood it. It was racism; there was no doubt about it; but it was a defensive, reflective kind of racism. And there are so many people of my color on earth, *so many millions of colored people . . . more than there are of white. . . .* The racism I saw that morning had had its origin not in the desire (I think) of the colored man to put the white man in an embarrassing position, to sting and hurt him; it was simply a question of color, which was an easy way of telling friend from foe. But the Indonesian official had not instituted this thing; it had been taught to him by faces as white as the American face that he had spurned. That was how the whites had felt about it when they had had all the power; all dark skins were bad and all white skins were good, and now I saw that same process reversed. . . .

Will Asians and Africans, being as human as white men, take over this vicious pattern of identification when they become, as they will, masters of this earth? Racism is an evil thing and breeds its own kind. Yet, it would be truly human if the Asians and Africans did, for they have much greater cause for doing so than the white man ever had. They would be acting out of a four-hundred-year tradition of racial conditioning. . . . After all, the colored races never did anything to the white races to call down upon their heads the centuries of brutality and exploitation that the whites have meted out to them. But the most important point is: Can the colored races, for the most part uneducated and filled with fear, forget so quickly the racist deeds of the white races as they strive to free themselves from the lingering vestiges of racial subjugation? I'm not advocating racism or even trying to justify it; racism is a loathsome thing. I'm just trying to explain how easy it is, and with what justification the colored races can and will, to some extent—depending upon how ignorant and emotionally wrought up the whites have kept them—practice racism, a racism that they have been taught too bitterly and too well.

It would be a naive and childlike white Westerner who, seeing the dreadful racist peril now confronting him, would say: "But I don't feel like that any more. I'm perfectly willing for racism to stop. I'll support any legislation to eradicate racism." But, unfortunately, life is not that simple. Contrite words cannot now stop profound processes which white men set in motion on this earth some four hundred years ago; four hundred years is a long time . . . time enough for habits, reactions, to be converted into culture, tradition, into a *raison d'être* for millions. . . .

In the future there will be white men who will look into black and yellow and brown faces, and they will say to themselves: "I wish to God that those faces were educated, that they had lived lives as secure and serene as mine; then I would be able to talk to them, to reason with them . . ." But then it will be too late.

In my goings and comings about Jakarta, meeting this person and that one, I was told that an Indonesian servant, when he is hired by, say, white Americans, is embarrassingly obsequious, that, upon entering a room, he will bow low, lifting both hands as though in prayer, and then walk with his right hand and its five fingers pointing toward the floor, crossing the room in the presence of his superiors. While serving food, the domestics will form a long line, then kneel and creep past the table, each holding a dish in his hands and wait with lowered eyes until the master has served himself. And they crawl away on their knees. These practices, I was told, were not originated by the Dutch. They constitute a heritage stemming from hoary Javanese feudal traditions. It need not be added that the Dutch did not find such tokens of groveling unpleasant, and these practices prevail today even in the homes of many upper-class Indonesians.

As humid Indonesian days unfold, I make many tiny discoveries. . . . Instead of toilet paper, the Indonesians use water; a small bucket of water is placed in each toilet. Toilet paper is hard to come by, having to be imported from Europe. Families not well-off enough to afford buckets will place several beer bottles of water discreetly beside the commode. . . .

Indonesian bathrooms are strange contraptions indeed; I tried futilely to determine how they originated. There is no bathtub as such. In middle-class Indonesian bathrooms there is a shower which works when there is enough water, which is rare. . . . Mostly you will find a walled-off enclosure about four feet high in which water is trapped as it drips from a faucet. Water pressure is lacking, and in this manner a reserve of water is kept on hand. It is necessary, most times, in order to bathe to take a tin pan and wash towel, soap yourself thoroughly, and, afterward, dip out of the walled enclosure enough water to dash over your head and body to rinse off the soapsuds.

The classic bathroom joke in Jakarta concerns an American businessman who got, by mistake, into one of those walled-off water-traps and actually took his bath, an act which necessitated the forgoing of all bathing for the Indonesian family in whose house he was an honored guest. The hygienic-minded American had polluted the supply of water for the entire family for the entire day.

Amid all of this disorder and uncertainty, it is odd how daily habits are adhered to; for example, shoes are regularly shined, even though gangs of bandits may be roaming the countryside. Slow-moving, barefooted boys slink into your room and appropriate your shoes and spend precious hours polishing them. Of course, it could be argued that there are not many shoes to be shined in a nation where most of the population goes barefooted, and that shoe-shining takes up but a tiny part of a servant's day. Even so, it indicates the degree to which certain parts of the population have been conditioned to Western habits. But, against this background, these habits take on a kind of caricatured aspect of the Western world. . . .

Since the state is weak and has but little authority, what keeps things going? The answer is: the animal habits which Indonesians share with the rest of mankind. The day is divided not so much into hours as into periods in which one sleeps, eats, works, etc.

"When will Mr. So-and-so be in?" I would ask.

"I really don't know, sir. But he'll surely be in about one. He has to eat, you know."

"Has Mr. So-and-so returned yet?" I'd ask.

"No, sir. But it's far past his bedtime and so he'll be in soon."

There are really no office hours; you must depend upon the biological functioning of the people to determine when you can see them.

My friend Lubis took me to see Dr. Mohammed Natsir, former Prime Minister, and one of the leading spokesmen for the idea of the Moslem state. He is young, about forty-seven, and is the head of Indonesia's largest political party, the *Masjumi*. I found him alert, friendly, open, relaxed, with a ready smile. He told me frankly that he was hopeful about the future, that there was absolutely no foundation for the widespread, irresponsible talk about a pending Communist coup, and that he was sure that Indonesia would have democracy, "not the kind of classical democracy known in the West, but still democracy. . . ."

"You make a distinction between East and West?" I asked.

"Of course. Our approach, because of our background, must be somewhat different," he said.

Mr. Natsir told me that he felt that the most important event of the twentieth century was the liberation of Asia and parts of Africa, but he did not think that Asia and Africa should form racial or political blocs against the West. He was positive that there did not exist in the general population a mood of hostility toward the white nations.

"We just want them to let us build up our countries," he said. "We want to keep our freedom. When we mobilize our people to reconstruct our countries, the white Westerners must not project out upon us their own sense of guilt. The whites cannot see us as we are because of what they have done to us. First, they sent us their missionaries; then they sent their mercenaries; and in the end they sent their military. . . . We call them the three M's of imperialism and we are on the lookout for them."

In talking to Mr. Natsir, I felt, as I was to feel when talking to many Indonesians, that concepts like Right and Left, and ideologies in general, did not figure decisively in his thinking. I had the feeling that the Indonesian Moslem had a personality that was intact, poised, healthy, and largely free from neurotic conflicts. These eighty million Indonesians, 90 per cent Moslem, had not been tampered with too much by missionaries as had all too many Africans. There was none of that uneasy shifting backward and forward between two worlds of values and two spheres of psychological being. Yet I was confronted with a religious statesman, a man who would perhaps some day rule or exert no small degree of influence upon his country.

"I'd like to try to give the Western reader some idea of this Moslem state which is the object of your policies," I told him.

"I've explained all about that in a speech I made in 1952 before the Pakistan Institute of World Affairs in Karachi," he said. "I'll give you a copy of that speech. But there is nothing in Islamic teachings that would clash against any ethical or moral precepts of any other religion. We believe in the Koran; it is our guide, our Bible, you might say."

"But you are classed as a colored man by the West," I told him. "And yet you are religious. Now, many people fear the world of Islam. And that world is colored."

"Yes," he said, smiling. "If the Moslems hope to cooperate with other peoples of the world in the interest of peace, we shall have to realize that an appreciation of the virtues of Islam is greatly lacking outside of the Islamic world, and that even amongst Moslems there are many misconceptions of the true aims and purposes of the Islamic teachings. Centuries of abject submission to foreign rulers have destroyed the prestige of the Moslems the world over as well as their sense of self-respect. Nevertheless, the Western world having once experienced the power of the sword of Islam has never lost sight of the potentialities contained in the Moslem world. The endeavors of the Moslems in the nineteenth century to achieve their resurrection in a united world of Islam (the Pan-Islamic movement) was met with suspicion and apprehension by the nations of the Western world as a menace endangering their power over colonies, the providers of precious indispensable raw materials for the prospering of economic life in the mother countries. . . ."

"Do your intellectuals feel this economic consideration?"

"How could we *not* feel it, since it was the main motive?" he asked me.

"Has the West changed its attitude and habits in this connection?" I asked him.

"It has had to," he said, laughing. "The course of history has brought about a resurrection of the Moslem world, and we are gradually coming into our own again. The Western world, after having belatedly found out that Islam is not the peril the world has to face, is now soliciting our cooperation to preserve peace and ward off the peril of a calamitous third world war. . . ."

"The West feels that Communism is the greater danger?"

"Yes. But the change of attitude on the part of the West has a negative foundation. From the point of view of Westerners, it is the choice of the lesser of two evils."

"In short, you feel that the approach of the West now is prompted more by fear of Communism than by love or understanding of the Moslem religion?"

"Correct; and we know it," he said emphatically. "And as long as we are in doubt on this point we shall always have our misgivings about the real aims of the West, of which we have had good reasons to be suspicious in our past history. In this case no real success can be expected from a cooperation founded on such weak grounds, with suspicion and distrust on either side ever lurking around the corner. The existing misapprehensions and misconceptions about Islam will have to be rooted out completely if that mutual suspicion and distrust is to be overcome."

"If that could be removed, if trust could be reinstated, then would you co-operate with the West?" I asked.

"If the West would meet us half way, yes," he said. "The part we shall be able to take in the co-operation, our own views and considerations must be fully taken into account.

We cannot be expected just to fall in line and act as we are told. The Islamic precepts and our position as Asiatic countries are decisive factors which cannot be neglected."

These are strong words, words colored with passion born of centuries of racial and religious oppression. Mr. Natsir was speaking for more than Indonesians; he was speaking for the world's four hundred million Moslems. Day by day I was learning to appreciate that one of the greatest realities of Asia was religion. . . .

"Just what kind of social structure would a Moslem state have?" I asked Mr. Natsir.

"There will be no need for Communism in Moslem countries," he said. "Pan-Islam will represent a world force, socialistic in nature, keeping a middle ground between Communism and Capitalism."

It was obvious to me that, if you tried to make this man choose between Communism and Capitalism, he'd feel that you were pushing him out of his natural mental orbit. He was more pro-Islam than anti-Communist or pro-Capitalist.

Later, in reading Mr. Natsir's political declaration made at Karachi in 1952, I learned that a Moslem state is not a state run by priests or a religious hierarchy. A Moslem state is a state for Moslems, but this does not mean that such a state is a theocracy. Moslems draw sharp distinctions between their kind of religious state and, say, a state in which a king rules by divine right. Every Moslem is a kind of priest; there is no separate church in a Moslem state, hence, there is no question of a separation of church and state. Again I was impressed by the firm rejection by the Asian mind of a division between the secular and the sacred. In the end, the Moslem state was a blur to me. I was told later that my inability to grasp the nature of the Moslem state was not just a personal shortcoming on my part; many young Indonesians were likewise baffled. Yet Mr. Natsir represented a substantial segment of Asian thought and he was not a man to be lured or bludgeoned into changing his stance by offers of machinery, nor would he budge because of fears of Red China. . . . The emotions of the Natsirs of Asia have been disciplined in a hard and bitter school; those emotions were wary, bruised, distrustful. . . .

PART II

Race and Religion at Bandung

I was now ready to go to Bandung to the conference. Rumors were rife. Everybody was guessing what each Asian and African nation was expecting to gain from its participation. There was no lack of easy speculation and interpretation: it was being said that Pandit Nehru was hoping to emerge from the conference as some kind of acknowledged leader or spokesman for Asia. Japan was expected to walk a tightrope, bowing and smiling to all sides among people over whom she once so brutally ruled, trying to place herself at the disposal of other Asian and African nations, offering her aid as a technical expert, hoping thereby to stimulate trade and retrieve her position as the real leader of Asia. (One Australian journalist commented bitterly: "Bandung means that Japan really won the war in the Pacific. . . .") Thailand was outdoing every other nation in an attempt to whoop up an immediate war against Red China, *now*. . . . Pakistan, tied to the West by treaties, would rather not have been at this conference at all, but came no doubt because she did not want to be accused of breaking Asian solidarity. . . . Sir John, representing a coalition government in which Communists and Trotskyites made up a vital element, was coming for much the same reasons, being as much concerned about his restless population at home as he was about Red China's teeming millions. Burma's U Nu, the popular Buddhist, it was openly said, would seek aid and support for his neutralist attitude. The entire Arab world, headed by Egypt's Nasser, would be seeking to air its direct grievance against Israel and its indirect case against France. The Philippines, a Westernized Asian nation anchored by the accident of geography amidst powerful Asian neighbors, linked to the West by treaties and to Asia by fear of what the future would bring, would be in the awkward position of having to carry water on both shoulders, would have to talk Right to keep faith with Washington and to act Left to prove that she was still free in her heart and understood the language of her disinherited Asian brothers. . . . About the Gold Coast, Liberia, and Ethiopia nobody had any real notions; indeed, it was rapidly becoming evident that Negro Africa was the weakest part of the conference. The Belgian Congo was not publicly mentioned, though that geographical prison was on the minds of many people who had never met a native from that sealed-off part of the earth. . . . I doubt if many of the delegates even knew that Spanish Africa existed. . . . The Portuguese and their slave system were remote from all minds. And the millions of blacks under French rule in Africa? Nobody but the North African delegates thought of the role that France played in trying to assimilate tribal Africans, pretending to be God to black men already conquered by the fear-systems of religion prevailing long before the logical and selfish French ever showed up. . . .

The main preconference speculation centered about Red China: How close really was Peking to Moscow? Would Chou En-lai grab the opportunity to use the conference as a whipping post for United States policy in Asia and the Pacific? Would jealous conflicts develop between Nehru and Chou En-lai? Were Asian and religious loyalties thicker than ideologies?

It was my impression that, with the exception of Nehru, Chou En-lai, and U Nu, no other delegations or heads of delegations came to Bandung but with the narrowest of parochial hopes and schemes. But when they got to Bandung, with their speeches in their pockets, something happened that no Asian or African, no Easterner or Westerner, could have dreamed of. . . .

The drive up the mountain slopes to Bandung lasted more than four hours and at no time were we out of sight of those brown, Javanese faces. The island of Java has more than fifty million people, a population density not to be matched anywhere else on earth: more than one thousand people to the square mile. In many respects the Javanese countryside reminded me of Africa; there were those same stolid peasants squatting by the side of the roads and staring off into space; there were those same bare-breasted young women with somber-colored cloths—sarongs—rolled and tucked about their waists; there were those barefooted men carrying burdens on poles slung over their shoulders (instead of on their heads as in Africa), making mincing little steps, almost like dancing a jig, so that the jogging of the elastic poles up and down would coincide with their footsteps; there was that same murderous sun that heated metal so hot that it would burn the skin; there was that same bright greenness of vegetation: beautifully terraced rice paddies filled with muddy water and rising in serried tiers toward blue and distant mountains; there were many white mosques and now and then the delicate Gothic spire of a Catholic Church looking fantastically out of place in this near-jungle scenery; and there was that bustling economic activity filling the visible landscape, that frantic buying and selling of matches and soap and tinned sardines, that fateful hallmark of those who have enjoyed the dubious blessing of having had their old, traditional and customary culture blasted and replaced by commercial and financial relations . . . There was that same red earth, that same attitude of the sleepwalker in the young men who strode along, that same gliding, slow-motion gesturing in the women and children, that fine gracefulness of stance that seems to be the physical trait of people who live in the tropics; only here in Java there was no jungle, no dense wall of dark green vegetation rising fifty or sixty feet into the moist and hot air. . . .

My friend Lubis was behind the wheel of the car, and the temperature dropped as we climbed into the mountains where volcanic craters could be seen crowned by haloes of white, fluffy clouds.

"I must take you to see a volcanic crater," Lubis said.

"I don't think so," I said.

"Why?" he asked, surprised.

"I'm looking for human craters," I said.

He laughed.

"Just how many people would you say are intellectuals in Indonesia?" I asked him.

"Well, somewhere between five and ten thousand," he answered.

"And, of that number, just how many, in your opinion, can really think?"

"Oh, I'd say about two thousand."

"The Dutch kept the people stupid, didn't they?"

"They did."

"Oh, those dear, damned, dull, dumb Dutchmen!" I sang out.

We laughed.

"Indonesia," said Lubis, "is an out-of-the-way place. The Dutch felt that they could do as they liked here and get away with it, and they did just that. They did it for three hundred and fifty years. Then the war came and spoiled their plans. There are Dutchmen who still dream of coming back, but that is impossible. They hate the role that America played in helping us to get our freedom. But, don't forget, there are some good Dutchmen, some who fought with us, some who became Indonesian citizens. I must be fair. . . ."

"This society has to be organized," I said.

"Absolutely," Lubis agreed.

"But who's going to do it? And how? And under whose ideology?"

"That's what the fight in Indonesia is all about," Lubis said. "We must work hard. Now, the Communists can do this job for us; they could put bayonets at our backs and make us work. But we must work no matter who is in control. Since we *must* work, why not work voluntarily? Why must we have a dictatorship?"

"Indonesia has taken power away from the Dutch, but she does not know how to use it," I commented. "This need not be a Right or a Left issue. Where is the engineer who can build a project out of eighty million human lives, a project that can nourish them, sustain them, and yet have their voluntary loyalty?"

We rolled into Bandung, a city of half a million people, and saw a forest of banners proclaiming Asian and African solidarity; bright posters welcomed delegations to the city. Stout, squat, white-helmeted troops lined the clean streets, holding Sten guns in their hands and from their white belts hand grenades dangled. . . . The faces of those troops were like blank masks, and they looked at you with black, cold, unresponsive eyes.

"Horrible, isn't it?" Lubis asked me.

"Not so horrible," I said. "You see, I've just come from Spain where you live under the muzzles of machine guns every hour of the day. You get used to it. The machine gun at the street corner is the trade-mark of the twentieth century. Open force is better than swarms of plain-clothes men. You know where you are with a machine gun."

Our car was stopped and we had to show our credentials, then we were waved on. I saw that the entrance to every hotel was under heavy guard. The city was organized up to the very hilt in the interests of security.

"They are taking no chances," I said.

"Since that plane carrying the Chinese delegation was downed," Lubis said, "they are frantic." He laughed softly. "Did you know this: a few days ago they rounded up every loose woman in the city and hustled them out? It was crazy. . . . The city is now ringed by crack troops. They don't want any unexpected visits from bandits. Incidentally, no deliveries of packages will be accepted at any hotel in which delegates or newspapermen are staying—"

"Why?"

"Such packages might contain bombs, my friend."

We drove past the conference building and saw the flags of the twenty-nine participating nations of Asia and Africa billowing lazily in a weak wind; already the streets were packed with crowds and their black and yellow and brown faces looked eagerly at each passing car, their sleek black hair gleaming in the bright sun, their slanted eyes peering intently, hopefully, to catch sight of some prime minister, a U Nu, a Chou En-lai, or a Nehru. . . . Then the air was pierced by a screaming siren, heralding the approach of some august representative of some colored Asian or African country. Day in and day out these crowds would stand in this tropic sun, staring, listening, applauding; it was the first time in their downtrodden lives that they'd seen so many men of their color, race, and nationality arrayed in such aspects of power, their men keeping order, their Asia and their Africa in control of their destinies. . . . They were getting a new sense of themselves, getting used to new roles and new identities. Imperialism was dead here; and, as long as they could maintain their unity, organize and conduct international conferences, there would be no return of imperialism. . . .

Lubis and I got out at my hotel and swarms of children with Oriental faces rushed forward with notebooks, calling out:

"Please sign! Autograph, please . . . !"

I didn't relish standing in that homicidal sun and I said quickly:

"Me, I no write." I pointed to Lubis. "He important man. Make him sign. Me, I no write."

I dashed for the shade of the hotel corridor and the children surrounded Lubis, held him captive for half an hour; he sweated and signed his name, cursing me for having gotten him into such a jam.

These children did not know who the personalities were; all they knew was that they were colored and important, and so they asked indiscriminately for signatures. . . . And during the coming week every one would sign his name, from Nehru, Chou En-lai, down to the humblest reporter from Paris, London, or Boston. . . .

Next morning, April 18, I'd no sooner climbed into the press gallery and looked down upon the vast assembly of delegates, many of them clad in their exotic national costumes, than I could sense an important juncture of history in the making. In the early and difficult days of the Russian Revolution, Lenin had dreamed of a gathering like this, a conglomeration of the world's underdogs, coming to the aid of his hard-pressed Soviets, but that dream had been a vain one indeed. And many Western writers, H. G. Wells, Lothrop Stoddard, etc., had long predicted the inevitable rise of these nations, but in their wildest intuitive flights they had never visualized that they would meet together in common cause. From a strictly Stalinist point of view, such a gathering as this was unthinkable, for it was evident that the Communists had no control here; this was no People's Front, no United Front, no Trojan Horse. . . . Every religion under the sun, almost every race on earth, every shade of political opinion, and one and a half billion people from 12,606,938 square miles of the earth's surface were represented here. . . .

The delegates began to file in. In came the Viet-Namese clad in Western dress. (I spied an Indo-Chinese friend I'd known years before in Paris and he seemed unchanged despite his background of war and suffering and revolution.) Three Gold Coast delegates entered, adding a blaze of brightness with their colorful togas. The Burmese entered wearing their soft white caps which had knots dangling at the sides of their heads; their skirts made even veteran newsmen lean forward and crane their necks. The Arabs, with their long white and black robes, seemed outlandish, like men from another world.

Nehru came in in his white Asian cap and the audience stirred. U Nu entered. Sir John of Ceylon entered. Then Ali Sastroamidjojo, Prime Minister of Indonesia, and the ideological father of the conference itself, entered, mounted the platform, and took the chairman's seat. Then came Mohammed Ali, Prime Minister of Pakistan. . . . At last Sukarno, President of the Republic of Indonesia, mounted the rostrum to deliver the opening address. . . .

He was a small man, tan of face, and with a pair of dark, deep-set eyes; he moved slowly, deliberately. He spoke in English with a slight accent; he knew words and how to use them, and you realized at once that this man had done nothing all his life but utilize words to capture the attention and loyalties of others. From the very outset, he sounded the notes of race and religion, strong, defiant; before he had uttered more than a hundred syllables, he declared:

"This is the first international conference of colored peoples in the history of mankind!"

He then placed his finger upon the geographical gateway through which the white men of the West had come into Asia:

"Sisters and Brothers, how terrifically dynamic is our time! I recall that, several years ago, I had occasion to make a public analysis of colonialism, and I drew attention to what I called the 'life line of imperialism.' This line runs from the Strait of Gibraltar, through the Mediterranean, the Suez Canal, the Red Sea, the Indian Ocean, the South China Sea, and the Sea of Japan. For most of that enormous distance, the territories on both sides of this life line were colonies, the people were unfree, their futures mortgaged to an alien system. Along that life line, that main artery of imperialism, there was pumped the lifeblood of colonialism."

In the third paragraph of his address, Sukarno evoked in a solemn manner a reality that Western statesmen refer to only in times of war or dire stress; he paid tribute to the many sacrifices which had made the conference possible. Implied in his recognition of sacrifice was an acknowledgment that it had been only through men willingly surrendering their lives in the past that a bridge had been made to this present moment. He said:

"I recognize that we are gathered here today as a result of sacrifices. Sacrifices made by our forefathers and by the people of our own and younger generations. . . . Their struggle and sacrifice paved the way for this meeting of the highest representatives of independent and sovereign nations from two of the biggest continents of the globe."

For Sukarno and national revolutionaries of his stamp, the present meeting was not merely a lucky stroke of politics, but a gathering whose foundations had been laid long before. He put his finger on the date in modern history when the real struggle against colonialism had begun in earnest:

"I recall in this connection the Conference of the 'League

Against Imperialism and Colonialism' which was held in Brussels almost thirty years ago. At that Conference many distinguished delegates who are present here today met each other and found new strength in their fight for independence."

It is hard for the Western world to realize how tenaciously these outsiders cling to and remember each link, each step in their life's struggles; to most of the delegates to whom Sukarno spoke, this meeting was the logical outcome of past sacrificial efforts. And why had they now come together? Sukarno said:

". . . we are living in a world of fear. The life of man today is corroded and made bitter by fear. Fear of the future, fear of the hydrogen bomb, fear of ideologies. Perhaps this fear is a greater danger than the danger itself, because it is fear which drives men to act foolishly, to act thoughtlessly, to act dangerously. . . . And do not think that the oceans and the seas will protect us. The food we eat, the water that we drink, yes, even the very air that we breathe can be contaminated by poisons originating from thousands of miles away. And it could be that, even if we ourselves escaped lightly, the unborn generations of our children would bear on their distorted bodies the marks of our failure to control the forces which have been released on the world."

What strength had Sukarno and Asian and African leaders like him? He was frank about it. He said:

"For many generations our peoples have been the voiceless ones in the world. We have been the unregarded, the peoples for whom decisions were made by others whose interests were paramount, the peoples who lived in poverty and humiliation. . . . What can we do? The peoples of Asia and Africa wield little physical power. Even our economic strength is dispersed and slight. We cannot indulge in power politics. . . . Our statesmen, by and large, are not backed up with serried ranks of jet bombers."

He then defined the strength of this gathering of the leaders of the poor and backward nations as:

"We, the peoples of Asia and Africa, 1,400,000,000 strong, far more than half of the population of the world, we can mobilize what I have called the *Moral Violence of Nations* in favor of peace. . . ."

And where was this moral violence coming from? Sukarno knew to what he was appealing, for he said:

"Religion is of dominating importance particularly in this part of the world. There are perhaps more religions here than in other regions of the globe. . . . Our countries were the birthplace of religions."

And what bound these diverse peoples together? Sukarno said:

"Almost all of us have ties to common experience, the experience of colonialism."

Sukarno was appealing to race and religion; they were the only realities in the lives of the men before him that he could appeal to. And, as I sat listening, I began to sense a deep and organic relation here in Bandung between race and religion, *two of the most powerful and irrational forces in human nature.* Sukarno was not evoking these twin demons; he was not trying to create them; he was trying to organize them. . . . The reality of race and religion was there, swollen, sensitive, turbulent. . . .

It was no accident that most of the delegates were deeply religious men representing governments and vast populations steeped in mystical visions of life. Asian and African populations had been subjugated on the assumption that they were in some way biologically inferior and unfit to govern themselves, and the white Western world that had shackled them had either given them a Christian religion or else had made them agonizingly conscious of their old, traditional religions to which they had had to cling under conditions of imperialist rule. Those of them who had been converted to Christianity had been taught to hope for a freedom and social justice which the white Western world had teasingly withheld. Thus, a racial consciousness, evoked by the attitudes and practices of the West, had slowly blended with a defensive religious feeling; here, in Bandung, the two had combined into one: *a racial and religious system of identification manifesting itself in an emotional nationalism which was now leaping state boundaries and melting and merging, one into the other.*

But let us follow the speakers who spell out this new thing that has come upon the world scene. Ali Sastroamidjojo, Prime Minister of Indonesia and spiritual architect of the multinationed gathering, was elected unopposed as President of the Conference. In his address he continued the theme:

"Among the main causes of the present-day tensions here is colonialism, the old scourge under which Asia and Africa have suffered for ages, which will be a subject of our special interest. It may be true that the larger part of mankind accepts the obvious truth that colonialism has to be considered as a thing of the past, but the fact is there that colonialism is still very much alive. When we look at the map of Asia and Africa we find many spots, and even whole countries, which are still fettered by the chains of colonialism. Moreover, in the flesh of several of us are still sticking the thorns, small or large, of colonial rule."

That the Asian-African Conference looked forward to convening again and broadening and deepening its scope was plainly stated:

"I hope that one day, and may it be soon, the opportunity will arise, or be created, to convene the representatives of independence movements in all colonial territories who are still struggling for the liquidation of colonial rule and for their national independence and sovereignty. We, the independent countries of Asia and Africa, have to do our utmost in supporting them in every peaceful effort which may achieve their freedom."

The degree to which resentment of practices of racialism still lives in the hearts of men who felt it for most of their lives comes through clearly in these words of Prime Minister Sastroamidjojo:

"Next to colonialism we meet racialism as an important source of tension. Racialism in fact is often, if not always, an aspect of colonialism based on feelings of superiority of the dominating group. Discrimination, however, based on differences of color is contrary to fundamental human rights. . . . How often are the timid attempts to have done with color bars outweighed by measures of ruthless discrimination? Is not Apartheid policy a form of absolute intolerance more befitting the Dark Ages than this modern world?"

Samdach Upayuvareach Norodom Sihanouk, heading the Cambodian delegation, added his concurrence by explaining that the Conference put:

". . . in concrete form, for the very first time, the solidarity of Asian and African peoples . . . it shatters the frontiers which separated two worlds: the Communist and the non-Communist. . . . I am proud of having had the privilege of leading my people in their struggle for independence and to have, after the Geneva Conference, determinedly steered our national policy towards . . . the community of neutral nations—among them: India and Burma."

Then Sir John Kotelawala, Prime Minister of Ceylon, expected by many to defend the Western world, continued the same theme of fear, mental pain stemming from conditions of previous servitude and the dread of another war. Said he:

"When the great powers of the West talk peace, their chances of agreement are weakened by the fact that each suspects the other's strength. We by contrast come to the conference table weak and relatively unarmed. We have no thermonuclear bombs in our pockets, no weapons of chemical or bacteriological warfare up our sleeves, no plans for armament factories or blueprints for ever more deadly methods of genocide in our brief cases."

Remembering the cynicism pervading the atmosphere of power politics, Sir John said:

"The old heresy dies hard—that if you want peace you must prepare for war. As a result, nations have armed themselves to the teeth against neighbors and have increased their might to a point where the least dispute can trigger a conflagration sufficient to involve the whole world. . . . The pass to which humanity has been brought by the domination and doctrine of force is the most vivid demonstration of the bankruptcy of force. Of what advantage is it to hold sway over vast territories, to have at one's command innumerable armies, to be able at the touch of a button to unleash the deadliest weapons science can invent, if, with all this, we are unable to rid ourselves of fear and hysteria and despair?"

And who is to stop this drift toward global destruction? Sir John has an answer. He says:

"We, the nations of the new Asia and Africa, whatever our language, whatever our faiths, whatever our form of government, whatever the color of our skins—black, brown, or yellow—have one thing in common: we are all poor and underdeveloped. Centuries of servitude and stagnation have left their mark, a dire heritage of poverty and ignorance, upon the masses of our peoples. . . . Where the wisdom of the West has failed, is it possible that the nations of Asia and Africa can hope to succeed? I think it is. Have the nations of this region in fact anything to offer? I think they have. Has the time come to offer it? I think it has. I say, then, in all seriousness and in all humility, that the peoples of this region have it in their power to apply to the problems of the present-day world, and for the first time in history, that traditional respect for the spiritual values of life and for the dignity of the human personality which is the distinguishing feature of all their great religions."

Egypt added her voice, new and revolutionary, to the assembly of nations that hate war and colonialism and racialism. Said Lieutenant Colonel Gamal Abdel Nasser:

"All over the world there is a growing sense of insecurity. The fear of war has been aggravated by the development of mass-destructive weapons capable of effecting total annihilation. The stakes are high in terms of the very survival of mankind."

Nasser too stressed the common feeling of identity born of a common heritage imposed by Western domination. He said:

"In this conference, we are meeting as representatives of the Asiatic and African countries. There is a striking similarity between the conditions prevailing in our countries, a similarity that operates as a unifying force; we have emerged from a long period of foreign influence, political as well as economic. . . . It is not surprising therefore that we should feel close together. . . ."

Nasser then struck at Israel as hard as he could:

"Under the eyes of the United Nations and with her help and sanction, the people of Palestine were uprooted from their fatherland, to be replaced by a completely imported populace. Never before in history has there been such a brutal and immoral violation of human principles. Is there any guarantee for the small nations that the big powers who took part in this tragedy would not allow themselves to repeat it again, against another innocent and helpless people?"

The Gold Coast, represented by Kojo Botsio, Minister of State, deepened the note of the new identification. Botsio said:

"It is, indeed, reassuring to us to be associated with the governments and peoples from whom we have drawn inspiration and guidance in our struggle for independence and whose experience of similar situations is recent and fresh enough to make them 'feel the stir of fellowship.' The struggles and sacrifices of these nations have in our day re-established and fortified the right of the people of all races to govern themselves; they are a shining example to all those laboring under racial discrimination, political subjection, and economic exploitation. . . . Although in our present transitional stage toward nationhood we are not yet responsible for our external affairs, nevertheless we were, on receipt of your invitation, most anxious not to miss the unique opportunity of being represented at this epoch-making conference. Many of the questions which will be discussed here are matters in which we have a natural and legitimate interest. . . ."

Prince Wan, representing Thailand, came before the assembly in a rather nervous attitude. Threatened with subversion at home and faced with hostile attitudes from its neighbors over the question of refugees and some three million Chinese owning dual nationality, Thailand put forward through Prince Wan a declaration of adherence qualified by reservations. Said Prince Wan:

"Truly in self-defense . . . and not for any aggressive or even provocative purposes whatsoever, Thailand has had to join with seven other powers in concluding a collective defense treaty . . . known as the Manila Pact.

"My Asian and African friends and colleagues will, no doubt, ask me how I justify the attitude of my government from the point of view of Righteousness or the Moral

Law . . . ?" Pleading self-defense, Prince Wan quoted Buddha: ". . . all warfare in which man tries to slay his brother is lamentable, but he does not teach that those who go to war in a righteous cause, after having exhausted all means to preserve the peace, are blameworthy. He must be blamed who is the cause of war."

(Prince Wan admitted "doubts in my mind," and those doubts must have been rather grave for, on May 3, 1955, Pibul Songgram, Premier of Thailand, in a New York *Times* story, said that: "I try as forcibly as I can to lead my country to secure peace in the world. They will always be at your side—in any way—to create the peace of the world.")

As though acting under the eye of the Almighty, Dr. Mohammed Fadhil al-Jamali of Iraq continued and deepened the theme of moral disapproval of the West and its ways. Said he:

"Unfortunately, colonialism is still well entrenched in many parts of the world. The people of North Africa, including those of Tunisia, Algeria, and Morocco, are still under the French yoke, and no amount of local sacrifices and world opinion seems to influence the French to move more rapidly in recognizing the rights of these people to independence and freedom.

"A typical example of outworn colonial policy is shown in South Africa where color prejudice and superiority of the white man have led to discrimination against Indians and natives, and to the segregation of the so-called colored people.

"It is our sincere hope that this Conference will prove in a very modest way to be a great moral force of ideological disarmament and moral rearmament. . . . May I conclude with the reading of a verse from the Holy Koran which I hope will be applicable to all of us here and to all those who are not with us but share our earnest desire for peace.

"'Allah will not change the condition of a people until they change from within themselves.'"

The same theme of anxiety sounded from the Chairman of the Ethiopian Delegation. He declared:

"This struggle against colonialism, which has characterized the life of each nation represented here, stresses a problem which the agenda before us underlines at several points. . . . Ethiopia's attitude toward theories of racialism is well known. We have opposed attempts to force these inhuman, scientifically discredited theories, to accomplish restrictive social, economic, and political ends in defiance of the provisions of the United Nations Charter and the Declaration of Human Rights."

Sami Solh, Prime Minister of Lebanon, head of its delegation, spoke bitterly regarding Arab refugees. He said:

"Heading these problems is that of martyred Palestine. Would the universal conscience accept any longer that one million refugees, driven out of their country, their homes, and deprived of their property, should live dispersed on the roads of exile? Would it accept that the decisions relative to this region as taken by that most solemn of Assemblies should remain unimplemented? Should we sacrifice one million victims on the altar of political opportunism?"

Only when Mr. Tatsunosuke Takasaki, principal Japanese delegate, rose to speak did the tone sink to the level of the rational. But even he had to speak in a confessional tone. He said:

". . . In World War II, Japan, I regret to say, inflicted damages upon her neighbor nations, but ended by bringing untold miseries upon herself. She has reestablished democracy, having learned her lesson at immense cost in lives and property. Chastened and free, she is today a nation completely dedicated to peace. As the only people who have experienced the horrors of the atomic bomb, we have no illusion whatever about the enormity of an attempt to solve international disputes by force.

"In the light of the foregoing statement, the Japanese delegation will submit to the Conference certain proposals on economic and cultural co-operation, together with a proposal for the maintenance of international peace."

Long heralded as the chief spokesman for the ideas of the West, Carlos P. Romulo, member of the Philippine cabinet, and chairman of the Philippine delegation to the Conference, made the most race-conscious and stinging speech of all. Indeed, the main burden of his address was an indictment of Western racialism. Here was a man who knew and loved America, who had the American outlook and attitude of pragmatism; but he had suffered under colonialism and he had sympathy for those who were not free. He said:

"In one sense this conference suggests that for the peoples of Asia and Africa the United Nations has inadequately met the need for establishing common ground for peoples seeking peaceful change and development. But I think that we must say also that if the United Nations has been weak and limited in its progress toward these goals, it is because the United Nations is still much more a mirror of the world than an effective instrument for changing it. It has been in existence only nine years and through that time always subject to all the pressures and difficulties of national rivalries and power conflicts, large and small."

This was straight, honest; then Romulo stated the mood of Asia:

"We do not have to be satisfied with the rate of progress being made."

Describing the nations who had sent delegates to the Conference, Romulo said:

"The majority of the independent nations represented here won their independence only within the last decade. Who would have been bold enough, twenty years ago, to predict that this would be so? Who will be bold enough now to say how soon or how slowly those peoples in Africa strong enough to win it will acquire the right to face their own problems in their own way on their own responsibility? The handwriting of history is spread on the wall; but not everybody reads there."

The Westernized Asian who spoke that line then struck at England, France, and Belgium:

"We know the age of European empire is at an end; not all Europeans know that yet."

Romulo stressed that there was not one way, but many, in which people could cast off the colonial yoke. He said:

"Political freedom has been won by many different means. The British surrendered power in Southern Asia because they knew they could no longer maintain it and were wise enough to base their action on reality. The French and Dutch had to be forced to the same conclusion."

He was certain that the old system has passed:

". . . everything we know and understand about history assures us that whatever travails the future holds, the old structure of Western empire will and must pass from the scene. Will it expire quietly and in dignity? Will it go out crashing violently?"

He waded boldly into the racial issue:

"I have said that besides the issues of colonialism and political freedom, all of us here are concerned with the matter of racial equality. This is a touchstone, I think, for most of us assembled here are the people we represent. The systems and the manners of it have varied, but there has not been and there is not a Western colonial regime which has not imposed, to a greater or lesser degree, on the people it ruled the doctrine of their own racial inferiority. We have known, and some of us still know, the searing experience of being demeaned in our own lands, of being systematically relegated to subject status not only politically and economically, and militarily—but racially as well. Here was a stigma that could be applied to rich and poor alike, to prince and slave, boss-man and workingman, landlord and peasant, scholar and ignoramus. To bolster his rule, to justify his own power to himself, the Western white man assumed that his superiority lay in his very genes, in the color of his skin. This made the lowest drunken sot superior, in colonial society, to the highest product of culture and scholarship and industry among subject people."

How has this affected the millions of the world's colored peoples?

"For many it has made the goal of regaining a status of simple manhood the be-all and end-all of a lifetime of devoted struggle and sacrifice."

Yet Romulo knows how easy it is to be a racist; and he sounds a warning to Asians and Africans to beware of becoming the kind of men whom they now condemn. He said pointedly:

"It is one of our heaviest responsibilities, we of Asia and Africa, not to fall ourselves into the racist trap. We will do this if we let ourselves be drawn insensibly—or deliberately—into any kind of counterracism, if we respond to the white man's prejudice against us as nonwhites with prejudice against whites simply because they are whites."

What, psychologically, did the policies of the whites do to the people of Asia and Africa?

"I think that over the generations the deepest source of our own confidence in ourselves had to come from the deeply rooted knowledge that the white man was *wrong*, that in proclaiming the superiority of his race, *qua* race, he stamped himself with his own weakness and confirmed all the rest of us in our dogged conviction that we could and would reassert ourselves as men. . . . Surely we are entitled to our resentment and rejection of white racism wherever it exists."

Then Romulo squared up to facts:

"Yet this white world which has fostered racism has done many another thing. A rich mythology of religious thinking and feeling, a rich heritage of art and literature came from them, and, above all, political thought and an astounding advancement of scientific knowledge also came from them.

"I ask you to remember," Romulo told his audience, "that just as Western political thought has given us all so many of our basic ideas of political freedom, justice, and equity, it is Western science which in this generation has exploded the mythology of race. . . ."

Following Romulo, other heads of delegations spoke: Liberia, Libya, Turkey, Pakistan, Syria, etc. But they added nothing new. It was clear that these speeches had not been arranged, or ordered; it was extremely doubtful if Romulo knew what the others had planned to say. . . . Hence, a certain amount of repetitiousness drove home the racial theme with crushing force. It was rumored that Nehru had objected to this battery of speeches and I can well believe it, but I doubt if even Nehru knew in advance what the over-all impression of that outpouring of emotion would be.

It is time now that we turn our attention to this Asian master, Nehru, and the man he was responsible for bringing to this massive international conference, Chou En-lai. . . .

PART III

Communism at Bandung

Communism at Bandung was conspicuous for its shyness, its coyness, its bland smile and glad hand for everyone. Chou En-lai, clad in a pale tunic, moved among the delegates with the utmost friendliness and reserve, listening to all arguments with patience, and turning the other cheek when receiving ideological slaps. In closed committee sessions Russia was attacked time and again and Chou En-lai refused to let himself be baited into answering. Russia had no defenders at Bandung. . . . Indeed, rumor had it that Chou En-lai had openly said that he did not agree with or support the Cominform; when pressed for his position, he would refer to the four points on the agenda and state that he was determined to keep within the limits of that agenda.

Yet we can guess at what must have been some of his unspoken reactions. Communism insists that it is a rational science, and Communists boast that their interpretation of history is materialistic. Then what could Chou En-lai have been thinking amidst this ground swell of racial and religious feeling? The speech that he had planned to deliver was passed out in printed form to the press, and he made another speech whose contents indicated that he had had strong reactions. He stated frankly:

"After listening to the speeches delivered by the heads of

many delegations, I would like to make some supplementary remarks."

The world had been led to expect that Chou En-lai would try to mobilize Asian support for his claim to Formosa, but he took a directly opposed line. He said:

"As for the tension created solely by the United States in the area of Taiwan, we could have submitted for deliberation by the Conference an item such as the proposal made by the Soviet Union for seeking a settlement through an international conference. The will of the Chinese people to liberate their own territory Taiwan and the coastal islands is a just one. It is entirely a matter of our internal affairs and the exercise of our sovereignty. . . . But we do not do this, because our Conference would be dragged into disputes about all these problems without any solution."

With that one gesture Chou En-lai surrendered his opportunity to use the conference as a forum for the ideas and policies of Red China. Why? He knew that the time for that was not ripe, that the distance that separated Red China from the religious nations of Asia and Africa was great indeed. Instead Chou En-lai chose another line, an attempt to identify himself with those millions with whom not many Western nations wanted or would accept identification. He said:

"The Chinese delegation has come here to seek common ground, not to create divergence. Is there any basis for seeking common ground among us? Yes, there is. The overwhelming majority of the Asian and African countries and peoples have suffered and still are suffering from the calamities under colonialism. This is acknowledged by all of us. If we seek common ground in doing away with the sufferings and calamities under colonialism, it will be very easy for us to have mutual understanding and respect, mutual sympathy and support, instead of mutual suspicion and fear, mutual exclusion and antagonism. That is why we agree to the four purposes of the Asian-African Conference declared by the prime ministers of the five countries at the Bogor Conference and do not make any other proposal."

It was that simple. Chou En-lai knew that he was addressing lonely men, men whose mentalities had been branded with a sense of being outcasts. It cost him nothing to make such a gesture, to speak words of compassion. He offered no programs of industrialization, no long-term loans, no mutual defense pacts. To the nations smarting under a sense of inferiority, he tried to cement ties of kinship. He said:

"We Asian and African countries, China included, are all backward economically and culturally. Inasmuch as our Asian-African Conference does not exclude anybody, why couldn't we ourselves understand each other and enter into friendly co-operation?"

A shrewd man speaking . . . Yet all was not easy in the mind of Chou En-lai. In Indonesia Moslems had butchered Communists, even though Communists held a balance of power in the present government. The rational Mr. Chou En-lai knew that religious feeling could rise threateningly against him, if it chose. It prompted him to say:

". . . I would like to talk about the question as to whether there is freedom of religious belief. Freedom of religious belief is a principle recognized by all modern nations. We Communists are atheists, but we respect all those who have religious belief. We hope that those with religious belief will also respect those without."

But what of subversion? More than ten million Chinese of dual nationality resided in many Asian countries and they constituted a problem. It was here that Chou En-lai made his smartest move and actually surrendered substantial concessions to his neighbor nations; he announced that he was signing a treaty with Indonesia, granting the minority of two million Chinese living in Indonesia the right to choose their nationality. . . . Brother Chou was most anxious to join this Asian-African church and was willing to pay for his membership. He stated that other Asian nations could avail themselves of similar treaty arrangements. It was a master stroke, and whatever misgivings existed melted not only into a passive acceptance of Red China, but into a kind of grudging admiration for Chou's good will.

It must not be thought that it was easy. Sir John and many others lashed out at Chou, blasted Russia's foreign policy, but Chou stood rocklike, insisting that he was as poor and hard-pressed as they were. In the end the photographers were able to snap pictures of Chou En-lai arm in arm with Sir John. . . . Needless to say, Nehru ran interference for Chou, fending off those who sought to question him too sharply. Yet, these simple moves do not explain it all.

Nehru's motives were clear: he wanted Asian unity. India was an Asian power and what happened in Asia should happen only with the consent of Asians. And such a state of affairs could not be brought about, as Nehru knew, without the co-operation of Red China.

There was an element of "Asianism" in the whole conference. They had, beforehand, excluded those issues upon which they could not agree, and they had before them an area in which it was obvious that they shared much in common. All Chou had to do was stand his ground and wait with outstretched hands, and they came to him. . . .

One must understand just what the two positions were at Bandung. The United States, though not present, had its spokesmen for the policy of a "containment of Communism." Communism was viewed in a rather naive light: eight hundred million people led by militant Communists under the command of Peking and Moscow. . . . But the Communists themselves viewed their position quite differently;

they had a historical perspective and they knew quite well from what quarter they could expect sympathy, recruits, in what parts of the world they could hope for an extension of their power. International Communism had, many decades before, turned its face away from Europe and had concentrated upon Asia, and now it had at long last begun to set its sights upon Africa, "the soft, rotten underbelly of imperialistic Europe," where there were no loyal European mass populations. Hence Chou En-lai, by promising to behave, had built a bridgehead that had found foundations not only in Asia but extended even into tribal black Africa. . . .

Hitherto international Communists had not been successful at all in Africa, where a tribal mass, wrapped in poetic dreams, had defied their efforts at ideological indoctrination. Only in the Union of South Africa, where a black industrial proletariat existed, had they made the slightest headway. Now, could the Chinese Communists do what Stalin had not done? Stalin had made many tragic mistakes with the Chinese Communists by his insisting upon the literal application of Marxist dogma. But Mao Tse-tung had organized what was at hand, that is, millions of starving peasants, plus Moslems, Buddhists, Protestants, and Catholics. Nothing succeeds like success and Stalin had had to accept what the Chinese had done, though at Yalta he told Roosevelt that the Chinese Communists were really not Communists. But, Communist or non-Communist, the Chinese were in the Red camp, the allies of Russia. And the question was: Could they do in the rest of Asia and Africa what they had done in China?

If there was no effective opposition to Chou En-lai at Bandung, among the Asian and African elite, how much more would there be among the illiterate millions sprawled over Asia and Africa? It would be safe to assume that, on the propaganda level, the opposition would be much, much less. For there does not exist any positive program from the Western powers in these areas. Western academic personnel is still discussing whether the Africans have the capacity for self-government, a psychological prejudice which no Communist worthy of his salt would ever carry as a handicap. And the delegates at Bandung felt that profound difference in approach.

Nkrumahism had already swept the Gold Coast where there was practically no industrialization; a strong, emotional, unorthodox nationalism had held the British at bay and had forced them either to fight a jungle war that would have been akin to the Kenya tragedy or to accept an illiterate and disciplined tribal nationalism. . . . The British, hungry for dollar exchange (cocoa), had accepted black nationalism. Will the Chinese revolutionaries, with their nonracist, pragmatic background of universalism, accept this new and unheard-of grafting of twentieth century political concepts upon truncated tribal societies? I believe that they will.

There must have been a lot of scratching of heads in Peking when the five Colombo Powers announced their determination to organize the Asian-African Conference. The Chinese must have known that, if they participated, they would be in the company of men who had perverted Marxism even more than they had. But what of that? Here was a chance for China to surround herself with men and nations who had suffered at the hands of the colony-owning Western states, and, since the United States had not disavowed its support of such states, China then could walk as a fellow guest into an anti-Western house built by a reaction to colonialism and racialism. . . . It was a gift from the skies. . . .

Surrounded thus by possible allies in case of war, posing as a champion of the oppressed, proudly identifying himself and his nation with the lowly of the earth, Chou En-lai publicly declared at Bandung:

". . . threats of war can frighten into submission no one who is determined to resist. They can only place the threat-makers in a more isolated and confused position."

With those words, an Asian politician had done what was believed impossible. Chou En-lai did not say that he knew the way of eternal salvation; he did not say that he had come to lift up "falling humanity"; he skirted any reference to virtue and morality; he simply said that he was willing to share the conditions of life of his black and brown and yellow brothers. But was he honest? If Chou En-lai were a trained and disciplined Bolshevik, then he was lying. And Chou En-lai is a trained and disciplined Bolshevik. Yet he had not said that he believed in what his Asian and African neighbors believed in; he had not pretended to accept their God. . . . All he had said was that he and his fellow Chinese were suffering, were backward, were afraid of war. . . . No one could recall having heard a Russian Communist speak like that; no one could recall if the Russian Communists had ever accepted a program drafted by others. One delegate, I was told, had come to Bandung violently pro-West, but had emerged from the closed sessions and had said: "I'm as violently opposed to Communism as ever. But I trust this man."

Chou En-lai was invited to Bandung by the authority of the five Colombo Powers. And whose voice is strong in that council? It is the voice of Nehru. . . . Now, at Bandung, Nehru was in the background, quiet, studied. There was widespread talk of rivalry between him and Chou En-lai, but I did not give much weight to that. These men were intelligent; they had talked over this conference long ago, had mapped out the boundary lines in advance; and that was why there were no serious conflicts at Bandung. . . .

Why did Nehru make such a strange pact? There are those who say that Nehru is a hypocrite, that he blows both hot and cold, that he says one thing today and another tomorrow. I talked with him and found no evidence of such aberrations. He was logical, quick, observant, and knowing. He is a great man. Of what does this greatness consist? It consists of his being what his country is: part East, part West. If one day Nehru says that the perplexities facing Asia are moral, then he is acting in a Western manner; if the next day he says that the world is gripped by a power struggle, he is looking upon life as an Asian. From his point of view, he is not merely playing with ideas; he is a reflection of what his India is, a halfway house between East and West.

Nehru's problem was: How can I find time to build up India? He knew that no Asian or African nation, though independent, was really free as long as it was backward and economically dependent. Then there was the fear that another war would result in the subordination of Asians and Africans again to Western rule. . . . Nehru sought to solve this question by forging a situation that would be a blend partly of power and partly of morality: the unity of Asia and Africa. What this vast combination lacked in terms of technical and military strength would be made up for in terms of numbers, that is, the body of mankind.

But such unity involved making indirect alliances with Red China, for there could be no unity in Asia without China. An alliance of Asians and Africans *without* China would be a hollow one; an alliance *with* Red China would be risky. But a multinationed agreement with China would, perhaps, give the other non-Communist nations a chance of standing together against China if she were caught cheating. . . . But would the other Asian and African nations join such a coalition?

It was at this juncture that Nehru, Sir John, Ali, U Nu, and Sastroamidjojo knew that they had trumps to play, cards that the West could not match: the fear of a new war, fear of racial prejudice, fear of poverty. . . . Get these hurt, frightened, lonely, suffering nations together and put the question to them. Nehru knew that these nations did not fear him or his people, did not fear Indonesia, Pakistan, etc.; the question was: Would they fear Red China? Trying for an alliance along the broadest possible lines, the Colombo Powers asked Chou En-lai to come in and behave. And Chou, being no fool, said yes.

But is there not something missing here? Weren't all these men deeply religious? Christians? Moslems? Buddhists? Hindus? They were. Would they accept working with Red China? Yes, they would. Why? Were they dupes? No, they were desperate. They felt that they were acting in common defense of themselves. Then, is Christianity, as it was introduced into Asia and Africa, no deterrent to Communism?

A quick examination of some of the delegations at Bandung revealed the solid presence of Christian influence. The five Liberian delegates were all members of the Y.M.C.A. Two members of the Indonesian delegation were Christians. The Philippine delegation was probably all Roman Catholic. The Ethiopian delegation was mostly Christian. The delegation from Lebanon was mostly Christian. . . . The rest of the delegations was composed mostly of Hindus, Moslems, Buddhists, etc. Obviously, religion, and particularly the Christian religion, was no bulwark against Communism in Asia. Indeed, a high official in the Indonesian government told me:

"In many instances Christianity provides Communism with its justification. Communism is paying the unpaid bills of the Christian church."

The more I examined the relationship between Communism and Christianity at Bandung, the more complicated I found that relationship to be. In the West one is inclined to feel that the two doctrines of life, Christianity and Communism, are opposed, but, at bottom, they are not as opposed as one would think. There are deep underground, emotional connections. Seen through Asian eyes, the two philosophies share much of the same assumptions of hope. As one writer has put it, Jesus Christ himself was one of the poorest men to claim divinity that the Asians ever heard of. So when a Communist comes into a colonial community, or a community still reacting in terms of the colonial situation (such as exists in Asia today), he can say: "I'll show you how to implement the Christian vision; I'll show you how to make Christianity come true, how to make the Kingdom of God real right here on earth. . . ." And the Asian Christian, longing for freedom from his white Christian masters, makes up his mind to follow the Communists.

Says Winburn T. Thomas, a missionary with twenty-two years of Asian experience, writing in the *Presbyterian Tribune*, February, 1954:

> **Strange as it may seem to Western observers, many Asians are both Christians and Communists. At one time, six of the seven leaders of the Travancore, India, Communist Party representatives were baptized Christians. There are two Communist Party representatives in the Indonesian parliament who also hold membership in the Batak Church.**
>
> **The sharp ideological lines and distinctions frequently drawn by Westerners are blurred in Asia. It is not uncommon for a Japanese to say that he is at once a Buddhist, a Confucianist, and a Christian. . . .**
>
> **The current phenomenon in China, with Christians giving thanks to the Communist Party and to the Peking government for its leadership of the church, goes beyond the traditional blurring of lines. Many Chinese do see basic conflicts between**

Christianity and Communism, yet are willing to co-operate with Mao Tse-tung in his new policies for the country. . . .

Summarizing, Thomas cites some of the following reasons to account for the situation:

Communist rule in China is Chinese. In this respect it differs from Japanese occupation.

During the period of colonial expansion, China was not taken over by any one Western nation. This was not due to innate strength on the part of the Chinese. The Western nations were unable to agree on how they would carve up the "sleeping giant" which was too large for any of them to take over alone. Yet unequal treaties were forced upon China beginning with the middle of the nineteenth century. Her cities became foreign concessions. White men were in charge of her customs.

The state of being a Christian does not, necessarily, condition an individual's feelings of nationalism and patriotism. . . .

The Chinese Christian thinks he reads in his Bible that all governments are the gift of God, and that political control has been vested in Mao's hands. . . .

The Communist government has had to raise to high position such men as Y. T. Wu, a Y.M.C.A. secretary, who is now head of the Protestant movement. He is national chairman of the Oppose-America, Aid Korea Three-fold Self-Reform Movement of the Church of Christ in China. He is editor of the *T'ien Feng* (*Heavenly Wind*), official publication of this body.

The Asian ground upon which the seeds of the Christian doctrine fell was far richer than the devout sowers dreamed. . . . The Asian mind is tenacious, pragmatic; when you speak of social justice and freedom to an Asian, he takes your words at face value; he does not suspect double talk. . . .

But religion alone, at Bandung, would not and could not have tipped the scales toward Chou En-lai. Fear was at Bandung. And among all the fears riding the delegates, there were some cardinal fears: fear of the vast and restless populations in their native lands; fear of the future; fear of their neighbors. . . . The delegates had to act and speak in a manner that assured them that they would be safe no matter what happened. Each address was directed to the voters at home, to the State Department in Washington, to Whitehall in London, to Peking, to Moscow, to their own Asian and African neighbors. An interview with a member of Romulo's delegation elicited the following attitude:

"We are worried. America is protecting us, but America does not really need us. She has atomic and hydrogen bombs. She can defend herself. Suppose America says that she has to retrench? Where would that leave us? We are a sentimentality for America. One day we will have to face these other Asian nations alone. . . . And that's what frightens me. . . ." He paused, scratched his head, and looked off. "Why are we at Bandung? Brother, in the past we have been objects to be moved here and there. We were handled as only those on the outside wanted us handled. We had no say in the matter. . . . Now, we want to show those people that we can manage our own lives. And this conference is a demonstration of that. We'll have our difficulties, but at least we want to try. And we are trying and we are not doing too badly. . . ."

Mrs. Gandhi, daughter of Nehru, told me a strange story that buttresses the above confession in a telling manner. She related how the Communist Parties of China and Russia had invited thousands of Indian students to visit Peking and Moscow to see the impressive strides that had been made in industrial development. These trips into Russia and China had been official excursions and the Indian students had been squired around. They had completed their tours by being definitely pro-Communist in sentiment. Upon their return to India, they had begun berating Nehru for not having done things as the Chinese and Russians had done them.

"These young people don't know that we are doing the *same* thing. Now we are making sure that our young people know what we are doing in our country. Many of them are surprised when they do see what we are doing. . . ."

She paused, then went on relentlessly:

"The Americans do not understand. The American press attacks us, day in and day out. Look, in India my father is respected. Look at me: I've served time in prisons. So has my father. We have suffered. We have lived in exile. These sufferings that we have endured have woven haloes about our heads for our masses. . . . They look to us. They respect us. They love us. And the love and the respect they have for us we use to keep unity while we build up our country. Yet the Americans attack us. Do they know what they are doing? Don't they know that if they destroy my father, they will be opening the gates to anarchy, to Communism even? Don't they know what they are doing, these Americans . . . ?"

And back of Sir John of Ceylon was also a nest of unrest. One day's visit in Colombo was enough to disclose dissatisfaction with the coalition government supporting him—a coalition composed of Communists, Trotskyites, and sundry other elements. . . . And what of Indonesia? There was hardly any government there at all, save for Sukarno's winged words of idealism, troops, and machine guns. . . .

The Gold Coast was harassed by widespread tribal revolts. And so it went. . . . I'm no expert regarding these politically turbulent areas of the world, but I'd suspect that the other Asian and African countries too had their millions of restless and demanding people.

Could these new statesmen look toward the West for the kind of help they wanted, help that would pull their debased populations quickly out of the mire of ignorance and poverty? A strange and new religion is in the hearts of these new Asian and African nationals. They feel that if they do not become quickly modern, if they do not measure up to the West almost overnight, they will be swallowed up again in what they feel to be slavery. And Chou En-lai stood there, bland, smiling, more liberal than any liberal ever seen on land or sea, preaching tolerance, assuring one and all that they need feel no shame, no sense of anxiety in the presence of his Communist-led six hundred million poor and backward Chinese. . . . From both Moscow and Peking the word had gone out: Be nice; no more clenched fists; give them all a glad welcome. . . . And all over Bandung the Communists were affable, shaking hands with their former enemies, waving aside all references to past hatreds and slanders, doing all in their power to heal old wounds. . . .

And under this vague drift toward collectivism was a powerful substratum of racial emotion. . . .

PART IV

Racial Shame at Bandung

Racial feeling manifested itself at Bandung in a thousand subtle forms. The Sten guns and the hand grenades of the brown Indonesian troops evoked deep fear in many white observers. Said one Englishwoman:

"I'd suggest that we evacuate Australia right now and settle the population in Canada."

As I watched the dark-faced delegates work at the conference, I saw a strange thing happen. Before Bandung, most of these men had been strangers, and on the first day they were constrained with one another, bristling with charge and countercharge against America and/or Russia. But, as the days passed, they slowly cooled off, and another and different mood set in. What was happening? As they came to know one another better, their fear and distrust evaporated. Living for centuries under Western rule, they had become filled with a deep sense of how greatly they differed from one another. But now, face to face, their ideological defenses dropped. Negative unity, bred by a feeling that they had to stand together against a rapacious West, turned into something that hinted of the positive. They began to sense their combined strength; they began to taste blood. . . . They could now feel that their white enemy was far, far away. . . . Day after day dun-colored Trotskyites consorted with dark Moslems, yellow Indo-Chinese hobnobbed with brown Indonesians, black Africans mingled with swarthy Arabs, tan Burmese associated with dark brown Hindus, dusty nationalists palled around with yellow Communists, and Socialists talked to Buddhists. But they all had the same background of colonial experience, of subjection, of color consciousness, and they found that ideology was not needed to define their relations. . . . I got the notion that ideologies were the instruments that these men had grown used to wielding in their struggles with Western white men and that now, being together and among themselves, they no longer felt the need for them. As the importance of ideology declined, I began to feel that maybe ideology was a weapon that suited only certain hostile conditions of life. Racial realities have a strange logic of their own.

Over and beyond the waiting throngs that crowded the streets of Bandung, the Conference had a most profound influence upon the color-conscious millions in all the countries of the earth. I cite the case of an American Negro who heard the "call of race" and came to Bandung. In his personality one can catch a glimpse of the befuddled hope that racial issues set in motion.

Mr. Jones was a light brown, short, husky man who, according to American nomenclature, was "colored." He was a mechanic in Los Angeles. He had never in his life written a line for publication, yet, when he heard that there was going to be a "big conference of all the colored nations on earth," this obscure man became deeply affected. By hook or crook he persuaded a newspaper to give him credentials, and he took all of his life's savings and those of his wife and set out for Bandung. . . . Mr. Jones was "colored," and being "colored" still means today in America that you can feel that you are in a lower category of the human race, that your hopes for freedom, for a redemption of your marked-off status, must be deferred. True, legislation against segregation was coming to Mr. Jones's aid, but he had become conditioned to feeling defensive about his complexion. In short, Mr. Jones felt that he belonged to a "colored" nation, that he was out of place in America. . . . So this brown man came thousands of miles to feel a fleeting sense of identity, of solidarity, a religious oneness with the others who shared his outcast state. . . . And brown Mr. Jones, watching the wily moves of tan Nehru and yellow Chou En-lai, understood absolutely nothing of what was going on about him. . . .

Do I cite an unusual case? Then I shall submit one from the very top levels of American Negro life.

Adam Clayton Powell is a Negro Congressman from New York; he is the pastor of one of the largest Protestant churches in the United States. Though classed by American standards as a Negro, Congressman Powell is actually a white man, much whiter in terms of skin color than many whites I've known. Hence, at Bandung, the Congressman had to explain that he was "colored," that his grandfather had been a branded slave.

Now, what Indonesia's President Sukarno had called "the first international conference of colored peoples in the history of mankind" deeply affected Congressman Powell, called to something buried not too far beneath his hard, practical mind; it awakened or reawakened his sense of racial and neonational romanticism. . . . So Congressman Powell flew to Bandung, coming as far as the Philippines in a United States bombing plane; there he teamed up with the Philippine delegation and, while en route to Bandung, began holding press conferences to "defend the position of the United States in relation to the Negro problem."

The Congressman gave us Americans a cleaner bill of racial health than we deserve, yet, at the same time, he stressed the colored population of the United States, putting the figure at 23,000,000, which included Mexicans, Puerto Ricans, Japanese, and maybe a few other races. It is to be recalled that, with the exception of Congressman Powell, no delegate or observer at Bandung raised the Negro problem in the United States—a problem which is child's play compared to the naked racial tensions gripping Asia and Africa. . . .

I'm not critical of Congressman Powell's efforts, though his activities were not my style, smacking much too much of high-pressure salesmanship and public relations—two hardy, frisky arctic animals utterly unknown in the tropical latitudes of Bandung. . . . The astounding aspect of Congressman Powell's appearance at Bandung was that he *felt the call*, *felt its meaning*. . . . At the very moment when the United States was trying to iron out the brutal kinks of its race problem, there came along a world event which reawakened in the hearts of its "23,000,000 colored citizens" the feeling of *race*, a feeling which the racial mores of American whites had induced deep in their hearts. If a man as sophisticated as Congressman Powell felt this, then one can safely assume that in less schooled and more naive hearts it went profoundly deep.

Just how conscious were the Asian statesmen at Bandung of the racial content of what they were organizing? I discussed this problem with none less than Nehru. That Asian statesman asked me what I thought of the reactions of the West to the Conference and I said:

"Mr. Prime Minister, the West has exploited these people for centuries and such gatherings as this evoke fear deep in their hearts. There are people who ask if this is not racism in reverse—"

"Yes," Nehru said. "The West feels what you say. But what the West feels can come about. Race feeling is in these people, and if the West keeps pressuring them, they will create racism in them."

By sheer chance I stumbled upon a little book that gave me great insight into how the Dutch created racial conditioning in Indonesia, just what the nature of Dutch and Indonesian relations were. This booklet was designed to teach the Indonesian language to Dutch officials, housewives, or just wandering tourists, European or otherwise. The first thing that one notices is that there are no Indonesian words in this booklet for polite talk, for civil intercourse; there is not a single sentence that would enable one to inquire of the feelings of another. Whether the author knew it or not, he was writing a book to instruct an army of invaders how to demean, intimidate, and break the spirit of an enemy people in a conquered, occupied country. . . . All sentences were rendered in terms of flat orders, commands; an exclamation point usually followed each sentence, implying that one actually shouted one's orders.

This booklet, entitled *Bahasa Indonesia*, a book of elementary Malay, was compiled by S. van der Molen (adapted for the use of English-speaking students by Harry F. Cemach). It was published by W. van Hoeve, The Hague, in 1949. For example, page 22, lesson 7, gave the following use of the Indonesian language. I cite the English equivalents of the Indonesian words which are printed in the left-hand column of each page:

Gardener, sweep the garden!
That broom is broken!
Make a new broom!
Sweep up in front first!
Washerwoman, here are the dirty clothes!

Don't ruin them, will you?
Babu, wash the clothes!

Then, on page 34, one gets in lesson 13, entitled "Hold the Thief!," a good look into the psychology of the Dutch as it related to the humanity of the Indonesian. I quote a part of it, thus:

Didn't you close the window last night?
All the silver is gone.
The drawers of the sideboard are empty.
During the night there has been a thief.
What did the thief steal?
Where is the gardener?
He went to the pawnshop.
He took two spoons and received five guilders.
All the other goods were still in his pack.
He was arrested by the police.
All my stolen property has been returned.

The masterpiece is in lesson 24, page 56; it is entitled "The Master Is Cross." Here it is, word for word:

Who is it?
Where do you come from?
Where are you going?
Why are you running about here?
What are you looking for?
Don't pass along here!
You must stay over there!
You are not clever enough.
You are stupid.
You'll get into trouble in a minute.
Be careful, don't do it like that!

Think first. Look for ways and means.
Are you ashamed?
I want information.
I don't understand.
I think you are lying.
I don't believe it!
Don't talk nonsense!
Speak straight out!
Don't be difficult!
Don't be afraid, answer!
Just why are you silent?
Why don't you dare?
I don't want to hear such nonsense! Be quiet!
Now that's enough!
That matter is already clear.

And today there are Dutchmen who complain that the Indonesians are "Dutch crazy," that is, when an Indonesian sees a Dutch face, he gets angry. . . . The mystery is how did it last for three hundred and fifty years? The sentences I have quoted above were designed to maintain "law, order, peace, and tranquility . . ." A reliable UNESCO official informed me that today the Belgians in the Congo use such methods of communication with their Congo natives and they characterize their attitude as "*dur, mais juste . . .*" And there are swarms of European social scientists in Asia and Africa culling for facts to find out why the natives rise suddenly and rush for the throats of Europeans.

One afternoon in Bandung a knock came at my hotel door; I rose and opened it and saw a tall white woman. She smiled shyly and said:

"Forgive me for bothering you. You are Richard Wright?"

"Yes. What is it?"

The woman looked off nervously, then smiled again, and asked:

"May I speak to you for a few moments?"

"Of course. Suppose we sit here on the veranda. Is that all right?"

"Oh, thank you," she said. "I know I'm intruding—"

"Not at all. Sit down. Now, what's on your mind?"

Seated, she smiled. Her hands were nervous and she knotted and unknotted her fingers.

"You are a journalist?" I asked her.

"Yes," she answered. "I want to ask you about something, but I don't know how to begin. You see, I've read your books and felt that you, of all people, could tell me something . . ."

"I'll try," I said.

"You see, my roommate is a Negro girl from Boston—"

"Hunh huh."

"She's nice, really. She's a journalist too. But—I don't know how to say it—" She broke off in confusion.

I studied her closely, but I could get no clue as to why she was so wrought up.

"You find this girl offensive," I suggested.

"Oh, no! It's not that. But—she's *strange*."

"In what way?"

"Believe me, it's not racial prejudice on my part—"

"You are American?"

"Yes. But I'm not prejudiced. I swear I'm not. I'm liberal—"

"I believe you," I told her.

"It has nothing to do with race," she said.

"Just relax and tell me what's the matter. What happened?"

She edged to the end of her bamboo chair and smiled again. Then suddenly she was serious, dead serious.

"It's at night. I don't understand it. She comes in late. . . . Oh, she's polite, all right. She pulls off her shoes and walks around in her bare feet; that's not to awaken me. She is black, real *black*, you see? Her skin is very shiny. I don't mind that.

When I first met her I thought she was very pretty; I do still. But when she thinks I'm sleeping, she does some strange things. . . . On her bare feet she creeps around like a cat. . . . Then one night I awakened and tried to see what she was doing; the room was dark. . . . I smelt something strange, like something burning. . . . She was in a dark corner of the room and was bent over a tiny blue light, a very low and a very blue flame. . . . It seemed like she was combing her hair, but I wasn't sure. Her right arm was moving and now and then she would look over her shoulder toward my bed. . . . I was scared. . . . Now, look, could she have been practicing voodoo, or something?"

"WHAT?"

"Voodoo," she repeated humbly.

"What makes you ask that?"

"Oh, maybe you think I'm crazy! But I want to understand. Why is she so secretive? Why does she creep around at night on her bare feet?"

I was baffled. *A blue light? A strange smell?* Was the woman telling me the truth?

"What else has this woman done?"

"Nothing. But she gives me the creeps, that moving around all night and that blue light and that odor. . . ."

"Did you try to get a look into her things?"

She hesitated, then looked off and said:

"I tried to find out what it was she was doing at all hours of the night. But I could find nothing but an empty tin can; it was marked *Sterno*. . . ."

I gaped as comprehension swept into my mind. Then I laughed out loud.

"Well, calm down. It's all very simple. The woman was straightening her hair. You said that she was using something that looked like a comb. . . . That can of Sterno was to heat her metal comb which she uses to straighten her hair. And she did not want you—"

"But why would she straighten her hair? Her hair seems all right."

"Her hair is all right. But it's not straight. It's kinky. But she does not want you, a white woman, to see her when she straightens her hair. She would feel embarrassed—"

"Why?"

"Because you were born with straight hair, and she wants to look as much like you as possible. . . ."

The woman stared at me, then clapped her hands to her eyes and exclaimed:

"Oh!"

I leaned back and thought: here is Asia, where everybody was dark, that poor American Negro woman was worried about the hair she was born with. Here, where practically nobody was white, her hair would have been acceptable; no one would have found her "inferior" because her hair was kinky; on the contrary, the Indonesians would perhaps have found her different and charming. (In fact, there are some Indonesians in some of the islands who have kinky hair!)

"So that's why she changed color so often," the woman spoke in a tone of quiet wonder.

"What did she do?"

"She would go into the bathroom, lock the door, and stay for an hour or more. . . . And when she came out, she'd be much lighter in color. When she went in, she was black, naturally black; but when she came out, she was much lighter, pale, sort of grey—"

"She uses chemicals on her skin," I told the woman.

"But why?"

"Negroes have been made ashamed of being black. Dark Hindus feel the same way. White people have made them feel like that. The American Negroes are black and they live in a white country. Almost every picture and image they see is white. The Hindus have been conditioned to regard white skins as superior; for centuries, all the authority and power in their country were in the hands of whites. . . . So these people grow to feel that their lowly position is associated with their being black. They have been told time and again that they are inferior. And this woman, your roommate, is trying to make herself look as white as possible. Can you blame her? It's a tribute that she pays to the white race. It's her way of saying: 'Forgive me. I'm sorry that I'm black; I'm ashamed that my hair is not like yours. But you see that I'm doing all that I can to be like you. . . .'"

"That's horrible," the woman breathed. "She crucifies herself—"

"Every day that woman commits psychological suicide," I tried to explain. "That is why twenty-nine nations are meeting here in Bandung to discuss racialism and colonialism. The feeling of inferiority that the white man has instilled in these people corrodes their very souls. . . . And though they won't admit it openly, they hate it."

"Now I remember something—"

"What?"

"One night she passed my bed; she stopped and said: 'I'm walking softly so that I won't awaken you.' And, you know what I said? I was half asleep and I mumbled: 'Don't bother, I see everything.' After that, she acted like she hated my very guts. . . ."

"She felt that you'd been spying on her shameful ritual of hair-straightening and skin-lightening."

"But what can I do?"

"Nothing," I told her. "This is much bigger than you or I. Your father and your father's father started all this evil. Now it lives with us. First of all, just try to understand it. And get all of that rot about voodoo out of your mind."

The woman stared and tears welled into her eyes.

"I'm ashamed," she whispered.

"The whole world ought to be ashamed," I told her.

She rose, reached out her hand to me, then she jerked it back. I wondered if I'd offended her with my frank talk about what the black woman had been doing.

"What's the matter?"

"That woman was telephoning today and I overheard what she was saying. . . . Say, now it comes clear. She was begging some Negro reporter to try to find a can of Sterno for her. And she wore a cloth about her head. She begged and begged for a can of Sterno. . . ."

"Maybe her Sterno is all gone."

"That's what she told the man—"

"Then that means that she cannot now straighten her hair. This heat and humidity will make it kinky again. And she doesn't want anybody to see her hair in its natural state—"

"God in Heaven, why doesn't she forget her hair? She's pretty like she is!"

"She *can't* forget it. The feeling that she is black and evil has been driven into her very soul. . . ."

The woman stood and stared off into space for a long time. I saw sweat beads on her forehead and nose. Then I heard the scream of a siren as some car belonging to the delegation of some Asian or African colored nation sped down the street, followed by a truckload of white-helmeted troops armed with Sten guns and hand grenades. The woman shook hands with me abruptly and said:

"Thank you. Goodbye."

"Goodbye," I said. "And tonight, for God's sake, try to sleep."

"I shall," she said and was gone.

Even among Indonesian intellectuals I found strong racial feelings. I spent an evening with a group of artists, poets, and writers who spoke of their attitudes toward the West quite freely. To my surprise, I was told that even in the city of Jakarta there were not many contacts between intelligent

Indonesians and Europeans and Americans. White missionaries had established some areas of contact; businessmen had created relations of a commercial nature; and of course the Communists maintained the closest and most intimate contacts of all. . . .

The only two public places where Indonesians and Europeans can meet on a basis of informal intimacy are the city's two main bars, but since Indonesians, because of religious reasons, are not great drinkers, they rarely frequent these bars. This lack of routine and steady contact stems, no doubt, from the heritage left here by Dutch rule.

"The Dutch, the Americans, and the English do not know us," a young and well-known poet told me. "Where can we meet them? In those two bars? No! We don't like night clubs. And our experience in meeting these Europeans has always turned out badly. When they leave Indonesia, they write false things about us. We are exotic children to them. Why, one white woman journalist went away and wrote an article saying that we grew banana trees in our homes! Can you imagine that?"

On many occasions I found that the moment a European or a white American entered a room in which I was talking to Indonesians, a sense of constraint and awkwardness at once came over the Indonesians, and the conversation would veer quickly from intimate descriptions of their personal feelings toward general topics.

In an intimate interview with one of the best-known Indonesian novelists I asked him point-blank:

"Do you consider yourself as being colored?"

"Yes."

"Why?"

"Because I feel inferior. I can't help it. It is hard to be in contact with the white Western world and not feel like that. Our people are backward; there is no doubt of it. The white

Western world is ahead of us. What we see of the white West is advanced; what we see of Asia is backward. So you can't help feeling inferior. And that is why I feel that I'm colored."

This writer heads a powerful cultural organization; he is devoutly religious and is highly respected among his colleagues. Yet he holds the most violent attitudes toward the Japanese.

"Those *yellow* monkeys!" He spat as he referred to them.

"But they are colored too," I reminded him.

"But we Indonesians are *brown*," he told me proudly.

Since all progress and social change are measured in terms of the degree to which Asian and African countries resemble Western countries, each tiny alteration wrought in the traditional and customary habits of the people evoke in them feelings of race consciousness. Said a young Indonesian bureaucrat to me:

"We Indonesians are just discovering the weekend. We used to hear about people going away for the weekend, but it was an experience we had never had. We saw American movies in which people went away from the city to the seashore or the mountains for weekends. Now we are doing what we saw those white Americans do in the movies. . . . Funny, isn't it? Under Dutch rule there was no such thing as a weekend for us. Either we were too busy working to make a living or we didn't have enough money for a weekend. Now we Indonesians can go and enjoy a cool weekend in the mountains like the Americans."

Even mild-tempered Buddhists echo this attitude of defensiveness toward the West in religious matters. Said U Mya Sein, Chargé d'Affaires of the Union of Burma Embassy in Indonesia, in an address before an audience of the Islamic University:

"When Western colonialism annexed Burma about a century ago, nearly one per cent of the then population were *bhikkus* or Buddhist monks. Gradually, however, Buddhism suffered a decline through neglect under conditions of colonialism. As a matter of policy, colonialists introduced non-Buddhist missionaries into Burma on the one hand and on the other deprived Buddhist monks and monasteries of the status enjoyed during precolonial days.

"Today, after regaining its independence from colonialism, Burma is returning to the traditions of Buddhism in everyday life. The Constitution of Burma provides for a Secular State although it endorses that Buddhism is [the religion held] by the majority (i.e. 90 per cent) of the nation."

Still another result of the Western impact upon the temperament of the Asian is the mushroom growth of a race-conscious and chaotic literature born of inferiority feelings; self-criticism runs rampant; extreme attitudes, smacking of omnipotence of thought, take the place of calm, constructive plans or projects. It is as if the Asian, smarting under his loss of face, were trying to offer to his new god of industrialization a sacrifice of ultramodernity of attitude and idea to redeem his state of racial degradation and humiliation. One hears the most abstruse ideas being debated by sweating brown or black or yellow men in sweltering bamboo houses. . . . Deprived of historical perspective, feeling his "racial" world broken, the new Asian makes a cult of action, of dynamism, to fill the void that is his; hence, motives for action are neurotically sought for. Racial insults, slights, and offenses, no matter how trivial, are hugged and nursed. If the past is shameful, and the future uncertain, then the present, no matter what its content, must be made dramatically meaningful. . . . Rendered masochistic by a too long Western dominance, carrying a hated burden of oversensitive racial feelings, he now rushes forward psychologically to embrace the worst that the West can do to him, and he feels it natural that the West should threaten him with atom or hydrogen bombs. In this manner he accepts the dreaded bombing long before it comes, if ever. Europeans told me that if an atom or hydrogen bomb ever fell on Asian soil from Western planes, every white man, woman, and child in sight would be slain within twenty-four hours.

The most racially pathetic of all the Asians is the Eurasian, those black-white men of Asia. . . . The West created this class as a kind of buffer between themselves and the illiterate yellow and brown and black masses, but now they want none of these Eurasians in their ordered Western societies. And the brown and yellow and black masses will have none of the Eurasians, for they, with their European dress, attitude, and manners, remind the masses too much of the white Europeans who once held them in subjection. Hated by both sides, shunned by all, the Eurasian ends by hating himself, alone in a lonely world.

"But why," an internationally important official asked me in worried tones, "do these people keep on talking and feeling this racial business when they are now free?"

"They can't forget it that quickly," I told him. "It lasted too long. It has become a way of life."

The Western world set these mighty currents in action, and it is not for that Western world to say when and how these currents, now grown turbulent and stormy, will subside and flow again in the normal channels of human intercourse.

The echo of racial consciousness assumes a truly agonizing ring when it is sounded by sensitive whites who try to penetrate the color curtain. A young, morally sensitive white Christian implored me to tell him how he could square the racial role he was forced to play with his love of the poor and the oppressed.

"I must earn my living; I have a wife and child," he explained. "Yet what I'm doing here is hurting these Indonesians. I try to make as many friends among the Indonesians as I dare, but I must be careful. My white comrades in the company where I work think that I'm odd, crazy. The company pays the Indonesian who works with me less than they pay me, yet that Indonesian is as efficient as I am. . . . I'm white and he is not; that is the only justification for this inequality in pay. And that Indonesian knows it and it makes him bitter. But if I so much as lift my voice about it, I'd be fired, blacklisted; I'd be guilty of the greatest sin that a white man could commit out here. I'm rewarded for doing wrong and penalized for doing right. Maybe you'd say, 'Leave.' But that's no solution. At least by remaining, I can talk to a few Indonesians. But that too is dangerous. . . .

"Here I must belong to my European circle; they want me to belong to their clubs and drink with them. The life we Europeans live out here is unnatural. For example, I cannot keep rabbits here like I did in Europe. Even for a European to keep a garden and do his own work in it makes him suspect. . . ."

It was hard for me to advise him. He was a Christian, and the Christian church has not found any practical answers to questions such as he had posed. For such moral problems the Communists have ready answers; they would have directed the man to remain on his job and organize, serve the interests of the Party, thereby enabling him to assuage the moral outrage done to his feelings. . . . But Christians have no Party, no practical cause to serve. Hence, such men carry out their colonial duties with loathing. Filled with a bad conscience, they find it impossible to defend the policies of the Western world.

"Have you tried to talk to some Indonesians?" I asked him.

"It's hard," he lamented. "A white man out here goes through agony before he can approach an Indonesian in an honest manner. First, he has to overcome his inhibitions. Then he has to be certain that the Indonesian he approaches has not been corrupted by the whites. There have been cases of Indonesians who have betrayed whites who sought their friendship, who tried to help them. Many Indonesians have seen whites sit behind big desks and earn good money, easy money; and, once some Indonesians reach such positions, they wish to keep them. They side with the whites."

It was not simple or easy.

PART V

The Western World at Bandung

The Western world was at Bandung in a way that could not be denied; it was on everybody's tongue, for the English language was the dominant language of the Conference. The Indonesians, having spurned the Dutch language as soon as they had heaved out the Dutch, had enthroned their own native tongue; but they knew that they had to have an auxiliary language, and English had been chosen. French was spoken by some of the delegates from North Africa, but that precise and logical tongue, which was once the lingua franca of all such international conferences, was all but dead here. Due to French intransigence toward all new nationalism, and thanks to French selfishness and chauvinism toward her millions of blacks in Africa, there were but few delegates at Bandung who felt the need for French. . . . Today, as never before, it can be seen that the future of national cultures will reside in the willingness of nations to take up modern ideas and live out their logic. The British, imperialists though they are, have been much more flexible than the French; they have not felt that they were compelled to insist on their own national ideas and have accepted the indigenous nationalisms of their subjects; hence, there were more free and independent former subjects of Britain participating in the Asian-African Conference than those of any other Western nation.

I felt while at Bandung that the English language was about to undergo one of the most severe tests in its long and glorious history. Not only was English becoming the common, dominant tongue of the globe, but it was evident that soon there would be more people speaking English than there were people whose native tongue was English. . . . H. L. Mencken has traced the origins of many of our American words and phrases that went to modify English to an extent that we now regard our English tongue in America as the American language. What will happen when millions upon millions of new people in the tropics begin to speak English? Alien pressures and structures of thought and feeling will be brought to bear upon this our mother tongue and we shall be hearing some strange and twisted expressions. . . . But this is all to the good; a language is useless unless it can be used for the vital purposes of life, and to use a language in new situations is, inevitably, to change it.

Thus, the strident moral strictures against the Western world preached at Bandung were uttered in the language of the cultures that the delegates were denouncing! I felt that there was something just and proper about it; by this means English was coming to contain a new extension of feeling, of moral knowledge. To those who had heard (or, more exactly, read) similar strictures leveled against the French and the English in bygone days by Frenchmen and Englishmen during the French and American Revolutions, these Bandung preachments had the tonal ring of a closing of a gap in history. For, if those past French and English revolutionaries had had the moral courage to have extended their new and bold declarations of a new humanity to black and brown and yellow men, these ex-colonial subjects would never have felt the need to rise against the West. . . .

The results of the deliberations of the delegates at Bandung would be, of course, addressed to the people and the statesmen of the Western powers, for it was the moral notions—or lack of them—of those powers that were in question here; it had been against the dominance of those powers that these delegates and their populations had struggled so long. After two days of torrid public speaking and four days of discussions in closed sessions, the Asian-African Conference issued a communiqué. It was a sober document, brief and to the point; yet it did not hesitate to lash out, in terse legal prose, at racial injustice and colonial exploitation.

I repeat and underline that the document was addressed to the West, to the moral prepossessions of the West. It was my belief that the delegates at Bandung, for the most part, though bitter, looked and hoped toward the West. . . . The West, in my opinion, must be big enough, generous enough, to accept and understand that bitterness. The Bandung communiqué was no appeal, in terms of sentiment or ideology, to Communism. Instead, it carried exalted overtones of the stern dignity of ancient and proud peoples who yearned to rise and play again a role in human affairs.

It was also my conviction that, if this call went unheeded, ignored, and if these men, as they will, should meet again, their appeal would be different. . . . IN SUM, BANDUNG WAS THE LAST CALL OF WESTERNIZED ASIANS TO THE MORAL CONSCIENCE OF THE WEST!

If the West spurns this call, what will happen? I don't know. . . . But remember that Mr. Chou En-lai stands there, waiting, patient, with no record of racial practices behind him. . . . He will listen.

The Bandung communiqué stressed economic cooperation among the Asian-African powers; did not condemn the acceptance of foreign capital; adjured the participating countries to aid one another technically; encouraged joint financial ventures; recognized the need for a greater flow of Asian-African trade; urged collective action to stabilize the prices of primary products; recommended that the participating nations process their own raw materials wherever possible; resolved to break the shipping monopoly of the Western maritime powers; agreed upon the necessity of establishing banks among themselves; advised for an exchange of information relating to oil, remittance of profits and taxation, all tending toward the formulation of common policies; emphasized that nuclear energy should be for peaceful purposes and urged its internationalized control; concurred in the decision to appoint liaison officers in the participating countries to facilitate a continued exchange of information; and stated that it did not consider that it was forming a regional bloc. . . .

This first section of the communiqué sounds innocent enough, but, to those who know the intricate and delicate economic structure of the Western world, it spells out what Jack London called the "Yellow Peril" and no less! For the "Yellow Peril," as Jack London conceived it, was not primarily a racial matter; it was economic. When the day comes that Asian and African raw materials are processed in Asia and Africa by labor whose needs are not as inflated as those of Western laborers, the supremacy of the Western world, economic, cultural, and political, will have been broken once and for all on this earth and a de-Occidentalization of mankind will have definitely set in. (Thus, in time, the whole world will be de-Occidentalized, for there will be no East or West!)

To have an ordered, rational world in which we all can share, I suppose that the average white Westerner will have to accept this ultimately; either he accepts it or he will have to seek for ways and means of resubjugating these newly freed hundreds of millions of brown and yellow and black people. If he does accept it, he will also have to accept, for an unspecified length of time, a much, much lower standard of living, for that is what a de-Occidentalization of present-day mankind will bring about. Indeed, if the above program were only slightly implemented among the billion and a half people involved, it would result in a need for radical reconstruction of the social and economic systems of the Western world.

On the cultural front, the Conference communiqué was no less ambitious; it called for a renewal, in "the context of the modern world," of the ancient Asian and African cultures and religions "which have been interrupted during the past centuries"; condemned colonialism without qualification; demanded the cultural liberation of Tunisia, Algeria, and Morocco from the hegemony of French rule; castigated racial and discriminatory practices of Europeans in Asia and Africa; urged Asian and African countries to place educational and cultural facilities at the disposal of their less developed neighbors; etc.

On the plane of human rights and self-determination, the communiqué endorsed the principles of human rights as set forth in the Charter of the United Nations; declared its support of those people now struggling for self-government; extended its sympathy to the victims of racial discrimination in South Africa and deplored such systems of racism; etc.

On the problems of so-called dependent peoples, the communiqué declared that all existing colonialism should be brought to a speedy end; and, for the second time, and in even sharper and blunter language, condemned the French government for not granting self-determination to Tunisia, Algeria, and Morocco; cited its support of the Arab people of Palestine and called for the implementation of the United Nations resolutions on Palestine; backed the claim of Indonesia to West Irian; appealed to the Security Council of the United Nations to accept Cambodia, Ceylon, Japan, Jordan, Nepal, and a unified Viet-Nam as members of the United Nations; etc.

In general terms, the communiqué deemed inadequate the representation of Asian-African countries on the Security Council of the United Nations; called for the prohibition of thermonuclear weapons and pressed for international control of such disarmament, and for the suspension of all further experiments with such weapons; etc.

It is to be noted that the emotional tone of the communiqué differed sharply from the highly charged speeches of the heads of delegations at Bandung. Indeed, it is to the credit of the taste of Nehru that he was violently opposed to those speeches but gave in when other heads of delegations insisted upon their right to make known their views upon world issues. And I suspect that Chou En-lai, materialistic and rational, was ill at ease when, on the final night of the conference, an Ethiopian delegate rose, mounted the rostrum, and, as though he were in a pulpit, preached for fifteen minutes an old-fashioned sermon about the "eternal values of the Spirit." And I dare say that Nehru, agnostic, poised, and civilized, must have winced more than once as that tide of fervent emotion spilled over him. . . .

What are the chances of the Asian-African nations implementing the contents of that communiqué? Frankly, I think that they are pretty good. The Western world erroneously thinks that its techniques are difficult to acquire; they are not; they are the easiest things that the East can take from the West. The hard things are the intangibles, such as the Western concept of personality, such as the attitude of objectivity. . . . But will the implementation of the communiqué solve the basic problems of Asia and Africa? I do not think so. Those problems have so vast and intricate a design and frame of reference, they have been left so long to rot, germinate, and grow complex, that I doubt seriously if such concrete and limited objectives can cope with them.

The question of time enters here. (Not the kind of time that the West speaks of, that is, how long will it take these people to master mechanical processes, etc. The West is much simpler in many ways than Asia and Africa, and Asians and Africans can understand our civilization much quicker than we can grasp their poetic and involved cultures!) The time I speak of is this: Can Asian and African leaders keep pace with the dynamics of a billion or more people loosed from their colonial shackles, but loosed in terms of defensive, irrational feelings? Bandung represented mankind negatively freed from its traditions and customs, and the conference at Bandung was the first attempt in history on the part of man as man to organize himself. . . . And he is not prepared to do so. He has been kept too long in ignorance and superstition and darkness. (But to use this as an excuse to keep him under tutelage longer will certainly not help matters any.) But now, there he is, free and on the stage of history!

Who can harness this force? While at Bandung listening to the delegates rise and make their speeches, I got a belated glimpse, couched in terms of concrete history, of the convulsive terror that must have gripped the hearts of the Bolsheviks in Russia in 1920. . . . Lenin, no matter what we may think of him today, was faced with a half-starving nation of 160,000,000 partly tribalized people and he and his cohorts felt that they could trust nobody; they were afraid of losing their newly gained power, their control over the destinies of their country. Now, today, there were one and one-half billion people loosed from domination and they too were afraid of losing their freedom, of being dominated again by alien powers, afraid of a war for which they were in no way prepared. What Lenin had faced in Russia in 1920 was here projected on a stage of history stretching over continents and augmented in terms of population a thousandfold!

Bandung was no simple exercise in Left and Right politics; it was no mere minor episode in the Cold War; it was no Communist Front meeting. The seizure of power was not on the agenda; Bandung was not concerned with how to take power. ALL THE MEN THERE REPRESENTED GOVERNMENTS THAT HAD ALREADY SEIZED POWER AND THEY DID NOT KNOW WHAT TO DO WITH IT. Bandung was a decisive moment in the consciousness of 65 per cent of the human race, and that moment meant: HOW SHALL THE HUMAN RACE BE ORGANIZED? The decisions or lack of them flowing from Bandung will condition the totality of human life on this earth.

Despite the hearty verbal endorsements of the Asian-African Conference by Moscow and Peking, the Communists at Bandung were more than usually silent. I think that that reticence stemmed from the fact that they understood all too well the magnitude of the problem confronting them. They did not want to disavow that problem, yet they could not actively seize hold of it; it was too big. . . . Pending their elaboration of a method or a theory of seizing hold of this vast multitude, they eyed it coldly and cynically to determine what "use" they could make of it. And they began making "use" of Bandung before the Conference was over. To evade or dodge enemies hot on their trail, they began "hiding" amidst this motley host, surrounding themselves with it for protection, etc.

I feel a difference between the Russian and the Chinese attitude toward Bandung. Committed to their strait-jacket dialectics, the Russians looked greedily at Bandung, but like a dog that had once eaten poisoned meat and wanted no more of it for the time being. The Russians had once lived through a situation like this and they had paid tragically for it. And it must be remembered that the Asians and Africans have no sturdy tradition in modern ideological socialism, no body of proven materialistic political thought, no background of trade-union consciousness on to which Stalinist-trained Russian Communists can easily latch. True, there are vast millions of Asians and Africans who are angry, frustrated, poor, and rendered restless and rebellious by their past relationship to the Western world. But this mystic-minded throng of colored men would not respond readily to the slogans born of Russian conditions of revolutionary struggle, and the Communists at Bandung knew it. . . .

The Chinese, I suspect, were more sanguine, but secretly so. They have had no little experience in organizing mystic-minded peasants. But these Asians and Africans were shy and had been warned. Hence, Chou's cautious approach. He committed himself to nothing but to play the role of a fellow traveler. He would be content for a while to snuggle as close as possible to this gummy mass and watch and wait. . . .

If the Asians and Africans cannot handle this, and if the Communists would merely play with it to gain time, to "use" it for their own advantages, who then can master this massive reality which has, like a volcanic eruption, shot up from the ocean's floor?

I know that there are Westerners who will decry my positing this unwieldly lump of humanity on their moral doorsteps when I state again and again that it was their past relationship to these baffled millions that made them angry and willful. I can only cite a British authority for my attitude. Says F. S. Furnivall in his *Colonial Policy and Practice* (Cambridge University Press, 1948), page 8:

> **. . . In policy, as in law, men must be held to intend the natural consequences of their acts, and it is from the results of colonial policy rather than from statements of its objects that its true character can be ascertained.**

But it is most difficult for a Westerner to understand or accept this; he insists upon the nobility of his intentions even when all the facts are dead against it. Whatever the Westerner *thought* he was doing when he entered these tropical lands, he left behind him a sea of anger. I'd call his attention to an objective observer's appraisal. Furnivall in *Colonial Policy and Practice*, page 299, judges the state of life among the natives after Britain and Holland had done their best. He says:

> **. . . they are the poorer for the loss of things that are bought without money and without price . . . they remain imprisoned in a dying civilization and their social life is impoverished and not enriched.**

Seeking intelligent reactions to the meaning of Bandung, I found a highly competent official who met my qualifications on grounds of elementary honesty; this particular man was a reformed American of the Old South. His grandfather had owned slaves and he was eagerly willing to own up to what had happened in history and was most committed to try to do something about it. I questioned him, narrowing my request for information to the situation obtaining in Indonesia, taking that baby nation and its case of measles as my point of departure.

"Let's start with Communism," he said. "It's no danger here, not yet. . . . What this country needs in order to make rapid progress is assistance; it needs it badly and in all fields. . . . Above all, it needs personnel trained in modern techniques. Now, I'd advocate that we Americans ought to take about a hundred and fifty Indonesian students each year and train them. . . . No political strings tied to that. In that way a body of trained and educated young men would be built up—"

"How long would this training process go on?" I asked.

"For fifty or a hundred years," he answered.

I stared at him in amazement.

"Have you got that much *time?*"

"What else can we do?" he asked, spreading his palms. "We can't interfere here. Our ethics prohibit such as that."

"Man," I said, "civilization itself is built upon the right to interfere. We start interfering with a baby as soon at it is born. Education is interference. I think you have a right to interfere, if you feel that the assumptions of your interference are sound."

"I'm a Jeffersonian Democrat," he said. "We will help, but we won't interfere."

"Does your concept of noninterference take into consideration what others might be doing?"

"What do you mean?" he asked.

"Well, there are people who have a conviction that one can educate people in how to build a nation," I began cautiously. "The Russians have institutes in which to train people in the principles of nation-building—"

"No institutes," he said with finality. "That's the beauty of our position. Look, when we select students to go to America, it is done on an informal basis. We don't have the right to try to mold and insist like that—"

"But suppose the Indonesians needed or wanted just that?"

The conversation broke down and I suspected that that man had suspicions of my political leanings. . . . We had at once clashed over two concepts of what was "good." He was insisting that Indonesians develop and progress precisely as Americans had done, and that this was "good" for them. I doubted if many Indonesians could have stated with any degree of accuracy what was "good" for them. They were much clearer about what they did not want than about what they wanted.

I did not question the man's intelligence, sincerity, or generosity, but I knew that he did not see the problem as I saw it, that he felt no sense of urgency, did not grasp the terrible reality that was sprawling so directly and dramatically before his eyes. He was inclined to take the high-flown rhetoric of Sukarno and others as mere spellbinding tricks and not as a true index of the nature of a reality that had to be grappled with.

In my search for a more modern and scientific attitude toward Asian problems, I was introduced to Mr. Benjamin Higgins, social scientist of the Center for International Studies, Massachusetts Institute of Technology. Mr. Higgins was the head of a field team which was gathering facts about colonial problems in the South Pacific and it was hoped that the facts found would enable new and effective solutions to problems to be worked out. Mr. Higgins was intelligent, quick, and admitted at once:

"The hour is late, very, *very* late."

"But not *too* late?" I asked.

"I don't know," he said.

In his most recent scientific paper, entitled *The "Dualistic Theory" of Underdeveloped Areas*, Mr. Higgins, an American liberal, takes issue with Dr. Boeke, a renowned Dutch social scientist and apologist for former Dutch colonial policy in Indonesia. Mr. Higgins brilliantly exposes Dr. Boeke's essentially reactionary position, which consists of such profound statements as:

> **We shall do well not to try to transplant the tender, delicate hothouse plants of Western theory to tropical soil, where an early death awaits them.**

Dr. Boeke feels that Eastern society is molded by "fatalism and resignation." In dealing with Indonesian personalities, Dr. Boeke recommends:

". . . faith, charity, and patience, angelic patience."

Mr. Higgins, with scientific precision, rips into Dr. Boeke's limited, prejudiced theories, branding them as "defeatist, and indeed dangerous, because it is precisely slow evolution that cannot succeed in face of all the obstacles."

What has Mr. Higgins, then, to offer? He outlines:

> **If truly ambitious programs of capital and technical assistance are undertaken, with full, wholehearted, and sympathetic co-operation of the underdeveloped countries themselves, I believe there is a good chance that the social and cultural obstacles may disappear without having to be attacked directly. However, this result will be attained only if the scale of such assistance is big enough both to provide a 'shock treatment,' and to turn the present large-scale disguised unemployment into an asset. The program must be big in relative terms (measured, let us say, in terms of the rate of per capita capital accumulation or rate of increase in man-hour production) as was the Industrial Revolution in Europe; which means, in view of the very much larger populations in the new underdeveloped areas, that it must be very much greater in absolute terms than anything that occurred in Europe in the eighteenth century or in the New World in the nineteenth and twentieth.**

Mr. Higgins is speaking in historical terms and what he here proposes makes a Marshall Plan sink into relative insignificance! He continues:

> **If the program of capital and technical assistance is big enough to produce a rate of increase in productivity high enough to outrun population growth for a time, there is good reason to suppose that the social and cultural barriers to further development will melt away.**

The transformation of the traditional and customary attitudes will come about in the following manner, according to Mr. Higgins:

> **. . . Similarly, the feudal attitudes towards entrepreneurship will tend to disappear, if trade and industry provide a route to the top of the social scale—even if it takes one or two generations—as it did in Europe and in the New World. If the economy is expanding and businessmen are being trained, opportunities for accumulation of wealth will be created; and if enough people in the underdeveloped areas become rich through trade and commerce, the feudal attitude towards "sullying one's hands in trade" will break down in the Orient as it did in Europe. Similarly, if standards of living are really improving, so that people have before their eyes a picture of families moving from one standard of living to a higher one through their own efforts, the "backward-sloping supply curve" will give way to a willingness to work harder, save more, and assume greater risks in hope of attaining a more ample life.**

I believe that this is today's typical Western attitude; and it is to be noted that there are no political considerations mentioned there. *But where are such skills and such vast sums of money coming from on the scale visualized by Mr. Higgins?* We are here dealing with one and one-half billion people living on 12,606,938 square miles of the earth's surface! Human engineering on the scale proposed by Mr. Higgins would bankrupt the United States in one year. . . . Mr. Higgins' vision is frontal and honest, lacking that unexpressed assumption of the biological inferiority of the Asian which buttresses Dr. Boeke's theories. But can such a project be implemented in terms of skilled men and money as we know these items today? The subcontinent of India alone contains half a billion human beings; as one official told me, rolling his eyes:

"There are just so many of them!"

Implied in Mr. Higgins' program is a picture of how he feels that America, the leader of the world, developed; and he now proposes to lure the Asian and African masses out of their torpor by presenting them with a highly visible and dramatic analogy, hoping that they will prefer concrete wealth, health, and other satisfactions to their static, traditional modes of living. I believe that the psychological assumptions involved here are correct; by and large, when and wherever they have been confronted with the choice, custom-bound, tradition-trapped men have voluntarily doffed their past habits and embraced new and exciting horizons. . . . The problem here is not whether these Asian masses can or will make progress; the problem is one, above all, of means, techniques, and *time*.

It is far preferable that the Western world willingly aid in the creation of Jack London's "Yellow Peril" in terms of Asians' and Africans' processing their own raw materials, which would necessitate a radical adjustment of the West's own systems of society and economics, than to face militant hordes buoyed and sustained by racial and religious passions. Industrialized Asia and Africa would be rational areas that could be dealt with; even the aims, then, of intercontinental wars would be clear, the military objectives of both sides understandable. But to wage war against racial and religious emotion is ultimately meaningless and impossible; atom and hydrogen bombs would only inflame racial and religious passions more, rendering the objects of military struggle ludicrous. It should be remembered that when Cortés captured Mexico City, his military prize consisted of a city whose streets were covered with heaps of Aztec dead whose religious fanaticism did not allow them to surrender. . . . William H. Prescott in his *History of the Conquest of Mexico* (Modern Library edition, New York), page 420, says:

> **. . . the Aztec, hitherto the proud lord of the land, was goaded by insult and injury, till he had reached that pitch of self-devotion, which made life cheap, in comparison with revenge. Armed thus with the energy of desperation, the savage is almost a match for the civilized man; and a whole nation, moved to its depths by a common feeling which swallows up all selfish considerations of personal interest and safety, becomes, whatever be its resources, like the earthquake and the tornado, the most formidable among the agencies of nature.**

But, one might ask, is it too late? Have racial and religious feelings already set in so deeply in Asia and Africa that it would be impractical to transform and attach them to secular and practical goals? What would be the ultimate results of welding this Asian consciousness with its present content of race and religion on to the techniques of the twentieth century? Was not Japanese Fascism the flower of such incongruous grafting of plants of different genres? There is no indication that the Japanese abandoned any of their earlier mystical notions when they embraced the disciplines of science and the techniques of modern industrial production. It is not difficult to imagine Moslems, Hindus, Buddhists, and Shintoists launching vast crusades, armed with modern weapons, to make the world safe for their mystical notions. . . .

One might argue, of course, that the present content of Western consciousness is not much better, that what I now cite as a peril from the East is exactly what the West did for four hundred years. Indeed, I'm inclined to believe that that is true. After all, the pot must not call the kettle black. . . . There is, however, one cardinal difference: a part of the Western world, out of the process of religious conquest by its Christian soldiers, did develop a secular outlook grounded in the disciplines of science and projected concretely in an astounding industrial universe which, like a web of steel, wraps our daily lives round. That secular outlook and that industrial atmosphere now dominate the center of gravity of the Western scene. And it is this fact that prompted Romulo, while bitterly denouncing Western racism, to remind the Asian-African delegates at Bandung in solemn tones:

". . . this white world which has fostered racism has done many another thing. . . . just as Western political thought has given us all our basic ideas of political freedom, justice and equity, it is Western science which in this generation has exploded the mythology of race. . . ."

Is this secular, rational base of thought and feeling in the Western world broad and secure enough to warrant the West's assuming the moral right to interfere *sans* narrow, selfish political motives? My answer is, Yes. And not only do I believe that that is true, but I feel that such a secular and rational base of thought and feeling, shaky and delicate as yet, exists also in the elite of Asia and Africa! After all, the elite of Asia and Africa, for the most part educated in the West, is Western, more Western than the West in most cases.

. . . And those two bases of Eastern and Western rationalism must become one! And quickly, or else the tenuous Asian-African secular, rational attitudes will become flooded, drowned in irrational tides of racial and religious passions.

Yet I do not think that any merging of these rational, secular areas of East and West can come about within the terms proposed by Mr. Higgins; those terms are allied too organically with personal and national interests, to the capricious ebb and flow of that most mercurial of all realities: capital. New terms will have to be found, terms that will fit the nature of the human materials involved. And I think that Bandung, however fumblingly and naively, presented those materials. . . . If Asians and Africans can sink their national and religious differences for what they feel to be a common defense of their vital interests, as they did at Bandung, then that same process of unity can serve for other ends, for a rapid industrialization of the lives of the people of Asia and Africa, for a shaking loose of the Asian-African masses from a static past.

Unless the Western world can meet the challenge of the miraculous unity of Bandung openly and selflessly, it faces an Asian-African attempt at pulling itself out of its own mire under the guidance of Mr. Chou En-lai and his drastic theories and practices of endless secular sacrifices. And there is no doubt but that Communism can dredge down and rake up the hidden reserves of a people, can shake them, rip them out of the traditional and customary soil in which they have stagnated for centuries. But can Stalinism repeat in Asia and Africa what it did in Russia, leaving aside for the moment the question of its aspects of limitless murder and terror, its wholesale sacrifices of human freedom and human life? It can, if the populations involved are made to feel that such a bloody path is preferable to a new loss of their freedom. (Men will give up their freedom to save their freedom, just as they will give up their lives to save their lives!) Indeed, I think that the very intensity of their racial and religious conditioning would lead these masses to accept such a desperate path, have prepared them to re-enact on a global scale ceremonies of collective crucifixion and rituals of mass rebirth. . . .

Seen through the perspective of Bandung, I think that it can be said that FEAR of a loss of their power, FEAR of re-enslavement, FEAR of attack was the key to the actions of the Russian Stalinists who felt that any and all efforts to modernize their nation would be preferable to a return of the *status quo*. . . . Today the Russians can feel bitterly, defiantly satisfied that they did what was brutally necessary, no matter how hard, inhuman, and terrible, to keep their power and industrialize their country. BUT MUST THIS TRAGIC METHOD, WITH ITS SECULAR RELIGIOSITY OF HORROR AND BLOOD, BE REPEATED ON THE BODY OF THE HUMAN RACE? Is there no stand-in for these sacrifices, no substitute for these sufferings?

AFTERWORD

> In the future there will be white men who will look into black and yellow and brown faces and they will say to themselves: "I wish to God that those faces were educated, that they had lived lives as secure and serene as mine; then I would be able to talk to them, to reason with them. . . ." But then it would be too late.
>
> —RICHARD WRIGHT, *THE COLOR CURTAIN*

> It was strange, but, in this age of swift communication, one had to travel thousands of miles to get a set of straight, simple facts. . . . Propaganda jams the media of communication.
>
> —RICHARD WRIGHT, *THE COLOR CURTAIN*

One

Published originally in 1956, *The Color Curtain* received favorable reviews, and its American edition went into two printings. But because of Wright's bold approach to issues of ideology and colonialism in the Cold War era, the book did not have the major impact it should have had on the reading public. This reprinting of *The Color Curtain* thus makes available an important work of Wright's that enables us to fully understand the range of his thinking, his deep involvement in world affairs, and his insights into issues that continue to be of concern and importance.

Michel Fabre notes that 1953 marks Wright's spiritual departure from Paris and the beginning of his growing involvement in Afro-Asian affairs (*The Unfinished Quest of Richard Wright*, 1973). In *The Color Curtain*—one of Wright's eight major works of fiction and nonfiction from the 1950s—he continues to explore his favorite themes of alienation and empowerment from the distinctive vantage point he had carved out of his exiled position in Paris where he had lived since 1947. For several years before his death in 1960 at age fifty-two, Wright had begun to see himself as an independent radical thinker, a kind of H. L. Mencken on the world stage, fighting "the battle of the Negro in the nation's thought" and challenging the West to live its highest ideals in dealing with its colonies and former colonies in Asia and Africa. Even before he and his inter-racial family felt confined by race and racism, he had become a major voice on African-American issues on the American scene and was learning to juggle these demands on his time and energy with the call of his craft. In the 1950s, he observed from Paris the slowly changing realities of American life, but remained unconvinced that they represented "qualitative" changes in public policy or social attitude.

Wright's interest in matters racial and American was still intense, and he wondered if, "armed with these gloomy insights from an exiled life, I could aid my country in its clumsy grappling with alien realities." These realities included the "naked and shivering world" of Asian and African nations just awakening to freedom. He saw the struggle for Civil Rights in the U.S. as inextricably linked to the full freedom for peoples of color throughout the world. So, while others participated in the boycotts and marches at home, he was convinced that he was fighting the same battles in global contexts by participating in debates on Negritude and Pan-Africanism and supporting movements for freedom in Africa and Asia. These new interests of Wright's had been shaped by his friendship with George Padmore, a West Indian exile who lived in London, and through his involvements in the journal, *Présence Africaine*. In an unpublished essay, "I Choose Exile," Wright had defended passionately his choice of living outside the U.S. by claiming his exile perspectives to represent the essence of Americanness, and he wondered in his correspondence why the exile of many white writers never received the kind of negative attention that his own did. While Wright was fully cognizant of racist and colonialist elements in the European psyche and conduct, his doubts about the American ability to completely overcome institutional racism were perhaps exacerbated by his own paranoia about the lingering specters of McCarthyism.

But the new role Wright was shaping for himself as a global intellectual was not unrelated to his earlier perspectives. By the late forties, it is clear that he had been thinking for some time about the relationship racism at home bore to the global realities of colonialism and capitalism, and had begun to view the American Negro as more than "America's metaphor." In 1946, he described the problem of 15 million black Americans as "symbolic" of the situation faced by over 1.5 billion people of color throughout the world. In a 1947 interview, he boldly declared the African-American to be "intrinsically a colonial subject, but one who lives not in China, India, or Africa but next door to his conquerors, attending their schools, fighting their wars, and laboring in their factories. The American

Negro problem, therefore, is but a facet of the global problem that splits the world in two: Handicraft vs. Mass Production; Family vs. the Individual; Tradition vs. Progress; Personality vs. Collectivity; the East (the colonial peoples) vs. the West (exploiters of the world)."

In contrast to Hugh Kenner's view of Robert Frost and William Faulkner as "homemade" artists, Wright emerged in the early 1950s as a literary descendant of the American expatriate writers of the 1920s whose craft and vision were shaped by European experience and influence. But he was also a descendant of slaves who made it his business to shape crosscultural perspectives on issues of identity, race, and colonialism—subjects neglected for the most part by the white Anglo-American modernists. In *The Outsider* (1953), Wright's critique of fascism, Marxism, and existentialism is achieved through the career of its protagonist, Cross Damon, who filters these Western philosophies through his African-American experience as a "man gifted with a double vision," as a center of "*knowing*," being "both *inside* and *outside* of our culture at the same time." At one level, Wright's later nonfiction represents an autobiographical movement toward connection and renewal that is implicit in Damon's final conversation with Ely Houston, the hunchbacked District Attorney who is both Damon's foil and his "double." It is not surprising that such a renewal in Wright's case would spring from his lifelong curiosity about far-off places and other peoples of color. In the late 1950s, since there is no evidence that Wright had abandoned the novel and the short story as his primary forms of expression and since there is a convergence of motifs—e.g. (ab)uses of power by and for the individual and the community—in his writings of all genres, his later nonfiction must be seen as a crucial part of his intellectual and artistic growth.

Wright's precocious fascination with distant social realities is evident in *Black Boy*: in Arkansas, the young Richard had pestered his mother with never-ending questions about "rifles" and "Germans" in World War I after a unit of black American soldiers marched past their home, causing him more terror than a chain-gang of men dressed in zebra stripes that he saw another day. In *Black Power* (1954), he views his Gold Coast trip as the fulfillment of his intense but unsatisfied curiosity as a boy about Africa. In the late 1930s, living in Chicago, as a member of the Communist Party, Wright had developed a serious interest in cultures and societies very different from the American life he had known. As early as 1941, he had considered going to the Soviet Union and China. In 1948–49, he had proposed a trip to Africa to report for the Associated Negro Press. Although neither of these trips materialized, Wright claimed that he was "temperamentally suited" to make such trips and report on their significance to fellow Americans.

Wright's vision in the 1950s is thus a fuller development of these early global interests. In his later nonfiction, he was particularly interested in exploring the paradoxical situation of blacks in the West, developing compelling parallels between their condition and those of Westernized Asians and Africans. He regarded *The Color Curtain* as a "companion volume" to *Black Power*, where he had subjected a slice of African reality to the same kind of serious analysis that Europe had received for centuries. In *White Man, Listen!* (1957), as he examined colonialism and its psychological effects upon ordinary people throughout the world, Wright had expressed the hope that the Westernized leadership of new African and Asian nations would help their masses to disengage from "the irrational ties of religion and custom and tradition" to empower themselves through the same processes of modernization and industrialization that provided the foundations of democracy and individual freedom in the West.

This Westernized leadership was now meeting at Bandung, Indonesia, on April 18–25, 1955, to consider how they could help one another in achieving the social and economic well-being of their large and impoverished populations. Wright notes several times in *The Color Curtain* how this first-ever gathering of twenty-nine African and Asian nations was generally ignored by the Western media and viewed with hostility and suspicion by government agencies in Europe and the U.S. For Wright, this meeting of leaders who represented well over a billion people, the "underdogs of the human race," was "a kind of judgement upon the Western world." Their agenda at Bandung included advancing shared social, economic, and political interests; finding solutions to problems of "national sovereignty and of racialism and colonialism"; and making joint contributions to "the promotion of world peace and co-operation."

Wright felt that his background as a black person from the American South and his experience with the Communist Party qualified him well as a reporter for the West on this unprecedented conference of nations that represented diverse races, religions, and ideologies but were brought together by their past experience of colonialism and continuing distrust of the West. Wright received financial support for his trip from the Congress for Cultural Freedom, but since he had an inkling of the Congress's links with the Department of State and the CIA, he made sure by prior agreement that this assistance would not in any way impair his freedom of speech as a writer and journalist.

Two

The Color Curtain is as much Wright's Asian book as *Black Power* had been his African book. The Bandung

Conference included representatives from both African and Asian nations, but none of the major black African leaders were actually present there and, as Wright noted, "Negro Africa" was the weakest part of the conference even in terms of awareness. The conference was dominated by Asian nationalist leadership from countries such as Indonesia, Ceylon (now Sri Lanka), Burma (now Myanmar), and the Philippines, but especially by the towering figures of Prime Minister Jawaharlal Nehru of India and Prime Minister Chou En Lai of People's Republic of China. As if to match the Asian dominance at the conference held in an Asian location, Wright's book is suffused with Asia, especially Indonesia, as seen through the filter of what Wright called the "Asian personality."

Wright showed his resourcefulness in briskly developing unorthodox techniques in approaching his new assignment in Asia. For his earlier trips to the Gold Coast and Spain, which formed the bases of *Black Power* and *Pagan Spain* (1957) respectively, Wright had done extensive library research. To prepare himself for his trip to Indonesia, he took the unusual step of developing a questionnaire with the help of sociologist Otto Klineberg. Between January and April 1955, he used this questionnaire to develop a comparative view of issues affecting individuals in modern life. He interviewed five individuals in Europe—four Asians and Eurasians and one Indonesian-born Dutch man—in order to gain some understanding of Asian attitudes and politics. While his quest for "the Asian personality" (like his concept of "the African personality" in *Black Power*) might appear to collapse significant differences that make up Asia, his methodological framework in *The Color Curtain* allows him to achieve a balanced perspective and avoid the worst pitfalls of homogenization. The extended interviews with diasporic Asians of diverse backgrounds residing in Europe are followed by interviews with Indonesian professionals, politicians, and journalists interspersed with detailed descriptions of Indonesian life and landscape. The effect of this creative mingling of detail is to evoke the reality of one particular nation, Indonesia (although he did not travel here as extensively as he had done in the Gold Coast), mediated through the strong sense of raw emotion and traces of self-hatred in "the Asian personality" that his interviews cumulatively convey.

Some of the questions Wright asked each of the five individuals he interviewed in Europe called for some very specific personal responses regarding their religious, educational, and family backgrounds, while others were aimed at gauging their general sense of the world in relation to "race," class, and colonialism. It is interesting, for example, to note how the Asian respondents almost invariably rejected the notion that specific geographical regions are intended only for specific peoples or "races," showing an early awareness of the dialogic, hybrid nature of national and ethnic identity in contemporary life.

Wright's poring over his interview notes during his journey by night train from Paris to Madrid conveys a sense of urgency about his project of travelling from West to East, underscoring the openness and spirit of inquiry that marked his desire to discover and connect to the "Asian personality." The five sections of the book together represent three clear movements. The excitement and exuberance of the new learner in the opening section gives way to more sober observations of Indonesian life and politics in the middle sections, building up our interest in the conference and preparing us for the controlled pessimism of his final thoughts. Each movement is shaped by a combination of rhetorical and literary strategies, including interviews with individuals, descriptions of personality and landscape, journalistic re-capturing of ideas and analysis—livened up occasionally by a novelistic treatment of event and character as in the "Sterno" episode in the chapter entitled "Racial Shame at Bandung" which returns to the motif of Asian self-hatred in the opening section.

Once again, as he had done in *Black Power*, Wright allows his readers a sense of participation in his own heuristic project, opening up the possibility of learning from travel in unknown surroundings. Thus Wright's later nonfiction marks a very different approach to travel literature, for example, from that represented in recent decades by V. S. Naipaul's brilliant trajectories of raw nerves and preconceived theories of whole and "half-made" societies. Wright's own ambivalences and resistances, which provided some of the drama in *Black Power*, seem closer to resolution now—there is in *The Color Curtain* a stronger sense of connection and empathy, of understanding and commitment. Also, the Richard Wright we encounter here is a more experienced explorer, who shows an ability to observe and absorb more quickly and a deeper faith in his own perspectives. His method in both *The Color Curtain* and *Black Power* is also illumined in some ways by the theory of writing he had outlined as early as 1935 in his unpublished essay, "Personalism." As a literary expression of "personal protest" which emphasizes "tendency rather than form or content," personalism is in a sense "anti-aesthetic" as it seeks "to make those who come into contact with it take sides for or against certain *moral* issues" (cited in Fabre, *op. cit.*). By placing himself as an explorer in a domain of "self-consciousness, of nervousness, of questioning, of seeking, of trial and of wandering," Wright draws the reader into a set of choices regarding the moral issues embedded in his narrative.

For Wright, some of these moral issues were defined by his interaction with the Indonesian people and landscape. Arriving in Jakarta on April 12, Wright was saddened by the harsh evidence of the 350-year colonial rule in the metropolis of 3 million people and the impoverished lives of its residents. The Dutch seemed to have exploited the rich resources of this island nation stretched over 3,000 miles of land and sea even more systematically than other colonial powers elsewhere in their Asian colonies. In the nineteenth-century, Netherlands Indies (the name the Dutch used for Indonesia) had for all practical purposes supported the industrialization of the Netherlands through its stupendous contributions of revenue. Through the introduction of extensive forced cultivation known as "Culture System," Holland had organized by 1830 an intensive exploitation of land and labor in Java, the most densely populated of the 15,000 islands, where the peasants were obliged to grow commercial crops for the colonizers on more than two-fifths of their land. In 1940, a couple of years before the ruthless Japanese occupation, the Dutch nationals—some 200,000 of whom resided in Indonesia—had investments worth $1,300 million in the colony. Sutan Sjahir, a respected Socialist leader and thinker, told Wright how the Japanese occupation had paradoxically strengthened the nationalist movement against Dutch colonial rule. The Dutch "caved in" to the Japanese, they "bowed" and "begged"; "Dutch fear of the Japanese was a powerful psychological element in our resolve to fight the Dutch for our freedom," Sjahir explains.

In 1955, however, Wright is struck more by the post-independence realities of poor housing and inadequate schooling, complicated by signs of neocolonial control. He notes how Jakarta, like Accra in the Gold Coast, "presents to Western eyes a commercial aspect, naked and immediate, that seems to swallow up the entire population in petty trade—men, women, and children. . . . [O]ne must sell to buy products shipped by Europe." He views the canals built by the Dutch in Jakarta as an imperial project inappropriate to Indonesian climate and landscape, observing how the poor urban residents use them for washing, bathing and defecation. He learns from journalist Mochtar Lubis about the nightmarish Chinese ghettoes, about bandits who pose a threat to safety and political stability, and about how the Indonesian rickshaws called *betjas* are shameful reminders of colonial rule.

Three

Early in the book, Wright's conversations with his wife make it clear how new and exciting the idea of Bandung was for him. But for many of its major participants, the project that Bandung represented had had a respectable history. While Wright might not have had a detailed knowledge of the backstage maneuverings before and during the conference, he proves himself a shrewd observer of the dynamic of idea and personality at Bandung in recognizing Jawaharlal Nehru as a pivotal presence. In fact, it was Nehru who served as a link between Bandung and its precursors and otherwise provided the foundational framework for the conference. At Bandung, Nehru made a case once again for non-alignment and neutrality as a way for African and Asian nations to stay clear of the Cold War tensions between the two super powers or otherwise mediate between their conflicting claims.

Nehru had been deeply influenced in his political thinking by his participation in February 1927 at the Congress of Oppressed Nationalities in Brussels, undoubtedly a major precursor to Bandung. It was at this conference that he, as a representative of Indian National Congress, met for the first time a wide array of representatives of colonial peoples and their European and Latin American supporters—

radical nationalists along with left-wing socialists and orthodox Communists. And it was at Brussels that the idea of forming a group of African and Asian nations for mutual cooperation was first conceived. Again, in March 1947, Nehru made his debut on the international scene by hosting in New Delhi the first Asian Relations Conference, an impressive gathering of scores of Asian nations. Echoing Emerson's "American Scholar" plea against European hegemony, Nehru caught the mood of the conference in his inaugural speech by asserting the place of Asia and Asians in the world political community, stressed Asia's "special responsibility" for Africa, and concluded with a plea for faith in the human spirit.

Many readers have noted how Wright's persona is a central presence in travel books such as *Pagan Spain*, *Black Power*, and *The Color Curtain*. When Wright writes about Africa and Asia, his emotional and political impulses are implicated at one level through his strong empathy with the Westernized leaders, the "tragic elite" to whom he dedicated *White Man, Listen!*, "men who are distrusted, misunderstood, maligned, criticized by Left and Right, Christian and pagan . . . and who . . . seek desperately for a home for their hearts: a home which, if found, could be a home for the hearts of all men." From Wright's portrait of Nehru in *The Color Curtain* and from their brief correspondence, it would appear that Wright felt a special affinity with Nehru. The two men shared an attraction to Marxism and socialism, but Wright, the independent artist, would have agreed with Nehru, the patrician aristocrat, who declared in his autobiography, *Toward Freedom*, that "communists often irritated me by their dictatorial ways, their aggressive and rather vulgar methods, their habit of denouncing everybody who did not agree with them." Based on his conversations at the conference, Wright found Nehru to be "logical, quick, observant, and knowing," someone who, like India, was "part East, part West." However, Wright hints that at Bandung Nehru was being used by the "coy" and smooth Communist, Chou En-lai, who made masterful moves to gain legitimacy for the People's Republic of China among resistant Third World nations, approaching the conference participants with "utmost friendliness and reserve . . . turning the other cheek when receiving ideological slaps."

Four

Wright understood the historic importance of Bandung and wanted his report to make up for its general neglect or misrepresentation in the Western media; for example, even the frequent dispatches and editorials in *The New York Times* in April 1955 appear to have swerved somewhat abruptly to match the official U. S. attitudes toward Bandung, from suspicion at its beginning to a final measure of satisfaction in the anti-Communist stances by nations such as Ceylon and Iraq. Wright notes early on how there was "something extra-political, extra-social" about the meeting—"it smacked of tidal waves, of natural forces." Wright bemoaned the Western media's capacity to distort the truth and noticed how poorly equipped Western journalists were to understand this event "initiated by someone else." For example, in pursuing their "tirade" against the exclusion of the U.S. and Europe from the conference, these journalists "seemed to have forgotten that for centuries Asian and African nations had watched in helpless silence while white powers" had "disposed of" their "destinies." Wright was not surprised at the "brooding, bitter, apprehensive" atmosphere surrounding the conference, fuelled by a "frenzied speculation" about the rising influence of Red

China over Nehru and a prediction by the U.S. Chief of Naval Operations that the Chinese Communists were about to attack Quemoy and Matsu in mid-April.

Throughout *The Color Curtain*, Wright shows great skill at staying away from topics—for example, Asian politics—that he was not well-equipped to deal with. He focused instead on issues such as the lures of racial and Communist ideologies where his insights were especially valuable in the 1950s and would still matter in any historical understanding of what is known today as Cultural Studies. Although not particularly well-informed about the intricacies of Asian politics and religions, Wright shows a sharp new understanding of the Asian personality, going well beyond the thoughts he expressed, say, after his meeting in New York with Vijaylakshmi Pandit, Nehru's sister, in 1945. Following his conversation with Mrs. Pandit about the effectiveness of non-violent means in seeking India's freedom, he had noted in his diary that the Asians lacked a "sense of personal worth" in their passivity and that he missed in them the "tension" he admired so much in the American and African-American personality. In 1955, Wright found the Asians he interviewed for *The Color Curtain* ready to "gush, erupt, and spill out" their racial feelings; he acknowledged that he had misjudged Asian feelings and found that "many Asians hated the West with an absoluteness that no American Negro could ever muster." The "racial tensions" that gripped Asia and Africa, observed Wright at Bandung, made "the Negro Problem" in the U. S. appear like "a child's play."

Like *Black Power*, *The Color Curtain* appears to have been deeply affected by Wright's subjective responses to Indonesia and the Bandung Conference, but he allows the reader once again to have access to other approaches or concepts which he might not fully endorse. For example, he concludes the long opening section, "Bandung: Beyond Left and Right," by recording an extended interview with Mohammed Nastir, a former Prime Minister who was a leading spokesperson for the idea of a Muslim state. Nastir projects "Pan-Islam" as "a world force, socialistic in nature, keeping a middle ground between Communism and Capitalism." Based on this interview, Wright felt that "the Indonesian Moslem had a personality that was intact, poised, healthy, and largely free from neurotic conflict. There was none of that uneasy shifting . . . between two worlds of values and two spheres of psychological being." One has only to recall Wright's lifelong exploration of "tension" and "twoness" as essential elements of a modern consciousness to know that he was not endorsing Nastir's views on either religion or the theocratic state. And yet, his treatment of Nastir's world view illustrates how on several occasions in *The Color Curtain*, he finds a way of locating himself outside the Western epistemologies with which he is generally associated in his travel books. His later nonfiction thus represents an early use of travel as knowledge and also anticipates the importance of positioning in current discourse on issues of culture and identity.

In the practiced method of layered texts such as *Black Power*, *Pagan Spain*, and *The Color Curtain*, Wright's own views thus get placed within a suggestive frame of other possible perspectives, achieving a measure of balance and the only kind of objectivity he thought possible. Objectivity, he tells us in *White Man, Listen!*, is a "fabricated concept, a synthetic intellectual construction," aimed at persuading others to apprehend "the same general aspects and tones of reality that comprise my world. By revealing the assumptions behind my statements, I'm striving to convert you to my outlook, to its essential humaneness, to the generality and reasonableness of my arguments."

His vision in *The Color Curtain* is ultimately fashioned by this kind of modified objectivity and his factual observations of Indonesian life and people are framed by his persuasive plea for full economic and political freedom for all. In his commentary on the conference itself, Wright stressed the potential unity among the participant nations based on their shared distrust of the West. Although he recognized the importance of religion in Asian and African lives, Wright dealt instead with what he grasped intuitively—the hostility of Asia and Africa to the West based on how they had been constructed by the West as the racial Other. As someone who had experienced the limits of ideology in his own checkered career with the Communist Party, Wright understood well why ideology mattered so little at the conference.

But while Wright warned the West against underestimating the enormity and depth of that feeling, he conveyed too his sense of the fragile nature of Asian-African unity based on "race" alone. A couple of years later, Wright was to declare in *White Man, Listen!* that the American Negro was "something not racial or biological, but something purely social, something made in the United States." In Indonesia, he was disturbed by evidence of "reverse racism" by which a government official gave him preferential treatment over a white American journalist. He was saddened too by the purely "racial" motives of Mr. Jones, a black man from Los Angeles, who had used his life's savings and his wife's to come to Bandung, "to feel a fleeting sense of identity, of solidarity, a religious oneness with the others who shared his outcast state." Wright notes how Carlos P. Romulo, the Philippines representative who had made the most race-conscious speech at the conference, reminds the delegates about "how easy it is to be a racist," warning Asians and Africans against becoming "the kind of men whom they now condemn."

So, for Wright in *The Color Curtain*, the future of Asia was best defined not through some fixed idea of ethnic purity or national exclusiveness, but in terms of how culture and politics are shaped by global issues as they affect the life-chances of ordinary human beings. For him, Chou En-lai's clever but effective moves at the conference (for example, in a speech aimed at gaining a Third World foothold, Chou stressed Asian-African unity instead of attacking the West or selling Communism to newly freed nations) symbolized both the understandable attraction and the risks that African and Asian nations faced in turning to Communism. Even though they desperately needed Western capital and technologies for development, these nations had genuine fears of being re-enslaved by the West through neocolonial methods. Wright reported on the Indonesian awareness of their uneasy relationship with the West; they would welcome Western technology and its advantages, but how could they fend off "the desire of the West to dominate"? While he warned the Western leadership about the possibility that Communism might spread in Asia and Africa unless they made the moral commitment needed to develop their former colonies, he refused to condemn Communism in any strong terms. In discussing the role of the West in Africa and Asia with a white American liberal, who considered himself a Jeffersonian Democrat, Wright favored constructive Western intervention—something he had shied away from in his advice to Kwame Nkrumah at the end of *Black Power.*

Wright emerges in *The Color Curtain* and other works of travel and political reflection as an independent observer of race and colonialism in world affairs who reserves the right to choose his targets in the West or elsewhere in search of an inclusive and humane vision of individual freedom and community life. When read in conjunction with *Black Power*,

White Man, Listen! and some passages not included in the published version of *The Color Curtain*, Wright's view of the West appears far more complex than the Cold War clichés and abstractions at the end of *The Color Curtain* that some readers have complained about. For example, here is part of what Wright says in a passage which he appears to have been persuaded to leave out from the concluding sections of the published book:

> **White Europe's impact upon the colored East sets in motion two contradictory currents: one is a reflex gesture on the part of the Easterner to recover what he has lost by his contact with the West—his language, his art, his religion and his traditional ways of seeing and doing; the other is a state of chronic anxiety, bordering on hysteria, to embrace as quickly as possible the new Western techniques of science and industry in order to defend himself. (Copyright © Ellen Wright; quoted by permission)**

It is such blending of psychology and political insight in his analysis of global affairs that makes *The Color Curtain* valuable reading even today and opens the possibility of viewing Wright's later nonfiction as a worthy precursor to the work of Frantz Fanon and Edward Said. Since Wright had constructed the worlds of his travel books from the 1950s with careful attention to artistic method and since he had poured into them his genuine passion and commitment as a black intellectual of the West, he was deeply disappointed by what he considered their often poor and hostile reception. Wright expressed his frustration at this in a letter to his Dutch friend, Margrit de Sablonière, when he wrote, "So far as the Americans are concerned, I'm worse than a communist, for my work falls like a shadow across their policy in Asia and Africa. . . . Truth-telling today is both unpopular and suspect" (30 March 1960).

Truth-telling will perhaps always be unpopular and suspect, but in *The Color Curtain*, as in all his later nonfiction, Wright did not hesitate to tell the truth as he saw it. These books are thus a crucial part of Wright's oeuvre, and one has to understand them in order to appreciate fully his deep concern and sensitive engagement with issues that continue to challenge us.

Amritjit Singh
Rhode Island College

White Man, Listen!

With a Foreword by John A. Williams

This book is dedicated to

My friend,
ERIC WILLIAMS,

Chief Minister of the Government of Trinidad and Tobago
and Leader of the People's National Movement;

and to

THE WESTERNIZED AND TRAGIC ELITE OF ASIA, AFRICA,
AND THE WEST INDIES—

the lonely outsiders who exist precariously
on the clifflike margins of many cultures—men who are
distrusted, misunderstood, maligned, criticized
by Left and Right, Christian and pagan—
men who carry on their frail but indefatigable shoulders
the best of two worlds—and who,
amidst confusion and stagnation,
seek desperately for a home for their hearts:
a home which, if found,
could be a home for the hearts of all men.

ACKNOWLEDGMENTS

For some of the many fragments of poems quoted in this volume I am indebted to the following authors:

Frank Horne, Langston Hughes, Robert E. Hayden, and Margaret Walker.

Particularly am I grateful to the editors of *The Negro Caravan*, Sterling Brown, Howard University; Arthur P. Davis, Virginia Union University; and Ulysses Lee, Lincoln University; for permission to quote from their most comprehensive anthology, *The Negro Caravan* (Dryden Press), fragments from the following authors' poems: Frances Ellen's Harper's *Bury Me in a Free Land*; Albery A. Whitman's *Rape of Florida*; George Leonard Allen's *Pilate in Modern America*; Frank Home's *Nigger*; Robert E. Hayden's *Gabriel*; Fenton Johnson's *Tired*; Claude McKay's *White Houses*; and Jean Toomer's *Song of the Son*.

I also wish to express appreciation to Harcourt, Brace and Company for permission to quote from W. E. B. DuBois's *A Litany at Atlanta*; to New Directions for permission to quote from Dylan Thomas's *Light Breaks Where No Sun Shines*; to Viking Press for permission to quote from James Weldon Johnson's *Saint Peter Relates an Incident*; to Random House for permission to quote James D. Corrothers'

At the Closed Gate of Justice; and to Harper & Brothers for permission to quote from Countee Cullen's *Heritage*.

Also Viking Press was kind enough to allow me to quote generously from my own book, *12 Million Black Voices*.

To Arna Bontemps and to Melvin Tolson I am indebted for their personal permission to quote lines from *Nocturne at Bethesda* and *Dark Symphony* respectively.

And may I take this opportunity to express publicly my thanks to Dr. Otto Klineberg for his invaluable aid, guidance, and advice in helping me to devise a questionnaire with which I armed myself upon my first foray to grapple with the Asian personality? Needless to say, the interpretations which I drew from the results of that questionnaire are mine and are not to be laid at his door.

R. W.

FOREWORD

"It can be said that the white man is at bay. Never have so few hated and feared so many."

These words, written by Richard Wright three years before his untimely death on November 28, 1960, in Paris, have more meaning today than when they were first set down. The white man, Wright meant, has been brought to bay by his own conscience, by the juggernaut, economics, and by the ceaseless pressure brought to bear upon his grim penchant for insisting that the world was his and his alone; the pressure has come from all over the world: China, Africa, Latin America, the rest of Asia, and in America itself. Nonwhite pressure.

It is good that WHITE MAN, LISTEN! is being reissued in this edition. The book tells us that the problems (and advantages) of race are not confined to the United States. There are facts here, not thin emotion; there are here the thoughts of a man exposed to as much of life as his energies would permit. WHITE MAN, LISTEN! may sound imperative; it is. But it is also a plea: *LISTEN!* please, *LISTEN!* No man may correct himself unless he knows an error has been made. Wright gives Caucasians around the world the chance to understand what their fathers and they have done not only to black and brown men, but to themselves. Wright cries to men to listen to a way to survive.

A man named James Meredith brought honor at last to the sullen, alien state of Mississippi, but Richard Wright also hailed from there. Self-educated and instinctively opposed to the way Negroes had to live in Mississippi and everywhere else in America, he left and made his way north to live in Chicago, New York, and, for a time, other cities. Intellectually he came to know that what was bad for the Negro was bad also for America: that what was a horror for an individual was a horror for the society.

Although Richard Wright had more than a dozen books published, he never in life (or death, as a matter of fact) gained his rightful place in American letters, except during brief, grudgingly illuminated moments. A most unusual phenomenon of the American literary society is that American Negro artists pass to success in single file and, more often than not, over one another's dead bodies. Richard Wright understood this very well, but even so he took a secret pride in venturing over the trail.

He deserved acclaim, not so much as a spokesman for the Negro people, and I don't know whether he thought himself one or not (I'm inclined to think that such a title would have disgusted him), but as an artist. He was a novelist who ranged from realism to surrealism; he was an essayist in the classic sense, posing a question and by logic answering it. He was a poet well versed in Haiku. He was a political analyst, a political writer as well. If he had to, he could write a good, tight news column, and then retreat to a corner and set down a poem in pyrrhic meter.

In *Native Son* Richard Wright jolted the American literary scene with Bigger Thomas, a hapless, bitter, damned, ignorant, brutal, ghetto-Condemned black Negro, who would have whipped half to death any one of Hemingway's soldiers and he-men on a southside Chicago street corner. Bigger was not romantic like Quee Queg in *Moby Dick*, nor was he legendary like John Henry. He was no Stepin Fetchit or Mantan Moreland. He was none of the shadow, soft and unobtrusive, mysterious, that we find in our literature. He was a Negro that few white people ever believed they would meet face to face, and yet, they faced him every day. He was real.

If Theodore Dreiser took his place in American literature by telling us of the damned relationship between American love and the American dollar in *An American Tragedy*; if Upton Sinclair and Frank Norris achieved their positions by giving us the first full-blown stink of the bottomside of capitalism in *The Jungle* and *The Pit*; if Sinclair Lewis could name the emptiness of America *Babbit*; then Richard Wright deserves a place beside them because he gave us a stunning view of the economic and spiritual poverty of millions of people. He deserves to be included among the American authors college students find in their literature books because he brought an entirely new dimension to American letters—a dimension that we have come to accept, after so long a time, as real.

Many black writers were influenced by Richard Wright, and this, too, I believe, is the sign of an artist, that he is in many ways emulated; the power of his words or the colors on his canvas impel others toward their own palettes or pens. There are still many writers, especially young Negroes, who reread Wright and find, in a vein of words which have been thought to be completely used up and digested, undiscovered diamonds. There were writers closer to Wright's own generation who were also influenced by him. One notices that while Wright's *The Man Who Lived Underground* is a short story, Ralph Ellison's *Invisible Man* is much like it in surrealistic tone, but brought to full fruition in the novel form. James Baldwin's *The Fire Next Time* has very strong similarities to

WHITE MAN, LISTEN! The difference here is that, while Baldwin attacks the white world only, Wright is just as quick to flay the black. It is Baldwin, of course, who has inherited what critics would consider Richard Wright's mantle.

One thought pervaded all of Wright's work: that the perennial human failing—man's gross inhumanity to man—had to be abolished. He explored this condition with foresight and explained it so accurately that, in many subtle ways, he was asked to keep his mouth shut. He went to Paris; he became an expatriate, although, because he was black, he was not considered in the same light as the white expatriates of twenty years earlier. This book, written as Africa came into independence, as the Montgomery boycott of 1955 was successfully concluded, will bear out his fantastic sense of perception. Because he could perceive by the acts of the past what the future would bring, many Asians and Africans violently disliked WHITE MAN, LISTEN! Wright was too honest to be altogether pro-African or pro-Asian.

For example, he could write with immense candor that he agreed "that some of the missionary work [in Africa] was good: I agree that his boiling down four hundred gods and six hundred devils into *one* God and *one* Devil was an advance." But Wright remained "numbed and appalled" to know that "millions of men in Asia and Africa assign more reality to their dead fathers than to the crying claims of their daily lives: poverty, political degradation, illness, ignorance."

Wright isn't any kinder to the white man who overran Africa and Asia. His opening paragraph in this book, a single, searing sentence, must rate among the most damning condemnations of white Christian civilization ever written. Like the flash of spear points, phrases dart from between the commas: "their countries filled with human debris," (much of which later helped settle America), and "waxing rich through trade in commodities," and "psychologically armed with new facts" (gained through the 800-year stay of the Arabs in Europe).

To be sure, in many, many places this book, like others Wright wrote, seems to echo the theory of dialectical materialism. It is highly probable that Wright, who left the Communist Party soon after he joined it, found this framework best to work in, even when stripped of its hard political limitations. For Wright the conflict between the oppressed and the oppressor, between capitalist and proletariat, if you will, always consisted of more than ideologies. Wright saw politics, finally, no matter who played them, as a weapon of oppression. If not constantly used, politics remained in the arsenal, available for any occasion. The Marxian framework—the conflict of the classes—could certainly be converted and used to describe the conflict of the colors.

WHITE MAN, LISTEN! is addressed to the men of the world. It is an appeal to them for vision and courage during this time of crisis. While this book begins with the power of a curse, it ends with the observation that the world is for a short time longer still man's to change so that it may be a fit place for him as we most honorably conceive him.

JOHN A. WILLIAMS
JANUARY, 1964

In every cry of every Man,
In every Infant's cry of fear,
In every voice, in every ban,
The mind-forg'd manacles I hear.

WILLIAM BLAKE

Light breaks where no sun shines;
Where no sea runs, the waters of the heart
Push in their tides . . .
Light breaks on secret lots,
On tips of thoughts where thoughts smell
    in the rain;
When logics die,
The secret of the soil grows through the eye,
And blood jumps in the sun . . .

DYLAN THOMAS

INTRODUCTION: WHY AND WHEREFORE

This book originated in a series of lectures delivered in Europe during the years 1950–56 in the cities mentioned below and under the following auspices: In Italy—in Turin, Genoa, and Rome—I lectured for the Italian Cultural Association; in Amsterdam, I addressed the Foundation for Cultural Co-operation (STICUSA, that is, *Stichting voor Culturele Samenwerking*); in Hamburg, I spoke under the joint auspices of the Congress for Cultural Freedom and the German publishing firm of Claassen Verlag; in Paris, I made two lectures for *Présence Africaine*; and, under the management of the great Swedish publishing house of Bonnier, I lectured in Stockholm, Uppsala, Oslo, Gothenburg, Lund, and Copenhagen. . . .

None of these lectures was composed under the spur of personal motivation; they were written in response to repeated requests and, for the most part, with deep reluctance, for I do not particularly relish public speaking and always find myself unconsciously practicing a kind of malingering in preparing what I have to say until the very last moment.

The idea of presenting these speeches in printed form never occurred to me until Bonnier suggested that they publish the four of them. It was then that I discovered that, by rearranging the order in which they were written, they made a comment, connected and coherent, upon white-colored, East-West relations in the world today.

The material dealt with in these addresses is admittedly explosive and blatantly unacademic, and the approach frankly subjective, though, as always, for the benefit of him who cares to read my lines attentively, I've scattered, with more than ample discursiveness, my value assumptions throughout the texts.

Upon rereading, I'm not inclined to want to alter anything in these discourses. With no attempt at special pleading or personal justification, I feel that responsibility, both political and social, informs every page, but that sense of responsibility has not made me curb my thoughts or censor my feelings. And I stand publicly behind every line I've written here.

When one is rash enough to commit oneself publicly upon issues as large and weighty as those contained in these lectures, one is naturally confronted with a cry for specifications, programs, platforms, and solutions; particularly is this comfort demanded with insistence by those who live uneasy lives in vast industrial civilizations where a hysterical optimism screens the seamier realities of life, hiding the quicksands of cataclysmic historical changes. In these pages, in which I've deliberately preserved the spoken tone, I'm much more the diagnostician than the scribbler of prescriptions. I'm no Moses and, as one great and shrewd American once said, if some Moses should lead you into the Promised Land, some other Moses, equally adroit and persuasive, could just as easily lead you out again.

To those who insist upon detailed and concrete plans of action, I can only urgently advise them to consult their congressman, their psychoanalyst, or, better still, if they are determined believers, their local priest. I can take this facetious method of answering with a good conscience because I'm convinced that we all, deep in our hearts, know exactly what to do, though most of us would rather die than do it.

I feel constrained, however, to ask the reader to consider and remember my background. I'm a rootless man, but I'm neither psychologically distraught nor in any wise particularly perturbed because of it. Personally, I do not hanker after, and seem not to need, as many emotional attachments, sustaining roots, or idealistic allegiances as most people. I declare unabashedly that I like and even cherish the state of abandonment, of aloneness; it does not bother me; indeed, to me it seems the natural, inevitable condition of man, and I welcome it. I can make myself at home almost anywhere on this earth and can, if I've a mind to and when I'm attracted to a landscape or a mood of life, easily sink myself into the most alien and widely differing environments. I must confess that this is no personal achievement of mine; this attitude was never striven for. . . . I've been shaped to this mental stance by the kind of experiences that I have fallen heir to. I say this neither in a tone of apology nor to persuade the reader in my ideological direction, but to give him a hinting clue as to why certain ideas and values appeal to me more than others, and why certain perspectives are stressed in these speeches.

Recently a young woman asked me: "But would your ideas make people happy?" And, before I was aware of what I was saying, I heard myself answering with a degree of frankness that I rarely, in deference to politeness, permit myself in personal conversation: "My dear, I do not deal in happiness; I deal in meaning."

RICHARD WRIGHT
PARIS

PART I

The Psychological Reactions of Oppressed People

Buttressed by their belief that their God had entrusted the earth into their keeping, drunk with power and possibility, waxing rich through trade in commodities, human and non-human, with awesome naval and merchant marines at their disposal, their countries filled with human debris anxious for any adventures, psychologically armed with new facts, white Western Christian civilization during the fourteenth, fifteenth, sixteenth, and seventeenth centuries, with a long, slow, and bloody explosion, hurled itself upon the sprawling masses of colored humanity in Asia and Africa.

I say to you white men of the West: Don't be too proud of how easily you conquered and plundered those Asians and Africans. You had unwitting allies in your campaigns; you had Fifth Columns in the form of indigenous cultures to facilitate your military, missionary, and mercenary efforts. Your collaborators in those regions consisted of the mental habits of the people, habits for which they were in no way responsible, no more than you were responsible for yours. Those habits constituted corps of saboteurs, of spies, if you will, that worked in the interests of European aggression. You must realize that it was not your courage or racial superiority that made you win, nor was it the racial inferiority or cowardice of the Asians and Africans that made them lose. This is an important point that you must grasp, or your concern with this problem will be forever wide of the facts. How, then, did the West, numerically the minority, achieve, during the last four centuries, so many dazzling victories over the body of colored mankind? Frankly, it took you centuries to do a job that could have been done in fifty years! You had the motive, the fire power, the will, the religious spur, the superior organization, but you dallied. Why? You were not aware exactly of what you were doing. You didn't suspect your impersonal strength, or the impersonal weakness on the other side. You were as unconscious, at bottom, as were your victims about what was really taking place.

Your world of culture clashed with the culture-worlds of colored mankind, and the ensuing destruction of traditional beliefs among a billion and a half of black, brown, and yellow men has set off a tide of social, cultural, political, and economic revolution that grips the world today. That revolution is assuming many forms, absolutistic, communistic, fascistic, theocratistic etc.—all marked by unrest, violence, and an astounding emotional thrashing about as men seek new objects about which they can center their loyalties.

It is of the reactions, tortured and turbulent, of those Asians and Africans, in the New and Old World, that I wish to speak to you. Naturally I cannot speak for those Asians and Africans who are still locked in their mystical or ancestor-worshiping traditions. They are the voiceless ones, the silent ones. Indeed, I think that they are the doomed ones, men in a tragic trap. Any attempt on their part to wage a battle to protect their outmoded traditions and religions is a battle that is lost before it starts. And I say frankly that I suspect any white man who loves to dote upon those "naked nobles," who wants to leave them as they are, who finds them "primitive and pure," for such mystical hankering is, in my opinion, the last refuge of reactionary racists and psychological cripples tired of their own civilization. My remarks will, of necessity, be confined to those Asians and Africans who, having been partly Westernized, have a quarrel with the West. They are the ones who feel that they are oppressed. In a sense, this is a fight of the West with *itself*, a fight that the West blunderingly began, and the West does not to this day realize that it is the sole responsible agent, the sole instigator. For the West to disclaim responsibility for what it so clearly did is to make every white man alive on earth today a criminal. In history as in law, men must be held strictly responsible for the consequences of their historic actions, whether they intended those consequences or not. For the West to accept its responsibility is to create the means by which white men can liberate themselves from their fears, panic, and terror while they confront the world's colored majority of men who are also striving for liberation from the irrational ties which the West prompted them to disown—ties of which the West has partially robbed them.

Let's imagine a mammoth flying saucer from Mars landing, say, in a peasant Swiss village and debouching swarms of fierce-looking men whose skins are blue and whose red eyes flash lightning bolts that deal instant death. The inhabitants are all the more terrified because the arrival of these men had been predicted. The religious myths of the Western world—the Second Coming of Christ, the Last Judgment, etc., have conditioned Europeans for just such an improbable event. Hence, those Swiss natives will feel that resistance is useless for a while. As long as the blue strangers are casually kind, they are obeyed and served. They become the Fathers of the people. Is this a fragment of paperback science fiction? No. It's more prosaic than that. The image I've sketched above is the manner, by and large, in which white

Europe overran Asia and Africa. (Remember the Cortés-Montezuma drama!)

But why did Europe do this? Did it only want gold, power, women, raw materials? It was more complicated than that.

The fifteenth-, sixteenth-, and seventeenth-century neurotic European, sick of his thwarted instincts, restless, filled with self-disgust, was looking for not only spices and gold and slaves when he set out; he was looking for an Arcadia, a Land's End, a Shangri-la, a world peopled by shadow men, a world that would permit free play for his repressed instincts. Stripped of tradition, these misfits, adventurers, indentured servants, convicts and freebooters were the most advanced individualists of their time. Rendered socially superfluous by the stifling weight of the Church and nobility, buttressed by the influence of the ideas of Hume and Descartes, they had been brutally molded toward attitudes of emotional independence and could doff the cloying ties of custom, tradition, and family. The Asian-African native, anchored in family-dependence systems of life, could not imagine why or how these men had left their homelands, could not conceive of the cold, arid emotions sustaining them. . . . Emotional independence was a state of mind not only utterly inconceivable, but an attitude toward life downright evil to the Asian-African native—something to be avoided at all costs. Bound by a charged array of humble objects that made up an emotionally satisfying and exciting world, they, trapped by their limited mental horizon, could not help thinking that the white men invading their lands had been driven forcibly from their homes!

Living in a waking dream, generations of emotionally impoverished colonial European whites wallowed in the quick gratification of greed, reveled in the cheap superiority of racial domination, slaked their sensual thirst in illicit sexuality, draining off the dammed-up libido that European morality had condemned, amassing through trade a vast reservoir of economic fat, thereby establishing vast accumulations of capital which spurred the industrialization of the West. Asia and Africa thus became a neurotic habit that Europeans could forgo only at the cost of a powerful psychic wound, for this emotionally crippled Europe had, through the centuries, grown used to leaning upon this black crutch.

But what of the impact of those white faces upon the personalities of the native? Steeped in dependence systems of family life and anchored in ancestor-worshiping religions, the native was prone to identify those powerful white faces falling athwart his existence with the potency of his dead father who had sustained him in the past. Temporarily accepting the invasion, he transferred his loyalties to those white faces, but, because of the psychological, racial, and economic luxury which those faces derived from their domination, the native was kept at bay.

Today, as the tide of white domination of the land mass of Asia and Africa recedes, there lies exposed to view a procession of shattered cultures, disintegrated societies, and a writhing sweep of more aggressive, irrational religion than the world has known for centuries. And, as scientific research, partially freed from the blight of colonial control, advances, we are witnessing the rise of a new genre of academic literature dealing with colonial and post-colonial facts from a wider angle of vision than ever possible before. The personality distortions of hundreds of millions of black, brown, and yellow people that are being revealed by this literature are confounding and will necessitate drastic alteration of our past evaluations of colonial rule. In this new literature one enters a universe of menacing shadows where disparate images coalesce—white turning into black, the dead coming to life, the top becoming the bottom—until you think you are seeing Biblical beasts with seven heads and ten horns rising out of the sea. Imperialism turns out to have been much more morally foul a piece of business than even Marx and Lenin imagined!

An agony was induced into the native heart, rotting and pulverizing it as it tried to live under a white domination with which it could not identify in any real sense, a white domination that mocked it. The more Westernized that native heart became, the more anti-Western it had to be, for that heart was now weighing itself in terms of white Western values that made it feel degraded. Vainly attempting to embrace the world of white faces that rejected it, it recoiled and sought refuge in the ruins of moldering tradition. But it was too late; it was trapped; it found haven in neither. This is the psychological stance of the elite of the populations, free or still in a state of subjection, of present-day Asia and Africa; this is the profound revolution that the white man cast into the world; this is the revolution (a large part of which has been successfully captured by the Communists) that the white man confronts today with fear and paralysis.

"Frog Perspectives"

I've now reached that point where I can begin a direct descent into the psychological reactions of the people across whose lives the white shadow of the West has fallen. Let me commence by presenting to you concept number one: "Frog Perspectives."

This is a phrase I've borrowed from Nietzsche to describe someone looking from below upward, a sense of someone who feels himself lower than others. The concept of distance involved here is not physical; it is psychological. It involves a situation in which, for moral or social reasons, a person or a group feels that there is another person or group above it. Yet, physically, they all live on the same general material plane. A certain degree of hate combined with love (ambivalence) is always involved in this looking from below upward and the object against which the subject is measuring himself undergoes constant change. He loves the object because he would like to resemble it; he hates the object because his chances of resembling it are remote, slight.

Proof of this psychological reality can be readily found in the expressions of oppressed people. If you ask an American Negro to describe his situation, he will almost always tell you:

"We are rising."

Against what or whom is he measuring his "rising"? It is beyond doubt his hostile white neighbor.

At Bandung, Carlos Romulo of the Philippines said:

"I think that over the generations the deepest source of our own confidence in ourselves had to come from the deeply rooted knowledge that the white man was *wrong*, that in proclaiming the superiority of his race, *qua race*, he stamped himself with his own weakness and confirmed all the rest of us in our dogged conviction that we could and would reassert ourselves as men. . . ."

The "we" that Romulo speaks of here are the so-called "colored" peoples of the world. It is quite clear here that it is against the dominance of the white man that Romulo measures the concept of manhood. Implied in his statement is the feeling or belief that the white man has, by his presence or acts, robbed the colored peoples of a feeling of self-respect, of manhood. Once more we are confronted with the problem of distance, a psychological distance, a feeling that one must regain something lost.

At Bandung, in 1955, President Sukarno of Indonesia spoke as follows:

"The peoples of Asia and Africa wield little physical power. Even their economic strength is dispersed and slight.

We cannot indulge in power politics. Diplomacy for us is not a matter of the big stick. Our statesmen, by and large, are not backed up with serried ranks of jet bombers."

Listen to the above words with a "third ear" and you will catch echoes of psychological distance; every sentence implies a measuring of well-being, of power, of manners, of attitudes, of differences between Asia and Africa and the white West. . . . The core of reality today for hundreds of millions resides in how unlike the West they are and how much and quickly they must resemble the West.

This "frog perspective" prevails not only among Asians and Africans who live under colonial conditions, but among American Negroes as well. Hence, the physical nearness or remoteness of the American or European white has little or nothing to do with the feeling of distance that is engendered. We are here dealing with values evoked by social systems or colonial regimes which make men feel that they are dominated by powers stronger than they are.

The "Whiteness" of the White World

This "frog perspective" which causes Asians, Africans, American or West Indian Negroes to feel their situation in terms of an "above" and a "below" reveals another facet of the white world, that is, its "whiteness" as seen and felt by those who are looking from below upwards.

It would take an effort of imagination on the part of whites to appreciate what I term "the reality of whiteness" as it is reflected in the colored mind. From the inside of an American Black Belt, from the perspective of an African colony where 90 per cent of the population is black, or from China, India, or Indonesia where the white man is a rare sight or a distinct minority, the Western white world shrinks in size. The many national states which make up that white world, when seen from the interior of colored life lying psychologically far below it, assumes a oneness of racial identity. This aspect of "whiteness" has been re-enforced by a "gentleman's agreement" (of centuries' standing) implemented by treaties and other forms of aid between the big colony-owning powers to support one another in their colonial difficulties. Of course, of late, there have been some exceptions to this rule. For example, today Germans are prone to boast that they and they alone among the European powers have no record of recent exploitation of Asians and Africans. The Americans can say that they were largely responsible for the liberation of Indonesia. And when the Germans and Americans say this they are expecting that Asians and Africans make a distinction between them and the other colony-owning European states. Yet this distinction is hardly ever made. Why? Because the "whiteness" of Europe is an old reality, stemming from some five hundred years of European history. It has become a tradition, a psychological reality in the minds of Asians and Africans.

I have on occasion heard an Englishman express horror at the French policy in North Africa; and I've heard Frenchmen condemn both the British and the American systems of racial practices. On the other hand, the Spanish claim that they and they alone treated the colored peoples fairly and justly: they married them, etc. In making these boastful claims of their virtues in dealing with their colored colonial subjects, all of these European nations forget that they are contending with a reality which they themselves created deep in the minds of their subject people.

Whose hands ran the business enterprises? White hands. Whose hands meted out the law? White hands. Whose hands regulated the money? White hands. Whose hands erected the churches? White hands. Thus, when the white world is viewed from inside the colored world, that world is a block-world with little or no divisions.

I've heard liberal-minded Frenchmen express genuine horror at the lynching of a Negro by Mississippi whites. But to an Asian or an African it was not a Mississippi white man who did the lynching; it was just a Western white man. It is difficult for white Western Europe to realize how tiny Europe is in the minds of most of the people of the earth. Europe is indeed one world, small, compact, white, apart. . . .

The Non-Western Sense of "Time"

In Asia and Africa white Westerners are always expressing astonishment at the fact that they are referred to by the native elite as "aggressors." Indeed, Westerners find that this accusative tone of the Asian-African elite is not limited to those living under colonial rule, but, strangely, also embraces those Asians and Africans who have already gained their freedom. The surprise of the West at this resentment reveals a singular poverty of imagination, for it indicates a failure on the part of the West to appreciate the magnitude, the intensity, and the depth of distortion which its impact has wrought upon the lives of its accusers.

The average European white lives far from the realities of colonial rule and, therefore, gives little or no thought to the plight of the Belgium Congo natives or the millions of blacks whose earthly destinies are dictated by Frenchmen; such repellent facts, if they are known at all, are casually rationalized under the well-intentioned but mystically enigmatic rubric: "Well, when they are as evolved as we are, they'll be free too." While the continued subjugation of millions of Africans constitutes a *fait accompli* for the bulk of Western whites, there exist legions of liberal-minded Westerners who would register genuine moral horror at what transpires in those geographical prisons known as colonies, if they ever saw one. Thus, intellectual isolation and moral laziness conspire to render the mentality of the Westerner stoutly resistant to the revolution launched by his own kind in the emotional life of the Asian-African elite, a revolution that has shaped its content and guided its orientation.

For example, practically the whole of the non-Westerner's conception of historic "time" is charged with a sense of hot urgency deriving from the fact that his feel of that "time" almost invariably refers to, just as it most certainly stems from, the date of the European occupation of his country. In their marathon and frantic discussions of their dilemma, the most habitual verbal reference on the lips of the non-Western elite is: *"After the coming of the white man . . ."* or, *"Before the coming of the white man . . ."* In the Asian-African mind there is a gaping historic "time" displacement whose vital dimensions and dynamism are unguessed at by whites who reckon their historic sense of "time" in more general and relaxed terms of such remote, non-racial, and "superhuman" events as the birth of Christ, etc. But the Asian or African, trapped in the net of European trade and religion and yet suspended in his own daily tribal rituals, cannot escape the profound, contrasting cleavages wrought in his world by Western pressure. Hence he feels that the historic "time" that has the most decisive meaning for him dates from his "awakening" consequent to white Western intervention in his existence.

Who and What Is a "Savage"?

Most Asians and Africans know that the word "savage" is frankly derogatory and is meant, when it is used, to demean them and create moral sanction in the public mind of the West for the continued dominance, political and/or economic, of Europe over them and their people. But, in my questioning of the Asian-African elite, I have found that the word "savage" had a far different, a psychologically double-edged, connotation and was not at all as simple as white Westerners would have it. In fact, Asian-African definitions of the word "savage" shed more light upon the mentality of the Europeans who used it than the objective reality that that word was supposed to describe.

An intuitive African scholar analyzed the word "savage" in the following terms:

"There *is* such a phenomenon as a 'savage,' but it's not what the Europeans think it is. Europeans are much too intimately involved in the creation of the 'savage' to be able to describe him objectively.

"You'll find our tribal life quiet, regimented; our villages are orderly, clean, our people obedient to tribal authority. If there's anything wrong in our tribal life, it's its deadly boredom broken only by religious ceremonies. . . . But, when Europeans yank a tribal man out of his tribe, shattering his orientation to his world, and inject him suddenly into a new and completely different sphere of living with other assumptions, that tribal man becomes emotionally confused, finds himself acting upon a wide range of conflicting values. His actions become erratic; he tries too quickly to fuse disparate elements into an impossible whole under the condescending monitoring of nervous Western tutors whom he seeks to please and, at the same time, struggles to keep peace in his own torn heart.

"Such behavior, when viewed by uncomprehending and unsympathetic outsiders, seems bizarre, contradictory, and it's undoubtedly from this artificially induced and warped behavior that the word 'savage' takes its meaning, for 'savages' are the products of a Western, a morally imperialistic, influence upon us, a wrong kind of an attempt to 'change' us. But the white missionary, who is largely responsible for the erratic behavior that goes by the name of 'savage,' can never understand that that which he calls our 'savage' behavior is the consequence of his zeal to 'save.' . . . Convinced that he is appointed by God for his mission, he is psychologically bound, in defense of his self-esteem, to brand any tribal man a 'savage' who fails to heed his call to salvation or to adjust to his standards, never suspecting that he is thereby unconsciously ridding himself of moral blame for his inept proselyting."

The Resentment of "Evolution"

Perhaps no word in the lexicon of the West is rejected more vehemently by the African living under French rule than the word *"evolué"* as it is applied to his gradual transition from the state of "savagery" to the level of "civilization." Above all, he resents bitterly the biological implications of the word, a reaction that few or no Europeans suspect. The word *"evolué"* means in French: to perform evolutions, to turn, etc. Perhaps the American-British socio-anthropological definition, *acculturation* (the approximation of one social group or people to another in culture or arts by contact) or its equivalent (maybe the word "absorption" would be better!) would evoke less offensive reactions. Or is the word *"evolué"* used, as many cynical French-African students contend, expressly to provoke psychological hesitancy, self-doubt—the necessary emotional reactions that would intimidate the black neophyte and create in him the feeling that he can never really make the "civilized" grade? The sheer vagueness of the word would seem to suggest this. And who is to determine when the African candidate has sufficiently *"evolué"* toward an acceptable level of "civilization"? Only when he rises *en masse* and, putting knives at the throats of his rulers, chases them out? To date that seems to have been the only *de facto* criterion.

The Projection of "Romance"

One sizzling April afternoon, in 1955, I sat in the press-room of the Bandung Conference listening to a hard-bitten young Indonesian national revolutionary as he related some of his hair-raising exploits at sea against the Dutch. As he talked a young white newspaperwoman entered on the far side of the room. At once my informant broke off his narrative, leaned forward, and pointed.

"You see that woman?" he asked me.

"Yes," I said.

"I was talking to her last night in a hotel bar," he said, settling back in his chair and laughing nervously. "Boy, is *she* in love with the island of Java! She raves about the red clay, the statuesque beauty of our naked peasants, the wild orchids, the soft breezes in the morning, the extinct volcanoes, the high and fluffy clouds, and the incredible blueness of our skies. . . . She says that our dances make her drunk with ecstasy. She swears that romance and poetry steep every moment of our lives, and that we oughtn't ever change our way of living in order to be like the West." He paused and stared. "There must be something lacking in the lives they live in the West that make them act like that." Suddenly he straightened in his chair and pulled aside the lapel of his Palm Beach coat and allowed the dun-colored tip of a hand grenade to peep forth. "Boy, if she'd known that I had one of these little babies nestling in each armpit, she would've fainted. . . . Ha ha ha . . . ! What do those people think we are?"

The Suspicion of "Stupidity"

"They want us to be stupid and they want to keep us stupid" is a statement I have heard scores of times both in Asia and Africa. What the Asian or African means by this is that he feels that the white West does not want him to develop to the same heights, or in the same way and manner, that the West has developed. Now, I cannot say if such an attitude is actually a reality in the minds of Western whites. I can only report that this suspicion that the white man wishes that the Asian and African remain in their tribal or "primitive" state is most certainly a reality in the Asian and African mind. When whites hold this outlook, the Asian and African feel that they detect an attitude of racial jealousy on the part of the white man.

"The moment that we become industrialized, they can no longer treat us as they did in the past" is another widespread statement among the elite of Asia and Africa. Put plainly, the Asian or African is prone to feel that the West strives to hinder the development of Asians and Africans who would compete with the white West on a plane of equality, or even some day attain a position of superiority. In short, the Asian and African feel that the race for industrialization is, in part, a "racial" race, that is, a "racial" competition. It is obvious that the concept of industrialization here has been wrenched by force of psychological reaction out of its normal historical context and harnessed to the dubious service of "racial" pride. In this direction it would be well to remember that the reality of an industrialized Russia figures symbolically and beckoningly large. Quailing before the tragic cost of Russia's industrialization, the elite of Asia and Africa frantically seeks for short cuts to avoid such wholesale expenditures of human life in order to become self-reliant and secure. Stalin's World War II motto of: "The side with the most motors will win" has sunk home in their hearts, but they can find as yet no humane method of arming themselves with the necessary motors.

This "suspicion of stupidity" causes the Asians and Africans to examine the most objective and liberal advice of white Westerners with care, probing for the "hidden jokers," searching for the "trap," the "gimmick," the "angle," that would keep the white West in a position of perpetual historical dominance. And many Western whites, who naively and unthinkingly accept their present status of dominance as natural, unwittingly feed the distrust and suspicion in Asian and African minds by superior attitudes borrowed from past historical contexts. Thus, longing ardently for conditions of industrialization, the Asian and African have come to feel that any display of industrial might and finesse on the part of the white West is for the purpose of intimidating them, of making them feel inferior. Missionaries who enter the continents of Asia and Africa with gleaming cars are resented; advertisements of television sets, washing machines, etc., are viewed with the necessary protective scorn; qualitative assessments of Western figures of production are sneered at at the very moment when the elite of Asia and Africa is desperately seeking ways and means of duplicating such figures in its own homelands.

Deceit? Hypocrisy? No. As this analysis of psychological reactions unfolds, you will see that such traits are thrown up by factors more powerful than the individuals involved, and it would be well to remember that I am here dealing with psychological "reactions" and not psychological "actions."

What Is a "White Man"?

The "white man" is a distinct image in Asian-African minds. This image has nothing to do with biology, for, from a biological point of view, what a "white man" is is not interesting. Scientifically speaking the leaders of Asia and Africa know that there is no such thing as race. It is, therefore, only from a historical or sociological point of view that the image of "white man" means anything. In Asian-African eyes, a "white man" is a man with blue eyes, a white skin, and blond hair, and that "white man" wishes fervently that his eyes remain forever blue, his skin forever white, and his hair forever blond, and he wishes this for his children and his childrens' children. Today I'm sure that the billion and a half colored people of Asia and Africa would be more than willing to sign a most solemn covenant guaranteeing that the Western "white man's" eyes shall remain forever blue, his skin forever white, and his hair forever blond. White Europe need not fear today regarding the purity of its blood stream. But what the Asian and African will not agree to is that the oil, the diamonds, the bauxite, the timber, the copra, the tin, the manganese, and the gold of this earth belong to the "white man" merely because his eyes are blue.

Any educated African, Asian, or American Negro who would seek to deny or negate the "whiteness" of white Europe would be branded by his colored brothers as being "white struck," as being "too Western," as having gone "white man." (The above phrases that I've used have occurred in correspondence which I've received from Africans, Asians, and American Negroes within the last few months.) Indeed, any man of color who seeks to give even an objective account of how "colored people" feel will often be accused of "mulatto thinking." Because I have sometimes questioned the modern serviceability of African culture, many Africans have criticized my thinking as "white thinking." Any Egyptian today who would marry a European would be considered disloyal by his compatriots.

This "whiteness" of the white world, this "frog perspective," this pathos of distance that I've been describing—these are not static qualities; they have their dynamic aspects which I shall now proceed to present to you.

Negative Loyalty

The foremost quality of action which one finds among so many colonial peoples is a kind of negative loyalty to the West among the educated elite. This negative loyalty is a kind of yearning under almost impossible conditions to identify with the values of the white world, since their own traditions have been shattered by that world. Perhaps this yearning to identify with the values of the white world is stronger among American Negroes and West Indian Negroes than any other sections of the colored people in the world. The reason for this is simple: The Negroes in America and in the British West Indies live within the confines of the white cultures that dominate them—cultures that limit and condition their impulses and actions.

Let me illustrate this from the American Negro point of view. The Negro American is the only American in America who says: "I want to be an American." More or less all the other Americans are born Americans and take their Americanism for granted. Hence, the American Negro's effort to be an American is a self-conscious thing. America is something outside of him and he wishes to become part of that America. But, since color easily marks him off from being an ordinary American, and since he lives amidst social conditions pregnant with racism, he becomes an American who is not accepted as an American, hence a kind of negative American.

The psychological situation resulting from this stance is a peculiar one. The Negro in America is so constantly striving to become an American that he has no time to become or try to become anything else. When he becomes a publisher, he is a "Negro" publisher; when he becomes a physician, he is a "Negro" physician; when he becomes an athlete, he is a "Negro" athlete. This is the answer to the question that so many people have asked about American Negroes: Why do not American Negroes rebel? Aside from the fact that they are a minority and their rebellion would be futile, they haven't got time to rebel. Why are Negroes so loyal to America? They are passionately loyal because they are not psychologically free enough to be traitors. They are trapped in and by their loyalties. But that loyalty has kept them in a negative position.

This negative loyalty is widespread also in Asia and Africa. The elite that I've met in Asia and Africa were striving desperately to build societies most nearly like those of the Western states. Nkrumah, Nasser, Sukarno, Nehru, are all Western-educated men striving to make a Western dream come true in non-Western conditions of life. They too share with the American Negro certain negative aspects of loyalty. Each of the four men I've named has come under heavy criticism by white Westerners. (This tragic problem of the elite I shall deal with a little later.)

The psychological dynamics of the Westernized non-Westerner, that is Western-trained and educated Asians and Africans, assume truly strange and compounded psychological patterns. The stance of negative loyalty leads to a whole variety of ironic attitudes. I shall describe this reality briefly under the heading of *acting*.

Acting

What? Am I saying that Asians and Africans and colored people in general are good actors? No. I'm not speaking of the theater. I'm saying that the situation of their lives evokes in them an almost unconscious tendency to hide their deepest reactions from those whom they fear would penalize them if they suspected what they really felt. Do I mean to imply that Asians and Africans and American Negroes are not honest people, that they are agents of duplicity? I do not. They are about as honest as anybody else, but they are cautious, wise, and do not wish to bring undue harm upon themselves. Hence, they act. Let me recite an experience of mine. I recently had lunch one day, in Paris, with an Englishman interested in Asia and Africa, and with a West Indian Negro social scientist. The Englishman kept asking me questions about Asians', Africans', and American Negroes' reactions to their plight, and I kept answering quite openly and frankly. I noticed, as I talked, that the West Indian Negro social scientist kept glowering at me, shaking his head, showing acute evidence of something akin to anger. Finally he could contain himself no longer and he blurted out:

"Wright, why are you revealing all of our secrets?"

Unwittingly, I had hurt that man. Desperately I sought to allay his feelings. I had thought that we were three free, modern men who could talk openly. But, no. The West Indian Negro social scientist felt that I was revealing racial secrets to the white race.

"Listen," I said, "the only secret in Asia and Africa and among oppressed people as a whole is that there is no secret."

That did it. He threw up his hands in disgust and exclaimed:

"You have now revealed the profoundest secret of all!"

The scope and intensity of this Asian-African and Negro acting depend on the degree of white hostility that they confront. In America, this acting is a perfected system; it is almost impossible for the white man to determine just what a Negro is really feeling, unless that white man, like a Gunnar Myrdal, is gifted with a superb imagination. In a recent interview William Faulkner, Nobel Prize winner, declared that he could not imagine himself a Negro for two minutes! A strange statement to come from a man with an undoubtedly rich imagination. The American Negro's adversary is next door to him, on the street, on the job, in the school; hence, acting has become almost a second nature with him. This acting regulates the manner, the tone of voice, even, in which most American Negroes speak to white men. The Negro's voice is almost always pitched high when addressed to a white man; all hint of aggressiveness is purged from it. In some instances an educated Negro will try to act as uneducated as possible in order not to merit rebuff from whites.

In Asia and Africa this acting exists, but in a looser form. Not being as intimately related to the Western white man in their daily lives as the American Negro, the Asian and African do not need to practice this dissimulation to the degree that the American Negro does. Yet it is there. There are Asians and Africans who, when confronting whites, will swear proudly that they have never felt any racial feelings at all, that such feelings are beneath them, and will proceed to act in a Western manner. Yet, when alone or among themselves, they will confess their feelings freely and bitterly. I believe that it was only at Bandung that the full content of Asian and African racial feelings were expressed publicly and for the first time in all their turgid passion. They were among themselves and could confess without shame.

This "acting" is one of the secrets that my West Indian social scientist did not want me to talk about. He felt that I was making the Negro, the Asian, and the African transparent, vulnerable to white attack. On the other hand, it is my conviction that the sooner all of these so-called secrets are out in the open, the sooner both sides, white and colored, realize the shadows that hem them in, the quicker sane and rational plans can be made. Let us go one step further into this business of secrets.

The educated Asian, African, or American Negro who longs to escape his debased position, who longs to have done with acting, who longs to convert his negative loyalty into something positive, will encounter ideology sponsored by labor leaders or revolutionaries, the most powerful and appealing of which is that of Marxism. In short, one minority section of the white society in or under which he lives will offer the educated elite of Asia and Africa or black America an interpretation of the world which impels to action, thereby assuaging his feelings of inferiority. Nine times out of ten it can be easily pointed out that the ideology offered has no relation to the plight of the educated black, brown or yellow elite. Yet, what other road is there out of his Black Belt? His captured homeland? His racial prison? But that ideology does solve something. It lowers the social and racial barriers and allows the trapped elite of Asia and Africa and black America the opportunity to climb out of its ghetto. In Asia almost all the national revolutionaries I met had received aid from the hands of Marxists in their youth. The same was true of the black politicians of the Gold Coast, even though Marxism did not even remotely pertain to their non-industrial society. The same is true of the Negro in the United States where there prevailed an absurd theory, Marxist in origin, that the Negro constituted a separate nation.

Ideology as Intimacy

The fear inspired by white domination breeds a tendency, as I have said, to make Asians and Africans act, pretend. And this same almost unconscious tendency to pretension will spur them to pretend to accept an ideology in which they do not believe. They accept it in order to climb out of their prisons. Many a black boy in America has seized upon the rungs of the Red ladder to climb out of his Black Belt. And well he may, if there are no other ways out of it. Hence, ideology here becomes a means towards social intimacy.

Yes, I know that such a notion is somewhat shocking. But it is true. And in your heart, you know it's true. Many an African in Paris and London, and many a Negro in New York and Chicago, crossed the class and racial line for the first time by accepting the ideology of Marxism, whether he really believed it or not. The role of ideology here served as a function; it enabled the Negro or Asian or African to meet revolutionary fragments of the hostile race on a plane of equality. No doubt the oppressed, educated young man said to himself: "I don't believe in this stuff, but it works." In the Gold Coast young revolutionary Africans told me that, as soon as they had gained their freedom, they were going to erect a statue to the English white woman, thereby celebrating friendships that had redeemed days and weeks of loneliness. "If it had not been for them, we would have lost," they told me.

Resistance

Now, the most natural reaction, the most human response, to the revelation I've just made is to reject it and declare that no such psychological reaction exists. And the tendency to deny psychological traits of the sort I've just revealed leads me to my next concept: Resistance. There is a state of mind among the elite of Asia and Africa and the Negroes of America to reject that which they imagine hurts, degrades, or shames them. It is painful to realize that one is not free enough to make clean and honest decisions, that one has to "use" ideologies for one's own personal benefit. It is a state of mind that compels people to protect themselves against truths that wound; it is a deep, unconscious mechanism that prompts one to evade, deny, or seek explanations for problems other than those that prevail, for one does not wish to acknowledge a state of affairs that induces a loss of face.

I had the experience in both Asia and Africa of receiving intimate, unprompted confessions of how Indonesians felt about the Dutch, of how the Africans felt about the British, but as soon as those confessions appeared in print, there were hasty and passionate denials on the part of the very men who had given me their confessions.

Oppressed people have two sets of feelings: one for home consumption and one for export. I must say in all fairness that this duality of attitude has really aided the Asian and African in his dealing with white Westerners. In almost every instance of colonial revolt, the white Westerner has had absolutely no inkling of the revolt until it burst over his head, so carefully hidden had the rebels kept their feelings and attitudes. In short, oppression helps to forge in the oppressed the very qualities that eventually bring about the downfall of the oppressor.

Flight into the Past

Not all evasion or resistance on the part of the subject people is so positive. Much of it is a flight into useless identification. One hears much in America about "Negro genius"; one hears much in Africa about vanished "glories of past empires"; in Asia one hears much of "our wonderful traditions that go back a thousand years." All of this, of course, is an attempt to prove that, though smarting under a sense of inferiority, they are the equals of those who oppress them. If the present is painful, then seek shelter in the warm womb of the past.

Let us push on into this uncharted area of human reactions and discover even more fantastic mental landscapes. Let us recall the "frog perspective"; let us recall the tendency to "act"; let us remember the will to resist the acknowledgment of facts that cause pain, and the tendency to retire to the haven of past "glories." In the light of all this, is it surprising that one discovers that religion among oppressed peoples is no longer a way of determining one's relation to the world, but has turned into a way of asserting pride? How can one's religion turn into pride?

The white West entered the vast continents of Asia, Africa, and even the Americas in the name of religion. (Of course, they took a lot of gold and silver and slaves while preaching religion, but it was in the name of religion that their actions were rationalized.) After five hundred years of white Western domination in the name of a superior religion, I found the ancient religions among the masses in those areas more or less intact. How is that possible? There was no doubt but that the missionaries had labored hard. There was no doubt but that the Asians and Africans had been converted by the hundreds of thousands to the Christian church. How was it then, that after five hundred years, the delegates at Bandung passed a resolution to resurrect their old religions and cultures and modernize them? Obviously, those religions were never really dead.

At the world conference of black writers, artists and intellectuals in Paris, in September 1956, the main and only resolution called for the rehabilitation of their ancient cultures and religions! And, more significant, at that conference African Christians launched an attack upon Christianity, calling for its de-Europeanization. In other words, the religious tie between Africa and Europe was under vigorous attack not by Communists, but by African Christians themselves. Why?

Well, let your minds go back a little. Remember the burden of the message carried by the Christian missionaries into Asia and Africa? The Asian and African felt that the Christianity in whose name he had been conquered was really his own religion slightly disguised! Here is how he looked at it. Christianity came from one and perhaps unrepeatable historical accident that was compounded in Rome from Greek science and love of human personality, from Jewish notions of a One and Indivisible God, from Roman conceptions of law and order and property, and from a perhaps-never-to-be unraveled amalgamation of Eastern and African religions with their endless gods who were perpetually sacrificed and their endless virgins who gave birth perennially.

(May I add here, quite frankly, that, in part, I agree that some of the work of the missionary was good: I agree that his boiling down four hundred gods and six hundred devils into *one* God and *one* Devil was an advance. But I don't think that the missionaries' efforts went far enough; they should have reduced the whole problem to a psychological project.)

When Christianity met the so-called pagan religions of Asia and Africa, there was a strange result. How could Asia and Africa reject a militant Christian religion, at least, upon its initial impact? There was too much in that Christian religion that the Asian and African had believed in long before the Christian religion ever came to their shores, for it had been from the shores of Asia and Africa that these powerful legends, myths, images, symbols, and rituals had originally come. But the return of Christianity to the place of its birth was no peaceful homecoming; it came with fire in its eyes, a sword in its hands, and with the will to conquer and despoil. Why, then, did the elite in Asia and Africa accept it? When I put this question to an African scholar in the Gold Coast three years ago, I got the following answer:

"We've got four hundred gods. Jesus Christ. God number 401."

What happened was quite simple. When the white Westerner, armed and powerful, received a submissive attitude from the Asian and African, he took it for granted that the Asian or African had accepted his religion. The Asian and African had pretended to accept it to stave off attack, to receive petty favors. But the building of railroads, factories, and mines in the colonies, and the introduction of wage-rate labor, and the general spread of secular ideas, ate slowly away at the native religions, not destroying them completely, but rendering them truncated.

Despite the fact that his old, ancestral religions were made useless, made a mockery, the Asian and African never really abandoned them. He kept his religion to show that he was still a human being. Religion became a matter of human pride. The white man said: "I have the only one and true religion." The Asian and African replied, silently to be sure, but nonetheless passionately, "We have a religion too."*

Industrialization Becomes Religion

But, in time, a new religion replaced the truncated one. The Asian and African saw that techniques and industrialization had enabled the white man to enter his land and, in hoping for freedom, he found that the only road out was to embrace techniques and industrialization. Indeed, indus-

---

* Under the religiously toned spur of a new Indian nationalism, the reverse process is under way in India today. Thousands of Hindu Christians are being de-Christianized in popular and public ceremonies.

trialization soon became the new religion, not because industrialization itself was loved or revered as a means of production, but because it was the only way to hoist the white man off his back.

Do you not see how facts change their aspects, their meaning, under the pressure of oppression? So strong and widespread is this tendency for facts to be seen by the oppressed from a special point of view that I've called this a Metamorphosis of Facts. Religion turns into pride. Industrialization turns into religion. Race consciousness emerges as shame and bitter defiance. And in many instances sexuality assumes the means by which status is gauged, permitting men or women to marry into certain social milieux where they will feel that their degradation will be redeemed.

Need I remind you that the emotional and psychological reactions of the oppressed are bewildering in their complexity? It simply means that oppression oppresses, that oppression takes its toll, that it leaves a mark behind. Now there are Asians and Africans, American and West Indian Negroes, who will wish to deny that oppression cuts as sharply and deeply into their hearts as I've outlined. But their denial of this is in itself proof of its truth, for their denial of what they feel under oppression is proof that oppression oppresses.

The Unity of Man

Environmental buffetings, crass racial distinctions, class discriminations, uprootings caused by migration, continual disillusionments, imprisonment for rebellious acts—all these hammer blows need not always produce shattered or mangled personalities. Sifting through such grinding social sieves are some whose characters are singularly free and whose apprehension of life is broad indeed. (I'm not implying that mistreatment and injustice ennoble character! Adversity, at times, crushes as well as molds; it would seem that if there is a latent predilection toward meanness, pressure will heighten it, and, conversely, if there is a tendency toward breadth and scope of outlook, pressure can release or aid its development.) It has been almost only among Asians and Africans of an artistic stamp and whose background has consisted of wars, revolutions, and harsh colonial experience that I've found a sense of the earth belonging to, and being the natural home of, all the men inhabiting it, an attitude that went well beyond skin color, races, parties, classes, and nations. On the other hand, I've heard Western whites declare frequently and with firm conviction that they felt that Africa was for the blacks, Asia was for the yellows and browns, and that Europe was for the whites, meaning, of course, that the past domination of Europe over those Asian-African areas was natural and justified by the racial structure of life and history itself, since both have reflected, during the past five hundred years, the supremacy of whites.

Amid some Asian-African scholastic circles, I found that Western scientific thought had encouraged some rare men toward a healthy skepticism not only of Christianity, but toward all traditional ideas. Striking advances in the realms of anthropology and Freudian psychology have stressed not as much the old-time diversities among men that the colonials and nineteenth-century scientists loved to insist upon, but the remarkable and growing body of evidence of the basic emotional kinship, empirically established, of all men and of all races. Today many of the scholars of Asia and Africa (a minority, to be sure, for I've found that psychological facts do not sit well upon the mentalities of oppressed people!) are beginning to feel a lessening of distance between themselves and the Western world. Indeed, I'd say that there exists in a given number of Asian and African intellectuals a profounder grasp of the psychology of the white Westerner than you would find among a comparable number of Western intellectuals toward the Asian and African. It is amusing and instructive to hear a Westernized African poet say, with pardonable superiority and pride born of detached insight:

"They call us uncivilized. But just read a volume of psychoanalytic case histories of white people! All of the culture of so-called barbaric Africa is reenacted on a couch in a psychoanalytic office when a New York white man pours out his dreams, paying $20 an hour for the honor of doing so. Our tribes say and do the same things each day for the fun of it."

In all fairness it must be emphasized that this as yet budding sense of "the unity of man" is confined to a minority of minorities; but, despite the fragility of this universal outlook, it indicates a political vista that needs must be mentioned here. The present leaders of the newly independent Asian-African states have come under daily and bitter criticism in the press of the Western world; they have been branded as "wild-eyed," "neutrals," "immoralists," and "unappreciative of the danger of Communism." What the Western press does not realize is that the delicately poised elite in these areas represents the only real bastions of Western thought beyond the confines of the West. If these few Western-minded leaders are overthrown, it is absolutely certain that their successors will be infinitely more anti-Western than they are. The closer the West approaches the Asian and African masses, the more exclusive, shy, evasive, and militantly racial and nationalistic it will find those masses to be. This is but another way of saying that the present Asian-African leadership is one that can continue to talk to the West in terms of Western concepts and within a Western frame of reference, no matter how many hot disputes may take place about ends and means.

I know that some romantic- and regressive-minded Westerners would prefer to deal with a more pliable and less intransigent Asian-African elite. But they will discover, to their sharp dismay, that this "softer" elite will have little or no influence over the illiterate masses who are still captured by their ancestral or mystical religious systems. Those Asian-African leaders who can grasp "the unity of man" are few, and the bare fact that there exist even a few possessing global and humane visions is really a kind of miracle (especially when one recalls the past recent history of the West in those areas!), a boon that the West should think hard upon before dismissing in disdain or racial scorn.

Lay Priests

The Asian-African leader is often far more conscious of his relation to his people than a Westerner is to his. The non-Westerner knows that he is functionally the direct descendant of the priest, the mystic, the saint, the chief, "the fathers of the people." Hence, though ofttimes lacking official sanction for his position, he wields a kind of power that the Western mind finds difficult to grasp. A Nkrumah, a Nasser, a Nehru, all of whom hold official offices, speak with an authority that goes beyond the mandates of elections; indeed, the official posts which they now hold were gained only after they had conquered the hearts of their people. And these Asian-African stand-ins for priestly powers know that when they meet Western engineers, bankers, industrialists, scientists, etc., they are regarded with distrust, suspicion, if not the downright scorn that is reserved for "eggheads."

The most powerful public organs in Asia and Africa are often not government-sponsored bodies at all, but are, on the contrary, *government-creating bodies*—the Western procedure being turned upsidedown in non-Western countries. The "leader" and his movement exercise a power that is above that of law. And it is safe to assume that this quasi-religious atmosphere will prevail until more secular ground has been won from the traditional institutions and a body of pragmatic experience has accumulated in the daily lives of the people.

The role of Asian-African "lay priests" is extremely difficult and complicated; they function in a situation that facilitates the mischief-making efforts of their Communist competitors who seek to win converts at their expense, promising quicker results, inflaming class feelings long before the issue of national independence is resolved. Educated for the most part in Russia, speaking the language of the common people, enjoying the most intimate contacts with the masses, projecting their missionary ideas in terms of the people's daily lives, the Communist agitator fills a vacuum by rushing in where more prudent nationalists would hesitate. The Asian-African nationalist elite often finds itself in an odd position of having to battle a species of home-grown Communism on the one hand, and a futile striving to win Western understanding, approval, and support on the other. Many times it turns from both sides in desperation, with an attitude of: "A plague on both your houses."

Post-Mortem Terror

I'd like now to move towards a more minute examination of this question and I'd like to confine my remarks mainly to consciousness of the elite of Asia, Africa, and the West Indies, for it is in this elite, educated in the West, and, for the most part, more Western than the West, that the truly tragic aspects of oppression can be seen and measured. I know that it is popular today to say that every square inch of human existence is wholly economic. That is easy, too easy. It's a good organizing slogan, but it is no guide when it comes to examining and weighing the human issues and attitudes involved.

As the waters of Western imperialism recede from the land masses of Asia and Africa, and when we begin to study the residue left behind, we shall find some strange formations indeed. The first curious fact that I'd like to call to your attention is that, though recently freed, many lands—Indonesia, Ceylon, Burma, India, the Gold Coast—are more profoundly upset, filled with more fear and unrest than obtained even when the colonizing power was there in all of its brutal glory. Why is this? Why is Indonesia not only socially and economically disorganized, but emotionally and psychologically upset? I've called this strange state of mind: Post-Mortem Terror. What do I mean by that?

It is a state of mind of newly freed colonial peoples who feel that they will be resubjugated; that they are abandoned, that no new house of the heart is as yet made for them to enter. They know that they do not possess the necessary tools and arms to guarantee their freedom. Hence, their terror in freedom, their anxiety right after their liberation, is greater than when under the dominance of the superior Western power. Many people have misread this phenomenon and said that the people were unhappy because the Western white man had gone. How silly. Their unrest stems from a fear that the white man will come back, and from the cold void in which they are suspended. Of course, this acute unrest, this thrashing about for a new security, is mainly confined to the elite that can see and know what the issues and odds are.

The Concept of Interference

What is the burden of consciousness of this elite? It looks at the powerful West and then looks at the weakness of its own lands and feels that some dire and drastic move must be made to equalize the situation. What move can they make? They wish to do all those things that will make their lands the equal of the Western lands, for only in that way can they feel safe. But what does that involve? This elite, you must remember, lives surrounded by powerful traditions stretching back into the remote past. It knows that any move it makes to extend the area of industrialization will be passively resisted by those of their own people who do not know the modern world as well as they do, who do not feel their sense of urgency.

Hence, this Asian-African elite, in its state of what I've called Post-Mortem Terror, wishes to *interfere* with the religion and traditions of its land and its people. They are impelled to interfere quickly, drastically, decisively, and break the force of religion and tradition and create secular ground for the building of rational societies. But something holds them back. What is it? Two forces hamper and hinder them. First, this elite was educated in the West and has grown used to gradual methods of social evolution. Second, the white Westerner stands looking critically at this new elite and warns: "Don't act like fascists toward your own people!"

I wonder if the white Western world can appreciate this agony. I've called it: "The Caul of Indecision."

The Caul of Indecision

Before this issue, the oppressed elite sweats. A man belonging to this elite argues. He questions himself. He fears the return of the West, yet he feels that he needs the

West. I will cite a few examples of how the elite seeks to solve this all important problem. In the United States just after World War I, Marcus Garvey rose to leadership among the American Negroes and proposed the creation of all-black nationalism based on color, racial pride; his aim was to settle the American Negroes again in Africa and build an industrial state. His scheme failed mainly for two reasons: it was premature, and the Negroes in America felt themselves more psychologically identified with America than with Africa.

In the Gold Coast we see Nkrumah trying to forge tribes into a unity based on modern political concepts, and we can see today the degree to which his efforts clash bitterly, bloodily, with the traditions and ambitions of Ashanti tribal life. Whether Nkrumah will be successful or not only the future will tell. (He has so far been successful.) In Indonesia the new government under Sastroamidjojo* has called for compulsory national service in order to step up the rate of industrialization and rehabilitation. In India, Nehru has had to set the guns of his police against the reactionary claims of tribes whose outlook falls far behind that of the Western-educated elite. These actions are tragic. Where does the white West stand in this matter? With the tribes! With superstition! With the noble savage! Imagine! The West sides with the tribes against the men whom it educated. They now find the naked tribal man a noble, wonderful creature. How selfish can you get? The West has had five hundred years to protect those tribes. I say let the elite try a bit.

But let's examine this tragic conflict between the Western elite of Asia and Africa and their own populations. It can be stated without fear of contradiction that it would not exist if that elite did not have bitter memories and fears of the Western white man. The reason for this brutal push of the elite against its own people stems from fear that if

---

* Since these lines were written, elective democracy has been suspended in Indonesia and a form of "guided" democracy has been enthroned in its place.

they do not quickly modernize their countries, the white man will return. So, instead of democracy obtaining in the newly freed areas, something hinting of dictatorship will no doubt prevail for a while—will prevail at least until fear of the West has died down.

Listen to what Gunnar Myrdal, executive secretary of the Economic Commission for the United Nations, says:

"If, as is assumed to be an urgent necessity in the underdeveloped countries, the movement toward industrialization is to be pushed ahead, the *state*[*] will have to intervene in the field of manufacturing . . . not only creating the external economies and supplying transport and power, but often also organizing the marketing of the produce of the expanding industrial sector, providing facilities for training workers, foremen, and technicians on all levels, as well as business executives, giving managerial advice, making capital available, often subsidizing or protecting new industrial enterprises, and sometimes actually establishing and operating them. At the same time it must have as its principal objective not only the development of industrialization to its practical limits, but also its direction, so that the growth is balanced and met by effective demand."

Sounds like the blueprint for a Soviet, huh? Is Gunnar Myrdal perverse in assigning so powerful a role to the state? Well, either plans like this are followed, or stagnation lingers on and bloody revolution comes. The road to freedom might well lead through stern mountain paths. And, mind you, Myrdal gives this advice to keep those men of the elite in Asia and Africa in the camp of democracy! Paradoxical, but it's true.

Did this notion of interfering with the lives of their own people stem from an innate cruelty on the part of the elite of Asia and Africa? No. And there's the joker. What this elite seeks to impose in Asia and Africa derives from the concepts they learned in Western schools. This elite learned

---

* My italics. R. W.

how Europe, during the Reformation, had rolled back the tide of religion and had established the foundations of the modern state, secular institutions, free speech, science, etc. And what this Asian and African elite is now trying to do, under conditions far more difficult than obtained in Europe, is to rebuild their lands quickly, in terms of self-defense.

Do I make this point clear? The sense of urgency that rides the elite of Asia and Africa so desperately stems from a feeling that if they do not measure up almost overnight, they will again be swallowed up in what they feel will be a new slavery. This was the fundamental mood of Bandung.

(Not long ago I had the opportunity to mention this widespread notion of interference to an audience in Paris, and some young man, imbued with absolutistic thought, rose and denounced me for advocating American intervention in Asia and Africa! Which goes to show how propaganda can mislead and blind people.)

The Cult of Sacrifice

Let us follow this tragic theme of the elite a little more. Since the newly freed Asian and African nations do not possess enough technical power, they must needs often reckon their strength in terms of human sacrifices. Indeed, sacrifice, deliberate and intentional, has become a means of political struggle. One of the cardinal traits of the national revolutionary is to anticipate in advance the cost of the liberation of his land in terms of human life and physical suffering. Since he is faced with a Western world that stubbornly clings to the idea that God Himself has given it the right to rule the "lesser breed," the elite of Asia and Africa has no other choice but the embracing of this melancholy outlook, as depressing as it is.

It is to be noted that at Bandung President Sukarno

pointed out in his opening address the role that sacrifice had played in the struggle against imperialist domination.

Indeed, this mentality of sacrifice lingers on even after the colonial area wins its freedom. In fact, in many instances the freed colonial subject will react in terms of his former situation. He feels that all his actions ought to carry punitive measures, penalties, so used has he grown to feeling and thinking of enduring chastisement for his rebellious acts. This almost masochistic tendency makes him rush forward to embrace all the threats that the white West could possibly hurl at him. Hence, military threats are discounted in their minds in advance. I found in Asia and Africa that the degree of suffering that a leader had undergone at the hands of Western whites was a definition of his standing as a hero. Mrs. Pandit told me at Bandung that it was the years that Nehru had spent in jail that were now enabling Nehru to hold the Hindu millions in a state of unity while the nation was being rebuilt. In Indonesia some of the highest posts of government could be won only by those men who had a past record of imprisonment. In the Gold Coast the party in power marched into the National Assembly wearing the caps that they had worn while behind jail bars.

But is all of this as negative as I have so far stated it? I've shown more or less the reaction of the Asian and African to the white West, its past domination and present pressures. Are there no positive elements of a psychological nature in this Asian-African reaction? There are indeed positive psychological motives. I shall attempt to list some of them.

The Nuclear Revolutionary Motive

At the top of this list I shall place what I have called the Nuclear Revolutionary Motive. Just what does this clumsy phrase mean? I shall here try to spell out something that has gone almost unnoticed in the Western world. What was the main impact of the West upon Asia and Africa? I know that Marxists will say that it was economic. Non-Marxists will say that it was Christianity. Academic men will try to persuade us that there was a mixture, a synthesis of East and West involved. Here, I propose to advance another concept to account for this impact of the West upon Asia and Africa, a concept that cuts down beneath the other answers. I maintain that the ultimate effect of white Europe upon Asia and Africa was to cast millions into a kind of spiritual void; I maintain that it suffused their lives with a sense of meaninglessness. I argue that it was not merely physical suffering or economic deprivation that has set over a billion and a half colored people in violent political motion. I further maintain that a mere class identification is not sufficient to describe manifestations such as Bandung, for it must be remembered that modern class relations and proletarian class consciousness do not exist in many of the societies of Asia and Africa.

The present-day attitude of the national revolutionary in Asia and Africa has the quality of a man who has been put to sleep for centuries and awakens to find the world of which he was once a functioning part roaring past him. He is bewildered, hurt, stunned, filled with a sense of self-hate at the trick he feels has been played upon him. He and his kind are many; his adversaries are relatively few in number. The world that such a man sees is devoid of meaning. He looks into this or that theory to find an idea of what has happened to him and his kind. And when he selects a theory, whether it be Marxism or any other revolutionary doctrine, he is not so much concerned emotionally with whether that theory is *right* or *wrong*, but whether it fits his feelings and most nearly describes what he sees and feels. Does it fill that aching void in him? Indeed, I'll go so far as to say that, psychologically, theories here are but excuses, justifications, rationalizations for actions. Here we come to that strange frontier where we can say that motive becomes ideology.

Have I been understood? What I'm saying is this: I'm presenting you with a picture that turns the usual view of this matter upside down. I state that emotion here precedes the idea, that attitudes select the kind of ideas in question. This is the void that the West has induced in the Asian and African elite and the filling of that void is with ideas THAT MOST NEARLY ANSWER THE NEED. The idea that is accepted usually depends upon which idea gets there first!

The dynamic concept of the void that must be filled, a void created by a thoughtless and brutal impact of the West upon a billion and a half people, is more powerful than the concept of class conflict, and more universal.

I know that there are those of you who will bridle at this assertion. Perhaps you will feel that I'm devaluing the passion felt by national revolutionaries, and that I'm painting the Western white man as a brutal idiot. I'm not trying to do any such thing. I say that, upon sound reflection, if you get rid of some of your preconceptions, you will see that this concept of the void-to-be-filled can be equated to a *raison d'être*, a justification for living.

It is interesting to recall that Khrushchev's recent visit to India resulted in the Russian Communist leader's making a significant admission. He said that Gandhi had made a most important contribution to the national liberation struggle in India. Now, many of us had known that little fact for a long, long time, but it took a personal visit of Khrushchev to find it out. In India millions felt that the British method of rule was nullifying their very sense of life, and they, under Gandhi's guidance, organized to oppose it. What happened? Gandhi did not get what he wanted. He organized India to *resist* British industrialization and ironically he thereby launched India upon the road of industrialization. Gandhi was dealing with processes that far outstripped his own imagination.

Let me call to your attention some of the traits of this void in Asia and Africa.

Men Without Language

The elite of Asia and Africa are truly men without language. I do not mean that they do not speak their own native tongues; I do not mean that they do not speak the language of the European countries that dominated their lands for so long. It is psychological language that I speak of. For these men there is a "hole" in history, a storm in their hearts that they cannot describe, a stretch of centuries whose content has been interpreted only by white Westerners. The seizure of his country, its subjugation, the introduction of military rule, another language, another religion—all of these events existed without his interpretation of them. Even when he sends his children to school in Europe he knows that they will be taught his country's past in a manner that he disapproves. Put differently, one can say that at this point the elite has no vocabulary of history. What has happened to him is something about which he has yet to speak.

One day in Indonesia an educator and writer said to me:

"How I envy you."

"Why?" I asked him.

"The English language is your mother tongue," he told me.

"That's true," I said.

"You can appeal, as a writer, to a vast, world-wide audience," he went on.

"Yes," I agreed.

"But, Goddammit, they taught us *Dutch!*" he stormed.

"What can I say in Dutch? To whom can I speak?"

He seethed. Both of us were historical victims of a sort. He had been taught Dutch and I had been taught English. This Indonesian writer and educator was leading the crusade for the rehabilitation of his old language, Bahasa Malay, as the national language of his country. This man felt it was preferable for his children to speak a language that would enable them to appeal eventually to seventy million Indonesians than to learn Dutch which would allow them communication with nine million people in a tiny dull European country called Holland.

It is almost impossible for a white Westerner to realize some of the facts that make non-Westerners angry and resentful.

The Zone of Silence

Ofttimes the elite is silent. There's a spell of quiet that comes over him when he sees that the point of view of the imperial power dominates the values of culture and life. The world confronting him negates his humanity, but he feels that it is useless to protest with words. Only a complete reversal of the economic and political situation can give him back his birthright, can enable him to speak, to allow him to grasp a language, a vocabulary, that he can feel is his own.

The State of Exaggeration

Obviously, any elite reacting to the kind of reality I've sketched here will find itself reacting violently. One of the aspects of life of the American Negro that has amazed observers is the emotional intensity with which he attacks ordinary, daily problems. When an American Negro tries to rent a house and is refused, he will react far more violently than a white who tries to rent the same house and is refused. Is this biological? No. The Negro can always feel that his refusal was based on color. The political rallies of the African Gold Coast reached an intensity of passion that actually frightened Europeans who did not realize that these political rallies were not just politics, but attempts at forging a new way of life. The devotion and fervor that characterized the organization at Bandung reduced Western observers to silence and fear. And the vast crowds that attended the recent Asian tour of Khrushchev and Bulganin rendered a homage to an industrialized Russia that was nonideological in origin.

Is it not clear that we are dealing here with attitudes that go beyond a mere reacting to local or limited events? These reactions go beyond mere politics; they involve the total attitudes of the men concerned.

Recoil and Self-Possession

In many instances racists or colonial administrators justified their harsh methods on the grounds that, once their rule was lifted, there would be a disorganized and aggressive surge forward on the part of the black and brown and yellow men. In the American South, the white racists contended that, once all Jim Crow laws were repealed, the blacks would leap through windows and rape their wives and daughters. But, in Alabama, when the United States Supreme Court declared the Jim Crow practices on the buses unconstitutional, there was no wild rush forward on the part of the Alabama blacks. Instead, those blacks put forward a demand that they be allowed to organize and operate their own bus companies! In this instance, how could the whites have so completely misread the reality that lay so plainly in the black minds? On one hand, the whites had projected out upon the blacks their own guilt, fears, and sexual preoccupations. On the other, the blacks wished a respite from their bruising contacts with whites, sought a period in which they could take stock of what they really wanted.

In the Gold Coast the Britishers were always alarmed when the Africans went off by themselves to hold their political rallies and were constantly asking: "What did they say? What are they planning? Don't they want partnership?"

At Bandung the proud Australians were in the embarrassing position of chiding Indonesians and Indians and Africans for having excluded them from the greatest international conference that ever took place in Asia in modern times.

I've been informed by reliable international experts that in New Delhi the white ambassadors of European nations fret and fume because they do not have easy access to a tan-skinned Nehru who spent a third of his adult life in prison under white jailers.

Because I've pointed out these tendencies to recoil and self-possession on the part of Asians and Africans, some critics have sought to brand me a racist. This is a primitive reaction and is akin to accusing a messenger who brings you bad news of having created the bad news he brings.

This Asian-African recoil and withdrawal have many determinations, the most distinctive and powerful of which is to reorganize their lives in accordance with their own basic feelings. The truncated religious structure comes again to the fore and reasserts itself, much to the astonishment of Europeans. The conference of black artists and writers recently concluded in Paris by *Présence Africaine* is a vivid example of this stocktaking on the part of the elite of the black world. It is a recoil and withdrawal prompted by psychological necessity, but it is far from being a negative gesture. It is a regrouping of psychological forces for constructive action—psychological forces that have been scattered and paralyzed for centuries.

The last psychological aspect I'd like to discuss with you shall be under the listing of:

The Mystique of Numbers

Lacking modern techniques and arms to secure them from invasion or resubjugation, the newly freed Asian and African elite shies off from the urgent and insistent suggestion of white Western social scientists to limit, reduce, or control their populations. We all know that modern medicines, modern methods of sanitation, and new techniques of production enable tropical populations to increase so rapidly that they quickly outstrip the capacity of the means of production—even when those means of production are being aided by outside forces. But when Westerners urge birth control and other methods of limiting populations upon Asians and Africans, they are heard with considerable reserve. I propose to discuss, however briefly, some of the psychological motives back of that reserve.

The most powerful element here, of course, is the religious background of Asia and Africa, a background of worshipful regard for ancestors. Children are not only new members of the community, but are viewed in the light of reincarnations of past family members. Hence, the Asian or African is likely to listen with a poker face to the white social scientist when he argues passionately for a reduction or a limitation of the population of his country.

Facing superior arms, the Asian-African elite is likely to feel that, the more of his kind there is around him, the better off he is. And, as the white social scientist points out the advantages in terms of higher standards of living that will accrue if he limits his population, the Asian or African will ask himself uneasily: "Why does he wish that we were not so numerous?"

The Asian-African suspects bad faith in this argument, and I believe that he is right. It can be argued that the West is ethically dubious when it urges upon Asians and Africans concepts or principles that the West discovered only accidentally and under conditions far different from those that obtain in Asia and Africa.

It is well-known that the populations of the West are relatively smaller than those of Asia and Africa. But those low populations of the West did not come about through deliberate efforts on the part of the West. They were the consequences of complicated social, economic, and cultural factors. It would be safe to say that there will be no limiting or control of Asian or African populations until there prevail in Asia and Africa more or less the same conditions that obtain in the West. And, when that time comes, there will be no need for Western social scientists to urge a reduction of populations upon Asian and African leaders.

An examination of the population problem will reveal a common attitude existing among all people apprehensive about their future and afraid of attack. The Russians boast of their 200 million. The Chinese boast of their 600 million.* Africa is proud of her 170 million. At Bandung no delegate rose to speak without paying tribute to the fact that the conference represented a billion and a half people. It can be seen that population here is regarded in the light of a protective weapon.

We have been tramping through an unknown country. In this chapter I've tried to indicate the main peaks and valleys. This listing of psychological reactions is by no means complete. In raising this subject I'm trying to spur others to plunge in and make explorations.

---

* In the torrid political debates of Hindus, Chinese, Africans, and Indonesians that rage in the cafés of Paris, one hears the frequent and defiantly masochistic declaration: "China could fight a war for twenty years and lose twenty million men and *still* have a population of six hundred million left!"

Psychological facts have about them an air of the derogatory. But this is only seemingly so. You must realize that what I've called Asian and African psychological facts are such only in a contingent sense. They are human reactions, and, as such, they belong to everybody. White men under the conditions I've described would have reacted more or less the same. I have not raised these questions in order to deny, demean, or criticize the reactions I've cited. These reactions are human, all too human.

I challenge Europe to be strong enough to admit and accept this revolution that she cast into the world, however unconsciously, stupidly, misguidedly, and clumsily she did it. Like a sleepwalker, Europe blundered into the house of mankind, nullifying ancient traditions that sustained and informed the lives of millions with meaning, shattering the mental crystallizations of centuries and sending black, brown, and yellow men hurtling toward horizons as yet distant and dim. The Western world has, through sheer selfishness and racial jealousy, lost a vital part of this revolution to Communism, for, when called upon to confess authorship of her own principles, she rejected them and called them forgeries.

The historical hour is late, too late for guns, too late for armies even. If we would have a free world, only an awakened and chastened Europe can sanction it, can give the word. Europe must admit the role she has played in history, the noble as well as the base aspects of that role. Europe must be big enough to accept its Descartes and its Cortés and what they did. Europe must be big enough to accept its Hume of England and its Leopold II of Belgium and what they did. It must possess enough stern responsibility to accept both its Goethe and its Hitler. Is the spirit of Europe big enough to admit and contain and resolve these contradictions? If it is, our world can be saved. If it is not, our world is lost. And the world that we save or lose is a bigger world than we are, and our last one.

It can be said that the white man is at bay. Never have so few hated and feared so many. What I dread is that the Western white man, confronted with an implacably militant Communism on the one hand, and with a billion and a half colored people gripped by surging tides of nationalist fanaticism on the other, will feel that only a vengeful unleashing of atom and hydrogen bombs can make him feel secure. I dread that there will be an attempt at burning up millions of people to make the world safe for the "white man's" conception of existence, to make the ideas of Mill and Hume and Locke good for all people, at all times, everywhere. There is no doubt that atom or hydrogen bombs can destroy much of human life on this earth. If the white West should attack the body of mankind in this fashion, it will not only sacrifice its own civilization, but will set off reactions of racial and religious hatreds that will last for generations. In trying in this manner to make the world safe for their own kind only, the white West will wipe out of men's minds the undoubtedly glorious contributions that it has made to human life on this earth. In that instance, the only possible winner can be Communism. And if Communism wins under such stupid conditions, its victory will have been given to it by the racial jealousies of the Western world, jealousies which make the West feel that it would rather have no world at all than to share it, living and letting live, giving and taking.

PART II

Tradition and Industrialization

The Historic Meaning of the Plight of the Tragic Elite in Asia and Africa

So great a legion of ideological interests is choking the media of communication of the world today that I deem it advisable to define the terms in which I speak and for whom. In the heated, charged, and violently partisan atmosphere in which we live at this moment, all public utterances are dragged willy-nilly into the service of something or somebody. Even the most rigorously determined attitudes of objectivity and the most passionate avowals of good faith have come to be suspect. And especially is this true of the expressions of those of us who have been doomed to live and act in a tight web of racial and economic facts, facts viewed by many through eyes of political or religious interest, facts examined by millions with anxiety and even hysteria.

Knowing the suspicious, uneasy climate in which our twentieth-century lives are couched, I, as a Western man of color, strive to be as objective as I can when I seek to communicate. But, at once, you have the right to demand of me: What does being objective mean? Is it possible to speak at all today and not have the meaning of one's words construed in six different ways?

For example, he who advocates the use of mass educational techniques today can be, and usually is, accused of harboring secret Soviet sympathies, despite the fact that his advocacy of the means of mass education aims at a quick spreading of literacy so that Communism cannot take root, so that vast populations trapped in tribal or religious loyalties cannot be easily duped by self-seeking demagogues. He who urgently counsels the establishment of strong, central governments in the so-called underdeveloped countries, in the hope that those countries can quickly pull themselves out of the mire and become swiftly modernized and industrialized and thereby set upon the road to democracy, free speech, a secular state, universal suffrage, etc., can be and commonly is stigmatized as: "Well, he's no Communist, *but* . . ." He who would invoke, as sanction for experimental political action, a desire to seek the realization of the basic ideals of the Western world in terms of unorthodox and as yet untried institutional structures—instrumentalities for short-cutting long, drawn-out historical processes—as a means of constructing conditions for the creation of individual freedom, can be branded as being "emotionally unstable and having tendencies that *could* lead, therefore, to Communism." He who would question, with all the good faith in the world, whether the philosophical ideas and assumptions of John Stuart Mill and John Locke are valid for all times, for all peoples, and for all countries with their vastly differing traditions and backgrounds, with the motive of psychologically freeing men's minds so that they can seek new conditions and instrumentalities for freedom, can be indicted as an enemy of democracy.

Confronted with a range of negative hostility of this sort, knowing that the society of the Western world is so frantically defensive that it would seek to impose conformity at any price, what is an honest man to do? Should he keep silent and thereby try to win a degree of dubious safety for himself? Should he endorse static defensiveness as the price of achieving his own personal security? The game isn't worth the candle, for, in doing so, he buttresses that which would eventually crush not only him, but that which would negate the very conditions of life out of which freedom can spring. In such a situation one's silence implies that one has surrendered one's intellectual faculties to fear, that one has voluntarily abdicated life itself, that one has gratuitously paralyzed one's possibilities of action. Since any and all events can be lifted by men of bad faith out of their normal contexts and projected into others and thus consequently condemned, since one's thoughts can be interpreted in terms of such extreme implications as to reduce them to absurdity or subversion, obviously a mere declaration of one's good intentions is not enough. In an all-pervading climate of intellectual evasion or dishonesty, everything becomes dishonest; suspicion subverts events and distorts their meaning; mental reservations alter the character of facts and rob them of validity and utility. In short, if good will is lacking, everything is lost and a dialogue between men becomes not only useless, but dangerous, and sometimes even incriminating.

To imagine that straight communication is no longer possible is to declare that the world we seek to defend is no longer worth defending, that the battle for human freedom is already lost. I'm assuming, however naively, that such is not quite yet the case. I cannot, of course, assume that universal good will reigns, but I have the elementary right, the bounden duty even, to assume that man, when he has the chance to speak and act without fear, still wishes to be man, that is, he harbors the dream of being a free and creative agent.

Then, first of all, let us honestly admit that there is no such thing as objectivity, no such objective fact as objectivity. Objectivity is a fabricated concept, a synthetic intellectual construction devised to enable others to know the general conditions under which one has done something, observed the world or an event in that world.

So, before proceeding to give my opinions concerning Tradition and Industrialization, I shall try to state as clearly as possible where I stand, the mental climate about me, the historic period in which I speak, and some of the elements in my environment and my own personality which propel me to communicate. The basic assumption behind all so-called objective attitudes is this: If others care to assume my mental stance and, through empathy, duplicate the atmosphere in which I speak, if they can imaginatively grasp the factors in my environment and a sense of the impulses motivating me, they will, if they are of a mind to, be able to see, more or less, what I've seen, will be capable of apprehending the same general aspects and tones of reality that comprise my world, that world that I share daily with all other men. By revealing the assumptions behind my statements, I'm striving to convert you to my outlook, to its essential humaneness, to the generality and reasonableness of my arguments.

Obviously no striving for an objectivity of attitude is ever complete. Tomorrow, or the day after, someone will discover some fact, some element, or a nuance that I've forgotten to take into account, and, accordingly, my attitude will have to be revised, discarded, or extended, as the case may be. Hence, there is no such thing as an absolute objectivity of attitude. The most rigorously determined attitude of objectivity is, at best, relative. We are human; we are the slaves of our assumptions, of time and circumstance; we are the victims of our passions and illusions; and the most that our critics can ask of us is this: Have you taken your passions, your illusions, your time, and your circumstances into account? That is what I am attempting to do. More than that no reasonable man of good will can demand.

First of all, my position is a split one. I'm black. I'm a

man of the West. These hard facts are bound to condition, to some degree, my outlook. I see and understand the West; but I also see and understand the non- or anti-Western point of view. How is this possible? This double vision of mine stems from my being a product of Western civilization and from my racial identity, long and deeply conditioned, which is organically born of my being a product of that civilization. Being a Negro living in a white Western Christian society, I've never been allowed to blend, in a natural and healthy manner, with the culture and civilization of the West. This contradiction of being both Western and a man of color creates a psychological distance, so to speak, between me and my environment. I'm self-conscious. I admit it. Yet I feel no need to apologize for it. Hence, though Western, I'm inevitably critical of the West. Indeed, a vital element of my Westernness resides in this chronically skeptical, this irredeemably critical, outlook. I'm restless. I question not only myself, but my environment. I'm eager, urgent. And to be so seems natural, human, and good to me. Life without these qualities is inconceivable, less than human. In spite of myself, my imagination is constantly leaping ahead and trying to reshape the world I see (basing itself strictly on the materials of the world in which I live each day) toward a form in which all men could share my creative restlessness. Such an outlook breeds criticism. And my critical attitude and detachment are born of my position. I and my environment are one, but that oneness has in it, at its very core, an abiding schism. Yet I regard my position as natural, as normal, though others, that is, Western whites, anchored in tradition and habit, would have to make a most strenuous effort of imagination to grasp it.

Yet, I'm not non-Western. I'm no enemy of the West. Neither am I an Easterner. When I look out upon those vast stretches of this earth inhabited by brown, black, and yellow men—sections of the earth in which religion dominates, to the exclusion of almost everything else, the emotional and mental landscape—my reactions and attitudes are those of the West. I see both worlds from another and third point of view. (This outlook has nothing to do with any so-called Third Force; I'm speaking largely in historical and psychological terms.)

I'm numbed and appalled when I know that millions of men in Asia and Africa assign more reality to their dead fathers than to the crying claims of their daily lives: poverty, political degradation, illness, ignorance, etc. I shiver when I learn that the infant mortality rate, say, in James Town (a slum section of Accra, the capital of the Gold Coast in British West Africa) is fifty per cent in the first year of life; and, further, I'm speechless when I learn that this inhuman condition is explained by the statement, "The children did not wish to stay. Their ghost-mothers called them home." And when I hear that explanation I know that there can be no altering of social conditions in those areas until such religious rationalizations have been swept from men's minds, no matter how devoutly they are believed in or defended. Indeed, the teeming religions gripping the minds and consciousness of Asians and Africans offend me. I can conceive of no identification with such mystical visions of life that freeze millions in static degradation, no matter how emotionally satisfying such degradation seems to those who wallow in it. But, because the swarming populations in those continents are two-time victims—victims of their own religious projections and victims of Western imperialism—my sympathies are unavoidably with, and unashamedly for, them. For this sympathy I offer no apology.

Yet, when I turn to face the environment that cradled and nurtured me, I experience a sense of dismaying shock, for that Western environment is soaked in and stained with the most blatant racism that the contemporary world knows. It is a racism that has almost become another kind of religion, a religion of the materially dispossessed, of the culturally disinherited. Rooted in my own disinheritedness, I know instinctively that this clinging to, and defense of, racism by Western whites are born of their psychological nakedness, of their having, through historical accident, partially thrown off the mystic cauls of Asia and Africa that once too blinded and dazed them. A deeply conscious victim of white racism could even be strangely moved to compassion for that white man who, having lost his mystic vision of a stern Father God, a dazzling Virgin, and a Dying Son Who promises to succor him after death, settles upon racism! What a poor substitute! What a shabby, vile, and cheap home the white heart finds when it seeks shelter in racism! One would think that sheer pride would deter Western whites from such emotional debasement!

I stand, therefore, mentally and emotionally looking in both directions, being claimed by a negative identification on one side, and being excluded by a feeling of repulsion on the other.

Since I'm detached from, because of racial conditions, the West, why do I bother to call myself Western at all? What is it that prompts me to make an identification with the West despite the contradiction involved? The fact is that I really have no choice in the matter. Historical forces more powerful than I am have shaped me as a Westerner. I have not consciously elected to be a Westerner. I have been made into a Westerner. Long before I had the freedom to choose, I was molded a Westerner. It began in childhood. And the process continues.

Hence, standing shoulder to shoulder with the Western white man, speaking his tongue, sharing his culture, participating in the common efforts of the Western community, I say frankly to that white man: "I'm Western, just as Western as you are, maybe more; but I don't completely agree with you."

What do I mean, then, when I say that I'm Western? I shall try to define what the term means to me. I shan't here, now, try to define what being Western means to all Westerners. I shall confine my definition only to that aspect of the West with which I identify, that aspect that makes me feel, act, and live Western.

The content of my Westernness resides fundamentally, I feel, in my secular outlook upon life. I believe in a separation of Church and State. I believe that the State possesses a value in and for itself. I feel that man—just sheer brute man, just as he is—has a meaning and value over and above all sanctions or mandates from mystical powers, either on high or from below. I am convinced that the humble, fragile dignity of man, buttressed by a tough-souled pragmatism, implemented by methods of trial and error, can sufficiently sustain and nourish human life, can endow it with ample and durable meaning. I believe that all ideas have a right to circulate in the market place without restriction. I believe that all men should have the right to have their say without fear of the political "powers that be," without having to dread the punitive measures or the threat of invisible forces which some castes of men claim as their special domain—men such as priests and churchmen. (My own position compels me to grant those priests and churchmen the right to have their say, but not at the expense of having my right to be heard annulled.) I believe that art has its own autonomy, a self-sufficiency that extends beyond, and independent of, the spheres of political or priestly power or sanction. I feel that science exists without any a priori or metaphysical assumptions. I feel that human personality is an end in and for itself. In short, I believe that man, for good or ill, is his own ruler, his own sovereign, his own keeper. I hold human freedom as a supreme right and good for all men, my conception of freedom being the right of all men to exercise their natural and acquired powers as long as the exercise of those powers does not hinder others from doing the same.

These are my assumptions, my values, my morality, if you insist upon that word. Yet I hold these values at a time in history when they are threatened. I stand in the middle of that most fateful of all the world's centuries: the twentieth century. Nuclear energy, the center of the sun, is in the hands of men. In most of the land mass of Asia and Africa the traditional and customary class relations of feudal, capitalistic societies have been altered, frequently brutally shattered, by murder and terror. Most of the governments of the earth today rule, by one pretext or another, by open or concealed pressure upon the individual, by black lists, intimidation, fiat, secret police, and machine guns. Among intellectual circles the globe over the desperate question has been raised: "What is man?" In the East as in the West, wealth and the means of production have been taken out of private hands, families, clans, and placed at the disposal of committees and state bureaucrats. The consciousness of most men on earth is filled with a sense of shame, of humiliation, of memories of past servitude and degradation—and a sense of fear that that condition of servitude and degradation will return. The future for most men is an apprehensive void which has created the feeling that it has to be impetuously, impulsively filled, given a new content at all costs. With the freeing of Asia and most of Africa from Western rule, more active and unbridled religion now foments and agitates the minds and emotions of men than at any time since 1455! Man's world today lies in the pythonlike coils of vast irrational forces which he cannot control. This is the mental climate out of which I speak, a climate that tones my being and pitches consciousness on a certain plane of tension. These are the conditions under which I speak, conditions that condition me.

Now, the above assumptions and facts would and do color my view of history, that record of the rise and fall of traditions and religions. All of those past historical forces which have, accidentally or intentionally, helped to create the basis of freedom in human life, I extol, revere and count as my fervent allies. Those conditions of life and of history which thwart, threaten and degrade the values and assumptions I've listed, I reject and consider harmful, something to be doggedly resisted.

Now, I'm aware that to some tender, sensitive minds such a decalogue of beliefs is chilling, arid, almost inhuman. And especially is this true of those multitudes inhabiting the dense, artistically cluttered Catholic countries of present-day Europe. To a richly endowed temperament such a declaration is akin to an invitation to empty out all the precious values of the past; indeed, to many millions such a declaration smacks of an attack upon what they have been taught to consider and venerate as civilization itself. The emotionally thin-skinned cannot imagine, even in the middle of our twentieth century, a world without external emotional props to keep them buttressed to a stance of constant meaning and justification, a world filled with overpowering mother and father and child images to anchor them in emotional security, to keep a sense of the warm, intimate, sustaining influence of the family alive. And I can readily conceive of such temperaments willing to condemn my attitude as being barbarian, willful, or perverse. What such temperaments do not realize is that my decalogue of beliefs does not imply that I've turned my back in scorn upon the past of mankind in so crude or abrupt a manner as they feel or think. Men who can slough off the beautiful mythologies, the enthralling configurations of external ceremonies, manners, and codes of the past are not necessarily unacquainted with, or unappreciative of, them; they have *interiorized* them, have reduced them to mental traits, psychological problems. I know, however, that such a fact is small comfort to those who love the past, who long to be caught up in rituals that induce blissful self-forgetfulness, and who would find the meaning of their lives in them. I confess frankly that I cannot solve this problem for everybody; I state further that it is my profound conviction that emotional independence is a clear and distinct human advance, a gain for all mankind and, if that gain and advance seem inhuman, there is nothing that can rationally be done about it. Freedom needs no apology.

Naturally, a man holding such values will view history in a rather novel light. How do these values compel me to regard the claims of Western imperialism? What virtue or evil do I assign to the overrunning of Asia and Africa by Western Christian white men? What about color prejudice? What about the undeniable technical and industrial power and superiority of the white West? How do I feel about the white man's vaunted claim—and I'm a product, reluctant, to be sure, of that white man's culture and civilization—that he has been called by his God to rule the world and to have all overriding considerations over the rest of mankind, that is, colored men?

And, since the Christian religion, by and large, has tacitly endorsed racism by the nature of its past historical spread and its present sway, how do I view that religion whose irrational core can propel it toward such ends, whether that religion be in Europe, Asia, or Africa? And, since tradition is generally but forms of frozen or congealed religion, how do I regard tradition?

I've tried to lead you to my angle of vision slowly, step by step, keeping nothing back. If I insist over and over again upon the personal perspective, it is because my weighing of external facts is bound organically with that personal perspective. My point of view is a Western one, but a Western one that conflicts at several vital points with the present, dominant outlook of the West. Am I ahead of or behind the West? My personal judgment is that I'm ahead. And I do not say that boastfully; such a judgment is implied by the very nature of those Western values that I hold dear.

Let me dig deeper into my personal position. I was born a black Protestant in that most racist of all the American states: Mississippi. I lived my childhood under a racial code, brutal and bloody, that white men proclaimed was ordained of God, said was made mandatory by the nature of their religion. Naturally, I rejected that religion and would reject any religion which prescribes for me an inferior position in life; I reject that tradition and any tradition which proscribes my humanity. And, since the very beginnings of my life on this earth were couched in this contradiction, I became passionately curious as to why Christians felt it imperative to practice such wholesale denials of humanity. My seeking carried me back to a crucial point in Western history where a clearly enunciated policy on the part of the Church spelt my and others' doom. In 1455 the Pope divided the world between Spain and Portugal and decreed that those two nations had not only the right, but the consecrated duty of converting or enslaving all infidels. Now, it just so happened that at that time all the infidels, from the white Western Christian point of view, were in Asia, Africa, the many islands of the Atlantic, the Pacific, and the then unknown Americas—and it just so happened that they were all people of color.

Further reading of history brought me abreast of a strong countercurrent of opposition to that Church that had imperialistically condemned all colored mankind. When I discovered that John Calvin and Martin Luther were stalwart rebels against the domination of a Church that had condemned and damned the majority of the human race, I felt that the impulses, however confused, animating them were moving in the direction of a fuller concept of human dignity and freedom. But the Protestantism of Calvin and Luther did not go far enough; they underestimated the nature of the revolution they were trying to make. Their fight against the dead weight of tradition was partial, limited. Racism was historically and circumstantially embedded in their rejection of the claims of the Church that they sought to defeat. Calvin and Luther strove for freedom, but it was inevitably and inescapably only for their kind, that is, European whites. So, while recognizing the positive but limited nature of Calvin's and Luther's contribution, I had to look elsewhere for a concept of man that would not do violence to my own concept of, and feeling for, life.

What did magnetize me toward the emotional polarizations of Calvin and Luther was the curious psychological strength that they unknowingly possessed, a strength that propelled them, however clumsily, toward the goal of emotional independence. These two bold European insurgents had begun, though they called it by another name, a stupendous *introjection* of the religious symbols by which the men of their time lived. They were proponents of that tide that was moving from simple, naive credence toward self-skepticism, from a state of sensual slavery to the sights, sounds, and colors of the external world toward a stance of detachment. By some quirk of mental strength, they felt stronger than their contemporaries and could doubt and even doff the panoply of religious rituals and ceremonies and could either live without much of them or could, gropingly to be sure, stand psychologically alone to an amazing degree. In the lives of Calvin and Luther there had begun a dual process: on one hand, the emptying of human consciousness of its ancient, infantile, subjective accretions, and, on the other, a denuding of an anthropocentric world of the poetry that man had projected upon it. A two-way doubt of the world and of man's own self had set in, and this putting man and his world in question would not pause until it had enthroned itself in a new consciousness. Western man was taking that first step toward a new outlook that would not terminate until it had flowered in the bleak stretches of an undiscovered America which, ironically, was peopled by red-skinned "savages" who could not dream of doubting their own emotions or questioning the world that impinged upon their sensibilities. (The partially liberated Pilgrims slew those religiously captured "savages"!) Not understanding the implications of the needs prompting them, Calvin and Luther did not realize that what they were trying to do had already been neatly, clearly, and heroically done before by the brave and brooding Greeks who, overwhelmed by contradictory experiences and the antinomic currents of their own passions, had lifted their dazed eyes toward an empty Heaven and uttered those bitterly tragic words that were to become the motto of abandoned Western man:

"What do we do now?"

The Protestant is a queer animal who has never fully understood himself, has never guessed that he is an abortive freeman, an issue of historical birth that never quite came to full life. It has been conveniently forgotten that the Protestant is a product and a result of *oppression*, which might well account for his inability to latch directly onto the Greek heritage and thereby save himself a lot of useless and stupid thrashing about in history. Stripped by the heavy, intolerant conditions of Catholic rule of much of his superfluous emotional baggage, the emerging Protestant rebel, harassed by his enemies and haunted by his own guilt, was doomed to *react* rather than *act*, to *protest* rather than *affirm*, never fully grasping what was motivating him until he had been swept by history so far beyond his original problem that he had forgotten its initial content of meaning. The Protestant was being called to a goal the terrifying nature of which he had neither the courage nor the strength to see or understand. The Protestant is the brave blind man cursed by destiny with a burden which he has not the inner grace to accept wholeheartedly.

The ultimate consequences of Calvin's and Luther's rebellious doctrines and seditious actions, hatched and bred in emotional confusion, unwittingly created the soil out of which grew something that Calvin and Luther did not dream of. (And this is not the last time that I shall call your attention to an odd characteristic of the Western world; the men of the West seem prone in their actions to achieve results that contradict their motives. They have a genius for calling things by wrong names; they seek to save souls and become involved in murder; they attempt to enthrone God as an absolute and they achieve the establishment of the prerequisites of science and atheistic thought; they seem wedded to a terribly naive and childlike outlook upon the world and themselves, and they are filled with consternation when their actions produce results that they did not foresee.) Determined to plant the religious impulse in each individual's heart, declaring that each man could stand face to face with God, Calvin and Luther blindly let loose mental and emotional forces which, in turn, caused a vast revolution in the social, cultural, governmental, and economic conditions under which Western man lived—a revolution that finally negated their own racial attitudes! The first and foremost of these conditions were the guaranteeing of individual conscience and judgment, an act which loosened, to a degree, the men of Europe from custom and tradition, from the dead hand of the past, evoking a sense of future expectation, infinitely widening man's entire horizon. And yet this was achieved by accident! That's the irony of it. Calvin and Luther, preoccupied with metaphysical notions, banished dread from men's minds and allowed them to develop that courageous emotional strength which sanctioned and spurred the amassing of a vast heap of positive fact relating to daily reality. As a result of Calvin's and Luther's heresy, man began to get a grip upon his external environment. Science and industry were born and, through their rapid growth, each enriched the other and nullified the past notions of social structures, negated norms of nobility, of tradition, of priestly values, and fostered new social classes, new occupations, new experiences, new structures of government, new pleasures, hungers, dreams, in short, a whole new and unheard of universe. A Church world was transformed into a worldly world, any man's world, a world in which even black, brown, and yellow men could have the possibility to live and breathe.

Yet, while living with these facts, Europeans still believed in and practiced a racism that the very logic of the world they were creating told them was irrational and insane!

Buttressed by their belief that their God had entrusted the earth into their keeping, drunk with power and possibility, waxing rich through trade in commodities, human and non-human, with awesome naval and merchant marines at their disposal, their countries filled with human debris anxious for any adventures, psychologically armed with new facts, white Western Christian civilization, with a long, slow, and bloody explosion, hurled itself upon the sprawling masses of humanity in Asia and Africa.*

Perhaps now you'll expect me to pause and begin a vehement and moral denunciation of Europe. No. The facts are

---

* *See* The Psychological Reactions of Oppressed People.

complex. In that process of Europe's overrunning of the rest of mankind a most bewildering mixture of motives, means, and ends took place. White men, spurred by religious and areligious motives—that is, to save the souls of a billion or so heathens and to receive the material blessings of God while doing so—entered areas of the earth where religion ruled with an indigenous absoluteness that did not even obtain in Europe.

Are we here confronted with a simple picture of virtue triumphing over villainy, of right over wrong, of the superior over the inferior, of the biologically fit blond beast over biologically botched brown, yellow, and black men? That is what Europe felt about it. But I do not think that that is a true picture of what really happened. Again I call your attention to the proneness of white Europe, under the influence of a strident, romantic individualism, to do one thing and call that thing by a name that no one but itself could accept or recognize.

What, then, happened? Irrationalism met irrationalism. The irrationalism of Europe met the irrationalism of Asia and Africa, and the resulting confusion has yet to be unraveled and understood. Europe called her adventure imperialism, the spread of civilization, missions of glory, of service, of destiny even. Asians and Africans called it colonization, blood-sucking, murder, butchery, slavery. There is no doubt that both sides had some measure of truth in their claims. But I state that neither side quite knew what was happening and neither side was conscious of the real process that was taking place. The truth lay beyond the blurred ken of both the European and his Asian and African victim.

I have stated publicly, on more than one occasion, that the economic spoils of European imperialism do not bulk so large or important to me. I know that today it is the fashion to list the long and many economic advantages that Europe gained from its brutal and bloody impact upon hundreds of millions of Asians and Africans. The past fifty years have created a sprawling literature of the fact that the ownership of colonies paid princely dividends. I have no doubt of it. Yet that fact does not impress me as much as still another and more obscure and more important fact. What rivets my attention in this clash of East and West is that an irrational Western world helped, unconsciously and unintentionally to be sure, to smash the irrational ties of religion and custom and tradition in Asia and Africa. THIS, IN MY OPINION, IS THE CENTRAL HISTORIC FACT! The European said that he was saving souls, yet he kept himself at a distance from the brown, black, and yellow skins that housed the souls that he claimed that he so loved and so badly wanted to save. Thank the white man's God for that bit of racial and color stupidity! His liberating effect upon Asia and Africa would not have been so thorough had he been more human.

Yes, there were a few shrewd Europeans who wanted the natives to remain untouched, who wished to see what they called the "nobility" of the black, brown, and yellow lives remain intact. The more backward and outlandish the native was, the more the European loved him. This attitude can be boiled down to one simple wish: The imperialist wanted the natives to sleep on in their beautifully poetic dreams so that the ruling of them could be more easily done. They devised systems of administration called "indirect rule," "assimilation," "gradual constitutional government," etc., but they all meant one simple thing; a white man's military peace, a white man's political order, and a white man's free trade, whether that trade involved human bodies or tin or oil.

Again, I say that I do not denounce this. Had even the white West known what it was really doing, it could not have done a better job of beginning to launch the liberation of the masses of Asia and Africa from their age-old traditions.

Being ignorant of what they were really doing, the men of Europe failed to fill the void that they were creating in the very heart of mankind, thereby compounding their strange historical felony.

There are Europeans today who look longingly and soulfully at the situation developing in the world and say: "But, really, we love 'em. We are friends of theirs!" To attitudes like that I can only say: "My friends, look again. Examine the heritage you left behind. Read the literature that your fathers and your fathers' fathers wrote about those natives. Your fathers were naive but honest men."

How many souls did Europe save? To ask that question is to make one laugh! Europe was tendering to the great body of mankind a precious gift which she, in her blindness and ignorance, in her historical shortsightedness, was not generous enough to give her own people! Today, a *knowing* black, brown, or yellow man can say:

"Thank you, Mr. White Man, for freeing me from the rot of my irrational traditions and customs, though you are still the victim of your own irrational customs and traditions!"

There was a boon wrapped in that gift of brutality that the white West showered upon Asia and Africa. Over the centuries, meticulously, the white men took the sons and daughters of the chiefs and of the noble houses of Asia and Africa and instilled in them the ideas of the West so the eventual Westernized Asian and African products could become their collaborators. Yet they had no thought of how those Westernized Asians and Africans would fare when cast, like fishes out of water, back into their poetic cultures. (These unemployed Asians and Africans eventually became national revolutionaries, of course!) Shorn of all deep-seated faiths, these Westernized Asians and Africans had to sink or swim with no guides, no counsel. Over and above this, the Europeans launched vast industrial enterprises in almost all of the lands that they controlled, vast enterprises that wrought profound alterations in the Asian-African ways of life and thought. *In sum, white Europeans set off a more deep-going and sudden revolution in Asia and Africa than had ever obtained in all of the history of Europe.* And they did this with supreme confidence. On one occasion Christian English gentlemen chartered a royal company for one thousand years to buy and sell black slaves! Oh, what hope they had!

I declare that merely rational motives could not have sustained the white men who damaged and destroyed the ancient Asian-African cultures and social structures; they had perforce to believe that they were the tools of cosmic powers, that they were executing the will of God, or else they would not have had the cruel daring to try to harness the body of colored mankind into their personal service. The sheer magnitude of their depredations and subjugations ought to have given them pause, but it never did to any effective degree. Only a blind and ignorant militancy could have sustained such insane ventures, such outlandish dreams. Indeed, one could say that it was precisely because the white Westerner had partially lost his rooting in his own culture that he could remain so insensitive to the dangerous unleashing of human forces of so vast and catastrophic a sweep. Had he been more at home in his own world of values, sheer prudence would have made him quail before the earth-shaking human energies which he so rashly and diligently cut loose from their moorings.

Today the intelligent sons and daughters of the old-time European freebooters, despoilers, and imperial pirates tremble with moral consternation at what their forefathers did. Says Gunnar Myrdal, in his *An International Economy*, page 168 (Harper and Brothers: New York, 1956):

> **"The horrible vision often enters my mind of the ultimate results of our continuing and rapidly speeding up the practice, well established in some countries during the era of colonialism, of tossing together ever bigger crowds of illiterate proletarians—these new proletariats being even more uprooted than they were in the stagnant villages where they lived in the remnants of some culture and some established mores."**

Who *took* here? Who *gave?* It is too complicated a process to admit of such simple questions. But the Europeans naively called it soul-saving, money-making, modern administration, missions of civilization, *Pax Britannica*, and a host of other equally quaint appellations. History is a strange story. Men enact history with one set of motives and the consequences that flow from such motivated actions often have nothing whatsoever to do with such motives. What irony will history reveal when those pages of Europe's domination of Asia and Africa are finally and honestly written! That history will depict a ghastly racial tragedy; it will expose a blind spot on the part of white Westerners that will make those who read that history laugh with a sob in their throats. The white Western world, until relatively recently the most secular and free part of the earth—with a secularity and freedom that was the secret of its power (science and industry)—labored unconsciously and tenaciously for five hundred years to make Asia and Africa (that is, the elite in those areas) more secular-minded than the West!

In the minds of hundreds of millions of Asians and Africans the traditions of their lives have been psychologically condemned beyond recall. Hundreds of millions live uneasily with beliefs of which they have been made ashamed. I say, "*Bravo!*" for that clumsy and cruel deed. Not to the motives, mind you, behind those deeds, motives which were all too often ignoble and base. But I do say "Bravo!" to the consequences of Western plundering, a plundering that created the conditions for the possible rise of rational societies for the greater majority of mankind.

But enough of ironic comparisons. Where do we stand today? That part of the heritage of the West that I value—man stripped of the past and free for the future—has now been established as lonely bridgeheads in Asia and Africa in the form of a Western-educated elite, an elite that is more Western, in most cases, than the West. Tragic and lonely and all too often misunderstood are these men of the Asian-African elite. The West hates and fears that elite, and I must, to be honest, say that the instincts of the West that prompt that hate and fear are, on the whole, correct. For this elite in Asia and Africa constitutes islands of free men, the FREEST MEN IN ALL THE WORLD TODAY. They stand poised, nervous, straining at the leash, ready to go, with no weight of the dead past clouding their minds, no fears of foolish customs benumbing their consciousness, eager to build industrial civilizations. What does this mean? It means that the spirit of the Enlightenment, of the Reformation, which made Europe great, now has a chance to be extended to all mankind! A part of the non-West is now akin to a part of the West. East and West have become compounded. The partial overcoming of the forces of tradition and oppressive religions in Europe resulted, in a round-about manner, in a partial overcoming of tradition and religion in decisive parts of Asia and Africa. The unspoken assumption in this history has been: WHAT IS GOOD FOR EUROPE IS GOOD FOR ALL MANKIND! I say: So be it.

I approve of what has happened. My only regret is that Europe could not have done what she did in a deliberate and intentional manner, could not have planned it as a global project. My wholehearted admiration would have gone out to the spirit of a Europe that had had the imagination to have launched this mighty revolution out of the generosity of its heart, out of a sense of lofty responsibility. Europe could then stand proudly before all the world and say: "Look at what we accomplished! We remade man in our image! Look at the new form of life that we brought into being!" And I'm sure that had that happened, the majority of mankind would have been Western in a sense that no atom or hydrogen bombs can make a man Western. But, alas, that chance, that rare and noble opportunity, is gone forever. Europe missed the boat.

How can the spirit of the Enlightenment and the Reformation be extended now to all men? How can this accidental boon be made global in effect? That is the task that history now imposes upon us. Can a way be found, purged of racism and profits, to melt the rational areas and rational personnel of Europe with those of Asia and Africa? How can the curtains of race, color, religion, and tradition—all of which hamper man's mastery of his environment—be collectively rolled back by free men of the West and non-West? Is this a Utopian dream? Is this mere wishing? No. It is more drastic than that. The nations of Asia and Africa and Europe contain too much of the forces of the irrational for anyone to think that the future will take care of itself. The islands of the rational in the East are too tenuously held to permit of optimism. And the same is true of Europe. (We have but to recall reading of ideas to "burn up entire continents" to doff our illusions.) The truth is that our world—a world for all men, black, brown, yellow, and white—will either be all rational or totally irrational. For better or worse, it will eventually be one world.

How can these rational regions of the world be maintained? How can the pragmatically useful be made triumphant? Does this entail a surrender of the hard-bought national freedoms on the part of non-Western nations? I'm convinced that that will not happen, for these Asian and African nations, led by Western-educated leaders, love their freedom as much as the West loves its own. They have had to struggle and die for their freedom and they value it passionately. It is unthinkable that they, so recently freed from color and class domination of the West, would voluntarily surrender their sovereignty. Let me state the problem upside down. What Western nation would dream of abdicating its sovereignty and collaborating with powers that once so recently ruled them in the name of interests that were not their own—powers that created a vast literature of hate against them? Such an act would be irrational in the extreme. And the Western-educated leaders of non-Western nations are filled with too much distrust of an imperial-minded West to permit of any voluntary relinquishing of their control over their destinies.

Is there no alternative? *Must* there be a victorious East or a victorious West? If one or the other must win completely, then the fragile values won so blindly and accidentally and at so great a cost and sacrifice will be lost for us all. Where is the crux of this matter? Who is to act first? Who *should* act first? The burden of action rests, I say, with the West. For it was the West, however naively, that launched this vast historical process of the transformation of mankind. And of what must the action of the West consist? The West must aid and, yes, abet the delicate and tragic elite in Asia and Africa to establish rational areas of living. THE WEST, IN ORDER TO KEEP BEING WESTERN, FREE, AND SOMEWHAT RATIONAL, MUST BE PREPARED TO ACCORD TO THE ELITE OF ASIA AND AFRICA A FREEDOM WHICH IT ITSELF NEVER PERMITTED IN ITS OWN DOMAIN. THE ASIAN AND AFRICAN ELITE MUST BE GIVEN ITS HEAD!

The West must perform an act of faith and do this. Such a mode of action has long been implied in the very nature of the ideas which the West has instilled into that Asian-African elite. The West must trust that part of itself that it has thrust, however blunderingly, into Asia and Africa. Nkrumah, Nasser, Sukarno, and Nehru, and the Western-educated heads of these newly created national states, must be given *carte blanche* to modernize their lands without overlordship of the West, and we must understand the methods that they will feel compelled to use.

Never, you will say. That is impossible, you will declare. Oh, I'm asking a hard thing and I know it. I'm Western, remember, and I know how horribly implausible my words sound to Westerners so used to issuing orders and having those orders obeyed at gun point. But what rational recourse does the West possess other than this? None.

If the West cannot do this, it means that the West does not believe in itself, does not trust the ideas which it has cast into the world. Yes, Sukarno, Nehru, Nasser and others will necessarily use quasi-dictatorial methods to hasten the process of social evolution and to establish order in their lands—lands which were left spiritual voids by a too-long Western occupation and domination. Why pretend to be shocked at this? You would do the same if you were in their place. You have done it in the West over and over again. You do it in every war you fight, in every crisis, political or economic, you have. And don't you feel and know that, as soon as order has been established by your Western-educated leaders, they will, in order to be powerful, surrender the personal power that they have had to wield?*

Let us recognize what our common problem really is. Let us rethink what the issue is. This problem is vast and com-

* Here is a paradox: Nehru is as powerful as an emperor; Nkrumah is a *de facto* dictator; yet both men are staunch democrats and are using their vast personal power to sponsor measures that will undermine their "cult of the personality"! The key to their motives is that they seek power not for themselves, but for their people!

plicated. Merely to grasp it takes an act of the imagination. This problem, though it has racial overtones, is not racial. Though it has religious aspects, it is not religious. Though it has strong economic motives, it is not wholly economic. And though political action will, no doubt, constitute the main means, the *modus operandi*, of its solution, the problem is not basically political.

The problem is freedom. How can Asians and Africans be free of their stultifying traditions and customs and become industrialized, and powerful, if you like, like the West?

I say that the West cannot ask the elite of Asia and Africa, even though educated in the West, to copy or ape what has happened in the West. Why? Because the West has never really been honest with itself about how it overcame its own traditions and blinding customs.

Let us look at some examples of Western interpretation of its own history. A Civil War was fought in America and American school children are taught that it was to free the black slaves. It was not. It was to establish a republic, to create conditions of economic freedom, to clear the ground for the launching of an industrial society. (Naturally, slavery had to go in such a situation. I'm emphasizing the positive historic aspects, not the negative and inevitable ones!) The French fought a long and bloody Revolution and French school children are taught that it was for Liberty, Equality, and Fraternity. Yet we know that it was for the right of a middle class to think, to buy and sell, to enable men with talent to rise in their careers, and to push back (which was inevitable and implied) the power of the Church and the nobility. The English, being more unintentionally forthright than others, never made much bones about the fact that the freedom that they fought for was a freedom of trade.

Do these misinterpretations of Western history by the West negate the power and net historical gains of the Western world? No. It is not what the West said it did, but what the results really were that count in the long run.

Why have I raised these points of Western contradictions? Because, when non-Westerners, having the advantage of seeing more clearly—being psychologically *outside* of the West—what the West did, and when non-Westerners seek to travel that same road, the West raises strong objections, moral ones. I've had a white Westerner tell me: "You know, we must stay in Africa to protect the naked black natives. If we leave, the blacks we have educated will practice fascism against their own people." So this man was in a position to endorse the shooting down of a black elite because that black elite wanted to impose conditions relating to the control of imports and exports, something which his country practiced every day with hordes of armed policemen to enforce the laws regulating imports and exports!

The same objections are leveled against Nkrumah in the Gold Coast, against Sukarno in Indonesia, against Nasser in Egypt, against Nehru in India. Wise Westerners would insist that stern measures be taken by the elite of Asia and Africa to overcome the irrational forces of racism, superstition, etc. But if a selfish West hamstrings the elite of Asia and Africa, distrusts their motives, a spirit of absolutism will rise in Asia and Africa and will provoke a spirit of counter-absolutism in the West. In case that happens, all will be lost. We shall all, Asia and Africa as well as Europe, be thrown back into an age of racial and religious wars, and the precious heritage—the freedom of speech, the secular state, the independent personality, the autonomy of science—which is not Western or Eastern, but human, will be snuffed out of the minds of men.

The problem is freedom from a dead past. And freedom to build a rational future. How much are we willing to risk for freedom? I say let us risk everything. Freedom begets freedom. Europe, I say to you before it is too late: Let the Africans and Asians whom you have educated in Europe have their freedom, or you will lose your own in trying to keep freedom from them.

But how can this be done? Have we any recent precedent for such procedure? Is my suggestion outlandish? Unheard of? No. A ready answer and a vivid example are close at hand. A scant ten years ago we concluded a tragically desperate and costly war in Europe to beat back the engulfing tides of an irrational fascism. During those tense and eventful days I recall hearing Winston Churchill make this appeal to the Americans, when Britain was hard-pressed by hordes of German and Italian fascists:

"Give us the tools and we'll finish the job."

Today I say to the white men of Europe:

"You have, however misguidedly, trained and educated an elite in Africa and Asia. You have implanted in their hearts the hunger for freedom and rationality. Now this elite of yours—your children, one might say—is hard-pressed by hunger, disease, poverty, by stagnant economic conditions, by unbalanced class structures of their societies, by surging tides of racial shame, by oppressive and irrational tribal religions. You men of Europe made an abortive beginning to solve that problem. You failed. Now, I say to you: Men of Europe, give that elite the tools and let it finish that job!"

FREEDOM IS INDIVISIBLE.

PART III

The Literature of the Negro in the United States

To most people the literature of the American Negro is fairly well-known. So for me to give you merely a bare, bald recital of what Negroes have written would, in my opinion, be shirking a duty and a responsibility. Indeed, it would be the easy and the lazy way out, and I don't like the easy and lazy ways out of things.

As we all know, anthologists are legion today; to make an anthology requires simply this: Get a big pile of books on a given subject together, a big pot of glue, and a pair of sharp scissors and start clipping and pasting.

I do most seriously want to tell you about Negro writing, but I also want to try to tell you what some of that writing means, how it came to be written, what relationship it had to its time, and what it means to us today. In short, I'd like to try to interpret some of it for you; but one cannot interpret without thinking, without comparing. And, for the most part, I'm going to use Negro poets and their poems as my examples; for poets and poems have a way of telling a lot in a compressed manner.

But, first, I'm going to try to deposit certain concepts in your mind about the world in which we live; then, using these concepts as a magnifying glass, we will look at some of the literary utterances of the American Negro. The concepts I shall deal with are familiar, though I doubt if they've been applied to American Negro expression before. Let me start by making a general comparison.

A few years ago I spent some months living in the heart of French Quebec, on an island in the St. Lawrence River, about fifteen miles from the city of Quebec. As you no doubt know, the Province of Quebec represents one of the few real surviving remnants of feudal culture on the American continent. It has a Catholic culture, a close, organic, intimate, mainly rural, way of life. For more than three hundred years, many of the customs and habits of life of French Canadians have not changed.

Never before had I the experience of living intimately in a culture so different from the Protestant, Puritan culture of my own native land. And, like most travelers, I saw French Canadian culture with two pairs of eyes: I saw the Catholic culture of French Quebec, and, at the same time, I saw how different that culture was from the culture of industrial, Protestant America.

Now you may feel that I'm going rather far astray in talking about Negro literature by describing a culture in which there are practically no Negroes, but I have my reasons for this.

In French Quebec the Catholic church dominates all personal and institutional and political phases of life from the cradle to the grave. There is no split between the personal and the political; they are one. In telling you these facts, please understand I'm making no judgment upon the culture of French Quebec. I'm merely trying to present a few facts for the purpose of establishing a basis of comparison. The people of French Quebec are at one with their culture; they express themselves in and through it. The personalities of the people I met were serene, even-tempered; no one strove too hard for a personal or an individualistic vision of life.

No one sought a separate or unique destiny; they were not a romantic people. The secular and the sacred are united in French Quebec; the social and the personal are integrated; the individual and his group are one.

How different this is from our culture! In America we are split up in almost every imaginable way. We have no central unity; our church and state are separate. With but a tiny area of agreement, each individual lives in his own world.

This break with the past was accomplished when we broke with the feudal world, and we call this Freedom, and it is the crowning development of the industrial West; it has given us the most powerful civilization the world has ever known. But, also, it has given us millions of wrecked lives, millions of oppressed. It has given us anti-Semitism, anti-Negroism. It has given us spectacular crime, corruption, violence, and a singular disregard for the individual. Yet I feel that we were right in breaking with the feudal world. We do not have and we do not need an official creed to which all must bow. Yet we have an industrial civilization that breeds restlessness, eagerness, an almost neurotic anxiety that there is a hidden meaning that each must wring from life before he dies lest he feel that he has failed.

How does this relate to the Negro in America? In this way: The Negro, like everybody else in America, came originally from a simple, organic way of life, such as I saw in French Quebec. And you must remember that your forefathers also came from the feudal cultures of Europe. It was from the total, oppressive cultures like those of French Quebec that men fled three centuries ago to settle in the New World. You are now adjusted to industrial life and perhaps you have forgotten that your forefathers once endured the agony of leaving their homes and native lands to settle in America. So, in historical outline, the lives of American Negroes closely resemble your own.

There are, of course, some few important differences; most whites left Europe voluntarily; the American Negro was snatched by force from the organic, warm, tribal culture of Africa, transported across the Atlantic in crowded, stinking ships, and sold into slavery. Held in bondage, stripped of his culture, denied family life for centuries, made to labor for others, the Negro tried to learn to live the life of the New World in an atmosphere of rejection and hate.

You see now why I feel that one ought to use the same concepts in discussing Negro life that one uses in discussing white life? It is the same life lifted to the heights of pain and pathos, drama and tragedy. The history of the Negro in America is the history of America written in vivid and bloody terms; it is the history of Western Man writ small. It is the history of men who tried to adjust themselves to a world whose laws, customs, and instruments of force were leveled against them. The Negro is America's metaphor.

Let me sum up the meaning of my comparison, for what it means will form the foundation of what I'll have to say to you about Negro literature. Let us imagine an abstract line and at one end of this line let us imagine a simple, organic culture—call it Catholic, feudal, religious, tribal, or what you will. Here are some of the features of that culture: It is bigger than the individual and the individual finds his meaning for living in it. The individual does not help to make up the rules or laws of that culture.

At the opposite end of our imaginary line, let us imagine another culture, such as the one in which we live. In contrast to entity, in which the personality is swallowed up, we have a constant striving for identity. Instead of pre-individualism, we have a strident individualism. Whereas French Quebec has holy days, we have holidays. Church bells toll the time of day in French Quebec; we look at our watches to see the hour. Fetes become festivals.

The distance between these two cultures is the distance between feudal Europe and present-day, vibrant, nervous, industrial America. And it is the distance between the tribal African culture of the Negro and the place which he now occupies, against such great and constant odds, in American life.

It will be along this imaginary line—between these two culture types—that I'll string the Negro writers I'll discuss. For the development of Negro expression—as well as the whole of Negro life in America—hovers always somewhere between the rise of man from his ancient, rural way of life to the complex, industrial life of our time. Let me sum up these differences by contrast; entity vs. identity; pre-individualism vs. individualism; the determined vs. the free.

Now, with this idea in mind, let me read you a short passage from the work of a world-famous Negro writer, a writer whose identity I shall withhold from you for a moment:

> **"Sire, I am sorry to tell your majesty a cruel fact; but the feeling in Dauphiné is far from resembling that of Provence. The mountaineers are all Bonapartists, Sire."**
>
> **"Then," murmured Louis XVIII, "he was well informed. And how many men had he with him?"**
>
> **"I do not know, Sire," answered the minister of police.**
>
> **"What! You do not know? Have you neglected to obtain information of this circumstance? It is true this is of small importance," the king added with a withering smile.**
>
> **"Sire, it was impossible to learn; the dispatch simply stated the fact of the landing and the route taken by the traitor."**
>
> **"And how did this dispatch reach you?" inquired the king.**

> **The minister bowed his head, and while a deep color overspread his cheeks, he stammered, "By the telegraph, Sire."**
>
> **Louis XVIII advanced a step, folded his arms over his chest as Napoleon would have done. "So, then," he exclaimed, turning pale with anger, "seven allied armies overthrew that man. A miracle of Heaven replaced me on the throne after twenty-five years in exile . . ."**

Did a Negro write that? It does not sound Negroid. And were Negroes ever in this world so intimately associated with any culture that they could write of kings and ministers and battles involving Louis XVIII?

Well, what I just quoted to you was a short passage from Alexander Dumas' *The Count of Monte Cristo*. Yes, it's true that Dumas was a Negro according to American racial codes, but his being a Negro was the least important thing about him. Why? Because there were no laws or customs barring him from the society in which he lived. He could attend any school he wanted to; he could go to any church he wanted to; he could engage in any profession he wanted to; he could live where he wanted to; he could marry whom he wanted to; and if he had the mind and talent, he could win fame if he wanted to. He did win fame. He was at one with the culture in which he lived, and he wrote out of the commonly shared hopes and expectations of his age.

Let me recall to you the imaginary, entity culture that we placed at one end of our line: a religious, tribal, feudal culture, a culture like that of French Quebec. I don't mean that a culture of this sort is an ideal for which we must strive; I put that culture at the end of an imaginary line to serve us as a guide, as a yardstick against which we could measure how well or ill men adjusted themselves.

We can say that Dumas was integrated with the culture of France and was a Frenchman.

Let me read you yet another passage from another Negro writer, a world famous one too:

> **The dawn was breaking. I was standing at my appointed place with my three seconds. With inexplicable impatience I awaited my opportunity. The spring sun rose, and it was already growing hot. I saw my opponent coming on foot, accompanied by just one second. We advanced to meet him. He approached holding his cap filled with cherries. The seconds measured twelve paces for us. I had to fire first, but my agitation was so great, that I could not depend upon the steadiness of my hands; and in order to give myself time to become calm, I ceded to my opponent the first shot. My adversary would not agree to this. It was decided that we should cast lots. The first number fell to him. He took aim and his bullet went through my cap. . . ."**

Is this Negro writing? It does not sound like the expressions of Negroes who live in America today. Did Negroes ever engage in duels? Well, what I have just read to you is a passage from a short story by Alexander Pushkin, a Russian Negro who was more a Russian than a Negro. Like Alexander Dumas, he had no cause to lament that he was a Negro; his writing does not carry any of the bitter and wild echoes of hate, frustration, and revolt found in the writings of American Negroes. Pushkin wrote out of the rich tradition of Russian realism, and he helped to further and enrich that tradition. He was one with his culture; he went to the schools of his choice; he served in an army that was not Jim Crow; he worked where he wanted to; he lived where he wanted to; and there was no sense of psychological distance between him and the culture of the land in which he lived.

Let me recall to you once again the concept we started with: Entity, men integrated with their culture; and identity, men who are at odds with their culture, striving for personal identification. The writings I've just read to you were the work of men who were emotionally integrated with their country's culture; no matter what the color of their skins, they were not really Negroes. One was a Russian, the other was a Frenchman.

Has any American Negro ever written like Dumas or Pushkin? Yes, one. Only one. As though in irony, history decided that the first Negro who was to express himself with any degree of competence on the soil of America should strike a universal note. Before the webs of slavery had so tightened as to snare nearly all Negroes in our land, one was freed by accident to give utterance in poetry to what she felt, to give in clear, bell-like, limpid cadences the hope of freedom in the New World.

One day, in 1761, a slave ship, having made the horrible voyage from Africa to America, dropped anchor in Boston harbor. As usual an auction was held, with the slaves stripped naked and made to stand in public upon blocks. Would-be purchasers probed their fingers about the bodies of the black men and women to determine if they were sound of limb. Finally, all the slaves, except a delicate twelve-year-old black girl, were sold. Because she seemed too frail to render a good day's hard work, no one wanted her. But a Boston tailor by the name of Wheatley bought her and took her home, where she was trained to be the personal servant of Mrs. Wheatley.

This nameless black child was given the name of Phyllis and was accepted into the Wheatley home as one of the family, enjoying all the rights of the other Wheatley children. She displayed a remarkable talent for learning and she was taught to read and write. Need I point out that this African-born child possessed dim recollections of her mother pouring out water to the rising sun, no doubt a recollection of some kind of tribal, African ceremony? Slavery had not yet cast its black shadow completely over the American scene, and the minds of white people were not so warped at that time as they are now regarding the capacities of the Negro. Hence, the Wheatley family was quite free of inhibitions about educating Phyllis; they proceeded to educate her in the so-called classical manner; that is, she got the kind of education that the white girls of her time received.

At an early age she was writing verse, influenced by the heroic couplets of Pope, the reigning English poet of that time. Closely bound to the Wheatley family, absorbing the impulses of the Christian community in which she lived, sharing the culture of her country in terms of home and school and church, her poetry showed almost no traces of her being a Negro or having been born in Africa. Indeed, so closely integrated was she with the passions and hopes of America that, in the War of 1776, she wrote a poem about George Washington. She was received by Washington at his military headquarters and the Father of Our Country complimented her upon her poetic utterances. In praise of Washington and in rebuke to imperialistic England, Phyllis Wheatley wrote:

Ah! cruel blindness to Columbia's state!
Lament thy thirst of boundless power too late.
Proceed great chief, with virtue on thy side,
Thy ev'ry action let the goddess guide.
A crown, a mansion, and a throne that shine,
With gold unfading, Washington, be thine.

There is a note of irony embedded in the life of this girl who wrote revolutionary poetry though her skin was black and she was born in Africa; she made a trip to England where the Countess of Huntingdon wanted to present her to the Court of George III, and only ill health robbed her of that honor. (This was, of course, after the Revolutionary War.)

Again let me recall to you the concept I mentioned before. Phyllis Wheatley was at one with her culture. What a far cry this is from the Negro Seabees who staged a sit-down strike a few years ago on the Pacific Coast when the war against Japan was at its hardest! What makes for this difference in loyalty? Are the three excerpts I've read to you the writing of Negroes? No, not by present-day American standards. Then, what is a Negro? What is Negro writing?

Being a Negro has to do with the American scene, with race hate, rejection, ignorance, segregation, discrimination, slavery, murder, fiery crosses, and fear. But we will examine that when we come to it.

At last we have found on the American scene, in the writing of Phyllis Wheatley, someone whom we can establish at the head of our imaginary line. Now we can use her as a guide, a yardstick to measure the degree of integration of other Negro writers.

Suppose the personalities of many Phyllis Wheatleys of America had been allowed to develop? What a different nation we might have been! What a different literary utterance the American Negro might have given voice to! But, as we move on to other Negro literary figures, a queer spell at once comes over the scene. We cannot examine other Negro literary figures without taking into account something terrible that was happening to Negroes in the United States.

Even though we had won the War of Independence, there was a reaction against the ideals of Patrick Henry and

Thomas Jefferson; the cotton gin was invented and vast new lands were opened up in the South. Slavery grew from a tentative gesture into the greatest single aggregate of political power in the nation. There followed decades of killings and burnings and lynchings and beatings and futile hope on the part of the Negroes. Stripped of his tribal African culture and not allowed to partake of the culture of the New World, the Negro was consistently brutalized, reduced to a creature of impulse who worked in the fields. Again and again he tried to revolt, hurling himself against his foes who outnumbered him, but in vain. It was but natural then that the nature of Negro literary utterance would change.

The next Negro literary figure I want to call to your attention is that of George Moses Horton, born in 1797 and died in 1883. The dates of his birth and death are important, for they span the bloodiest period of the history of the Negro in America. Born in North Carolina, he was a slave of the Horton family; but his relationship to that family differed greatly from that of the Phyllis Wheatley relationship to the Boston family in which she was reared. Horton was passed around from one member of the Horton family to another; finally, in 1865, his master allowed him to hire himself out. While working around the home of a university president, he learned to read and write; for years he was a village character, regarded with amusement by the white students. He hired himself out as a writer of verse, charging twenty-five and fifty cents for a poetic job.

Finally some of his verse crept into print; not too much is known about this obscure wanderer's life, but we can guess at what he really felt from the following lines:

Alas! and am I born for this,
To wear this slavish chain?
Deprived of all created bliss,

Through hardship, toil and pain!
Oh, Heaven! and is there no relief
This side the silent grave—
To soothe the pain—to quell the grief
And anguish of a slave?

The poem runs on, lamenting, fighting, imploring. Something has happened since Phyllis Wheatley wrote. Entity has turned into a kind of sullen, raging sense of rebellious identity. Horton certainly was not at one with his culture, but neither had he completely broken away. He writes in English and tries to express himself in the poetic traditions of his time, but there is now a sense of psychological distance between him and the land in which he lives. Horton was an emotionally trapped man; he lived in a culture of which he was not really a part; he was a split man, believing and feeling something which he could not live; he was an agonizingly self-conscious man, always longing to perform an act against which there existed a dreadful taboo!

We are now, it seems, approaching the literature of the American Negro and I think that you can readily see what it is that makes the difference between American Negro writing and just plain American writing. Horton's writing does not stem from racial feeling, but from a social situation; and Horton's cry for freedom was destined to become the tradition of Negro literature in the United States. Almost unbrokenly this tradition of lament was to roll down the decades, swelling, augmenting itself, becoming a vast reservoir of bitterness and despair and infrequent hope. This tradition of bitterness was to become so complex, was to assume such a tight, organic form, that most white people would think, upon examining it, that all Negroes had embedded in their flesh and bones some peculiar propensity toward lamenting and complaining.

From now on we plunge into a welter of crude patterns of surging hate and rebellion; from Horton's time on but few Negroes would even possess the opportunity to live in stable family units.

Another Negro poet, James M. Whitfield, born in 1830 and died in 1870, was a barber by trade. Whitfield was born in Boston, then moved to Buffalo, New York; and not too much is known about how he came to write. His first poetic utterances were so favorably received that he quit barbering and took to the public platform; and his poems continue the tradition of Horton:

America, it is to thee,
Thou boasted land of liberty,—
It is to thee that I raise my song,
Thou land of blood, and crime, and wrong.
It is to thee my native land,
From which has issued many a band
To tear the black man from his soil
And force him here to delve and toil
Chained on your blood-bemoistened sod,
Cringing beneath a tyrant's rod . . .

As you see, the fact of separation from the culture of his native land has now sunk home into the Negro's heart; the Negro loves his land, but that land rejects him. Here we can witness the slow emergence of a new type of personality; here is the beginning of insecurity as a way of life; of violence as a daily companion.

The next Negro poet to attract attention in America was a woman, Frances Ellen Harper; living from 1825 to 1911, her life spanned slavery, war, emancipation, and freedom; and when she put her pen to paper her eyes were filled with more scenes of violence than perhaps many of our soldiers saw in the war just ended. In a poem entitled "Bury Me in a Free Land," she says:

Make me a grave where'er you will
In a lowly plain, or a lofty hill;
Make it among the earth's humblest graves,
But not in a land where men are slaves.
I could not rest if around my grave
I heard the steps of a trembling slave;
His shadow above my silent tomb
Would make it a place of fearful gloom.

Truly, you must now know that the word Negro in America means something not racial or biological, but something purely social, something made in the United States. Poems such as the above seem to imply that the eyes of the American Negro were fastened in horror upon something from which he could not turn away. The Negro could not take his eyes off the auction block: he never had a chance to; he could not stop thinking of lynching: he never had a chance to. The Negro writer had no choice in his subject matter; he could not select his experiences. Hence, the monotonous repetition of horror that rolls in verse from one generation to another.

Let us pursue this melancholy tale.

Albery A. Whitman, born 1851 and died 1902, spanning with his life slavery, war, freedom, also spoke a tongue that denied him, belonged to a culture that rejected him, walked upon a soil that mocked him, and lived and labored among men who hated him.

In his poem "The Rape of Florida," he says:

So fared the land where slaves were groaning yet—
Where beauty's eyes must feed the lusts of men!

'Tis as when horrid dreams we half forget,
Would then relate, and still relate again—
Ah! cold abhorrence hesitates my pen!
The heavens were sad, and hearts of men were faint;
Philanthropy implored and wept, but then
The Wrong, unblushing trampled on Restraint,
While feeble Law sat by and uttered no complaint.

In the verse of Whitman we see the beginnings of complexity; he too wrote of wrong, but there was in his rhymes a desire to please. But the split in Negro personality deepened despite the fact that men like Whitman strove to weave color and drama and movement into their poems. A tradition of bitterness has set in; the basic theme is now set, and there is no escape from it. All black lips that now sing pay tribute to the power of oppression. It is true that there was an urge in some black singers to write so that the whites would buy their poems; but in them no less than in others this sense of distance could not be ignored. So, self-consciously, while hiding what they saw and knew to be true, knew to be the real meaning of their lives, some Negro poets deliberately put forth the lighter, the more lyrical, side for *white* consumption.

The most gifted, vivid, and popular black poet to pay tribute to this contradiction was Paul Laurence Dunbar. During his tragically brief career (1872–1906), no sweeter verse than his was written in America:

Ere sleep comes down to soothe the weary eyes,
Which all the day with ceaseless care have sought
The magic gold which from the seeker flies;
Ere dreams put on the gown and cap of thought,
And make the waking world of lies—
Of lies most palpable, uncouth, forlorn,

That say life's full of aches and tears and sighs,—
Oh, how with more than dreams the soul is torn,
Ere sleep comes down to soothe the weary eyes.

Dunbar was the first Negro singer to be really helped by whites; he was fostered by William Dean Howells and his verse was published in the leading periodicals of his time. He labored hard to fill the many commissions that poured in upon him; but through his lyrical songs now and again there broke a sense of the paradox that was his life, as in the following poem:

I know why the caged bird sings, ah me,
When his wing is bruised and his bosom sore,—
When he beats his bars and would be free;
It is not a carol of joy or glee,
But a prayer that he sends from his heart's deep core,
But a plea, that upward to Heaven he flings—
I know why the caged bird sings!

Then there were times when he spoke out what was in his heart:

We smile, but, Oh great Christ, our cries
To thee from tortured souls arise.
We sing, but oh the clay is vile
Beneath our feet, and long the mile;
But let the world dream otherwise,
We wear the mask.

Dunbar wrote many novels and poems which had wide sales. But there was a fatal conflict in him; he drank heavily to drown it, to resolve it, and failed. He tells us but little of what he really felt, but we know that he tried to turn his eyes as much as possible from that vision of horror that had claimed the exclusive attention of so many Negro writers, tried to communicate with his country as a man. Perhaps no other Negro writer ever demanded more of himself than Dunbar did, and that he achieved so much, that he did manage to wring a little unity out of the blatant contradiction that was his life, is truly remarkable.

The black singers who followed Dunbar, however, cared less about what their *white* friends thought and more about what *they* felt, and they resumed the tradition, sensing that the greatest and deepest meaning of their lives lay in it, that all that was truly human in them had to be wrung from its dark and painful depths.

But let us catch up with ourselves. Expression springs out of an environment, and events modify what is written by molding consciousness. From 1761 to 1900, roughly speaking, a kind of unity knit Negro expression together. But, starting with emancipation, many kinds of stratification took place in Negro life; Negroes became separated from Negroes, the rich from the poor, the ignorant from the educated, the city Negro from the country Negro, and so on.

While this stratification was taking place among Negroes, white attitudes gradually hardened and a still further atomization of Negro life took place, creating personality types far below even those that existed in slavery. Around the turn of the century, two tendencies became evident in Negro expression. I'll call the first tendency: The Narcissistic Level, and the second tendency I'll call: The Forms of Things Unknown, which consists of folk utterances, spirituals, blues, work songs, and folklore.

These two main streams of Negro expression—The Narcissistic Level and The Forms of Things Unknown—remained almost distinctly apart until the depression struck our country in 1929, when once again there surged up a tendency toward unity in Negro thought and feeling, though the traditional sense of distance still prevailed. This division in Negro life can be described in psychological as well as in class terms. It can be said there were Negroes who naively accepted what their lives were, lived more or less unthinkingly in their environment, mean as they found it, and sought escape either in religion, migration, alcohol, or in what I've called a sensualization of their sufferings in the form of jazz and blues and folk and work songs.

Then there were those who hoped and felt that they would ultimately be accepted in their native land as free men, and they put forth their claims in a language that their nation had given them. These latter were more or less always middle class in their ideology. But it was among the migratory Negro workers that one found, rejected and ignorant though they were, strangely positive manifestations of expression, original contributions in terms of form and content.

Middle-class Negroes borrowed the forms of the culture which they strove to make their own, but the migratory Negro worker improvised his cultural forms and filled those forms with a content wrung from a bleak and barren environment, an environment that stung, crushed, all but killed him.

But, before I tell of these migratory voices, let me explain what I mean by the Narcissistic Level of expression that prevailed among middle-class Negro writers, say, from 1900 to 1925.

Remember Phyllis Wheatley and how she was at one with her country? After her time that oneness was no longer possible with Negroes; race hate and Jim Crowism would not let them feel it.

But there were some few Negroes who, through luck, diligence, and courage, did rise and make the culture of their nation their own even though that nation still rejected them; and, having made the culture of their nation their own, they hurled pleading words against the deaf ears of white America until the very meaning of their lives came to be in telling how and what the rejection which their country leveled against them made them feel. You remember the Greek legend of Narcissus who was condemned by Nemesis to fall in love with his own reflection which he saw in the water of a fountain? Well, the middle-class Negro writers were condemned by America to stand before a Chinese Wall and wail that they were like other men, that they felt as others felt. It is this relatively static stance of emotion that I call The Narcissistic Level. These Negroes were in every respect the equal of whites; they were valid examples of personality types of Western culture; but they lived in a land where even insane white people were counted above them. They were men whom constant rejection had rendered impacted of feeling, choked of emotion. During the first quarter of this century, these men, Trotter, DuBois, Washington, etc., fought as the Negro had never fought before for equal rights, but they fought in vain. It is true that when their voices reached the ears of many philanthropic whites, they did win a few concessions which helped Negro institutions to exist. But the irony in the efforts of these Negroes was that the gains they won fastened ever tighter around their necks the shackles of Jim Crowism. For example, every new hospital, clinic, and school that was built was a *Negro* hospital, a *Negro* clinic, a *Negro* school! So, though Negroes were slowly rising out of their debased physical conditions, the black ghettos were growing ever larger; instead of racial segregation lessening, it grew, deepened, spread. Today, Jim Crow institutions have fastened themselves organically upon the free soil of the nation and the Black Belt is commonplace.

While this was happening in the upper levels of Negro life, a chronic and grinding poverty set in in the lower depths. Semi-literate black men and women drifted from city to city, ever seeking what was not to be found: jobs, homes, love—a chance to live as free men. . . . Millions swarmed from the plantations to the small towns and cities of the South; and then from the southern towns and cities they flooded the northern industrial centers. Bereft of family life, poverty-stricken, bewildered, they moved restlessly amidst the highest industrial civilization the world has ever known, in it but not of it, unable to respond to the vivid symbols of power of an alien culture that met their eyes at every turn.

Because I feel personally identified with the migrant Negro, his folk songs, his ditties, his wild tales of bad men; and because my own life was forged in the depths in which they live, I'll tell first of the Forms of Things Unknown. Numerically, this formless folk utterance accounts for the great majority of the Negro people in the United States, and it is my conviction that the subject matter of future novels and poems resides in the lives of these nameless millions. There are two pools of this black folk expression: The sacred and the secular. (Let me recall to you quickly that we are now far beyond the world of Phyllis Wheatley; she was an integrated individual, at one with her culture; we are now dealing with people who have lost their individuality, whose reactions are fiercely elemental, whose shattered lives are burdened by impulses they cannot master or control.) It is from the sacred songs of the plantation that we get the pathos of:

Sometimes I feel like a motherless child
Sometimes I feel like a motherless child
Sometimes I feel like a motherless child
A long ways from home . . .
A long ways from home . . .

And then there is the nostalgia for another world, an unappeasable longing to escape a painful life:

Swing low, sweet chariot,
Coming for to carry me home . . .

And here is a paradoxical note of triumphant defeat:

Steal away, steal away, steal away to Jesus,
Steal away, steal away home,
I ain't got long to stay here . . .

And here is militancy disguised in religious imagery:

Joshua fit the battle of Jericho,
Jericho, Jericho,
Joshua fit the battle of Jericho,
And the walls came tumbling down . . .

And tender, timid despair:

Oh, they whipped him up the hill, up the hill,
up the hill
Oh, they whipped him up the hill, up the hill,
up the hill
Oh, they whipped him up the hill, and he never
said a mumbling word,
He just hung down his head, and he cried . . .

Outright rebellion is couched in Biblical symbols; is it not plain that the Negro is a Negro even in his religion, that his consciousness of being a rejected American seeps into his worship, his prayers . . . ?

If I had-a my way,
I'd tear this building down.
Great God, then, if I had-a my way

If I had-a my way, little children,
If I had-a my way,
I'd tear this building down . . .

These authorless utterances sprang spontaneously from the lips of slaves and they remain the single most significant contribution of folk and religious songs to our national culture. It was through the door of religion that the American Negro first walked into the house of Western culture, and it was through religious symbols that he has given voice to his most poignant yearnings. And yet, instead of his songs being mystical or metaphysical, they are simply and directly wish fulfillments, projections of his longings to escape his chains and blows.

And even when the Negro turns from the sacred to the secular, he seems unable to escape the burdens and consciousness of his racial plight that determines all, making him feel that he is a Negro before he is a man. Recognition of wrong comes even in lilting ditties:

We raise the wheat,
They give us the corn;
We bake the bread,
They give us the crust;
We sift the meal,
They give us the husk;
We peel the meat,
They give us the skin;
And that's the way
We skin the pot,
They give us the liquor,
And they say that's good enough for nigger.

We get hints of probable dirty work of slaves against their masters in this humorous ditty which tells of a master who promised freedom to a slave, and it brought about an attempt on the part of the slave to hasten his day of liberation:

Yes, my old master promise me;
But his papers didn't leave me free.
A dose of poison helped him along.
May the Devil preach his funeral song.

Even at the very bottom of Negro life there existed a knowledge of the dual existence they were forced to live; in this work song, a laborer states the problem:

Me and my captain don't agree
But he don't know, 'cause he don't ask me
He don't know, he don't know my mind
When he sees me laughing
Laughing to keep from crying
Got one mind for white folks to see
Another for what I know is me . . .

The impulses that prodded so many millions of southern Negroes to leave the plantations for the cities of the South, and the dissatisfaction that drove so many other millions from the cities of the South to the industrial centers of the North are summed up in the "Backwater Blues" as sung by Bessie Smith:

Then I went an' stood up on some high ol' lonesome hill
I went an' stood up on some high ol' lonesome hill
An' looked down on the house where I used to live
Backwater blues done cause me to pack mah things and go

Backwater blues done cause me to pack mah things and go
Cause mah house fell down an' I cain' live there no mo'

Many of them knew that their hope was hopeless, and it was out of this that the blues was born, the apex of sensual despair. A strange and emotional joy is found in contemplating the blackest aspects of life:

I'm going down to the river, set down on the ground
I'm going down to the river, set down on the ground
If the blues overtake me, I'll jump overboard and drown

And what the psychoanalysts call ambivalence is put forward by illiterate Negroes in terms that would have shocked Dr. Freud:

I'm going to buy me a shotgun long as I am tall
I'm going to buy me a shotgun just as long as I am tall
I'm going to shoot my woman just to see her fall . . .

In "Dink's Blues" we hear a death-wish vented against white people:

I wish to God that east-bound train would wreck
I wish to God that east-bound train would wreck
Kill the engineer, break the fireman's neck . . .

Lower-class Negroes cannot be accused of possessing repressions or inhibitions! Out of the folk songs of the migrant Negro there has come one form of Negro folklore that makes even Negroes blush a little among themselves when it is mentioned. These songs, sung by more adult Negroes than would willingly admit it, sum up the mood of despairing rebellion. They are called *The Dirty Dozens*. Their origin is obscure but their intent is plain and unmistakable. They jeer at life; they leer at what is decent, holy, just, wise, straight, right, and uplifting. I think that it is because, from the Negro's point of view, it is the right, the holy, the just, that crush him in America. I'm sure that we've reached that point in our public life where straight, documentary facts can be presented without someone saying that they are in bad taste. I insist upon presenting *The Dirty Dozens* because they possess a meaning far beyond that of the merely risqué.

But first, picture to yourselves a vast mass of semi-literate people living amidst the most complex, the most highly industrialized, nation on earth, and try to understand these contradictions: The Negro's shattered families lived amidst the most stable families of the land; his broken speech was uttered in the same neighborhoods where white people spoke flawlessly. The Negro had but to turn his eyes from his unpainted wooden shack and he saw the painted homes of whites. Out of this organic contradiction, the Negro hurled his hardest words against the white world in which he lived. He had no family life; well, why worry about that? Was it not the family life of whites above him that was crushing him? These Negroes seemed to have said to themselves: "Well, if what is happening to me is right, then, dammit, anything is right."

The Dirty Dozens extol incest, celebrate homosexuality; even God's ability to create a rational world is naively but scornfully doubted, as in the following ditty:

God made Him an elephant
And He made him stout

But He wasn't satisfied
'Til He made him a snout
And He made his snout
Just as long as a rail
But He wasn't satisfied
'Til He made him a tail
He made his tail
Just to fan the flies
But He wasn't satisfied
'Til He made him some eyes
He made his eyes
Just to look on the grass
But He wasn't satisfied
'Til He made his yes yes yes
He made his yes yes yes
But He didn't get it fixed
But He wasn't satisfied
'Til He made him six
He made him six, Lord,
And He made them well
So you know by that
That the elephant caught hell . . .

This is not atheism; this is beyond atheism; these people do not walk and talk with God; they walk and talk about Him. The seduction of virgins is celebrated with amoral delight:

Why your little sister
  Why she ask me to kiss her
I told her to wait
  'Til she got a little bigger
When she got a little bigger
  She said I could kiss her

You know by that, boys,
That I didn't miss her
Now she's a dirty mistreat
A robber and a cheat
Slip her in the dozens
Her papa is her cousin
And her mama do the Lordy Lord . . .

That white men who claimed that they followed the precepts of Christ should have been guilty of so much cruelty forced some nameless black bard to utter:

Our Father, who art in heaven
White man owe me 'leven, and pay me seven,
Thy kingdom come, thy will be done
And ef I hadn't tuck that, I wouldn't got none.

Do you catch the echoes of Communism here? If you do, you are suffering from an auditory illusion; for that irreverent ditty was written long before Communism was conceived of, long before Karl Marx wrote *Das Kapital*. If there's any Communism in that verse, it is of a divine origin.

A Negro woman exults consciously and publicly in the disorganization of life which America forces her to live:

My floor is dirty and my house ain't never clean
My floor is dirty and my house ain't never clean
Ain't got no husband but I got a dozen married men . . .

Still another woman's knowledge of the sexual prowess of all the men living in her neighborhood reveals a compulsive promiscuity which she unshamedly and lyrically advertises:

There's nineteen men livin' in mah neighborhood
Nineteen men livin' in mah neighborhood
Eighteen of them are fools, an' de other ain' no dog-gone good

Well, what do you want? What can you expect from men and women who have been driven out of life?

But there are times when these torrid moods of meanness are lifted by gifted writers to the level of social and political direction, as in the bitter, fighting lyrics of Warren Cuney, who sums up what Jim Crowism in wartime means to Negroes:

Well, airplanes flying across the land and the sea
Everybody's flying but a Negro like me
Uncle Sam says your place is on the ground
When I fly my airplanes I want no Negroes around
The same thing for the navy when ships go to sea
All they got is a mess-boy's job for me . . .

But what was happening, so to speak, upstairs, when the Negro migrants were venting their spleen against the world? If you remember, we left the Negro middle-class writers standing before the Chinese Wall of America, narcissistically preoccupied with their feelings, saying, "If you prick me, I bleed; if you put fire to me, I burn; I am like you who exclude me. . . ." Perhaps the most graphic and lyrical of these men was W. E. B. DuBois; indeed, one might say that it was with him that the Negro complaint reached almost religious heights of expression. DuBois prays to God in public:

Listen to us, Thy children: our faces dark with doubt are made a mockery in Thy sanctuary. With uplifted hands we front Thy heaven, O God, crying;
We beseech Thee to hear us, good Lord!

And then, vehemently, in Old Testament style:

> **Doth not this justice of hell stink in Thy nostrils, O God? How long shall the mounting flood of innocent blood roar in Thine ears and pound in our hearts for vengeance? Pile the pale frenzy of blood-crazed brutes who do such deeds high on Thine altar, Jehovah, and burn it in hell forever and forever.**
>
> **Forgive us, good Lord! we know not what we say!**

Moods such as these have suffused the many books of DuBois, and where the mood is absent *per se*, we find it projected in terms of history, fiction, verse. Here we see the outright curse of the Negro migrant lifted to a hymn of bitterness; here we see the long, drawn-out moan of the blues turned into a phrase of lament; here we see the brutal cynicism of illiterate Negroes converted into irony; here we watch the jerky lines of *The Dirty Dozens* transmute themselves into the surging rhythms of free verse; here indeed we see Pushkin and Dumas turned into raging, livid demons! Poor Phyllis Wheatley would have burned to a cinder if such searing emotions had ever entered her frail body.

Following DuBois, James Weldon Johnson lifted his voice; listen to Johnson, as conservative a Negro as ever lived in America; but his eyes were riveted upon this:

> *Quick! Chain him to that oak! It will resist*
> *The fire much longer than this slender pine.*
> *Now bring the fuel! Pile it 'round him! Wait!*
> *Pile not so fast or high, or we shall lose*
> *The agony and terror in his face.*
> *And now the torch! Good fuel that! the flames*
> *Already leap head-high. Ha! hear that shriek!*
> *And there's another! wilder than the first.*

Fetch water! Water! Pour a little on
The fire, lest it should burn too fast. Hold so!
Now let it slowly blaze again. See there!
He squirms! He groans! His eyes bulge wildly out,
Searching around in vain appeal for help!

Was it otherwise with other writers? No. You've seen the images of horror that a conservative like James Weldon Johnson evoked. Yet, I, coming from an entirely different social stratum, wove the same vision of horror into another pattern in a poem called "Between the World and Me":

And one morning while in the woods I suddenly
stumbled upon the thing,
Stumbled upon it in a grassy clearing guarded by scaly
oaks and elms.
And the sooty details of the scene rose, thrusting
themselves between the world and me . . .

There was a design of white bones slumbering forgot-
tenly upon a cushion of gray ashes.
There was a charred stump of a sapling pointing a
blunt finger accusingly at the sky.
There were torn tree limbs, tiny veins of burnt leaves,
and a scorched coil of greasy hemp;
A vacant shoe, an empty tie, a ripped shirt, a lonely
hat, and a pair of trousers stiff with black blood.
And upon the trampled grass were buttons, dead
matches, butt-ends of cigars and cigarettes, peanut
shells, a drained gin-flask, and a whore's lipstick;
Scattered traces of tar, restless arrays of feathers, and
the lingering smell of gasoline.
And through the morning air the sun poured yellow
surprise into the eye sockets of a stony skull . . .

And while I stood there my mind was frozen with a
cold pity for the life that was gone.
The ground gripped my feet and my heart was circled
with icy walls of fear—
The sun died in the sky; a night wind muttered in the
grass and fumbled with leaves in the trees; the
woods poured forth the hungry yelping of hounds;
the darkness screamed with thirsty voices; and the
witnesses rose and lived:
The dry bones stirred, rattled, lifted, melting
themselves into my bones.
The gray ashes formed flesh firm and black, entering
into my flesh.
The gin-flask passed from mouth to mouth; cigars
and cigarettes glowed, the whore smeared
the lipstick red upon her lips.
And a thousand faces swirled around me, clamoring
that my life be burned . . .

And then they had me, stripped me, battering my
teeth into my throat till I swallowed my own blood.
My voice was drowned in the roar of their voices,
and my black wet body slipped and rolled in their
hands as they bound me to the sapling.
And my skin clung to the bubbling hot tar, falling
from me in patches,
And the down and the quills of the white feathers
sank into my raw flesh, and I moaned in my agony.
Then my blood was cooled mercifully, cooled by a
baptism of gasoline.
And in a blaze of red I leaped to the sky as pain rose
like water, boiling my limbs.
Panting, begging, I clutched childlike, clutched to the
hot sides of death.

Now I am dry bones and my face a stony skull staring in yellow surprise at the sun . . .

Did ever in history a race of men have for so long a time the same horror before their eyes? I know that for short periods horrors like this have come to men, but they ended at last; I know that in war horror fills the minds of all, but even wars pass. The horrors that confront Negroes stay in peace and war, in winter and summer, night and day.

Futility now enters the heart of the urban Negro; from the teeming city of Chicago Fenton Johnson comes with testimony:

I am tired of work; I am tired of building up somebody else's civilization.
Let us take a rest, M'Lissy Jane.
I will go down to the Last Chance Saloon, drink a gallon or two of gin, shoot a game or two of dice and sleep the rest of the night on one of Mike's barrels . . .

Then again racial bitterness enters:

Throw the children into the river; civilization has given us too many. It is better to die than grow up and find out that you are colored.
Pluck the stars out of the heavens. The stars mark our destiny. The stars marked my destiny.
I am tired of civilization.

And then Claude McKay reaches a white-hot pitch of passion with:

Your door is shut against my tightened face,
And I am sharp as steel with discontent;

But I possess the courage and the grace
To bear my anger proudly and unbent.
The pavement slabs burn loose beneath my feet,
A chafing savage, down the decent street;
A passion rends my vitals as I pass
Where boldly shines your shuttered door of glass.
Oh, I must search for wisdom every hour,
Deep in my wrathful bosom sore and raw,
And find in it the superhuman power
To hold me to the letter of your law!
Oh, I must keep my heart inviolate
Against the potent poison of your hate!

Remember that white faces were hovering in the minds of black men when they wrote those lines; this is their judgment upon you and your world. Are we not a long, long way from the innocence of Phyllis Wheatley? To say that Claude McKay is a rebel is to understate it; his rebellion is a way of life.

Even when Negro poets become sensually lyrical now, they cannot escape the horrible vision of their life in America, as we can see in these lines of Jean Toomer:

O Negro slaves, dark purple ripened plums,
Squeezed, and bursting in the pine-wood air,
Passing, before they strip the old tree bare
One plum was saved for me, one seed becomes
An everlasting song, a singing tree,
Caroling softly souls of slavery
What they were, and what they are to me,
Caroling softly souls of slavery.

Even at the apex of lyrical utterance, color and race form the core of meaning for Countee Cullen, as in "Heritage":

What is Africa to me:
Copper sun or scarlet sea,
Jungle star or jungle track,
Strong bronzed men, or regal black
Women from whose loins I sprang
When the birds of Eden sang?

The conflict between the human needs of the Negro and what is demanded of him by white America reaches a point that all but overwhelms the poet:

All day long and all night through,
One thing only must I do:
Quench my pride, and cool my blood,
Lest I perish in the flood. . . .

No less than a black clergyman, James D. Corrothers, likens the plight of the Negro to that of Christ:

To be a Negro in a day like this
Demands forgiveness. Bruised with blow on blow,
Betrayed, like Him whose woe-dimmed eyes gave
bliss
Still must one succor those who brought one low,
To be a Negro in a day like this.

George Leonard Allen again stresses the Biblical theme in an attempt to awaken compassion by reminding America that she acts like Pilate toward her darker brother:

Lord, 'twas not I that slew my guiltless brother
Without a cause, save that his skin was black!
Not my fierce hate, but that of many another
Stole what man's puny strength cannot give back!

In a bitter, masochistic mood of self-laceration a black poet, Frank Home, tries to see his people and himself through white American eyes:

Little Black Boy
Chased down the street—
"Nigger, nigger, never die
Black face and shiny eye,
Nigger . . . nigger . . . nigger."

A mood of poignant nostalgia makes Arna Bontemps evoke:

The golden days are gone. Why do we wait
So long upon the marble steps, blood
Falling from our open wounds? and why
Do our black faces search the sky?

But despair is not the entire picture. Each new generation of Negro writers lived in an environment that was almost the same until World War I; but that war provided the first real break in this continuity of hopelessness. Out of the restlessness left in the wake of World War I, Soviet Russia rose and sent out her calls to the oppressed. Until that time the American Negro had to depend upon white Americans for a definition of his problem, of his position, had to accept the friendship of white liberals. For three centuries white America told the Negro that nowhere on earth would he be as highly regarded as in America; and the Negro had to fight and plead within the frame of reference of that charitable advice. But suddenly that spell was broken forever. Alien ideologies gripped men's minds and the most receptive minds in our land were those of rejected Negroes. Color consciousness lost some of its edge and was replaced in a large measure by class consciousness; with the rise of an integral working-class movement, a new sense of identification came to the American Negro.

Then, for the first time since Phyllis Wheatley, the Negro began to make a wholehearted commitment to a new world; after wandering for three hundred years, he found a new sense of oneness, a new integration; it was possible once more for him to write out of the shared hopes and aspirations of millions of people. Phyllis Wheatley visited the headquarters of George Washington, the father of our republic; Langston Hughes visited the headquarters of Lenin, the father of the Soviet Republic!

In the work of poets like Davis, Tolson, Hughes, Brown, Walker, Brooks, and Bontemps this new vision was reflected. One of the first lyrical-sounding voices of this new period was that of Langston Hughes; here, in plain images, we get, not complaints and pleas, but statements and demands:

Let America be America again,
Let it be the dream it used to be,
Let it be the pioneer in the plain,
Seeking a home where he himself is free. . . .

Out of a mood of bitter, political anger, he says:

Good morning, Revolution,
You're the very best friend I ever had;
Come on; let's pal around together . . .

Poet Robert E. Hayden imagines the dying testimony of Gabriel, an executed slave, in these lyrical but bitter terms:

I see a thousand
Thousand slaves

Rising up
From forgotten graves
And their wounds drip flame
On slavery's ground,
And their chains shake Dixie

With a thunder sound.
Gabriel, Gabriel
The end is nigh,
What do you wish
Before you die?
That rebellion suckle
The slave-mother's breast
And black men
Never, never rest
Till slavery's pillars
Lie splintered in dust
And slavery's chains
Lie eaten with rust.

Sterling Brown hints at what the Negro would do if the numerical odds were more nearly equal:

They don't come [at us] by ones
They don't come by twos
But they come by tens
They got the judges
They got the lawyers
They got the law
  They don't come by ones
They got the sheriffs
They got the deputies
  They don't come by twos
They got the shotguns

They got the rope
We get the justice
In the end
And they come by tens. . . .

Out of the Deep South, out of Texas, Melvin Tolson lifts his voice higher than that of Martin Dies and says:

Out of the dead-ends of poverty,
Through the wilderness of Superstition,
Across the barricades of Jim Crowism . . .
We advance!
With the peoples of the world . . .
We advance!

Margaret Walker, a Negro girl who started writing at about the age when Phyllis Wheatley began writing, says in images that Phyllis Wheatley could not imagine:

Let a new earth rise. Let another world be born. Let a bloody peace be written in the sky. Let a second generation full of courage issue forth, let a people loving freedom come to growth, let a beauty full of healing and a strength of final clenching be the pulsing in our spirits and our blood. Let the martial songs be written, let dirges disappear. Let a race of men now rise and take control!

Out of this sense of identification with the workers of other lands, I too wrote:

I am black and I have seen black hands
Raised in fists of revolt, side by side with the white
fists of white workers.

And some day—and it is only this which
sustains me—
Some day there shall be millions of them,
On some red day in a burst of fists on a new horizon!

Now, I'm not naive. I know that many of you are shaking your heads and wondering what value there is in writing like that; you may feel that we ought to write like Phyllis Wheatley, Alexander Dumas, or Alexander Pushkin. Well, we simply cannot; our world is not their world. We write out of what life gives us in the form of experience. And there is a value in what we Negro writers say. Is it not clear to you that the American Negro is the only group in our nation that consistently and passionately raises the question of freedom? This is a service to America and to the world. More than this: The voice of the American Negro is rapidly becoming the most representative voice of America and of oppressed people anywhere in the world today.

Let me remind you that during the past twenty-five years the great majority of the human race has undergone *experiences comparable to those which Negroes in* America have undergone for three centuries! These people, Russians, Germans, French, Chinese, Indians, Danes, Spaniards, suddenly heard a voice speaking of their wrongs. From the Argentine, Brazil, Sweden, Norway, England, France, and India have come questions about the American Negro; they want to know how we live; they want our testimony since we live here amidst the greatest pretense of democracy on earth. And we Negroes are answering, straight, honestly.

So, the voice that America rejected is finding a home at last, a home such as was never dreamed of.

But our hope is steeped in a sense of sober tragedy. In the final pages of a book I wrote called *12 Million Black Voices*, I tried to indicate the quality of that hope when I said:

"We black folk, our history and our present being, are a mirror of all the manifold experiences of America. What we want, what we represent, what we endure, is what America *is*. If we black folk perish, America will perish. If America has forgotten her past, then let her look into the mirror of our consciousness and she will see the *living* past living in the present, for our memories go back, through our black folk of today, through the recollections of our black parents, and through tales of slavery told by our black grandparents, to the time when none of us, black or white, lived in this fertile land.

"The differences between black folk and white folk are not blood or color, and the ties that bind us are deeper than those that separate us. The common road of hope which we have all traveled has brought us into a stronger kinship than any words, laws, or legal claims.

"Look at us and know us and you will know yourselves, for *we* are *you*, looking back at you from the dark mirror of our lives!

"What do we black folk want?

"We want what others have, the right to share in the upward march of American life, the only life we remember or have ever known.

"The Lords of the Land say: 'We will not grant this!'

"We answer: 'We ask you to grant us nothing. We are winning our heritage though our toll in suffering is great!'

"The Bosses of the Buildings say: 'Your problem is beyond solution!'

"We answer: 'Our problem is being solved. We are crossing the line you dared us to cross, though we pay in the coin of death!'

"The seasons of the plantation no longer dictate the lives of many of us; hundreds of thousands of us are moving into the sphere of conscious history.

"We are with the new tide. We stand at the crossroads. We watch each new procession. The hot wires carry urgent appeals. Print compels us. Voices are speaking. Men are moving! And we shall be with them. . . ."

I am leaving off my interpretation of the literature of the American Negro at a point which antedates the present by some years. After World War II a list of new names and new themes entered the body of American Negro expression, but not enough time has elapsed for me to subject that new phase of expression to the same kind of analysis that I've used in the foregoing. Not enough perspective exists for me to feel the new trends. Yet the sheer absence of some of the old qualities is enough to allow one to draw some inferences. For example, in the work of Chester Himes, Ralph Ellison, James Baldwin, Ann Petry, Frank Yerby, Gwendolyn Brooks, etc., one finds a sharp loss of lyricism, a drastic reduction of the racial content, a rise in preoccupation with urban themes and subject matter both in the novel and the poem. Why is this?

Again I remind you that an understanding of Negro expression cannot be arrived at without a constant reference to the environment which cradles it. Directly after World War II, the United States and Soviet Russia emerged as the two dominant world powers. This meant a lessening of the influence of the ideology of Marxism in America and a frantic attempt on the part of white Americans to set their racial house somewhat in order in the face of world criticism. America's assumption of world leadership brought her racial problem to the fore in the mind of the world and the resulting shame and self-consciousness on the part of white Americans have resulted in several dramatic alterations in the Negro's relationship to the American scene. The recent decision of the United States Supreme Court to integrate the schools of America on a basis of racial equality is one, but by no means the chief, change that has come over the American outlook. Naturally this effort on the part of the American nation to assimilate the Negro has had its effect upon Negro literary expression.

I've heard some people express the view that they do not like the new literary expression of the Negro as much as they admired the old. This is a sentimental approach. What I've discussed with you in this lecture certainly should have proved that the mode and pitch of Negro literary expression would alter as soon as the attitude of the nation toward the Negro changed.

At the present moment there is no one dominant note in Negro literary expression. As the Negro merges into the main stream of American life, there might result actually a disappearance of Negro literature as such. If that happens, it will mean that those conditions of life that formerly defined what was "Negro" have ceased to exist, and it implies that Negroes are Negroes because they are treated as Negroes. Indeed, I'd say to you here who listen to my words that I could convert any of you into Negroes, in a psychological sense, in a period of six months. That is, I could, by subjecting you to certain restrictions, hatreds, hostilities, etc., make you express yourselves as the American Negro formerly did.

One last thought. . . . As Negro literary expression changes, one feels that American liberal thought has sustained a loss. What, then, was the relation of Negro expression to liberal thought in the United States? The Negro was a kind of conscience to that body of liberal opinion. The liberals were ridden with a sense of guilt, and the Negro's wailing served as something that enabled the liberal to define his relationship to the American scene. Today the relationship between liberals and Negroes is hard to define. Indeed, one feels that the liberals kind of resent the new trend of independence which the Negro exhibits. But this is inevitable; the Negro, as he learns to stand on his own feet and express himself not in purely racial, but human terms, will launch criticism upon his native land which made him feel a sense of estrangement that he never wanted. This new attitude could have a healthy effect upon the culture of the United States. At long last, maybe a merging of Negro expression with American expression will take place. As that process develops and continues, you may watch it, using the few concepts that I've discussed with you. In that case I feel that its human drama will have, perhaps, some meaning for you.

If the expression of the American Negro should take a sharp turn toward strictly racial themes, then you will know by that token that we are suffering our old and ancient agonies at the hands of our white American neighbors. If, however, our expression broadens, assumes the common themes and burdens of literary expression which are the heritage of all men, then by that token you will know that a humane attitude prevails in America towards us. And a gain in humaneness in America is a gain in humaneness for us all. When that day comes, there will exist one more proof of the oneness of man, of the basic unity of human life on this earth.

PART IV

The Miracle of Nationalism in the African Gold Coast

Time: *The middle of the twentieth century.*

Place: *The hot and lush high rain forest of British West Africa.*

Characters: *Black students, black workers, black doctors, black judges, black knights of the British Empire, black merchants, black schoolteachers, black politicians, black mothers, black cooks, black intellectuals, detribalized and disinherited; and a white British colonial Governor, white merchants and businessmen, white British civil servants, white missionaries, white British army officers, and white CID men.*

I've commenced as though I were about to present a drama. But it's not quite that. Yet, in a sense, what I'm about to relate is a phase of the prime, central and historical drama of the twentieth century, the most common and exciting drama that we know. All of us are caught up in its stupendous and complicated unfolding; all of us play some kind of role, passive or active, in it; and yet most of us are totally unaware that we do so.

What I have to tell you shall be in the form of a story, a simple story. That is, the story is simple in outline, but its scope and meaning and content are extremely intricate. What makes this story even more involved than the telling of it is that, though it deals in the main with black people in the faraway depths of Africa's fetid jungles, though it is about life couched in a strange guise, though it's about men Whose skin color and whose shape of nostrils and whose curl of hair and whose accents of speech and whose outlook upon life differ drastically and markedly from yours, this story involves you, you white men of Europe; it is, in an odd sense, *your* story—a tale of yourselves projected in a drama whose setting is fantastic and whose characters are draped in external aspects of life alien to you. As you watch this story unfold and roll toward its unexpected denouement, you will be observing actions whose motives are akin to yours, attitudes mainly derived from your assumptions, decisions whose resolutions partake of your will, and ideals whose emotional coloration reflect values that have long shone in the ardent hearts of Western man. Indeed, I'd go so far as to say that, had you been the personages in this drama, you would undoubtedly have acted more or less as these black men acted. In fact, I'm sure that, had it not been for your historical attitudes and deeds, and the historical attitudes and deeds of your fathers and your fathers' fathers, this story would not have happened.

One swelteringly hot night, in 1948, a group of six black men, each coming stealthily from his home and traveling by a separate, secret route, met at an agreed-upon spot in an African jungle. All six of these men were members of what was then called the United Gold Coast Convention, a nationalist organization composed almost exclusively of the black bourgeoisie, that is, black doctors, black merchants, black lawyers, black businessmen, etc., who resided in an area of British West Africa which Europeans had fondly christened, because of the fabulous booty in gold and slaves that it had yielded them, the "Gold Coast."

The avowed aim of that organization was self-government. Under the justification that it was allowing the Gold Coast people to prepare themselves for eventual nationhood, the British permitted this organization to exist more or less legally, though no one could really tell how long the organization would be tolerated or at what point it would or could be characterized by the British CID (Criminal Investigation Division of Scotland Yard) as Communistic or subversive.

The six men meeting clandestinely in that jungle that night, though members of the organization, were in deep and passionate disagreement with that organization's aims. They were ex-tribal men and they felt that that organization was too snobbish, too British in tone and outlook, too hedged about with property, educational, social, and class qualifications. In short, they felt that it was a kind of exclusive club. Though that organization's membership consisted entirely of *black* men, these six blacks felt that it fostered values, attitudes, and standards alien and offensive to their hearts, that is, *British* values of extreme individualism, of invidious class and social distinctions, of divisive Anglo-Saxon manners that facilitated British tactics of divide and rule. They resented being told from the *outside* what was "good" for them; they felt outraged at the thought of someone above them monitoring the pace and pitch of their social, economic, and political progress. They wanted the right to choose what they felt they needed most and they were convinced that their wisdom was better for their people than the cold, dry, abstract notions of professors in British universities. These men knew that the Western world considered those aspects of the tribal life of their country that most resembled Western mores as "good" and those aspects that differed from Western mores as "bad."

Though these men wore Western clothes, they had not learned—and did not wish to learn—to look down in disfavor upon the naked, ignorant tribal masses that comprised their racial, cultural, and blood kin. They were of the conviction that the struggle to free their country from alien rule should involve the whole population—every man, woman, and child in it regardless of religious, family, or class loyalties—and not just the black, British-educated elite. These six black men were, therefore, as much opposed to the rich British blacks as they were to the rich British whites. They wanted freedom, their own flag flying over their ancestral homeland, the right to restore the ancient names of their land, their towns, their rivers. In short, they wanted the right to control their total destiny, and they wanted that right for more than just a few of their kind who had been hand-picked by Britishers actuated by racial, religious, and imperialistic motives. To be sure, these six blacks had read attentively their John Stuart Mill, their John Locke; but there was something in their hearts that made them detached from, and suspicious of, the preachments and postulates of those British prophets of freedom and democracy.

So the gathering together that night of these six men in secret constituted an act of treason not only toward the British, but toward a decisive section of their own people, the best qualified and wisest of their own leaders. What did the six men want? They were striving for a total transformation and redemption of the situation in which they found themselves. They were politicians, these men, but their policies, because of the situation in which they found themselves and because of their peculiar outlook upon life, bordered upon the intensity of the religious.

No record was kept of that meeting that night in that jungle, but, since I've talked to all of the men involved and feel I know them, I think I can paraphrase what they said. Will you allow me to state their case, using my memory and imagination to put words in their mouths?

Black man number one: "I want no freedom based upon the assumptions of the British. Such a freedom simply means exchanging a set of white masters for a set of black masters. If I'm against British rule, then I'm against the rule of her stooges."

Black man number two: "All day and all night they talk to us about 'sound and solid development, sound and solid education.' All right. The British, in 104 years, provided an abortive sort of education for less than 10 per cent of our people; that is, less than 10 per cent of our population received an elementary and badly taught knowledge of reading, writing, and arithmetic. Now, if that British educational timetable were followed by the black bourgeois elite when it came to power, it would take one thousand years to make our society partially literate. I say to hell with John Stuart Mill and John Locke. Let's make our own philosophy, based upon our own needs.

"Who says that we black men must duplicate and ape the development of the white man? Aren't we in the position of studying the white man's mistakes, taking advantage of them, and making even faster progress than he made? To imitate the white man means that we are still slaves in our hearts. I say, let us be free; and freedom means mapping out our own road for ourselves, making our own mistakes and being responsible for them."

Black man number three: "Since more than 90 per cent of our people are illiterate, it cannot be said that Britain has any loyal masses in the Gold Coast. Why, then, is she here? She wants the bauxite, the gold, the timber, the manganese, the diamonds. I say, let's so organize our people and so pool these raw materials that we can bargain them for what we need most from the outer world. Why in hell should white men come in here and take our raw materials at prices that *they set*, and then sell us imported European goods at prices that *they determine*?"

Black man number four: "How are we going to organize our people? As the European Socialist organizers organized theirs? Or as the Russian Communists organized and trained their people for revolution? Obviously not. We have practically no industrial proletariat and, hence, Marxist ideology is, in the long run, of little or no interest to us. I say let us organize our people on the basis of a struggle for national freedom and of their being proud of their ancestor-worshiping traditions. Now, gentlemen, I realize that we do not believe in such mumbo jumbo, and all the childish rituals that such traditions imply. But we have no other basis upon which to make a call for unity. So we must say to our people: 'Let's heave out the British and save our culture and traditions.' But we, we who have been educated in the West, know well that the moment we start organizing our people to defend and protect their ancient traditions, those traditions must of necessity begin to weaken, will be destroyed. And that is exactly what we want. So let us do two things at once: Organize the tribes and pit them in struggle against the British, and, in organizing our tribes to do that job, we launch them toward taking the first step toward a secular life, toward a new outlook."

Black man number five: "I agree. We are *outsiders* in our own land. So let us stand *outside* of the tribal life, in which we do not believe, and organize it. That means that, in order to go forward, we must go backward a step or two. We must all, from this night forward, doff our Western clothes and wear the clothes of our tribes. We must do this in order to win the confidence and allegiance of the masses. But we must go further than that; we must cut off the avenue of retreat to the past so that our people will *never* go back, *can* never go back. Though dressed in tribal clothes, we must always use the most modern methods in organizing. We are going to latch our tribal people directly onto the techniques of the twentieth century. We're going to *change* our people!"

Black man number six: "We need really fear no competition from outsiders, from potential rivals, such as Communists. During the last fifty years there has not come from Russia one volume dealing with the manner and techniques of organizing tribal men. So let us make our main slogan: SELF-GOVERNMENT NOW! In that way, no one can top our appeal to our people. One other thing. We must have unity. We must have an iron discipline. He who breaks the unity of our ranks will have to be tossed beyond the pale. The basis for that is already in our tribal life. It is not only a political party that we must organize; it is a brotherhood. We must share and share alike in all things. So tight must our unity be that no enemy can sneak into our ranks. The whole might of Britain cannot break a political unity based upon tribal brotherhood and cemented in blood loyalty."

That must have been how much of the discussion went. These men were desperately angry and serious. The hot emotions that bubbled in their hearts bordered upon violence, made them tense and anxious. Their impulses were turgid and blind. Yet, despite their fury, their manner was controlled, calm. These men were spiritually homeless and they were ardently seeking a home for their hearts.

But there were no fetish priests present. The traditional big black pot with a roaring fire beneath it, the kind of pot which white Westerners like to imagine that missionaries are parboiled in, was absent from that jungle meeting. These black men did not even believe in spirits; indeed, they didn't even lend credence to what is popularly called the "Other World." The truth is that these six desperate black men were all educated products of Western universities; upon all of them had been conferred degrees in law, literature, and political science from the universities of France, England, and America. Why, then, were they angry? Why were they meeting secretly in the dead of the night in a jungle where the only sounds were the muted cries of wild beasts?

These men were meeting to plot what they felt to be the freedom of their country, their nation. What? What "nation"? What "country"? When were there ever nations in Black Africa? History dimly tells us that maybe there existed some few Sudanic black kingdoms some hundreds of years ago, but surely no black nations in the modern sense of that term existed in Africa in historically recent times. Then what did these six black men mean by the "freedom of their country," their "nation"?

You can see that, from the outset, this simple story takes on historical, cultural, and psychological complexities and obscurities. From where did these six black men ever get the notion of building something that had never existed before in Africa? Were they irrational? Were they dreaming? Or were they merely wishing? It was infinitely more recondite than that. But, even so, did not their sanguine desire for nationhood clash mockingly with the impersonal, indifferent jungle density that lay all about them? Was not there something ironically incongruous in their yearning to belong to a modern nation when their black brothers and sisters, millions upon millions of them, lay sleeping a sleep that was sounder than that sleep of which dreams form the mysterious curtain?—a sleep of ancestor-worshiping religion which made their invisible fathers, long dead, more real and more powerful than the earth upon which they walked—that earth which they tilled—that earth that sustained them from day to day? How foolhardy were these six men, lonely and glutted with bitter pride, to dare even to think of pitting themselves against the mental crystallizations of thousands of years! Who were their friends? Surely not the British, not the Western businessmen, not the Protestant or Catholic missionaries. And who were their allies? Surely not the Communists, for the Communists had long ago adamantly decreed that there had to exist an industrial proletariat to lead the revolution. Who understood them? The sociologists? If so, I've yet to read an account from them of how these men really feel. The psychoanalysts? Vaguely, perhaps; but surely not in terms of any concreteness that would serve to make their turbulent state of mind sympathetically known. What audacity did these six black men have to think of challenging the deep-rooted traditions which even white missionaries and white social scientists of the Western world had failed to change or modify during long centuries of effort? Don Quixote was a sane and balanced man compared to these six black revolutionaries!

But, stop and think a moment. Their dreaming and plotting for the "freedom of their country" flew into the face of even sterner realities than the religion of their people. These men lived in the Gold Coast, an area about the size of England; it was administered by a much-vaunted British civil service behind which, protecting it, was the ever-present threat of force represented by British district commissioners, soldiers, police, etc. And, beyond this show of force, lurked the British navy and army, which could, upon the whim of a moment's notice, change the government or suspend the constitution. The stealthy British CID was omnipresent, smelling out the least vestiges of subversion.

How in the name of common sense, then, could these six black men, unarmed and penniless, even think of establishing a nation of their own in the teeth of British opposition and the stagnant traditions of their own people? What an absurdity! Were they not like unto children? One laughed at men like that. Or one pitied them. They would never succeed. Their situation was more than hopeless. Hadn't they better come to terms with their people, quell their hot passions, obey the wisdom of the British and live peaceful, useful, good, sound lives? Why attempt the impossible? Oughtn't they progress slowly, soundly, according to the way in which the Western world had progressed? Oughtn't they to think of taking decades to build a nation, yea, centuries even?

Yes, these men knew all of these cogent arguments, but they had long ago firmly decided that they could no longer wait. They were being prompted and spurred by elements, strange and compounded, that lay deep in their own personalities. They were hungering for something that had not come into reality and they had gotten the impulse of that hunger from the white men who had ruled them, from the white missionaries, the white military, the white mercenary—the three white groups which the Asians and Africans call the three M's of imperialism. These six men had been swept out of the orbit of influence of their tribal life and into the sphere, no matter how loosely, of the Western world. At long last the colonizing efforts of your forefathers were bearing their strange fruit. Hence, these men, though black, were not really, in a strict sense of the word, traditional Africans at all. They were black and they lived in Africa; but, at heart, they were really more akin to Europe than to Africa. Their outlook upon the world and their feel of life had been toned by Western values.

If we are prepared to understand how Westernized these six black men were—and their Westernization would have to differ profoundly from yours, for they had become Westernized under corrosive conditions of partial servitude—then we are ready to understand something else about them that is even more surprising.

These men were caught in a psychological trap; they were living in a situation in which they did not really belong. They had been plucked by the hand of the white man out of their tribal societies, educated in Western institutions, and then thrown back into the jungle to sink or swim. They knew the West from the *outside*; and now they saw and felt their own society from the *outside*. They shared a third but not quite yet clearly defined point of view.

Living the daily life of the tribe and with their heads filled with Western values, these men saw the Gold Coast in what light? To understand how they saw life, you must open your minds and imagination. Though the guns of the British navy and the tanks of the British army were pitted against their aspirations, and though the stagnant traditions of their people loomed as an almost insuperable barrier to the realization of their demands, these men, from the angle of vision afforded by their unique position, saw something in the structure of the society of the Gold Coast colony that made the task that they had in mind much easier and simpler than you would suppose.

True, they knew that they could not face the invincible might of the British army, navy, and air force and win. That was out of the question. And they knew well that the ancient traditions of their people were strong and deeply entrenched. But these men, as I have said, were Westernized. THEY HAD ANALYZED THE RELATION OF BRITAIN TO THEIR ANCESTRAL HOMELAND. They knew exactly where Britain was strong and where she was weak, how British minds worked and what British values were. They knew how to distinguish between what the British said and what they really meant; standing *outside* of Britain, they knew the sharp difference between British professions of idealism and British behavior. They had long grown used to hearing the British say one thing and do the opposite. They knew, at bottom, that the British respected only strength, would react, in the main, only to a *fait accompli*. They were no fools, these black men; they were hard, tough; and they were willing to sacrifice their very lives to test the validity of the reality that they had discovered through Western instrumentalities of thought.

As we know, the population of the colony was more than 90 per cent illiterate. In the urban parts of the colony, due to Western influence, there had set in a deep and chronic disorganization of family tribal life, and the British, who had wrought this atomization of family life, seemed happily ignorant of it. Hence, there existed large masses of tribal individuals who owed no deep allegiances to anybody or anything—masses that were free to be organized—masses that constituted an ironic British gift to the black national revolutionary. And the traditional tribal structure, though intact as a functioning frame of emotional reference from day to day, had been dealt a mortal blow by the religious, mercantile, and military interests of the West. In sum, a kind of void, emotional and psychological in nature, existed in the social structure, and only a few Africans even, seemed aware of it.

But, ah, you may say, you are overlooking something of vital importance. Britain is strong in Africa because of the work, sacrificial and dedicated, of her many missionaries. Christianity has friends among the masses of Africans.

Well, maybe yes and maybe no. Let's take a quick and close look and see how Christian values resided in the tribal heart. The first thing to be noticed is that the very essence of the African drive for nationalism stemmed from the influence of Christianity itself! Had the missionary not gone meddling in Africa, the mores of the millions of blacks would have remained intact. What the missionary failed to do was replace effectively what he had torn out of the African heart. That void that he had created could be felt in all of its terrible intensity only by the African who endured it, and it was that African who was now moving resolutely toward setting his emotional house in order.

Before the coming of the missionary, the African's tribal life had been wholly religious; the introduction of Christianity had reduced the volume, if I may be permitted to put it that way, of religion, not increased it. Hence, the African's contact with Christianity had freed him for action. But what kind of action? That was the question. So these black Christian friends of Britain were filled with ambivalence; they felt that they had been seduced by Britain and then abandoned by her, and now they hated her as much as they loved her.

The white missionaries, the white military, and the white mercenaries, because of racial antipathies, kept apart from the natives, refusing to live or mingle with them on a basis of social equality. And the few educated blacks who collaborated with the British also lived aloof from their own black brothers. The white British civil service, in which a few qualified blacks participated, also quarantined itself from the native population. Thus, upon the most casual inspection, more than 90 per cent of the native population lived remote from the British. Psychologically, Britain existed somewhere on Mars as far as the native Gold Coaster was concerned. Britain was an image, dim and misty, or completely nonexistent, in their minds. Even to say that 90 per cent of the population was loyal or disloyal to Britain was to talk in terms of unrealities. The truth is that the masses of the Gold Coast people didn't feel anything for or against Britain; they lived, labored, procreated, and died. This stagnant state of affairs was called *Pax Britannica*, and it had been most carefully, deliberately, and profitably arranged.

Why was Britain, then, in the Gold Coast at all, since her relationship to the bulk of the population was so tenuous and remote? I'll answer that question, though I know that my answer will make many of you bristle. And I'll tell you what those six black revolutionaries thought and felt about why Britain was there. The absolute consensus of attitude of the black life in the Gold Coast, Left and Right, Christian and pagan, insurgent and conservative, was that Britain was there to get what she could of the natural resources of the colony. These six black men did not contemplate this bald and cynical fact with any degree of hate or bitterness; the awful thing was that they were calm about it; it seemed natural to them that Britain should do this, and a British education had enabled them to arrive at this negative interpretation of Britain's role. Were these black men, then, aware of any contradiction in Britain's attitude toward them? They were. One African explained his bafflement about the British by saying:

"They send us to universities and urge us to study, but the moment they grant us a degree, they become afraid of us."

Another young African expressed himself as follows:

"They continuously stress that we become qualified, but when we become qualified, they tell us that they like the uneducated native better, that the naked tribal man is noble and unspoiled."

But why had Britain bothered to educate a few Africans in the Gold Coast at all? Should not these blacks have felt grateful for that British effort? Strangely, they felt no such thing. They had intuitively grasped that there was something odd about the desire of the British missionary to remold their minds into the patterns of white men's minds.

The missionaries had explained that their preoccupation with the native was prompted by "love," and the African, living a deeply communal existence, had never been able to fathom that aloof, nervous, and condescending "love." They sensed that it was a self-centered concentration of the white man upon himself rather than upon them that caused him to propound his doctrines. In short, they felt a kind of psychological selfishness and guilt in the white man. Now, you can be sure that the British felt no such selfishness or guilt, but I'm only informing you what the blacks felt about it, and how they felt is the decisive thing here. You're entitled to your view and the blacks are certainly entitled to theirs.

The first step, therefore, that these six black men resolved to take was to deny to Britain the right to take the raw materials from the colony. A tall order, that, for six black penniless men to execute. Yet, a further analysis of the relation of Britain to the Gold Coast quickly revealed that, though that task was difficult and improbable, it was not at all impossible. These six black then knew their Marxism, but it is important to remember that they were not really Marxists. They handled Marxist thought self-consciously, standing *outside* of it, so to speak; they used it as an instrumentality to analyze reality, to make it meaningful, manageable. (But the moment they felt that that Marxist thought was no longer useful, the time when it no longer applied to their problems, they could drop it. Marxist ideology was a tool to them, a tool to be used and then cast aside. Need I remind you again that these men were *free* in their hearts? By enslaving them, Britain had liberated them. These men did not regard any system of ideas as creeds in which one had to believe; ideas were weapons, techniques. Ah, you British Prime Ministers, do you think you are masters of reality, of men? You must need have such confidence, or your empire building could not have been done. But life is more complicated than even a British Prime Minister thinks! You set out to civilize men and you produced personality types never hinted at even in your nightmares.) The Achilles' heel of Britain in the Gold Coast was, according to the analysis of these black nationalists, economic, and, if they could only somehow bruise that economic heel, half of their battle would be won.

Oh, do you suspect the cunning hand of Moscow here? If you do, you only confirm that your conditioning and reactions are traditional, popular, and natural. When the British—to anticipate my story a bit—heard of what these six black men proposed to do, they sent in their CID spies to rout out all the Red cells that could be found. For long months the CID searched, questioned, censored the mails, imposed curfews, and probed, but not a single Red cell did it discover.

But how could these six black men paralyze the economic life of the Gold Coast and deny to Britain the raw materials that she wanted? Well, again, a most casual analysis of the relation of the British to the native revealed fatal weak spots. The only good roads that existed in the colony ran from the mines and timber mills to the seaports, and there were but few of them. And the actual number of loyal, educated blacks in the colony was some few score. In the last analysis, the relation of Britain to the Gold Coast depended upon the functioning loyalty of these few score. It was as delicate as that. Suppose, then, that those few score black bourgeois men were discredited, were driven from their positions of influence and favor, what would happen? The answer was so simple as to be startling. The British would be compelled to depend upon those tough-minded revolutionary blacks, whether they liked them or not, who had organized and thus had control of the native masses. So the strategy was obvious: Knock out the few educated bourgeois blacks who were loyal to the white British administrators, and those administrators would then be faced with a mass of four and a half million tribal blacks many of whom could not even speak English and whose loyalty was more to their dead fathers than to the power of Britain. The British would then be faced with a choice: They would either have to deal with the new spokesmen of these four and a half million tribal-minded men, or shoot their spokesmen and then rule the black masses by sheer naked force.

But can bombs produce cocoa? Can machine guns cut timber? Can bayonets dig the gold out of the mines? Can tanks unearth the bauxite? The answer to these questions was the crux of what those six black men had to decide that night in the jungle, and they decided that Britain badly, desperately, needed the gold, the timber, the bauxite. They guessed right. For, when the chips were down, the British said: "Let's talk business." The British turned their backs upon poor Jesus Christ hanging there upon the Cross and took out their fountain pens and sat down at tables with the black revolutionary leaders and began to add, divide, subtract, and multiply.

Now I come to an odd part of my story. Those six sweating black men in that jungle, discussing and planning and plotting the freedom of a nation that did not exist, resolved to bind themselves together; they agreed to call themselves: *The Secret Circle.** Then they swore fetish, a solemn oath on the blood of their ancestors to avoid women, alcohol, and all pleasure until their "country" was free and the Union Jack no longer flew over their land. They swore fetish to stick together.

What? Fetish? Ah, you will say: "These black men were not as Western as you claimed." Yes, they swore fetish. Well, why not? They were scared of the British. They were scared of their own people—their brothers and sisters who would

---

* In *Black Power* (Harper & Brothers, New York: 1954), in which the author rendered an account of the nationalistic revolution in the Gold Coast, all mention or description of this highly interesting and indigenous African political cell was deliberately withheld for fear that the politically reactionary or ideologically immature would confuse it with Russian Communism and call for the suppression of the African's first modern bid for freedom. R. W.

not understand what they were trying to do. And, above all, they were scared of one another. Suppose one of their number informed the British of what they were planning? All of them would either be killed or imprisoned. Hence, though Westernized, these men swore a blood oath to stick together, not to betray one another. We now come to a twilight zone in my story, a zone that will make the reality here more complicated still. I have contended that these men were Westernized. They were. But they lived amidst tribal conditions of life and they reacted to ancestor-worshiping values each day. Thus their world was compounded half of Europe and half of Africa. When they desired to see reality in terms of its external and objective aspects, they thought and felt Western; when they had to deal with their own emotions, they felt and thought African. They lived in two worlds. BUT THEY DIDN'T REALLY AND DEEPLY BELIEVE IN EITHER OF THOSE WORLDS. THE WORLD THAT THEY REALLY WANTED, THE WORLD THAT WOULD BE THE HOME OF THEIR HEARTS, HAD NOT YET COME INTO BEING. So, while standing *outside* of both worlds, so to speak, they were manipulating aspects of both worlds to create the one and single world that they really wanted.

Now I know that you've heard that, when you educate an African, he talks like a European but feels like an African still. White racists contend that a Western education with an African goes only skin deep. All of this is much too simple. The African, when educated in the West, is really neither European nor African. The truth is that he has yet to make himself into what he is to be. So there is really nothing so astonishing about our six black men swearing a blood oath to be loyal to one another; it is no more astonishing than when Western white men cross themselves just before they send a bombing mission to seize the Suez Canal, or when the President of the United States gets on his knees and prays to God just before he issues the order to drop the atom bomb on Hiroshima.

Both the African and the white Westerner are partly rational and partly irrational: that is, all men are somewhat infantile. The other man's God is our devil, and our God is usually his devil. What makes other men seem outlandish to us is our lack of imagination. We all, both black and white, both Easterners and Westerners, have our blind spots. Conditions of life shape our attitudes and give us our values.

This incongruity, this mixing of tribal and Western values, runs like a red thread through the whole story I'm to tell you. Watch this curious intertwining of tradition with modernity; study these Western blacks dealing self-consciously with their tribal religions; contemplate polygamy blending with Puritanism; marvel at the sprouting of socialist thought in a jungle where no working-class ideology existed to support it; try to grasp this strange transition of politics turning into a passion whose intensity partook of the religious.

My story of Gold Coast nationalism can now run swiftly, for I'm reasonably sure that you sense or feel the substratum of emotion, idealism, and self-vindication out of which this nationalism was forged. In most discussions of movements of this sort, you'll hear descriptions of constitutions, of the principles of democracy, etc. In short, you'll hear Westerners, who feel that only their assumptions are valid for all people, at all times, and everywhere, tell you how the lower orders of mankind are gradually beginning to resemble them. In contrast to that approach, I emphasize the primal impulses that give birth to such movements toward freedom. I'm telling this story, if you don't mind, from the black man's point of view.

One of the men who comprised *The Secret Circle* was named Nkrumah. Educated both in Britain and America, he had been sent for by the heads of the United Gold Coast Convention to act as secretary, and it was he who objected most strongly to the snobbish and reactionary leanings of the educated black elite. Resolved now upon a course of bold action to organize the energies of the entire population, Nkrumah launched a drive to broaden the basis of the United Gold Coast Convention. Nkrumah became the leader of *The Secret Circle*. How did that happen? Did he declare himself as leader and impose himself upon them? No. His followers declared him leader. Naturally, he was qualified for this role by his superb organizing and speaking abilities; but, by his colleagues fastening their hopes upon him, he was lifted to the position of almost a deity. Listen carefully to what I'm explaining and perhaps you'll get some insight into the tendencies toward, and origins of, authoritarian or dictatorship governments. The concrete nature of the situation throws up such phenomena. The "cult of the personality" was not invented in Moscow. The longing for someone to be The Leader stems from the very nature of the human material involved. We can say that Nkrumah and his talent for leadership were captured by his followers. He could not say yes or no. These masses needed someone upon whom they could project their hopes, and Nkrumah was chosen. There came moments when, had he refused to act, they would have killed him. Do you recall the story of the Dying God? Gods must serve men, or they are killed.

Nkrumah's labor to strengthen the popular basis of the United Gold Coast Convention coincided with the spontaneous efforts of a subchief (of a tiny state called Ga) to lower the price of imported goods. Early in 1948 a colony-wide boycott was launched against foreign merchants. Now, let me explain that the boycott against foreign merchants and the efforts of Nkrumah were not allied. They were independent ventures, but both were heading in the same direction. This is not going to be the last time that I shall call your attention to spontaneous factors leaping up from the life of the Gold Coast natives and coinciding with the leadership of Nkrumah. More than anything else, these spontaneous features of support proved to *The Secret Circle* that they were headed in the right direction, that their analysis of Gold Coast reality was correct. One had only to give a determined push against the structure of political and economic rule of the British and that rule went toppling.

The boycott was effective and, within one month, the European business firms were on their knees. The members of the Government and the heads of European business firms met and pledged an immediate reduction in the retail prices of imported goods. But, during the days that followed, when the populace went shopping in the stores that sold imported goods and naively expected to find a reduction in retail prices, they found the old prices intact. A mounting anger swept the colony. Spontaneous demonstrations flared against the firms selling European goods. In the afternoon of February 28, 1948, a delegation of ex-servicemen, chanting slogans and waving banners, marched on the Governor's castle in Christianborg to present their grievances. The police ordered the demonstrators to disperse and they refused. The police opened fire and killed three black veterans of British campaigns in India and Burma. The news of this killing spread, and an infuriated populace began to loot the foreign firms. Arson and street fighting ensued and, during the following days, violence gripped the southern half of the colony. Twenty-nine people were killed and about two hundred and thirty-seven were injured.

From this it seems that the analysis of the reality of the Gold Coast made by *The Secret Circle* was sound. They had not discussed democracy; they had not talked of trial by jury; they had not debated the merits of free speech. They had assumed that they and their people were being cheated, that the whole of their lives had been caught in an economic trap which allowed the British to buy from them at low prices and sell to them at high prices! And the moment the finger of *The Secret Circle* touched that sore spot, an explosion resulted.

And what did the British think of all this? It was all a plot sponsored by the men in Moscow, of course. Surely the nobility of their intentions could not set off reactions of hate and violence of that magnitude. Therefore, find the Red culprit! They, the British, were doing good, saving the heathen, uplifting fallen humanity, etc. So find the devils who were meddling with their civilizing mission!

The Governor declared a state of emergency. A curfew was imposed. The leaders of the United Gold Coast Convention sent cables to London petitioning the British Colonial Secretary to create a commission of inquiry to study the underlying causes of the disorders; they also demanded an interim government. The Governor countered this move by arresting the leaders of the United Gold Coast Convention and banishing them to the barren Northern Territories where they were incarcerated separately for fear that they would meet and plot. But the British had never really understood the mentality of the people they were governing; the black leaders immediately called upon the loyalty of their black guards and established instant communication with one another and their followers. The tribal brotherhood forged by *The Secret Circle* was proving too much for the British. Another government, as yet unrecognized and invisible, had come to exist in the Gold Coast and the British were oblivious of its reality and power. Yet they were alarmed, and feared that the local black soldiers and police were not loyal, so they imported troops from Nigeria.

As a result of the appeals made by the new revolutionary leadership, the core of which was *The Secret Circle*, the British Colonial Secretary in London appointed a commission to investigate the causes of the sudden flare-up in violence and to recommend constructive measures. The commission was named after its chairman, Aiken Watson, and it took testimony in April of 1948; the arrested leaders were released so that they could give evidence. In June of that year the commission issued a report that declared the old constitution outmoded, urged a new constitution embodying the aspirations of the people, and endorsed a ministerial type of government patterned on those obtaining in the dominions. Thus, the commission confirmed the diagnosis of Gold Coast reality that had been made by *The Secret Circle*.

But, when the Governor, in December 1948, appointed a constitutional committee of forty Africans under the chairmanship of a famous black jurist, the now Sir Henley Coussey, apprehension set in. The constitutional committee was composed entirely of upper-class chiefs and lawyers, and the younger nationalist elements of the population were completely ignored. The pattern of British class snobbery that *The Secret Circle* so loathed was about to be saddled upon them again in a new manner. Nkrumah's immediate following urged him to leave the United Gold Coast Convention and set up a rival organization that would embody the real aims and feelings of the masses. But Nkrumah hesitated. He did not wish to split the unity of the people.

When the constitutional committee began its work on the twentieth of January 1949, trade unionists, students, the women traders of the streets, and the nationalist elements launched a vehement protest against the exclusion of their representatives. Nkrumah hastily organized a committee of youths, and sent a team of young men touring the country to raise three demands: (1) universal adult suffrage; (2) a fully elected legislature with a fully representative cabinet; and (3) collective ministerial responsibility.

The fat was in the fire. Naturally these demands were beyond the aims of the black bourgeois leaders of the United Gold Coast Convention. And Nkrumah had been pushed by his followers to take this extreme step. He had had either to take it or forfeit his leadership; though the leader, he was really a kind of captive, a prisoner of the hopes and passions of his people. This is an important point to remember, for all else in this story—and its aftermath has yet to be enacted—rests upon it or will be influenced by it. Politics in these non-Western societies proceeds in a manner quite unknown to us where wages, parties, newspapers, printing, plumbing, and public opinion shape the deeds of men.

The rich black doctors, lawyers, and politicians reacted with fury, as was to be expected. What was this man, Nkrumah, doing? The naked ignorant masses had no part in politics and government. The right to vote, they argued, ought to be conditioned by how much money or property you had, for money and property indicated how much you knew, how dependable and responsible you were. Hadn't John Stuart Mill and John Locke said so? And was not England great as proof of what Mill and Locke had said? Who would dare gainsay the august wisdom of the savants of the mighty British? A tramp like Nkrumah and his wild-eyed boys of the streets of the disorganized harbor towns? How absurd! But they failed to take action against Nkrumah in time, for they were convinced that, if they only talked to him in a fatherly manner, he would change. These rich and sedate blacks were the psychological prisoners of their assumptions; they felt that even the sun agreed that their ideas were the only good and valid ones. They enjoined Nkrumah to stop his agitating, and Nkrumah, deciding to cast his lot with his people, countered by going even further into radical departures. In his newspaper, *The Accra Evening News*, which had been launched in September 1948, he vehemently demanded a democratic constitution. The rich blacks reaffirmed their disdain for the masses. The differences could not be bridged. Nkrumah, urged by his supporters, resigned from the United

Gold Coast Convention and launched and announced, in August 1949, the Convention People's Party and stated his intention of staging "Positive Action" based on non-violence—a political stroke that fitted the mood of the country.

It was a gesture that called for tribal unity, brotherhood, sacrifice, and a rebirth of the ancient sense of the people's continuity of being in its traditional form. But, at the same time, Nkrumah announced the following modern socialistic aims: Housing, technical education, road building, health measures to reduce infantile mortality, the liberation of women from traditional fetters, the building of co-operatives, and a campaign of mass education to wipe out illiteracy. A mixture, eh? It was. The tribal traditions were emphasized at the very moment when they were being organized toward goals that would eventually nullify them! No wonder the British and the rich blacks were dizzy with bewilderment. The ancient national dress of the Gold Coast, togas draped about the body in Roman style, was worn with a new pride now in every village and street of the country. And yet the methods of urging the population to struggle for national freedom and socialism were couched in terms of fleets of trucks with loudspeakers, brass bands, pamphlets, and mass meetings where oxen were sacrificially slain to appease the spirits of the dead ancestors! The chiefs, under their brilliant umbrellas, dribbled palm wine and gin upon the earth as they recited libations to the departed in the name of socialism! Men with six wives came forward and saluted and endorsed a social order that would reduce the number of their wives to only one! (Yet these men had no intention of giving up their many wives.) Women, hitherto regarded as chattels, came out of their compound kitchens and danced and sang in the streets. The Gold Coast African greeted the dawn of the twentieth century in his community by pounding his tom-toms with wild frenzy.

Disorder? Irrationality? Foolishness? The antics of children? No wonder the British recoiled with consternation, and no wonder the rich black nationalists sided with the British in sheer horror and fear. But let us take a closer look at this disorder, this irrationality, this foolishness, these antics of children. *What else could have happened but what did happen?*

In terms of Western assumptions, there existed no foundations for classical democracy in the Gold Coast; that is, if one defined democracy only and merely as a voting choir of literate property owners who believed that there was only one God, only one Jesus, and only one Holy Ghost. That, in all honesty, has to be admitted. But, in 104 years of British rule, and during a stretch of historic time dating back to the fifteenth century, France, Denmark, Sweden, Germany, and Portugal had held sway over the people of the Gold Coast and had made no effort to establish any such foundations for democracy. Hence, the easiest criticism to hurl today at the inhabitants of the Gold Coast is: "You are not ready for self-government!" And the Gold Coaster can reply: "Whether we are ready or not, in accordance with your notions, is not important. We're acting." And that is exactly what Nkrumah had decided to do.

Nkrumah was—and all the basic facts were with him—proceeding upon the assumption that the subjective lives of his people had been smashed, that the missionaries had rendered the lives of his people meaningless, that the merchants had trapped them in a manner that rendered them more and more impoverished, emotionally and materially, each day, and that the guns of the British, though they were there in the name of public order, were weapons that intimidated the very foundations of the personalities of the people toward whom they were pointed. Nkrumah's drive for self-government was more than merely a scheme to grab selfishly at the reins of political power. It was a mandate to his people that they were not intrinsically inferior, no matter what their present condition of life was, to the rest of the human race—an implication that British rule had long sought to implant in them. More, Nkrumah gave sanction to his people that, though their outlook upon life and their tribal customs differed drastically from those of the Western white man, their customs and outlook did not justify their being conquered and held abjectly as economic hostages for centuries. He encouraged his people to believe that, though they were lagging behind in the race for progress, they needed no *outside* tutors to intimidate them with guns while monitoring their daily lives.

What was, then, Nkrumah's task? Merely to ask that question is to step beyond the confines of this story. But we must hint at it. Nkrumah's task was much, *much* more than merely to drive out the British. He was calling his people from their Eden-like allegiances to their dead fathers and inspiring them to believe that they could master the ideas and techniques of the twentieth century. He was attempting to empty out the rich increment of the overburdened emotional consciousness of his tribal brothers and fasten that consciousness onto the brute, stark, workaday world in which it existed; and, at the same time, incite that consciousness to manipulate that world in the interests of his own deepest humanity.

On September 15, 1949, certain British officials actively entered the fight against Nkrumah by filing a series of libel suits, charging him with contempt of court. He was fined £300, a truly staggering blow for a newly created movement supported by penniless tribal people. But, within a matter of hours, the sum was raised voluntarily by the people of the streets. This act, more than anything else, convinced Nkrumah and his aides that their people were back of them, and they intensified their drive for self-government.

In October of 1949, the Coussey Committee's report was announced and Nkrumah called a monster mass meeting in Accra to study the constitutional proposals and decide to what extent they were acceptable. More than 80,000 people attended that meeting. The vast crowd objected to the three ex-officio members representing British vested interests being included in the cabinet; it protested against the suffrage age limit being set at twenty-five; it demanded a legislature composed of fully elected members instead of, as the report recommended, some being nominated and some being elected. The mass meeting advocated countrywide civil disobedience and non-co-operation if the British refused these demands.

During the first days of January of the following year, 1950, the Government invited the leaders of the Convention People's Party to a conference to discuss their proposals for constitutional change. The Government asked the nationalist leaders to postpone their campaign for civil disobedience until the Government had time to study what course to take. Nkrumah felt that such an attitude on the part of the Government indicated a ruse to stall for time; accordingly, twenty-four hours later, Nkrumah announced that "Positive Action" would begin.

On the morning of January 8, 1950, a colony-wide strike paralyzed the Gold Coast: not a train ran; buses and transportation trucks stood still; only water, electricity, health, and medical services, were allowed to function. For twenty-one days, despite threats of dismissal of workers from jobs, martial law, warnings, curfews, and the full evocation of the emergency powers of the Governor, "Positive Action" and civil disobedience held away in the Gold Coast. When it became evident that such action could continue indefinitely, the Governor again ordered the arrest of Nkrumah and the leaders of the Convention People's Party on charges of sedition. The trial lasted two months and ended with the conviction of all the leaders and their being sentenced to prison for terms varying from three months to four years.

During 1950, elections for town councils were held in the three largest cities of the Gold Coast: Accra, Kumasi, and Cape Coast. Though in prison, the leaders of the condemned party swept the polls, gaining decisive majorities wherever they had candidates running. When general elections were announced, the imprisoned leaders organized and conducted their campaigns from their prison cells! How was that possible? It was easy in the kind of tribal brotherhood that Nkrumah had established in his organization. The black jailers assigned by the Governor to guard the prisoners became the prisoners' messengers! They could not refuse to serve; first, they hotly wanted to see their land free of alien domination; second, they were bound by tribal loyalties to help their own brothers. Hence, the Convention People's Party was able to put up candidates in all of the country's constituencies. And from the leaders' prison cells political orders scribbled on toilet paper were smuggled out to the public by the men assigned to guard the prisoners! THESE MEN WERE ALREADY FREE! BUT THEY HAD TO PROVE IT WITH SACRIFICES! Were they willing to make those sacrifices? They were.

It was in prison that the greeting of "Freedom" was conceived and the salute of the elbow-resting-on-the-hip-and-the-right-palm-fronting-outward was invented. Nkrumah himself, while in his cell, wrote the party's song that would eventually be sung by the newly freed nation.

On February 8, 1951, the Convention People's Party swept the nation, winning thirty-five out of the thirty-eight seats. The people of the Gold Coast had elected as heads of the new government men who were in prison cells and the British had a new headache on their hands.

A few days later Nkrumah and his aides were told to dress in civilian clothes, an order that aroused their suspicions, for they thought that the British did not want the populace to see their newly elected leaders being transferred to another prison. But, no. It was freedom, an act of "grace," as the British quaintly called it for public consumption. But, privately, when speaking to the nationalist leaders themselves, the Governor admitted: "You chaps out-organized us." That was all. There was no mention of virtue; no talk of metaphysics; he didn't charge the African leaders with having progressed too fast. In short, his attitude said: "Well, you proved you were men. All right, you have the government." It was as simple as that.

Though Nkrumah had branded the constitution as being "bogus and fraudulent," he decided that his party would take a leading role in the new government for the following reasons: "We are going into the Government to show the world that the African can rule himself. We want the chance to fight for the political, social, and economic improvement of the country from both within and without the government."

This is a happy note upon which to end this story, but if I terminated my remarks here, I'd not be true to you or to the efforts of the Gold Coast Africans. Soon after he had taken over the government, Nkrumah had trouble. Some sections of the once-powerful tribes of the Ashanti and a few elements among the backward natives of the Northern Territories, incited by disgruntled political leaders, threatened secession. Self-government and freedom were proving to be a hard and lonely road, a cold and anguishing life. They suddenly longed for the father-image of the white man, for their warm and ancient days. They rebelled, rioted, shouted slogans against the new government, and called for a federal constitution that would enable them to follow their ancient folkways. Nkrumah stood firm against these new onslaughts from his own people and insisted that they march ahead. After much agitation, elections were held, in 1956, on the issue of whether there should be a strong central government or a loose federation of small local states, each with its own autonomous folkways. The idea of a strong central government, oriented towards an industrial future, won, as it should have.

In March 1957, the Gold Coast, under the leadership of Nkrumah, assumed independent status with full responsibility for its present and future, and its name was changed to Ghana.

Let us pause here and glance back over this story. In one sense, it is a glorious tale of men succeeding against almost impossible odds. But in another sense it is a stupid and tragic story. WHAT WAS THE FIGHT IN THE GOLD COAST ALL ABOUT? The issue was something so simple and human that one is almost ashamed to mention it. One set of men, black in color, had to organize and pledge their lives and make grievous sacrifices in order to prove to another set of men, white in color, that they were human beings! What a perversion of the energies of human life! What a reduction of human dignity comes about when men must consecrate their end-all and their be-all merely to prove that they are human beings. Suppose all of that energy had been put to embellishing the life of that country? What life-furthering gains there could have been!

But the black men involved had no choice. To maintain their position of psychological luxury stemming from the cheap and vulgar superiority of race domination, the white British had branded the black Gold Coasters as inferior, and those black men had no choice but to accept that challenge before they could do anything else. This useless struggle of having to prove one's humanity, which is a kind of *supra* racism, is the blight that the Western white man has cast upon the colored masses of Asia and Africa.

But the struggle in the Gold Coast is not over. The European has been driven from power there, but can the African drive out of himself that religious weakness that enabled the European to enter his land so easily and remain there as master for centuries? Can the African get *Africanism* out of Africa? Can the African overcome his ancestor-worshiping attitudes and learn to doubt the evidence of his senses as Descartes taught the Europeans to do, and master the techniques of science and develop a spirit of objectivity?

I can say one thing with certainty: The Gold Coast African now knows what he needs most to do. He needs to trade with the world; he needs the learning of the world; he needs the industrial disciplines and scientific facts of the world. What he does not need is bossing, white masters, racial snobbery, and the white man's concept of what is "good" for him.

Let us pause here and ask some pertinent questions. If the people of the Gold Coast had accepted the advice of the British, could they have won their independence so quickly and effectively? The answer is a categoric no. Only Africans, giving African solutions to African problems, could have accomplished that miracle. What politicians or academic spokesmen of the Western world would have dared, even merely imaginatively, to envisage the confounding unity of so many disparities which Nkrumah forged into so masterful a whole? None. What Nkrumah did had not only been declared impossible, unsound; but it was immoral. Why? For the simple reason that it had never been done before.

Do you know that even scientists and academic people, too, have their mysticism, their superstition? According to their feelings, that which has never happened before must somehow be wrong; and especially is this the attitude they hold in the sphere of human relations. It is for this reason that, no matter what happens in the Gold Coast, the Africans there are stoutly determined to decide for themselves what is good or bad for them.

The new government plans to construct a gigantic hydroelectric project by damming up rivers and creating one of the world's largest inland lakes. The idea is to use the electric power to manufacture aluminum out of bauxite, of which there is enough to last two hundred years. What do they plan to do with the aluminum? They want to swap it for atomic piles! In short, the Gold Coast is planning to launch itself directly into the twentieth century, with its present tribal structure and all. Well, why not? Why should the people of the Gold Coast repeat the slow, costly, and stupid industrial growth of the Western world?

Of course, the academic people have declared that that is wrong. Why? Well, it has just never happened before, so it's wrong. I say that, as yet, the world does not know what is "right" or "wrong" in such matters. I say that Nkrumah is right to plunge ahead and experiment. If such experiments are honestly and intelligently conducted, one cannot really lose. Even if failure attends the enterprise, one will have learned something, and a few new facts about man's life on earth will have been added to our stock of human knowledge.

Whenever and wherever I've explained this problem, I've been deluged with questions from Western whites:

"How can we help the Africans? Can we go to Africa and work with them? Will the Africans accept us?"

Yes, you can work with and help the Africans, and they will accept you if you can work with them in the spirit of civil *servants* rather than civil *masters*.

But, in my opinion, the greatest aid that any white Westerner can give Africa is by becoming a missionary right in the heart of the Western world, explaining to his own people what they have done to Africa. To those of you who fervently long to go to Africa, I say, beware. Africa is a most dangerous psychological trap. The millions of naked blacks living there in poetic dreams beckon seductively to the white misfits, the white failures, the white psychological cripples of the Western world. If you can't adjust to the exacting conditions of life in New York, or London, or Paris, or Berlin, then go to Africa and play God to simple-minded men. Only a mentally stunted and botched white man would want to obtain that kind of cheap salvation. Every white man desiring to go to Africa ought to be subjected to a most rigorous psychoanalytic examination to determine whether he is really emotionally fit to do so. Until today, the most tenacious enemies of Africa have been emotionally deformed white men hanging like millstones about Africa's neck.

What Africans need, above all, is an understanding on the part of others of what has happened to them. They know now, in part, what has happened to them, but the white men who caused that catastrophe do not know it. More than techniques, which they need, more than Point Fours, which they need, more than loans and gifts, which they need and can use, Africans need a simple acknowledgment from the white West of what it did. And that terribly human gesture, to be frank—men being what they are—is about the last thing that the white West can give Africa. It's too human a thing to ask, and, even if the West could give it, it would help the West even more than it would help Africa. For one thing, it would mean that the white man would not again, acting upon a ridiculous delusion, attempt to conquer lands in the name of a superior god or race. And that assurance would leave the newly freed African in psychological peace for a while to find himself and rebuild his shattered existence.

Can this happen? Is the West free enough of its own fears to let these people know that they will not be resubjugated? That is the question.

The Secret Circle that launched this revolution looked at their people through Western eyes, or they could not have pitted their puny strength against the might of Britain and the traditions of their people. Being Western, they were rightfully impatient; they wished to move ahead fast and create that world that would make them feel at home; they wanted to know that the earth upon which they lived and the men about them were not hostile. Western white men can understand these nationalist Africans if racial jealousy can be drained out of their hearts and if moral imperialism can be purged from their sensibilities.

If my words have any weight with you, I say, when you look at these black nationalists, you are looking at yourselves in another guise. But need that fact upset you? Need it incite you to anger? In order to contemplate one's life in an alien guise, one must have a clean heart, or else one is prone to project out upon that alien life one's own dirt, one's own spite, one's own self-hate, one's own inhibited impulses. Too long has Africa been made into a psychological garbage heap where white men dumped that part of themselves that they did not like. A free Africa will not only mean a chance of life for millions of people who have been victimized for centuries, but it will be a sign, too, that at long last the white man has grown up and has no longer any need to crucify others in order to feel normal. In sum, a free Africa presupposes a free mankind.

But, let me repeat one word of warning: The white man injected race feeling in Africa. And the easiest, the cheapest, the most vulgar, and the least worthy road that the African can travel is to become a racist like the white man, which would mean that the African has learned his lesson too bitterly and too well. To steer clear of the foul road of racism is not left to the decision of the African; too much pressure upon him can take him down that road, and, if he goes, and if the Asians follow him, then the vile logic of racism, which the white man helped to sow in this world, will grow and bear its blighted fruit.

We have it within our will and power to see that that does not happen.

Would it not be better to have continents of Asians and Africans wedded to practical goals than have them arming and mobilizing to make the world accept them as men? We make the world in which we live. So far we've made it a racist world. But surely such a world is not worthy of man as we dream of him and want him to be.

Insights, Interviews & More . . .

About the author

A Chronology of Richard Wright

The Granger Collection, New York

1908

Born Richard Nathaniel Wright, September 4, on Rucker's Plantation, a farm near Roxie, Mississippi, 22 miles east of Natchez, first child of Nathan Wright, an illiterate sharecropper, and Ella Wilson Wright, a schoolteacher. (All four grandparents had been born in slavery. Father was born shortly before 1880, the son of Nathaniel Wright, a freed slave who farmed a plot of land he had been given at the end of the Civil War. Maternal grandfather, Richard Wilson, born March 21, 1847, served in the United States Navy in 1865, then became disillusioned because of a bureaucratic error that deprived him of his pension. Maternal grandmother, Margaret Bolton Wilson, of Irish, Scottish, American Indian, and African descent, was virtually white in appearance. A house slave before the Emancipation, she later became a midwife nurse, a devoted Seventh-Day Adventist, and the strict head of her Natchez household, which included eight surviving children. Mother, born 1883, married Nathan Wright in 1907 despite her parents' disapproval, and then gave up school teaching to work on the farm.)

1910

Brother Leon Alan, called Alan, born September 24.

1911–12

Unable to care for her children while working on the farm, mother takes Wright and his brother to live with Wilson family in Natchez. Father rejoins family and finds work in a sawmill. Wright accidentally sets fire to grandparents' house.

1913–14

Family moves to Memphis, Tennessee, by steamboat. Father deserts family to live with another woman, leaving them impoverished. Mother finds work as a cook.

1915–16

Wright enters school at Howe Institute, Memphis, in September 1915. Mother falls seriously ill in early 1916. Grandmother comes to care for family. After grandmother returns home, mother puts Wright and his brother in the Settlement House, Methodist orphanage in Memphis, where they stay for over a month. Spends relatively pleasant summer at 1107 Lynch Street in Jackson, Mississippi, where maternal grandparents now live, before going with mother and brother to Elaine, Arkansas, to live with his favorite aunt, Maggie (his mother's younger sister), and her husband, Silas Hoskins, a saloonkeeper.

1917–18

After Hoskins is murdered by whites who want his prosperous liquor business, terrified family flees to West Helena, Arkansas, then returns to Jackson with Aunt Maggie to live with the Wilsons. After several months they go back to West Helena, where mother and aunt find work cooking and cleaning for whites. Aunt Maggie leaves with her lover, "Professor" Matthews, a fugitive from the law (they eventually settle in Detroit).

1918–19

Wright enters local school in fall 1918. Mother's health deteriorates early in 1919 and Wright is forced to leave school to earn money. Delivers wood and laundry and carries lunches to railroad workers. Family moves frequently because of lack of rent money; Wright gathers stray pieces of coal along railroad tracks to heat their home. Mother suffers paralyzing stroke, and grandmother comes to bring the family back to Jackson. Aunt Maggie helps care for mother, then takes Leon Alan back to Detroit with her; other aunts and uncles help pay for mother's treatment. ▶

A Chronology of Richard Wright *(continued)*

1919–20

Wright moves into home of aunt and uncle, Clark and Jody Wilson, in nearby Greenwood, Mississippi, where he is able to attend school. Finds household calm and orderly but his aunt and uncle cold and unsympathetic, and is terrified by episodes of sleepwalking. Returns to grandparents' home in Jackson. Mother begins to show signs of recovery from paralysis, then has relapse caused by a cerebral blood clot that leaves her virtually crippled. Her illness impoverishes the family, already hurt by the rheumatism that makes Grandfather Wilson unable to work.

1920–21

Enters Seventh-Day Adventist school taught by his youngest aunt, Addie. Only nine years older than Wright, she is a rigid disciplinarian often at odds with him. Wright rebels against the rules and practices of the religion, including its diet, which forbids eating pork. Finds himself opposed to his family in general, except for his mother, who is too sick to help him.

1921–22

Enters the fifth grade of the Jim Hill School in Jackson, two years behind his age group. Does well, quickly gains in confidence, and is soon promoted to the sixth grade. Begins friendships, some of them lasting into his adulthood, with a number of other students, including Dick Jordan, Joe Brown, Perry Booker, D. C. Blackburn, Lewis Anderson, Sarah McNeamer, and Essie Lee Ward. Takes job as a newsboy, which gives him the chance to read material forbidden at home because of religious prohibitions. Family life continues to be difficult, although his mother's health improves slightly. Travels briefly during summer in the Mississippi Delta region as "secretary-accountant" to an insurance agent, W. Mance. The trip allows him to know better the rural South, but he is dismayed by the illiteracy and lack of education he encounters among blacks.

1922–23

Enters the seventh grade. Grandfather Wilson dies November 8. After many arguments, grandmother reluctantly lets Wright take jobs after school and on Saturday (the Seventh-Day Adventist sabbath). Runs errands and performs small chores, mainly for whites. For the first time has enough money to buy school books, food to combat his chronic hunger, and clothing. Baptized in the Methodist Church, mainly to please his mother. Avidly reads pulp magazines, dime novels, and books and magazines discarded by others. Uncle Thomas Wilson, his wife, and their two daughters come to live with the family in spring 1923. Mother's health worsens. Wright works during the summer at a brickyard and as a caddy at a golf course.

1923–24

Enters eighth grade at the Smith Robertson Junior High School, Jackson (a former slave, Smith Robertson had become a successful local barber and a community leader; the school, built in 1894, was the first black institution of its kind in Jackson). Until he can afford a bicycle, Wright walks several miles daily to and from the school. Makes new friends at school, including Wade Griffin, Varnie Reed, Arthur Leaner, and Minnie Farish. Begins working for the Walls, a white family he finds kindly (will serve them for two years). Later remembers writing his first short story, "The Voodoo of Hell's Half-Acre," in late winter (story is reported to have been published in the spring as "Hell's Half-Acre" in the Jackson *Southern Register*, a black weekly newspaper; no copies are known to be extant). Brother Leon Alan returns from Detroit. Wright is initially pleased, but their relationship soon disappoints him. Works for the American Optical Company, cleaning workshop and making deliveries.

1924–25

Enters ninth grade at Smith Robertson Junior High School, and graduates on May 29, 1925, as valedictorian. Rejects graduation speech prepared for him by the principal and instead delivers his own, "The Attributes of Life." Works as a delivery boy, sales clerk, hotel hallboy and bellboy, and in a movie theater. Begins classes in fall at newly founded Lanier High School, but quits a few weeks later to earn money. Leaves Jackson for Memphis, Tennessee, where he boards with a family at 570 Beale Street.

1926

Works for low pay as a dishwasher and delivery boy and at the Merry Optical Company. Reads widely in *Harper's*, *Atlantic Monthly*, *The American Mercury*, and other magazines. Moves to 875 Griffith Place. ▶

A Chronology of Richard Wright *(continued)*

1927

Joined by mother, who is still in poor health, and brother; they take an apartment together at 370 Washington Street. After reading an editorial highly critical of H. L. Mencken, long noted as a critic of the white South, Wright seeks out Mencken's *Prejudices* and *A Book of Prefaces* and is particularly impressed by Mencken's iconoclasm and use of "words as weapons." These books serve as guides to further reading, including works by Theodore Dreiser, Sinclair Lewis, Sherwood Anderson, the elder Alexandre Dumas, Frank Harris, and O. Henry. Aunt Maggie, who has been deserted by "Professor" Matthews, joins family in the fall. In December, Wright and Maggie, who hopes to open a beauty salon, move to the South Side of Chicago, while mother and Leon Alan return to Jackson. Sees his aunt Cleopatra ("Sissy"), but is disappointed to find that she lives in a rooming house, not an apartment, and moves into a rooming house with Aunt Maggie.

1928

Works as delivery boy in a delicatessen, then as a dishwasher. Wright finds Chicago stimulating and less racially oppressive than the South, but is often dismayed by the pace and disarray of urban life. Passes written examination for the postal service in the spring, then begins work in the summer as a temporary employee at 65 cents an hour. Rents an apartment with Aunt Maggie and is joined by mother and brother. In the fall Wright fails the postal service medical examination required for a permanent position because of chronic undernourishment and returns to dishwashing. Disputes over money and his reading cause tension with Aunt Maggie. Wright takes another apartment for family and invites his aunt Cleopatra to move in with them.

1929

After undertaking a crash diet to increase his weight, Wright passes the physical examination and is hired by the central post office at Clark Street and Jackson Boulevard as a substitute clerk and mail sorter. Moves with family to four rooms at 4831 Vincennes Avenue, which allows him to read and write in relative comfort. Dislikes the post office bureaucracy, but becomes friendly with many fellow workers, both black and white. Among his friends are schoolmates from the South, including Essie Lee Ward, Arthur

Leaner, and Joe Brown. Writes steadily and attends meetings of a local black literary group, but feels distant from its middle-class members. Attracted by the Universal Negro Improvement Association, a group inspired by Marcus Garvey, but does not join it.

1930

Volume of mail drops in decline following the 1929 Wall Street crash; Wright has his working hours cut back before losing his job altogether. South Side sinks into economic depression. Works temporarily for post office in the summer. Mother suffers a relapse, aunt Cleopatra has a heart attack, and brother develops stomach ulcers. Begins work on *Cesspool*, novel about black life in Chicago. Enrolls in tenth grade at Hyde Park Public School, but soon drops out.

1931

Reads books recommended by friend William Harper (who will later own a bookstore on the South Side). Wright is particularly impressed by Dreiser and Joseph Conrad, and continues to write. Short story "Superstition" is published in April *Abbott's Monthly Magazine*, a black journal (magazine fails before Wright is paid). Through a distant relative, finds job as a funeral insurance agent for several burial societies. Also works as an assistant to a black Republican precinct captain during the mayoral campaign, and at the post office in December. Becomes interested in views of Communist orators and organizers, especially those in the League of Struggle for Negro Rights.

1932

Sells insurance policies door-to-door and works briefly as an assistant to a Democratic precinct captain. Family moves to slum apartment as Wright is increasingly unable to sell policies to blacks impoverished by the Depression. Asks for and receives relief assistance from the Cook County Bureau of Public Welfare, which finds him a temporary job as a street cleaner. Works at the post office during the Christmas season.

1933

Digs ditches in the Cook County Forest Preserves, then works at Michael Reese Hospital, caring for animals used in medical research. Recruited by ▶

A Chronology of Richard Wright *(continued)*

fellow post office worker Abraham Aaron to join the newly formed Chicago branch of the John Reed Club, a national literary organization sponsored by the Communist party. Welcomed and encouraged by the almost entirely white membership of the club, Wright begins to read and study *New Masses* and *International Literature*, the organ of the International League of Revolutionary Writers. Writes and submits revolutionary poems ("I Have Seen Black Hands," "A Red Love Note") to *Left Front*, the magazine of the midwestern John Reed Clubs. Elected executive secretary of the Chicago John Reed Club and organizes a successful lecture series which allows him to meet a variety of intellectuals. Gives lecture at open forum on "The Literature of the Negro."

1934

Hoping to consolidate his position in the John Reed Club, Wright joins the Communist party; is also impressed by the party's opposition to racial discrimination. Publishes poetry in *Left Front*, *Anvil*, and *New Masses*. Becomes a member of the editorial board of *Left Front*. Enjoys literary and social friendships with Bill Jordan, Abraham Chapman, Howard Nutt, Laurence Lipton, Nelson Algren, Joyce Gourfain, and Jane Newton. Grandmother Wilson comes to Chicago to join the family; they move to apartment at 4804 St. Lawrence Avenue, near the railroad tracks. Mother's paralysis returns after attack of encephalitis. Wright is laid off by the hospital in the summer, and again works as a street sweeper and ditch digger before being hired to supervise a youth club organized to counter juvenile delinquency among blacks on the South Side. Attends Middle West Writers' Congress in August and the national congress of John Reed Clubs in September. Dismayed by party decision to cease publication of *Left Front* and to dissolve the John Reed Clubs in 1935 as part of its Popular Front strategy. Meets Jack Conroy, editor of *Anvil*. Reading in Chicago by this time includes Henry James (especially the Prefaces to the New York Edition), Gertrude Stein (notably her *Three Lives*, with its portrait of a black character, Melanctha Herbert), Faulkner, T. S. Eliot, Sherwood Anderson, Dos Passos, O'Neill, Stephen Crane, Dreiser, Whitman, Poe, D. H. Lawrence, Conrad, Galsworthy, Hardy, Dickens, George Moore, Carlyle,

Swift, Shakespeare, Tolstoy, Dostoevsky, Turgenev, Chekhov, Proust, Dumas, and Balzac. Lectures on the career of Langston Hughes to the Indianapolis John Reed Club in November and contributes fee to new publication *Midland Left*.

1935

Publishes leftist poetry in *Midland Left*, a short-lived journal, *New Masses* ("Red Leaves of Red Books" and "Spread Your Sunshine"), and *International Literature* ("A Red Slogan"). Family moves to 2636 Grove Avenue. Begins submitting novel "Cesspool" to publishers (later retitled *Lawd Today!* by Wright; it is rejected repeatedly over the next two years, then published posthumously as *Lawd Today* in 1963 by Walker and Company). Wright attends the first American Writers' Congress, held in New York in April. Speaks on "The Isolation of the Negro Writer," meets Chicago novelist James T. Farrell, and becomes one of fifty members of the national council of the newly formed League of American Writers. Works on story "Big Boy Leaves Home." Publishes "Between the World and Me," poem about lynching, in July–August *Partisan Review*. Falls seriously ill with attack of pneumonia during the summer. Article "Avant-Garde Writing" wins second prize in contest sponsored by two literary magazines but is never published. First piece of journalism, "Joe Louis Uncovers Dynamite," describing the reaction of Chicago blacks to the Louis-Max Baer fight, published in *New Masses*. Grandmother Wilson dies. Family, with Wright still virtually its sole support, moves to 3743 Indiana Avenue. Wright is hired by the Federal Writers' Project (part of the Works Progress Administration) to help research the history of Illinois and of the Negro in Chicago for the Illinois volume in the American Guide Series. Discusses influence of Hemingway with fellow writers in federal project.

1936

Publishes "Transcontinental," a six-page radical poem influenced by Whitman and Louis Aragon, in January *International Literature*. Becomes a principal organizer of the Communist party–sponsored National Negro Congress (successor to the League of Struggle for Negro Rights), held in Chicago in February, and reports on it for *New Masses*. Transferred in spring to the Federal ▶

A Chronology of Richard Wright *(continued)*

Theatre Project, where he serves as literary adviser and press agent for the Negro Federal Theatre of Chicago and becomes involved in dramatic productions. Finishes two one-act plays based in part on a section of his unpublished novel. In April, Wright takes a leading role in the new South Side Writers' Group (members will include Arna Bontemps, Frank Marshall Davis, Theodore Ward, Fenton Johnson, Horace Cayton, and Margaret Walker). Takes an active role in the Middle West Writers' Congress, held in Chicago June 14–15. Because of what he later describes as a Communist plot against him on the Federal Theatre Project assignment, Wright returns to the Writers' Project, where he becomes a group coordinator. Story "Big Boy Leaves Home" appears in anthology *The New Caravan* in November and receives critical attention and praise in mainstream newspapers and journals.

1937

Publishes poem "We of the Streets" in April *New Masses* and story "Silt" in the August number. Breaks with the Communist party in Chicago, basically over the question of his freedom as a writer. Brother finds job with the Works Progress Administration and assumes some responsibility for support of the family. Wright ranks first in postal service examination in Chicago, but turns down offer in May of permanent position at approximately $2,000 a year in order to move to New York City to pursue career as a writer. Stays briefly with artist acquaintances in Greenwich Village, then moves to Harlem; by mid-June he has a furnished room in the Douglass Hotel at 809 St. Nicholas Avenue. Attends Second American Writers' Congress as a delegate and serves as a session president; stresses the need for writers to think of themselves as writers first and not as laborers. Becomes Harlem editor of the Communist newspaper *Daily Worker* and writes over 200 articles for it during the year, including pieces on blues singer Leadbelly and the continuing Scottsboro Boys controversy. With Dorothy West and Marian Minus, helps launch magazine *New Challenge*, designed to present black life "in relationship to the struggle against war and Fascism." Wright publishes "The Ethics of Living Jim Crow—An Autobiographical Sketch" in *American Stuff: WPA Writers' Anthology* (essay is later included in the second edition of *Uncle Tom's Children* and incorporated into *Black Boy*). In November, publishes influential essay "Blueprint for Negro Writing" in *New Challenge*, criticizing past black literature and urging a Marxist-influenced approach that would transcend nationalism. Lacking party support, *New Challenge* fails after one number. Befriends 23-year-old Ralph Ellison. Wright's second novel, *Tarbaby's Dawn*, about a black adolescent in the South, is rejected by publishers (it remains unpublished). Learns that story "Fire and Cloud" has won first prize ($500) among 600 entries in *Story Magazine* contest. Wright joins the New York Federal Writers' Project (will write the Harlem section for *New York Panorama* and work on "The Harlems" in *The New York City Guide*).

1938

Rents furnished room at 139 West 143rd Street. Engages Paul Reynolds, Jr., as literary agent. Reynolds makes arrangements to place *Uncle Tom's Children: Four Novellas* ("Big Boy Leaves Home," "Down by the Riverside," "Long Black Song," and "Fire and Cloud") with editor Edward Aswell at Harper and Brothers, beginning Wright's long association with Aswell and Harper; book is published in March and is widely praised. Sends Aswell outline of novel about a black youth in Chicago. Announces plans to marry daughter of his Harlem landlady in May, but then cancels wedding, telling friends that a medical examination had revealed that the young woman has congenital syphilis. Moves into home of friends from Chicago, Jane and Herbert Newton, at 175 Carleton Avenue in Brooklyn. Story "Bright and Morning Star" appears in May *New Masses*. Writes about the second Joe Louis–Max Schmeling fight in the June *Daily Worker* and July *New Masses*. In June, replaces Horace Gregory on the editorial board of the literature section of *New Masses*. Works steadily on new novel; often writes in Fort Greene Park in the mornings, and discusses his progress with Jane Newton. Asks Margaret Walker to send him newspaper accounts of the case of Robert Nixon, a young Chicago black man accused of murder (executed in August 1939). Moves in the fall with the Newtons to 522 Gates Avenue. Congressman Martin Dies, chairman of the House Special Committee on Un-American Activities, denounces "The Ethics of ▶

A Chronology of Richard Wright *(continued)*

Living Jim Crow" during an investigation of the Federal Writers' Project. Finishes first draft of novel, now titled *Native Son*, in October and receives $400 advance from Harper in November. "Fire and Cloud" wins the O. Henry Memorial Award ($200). Travels to Chicago in November to research settings and events used in *Native Son*. Moves with Newtons to 87 Lefferts Place.

1939

Meets Ellen Poplar (b. 1912), daughter of Polish Jewish immigrants and a Communist party organizer in Brooklyn. Completes revised version of novel in February and shows it to Reynolds. Awarded Guggenheim Fellowship ($2,500) in March and resigns from the Federal Writers' Project in May. Discusses black American writing with Langston Hughes, Alain Locke, Countee Cullen, and Warren Cochrane during meeting of Harlem Cultural Congress. After Newtons' landlord evicts them, Wright moves to Douglass Hotel at 809 St. Nicholas Avenue in May, renting room next to Theodore Ward, a friend from Chicago. Becomes close to Ellen Poplar and considers marrying her, but also sees Dhima Rose Meadman, a modern-dance teacher of Russian Jewish ancestry. Plays active role at Third American Writers' Congress. Finishes *Native Son* on June 10. Ward dramatizes "Bright and Morning Star." The story is included in Edward O'Brien's *Best American Short Stories, 1939* and *Fifty Best American Short Stories (1914–1939)*. Begins work on new novel, *Little Sister*. Marries Dhima Rose Meadman in August in Episcopal church on Convent Avenue, with Ralph Ellison serving as best man. Lives with his wife, her two-year-old son by an earlier marriage, and his mother-in-law in large apartment on fashionable Hamilton Terrace in Harlem. Attends Festival of Negro Culture held in Chicago in September. Moves to Crompond, New York, to work on *Little Sister* (it is never completed).

1940

Visits Chicago in February and buys house for his family on Vincennes Avenue. Has lunch in Chicago with W. E. B. Du Bois, Langston Hughes, and Arna Bontemps. *Native Son* published by Harper and Brothers March 1 and is offered by the Book-of-the-Month Club as one of its two main selections. In three weeks it sells 215,000 copies. Wright delivers talk "How 'Bigger' Was Born" at Columbia University on March 12 (later published as a pamphlet by Harper, then added to future printings of *Native Son*). *Native Son* is banned in Birmingham, Alabama, libraries. Takes his first airplane flight when he accompanies *Life* magazine photographers to Chicago for an article on the South Side; tours the area with sociologist Horace Cayton, beginning long friendship (article is later canceled). Sails in April for Veracruz, Mexico, with wife, her son, mother-in-law, and wife's pianist. Rents ten-room villa in the Miraval Colony in Cuernevaca. Takes lessons in Spanish and studies the guitar. Reunited with Herbert Kline, friend from the Chicago John Reed Club, who is filming documentary *The Forgotten Village* with John Steinbeck; Wright travels with them through the countryside and takes an interest in the filming. Signs contract with John Houseman and Orson Welles for stage production of *Native Son*. Marriage becomes strained. Wright leaves Mexico in June and travels through the South alone. Visits his father, a poor and broken farm laborer, in Natchez, but is unable to make anything other than a token reconciliation with him. Goes to Chapel Hill, North Carolina, to begin collaboration with Paul Green on stage adaptation of *Native Son*. Meets producer John Houseman and drives to New York with him. Travels to Chicago to do research for book on black American life featuring photographs selected by Edwin Rosskam. Wright and Langston Hughes are guests of honor at reception given by Jack Conroy and Nelson Algren to launch magazine *New Anvil*. Returns to Chapel Hill in July to continue work with Paul Green. Elected vice-president of the League of American Writers. Harper reissues story collection as *Uncle Tom's Children: Five Long Stories* with "Bright and Morning Star" added and "The Ethics of Living Jim Crow" as an introduction. Starts divorce proceedings. Moves in with the Newtons, now at 343 Grand Avenue in Brooklyn; in the autumn Ellen Poplar moves into the Newton house. In September Wright is elected a vice-president of American Peace Mobilization, a Communist-sponsored group opposed to American involvement in World War II. Works with Houseman on revising stage version of *Native Son* (both Wright and Houseman think that Green has diverged too much from the novel); Houseman agrees that Orson Welles, who is finishing *Citizen Kane*, should direct. Story ▶

A Chronology of Richard Wright *(continued)*

"Almos' a Man" appears in *O. Henry Award Prize Stories of 1940.*

1941

In January the National Association for the Advancement of Colored People awards Wright the Spingarn Medal, given annually to the black American judged to have made the most notable achievement in the preceding year. Rehearsals for *Native Son* begin in February. Marries Ellen Poplar in Coytesville, New Jersey, on March 12. They move to 473 West 140th Street. *Native Son*, starring Canada Lee, opens at St. James Theatre on March 24 after a benefit performance for the NAACP. Reviews are generally favorable, though the play is attacked in the Hearst papers, which are hostile to Welles following *Citizen Kane*. Production runs in New York until June 15. Welles's striking but costly staging causes production to lose some money, but it recovers during successful tour of Pittsburgh, Boston, Chicago, Milwaukee, Detroit, St. Louis, and Baltimore. Wright asks the governor of New Jersey to parole Clinton Brewer, a black man imprisoned since 1923 for murdering a young woman, arguing that Brewer, who had taught himself music composition, has rehabilitated himself (Brewer is released July 8; Wright had previously sent one of his pieces to his friend, record producer and talent scout John Hammond, who arranged for Count Basie to record it). Begins novel *Black Hope* (never completed). Introduces Ellen to his family in Chicago during visit in April. Signs appeal of forty members of the League of American Writers against American intervention in the war that appears in *New Masses* May 27, and publishes "Not My People's War" in *New Masses* June 17. After Germany invades the Soviet Union, June 22, American Peace Mobilization changes its name to American People's Mobilization. Wright travels to Houston with Horace Cayton and John Hammond to accept Spingarn award from NAACP convention on June 27. Delivers enthusiastically received speech, in which his criticism of Roosevelt administration racial policies is muted in response to Communist party pressure. Lectures at Writers' Schools sponsored by the League of American Writers. Wrights move to 11 Revere Place, Brooklyn, in July. At John Hammond's request, Wright writes "Note on Jim Crow Blues" as a preface to the blues singer Josh

White's *Southern Exposure*, an album of three recordings attacking segregation. Hammond then produces recording of Paul Robeson singing Wright's blues song "King Joe," accompanied by the Count Basie orchestra. *12 Million Black Voices: A Folk History of the Negro in the United States*, with photographs selected by Edwin Rosskam (one taken by Wright), published by Viking Press in October to enthusiastic reviews. Wright reads *Dark Legend*, a psychoanalytic study of matricide by psychiatrist Fredric Wertham, then writes to Wertham about Clinton Brewer, who had murdered another young woman within months of his release. Wertham intervenes in the case and helps save Brewer from execution. (Wright and Wertham begin close friendship, and Wright becomes increasingly interested in psychoanalysis). Finishes draft of novel *The Man Who Lived Underground*. Signs petition "Communication to All American Writers" in December 16 *New Masses*, supporting America's entry into the war after the December 7 Japanese attack on Pearl Harbor.

1942

Mother and Aunt Maggie rejoin Addie in Jackson, Mississippi (brother remains in Chicago, though house on Vincennes Avenue is sold two years later). Daughter Julia, Wright's first child, born April 15. Wrights move in summer to 7 Middagh Street, a 19th-century house near the Brooklyn Bridge shared by George Davis, Carson McCullers, and other writers and artists. Excerpts from *The Man Who Lived Underground* appear in *Accent*. As the sole support of his family, Wright is classified 3-A and not drafted. Unsuccessfully tries to secure a special commission in the psychological warfare or propaganda services of the army. *Native Son* returns to Broadway in October (runs until January 1943). Publishes "What You Don't Know Won't Hurt You," article describing some of his experiences as a hospital janitor in Chicago, in December *Harper's Magazine*. Breaks quietly with the Communist party over its unwillingness to confront wartime racial discrimination and its continuing attempts to control his writing.

1943

Accompanied by Horace Cayton, Wright goes to Fisk University, Nashville, in April to deliver talk on his experiences with racism. Strong reaction from the audience leads Wright to begin autobiography ▶

A Chronology of Richard Wright *(continued)*

American Hunger. Neighbors and associates are interviewed by the Federal Bureau of Investigation. (Files obtained under the Freedom of Information Act in the 1970s show that the FBI began an investigation in December 1942 to determine if *12 Million Black Voices* was prosecutable under the sedition statutes. Although the sedition investigation is concluded in 1943, the FBI will continue to monitor Wright's activities, chiefly through the use of informers, for the remainder of his life.) Wrights move in August to 89 Lefferts Place in Brooklyn Heights. Helps organize the Citizens' Emergency Conference for Interracial Unity in response to widespread riots in Harlem following the wounding of a black soldier by white police in August. Finishes *American Hunger* in December.

1944

Writes film scenario "Melody Limited," about group of black singers during Reconstruction (scenario is never produced). Becomes friends with C. L. R. James, a Trinidad-born historian and Trotskyist, with whom he plans a book, *The Negro Speaks*, and a journal, *American Pages* (neither of these projects appear), and James's wife, Constance Webb. Writes series of radio programs on the life of a black family for producer Leston Huntley and is frustrated when Huntley is unable to place the series, in part because of criticism by middle-class blacks. Attends party held in honor of Theodore Dreiser on June 2, where Wright and Dreiser discuss the influence of life in Chicago on their attitudes. Deepens friendship with Dorothy Norman, New York *Post* editorial writer and editor of *Twice a Year*, who introduces him to existentialist philosophy and literature. Book-of-the-Month Club tells Harper that it will accept only the first section of *American Hunger*, describing Wright's experiences in the South; Wright agrees to this arrangement. Changes title to *Black Boy*. (Second section, telling of Wright's life in Chicago, is published as *American Hunger* by Harper & Row in 1977.) Wrights vacation in August outside Ottawa and in the nearby Gatineau country in Quebec. Excerpts from second section of autobiography appear as "I Tried to Be a Communist" in *Atlantic Monthly*, August–September, making public Wright's break with the Communist party. He is denounced by various party organs, including *New Masses* and the

Daily Worker. Helps the Chicago poet Gwendolyn Brooks to place her first book, *A Street in Bronzeville*. Expanded version of *The Man Who Lived Underground* is published as a novella in *Cross Section*.

1945

To circumvent racial discrimination, Wrights form the "Richelieu Realty Co." and use their lawyer as an intermediary in buying a house at 13 Charles Street in Greenwich Village. (Residence is delayed by their waiting for a Communist tenant hostile to Wright to leave and by redecorating.) Reviews books for *P.M.* newspaper; his highly favorable review of Gertrude Stein's *Wars I Have Seen* leads to correspondence with her. *Black Boy: A Record of Childhood and Youth* published by Harper and Brothers in March to enthusiastic reviews. The book is number one on the bestseller list from April 29 to June 6 and stirs controversy when it is denounced as obscene in the U.S. Senate by Democrat Theodore Bilbo of Mississippi. Takes part in several radio programs, including the nationally influential *Town Meeting*, where he argues the negative on the question "Are We Solving America's Race Problem?" In the summer, Wrights vacation on island off Quebec City, and Wright lectures at the Bread Loaf writers' school in Middlebury, Vermont. Writes long introduction to *Black Metropolis*, a sociological study of black Chicago by Horace Cayton and St. Clair Drake. Befriending a number of younger writers, white and black, Wright helps the 20-year-old James Baldwin win a Eugene F. Saxton Foundation Fellowship. Publishes a favorable review of Chester Himes's first novel, *If He Hollers Let Him Go*, and lends Himes $1,000. In the fall, Wrights move to an apartment at 82 Washington Place in Greenwich Village to be closer to a school for Julia. Wright undertakes four-month lecture tour but stops after six weeks because of exhaustion.

1946

Serves as honorary pallbearer at funeral on January 12 of poet Countee Cullen, attending service at Salem Methodist Church in Harlem and burial at Woodlawn Cemetery in the Bronx. By January 19, *Black Boy* has sold 195,000 copies in the Harper trade edition and 351,000 through the Book-of-the-Month Club, making it the fourth best-selling nonfiction ▶

A Chronology of Richard Wright *(continued)*

title of 1945. Wright, his psychiatrist friend Dr. Fredric Wertham, and others found the Lafargue Clinic, a free psychiatric clinic in Harlem. Meets Jean-Paul Sartre in New York. Receives invitation to visit France, but requests for a passport meet with opposition. Wright goes to Washington for an interview and enlists the aid of Dorothy Norman (who appoints him coeditor of *Twice a Year*), Gertrude Stein, and French cultural attaché, anthropologist Claude Lévi-Strauss, who sends him an official invitation from the French government to visit Paris for a month. Wright leaves New York on May 1. In Paris, welcomed by Gertrude Stein and by almost all the important French literary societies and circles. (Stein dies on July 27 after operation for cancer.) Meets Simone de Beauvoir and André Gide, whose *Travels in the Congo* has impressed Wright, as well as Léopold Sédar Senghor of Senegal, Aimé Césaire of Martinique, and others in the *Négritude* movement. Assists Senghor, Césaire, and Alioune Diop of Senegal in founding the magazine *Présence Africaine* and attends its first board meeting at the Brasserie Lipp. Donates a manuscript to an auction for benefit of experimental dramatist Antonin Artaud. "The Man Who Killed a Shadow" published in French in *Les Lettres Françaises* (first appears in English in 1949 in magazine *Zero*). Leaves Paris in late December and travels to London.

1947

Meets the Trinidad-born intellectual George Padmore and dines with members of the Coloured Writers' Association, including its president, Cedric Dover, author of *Half Caste*, and the colored South African journalist and novelist Peter Abrahams. Returns to New York in January. Moves with family into their Charles Street house in Greenwich Village. Helps to welcome Simone de Beauvoir to New York in the spring. Refuses offer from Hollywood producer to film *Native Son* with character Bigger Thomas changed to a white man. Wright's works are being translated into French, Italian, German, Dutch, and Czech. Decides to return to Europe permanently with his family, partially in response to the racial hostility they are encountering in New York. Sells Greenwich Village house in June. Vacations at a cottage at Wading River, Long Island, owned by a friend. Buys an Oldsmobile sedan to take to Europe. Wright, his wife, and daughter reach Paris in August. They rent rooms from a friend, Odette Lieutier, in her apartment on the rue de Lille, then move into an apartment at 166 avenue de Neuilly. Albin Michel publishes French translation of *Native Son* in autumn.

1948

Begins to read more deeply in existentialism, including Heidegger and Husserl. Sees much of Sartre and Simone de Beauvoir. Wright is particularly impressed by Camus's *The Stranger*, and begins work on an existentialist novel, eventually titled *The Outsider*. Gallimard translation of *Black Boy* wins French Critics' Award. Wright establishes friendships with the Reverend Clayton Williams, pastor of the American Church, and with Harry Goldberg of the American Library. Becomes unofficial spokesman for African-American colony in Paris, which includes James Baldwin. Visits Italy for the publication there of *Native Son*. Meets with Carlo Levi and Ignazio Silone, who later introduces him to Arthur Koestler in Paris. Interviewed by his Italian translator, Fernanda Pivano, Wright says he likes to read *Metamorphosis*, *Moby-Dick*, *Ulysses*, and *The Sound and the Fury*. Travels through Belgium to London, where he sees a performance of *Native Son* and renews friendship with George Padmore, who stirs Wright's interest in the question of colonialism in Africa. Moves with family to 14 rue Monsieur le Prince in the Latin Quarter in May. Ellen returns to New York in June to select furniture and other possessions for their new life in France. Wright is beset by recurring sinus problems and influenza. His tonsils are removed. Aids Sartre and Camus in the leadership of the Rassemblement Démocratique Révolutionnaire (RDR), an organization of intellectuals critical of both the Soviet Union and the United States. Wright plays prominent role in its writers' congress, held in Paris on December 13, delivering lengthy speech (translated by Simone de Beauvoir). Spends $6,000 to buy Paul Green's share of film rights to *Native Son* in hopes of making screen version with French director Pierre Chenal.

1949

Daughter Rachel born January 17 at the American Hospital. Wright travels again to Rome and to Switzerland, for the publication of *Black Boy*. In ▶

A Chronology of Richard Wright *(continued)*

April, James T. Farrell and Nelson Algren visit him in Paris. Suspects socialist David Rousset of trying to shift the RDR toward a more pro-American, anti-Soviet stance. Refuses to attend large RDR rally held on April 30 (organization soon splits and dissolves). In May, visits London to consult with Richard Crossman, who is including "I Tried to Be a Communist" with similar essays by Koestler, Gide, Silone, Stephen Spender, and Louis Fischer in collection *The God That Failed* (published later in year, book is widely reviewed). Continues work on his existentialist novel. Assists George Plimpton and others in launching of *Paris Review*. James Baldwin's essay "Everybody's Protest Novel," attacking Stowe's *Uncle Tom's Cabin* but including criticism of *Native Son*, sours relationship between Wright and Baldwin. Wright writes screenplay for *Native Son*, adding several dream sequences to the story, then revises it with Chenal. After Canada Lee withdraws from project because of new commitments and worsening health, Wright undertakes to play the main role of Bigger Thomas. Sails for the United States in August, briefly visiting New York before going to Chicago for filming of exteriors for *Native Son*. Sees old friends Horace Cayton, St. Clair Drake, and others. Leaves New York in September for Argentina, where film is being made (Chenal had worked there during World War II, and political pressure had blocked access to French studios). Makes brief stops in Trinidad, Brazil, and Uruguay before arriving in Buenos Aires in October. Loses 35 pounds in preparation for the role by following strict diet and exercise program. Continues working on screenplay with Chenal.

1950

Production is delayed by financial problems. Wright finds atmosphere of Argentine life under the Perón dictatorship oppressive. Filming ends in June. Wright leaves Buenos Aires in July. Stops briefly in Brazil and Trinidad, spends two weeks in Haiti, then returns to Paris by way of New York, where he visits Fredric Wertham and the Lafargue Clinic. In Paris, begins work on screenplay about Toussaint L'Ouverture of Haiti. Works with Aime Césaire on "Revelation of Negro Art," an exhibition that includes works from the Musée de l'Homme and song and dance performances at the Cité Universitaire. Vacations in the fall in the Swiss and French Alps, visiting Basel,

Zurich, and the Aoste Valley, where he is a jury member with Paul Eluard, Louis Bromfield, and others for international San Vicente literary prize. Founds and becomes president of the Franco-American Fellowship, intended to protest official American policies and oppose racial discrimination by American companies and organizations active in France. Fellowship members take precautions when meeting in anticipation of surveillance by the American government (files released in the 1970s show that the Fellowship was monitored by informers employed by the Central Intelligence Agency and the FBI).

1951

Lectures in Turin, Genoa, and Rome in January. *Sangre Negra* (the film version of *Native Son*) opens to acclaim in Buenos Aires on March 30. American distributor cuts almost 30 minutes from film under pressure from New York state censors (original length was approximately 105 minutes); shortened version opens in New York on June 16 to unfavorable reviews. (Several states ban the film, but it is shown in Beverly Hills and, in spring 1952, in Mississippi, where members of Wright's family see it.) A partially restored print is warmly received at the Venice Film Festival in August. The Milan press praises Wright's acting; in general, his performance is deemed sincere but awkward, especially by American critics who compare it with Canada Lee's stage version. Wright visits the sociologist Gunnar Myrdal in Geneva, beginning a long friendship. With Jean Cocteau, inaugurates the Cercle International du Théâtre et du Cinéma. *New Story Magazine* accepts excerpts from Jean Genet's *Our Lady of the Flowers* on Wright's recommendation. Baldwin's essay "Many Thousands Gone," an explicit attack on Wright in *Partisan Review* (November–December), leads to painful break between the writers. Submits screenplay about refugees forced to choose between sides in the Cold War to the French Association of Film Writers.

1952

Travels to England in February. Spends several months in London and Catford, Surrey, completing the first full version of *The Outsider*. Vacations with his family in Corrèze at the end of August and continues to revise and cut novel. Refuses suggestion by John Fischer, his new Harper editor, ▶

A Chronology of Richard Wright *(continued)*

that he come to the United States for the publication of his book, citing the risk that he would be subpoenaed by an anti-Communist congressional investigating committee. Begins work in December on a novel about a white psychopathic murderer, based in part on his experience with Clinton Brewer.

1953

Begins correspondence with Frantz Fanon. *The Outsider* published by Harper and Brothers in March. Reviews are mixed; sales are initially brisk but eventually disappointing in comparison to *Native Son* and *Black Boy*. Wright composes an introduction to *In the Castle of My Skin*, first novel by the young Barbados writer George Lamming. Friendship with Sartre cools as Sartre moves closer to Communism. Wright's circle of friends remains wide, including Americans such as Chester Himes and William Gardner Smith, but he begins to withdraw from official organizations and to avoid formal gatherings. He is a regular at favorite cafés such as the Monaco and Tournon, where he entertains a steady stream of visitors from America, including Elmer Carter, Dorothy Norman, Nelson Algren, E. Franklin Frazier, and Louis Wirth. Discusses treatment of Algerians in France with Ben Burns, editor of *Ebony* magazine, during his visit. Wright tells Burns that he avoids criticizing French policies for fear of being deported. Ellen Wright begins work as a literary agent with Hélène Bokanowski, a prolific translator of Wright's work. From June to August, Wright travels in the Gold Coast (then a British colony with limited self-government, after 1957 the independent country of Ghana) to collect material for a book on Africa. Boat stops briefly in Freetown, Sierra Leone, en route to Takoradi; from there travels by road 170 miles to Accra, his main stop. Meets Prime Minister Kwame Nkrumah and other members of the pro-independence Convention People's Party, as well as Osei Agyeman Prempeh II, king of the Ashanti, and other traditional leaders. Excursions take him from Accra to Cape Coast, Christianborg, and Prampram; visits slave-trading fortresses and dungeons. Travels almost 3,000 miles in a chauffeur-driven car, touring the interior through Koforidua to Mampong, and the Secondi-Takoradi to Kumasi regions. In general, Wright is fascinated by Africans but is reinforced in his sense of self as a Western intellectual. Visits England to discuss his impressions with George and Dorothy Padmore before returning to Paris in September to begin work on book about his trip. Undergoes surgery for hernia.

1954

Revises book on Africa. Decides to write an account of Spanish life and culture. Drives his Citroen almost 4,000 miles between August 15 and September 9 on a route that includes Barcelona, Valencia, Saragossa, Guadalajara, Madrid, Córdoba, Seville, Granada, and Málaga. On September 16 State Department and FBI officials interview Wright in Paris about his relationship to the Communist party when he goes to renew his passport. *Black Power: A Record of Reactions in a Land of Pathos*, about his African trip, published by Harper and Brothers September 22. Receives mixed reviews in America, but is widely praised in France. *Savage Holiday*, novel about psychopathic murderer, is published as a paperback original by Avon after having been rejected by Harper. Book attracts little attention in the United States but is well received as *Le Dieu de Mascarade* in France. Visits Geneva with Gunnar Myrdal for further research on Spain at the United Nations library. Lectures on Africa in Amsterdam in October, where he meets Margrit de Sablonière, his Dutch translator, and begins an important friendship with her. Retúrns to Spain on November 8. Hires a driver and travels through Irun and on to Madrid, where he stays before returning to Paris in mid-December.

1955

An old Chicago friend, the cartoonist Ollie "Bootsie" Harrington, arrives to live in France. Wright secures funding for his attendance at forthcoming conference of non-aligned nations in Bandung, Indonesia, from the Paris office of the Congress for Cultural Freedom, an international alliance of anti-Communist intellectuals. Returns to Spain February 20, and spends several weeks there, including Holy Week in Granada and Seville. Leaves Spain on April 10 for Indonesia. At Bandung, Wright shares room with missionary Winburn T. Thomas. Leaders attending conference include Nehru (with whom Wright speaks), Sukarno, Sihanouk, Nasser, and Zhou Enlai. Remains in Indonesia at home of Thomas until May 5, working on notes of his impressions, then ▶

A Chronology of Richard Wright *(continued)*

returns to Europe via Ceylon and Kenya. Begins writing an account of the conference. Spends July to October with family at their new country home, a small farm in village of Ailly in eastern Normandy. Plans series of novels dealing with the conflicts between individuals and society (including one set in Aztec Mexico), but abandons the project on the advice of Reynolds and Aswell (now with McGraw-Hill). Returns to Paris when daughter Rachel falls ill with scarlet fever, then goes back to Ailly when her continued quarantine makes work at home difficult. *Bandoeng: 1.500.000.000 hommes.* French translation of book on nonaligned conference, published in December.

1956

Prepares manuscript of book on Spain in February and March, often living alone at Ailly, where he enjoys hours of gardening. Fearing deportation, remains silent on Algerian war of independence while in France (will offer guarded criticism of war when in other European countries). *The Color Curtain: A Report on the Bandung Conference*, with an introduction by Gunnar Myrdal, published March 19 by World Publishers in America and receives favorable reviews. Revises and cuts book on Spain. Adapts Louis Sapin's play *Papa Bon Dieu* as *Daddy Goodness* but is unable to have it produced. First Congress of Negro Artists and Writers, sponsored by *Présence Africaine* and which Wright had helped plan, meets in Paris in September, attended by delegates from Africa, the United States, and the Caribbean. Wright speaks on "Tradition and Industrialization: The Tragic Plight of the African Elites" and participates in several sessions. Suspects that *Présence Africaine* is being secretly taken over by the French government through anti-nationalist Africans and considers withdrawing from its activities. Lectures in Hamburg on "The Psychological Reactions of Oppressed Peoples" and tours the city with Ellen. Attends a meeting in London of the Congress for Cultural Freedom, organized by Arthur Koestler. Travels alone to Stockholm in late November for the Swedish publication of *The Outsider*; it sells 35,000 copies in four days (*Native Son* had sold 75,000 copies and *Black Boy* 65,000). Lectures in Sweden, Norway, and Denmark before returning to Paris in early December. Agrees to help found the American Society for African Culture, inspired by the French Société Africaine de Culture. Returning to native material, Wright begins work on novel set in Mississippi.

1957

Aunt Maggie dies January 20 in Jackson, Mississippi, where she had been taking care of Wright's mother (Wright has continued to help support them through the years). Mother moves in with a niece, then goes to Chicago at the end of June to live with Leon Alan. *Pagan Spain* published by Harper in February to good reviews but weak sales. Works at Ailly on new novel. Travels throughout Italy with Ellen during the spring. Visits West Germany in July to interview black American servicemen stationed there. *White Man, Listen!*, a collection of essays drawn from Wright's lectures, published October 15 by Doubleday (where Edward Aswell is now an editor). The book is especially well-received by the black press in the United States.

1958

Finishes *The Long Dream*, Mississippi novel, and begins *Island of Hallucinations*, sequel set in France. Seeking to renew his passport, he is again compelled to report to the American embassy in February and sign a statement admitting his past membership in the Communist party. Becomes increasingly alienated from the black community in Paris, which is torn by suspicion and dissension; finds himself the object of resentment, including rumors that he is an agent of the FBI or the CIA. Depressed and isolated from other blacks, Wright suspects that he is being persecuted by agents of the U.S. government. Takes part in a session of the Congress for Cultural Freedom, and in seminars on American literature sponsored by the American Cultural Center in Paris. Supports Sartre and Simone de Beauvoir in their opposition to the new regime of General de Gaulle. Works on new novel at Ailly during summer. *The Long Dream* published by Doubleday in October to often hostile reviews and flat sales. When Leon Alan telegraphs that their mother is seriously ill, Wright is forced to borrow extra money from Reynolds to send to his brother. Edward Aswell, his long-time editor, dies November 5. Considers moving to England and enlists aid of Labour member of Parliament John Strachey, who obtains assurances from the Home Secretary that Wright's application for residence will be fairly considered. Wright ►

A Chronology of Richard Wright *(continued)*

distances himself from various organizations he had previously supported, including *Présence Africaine* and the Société Africaine de Culture.

1959

Mother dies January 14. Wright sends the manuscript of *Island of Hallucinations* to Reynolds in February. Later in the month, he spends a day with Martin Luther King, Jr., who is passing through Paris en route to India. Timothy Seldes (Aswell's successor at Doubleday) asks for major revisions in *Island of Hallucinations*; Wright puts book aside (it is never completed). Discouraged by financial worries, weak reviews, poor health, and frustrating state of his novel, Wright continues to curtail his public activities. Declines to attend the second Congress of Black Writers and Artists in Rome. Plans a study of French Africa. After Doubleday promises a $2,500 advance, Wright asks the American Society for African Culture for an additional $7,500, but is turned down; believes CIA infiltration of the organization is responsible for his rejection. Tired of what he considers to be growing American political and cultural influence in French life and in the wake of increased attacks by other expatriate black writers, Wright prepares to leave France and live in England. Sells farm at Ailly. His play *Daddy Goodness* is produced in Paris in the spring. Wright falls ill in June with attack of amoebic dysentery, probably picked up in Africa. Illness persists despite treatment at American Hospital. Vacations at the Moulin d'Andé near Saint-Pierre du Vauvray in Normandy. With daughter Julia now at the University of Cambridge, his wife Ellen and daughter Rachel establish themselves in London. Ellen works there as a literary agent and looks for a permanent home for the family. Wright begins writing haiku (eventually completes some 4,000 pieces). Harassed by British passport officials during visit to England in September. Sees George Padmore, who dies not long after Wright's visit. Wright returns to England for the funeral. Tries to obtain resident visa from the Home Office, but is denied one without explanation. Alone in Paris, he sells home on rue Monsieur le Prince and moves to a two-room apartment on rue Régis. Recovers from dysentery but continues to have intestinal problems. Among his close friends at this time are Michel and Hélène Bokanowski, Colette and Rémi Dreyfus, Simone de

Beauvoir, Ollie Harrington, and the Reverend Clayton Williams. "Big Black Good Man" is included in *Best American Stories of 1958*.

1960

The Long Dream, adapted by Ketti Frings, opens on Broadway February 17 to poor reviews and closes within a week. Translation of *The Long Dream* well-received in France, but earnings are not enough to quell Wright's deepening anxiety about money. In April, driving his own Peugeot, Wright accompanies his gastroenterologist, Victor Schwartzmann, and Dr. Schwartzmann's father to medical conference in Leiden, Holland, where he visits Margrit de Sablonière. Selects and arranges 811 haiku for possible publication. Declines offers from Congress for Cultural Freedom to attend conferences on Tolstoy in Venice and New Delhi, believing that the organization is controlled by the American government (the Congress is later shown to have received substantial covert funding from the CIA). Records series of interviews concerning his work in June for French radio. Spends much of summer at Moulin d'Andé, where he begins new novel, *A Father's Law*. Falls ill on return to Paris in September. Julia Wright decides to study at the Sorbonne and visits her father before returning to England to pack her belongings. In September, Dorothy Padmore comes to visit. Later, old Chicago friend Arna Bontemps makes his first visit to Paris. Wright delivers lecture on November 8 at the American Church on the situation of black artists and intellectuals. Accuses the American government of creating and manipulating dissension among them through spies and provocateurs. Continues to suffer from intestinal difficulties and dizzy spells. Finishes complete proofreading of collection of stories, *Eight Men* (published by World Publishers in 1961). Welcomes Langston Hughes to his home for a brief but enjoyable visit on the morning of November 26, then enters the Eugene Gibez Clinic for diagnostic examinations and convalescence. Dies there of a heart attack shortly before 11:00 P.M., November 28. Cremated, along with a copy of *Black Boy*, at the Père Lachaise cemetery December 3, where his ashes are interred.

Richard Wright: Field Notes and Photos

Yale Collection of American Literature, Beinecke Rare Book and Manuscript Library

"Chief sitting under an umbrella, holding a ceremonial sword."

Yale Collection of American Literature, Beinecke Rare Book and Manuscript Library

"Chief being carried on a platform under an umbrella."

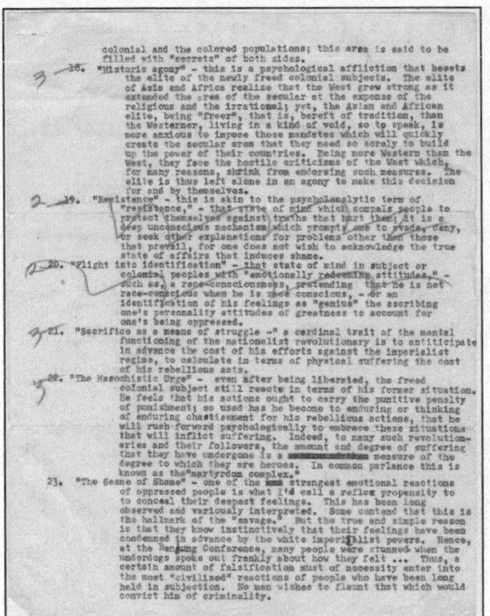

colonial and the colored populations; this area is said to be filled with "secrets" of both sides.

18. "Historic agony" - this is a psychological affliction that besets the elite of the newly freed colonial subjects. The elite of Asia and Africa realize that the West grew strong as it extended the area of the secular at the expense of the religious and the irrational; yet, the Asian and African elite, being "freer", that is, bereft of tradition, than the Westerner, living in a kind of void, so to speak, is more anxious to impose those mandates which will quickly create the secular area that they need so sorely to build up the power of their countries. Being more Western than the West, they face the hostile criticisms of the West which, for many reasons, shrink from endorsing such measures. The elite is thus left alone in an agony to make this decision for and by themselves.

19. "Resistance" - this is akin to the psychoanalytic term of "resistence," - that state of mind which compels people to protect themselves against truths that hurt them; it is a deep unconscious mechanism which prompts one to evade, deny, or seek other explanations for problems other than those that prevail, for one does not wish to acknowledge the true state of affairs that induces shame.

20. "Flight into identification" - that state of mind in subject or colonial peoples with "emotionally redeeming attitudes," - such as, a race-consciousness, pretending that he is not race-conscious when he is race conscious, - or an identification of his feelings as "genius" the ascribing one's personality attitudes of greatness to account for one's being oppressed.

21. "Sacrifice as a means of struggle -" a cardinal trait of the mental functioning of the nationalist revolutionary is to antiticipate in advance the cost of his efforts against the imperialist regime, to calculate in terms of physical suffering the cost of his rebellious acts.

22. "The Masochistic Urge" - even after being liberated, the freed colonial subject still reacts in terms of his former situation. He feels that his actions ought to carry the punitive penalty of punishment; so used has he become to enduring or thinking of enduring chastisement for his rebellious actions, that he will rush forward psychologically to embrace these situations that will inflict suffering. Indeed, to many such revolutionaries and their followers, the amount and degree of suffering that they have undergone is a measure of the degree to which they are heroes. In common parlance this is known as the "martyrdom complex."

23. "The Sense of Shame" - one of the strangest emotional reactions of oppressed people is what I'd call a reflex propensity to to conceal their deepest feelings. This has been long observed and variously interpreted. Some contend that this is the hallmark of the "savage." But the true and simple reason is that they know instinctively that their feelings have been condemned in advance by the white imperialist powers. Hence, at the Bandung Conference, many people were stunned when the underdogs spoke out frankly about how they felt ... Thus, a certain amount of falsification must of necessity enter into the most "civilized" reactions of people who have been long held in subjection. No man wishes to flaunt that which would convict him of criminality.

"Development notes" for *White Man, Listen!*

Yale Collection of American Literature, Beinecke Rare Book and Manuscript Library

- 2 -

He smiled at me and said, grasping my hand:

"You are known all over the world."

I felt my tension slackening. I'd heard that in the cabinet of the present President of Indonesia that there were several Communists and I did not know if I was speaking to a Communist or not ... We sat down. We talked in generalities for a few moments, paying each other compliments. I told him when I expected to go to Jakarta, that is, on or about the 10 or 11th of April. He said that he saw no objection to my going and called the young lady who had received me and told her to get me the application blanks. She brought in four sets which had four pages each. With the application blanks lying on a table in front of me, we chatted about world conditions and the talk assumed a familiar ring, colords vs. whites.

"How many millios of colored people in all will be represented there?" I asked.

"About a billion or more," he answered, smiling.

"That's the human race," I said.

He burst into laughter and said:

"Yes."

"Just what will they discuss?"

"That would be hard to tell at this time," he told me.

Entry from the "Travel Diary," for *The Color Curtain*.

Yale Collection of American Literature, Beinecke Rare Book and Manuscript Library

Have You Read?
More by Richard Wright

Other classic works by Richard Wright available from Harper Perennial:

THE MAN WHO LIVED UNDERGROUND

The novel Richard Wright was unable to publish during his lifetime—an explosive story of racism, injustice, brutality, and survival, written between his landmark books *Native Son* (1940) and *Black Boy* (1945). Fred Daniels, a Black man, is picked up by the police after a brutal double murder and tortured until he confesses to a crime he did not commit. After signing a confession, he escapes from custody and flees into the city's sewer system.

"Not just Wright's masterwork but also a milestone in African American literature. . . . One of those indispensable works that reminds all its readers that, whether we are in the flow of life or somehow separated from it, above- or below ground, we are all human."

—Gene Seymour, CNN

A FATHER'S LAW

Richard Wright wrote *A Father's Law* in a six-week period near the end of his life. He never finished the novel and never managed to correct the typescript.

But his daughter Julia Wright, now his literary executor, was with him while he wrote in a remote farmhouse in the French countryside. She has written an introduction that explains how the book came to be written and why she believes it is an important addition to the Wright corpus.

"It comes from his guts and ends at the hero's 'breaking point.' It explores many themes favored by my father like guilt, the difficult relationship between the generations, the difficulty of being a black policeman and father, the difficulty of being both those things and suspecting that your own son is the murderer. It intertwines astonishingly modern themes for a novel written in 1960."

—Julia Wright

EIGHT MEN

Each of the eight stories in *Eight Men* focuses on a Black man at violent odds with a white world, reflecting Wright's views about racism in our society and his fascination with what he called "the struggle of the individual in America." These poignant, gripping stories will captivate all those who love Wright's better-known novels.

"There is not a touch of phoniness or fakery in the book. All eight men and all eight stories stand as beautifully, pitifully, terribly true. . . . All the way through this is fine, sound, good, honorable writing, rich with insight and understanding, even when occasionally twisted by sorrow."

—*New York Times Book Review*

NATIVE SON

Right from the start, Bigger Thomas had been headed for jail. It could have been for assault or petty larceny; by chance, it was for murder and rape. *Native Son* tells the story of this young Black man caught in a downward spiral after he kills a young white woman in a brief moment of panic. Set in Chicago in the 1930s, Wright's powerful novel is an unsparing reflection on the poverty and feelings of hopelessness experienced by people in inner cities across the country and of what it means to be Black in America.

"The most powerful American novel to appear since *The Grapes of Wrath* . . . so overwhelming is its central drive, so gripping its mounting intensity."

—*The New Yorker*

UNCLE TOM'S CHILDREN

Set in the deep South, each of the powerful novellas collected in Wright's first book shines an unflinching light on the lives of Black people in the postslavery era, exploring their resistance to white racism and oppression.

"I found these stories both heartening . . . and terrifying as the expression of a racial hatred that has never ceased to grow and gets no chance to die."

—Malcolm Cowley, *The New Republic*

Have You Read? *(continued)*

PAGAN SPAIN

Richard Wright chronicles his trip to Spain in 1954, capturing the beauty and tragedy of the country under the rigid rule of Francisco Franco.

"A book which required courage to write—and even greater courage to publish."
—Joseph G. Harrison, *Christian Science Monitor*

BLACK POWER: THREE BOOKS FROM EXILE: BLACK POWER; THE COLOR CURTAIN; AND WHITE MAN, LISTEN!

Three late books by Richard Wright—*The Color Curtain; Black Power; White Man, Listen!*—are gathered in one volume for the first time, with an introduction by Cornel West. *Black Power* is an impassioned chronicle of Wright's trip to Africa's Gold Coast before it became the free nation of Ghana. *White Man, Listen!* is a stirring collection of essays on race, politics, and other essential social concerns, and *The Color Curtain* is an indispensable work urging the removal of the color barrier. It remains one of the key commentaries on the question of race in the modern era.

"The time is ripe to return to [Wright's] vision and voice in the face of our contemporary catastrophes and hearken to his relentless commitment to freedom and justice for all."
— Cornel West (from the Introduction)

BLACK BOY

Black Boy is a classic of American autobiography, a subtly crafted narrative of Richard Wright's journey from innocence to experience in the Jim Crow South that remains a seminal work in our history about what it means to be a man, Black, and Southern in America.

Superb. . . . A great American writer speaks with his own voice about matters that still resonate at the center of our lives." —*New York Times Book Review*